D1268066

POWERHOUSE FOR GOD

Speech, Chant, and Song
in an Appalachian Baptist Church

POWERHOUSE FOR GOD

By Jeff Todd Titon

University of Texas Press, Austin

First edition, 1988

Requests for permission to reproduce material from
this work should be sent to:
 Permissions
 University of Texas Press
 Box 7819
 Austin, Texas 78713-7819

Library of Congress Cataloging-in-Publication Data

Titon, Jeff.
 Powerhouse for God.
 Bibliography: p.
 Includes index.
 1. Fellowship Independent Baptist Church (Stanley,
Va.) 2. Stanley Region (Va.)—Religious life and
customs—Case studies. 3. Languages—Religious
aspects—Christianity—Case studies. 4. Music—
Religious aspects—Christianity—Case studies. I. Title.
BX6480.S8434T57 1988   398'.355'0975595   87-30024
ISBN 0-292-76485-5

*This publication has been supported by the National Endowment for the
Humanities, a federal agency which supports the study of such fields as
history, philosophy, literature, and languages.*

A portion of the Introduction is reprinted from "Folklife Stories and Religion," *Mid-America Folklore*, vol. 13, no. 2 (Summer–Fall 1985). Portions
of Chapter 5 are reprinted from "God'll Just Bless You All over the Place,"
Appalachian Journal, vol. 14 (Summer 1987) and "A Song from the Holy
Spirit," *Ethnomusicology*, vol. 24 (1980). Portions of Chapter 9 are reprinted from "The Life Story," *Journal of American Folklore*, vol. 93
(1980). I am grateful to the editors of these publications for permission to
reprint this material and to the Virginia State Library for permission to
reprint portions of the John W. Keyser diary, Personal Papers Collection,
Accession 24023, Archives Branch, Virginia State Library and Archives,
Richmond, Virginia.

For Paula and Emily

Contents

PHOTOGRAPHS

(All photographs are by the author unless otherwise indicated in captions.)

FIGURES

(All transcriptions are by the author.)

TABLES

Acknowledgments

When I am asked to identify myself professionally I usually say that I am both a folklorist and an ethnomusicologist. For fifteen years I taught both subjects at Tufts University, in a joint appointment in the English and music departments. This book is based more in the field of folklife than ethnomusicology. Yet I hope my colleagues in music will read it, for in my mind it represents me as both a folklorist and an ethnomusicologist. Readers hoping for a generative model of gospel hymnody, on the order of the model I derived for blues melodies in my first book (Titon 1977), will be disappointed. The fact is that blues provided a relatively fixed form, and the number of melodic families was small. Gospel hymnody, on the other hand, draws on the entire body of American folk and popular song, an enormous subject; and a generative model offering that melodic grammar is well beyond my scope. If the musical analysis is of a different sort here, it does not mean I have changed my mind about the worth of generative models in musical analysis; but I will leave the working-out of such a model for gospel hymnody to a computer and very patient programmers and data-enterers.

People in the field of music who read this book will recognize that it represents my view—scarcely a novel view—that music is a part of a system of communication involving speech, chant, and song; and that one way of coming to understand musical performances—the best way, I believe—is to see them as part of a system of performances, some musical, some nonmusical. For that reason I looked hard at all the performance genres; not only singing, but praying, preaching, teaching, and testifying. In so doing, I found that while the performers make distinctions among genres, they hold a special theory of language and communication that underlies and unites all genres (see Chapter 4). What began originally as a field study involving music and culture among a contemporary folk group expanded, first, to a study of speech as well as chant and song; and second, to a study of the historical and religious traditions of the performers. Finally, as the subject grew, I became interested in the people themselves, and in answering "why" questions rather than just the usual "what" and "how."

This led me to concentrate on the biography of the pastor (Chapter 9) and to ground the rest of the book on the interplay between language and life. I am not advocating this interdisciplinary approach for all studies; I simply put this book forth as an expression of one person's path trying to understand other people's paths that are at once very different from and yet, I increasingly realize, very much the same as my own.

This study took nearly ten years to research and write, chiefly because of the large amount of field documentation and transcription, the time depth I wanted, and the need to fashion a suitable methodology; but the long gestation period was also the result of much pleasurable reading and discussion with colleagues in fields I found relevant to this work—particularly folklore, social history, American studies, philosophy, linguistics, literary criticism, religious studies, cultural geography, and ethnomusicology.

At Tufts I spent several years teaching in the American Studies Program, and it was in that context that I was best able to explore the various disciplines that have contributed to this study. Faculty seminars and team-taught courses provided a congenial yet demanding atmosphere in which I was able to present, modify, and re-present much of the material in this book. In particular I am grateful to my colleagues in the team-taught course "History and Ecology in America": physicist Ronald K. Thornton, historian John Brooke, anthropologist Barbara Tedlock, and literary critic Jesper Rosenmeier. I am especially grateful to my long-time friend, cider-making partner, and colleague, Daniel C. Dennett, for his tough-minded criticism of my ideas as they have developed over the years. And I owe an unrepayable debt of thanks to my friend and colleague Maryanne Wolf, whose curiosity, sympathy, and kindly yet probing questions got me through many a tough part of this project.

My other intellectual debts are many, and I would like to identify a few people from whom I have learned a great deal and whose stamp seems to me all over this book. In Georgia, as a teenager, I read James Agee and Walker Evans' *Let Us Now Praise Famous Men*. It was on my parents' bookshelf and, bored with my school assignments, I picked it up and read it furiously at one sitting. At the time it turned me into a documentary photographer; I know now that it also influenced me to do my fieldwork among so-called "ordinary" people, whether blues singers or Baptists, and it taught me how to "see" detail in daily life.

Not long after beginning as an assistant professor I met the poet Kenneth Irby, a man who could converse about Charley Patton as easily as about Charles Olson, a man whose intense seriousness about what mattered most took him on an intellectual search that served (and still serves) as an example for me and countless others who have known him. I was fortunate enough to be his colleague for four years. It was through him that I learned about Carl Sauer, the "father" of cultural geography in America, and I read his works eagerly and came to see how important human ecology and cultural geography were for my own particular interests. And it was through him that I met the anthropologist Dennis Tedlock. For several years Dennis and I discussed our fieldwork and "texts" and problems of interpretation. At a time when few others were paying attention to the poetic features of the spoken and sung word, his gentle words on the documentation, re-presentation, and interpretation of oral poetry helped me stay my course.

I gladly give thanks to others: Albert Lord, who had me guest-lecture several times in his courses and who answered my many questions about his theories concerning oral poetry; Daniel Patterson, whose untiring work in southern culture and southern religion serves as an example to all of us; Elizabeth Ammons, through whom I learned much about feminist theory (and practice) and learned to see some of the implications of the thoroughly patriarchal society I describe in this book; Cameron Nickels, a close friend and fellow-musician when we were together in the American Studies graduate program at the University of Minnesota, who in 1971 first brought my attention to Brother John when he sent me a tape recording he had made of an afternoon's singing and preaching from a radio station not far from James Madison University, where he taught American literature; Kenneth George, my former student, who in 1975 was the first to interview Brother John, and with whom I shared fieldwork in the summer of 1977 and countless discussions over the meaning of what we were documenting; Thomas Rankin and Barry Dornfeld, also former students, and collaborators on the *Powerhouse for God* film project, who spent most of the fall of 1985 with me in the church community; William Clements, who generously shared with me his pioneering work in folk-cultural studies of American Protestantism at a time when almost no other folklorists were paying attention to this phenomenon; Steven Feld, whose continuing investigation of the relationship between fieldworker and informant promises to teach us terribly important things about ourselves; and Henry Glassie, whose work in folklore has always served as an inspiration to me, and whose *Passing the Time in Ballymenone* is as "complete" a work as anything I have ever read.

Others I must mention (they will know why) include Samuel Jenkins, David Perry, Alan Jabbour, Loyal Jones, Carl Fleischhauer, Bess Hawes, Andrew Woolf, Alan Lomax, Edward (Sandy) Ives, David Gow, Tom Bassett, Patricia Caldwell, Elaine Lawless, Paul Hester, Philip Rhodes, J. Roderick Moore, Vaughan Webb, Jeffrey Rubin, David and Melynn Byerly, Allen Smith, Dale Cockrell, Judith McCulloh, Charles Wolfe, David Whisnant, Clifford Clark, and Robert F. Berkhofer, Jr. Statistician Frank Wolf of Carleton College was kind enough to spend several hours consulting with me on the food energy production and consumption formula in Chapter 2. Charles Perdue and Nancy Martin-Perdue, who are undertaking a mammoth research project on families on the other (eastern) side of the Blue

Ridge, helped me get started with the population census, marriage books, will books, deed books, and other keys to the history of the nineteenth-century ancestors of the present-day church members, and they alerted me to the U.S. Census of Agriculture's household-by-household farm inventories.

I am grateful to Luther Miller, County Clerk of Page County, Virginia, for his help during the many visits I made to the courthouse. Charles Anibal of the Shenandoah National Park and local historian Dorothy Noble Smith helped me research the oral histories and material culture of the people who lived on what is now park land. John Waybright, editor of *The Page News and Courier,* took a kind interest in this project and showed me nineteenth-century local newspapers. I am grateful to the staffs at the National Archives, the Virginia State Library in Richmond, and several county courthouses in Virginia, where I did research about the nineteenth-century ancestors of the people in this book.

At various times during the research and writing of this book I was supported by grants and fellowships from the National Endowment for the Arts, the National Endowment for the Humanities, the Virginia Council for the Humanities, and the Howard Foundation; I am grateful also to Tufts University for paid and unpaid leave to work on this project, and to Brown University for a grant to pay for printing my photographs and drawing the maps.

Finally, I am immensely grateful to Brother John Sherfey and his family, and to all the members of the Fellowship Independent Baptist Church of Stanley, Virginia, the subjects of this book, who willingly and trustingly gave of their time and friendship, and who taught me so much about them and about myself.

J.T.T.

December 1985

NOTE: A documentary 2-LP record, *Powerhouse for God,* features selections from the 1977 and 1978 field tape recordings for this project. It may be purchased from the publisher, University of North Carolina Press, Box 2288, Chapel Hill, North Carolina 27514.

A 1-hour color documentary film, *Powerhouse for God,* by Barry Dornfeld, Thomas Rankin, and Jeff Todd Titon, shot in 1985 and 1986, is available in film and videotape formats. For information, write to Jeff Todd Titon, Department of Music, Brown University, Providence, Rhode Island 02912.

POWERHOUSE FOR GOD

"There's power in the word, see. And if people believe that, and live that, you can have a power-house for God. But until they believe it, then it's nothing at all; it's just like a mere book."

—Brother John Sherfey

Jeff Titon and Brother John Sherfey. Photo by Thomas Rankin.

Prologue

We made our way into the fried chicken restaurant on a hot July afternoon in 1977: a dozen Sherfeys, four Hurts, three folklorists. Women and children sat at three center booths while Brother John Sherfey, Brother Belvin Hurt, Carl Fleischhauer, Ken George, and I squeezed into a window booth. We could look out and see the rest of the Luray, Virginia, shopping center.

Carl had come to visit. He'd heard our recordings of Brother John's powerful singing and preaching and, as media specialist at the American Folklife Center at the Library of Congress, he'd loaned us a professional tape recorder for our summer's project documenting songs, sermons, prayers, testimonies, and life histories from Brother John and his congregation. This in-depth study of one church was part of a larger survey of American religious folklife at the grass-roots level that I had begun almost a decade earlier. Of the hundreds of preachers and congregations I had heard, Brother John's friendly sincerity, intensity, and old-fashioned singing and preaching impressed me the most.

Giving the waitress a large order, Brother John announced that he was hungry. "The only thing I'd rather do than eat is preach," he said, "and you can tell by looking at me that I love to eat." At six feet and 240 pounds, Brother John might have been taken for a retired football lineman, perhaps an offensive guard. His eyes and hair were gray, and his direct gaze inspired confidence. He did not stare you down but met your glance with a clear and friendly look. Sister Ethel Painter came over and said John looked like he could wrestle a lion. But he seemed shy near the man from Washington.

Sensing his shyness, Carl spoke about the beauty of the Blue Ridge, contrasting it with crowded Washington. He asked about the cost of land and houses near Luray, adding that the price of rental housing in Washington was more than most people could easily afford. Brother John agreed, saying he rented an apartment for his family in Falls Church, Virginia, the Washington suburb where they lived. He commuted four hours round-trip to pastor his Blue Ridge Mountain church on weekends.

"Now, is the place you work in Falls Church?" Carl asked.

"No, it's in Rockville. Rockville, Maryland," Brother John said.

"What kind of place is it?" Carl went on. "Is it a factory?"

"No, it's an oil company."

"Oil company?"

"Mm-hmm. Alcoa Oil Company. We deliver fuel oil, gasoline, furnace oil, diesel fuel. Course I don't. I work on the trucks. Or try to. They work on me more'n I work on them."

Carl laughed. The chicken had come, and everybody was passing around the extra orders of coleslaw and mashed potatoes. "Well, machinery is exasperating sometimes," said Carl.

I looked over at Ken and he smiled. The tape recorder Carl had loaned us for the summer was giving us trouble, and part of the reason Carl had come down was to exchange the troublesome recorder for a new one. We were using a machine worth $5,000 that cost me $500 to insure, and wishing we had something a little less delicate. Luckily, I'd brought a couple of less-expensive, back-up recorders. One was lying on the table now, recording the conversation.

"I, ah, that's a source of frustration I guess always, trying to get machines to stay working," Carl remarked.

"Yeah, I know what you mean. I have a terrible time with them things sometime," John said.

"If there are smaller devils, you know, little bitty ones that get around and trouble things I'm pretty sure they can be found in machines," said Carl. "Just annoyances."

"They's something all the time to keep you tore up, you know," John replied. "What's so funny, though, is you can work and work and work and try to get a nut on a bolt or, you know, a lot of places that are hard to get to, and I have big hands anyway, you know, and I'll worry with it until finally at last it's just a-gittin' to me and I'll just lay it down, walk off and leave it."

"That's right," said Brother Belvin.

"Go on somewhere and drink me a cup of coffee and mess around a little while, and have a little talk with the Lord, and come back, pick that nut up, you know, and reach there and it goes in."

"I know what you mean," Belvin said.

"I've done that so many times," John continued. "I was telling that over in church here awhile back. That boy of mine just laughed. He thought that was the funniest thing he ever heard, you know? Somebody done something like that!"

"I've done that many times," Belvin said. "Yes sir, that'll work."

John decided to go ahead and tell the story now. "Yes, well, the reason was that I was working, and every time I'd start to put the wrench on something I'd drop it, you know?" He paused. "It kept up a little. Finally at last I just picked my tools up, I carried them over, and I laid them in my toolbox. Locked the toolbox. Washed and cleaned up and went to the car and went down to punch out. The boss said, 'You're leaving?' I said, 'Yep, I'm taking off.' I said, 'Everything I start to do goes wrong. I'm gonna wait till tomorrow.' He said, 'I don't blame you.'"

"Hunh!" exclaimed Belvin.

"I went on home. Went back the next morning and everything just fell right in place," he wound up, chuckling. "Well, you get tired, you know," he said.

"That's right," I said. While Carl and John continued their conversation, I thought about the story John had told.

It was a good story, a funny story, but it was more than that. John was trying to tell Carl the sort of person he was. Carl had asked him what kind of work he did when he wasn't preaching. We—or he—had told Carl he wasn't a full-time preacher. John could have simply said, "I'm a mechanic. I work on oil trucks for a company in Rockville, Maryland." Instead, he told a revealing story. To him the story must have been more important, and interesting, than a mere answer to a question. The story showed that he did not identify himself as a mechanic, but as a man with a certain attitude toward mechanical work. The difference is crucial.

After all, John had introduced himself as someone who had a hard time with his job. The trucks "work on me more'n I work on them," he began diffidently. But in the story he showed how he got the better of his frustrations, and the truck too. Not only that, but he got a half-day vacation, and had his boss sanction it.

I thought about the five of us sitting there. I had wondered how Carl was going to take to John. Probably John had wondered as well. Here was a man from Washington, connected with the Library of Congress, come all the way from the nation's capital to see a country preacher. Did he want to be saved? Had the Lord led him here? It was important that Carl know who John was. He wasn't just a preacher; he wasn't just a mechanic. He was a man with a view of himself and a view of life. So there we sat, the five of us, three folklorists outnumbering two Baptists, making small talk after the worship service, eating lunch, hoping to agree with one another.

John's story gave us that chance. Carl encouraged him to begin, agreeing that machinery was exasperating. Belvin kept seconding John's statements as he went along. Belvin is a farmer as well as a sometime preacher and knows the frustrations of keeping machines in repair. And, as a man of God, he could support John's claim that going off to "have a little talk with the Lord"—to pray—helps a man work calmly and confidently. Ken and I spoke little, but we listened hard and nodded in agreement. This was a satisfying picture of the man we'd decided to spend our time with that summer of 1977.

John had identified himself as a worker, not a boss. Yet despite that subservient position, with God's help he could be happy. More, he could be a

victor, not a working-class victim. The way he told it, he turned his boss
from potential obstacle into sympathetic coworker. Whether that part of
the story is actually true doesn't make much difference. Even if it is John's
wishful thinking embellishing the story a bit, it reveals the way he wants
to see himself. He sees himself triumphing over trucks, bosses, frustrations, and time. He punches out on the time clock and steps off the "time
is money" treadmill. He doesn't agree with that proverb. He won't be a cog
in a machine at the expense of the quality of his working life. He knows
the machine won't be efficient anyway unless he's treated decently and
respected as a man, not just a mechanic. He uses the word *time* on four
occasions in the conversation.

Here I was, a scholar studying religious language, concentrating on its
use in worship, when I noticed that John's language, in what seemed a
very ordinary situation, had established and maintained (during our lun-
cheon conversation) a kind of community among us. In other words, while
John's story told us what sort of person he thought he was, it also put us
into a face-to-face relationship as sympathetic friends. This is quite an ac-
complishment for language, and one of the things it does best: define and
establish identities and communities. Religious language, I am convinced,
does the same.

Introduction

This book belongs to a small but growing number of interpretative works in American culture that are based in the field of folklife. Although the study of folklife has a long history in Europe, particularly in Scandinavia, it has come into prominence in the United States only in the past twenty years. British folklorist J. Geraint Jenkins writes that folklife's chief aim "is to study ordinary people. . . . to record details of their life, their skills, their homes, their fields, their customs, their speech, and their leisure activities. The student of folklife searches for the key to the world of ordinary people; he attempts to throw light on their ill-documented day-to-day life. . . . Folklife is therefore an holistic approach to the study of an organic community" (Jenkins 1972:498). Its main American proponent, Don Yoder, defines folklife as "a newer holistic approach that analyzes traditional cultural elements in a complex society—whether these elements are defined as folk, ethnic, regional, rural, urban, or sectarian—viewing them in the context of that larger unifying society and culture of which all subgroups and traditions are functioning parts. It can focus upon the individual, the group, single cultural traits or complexes, or the culture as a whole" (Yoder 1976:13).

In calling folklife a "newer holistic approach" Yoder contrasts it with the text-centered approach of folklore. Students of folklife do examine texts—tales, legends, beliefs, ballads, barns, etc., but that is not the ultimate orientation; rather, folklife is aimed, in the words of Richard Weiss, at "the study of the interrelationships between the folk and folk-culture, in so far as they are determined by community and tradition" (quoted in Yoder 1976:4). Folklife, in other words, involves the study of people as well as the collection and analysis of texts. No other field of study is so well situated at the locus of my interest: that is, at the meeting place between traditional ways of life and artfully performed language.

The focus of this book is on one such "key to the world of ordinary people": religious thought and behavior. More specifically, my focus is on language in the practice of religion—song, prayer, preaching, teaching, and testimony—and its place in the lives of a Baptist folk group in Virginia's northern Blue Ridge Mountains. On reflection, these ordinary people turn out to be not so ordinary after all, for they have sought and found a solution to the problem of meaning in life. The book does not advocate their particular religion, but I must admit I find much to admire in their efforts to preserve old values and ways of life, to act on the basis of those values and create a community for good, and in so doing to resist certain aspects of modernization. The book is based on fieldwork conducted from 1975 through 1985 by Kenneth M. George and myself. It contains a great many verbatim texts, examples of this largely spontaneous religious language, set in the context of their use, and illuminated by the members of the group's statements about it: how they intend it, how they interpret it, and how it affects them. Alongside their interpretations and exegeses, there is mine: throughout the book I am concerned with the way religious language helps them live their lives and understand who they are.

The members of the Fellowship Independent Baptist Church, near Stanley, Virginia, call themselves old-fashioned, meaning that they believe they practice the religion of their mountain-farming forefathers. I selected this church for several reasons, but the three most important are that they represent a major strain in Appalachian religion, that they are outstanding performers of religious language, and that they are able to articulate clearly and eloquently their beliefs about language and behavior. Their doctrine falls squarely within what Samuel S. Hill, Jr., has termed "popular southern Protestantism," the dominant regional religion in the South from about 1800 to the present, which traces its beliefs, practices, and emphasis to fundamentalism, frontier revivalism, and, ultimately, the radical wing of the sixteenth-century continental and the seventeenth-century English Protestant reformations (Hill 1967 : 23–31, 137). The heart of the doctrine is that one becomes a Christian not through gradual maturation and intellectual enlightenment, but by choosing to yield to God and experiencing a new birth, suddenly and totally. Conversion begins with an agonizing spiritual crisis, called conviction, during which one feels condemned to hell for one's wicked deeds and sinful nature. The new birth results from sincere repentance and a spoken prayer to Jesus as Savior for forgiveness.

Certain beliefs of the members of the congregation of the Fellowship Independent Baptist Church, and of many other folk Protestant congregations (see Chapter 3 for a discussion of the difference between "folk" and "established" religion), have special consequences for language. Except for song, almost all of their language during worship is spontaneous. The church members say it is led by the Holy Spirit and that at moments of particular intensity it is understood as the direct utterance of the Lord. Such moments are apparent even to an outsider because the words become louder, faster, and shift from speech to chant. Language led by the

Spirit is said to have the power to change things. During worship the church becomes, in the words of the pastor, Brother John Sherfey, a "power-house for God."

By focusing on language, tradition, and meaning, I hope to offer a corrective to the dominant sociological and historical view of Appalachia as a backward and deviant culture of poverty whose intense religious practices express disorganization and alienation in the face of modern life. In this view, which derives from the writings of Marx and Durkheim, Appalachian mountain religion is seen as a compensation for material poverty (see Photiadis 1978). Desiring but unable to realize the American dream of success, wealth, and happiness, the Appalachian poor are said to have created a delusion—an emotionally charged, intellectually impoverished, highly demonstrative spiritual realm—where they assert power denied to them in the economic sphere. But in my view they are better understood as adapting inherited traditions, not creating pathetic delusions.

I believe that much within twentieth-century Appalachian religion stems from a nineteenth-century agrarian folklife tradition emphasizing diversity, versatility, and dependence—on family, friends, neighbors, and God. Moreover, after research into the nineteenth-century economy and ecology of mountain farming in the northern Blue Ridge, I am convinced that Appalachian poverty, far from being rooted in the region since settlement, is a newer development belonging mainly to the twentieth century. The mountain folk were not so much "left behind" by the modern industrial state as victimized by it.

The old-fashioned Baptists I have come to know reject much of the modern world, but alienation does not describe their situation. They do not think of themselves as adrift or cut off. Nor do I. Neither confused nor disorganized, their religious folk culture is a deliberate, intentional, patterned, and subtle adaptation to the modern world. Through language and action they establish, maintain, modify, dissolve, and re-form communities—the family, the congregation, the true church everywhere. And through language they continually assert their identity as members of these communities. Of course, they have difficulties. But if they are alienated, it is because they are human, not because they are different.

Folklife: Affect, Performance, Community, Memory

Most definitions of folklore and folklife begin by identifying folk genres (folktale, folksong, folk beliefs, folk crafts, folk architecture, etc.). Individual items of folklore—this story, that song—exist in different versions, the result of variation over time and place. Texts, in other words, are variable rather than fixed. As Charles Seeger remarked, we can locate Beethoven's *Fifth Symphony* in its score, but we cannot locate "Barbara Allen" in any single text—it exists as several variants (Seeger 1950:828). Barre Toelken, whose definition of folklore draws on recent work and has been influential in the field, stresses the dynamic, or innovative aspects of variation within folk tradition, and the informality of folk performance—it is usually face-to-face, oral, and gestural, rather than technical, bureaucratic, or school-based (Toelken 1979:28–29). The folk are regarded today as not just the rural and old-fashioned, but any group—they can be urban, well-educated, and modern—who share folklore.

To these generally accepted notions I add Henry Glassie's premise that folklife centers on *affect,* the power to move people (1982:xvi; see also Armstrong 1971). Affect is at the center of the barn, the ballad, the folktale, the religious rite—the various and sundry activities folklorists study. Affect cuts across them all, is the common element. It binds the folk to the lore even as it brings the folklorist to both the folk and the lore.

Affect is brought into being by *performance* (Jansen 1957; see also Hymes 1974; 1981; and Bauman 1984). Songs and prayers, for example, are performed, and the concept of performance carries implications worth exploring. First, a performance is intentional. The people who perform songs, prayers, sermons, and testimonies intend something by those performances. They intend to move people, and to do so in specific ways. Hymns are performed with the intention to give assurance to the converted and to bring the unconverted to repentance, for example.

Second, a performance is rule-governed. In other words, certain rules or principles operate in any performance to guide exactly how it goes along. When members of the Fellowship Independent Baptist Church pray in the worship service, they do so out loud. One of the rules (or principles), then, is that one prays aloud. Sometimes, performers can articulate the rules and give reasons for them. I asked Brother Jesse Comer about praying aloud. He said, "A spoken prayer is saying something openly that you're not ashamed of, that the whole world would hear you. I'm not saying that the man . . . that is praying silently is not doing what the Lord is leading him to do. But I believe that if he or she would do it openly, they would get a greater blessing out of it by far" (Comer interview, 1977, p. 12). By "blessing" he means the intensely felt presence of the indwelling Spirit, something that often produces tears or shouts—signs, to be sure, of affect. One performs to affect oneself as well as others. More rules concerning prayers have to do with the proper subject matter, how one takes up a reverent posture, and the proper behavior afterward: at moments of great intensity, men hug men, one of the few times that male touching is encouraged in this culture. Performance is organized, coherent, and purposeful. In order to be that way it must proceed from a set of rules or principles. The rules are not written in a constitution, of course; they are tacitly understood by the performers, and they are learned by imitation. The church members do not find out how to pray in a revelation. They stress that the newly converted Christian must be taught and learn like a new-born baby. Of course, he or she may well have grown up going to church and have seen and heard how it is done, and thereby have a head start. The rules and principles, then, are absorbed through practice and, at times, experiment.

Third, performance is not only intentional and rule-governed; it is also interpreted. Performers interpret their performance as they go along; they understand what goes on, and their continuing performance is based in part upon their interpretation. Sharing knowledge and understanding, performers (and audience, if separate) determine the meaning and significance of the performance. Interpretation also involves evaluation—how effective is the performance? Evaluation frequently feeds back into performance: a poor one may be improved or even broken off.

Last, performance is keyed or marked. People who perform call attention to it as performance. "Now, church, we're going to pray" sets the event off from the current state of affairs. Beginnings and endings ("Amen") of performances are marked, and middles, too: extraordinary tones of voice, stylized movements, intent concentration, and so forth.

In Figure 1, a model for folklife studies, I have situated affect within performance within community within memory by making concentric circles. My intention in doing so (the intention of *this* performance) is to move the reader toward a holistic understanding of folklife and ethnomusicology as fields of inquiry. Performance is situated within a *community*, what folklorists call a folk group: those people who share affective performance and interpretation. The Fellowship Independent Baptist Church is such a folk group. A family is a folk group. Basketball players comprise a folk group. And so on. The performances shared by folk groups have certain characteristics that make them folklore. For one thing, the communication is face-to-face; personal presence is very important because communication is multileveled, not just verbal. One person sitting and watching something on television does not comprise a folk group; but a few people listening to a record and interacting over that record form a small, face-to-face community so long as they share an aesthetic and interpretative framework. Second, because of the shared framework and personal presence, there is a certain informality, and this is missing in encounters with people who are differently attuned.

Finally, affective performance in a community is situated in *memory*. I do not mean a collective or folk memory, but the memories of persons in the community. When memory is made public and shared it can become community history—from the inside, of course. Brother John, pastor of the Fellowship Independent Baptist Church, tells stories from the pulpit about his early life, thus creating a public figure, an example, himself—as his memory would have it. Thus performed, these stories affect the congregation, reside in their memories, and stand as true examples of divine providence: God's working through history on the level of individual lives—the pastor's and their own.

Then there is another kind of history, the history of traditions, not the history that rises from stories. Performance changes, rules change, interpretation changes over time, affected by changes in culture and society, in personal fortunes and individual aspirations. And viewed from outside the community, this community, the folk group, is in history, much as it may view itself, as some religious groups do, as apart from the world. The people in the folk group are born and they die. They take part in the social, political, economic institutions and processes that surround them, and they are affected by these, too. They are people of history, and history contributes tradition. These intentions, these rules, these interpretations of performance themselves have a history; they are not eternal but have changed through time. Moreover, they change (or remain the same) in response to the community's perception of history. Much of the Fellowship Independent Baptist Church's religious folklife is a response and reaction to history: not only their perception of the current state of the world, but their mind-set as descendants of mountain farmers with a particular history in this section of the Blue Ridge.

The Interpretative Dialogues

Outside of this, interacting with, apprehending, recording, transcribing, interpreting, and presenting (to colleagues, students, and the public at large) the folklife stands the folklorist. He or she is (I am) engaged in a two-way dialogue: with the members of the church on the one hand, and with the readers on the other. I am at once a participant-observer, translator, presenter, and interpreter. I select and present the church members' texts and interpretations, and then I interpret these. This dialogical hermeneutic is a performance in itself, intended not only to inform but also to move the reader; yet the dialogical hermeneutic is difficult and unfamiliar.

If I thought my task simply involved collecting examples of language in religious practice, and statements about such language, then writing these down, presenting them, and interpreting them, I would happily subject my texts to the various strategies of criticism designed for the written word, whether structural, post-structural, deconstructional, hermeneutical, semiotic—whatever seemed most promising. But the spoken (and chanted and sung) word, particularly in the context of ritual, constitutes, as critics as different as Jacques Derrida and Paul Ricoeur proclaim, a different kind of event from the act of writing. It is a different kind of performance, and operates by different rules (Ricoeur 1976:25–44; see also Norris 1982:24–41). Let me reiterate that the performed word is interpreted by performer and audience right in the midst of performance. In

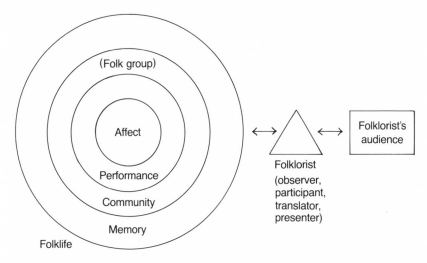

Figure 1. A model for folklife studies.

fact, much of the language in religious practice at the Fellowship Independent Baptist Church *is interpretative itself,* interpreting texts. Sunday school, for example, and sermons are at once performances and interpretations of the Bible. Testimonies interpret the events of daily life. What is more, certain other language spoken in the church is understood as interpretation of performance, as when Brother John tells the congregation what he thinks the words of a hymn just sung mean.

What to do with all this language and interpretation? Recording and transcribing texts is a necessary step; the words must be caught for study (see Tedlock 1983:4–11). In fact, this book contains a great many texts, and there are two good reasons for that. Until the late 1960s, when they became preoccupied with theory, folklorists published a much higher percentage of texts in their work. Certainly I hope this book will be taken as a contribution to the current discussions of theory in folklore and folklife. But very few accurate texts of this nature have been published before, and most of those that have been published have been wrenched from their religious context. We know that much in this language derives from practice in the nineteenth century and even earlier, but we have very few trustworthy texts for comparison. Furthermore, we know from the history of folklore as a discipline that the usefulness of accurate texts outlives the theoretical framework in which they are presented. So this work also looks forward to the future in the way that the field collections of ballad and folksong did when they were published more than a half-century ago.

In this book, everything in quotation marks attributed to a church member is a verbatim transcription from field tape recordings. All texts of hymns, prayers, sermons, testimonies, and conversion narratives are also my verbatim transcriptions. Most transcriptions are in conventional prose, some are in music notation, and others are in ethnopoetic transcription following a system derived from Dennis Tedlock and adapted by Ken George and myself (Titon 1976b; Titon and George 1977). Duplicates of the field tapes—some 200 hours of worship services, hymn sings, prayer meetings, religious radio broadcasts, interviews and conversations—are on deposit in the Library of Congress Archive of Folk Culture, and in the University of North Carolina Folklore Archives. Excerpts may be heard on this book's companion record album, *Powerhouse for God*, published by and available from the University of North Carolina Press. A documentary film/videotape is available; for information, write to Jeff Todd Titon, Department of Music, Brown University, Providence, Rhode Island 02912.

The task of interpretation involves understanding the significance and meaning of the texts in the context of their performance and in the context of the wider world. Ordinary procedures of literary criticism will not do. Literary critics assume that meaning is revealed to the intelligent reader in an encounter with the written text. Properly trained and familiar with the conventions of the text at hand, the critic derives a sensible interpretation. For written literature this is well and good. But the meaning of language performed orally in a folk group is often so context-bound that attempts to work primarily from the transcribed texts are misguided. In other words, in the church context, with a particular group of worshipers, meaning is personal and even eccentric. The text of a song, for example, may reveal a certain meaning, but in performance it may have quite a different meaning. The text may be associated with a departed loved one, for instance, and the church members will locate its meaning there rather than in its words. Or a performance may signify in bringing a blessing (tears, shouts) to a person singing or praying, quite apart from the words that are uttered and their sensible "meaning." For the folklorist or ethnomusicologist, the beginning of understanding involves *being there*, listening to interpretative remarks made by the performers, and moreover eliciting interpretative statements from them in conversation or dialogue. Working from the text alone is misleading.

Over against dialogue, Tedlock (1983:321–38) identifies a misguided, "analogical"[1] interpretative tradition, in which the anthropologist (read folklorist), after collecting these performed texts and native interpretations, simply replaces them with his or her own claims about what is "really" happening. The folklorist also claims, implicitly, to "know more" than the folk; he or she has had a scientific education and can see their behavior "objectively." Another analogical tradition is the anthropologist's

1. Tedlock means single-voiced, but when I use the term in this book I mean analogy-based, as in "analogical thinking."

confessional, a genre characterized by autobiographical writing on anxieties, tribulations, and mistakes while doing fieldwork. Both are analogical because they are written in one voice: the anthropologist's. These analogical traditions, Tedlock believes—and I agree—are mistaken because, among other things, they are not faithful to the phenomenon of understanding as it occurs; namely, in the dialogue between the folklorist and the folk, the "other." Nor are they faithful to the constant reinterpretation that occurs as the folklorist (and the other, be it said) "learns more" while time passes and one thinks about what one has seen and heard. Tedlock calls for a "dialogical" method of interpretation in which the dialogue is carried from the field to the scholar's published account. "The anthropological dialogue creates a world," he writes, "or an understanding of the *differences between* two worlds, that exists between persons who were indeterminately far apart, in all sorts of different ways, when they started out on their conversation" (ibid.: 323; italics in original). This is the world, the intersubjective reality, that the fieldworker comes to know; and this is the only world one can truly reconstruct in one's interpretative writings—if one comes to any understanding at all.

Hermeneutic phenomenology, then, seems to me to be the best available framework, as today's folklorist contemplates the affective performance of folklore within a community within memory and history. But to my knowledge no folklorist or ethnomusicologist has attempted an interpretative work from this standpoint. There are no rules—at least, not yet. But there might well be some conventions. In these published accounts, the "folk" will be allowed to speak for themselves, and they will speak—as they do—to each other *and* to the folklorist; that is, their words will be reported as close to the original as possible. The "folk" texts and the folk interpretations of texts will be presented as one part of the dialogue. The folklorist takes up the other side of the dialogue, and will be presented in dialogue with the folk: that is, his or her questions and responses and interpretations in performance will be presented as well. This hermeneutic practice has an additional implication, based on the principle of the hermeneutic circle: the folklorist keeps returning to the "folk" *where they are* to continue the dialogue. That is, one goes back to visit, not to do "follow-up fieldwork" and verify conclusions, but to continue the dialogue, knowing that the conclusions will never be conclusive.

And then, as I wrote above, there is yet another dialogue, and this is between the scholar and his or her colleagues, students, and the interested public. Here is another set of rules and conventions; but here, after all, the scholar has had education, training, and experience, and should feel on surer ground.

I believe that the folklorist's ultimate object of study is folk "art" (with art understood as the art of living, the shaping, forming, designing that people give to their daily lives). Folk art has no meaningful existence apart

from a human community with a shared set of traditions, aesthetic preferences, and worldview. Folk art ultimately resides not in objects or song or
story, nor in the process of their coming into being, but in the mind-set
that finds expression in these particular activities and, finally, in the well-
lived traditional life.

Language and Life

I center this book on language and life, the junction between how people
communicate who they are and how they live, all in the richly expressive
context of a highly articulated ideology: religion. In my mind, the symbolic
center is the congregation gathered in church for Sunday worship: speaking, chanting, singing. The worship service is the core. Radiating from
and into it are language and life (Figure 2). Language radiates along two
vectors, in the upper half of the figure. First, language about worship and
belief: here, the articulated intention, affect, and interpretation of language in religious practice is a metalanguage, or a language about language. Second, another metalanguage: language about life—that is, the
church members' stories and conversations about their lives and others'.
In the lower half of the figure, ways of life radiate along two vectors. First
is the pattern of worship and belief proper: this congregation as situated in
a historical religious context. Second is the pattern of these people's lives
overall: this congregation as situated in a historical and geographic context; that is, the pattern inscribed on the landscape, in their particular
place (region, locale, in fact an area comprising not much more than five
mountain "hollows" and twenty square miles in southeastern Page County,
Virginia).

I have organized the chapters in this book to follow from the radiant core
of the worship service as the juncture of language and life, since this core
forms the central object of inquiry: just what (if anything) takes place, is
transacted, communicated, signified, negotiated, mediated, accomplished
during this ritual? The center of the book, then, takes up the actual language in the religious practice of the worship service, first in general
(Chapter 4), then examining texts and beliefs about texts, organized according to genre: song (Chapter 5), prayer (Chapter 6), and teaching and
preaching (Chapter 7). Prior to that I discuss the history and cultural geography of the community (Chapter 2) and place their way of worship
within the historical traditions of southern folk Protestantism (Chapter 3).
After the center, in Chapters 8 and 9, I explore the members' reflective
language about their lives—Chapter 8 on conversion and testimony, and
Chapter 9 on the pastor's life story (which may be heard as Side D of the
record *Powerhouse for God*)—to examine how language makes sense of
experience and gains, for these people, through continual practice, a confirmation of their identity. Finally, because language establishes commu-

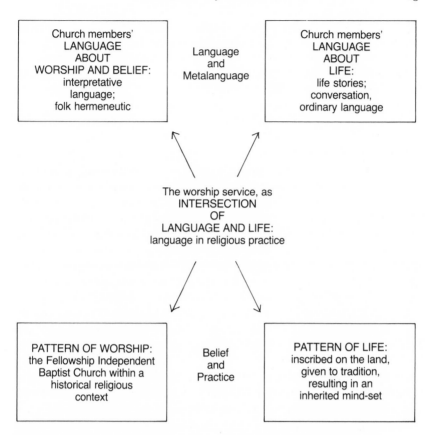

Figure 2. The worship service at the intersection of language and life.

nity as well, I frame the book with a first chapter that describes their homecoming worship service and an epilogue that offers a secular counterpart, the annual homecoming parade held in the nearby town of Stanley.

The Fieldwork of Documentation

When I presented parts of this book as work in progress at folklore and ethnomusicology conferences over the past several years, other scholars, many doing their own fieldwork with religious groups, asked me how the people in the church community I worked with reacted to me. The question arose often, and I learned that those who were contemplating or already engaged in fieldwork with religious folk groups anticipated problems in the field or were having them. I think I was most fortunate in choosing to work with a pastor whose acceptance of our documentary project—that is, mine and Ken George's and, be it said, the church members'—was based on his firm belief that his life should be publicly accessible because he is a living witness for God. In any event, although Ken and I had a few difficult moments during the fieldwork, and although some of the members of the congregation were skeptical of our motives, for almost all of our time in the church community we enjoyed their full cooperation; so much so, in fact, that those few difficult times came as a shock.

Ken and I had both visited Brother John, spoken with him at home, and attended services at the church prior to my writing him early in 1977 to ask his permission for us to come spend the summer with them. In my letter I stated that the purpose of our visit was documentation, and that we hoped he would permit us to tape-record, videotape, and photograph their worship services. I said that the American Folklife Center of the Library of Congress had loaned us a high-quality tape recorder for the documentation, and that copies of the tapes would go into the Library of Congress and the University of North Carolina Folklore Archives, and that we would also give a set of the tapes to the church to use as they saw fit.

Brother John read the letter in church and discussed it with the members, many of whom had met Ken and me on our previous visits. He said he did not understand why Ken and I and the Library of Congress would be interested in a country preacher and church, but he felt that since we were interested in documenting the services, and since he was commanded by God to witness for his beliefs to anyone who would listen, he thought the documentation would be a wonderful work in helping to spread the gospel. The members agreed with Brother John and invited us to begin the project whenever we wished.

When we came into their community I presented myself as a college professor and Ken presented himself as a graduate student. Documentation was part of our scholarly work. It was possible, I told Brother John, that a record album might be released offering highlights from the summer's recordings, but I did not want to give him false hope. Privately I was a little more optimistic, and when a year later I began negotiating with the University of North Carolina Press for the release of the *Powerhouse for God* record album, I kept Brother John up to date as it moved through its various stages. (After I selected the recordings and wrote the notes for the booklet I sent him a copy for corrections and approval. The only correction he wanted made was an indication that during a sermon he had incorrectly referenced a Bible verse. He wanted the correct verse indicated as well, and it was.) I said that aside from the tapes which would be available to the public at the Library of Congress and the University of North Carolina at Chapel Hill, I would try to write and have published a book about the church; and when, later in the summer, I received a letter from an editor at the University of Texas Press, asking me (as a recent fellowship recipient) if I anticipated a book coming from my project, I told Brother

John about the letter and said I had replied and stated that I hoped this book would result. And when Texas gave me an advance contract for the book in the spring of 1978 after I had sent them a proposal along with what one editor referred to as "a steamer trunk" of documentation— mostly prose and ethnopoetic transcriptions of prayers, sermons, testimony, life histories, and so forth—I told Brother John that I had a publisher interested in the book if only I could write it.

My point is that Ken and I were deliberately conservative, determining that documentation was our chief purpose, that publication might or might not result, and that scholarly analysis was a more distant goal. Ken told Brother John he was writing his M.A. thesis based on this field documentation project, and when he finished it he sent Brother John a copy, which he read (George 1978). We adopted this careful, conservative attitude partly because we knew the church members were scrutinizing us, but chiefly because we wanted to be honest in our dealings with them. Moreover, we believed that high-quality documentation of this eloquent but (to the scholarly world) little-known language in religious practice would make a contribution to knowledge in and of itself. Many times when researching the scholarly literature on religion I had become frustrated because of the lack of verbatim (or even paraphrased) transcriptions. Would that there had been more (some, even) documentation and less explanation.

Most important, we had an advocate in Brother John, and he continually reminded the visitors and congregation why we were there and what we were doing. Of course with our microphones, cables, tape recorders, cameras, and videotape portapak mounted on its tripod near the front of the sanctuary we were impossible to ignore. I do not want to give the impression that every pastor and church I have done fieldwork with has welcomed me with gracious gratitude. A few were suspicious, and in one or two services I felt uncomfortable. But I would not have chosen Brother John and his congregation had I not felt at ease with them. And by the time I chose them I had already done survey fieldwork in religious folklife for eight years, attending services and talking to people about their lives and beliefs in Minnesota, Michigan, Indiana, Massachusetts, Maine, Virginia, and Georgia.

And yet despite this preparatory period I was still naïve about the congregation's reaction to us during the eight consecutive weeks we were there in the summer of 1977. If anybody had asked me about it I would have said the congregation accepted us at face value and agreed with Brother John that they should be pleased to witness publicly for their beliefs. True, one or two people had left the congregation just before we arrived. Word had gotten to us about this, and, worried, we asked Brother John, who told us not to take it seriously. They were looking for an excuse to leave and found it, he said. One of them thought he would be hypnotized by the camera, John said, chuckling. We agreed that was pretty strange and, although it troubled us to think we had caused a couple of people to leave, we kept on.

I failed to give enough thought to the likelihood that the members of the congregation would talk about us among themselves even after going along with our wishes. I look back over my field notebooks for signs of awareness and find almost nothing. An entry dated June 26 reads, "All extremely friendly." June 28, after attending a prayer meeting: "They were nervous about the recorder during the singing. As there were only 8 (& me) present I was conspicuous." They found out I played guitar and asked me to accompany their singing, but I refused, not wanting to intrude myself into what I was documenting.

Besides the worship services we wanted to document the life histories and religious beliefs of the church members. We had already found conversations with Brother John about his life and beliefs extremely interesting, not only in themselves but as a gloss on the church rituals. I would ask him to interpret the purpose and meaning of the various worship activities—song, prayer, testimony, and so forth—and he was most articulate in doing so. We told him we would like to talk with other church members, and he suggested I stand up during the testimony period and invite members of the congregation to talk with us. I did that on July 3, and Brother John spoke immediately afterward, saying how much he had enjoyed talking to us, and encouraging others to do so. After services we got the addresses of about ten volunteer families—perhaps half the congregation—and accepted Brother Rastus Lam's invitation to see him at his home in the middle of the week.

We were totally unprepared, then, for what happened when we went to Brother Vernie and Sister Hattie Meadows' home on July 15. Sister Hattie declined to speak with us, and Brother Vernie was not very talkative; he volunteered little and was cautious, speaking only in answer to questions. When we were through, Sister Hattie emerged and the two of them said, "Now do you mind if we ask you some questions?" "Go right ahead," we said.

"Are you Moonies?" she asked. Once our surprise had worn off, we said we were not Moonies. Nor were we Communists, nor had we come as wolves in sheeps' clothing to change or convert them to our way of life. We reaffirmed our purposes, and they believed us. We then asked how widespread this doubt was. Sister Hattie said some people had been wondering, and a few were so suspicious of us they stopped attending. She added that it was only a few, and that they did not attend regularly. These were the ones who had left the congregation before we began the project. Still, it was a setback for us to be asked those questions, and it made us realize that no matter how clear we were about why we were there, they would speculate about our motives. And God's: some felt that God had led us there for a mysterious purpose.

It is a sign of the church members' independence that all did not simply accept our word or the word of their pastor and, during the summer that we were among them, the speculation about our motives continued. How could it not have? We had wanted to show the documentary videotapes to the congregation so they could see what we were recording. On July 20 we visited Sister Ella and Brother Earl Turner, had supper with them, and showed them some of the tapes. Brother Thurston and Sister Bea Hughes came over to join us for the viewing. We arranged to show highlights of the tapes at the church on the evening of July 30, and most of the congregation turned out to see them. Here is a portion of Sister Edith Cubbage's testimony from the morning worship service the next day in which she mentions the gossip about us and the videotapes and states her own attitude toward it and toward us:

> I know we got a God that's big enough to be over all things and that's the reason why I don't care what people says about me nor what they do 'cause they're going to answer for it. Just like you say about they won't come to church on account of these boys [i.e., Ken and me]: these boys can't send them to hell. These boys can't do nothing to 'em. It don't make no difference what they do, if they do something wrong they're going to answer for it. I'm not going to answer for it. And if they's good it's the good of the Lord. And I say if it's the good of the Lord just keep it up but if it's of the devil quit it. That's all I can say. And I want you all to pray for me. And if they're living and doing what's right and it's the right thing to do I say it's good to do it. But if it ain't, if it's of the devil, I pray they tear it down. And I'll be honest about it and I don't care who knows it and I don't go back and talk about nobody behind their back. What I say I'll say it to their face and if God tells me to say it I'll say it.
>
> And I want you all to pray for me 'cause I don't believe these boys is a bit more than we are 'cause they're made by God just like we are. Not unless the Communists has taken them over and they would be of the devil. But they can't be nothing but God's children. They ain't nobody can take this, just like I told you time and again, there's no man or woman can take what God's give me. And I know what he's give me and I'm not going to speak ill of them. And I'm so proud of that. You know, well, they say they don't like their [videotape] screen. I'm not bothered about being on that screen.
>
> [*Weeping:*] I'm on a bigger screen than that when God looks down on us and sees everything. Don't make no difference what kind of clothes I got on or what I got on, he knows what's in my heart. And why do I care about man? And they say you're going crazy when you do like that but I don't care. If the Lord gives it to me to go through here and to holler I got to

holler, and if he says keep talking I've got to keep talking. I don't care what they say.

After Sister Edith's testimony, Brother John replied:

> You that weren't here last night, they showed the radio program, how that everything's done there was showed on the screen. And also your testimonies, and had different people testifying. And singing and preaching. And I think it's a great thing. Jeff told 'em here last night, explained to 'em just exactly what it's all about, and so I thank God for it, I thank God that they thought enough of this hillbilly preacher, this country preacher. And we appreciate them taking that much interest and coming here and coming back to show you these films. And it's for a good cause and God'll bless you. And it don't bother me. Some of 'em says it bothers 'em, you know, and all. Well, you know what, some of 'em just don't want to be bothered in the first place. Amen, brother, if they leave the church over that they didn't leave over that. They just wanted an excuse to leave anyhow. That's exactly how I feel about it, bless God, and I'll just tell them the same thing: I think they's hunting for something to leave for, and they couldn't find it, so finally this came along and that give 'em an opening. You got people that's always hunting for something anyhow. So bless God let's just stay true to God and God'll bless us and give us the victory. Amen.

Brother John had encouraged us all along, and his support enabled us to continue. After we showed the videotapes, Brother John surprised us by asking the congregation to contribute a love offering for us; we accepted the forty dollars they collected and used it to buy the church a cassette tape recorder. Subsequently they made use of the recorder and the cassette copies of all the tapes we made that summer in the form of a lending library for their members. People who were recovering from illness listened to the tapes at home. A couple of years later I learned on a visit to the church that the recorder and some of the cassettes were in one member's home that was robbed while she and her family were at the hospital in Harrisonburg. The house was ransacked and everything of value in the bedroom was taken except for the recorder and cassettes, which were lying undisturbed on the bedside table where she had put them. A year earlier when I had returned for a visit Sister Ella had mentioned the tapes in her testimony:

> The other evening I got a telephone call. I had the tape player on where we took the tape from here. I just have to tell this. It's really good. She went on talking, it was still a-playing. "What station is that on?" she said. She wanted to know what station it was on so she could hear it. So just thank the Lord . . . We told her we had taped it, it was on tape . . . But she was really interested in it. And let's pray for her that if she's not right she'll get saved before it's too late. (Ella Turner, morning service, April 2, 1978)

Brother John said, "Are you talking about the tapes that Jeff and them made?"

"That's right," she replied.

"That's what I thought you was talking about. I just wanted to clarify that, that that's what it was. It was some of those tapes that was made here at the church when Jeff and them were here last summer. He made 'em and we been playing 'em and so who knows what might come out of it yet. People may get saved from a long ways and it'll be a great blessing. If one soul is saved it's worth it all. One soul."

Ken and I left as we had planned after spending eight weeks among the church community that summer. The congregation had, I think, pretty well gotten used to us. We enjoyed their fellowship outside of church. They had become interested in our lives as we had in theirs. They fussed a little over us at the last service, shaking hands and hugging us, thanking us for having visited them, knowing that they would continue after we left. Brother John summed up our feelings when he spoke from the pulpit at the end of the service:

And again let me say we appreciate these young men and I appreciate the work they've done. And I hope the radio audience was listening today that could hear why they were here and what they were doing here and I hope they heard it. They're leaving Tuesday, Jeff told me, going back to their colleges. Ken's in North Carolina at Chapel Hill and Jeff's in Massachusetts. So they'll be leaving Tuesday, going back. You that've had 'em in your homes, they really appreciated it. They told me this evening, I sat and talked to 'em, Pauline and I did, from the time we went off the radio until about fifteen after five. And we had a wonderful talk and discussion and a wonderful meal together and so I appreciate 'em. They enjoyed their meals with you, enjoyed visiting with you, talking with you, and they love you. They told me that they loved you and I believe that. I ain't got no more sense than to believe it and I want you to pray for 'em as they go that God will use them and that God will keep on blessing them in their work. They've certainly been a blessing to me. Not just because I'm going into Congress but I count that an honor and a privilege to get to go into the Library of Congress. Praise God and one day before much longer if I can get my boss to let me off I'm going to call Carl and I'm going over and I'm going through it and I'm going to see it and then I'm going to come back and tell you about it. And you can go look too, if you want to. Amen, ain't going to cost you nothing to get in as I know of. Carl told me anytime I wanted to go through just give him a call and make sure he was there and he'd show me through. So I'm going. And I appreciate it, I really do. It's been a pleasure, boys, to work with you and we certainly hate to see you go, and we hope you'll come back.

And we did come back. I visited Brother John and the church at least once a year for the next seven years, and I have thoroughly enjoyed these visits. As I write this, in the fall of 1985, Barry Dornfeld, Tom Rankin, and I have completed three months of shooting for a documentary film about Brother John and his family and the church. As he did when we proposed the first project, Brother John took it up with the congregation, they discussed it, approved it, and cooperated generously.

I. Homecoming

The church stands in Virginia's northern Blue Ridge at the base of Roundhead Mountain, between the mountain farms and the town of Stanley. Its entrance looks out across the county road to the ridges and valleys in southeastern Page County (Figure 3), old mountains worn through the millennia, the eroding rivers reduced to rocky runs between the steep, wooded cliffs. Almost all of the members of this church were born and raised on nearby mountain farmsteads, where the names on the land tell about the topography and of the English and Pennsylvania Germans who settled there in the nineteenth century: Pine Grove Hollow, Hawksbill Creek, Lucas Hollow, Tanner's Ridge, Long Ridge, Naked Creek, Basin Hollow, Stony Run, Piney Mountain, Cubbage Hollow, Dog Slaughter Ridge, Jack's Prong, Line Run, Dovel Hollow, Jollett Hollow, Big Meadows, Weaver Hollow, Honeyville.

The members of the congregation built their own church. Some among them are carpenters, bricklayers, painters, and electricians; most have done construction work at one time or another in their lives. The concrete block foundation, brown brick walls, and asphalt-shingled gray roof of the church are similar to their counterparts on the ranch houses, branch banks, post offices, and fast food restaurants that these men have built for a living. But its rectangular dimensions, twin gables, modest steeple, unadorned windows and door, and plain interior mark it as a country church. The exterior measures thirty-two feet long, seventy feet wide, and twenty-three feet to the peak of the gable above the entrance. Over the entrance door and flat against the gable is a slim wooden cross. A small tower sits on the roof about ten feet behind the gable; projecting upward from the tower is a five-foot spire; perched atop the spire is a small red cross. Abutting the front entrance is a concrete slab covered with a green carpet that serves as a patio. This patio is encircled by a grass lawn extending nearly one hundred feet to the newly paved county road. A graveled parking lot rings the sides and rear of the building, where the ground slopes downhill to Stanley. The lot is surrounded in turn by a thin band of shortleaf pines, oaks, and maples. Near the county road at the edge of the church lawn stands a sign attached to an L-shaped brick sidewall. A blue spruce grows on one side of the sign, a loblolly pine on the other, each about three feet higher than the sidewall. The hand lettering on the sign, identifying the edifice as the Fellowship Independent Baptist Church, is the only amateur touch in the entire construction. Awkward and unbalanced, the sign's letters are squeezed, the result of improvisation rather than careful planning. The pastor's name is misspelled. Yet the sign has character and determination, and it gives off vitality and spontaneity, qualities absent from the symmetrical perfection of professional sign lettering.

At nine-thirty in the morning on this, the first Sunday in August in the year 1977, the still air is already hot, and the weather forecast calls for afternoon temperatures in the high nineties. But today is homecoming day at the church, and the people will willingly put up with the heat. Homecoming is an all-morning, all-afternoon memorial service, with dinner on the grounds where the parking lot meets the woods. The Puritan ancestors of this congregation abolished the church year, with its cycle of feasts and fasts and holy days, leaving the recurring Sunday worship to mark the outstanding observances, such as Christmas and Easter. But in this congregation the annual homecoming service is the most meaningful holy day of all, for it is a celebration prefiguring the heavenly homecoming when they will join the saved among their departed loved ones and be eternally united as brothers and sisters with Jesus and as children of God. Tears of joy will overflow; shouts of "Glory!" will fill the air. Homecoming is a powerful time.

First to arrive is Brother Rastus Lam. He checks the inside of the church to see that it is clean and orderly, then climbs back into the cab of his blue pickup truck. Brother Vernie Meadows and his wife, Sister Hattie, arrive. Rastus climbs down to greet them, walking slowly, using a crutch. His leg, he tells them, is still stiff. It has bothered him ever since he took his ten-year-old grandson hunting last fall, slipped, and broke his ankle in the mountains up on Long Ridge near the old homeplace. Rastus is seventy-one, once a farmer, now retired after nearly thirty years of work as a rigger for the Merck Chemical Company in their plant south of Elkton. At six feet, seven inches, he is one of the tallest men in Page County—as a young man, he *was* the tallest—and one of the kindliest. His wife stays out of church, and it troubles him greatly, but he has lived out his three-score years and ten, made things right with the Lord, and is unafraid to die. (He will die thirteen months hence.) Brother Clyde Cubbage arrives with his wife, Sister Edith. Since boyhood Clyde and Rastus have walked the ridges and valleys of the nearby mountains together, knowing the land and its ways; but now Clyde is blind—has been for ten years—and Rastus hobbles with his crutch. Edith and Hattie greet with an enthusiastic hug. Embracing is common among the womenfolk. The men, normally shy of touching other than in shaking hands, drop their shyness and embrace in

Rear view of Fellowship Independent Baptist Church, Stanley, Virginia, 1978. Roundhead Mountain is in the background.

Fellowship Independent
Baptist Church
Sunday School ~ 10: A.M.
Worship Service ~ 11: A.M.
Eve. Service   6:30 P.M.
Prayer Service Tue. 7:30 P.M.
Your End Of a Search For A
Gospel Church
Pastor ~ John Sherfy
Everyone Welcome

Sign in front of church, 1978.

moments of great joy, as when someone is saved at the altar.

Brother John Sherfey, the pastor, arrives with his wife, Sister Pauline, their sons, Brother Donny and Brother Charles, their sons' wives, Sister Jeannie and Sister Pammie, and the grandchildren. They have driven in two cars to Stanley from their homes in the Washington, D.C., suburbs. John's mother, Sister Josie Sherfey, and his sister, Sister Elsie Sherfey McNally, will drive north from their homes in Tennessee and North Carolina for the homecoming. Elsie, in the hospital with spine trouble, got special permission from her doctor to come. Others arrive: Sister Janice Turner from Newport; Brother Jesse Comer from Comertown; Brother Belvin Hurt and his daughter, Sister Delores Hurt, from Etlan, over the mountain in Madison County; the Caves—Sister Betty and Brother Arthur, and Sister Rosalee and Brother Welford—also from hollows on the other side of the peaks of the Blue Ridge; Brother Tom Breeden, Brother George Shaffer, and Brother Oscar Jenkins; and Brother Thurston Hughes from Luray.

All linger outside the church for awhile in fellowship, talking about the parched cornfields (Page County is in the midst of a year-long drought), yesterday's brief but welcome thunderstorm, their fall garden plantings, the health of their friends who are ill, and their own health. Rastus gives away extra eggs. He gives some to me. The grocery store will no longer take them in exchange for salt and staple goods; the grocer is tied up with a contract and the eggs are trucked in. Rastus keeps his hens anyway; he likes having them about, he likes fresh eggs, and he likes giving away extras at church. The women look to the long table where they will spread the home-cooked dinner a little after noon. Brother Earl drives up without his wife, Sister Ella, daughter of Sister Edith. She is recovering at home, just out of the hospital in Harrisonburg; her children are at home looking after her. Perhaps Earl will stand in for her during the healing prayer. Certainly he will ask the congregation to pray for her.

Shortly before ten o'clock the brothers and sisters enter the church. Inside is a vestibule with bathrooms on either side, a stairway to the basement where Sunday school classes are held for the children, and a water fountain. Brother John says it is the best water in Stanley. "Holy water," he adds, smiling. A plain-faced wooden door on the far end of the vestibule opens into the large room used for worship. Here begin the sixteen rows of solid oak benches, each twenty feet long and with a back hewn from a single tree. No cushions soften the seats; church is not a place to relax in. Separated by a center aisle, the benches extend three-quarters of the length of the room, ending in the altar area, a space running the width of the room and occupied by a small table on each side and a larger altar table in front of the pulpit stand. The altar area is marked also by two carpeted

Figure 3. Page County, Va.

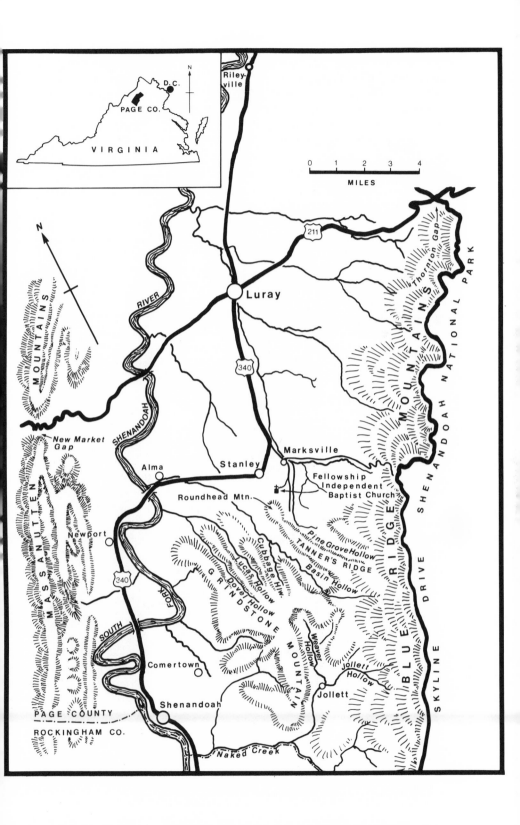

Brother Rastus Lam, 1977.

Fellowship before church, 1985. *Left to right:* Sister Cora Stallard, Brother John Sherfey, Sister Hattie Meadows, and Brother Allen Dove.

stairs leading to rails on each side of the pulpit stand, separating the altar from the choir stand to the left and from the benches to the right. Behind the pulpit stand are three large carved oak chairs. On the wall behind these chairs, behind the pulpit, a large tapestry faces the congregation. It depicts the Last Supper. To the left and right of the tapestry are oak billboards with movable numbers showing church attendance, the amount of the offering, and the number of Bibles brought to church. The sides are paneled to window-level in walnut panelboard. The windows are plain and double-hung. The walls and ceilings are white plaster. The interior is lit with recessed ceiling lights and daylight from the side windows. If the congregation could look through the wall behind the pulpit they could see the town of Stanley, but as this wall has no windows the town is shut out.

The building is arranged to house a community of worshipers, not an altar or shrine with cult objects. The concept is an auditorium: a large room filled with seats and dominated by a raised speaker's platform. Here are no distant vistas or balconies from which to view grand spectacles. No two-room, nave-sanctuary plan separates the group into a rite-performing priesthood and a passive congregation. But as one moves toward the altar the space is charged with greater sacred power, or so it seems; for here communal prayer, the most intense religious expression in this congregation, takes place. The choir stand seemingly elevates and separates part of the congregation, suggesting a hierarchy among worshipers. But in this church they keep no choir, and today no one sits in the choir stand.

The hugging, handshaking, and conversation continue inside the church as the people prepare for worship. Brother Allen Dove and his wife, Sister Goldie, take their accustomed place on the third bench, just right of center. Brother Jesse sits as always on the first bench just to the left of center. Not everyone sits in the same spot week after week; Brother Vernie, it is said, is the sort who will move around in the church, and he does. But most sit in the same place one Sunday after the next. Some husbands sit next to their wives; others do not. Children always sit next to their mother or an aunt. Members and those who come frequently but have not joined this church officially cluster on the left side in the front ten or so benches. Visitors find it less crowded on the right. Prominent visitors somehow position themselves in the front few benches on the right even though nobody leads them there. Among the regulars there is no hierarchy of seating. Saintliness, eminence, and length of time since conversion or in church office are not mapped, in this quadrant, among the saved, all of whom are equal in the sight of the Lord. One person stands out: Brother John, the pastor, songleader, and most gifted speaker among them. He steps behind the pulpit to signal the start of the service. He says he is glad to see everyone; he welcomes guests by name and mentions their hometowns. He predicts everyone will "have a good time in the Lord" this morning.

The service begins with congregational hymns, but a visitor from one of the liturgical churches would search in vain for a printed program or a billboard with the order of worship and the numbers of the hymns. Here it is more natural to remember the order of worship, but this is not merely out of convenience. The language of worship, the church members believe, ought to be determined at the moment of delivery by the indwelling Holy Spirit and not beforehand. Liturgical books are therefore out of the question; only the Bible and their hymnal are appropriate. The Spirit leads the people to select whatever hymns are needed. Anyone can select a hymn by calling out its number in the hymnal just after the previous hymn is sung. Probably someone has a special need which will be met with the comfort of its words. That person's need is unknown to the person who selected the hymn, but that is the way the Spirit works.

Brother John selects the first hymn: "I Will Never Turn Back" (Figure 4). As he sings out the first phrase, all join in, singing the melody in unison. John stands erect like the soldier of the cross that he is, marking the beat with quick vertical movements of his left hand, up on the up-beat and down on the down-beat, while with his right he holds the hymnal and reads the words. He knows the tunes from memory; like the members of the congregation, he cannot read the tunes at sight. But his pitch is true,

---

1. Once I wandered in darkness unsaved,
   Till the Savior came knocking at my heart,
   And I opened the door, let him in;
   Now rich blessings to me he imparts.

Cho. I will never turn back (Never turn back, never turn back);
   He's my light every day (He is my light every hour and day);
   No, I'll never turn back (Never turn back, never turn back),
   For my Savior is leading the way.

2. Of his love I will sing every day,
   Yes I'll sing of his wondrous power to save,
   For my Savior is leading the way,
   To those mansions of glory above.   *[Cho.]*

3. In his service each day may I be,
   Leading sinners to Jesus to be healed,
   Through the blood flowing from Calvary,
   Till the light of his love is revealed.   *[Cho.]*

4. Healing body and soul by his blood,
   And he keeps me each moment by his power,
   I will walk in the light of his word,
   And be ready to go any hour.   *[Cho.]*

I Will Never Turn Back

Actual Key: F♯

Once I wan-dered in dark - ness un-saved ____ till the

Sav - ior came knock-ing at _ my heart. _ And I o - pened the door _ let him

in; Now rich bless - ings to me __ he im - parts.

[Cho.] I will nev - er turn back; ____ He's my

light— _ ev' - ry day ____ No, I'll nev - er turn

back ____ for _ my Sav - ior is lead - ing the _ way. ____

Supplementary notation for music (here and after):

⌢   Pitch held slightly longer than notated.
⌣   Pitch held slightly shorter than notated.
↑   Pitch slightly higher than notated.
↓   Pitch slightly lower than notated.
↗• Vocal glide from one pitch to next. Not a phrase marker.
⟋• Vocal glide from indefinite lower pitch to notated pitch.

Figure 4. "I Will Never Turn Back," as sung by John Sherfey, homecoming service, August 7, 1977. Fellowship Independent Baptist Church, Stanley, Va. Transcribed by author. Lyrics and music by R. N. Brisham.

he keeps a strong and steady beat, he sings loud, and he pitches the melody in a comfortable range. His skills are all the more needed because the music has no instrumental accompaniment.

Scarcely a second passes after "I Will Never Turn Back" before Sister Janice cries out, "107!" All turn to "I Must Tell Jesus," a difficult tune in 9/8 meter, with plenty of breath needed for the chorus (Figure 5). Brother John's untrained voice soars effortlessly and unselfconsciously, embellishing the melody with the rising glides, catches, and grace notes typical of traditional Anglo-American folksingers from the South. It is just the way he sings, he told me, adding that when he was a boy his father led the singing at the Howard's Creek Union Baptist Church.

Congregational hymn-singing, 1977.

Brother John Sherfey leads a congregational hymn, 1977.

I Must Tell Jesus

Figure 5. "I Must Tell Jesus," as printed in *Church Hymnal* (Hall, ed. 1951) and as sung by John Sherfey, homecoming service, August 7, 1977, Fellowship Independent Baptist Church, Stanley, Va. Transcribed by author. Lyrics and music by E. A. Hoffman, 1893.

1. I must tell Jesus all of my trials,
   I cannot bear those burdens alone;
   In my distress he kindly will help me,
   He ever loves and cares for his own.

Cho.   I must tell Jesus, I must tell Jesus,
       I cannot bear my burdens alone;
       I must tell Jesus, I must tell Jesus,
       Jesus can help me, Jesus alone.

2. I must tell Jesus all of my troubles,
   He is a kind, compassionate friend;
   If I but ask him, he will deliver,
   Make of my troubles quickly an end.   [Cho.]

3. Tempted and tried I need a great Savior,
   One who can help my burdens to bear;
   I must tell Jesus, I must tell Jesus,
   He all my cares and sorrows will share.   [Cho.]

4. O how the world to evil allures me,
   O how my heart is tempted to sin;
   I must tell Jesus and he will help me
   Over the world the victory to win.   [Cho.]

Sister Hattie calls out "401," a hymn John recognizes by number. "Amen," he says, "how true that is. Thank God one day we're going someplace where the clouds will never hover. . . . This is an old song, one Daddy used to sing a lot when he was a-living, 'The Uncloudy Day.' You don't hear this song sung too much anymore. I heard it this past week but they kind of jazzed it up. To me, take these old songs and jazz them up, you lose the true meaning of the song. Same way with the gospel: if you jazz it up and change it around you, you lose the meaning of the word of God. So I believe we ought to take it just like it is." John acts as an interpreter, commenting before or after any act of worship, to remind, instruct, and gain assent from the congregation's shouts of "Amen!" "The Unclouded Day" (Figure 6) is the day of eternal life in heaven, an appropriate theme for the service. Brother Rastus calls out Number 71, "Sweet Hour of Prayer," a slow and stately hymn (Figure 7) and a favorite of the pastor and congregation. When they have sung it, Brother John says a few words about the last stanza: "Won't that be a glorious time, children of God, when you can drop this robe of flesh, this old house that you live in now, you can just drop this back to the ground, praise God, and go on home to be with the Lord, live with him forever and ever. The Bible says to live in his presence. And so thanks be to God we can bid this old world goodbye. Sin and destruction, we can bid it goodbye forever and forever."

---

    1. Oh they tell me of a home far beyond the skies,
       Oh they tell me of a home far away;
       Oh they tell me of a home where no storm clouds rise,
       Oh they tell me of an uncloudy day.

Cho.   Oh the land of cloudless day,
       Oh the land of an uncloudy sky;
       Oh they tell me of a home where no storm clouds rise,
       Oh they tell me of an uncloudy day.

    2. Oh they tell me of a home where my friends have gone,
       Oh they tell me of that land far away;
       Where the tree of life in eternal bloom
       Sheds its fragrance through the unclouded day.
Cho.

    3. Oh they tell me of the king in his beauty there,
       And they tell me that mine eyes shall behold
       Where he sits on the throne that is whiter than snow
       In the city that is made of gold.
Cho.

    4. Oh they tell me that he smiles on his children there,
       And his smile drives their sorrows all away;
       And they tell me that no tears ever come again
       In that lovely land of unclouded day.   *[Cho.]*

The Unclouded Day

Figure 6. "The Unclouded Day," as sung by John Sherfey, homecoming service, August 7, 1977. Fellowship Independent Baptist Church, Stanley, Va. Transcribed by author. Lyrics and music by J. K. Alwood.

Sweet Hour of Prayer

AS PRINTED:

Sweet hour of prayer, sweet hour of prayer, May

AS SUNG:

Actual Key: C♯

I thy con - sol - a - tion share Till from Mount

Pis - gah's loft - y height, I view my home _ and

take my flight. This robe of flesh I'll drop, and

rise to seize the ev - er last - ing

prize, and shout while pass - ing thru the

air, "Fare - well, fare - well __ Sweet hour of prayer."

1. Sweet hour of prayer, sweet hour of prayer,
   That calls me from a world of care,
   And bids me at my father's throne,
   Make all my wants and wishes known.
   In seasons of distress and grief,
   My soul has often found relief,
   And oft escaped the tempter's snare,
   By thy return, sweet hour of prayer.

2. Sweet hour of prayer, sweet hour of prayer,
   Thy wings shall my petition bear,
   To him whose truth and righteousness,
   Engage the waiting souls to bless;
   And since he bids me seek his face,
   Believe his word and trust his grace,
   I'll cast on him my every care,
   And wait for him, sweet hour of prayer.

3. Sweet hour of prayer, sweet hour of prayer,
   May I thy consolation share,
   Till from Mount Pisgah's lofty height,
   I view my home and take my flight.
   This robe of flesh I'll drop, and rise
   To seize the everlasting prize,
   And shout, while passing through the air,
   "Farewell, farewell, sweet hour of prayer."

Figure 7. "Sweet Hour of Prayer," as printed in *Church Hymnal* (Hall, ed. 1951) and as sung by John Sherfey, homecoming service, August 7, 1977, Fellowship Independent Baptist Church, Stanley, Va. Transcribed by author. Lyrics by W. W. Walford; music by William B. Bradbury.

Brother John stays behind the pulpit and asks, "Anybody have a prayer request on your heart?" People speak up one at a time. Brother Earl: "Brother John, I'd like for you all to remember Ella this morning." John: "Amen, Brother Earl's wife. She's home sick this morning, she just got out of the hospital. She was in the hospital last Sunday but she's home today unable to come to church, so let's remember her when we pray." Others request prayer for themselves and for people they name and talk about: some are ill, others unsaved. The people take their time. In the silence following each request, John asks if anyone else has a prayer request "on their heart," the seat of the indwelling Spirit. Five or ten seconds pass, then someone—anyone—speaks up.

Sister Goldie asks for strength after the death of someone dear, an experience everyone in the congregation has shared, and something which touches the center of Brother John's faith. Twenty-five years ago God took away his five-year-old son, Buddy Wayne. Brother John reflects a moment, then speaks.

"Death comes, and sorrows hang around for a long, well, they never, I don't think they ever go. I know every time I think about the death has hurt our family, it brings back sorrows, and certainly that's something you'll never get rid of. It gets to the place it don't torment you as much, but it's always there. And also in my home I think a lot about what David said. David, when he transgressed the law of God, sinned against God, David had to pay the price.

"You remember the penalty David paid. God took his son away from him, wouldn't let him keep it. And so, but old David, he done some repenting. And he done some talking to God. He said, 'I can't call him back to be with me but,' he said, 'this one thing I know, that I can be with him.' And I have the same thing in my home."

Here Brother John chokes back tears and continues in a husky voice. "I transgressed the laws of God, I done wrong. God took Buddy Wayne away from me, just as sure as I'm standing here, for the life I was living. But thanks be to God one day I'll see Buddy again. I'll take him up in my arms again just like I did when he left this walk of life. And this homecoming, that's what this is all about, in remembrance of those that's gone on, a memorial day, and I hope and pray you'll remember that. And if you have a loved one that's gone on, it's for you also."

Brother John asks all "who can and will to gather around the altar to pray." Most rise and come forward to kneel, head down, hand shielding the face. Others kneel at their benches. John asks Brother Jesse to lead them in prayer. "O heavenly father," he begins, and suddenly everyone prays out aloud as the Spirit moves, all at once. To an outsider this altar prayer is a confusion of voices, bedlam. To the congregation it is an invocation of the Holy Spirit and a confirmation of its presence, for the Spirit gives them words to pray. The sound swells louder, and some shift from

Congregational hymn-singing, 1985.

speech into a tonal chant, each burst of words punctuated by a gasp (+hah+) before sucking in air. After nearly five minutes, the sound fades, and the altar prayer (Figure 8) is over when the last person is through. Everyone rises and walks slowly back to the benches, feeling the power of the Spirit.

Brother Belvin and his daughter, Sister Delores, come forth and stand at the pulpit. It is time for the special-hymn singing. "Specials," as they are called, give soloists and small groups (usually family duos, trios, or quartets) a chance to sing and witness. Sister Delores is twenty-one and sometimes jokes that she is an old maid already, for most of her friends got married in their teens. (She will marry at twenty-three.) But if she is single, it must be by choice, for her sweet disposition, sandy hair, regular features, slender figure, and bright smile would be the envy of any college cheerleader or homecoming queen. Today she is a homecoming queen, like all the other sisters.

Brother Belvin, her father, farms part-time and drives a school bus. "Don't like to drag a service," he says. "I'm going to do what I'm going to do for the Lord. . . . Bless your heart it's happiness to be a Christian, and joy to meet with our loved ones. And we can come together wherever it's at, and shake one another's hand and look at one another's shiny eyes one

The altar prayer, 1977.

. . . we pray that you'd bless the minister as he breaks the bread of life this morning. Lord father encourage the preachers all over the land today. Give them souls for their labor along the way as they work Lord that their work might not be in vain but they might see things done for the glory of God. Lord bless this little church to be a soul-saving station in this community with an outreach far and wide that we might see souls come to know Jesus before it's eternally too late. Lord remember all the names in the little box, Lord, here on the table today. Those that are sick, those that are lost, Lord we pray that you Lord touch those hearts and heal those bodies today wherever they might be. Now Lord take over in this service, in the remainder today, the homecoming, the preaching, the singing, everything that's said and done, and we'll give you the praise, honor, and all the glory for it, because we ask it all in Jesus' name, amen.

Figure 8. Close of Jesse Comer's altar prayer, homecoming service, August 7, 1977, Fellowship Independent Baptist Church, Stanley, Va. Transcribed by author.

more time this side of eternity. Well, neighbor, that's a blessing to meet one another and have a good time in the Lord Jesus Christ. . . . Look at [people] just like you were going to look at 'em the last time, in their box. Neighbor, that's the way we ought to look at things." Brother Belvin's language is filled with striking, homely images. His daughter sets a sheet of paper on the lectern with the words to their song, "I'm So Glad He Found Me," a pop gospel song known to most of the singing groups in the congregation. She searches under her breath for a suitable key, then leads out smartly, her father singing along an octave below (Figure 9).

Delores has an unmistakable mountain voice, harsh and strong, with a powerful lower register that seems to launch each syllable into the congregation below. After they finish, others come forward to sing specials, and after all those who want to sing have had a chance to do what they can for the Lord, Brother John asks his sister Elsie if she feels well enough to sing. She says yes and, stepping to the pulpit, she is joined by Brother John and his two sons, Brother Donny and Brother Charles. They are a

Sister Delores and Brother Belvin Hurt sing a special-hymn, 1977.

I'm So Glad He Found Me

1. I was on the mountain, wandering from the fountain,
    When I heard my Savior speak to me;
    "Come to me relenting, of your sins repenting,
    And I will take you out where you can see."

Cho.   And I'm so glad he found me, in love he bound me,
    put his arms around me,
    Led me to the shelter, and now I'm one of his own;
    And oh the joy of knowing, with hearts a-glowing,
    someday I'm going
    To my home in glory and walk the streets of gold.

2. Now I will love him ever and part from him no never,
    For he's the dearest friend I ever knew,
    And when I see him yonder, love with him grows fonder,
Cho.   In that lovely land beyond the blue.

Figure 9. "I'm So Glad He Found Me," as sung by Belvin and Dolores Hurt, homecoming service, August 7, 1977, Fellowship Independent Baptist Church, Stanley, Va. Lyrics transcribed by author.

singing family: Sister Pauline, Sister Jeannie, and Sister Pammie also sing in the family trios, quartets, and quintets whenever they wish, and the grandchildren, Tammy and Denise, sing with their father, Brother Donny. John introduces their song, "When I Get Home," as a composition by Roscoe Reed in memory of the great gospel singers who have gone on to meet the Lord, but as each listener leans forward and catches the words (Figure 10), the song becomes a projection of the heavenly homecoming for all of the congregation and their saved loved ones, and the brothers and sisters shout "Glory!" or "Hallelujah!" when the Spirit strikes and they get a blessing and are overcome with joy.

Brother John asks Sister Elsie if she will testify. "I don't like to turn down an opportunity to say that I'm glad I'm saved," she says, witnessing for the Lord. "I've been borned again by the Spirit of God, and I know this morning that I'm one of his. I've felt him in many ways in this walk of life, but it's always good to stand and say that I'm saved this morning. And I require the prayers of each and every one of you here that I'll grow stronger. But as I said before when I made a request for prayer, I know that through the works of doctors and the works of the Lord that I'm going to be well again, and I thank God that I had a doctor that would agree to give me a pass to come over and visit with John. I have to be back in the hospital tonight at eleven o'clock, so you all pray for me and I'll pray for you."

Singing a special-hymn, 1985. *Left to right:* Brother Donny, Brother Charles, Sister Pammie, Sister Jeannie, and Brother John Sherfey.

1. Since I heard about a better home,
   I will leave this old world with all its own;
   Just slip away most any day to heaven's shore;
   I'll find sweet rest beyond the gates forevermore.

Cho. Yes I'll reach home O praise the Lord some sweet day (after while),
   When I walk up that great Milky Way (bye and bye);
   Goodbye old world, good morning there before the throne;
   What a singing there will be when I get home (eternal home)!

Figure 10. "When I Get Home," as sung by John Sherfey, Elsie Sherfey McNally, Charles Sherfey, and Donny Sherfey, homecoming service, August 7, 1977, Fellowship Independent Baptist Church, Stanley, Va. Transcribed by author. Lyrics and music by Roscoe Reed.

(**Figure 10** *continued on following pages*)

When I Get Home

2. When I move up there to settle down,
   When I step inside the gates to look around,
   I want at least a million years to view the throne;
   So many friends I want to see when I get home.

   Cho.

3. O Lord hear my prayer before I leave;
   May I live so my friends will follow me;
   My little home you gave to me while here below,
   I'd like to meet each one of them when life is through.

   Cho.

Figure 10, *continued.*

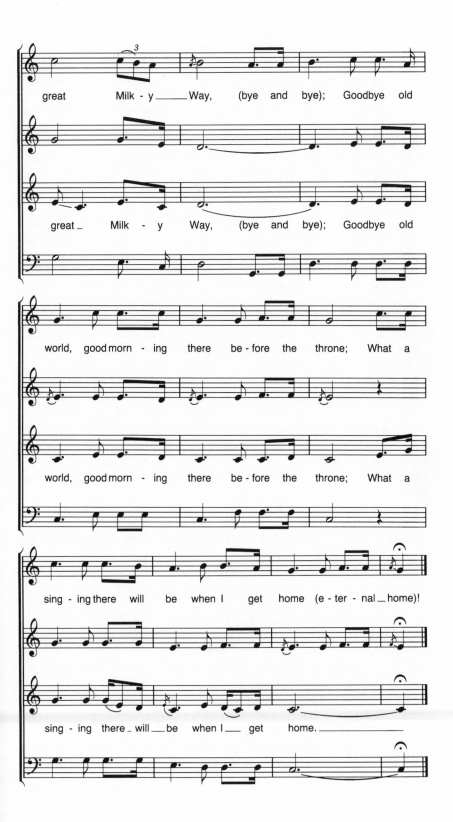

great Milk - y _____ Way, (bye and bye); Goodbye old

great _ Milk - y Way, (bye and bye); Goodbye old

world, good morn - ing there be - fore the throne; What a

world, good morn - ing there be - fore the throne; What a

sing - ing there will be when I get home (e - ter - nal _ home)!

sing - ing there _ will _ be when I _ get home. _____

Brother John comes down now to the altar. "I believe God's able to heal," he says, "and to make us whole of whatever disease it may be. And I'm a firm believer in that. James, Chapter 5, says, 'Is any sick among you? Let him call for the elders of the church, let them pray over him, anointing him with oil in the name of the Lord, and the prayer of faith will save the sick.'" John asks Brother Donny, Brother Charles, Sister Jeannie, and Sister Pammie to stand at the pulpit and sing the first verse and chorus of "The Healer." Three people who wish prayer come forward to the altar, where the deacons place a drop of olive oil on each of their foreheads while the family quartet sings. The song finished, Brother John grasps the Bible and says, "How many believes this to be the word of God that I hold in my hand?" In trance-like voices they murmur yes, they believe. "I want you to pray with me right now, faith-believing," says Brother John. All gather close, shutting eyes, praying all at once, aloud, as the Spirit moves them. Brother John's prayer is loudest and can just be heard above the rest (Figure 11) but the Lord understands all. The deacons and those prayed over return to their benches while the family quartet repeats the chorus of "The Healer." Nobody testifies to a miraculous instantaneous healing. Healing is dependent on the Lord's will; it cannot be commanded by this healing prayer.

Behind the pulpit once more, Brother John asks for the morning offering, and Brother Vernie improvises a prayer of thanksgiving. The ushers pass the plates as the congregation stands and sings "Amazing Grace," led by Brother John (Figure 12). Normally the morning collection comes to around $100, but this morning it is $200 because of the larger number of people. But even the smaller amount is enough to pay the mortgage and utilities.

The ushers tally the collection and put the amount on the billboard for all to see. Brother John welcomes the late arrivals and says the time has come for the message (sermon). He calls it a message because it comes from God; he is only its mouthpiece. The Lord has impressed on his mind a passage from the Bible that is appropriate to the homecoming, First Thessalonians 4: 13–18, and he begins by reading it aloud. (The entire sermon is transcribed in Chapter 7.) After the passage, he speaks to the congregation.

"I don't know of anything, beloved," he says, "in my life that's any more comforting this morning than to know, praise God, that there is a homecoming day for God's people. Now, beloved, we call this a homecoming day. We have our homecoming here at this church on the first Sunday in August each year. And, beloved, this *is* a homecoming. But, my brothers and sisters, I'm looking forward on to the great final homecoming of God's people. Beloved, that's the one when we'll meet in the air with the Lord Jesus Christ, my beloved friends."

The message is wholly extemporaneous and lasts for about twenty-five minutes. Brother John returns to the idea of the homecoming again and again as he explains the Bible passage. He paints a word-picture of the city of God and the arrival of the saints, and he imagines himself marching through heaven.

"I want to tell you something. When that day comes, brother, there'll be some shouting in the air. Amen? These Baptists so dead they can't shout will shout then, praise God. Some say, 'Preacher, I don't believe in shouting in the church and I don't want to shout in heaven, then.' I believe in it here and I'll believe in it when I meet Jesus. I'll believe in it when I meet all of God's people on the other side. And when I start marching down through heaven singing that song, 'Raise the bloodstained banner,' I'll march through, have on the most beautiful robe. [*Weeping:*] Elsie, I love the suit—her and James give me this suit—but, praise God, I'll get my robe on without a spot, without a wrinkle. You talking about an old boy a-marching, honey! [*Shouts:*] Whoo! Glory to God! I'll march, brother, right down through the portal of glory!"

Weeping and shouting like this might be indecorous in a mainline church, but this congregation feels and expressively demonstrates its joy. Brother John is not boasting; all the listeners imagine themselves in their glorified bodies with white robes, marching with Jesus through the city of God. Under a special anointment of the Spirit, Brother John begins to chant the message:

+hah+ the victory through Jesus Christ our Lord +hah+
Brother I'm saying to you today +hah+
the victory's in Jesus this morning. +hah+
It's not because you're Baptist. +hah+
It's not because you're Pentecostal.
It's not because you're Methodist. +hah+
But it's [*claps hands*] because you're saved +hah+
by the power of God +hah+
and filled with the Holy Ghost +hah+
brother that you're in his care today

Listening to this fevered chant, members of the congregation cry out, "Glory to God!" "Hallelujah Jesus!" "Amen!" and even wordless vocables: "Ahhh!" Brother John's periods of chant alternate with periods of speech, when he talks and draws on familiar analogies from childhood, home, and farm life to make the message plain. He says the church has a race to run and likens it to running a sack race. He says when the power of God gets hold of him he feels like the fast-moving cog on a mowing machine. He concludes the message by telling of a vision he had of heaven.

"I think I told you this before, a long time ago," he begins. "Pauline remembers very well. I, some of you's maybe never heard me tell this. I just feel like telling you this morning. I was laying flat on my back in the bed. I don't know what happened. I can't tell you. I'm like Paul; I was caught up

HEALING PRAYER

KEY: *Drop to next indented line: pause about ½ to ¾ second.*
Return to left margin: read without pause.
Boldface: increase volume, compress intonation range.
Raised words: pitches about a neutral third above reciting pitch.
All others in chant section at reciting pitch.

[*Speech:*]

O God our heavenly Father Lord as we come before the throne of grace,
Father we come Lord this morning as humble, God, as we know how.
Father we know this morning Lord that in our hands we can bring
nothing, but O God,
    Jesus that through you, Lord you can do all things, you can do miracles.
Lord, we've seen the miracles performed, our Father, so many times.
We've all needs this morning that's walked down this aisle,
Said, "Brother John I want you to pray for me and they'll be healed."
God we know this morning that your power is so real and God that
you're able
    [*Transition to chant:*]

Our Father to touch to the uttermost +hah+
Our Father regardless of what the infirmity
Might be in their bodies this morning, God we pray
+Hah+ Lord that right now thou would heal +hah+

    [*Chanted:*]

        heal   **touch**
+Hah+ would   **and**   **O Jesus +hah+**

Upon their bodies Lord right now +hah+

    name   **Christ**
In the   **of Jesus**   **Father**

    touch
+Hah+ Lord   **'em and make 'em whole +hah+**

Our Father God that we hold on to +hah+

  bey
O   **the Holy Spirit +hah+**

    O   **a**
And   **God that they'll be** **ble +hah+**

Figure 11. Healing prayer, spoken and chanted by John Sherfey, homecoming service, August 7, 1977, Fellowship Independent Baptist Church,
Stanley, Va. Ethnopoetic transcription by author.

    lift up
To   **holy hands** +hah+

And shout the praises of God +hah+

             their
+**Hah**+ **because**   **bodies** +hah+

Have   **made whole**
     been   *[claps hands]* +hah+

              through the blood
+**Hah**+ *[claps hands]*   **of the Holy Ghost** +hah+

Of the Lord Jesus Christ +hah+

Lord you touch 'em and pray for 'em +hah+

    [Speech:]
And to know that right now in the name of Jesus
We make this prayer.
Amen.
Go in peace.

Healing prayer, 1977.

Amazing Grace

1. Amazing grace, how sweet the sound,
   That saved a wretch like me!
   I once was lost, but now I'm found,
   Was blind, but now I see.

2. 'Twas grace that taught my heart to fear,
   And grace my fears relieved;
   How precious did that grace appear,
   The hour I first believed.

3. Thru many dangers, toils and snares,
   I have already come;
   'Tis grace that brought me safe thus far,
   And grace will lead me home.

4. When we've been there ten thousand years,
   Bright shining as the sun;
   We've no less days to sing God's praise,
   Than when we first begun.

Figure 12. "Amazing Grace," as printed in *Church Hymnal* (Hall, ed. 1951) and as sung by John Sherfey, homecoming service, August 7, 1977, Fellowship Independent Baptist Church, Stanley, Va. Transcribed by author. Lyrics by John Newton; music by William Walker.

Brother Jesse Comer collecting the morning offering, 1977. Photo by Paul
Hester.

into the third heaven. But I seen something I can tell you about. I can see
something I can tell you about. Whether in the flesh or out of the flesh I
don't know, in the Spirit or out of the Spirit I don't know. I can't tell you.
But I was laying flat on my back. Brother and I thought I was dead. I
thought I was gonna die that time.

"And I was laying there that day and something happened to me, I don't
know what happened. But I do know one thing. I got up in about twenty
feet. I was climbing this narrow path. Somebody said it was a vision. I
don't know whether it was or not, but I was going this narrow path and
just room for me to walk on it. And somebody caught me around the shoulders and tried to throw me off, and I remember very well I did thisaway [*rolls
shoulders to left*] and they went down into the pit a-hollering. They went
out of sound, out of—they just kept a-going. . . .

"And when I got in twenty feet of that door, the beautiful gate, and I got
in twenty feet of it, Jesus and Buddy Wayne walked by. Buddy Wayne was
on and he walked this way. The most beautiful hill I ever seen in my life.
[*Weeping:*] I haven't got there yet—I'm still trying to make that twenty

Brother John preaching, 1985.

feet—but bless God I'll soon make that twenty feet, amen? Praise God this morning. And when Buddy Wayne spoke to me, that's when I come out of whatever I was in. I come out of it, and thanks be to God this morning I'm still traveling that narrow path. And I'm gonna keep on traveling it. Praise God this morning. God is so real. I feel him in my soul."

The message concluded, Brother John offers an extemporaneous prayer on behalf of the congregation, then invites any among them who are unsaved, or who "once knew the Lord but then strayed away," to come forward to the altar for prayer. Brother Donny leads the congregation in an altar-call hymn, "Lord, I'm Coming Home" (Figure 13). They sing two verses and two choruses, keeping harmony by ear. No one comes forward. Brother John asks if anyone has a word on their heart before they dismiss for dinner on the grounds. No one does. He says again how happy he is to see everyone, how glad he was to feel the presence of the Lord in the ser-

Lord, I'm Coming Home

1. I've wandered far away from God,
   Now I'm coming home;
   The paths of sin too long I've trod,
   Lord, I'm coming home.

2. *Cho.* Coming home, coming home,
   Never more to roam;
   Open wide thine arms of love,
   Now I'm coming home.

3. I've wasted many precious years,
   Now I'm coming home;
   I now repent with bitter tears,
   Lord, I'm coming home.

4. *Cho.*

Figure 13. "Lord, I'm Coming Home," as sung by Donny Sherfey, home-coming service, August 7, 1977, Fellowship Independent Baptist Church, Stanley, Va. Transcribed by author. Lyrics and music by William J. Kirkpatrick.

Sister Jeannie singing an altar-call hymn, 1985.

Fellowship after the service, 1977. *Left to right:* Brother Allen Dove, Brother Vernie Meadows.

vice. Everyone murmurs assent. He says he looks forward to the dinner, rubs his belly, and says everyone knows he loves to eat. The only thing he'd rather do than eat is preach, he says. He reminds the children not to play inside the church while everyone else is finishing up dinner, and he invites everyone to return for the afternoon service. It will be a song service, with a special performance by a professional gospel group. John will give another altar call, and the day will close with testimonies from many in the congregation, each telling what the Lord has done in his or her life.

In this homecoming celebration the church is heroic and triumphant. The return is understood on a personal and communal level. It is a reunion in fellowship with their Christian loved ones, their brother Jesus, and their father God. But unlike other homecoming celebrations, this takes place in the middle of the journey, in the midst of the battle. It is a celebration for the living, not the dead. It revives, sustains, and prefigures the final victory.

2. Land and Life

With grateful acknowledgment to the historical geographer Carl Sauer, I borrow this chapter's title from his book of the same name. My thesis is not environmental determinism but an assertion of human ecological interdependence among where people live, how they work, how they interact, and what they believe. My methods in this chapter are mainly social history and cultural geography, and by them I will attempt to show the interdependence of household economy, family, and mind-set among the mountain-farming ancestors of the present-day Fellowship Independent Baptist Church congregation. I claim that this mind-set is a product of tradition, and that in the religious sphere it finds its most telling and poignant and characteristic expression in the beliefs and activities surrounding preparation for the heavenly homecoming reunion.

The chapter may appear complex, but its thread is simple, and involves moving back, then forward, in time. I begin with the present, a visit to Brother Rastus Lam and an observation of his life as a pattern inscribed on the landscape. Through oral history I trace that pattern back to the beginning of this century. I note what historians say about the earlier history of these mountain farmers and how it seems at variance with the facts I discovered in the public archives. The bulk of the chapter takes us back to the earliest settlers in the region and then moves forward in an attempt to present a more balanced picture of the mountain farmers in the context of the neighboring valley culture. Then I draw the picture forward again to time present.

Throughout the chapter I intersperse passages and sections concerned with the chapter's basic themes: the land, the household mode of production, food and foodways, family, authority, parents and children, social relations, commerce, and the mountain mind-set. In the metaphor of husbandry—an idea borrowed appreciatively from Wendell Berry—I find the linking pattern among the material, social, and ideational spheres: between farmstead, family, and religion.

A Visit to Brother Rastus

I knew that most of the older members of the church had been mountain farmers; but because they had migrated down from the mountains many decades earlier to join the cash-wage economy as carpenters, bricklayers, factory workers, and so forth, I underestimated the persistence of the mountain-farming mind-set amidst the conditions of modern town life. Not until Ken George and I visited Brother Rastus at home did I begin to realize its full import. I have reconstructed the following narrative from my field notes. The visit took place on the hot summer afternoon of July 8, 1977. We had been in the community for two weeks. Rastus had been especially kind to us, friendly and gentle. We had stood up in the church and said that as part of the documentation project we would like to speak with members of the congregation individually about the history of their lives and their beliefs. Rastus had been among the first to invite us to come visit him at home for that purpose and we were glad to be seeing him. At noon the sky was clear but a light haze hung over the nearby Massanutten Mountains. We left the main highway and drove on a dirt road climbing a hill past a few scraggly cornfields. The temperature was ninety-five degrees and climbing. Drought and heat had parched and stunted the corn.

We turned onto another dirt road and wound past a few small, wooden houses where two of Brother Rastus' married sons lived. Rastus had bought one hundred acres of land here on Mill Creek in 1950, and gradually sold most of it and settled his sons on the rest of it. Rastus came out past the screen door of his house to greet us as we pulled into the driveway. He wore a yellow shirt and blue denim bib overalls and black and white sneakers. He greeted us warmly, putting a large hand on my shoulder.

To a folklorist, none of the "things" people choose to surround themselves with is insignificant; types of clothing, food, and shelter form a pattern whose sign language, so to speak, tells us about the person's notions of how to live a satisfying life. And so Ken and I began by asking Rastus about his house. It was on the property when he bought it, he said. I saw that it was a two-story, rectangular building of about 1,100 square feet. Balloon-framed, it sat on a cement foundation, plasterboarded on the inside and weatherboarded on the outside. Over the weatherboards Rastus had nailed felt siding that is supposed to look like brick but looks like felt that is supposed to look like brick.

We turned about and saw the large kitchen garden, an acre or so planted in feed corn, and some outbuildings that Rastus had constructed: a hog pen, a chicken coop, and a meat house/potato cellar. Brother Rastus said he had learned "light carpentry" from his father, Alexander Lam (b. 1861), who had built the house on Tanner's Ridge that Rastus grew up in. Made almost entirely of American chestnut, it was a timber-framed cabin with vertical board siding; wood shingles covered the roof. Rastus' house was modern by comparison, but more important than the contrast in material and appearance was the continuity in building for oneself, an inherited tradition of self-reliance.

Rastus showed us his half-dozen hogs and pointed to about a dozen hens. He told us he butchers his hogs in the late fall, then salts and smokes them and hangs them in the meat house. His sons help with the butchering. He said he loves to hunt deer and rabbits and he eats what he kills. It was while he was taking his young grandson hunting last fall that he slipped on some leaves and fell and broke his ankle. His wife puts up vegetables from their garden and he buries the root crops in the potato cellar. Except for milk they seldom buy food at the store. Rastus grew up on a farm, worked for many years in a factory, and in retirement returned to farming after a fashion to supply some of his needs.

He invited us inside, and we went in through the kitchen/dining room to the living room. Rastus walked slowly with his crutch, introduced us to his wife, Ruth, and motioned for us to sit down on the brown-cloth-covered couch in the corner. We walked on a floor of green plastic tile squares that Rastus had placed over the original wood floor ten years earlier. A television with small, framed photos of Rastus' children on top was in another corner of the room, a gray upholstered chair above which hung a calendar with a lithograph of Jesus was in another corner, and nothing was in the last corner. On the wall behind the couch hung a wooden-cased, spring-wound clock.

Ken and I asked Brother Rastus if he minded whether we would tape-record him when he told us about his life. "I got nothing to be ashamed of," he said. "Go right ahead." He meant that his conscience was clear because he had made things right with the Lord. We set up the recorder and microphone, tested it to make sure it was working, and played back a little for Rastus to hear. Satisfied, he spent the next two hours reminiscing and answering our questions.

After the interview we returned to the kitchen, where Ruth had prepared dinner for us. We had not expected a meal and had, in fact, had a snack before the visit. Their kitchen was filled with appliances: two sinks, many storage cabinets, a large, modern refrigerator-freezer, a separate freezer, another refrigerator (an older one), and a wood cook stove. The appliances spilled out onto the screened-in porch, effectively a summer kitchen, where they kept yet another refrigerator and an electric stove.

We sat down to eat at a large, gray-plastic-covered table on top of which Ruth had seemingly laid the contents of at least two of the refrigerators. More was stacked on a cart she wheeled up alongside. Hamburgers, onions, potatoes, potato salad, cabbage, green beans, home-baked bread, apple-sauce, lemonade, ham, ham salad, chicken, chicken salad, eggs, egg salad, and an abundance of other prepared foods were laid out in their plastic refrigerator containers that doubled as serving dishes. Rastus said

Brother Rastus at home, 1977.

Brother Rastus in his meathouse, 1978.

grace and the three men ate while Ruth stood, serving. She would eat when we had finished, she explained. The temperature had reached the high nineties, the air was heavy in the house, and the smells of the foods mingled in the air. We ate and chatted and praised Ruth's cooking and remarked about the great variety of dishes in front of us.

As we left, I thought about Brother Rastus and the pattern of his life. I have thought about it a great deal since. We visited him to talk, and talk we did. But as I think about the visit now, I am struck by what the Lams "told" us, by the things they surrounded themselves with. And surrounded us: the meal was memorable, and in retrospect I am convinced that the huge spread, like the homecoming dinner on the church grounds, signified abundance, plenty, the bounty of the earth nurtured by careful husbandry. Ken and I were puzzled at the time by the Lam family's "subsistence" farming on their small acreage when it was uneconomical and hence seemingly irrational. If the Lams were not behaving in their economic best interests—after all, they could buy their food at the store for less than it cost them to raise it—what other interests and needs were they serving?

Old-Fashioned by Intent

The signs of the congregation's present life, as I saw them, centered on food, farming, and family, and the relation of these to religion and especially to religious language. The pattern of Brother Rastus' life was inscribed for all to see on the landscape: his house, innocent of "style"; his household industry, food production for the family, with its complement of devices—cornfield, hogpen, meat house, kitchen garden, root cellar, chicken coop, summer canning and freezing, household appliances; the television and telephone, connections to the outside world; refrigerators and freezers to complement the household industry; his sons, settled with their wives and Rastus' grandchildren on adjacent land; his Bible, a teacher in this life and hope for the future.

Brother Rastus' life—indeed, the lives of virtually all of the members of the Fellowship Independent Baptist Church—was old-fashioned, rural, and out of touch with the American mainstream. The historians and sociologists I had read (see below, "Getting behind 'History'") had told me that Appalachian mountain people like Rastus were old-fashioned because civilization had passed them by and they could not adapt. Appalachian religion, the sociologists wrote, with its denominational factions, theological disputatiousness, miracle healing ceremonies, its shouts and sobs and "running fits" and holy dancing, was an emotional outlet for frustration born of alienation, a kind of compensation for inability to adjust to modern industrial life.

Yet despite their impeccable credentials as old-fashioned Appalachian mountaineers, Rastus and the other members of the Fellowship Independent Baptist Church did not fit the sociologists' portrait. Denominationalism was not an important issue in this section of the Blue Ridge; a person could be saved as a Baptist, a Methodist, a Pentecostal, and so forth. Churches served communities, not denominations. As for theological wrangling, aside from a few issues (perfectionism—the idea that a Christian could become free from sin and never sin again—or, as Brother John puts it, "Once in grace, always in grace"—was one of the few), almost all of the "fighting" done by this church was in opposition to the world of sin and the devil. True, emotionalism ran high during services, and shouts and weeping punctuated the hymns and sermons and testimony, but to me there was nothing frightening about shouts of glory or tears of joy. And as for miraculous healing, the congregation believed in it and practiced a healing ceremony as directed in the Bible, but they did not faint or expect results every time. Sister Edith insisted that such ceremonies were petitionary; she rejected the idea that one could command God. "God's our command," she said (Cubbage interview, p. 22).

It occurred to me that there was another, simpler and better explanation for the lifeways of these church members: that they were traditional, inherited, and deliberate. Folklorists are keen on tradition, so it was natural for me to look in that direction. I spent the first few years of the research project behind this book getting acquainted with Brother John and his congregation and their way of life, documenting their worship services, and learning through conversations and interviews about the history of their individual lives. As I became convinced that tradition, not alienation, was at the root of their religious community, I spent more and more time on tradition. From their life stories I found out a great deal about family traditions, and I learned that most of the older members of the church had been born and raised on mountain subsistence farms.

Oral History: Mountain Farming

Brother Vernie Meadows, a deacon in the Fellowship Independent Baptist Church, grew up on a mountain farm on Naked Creek near Long Ridge (see Figure 14). He began his recollection of mountain farming by contrasting it with farming in the valley:

> You can raise most anything in the mountains; it's just a little harder to produce, to gather. It's hilly and rocky. Well, we farmed mostly for our own use. It's a nice life to live, farming. But it ain't like it used to be. You can't raise like you used to, on account of beetles. Stuff gets in your crop, you know. It's much more expensive than it used to be. Used to be all you had

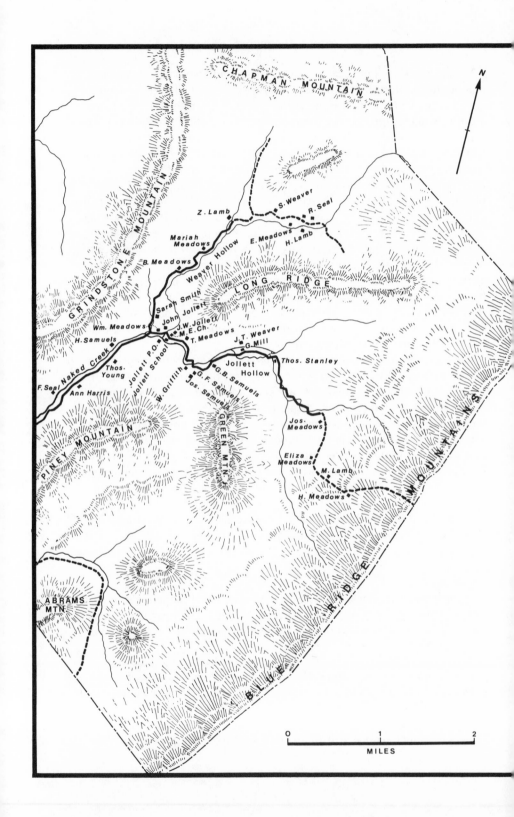

to do was plant it and work it a couple of times and then gather it. But now you got a big expense. (Meadows interview, 1977, p. 6)

Mountain farming is a thing of the past for Brother Vernie, but his memory paints an idyllic picture: almost anything would grow, the crop needed little attention, and all that was necessary was to gather it in at the harvest. This memory is typical among the church members but not all share it; Brother John, for example, found farming tiresome. Mention a root cellar and a meat house and he shudders; he is happy to buy frozen vegetables and canned ham at the grocery store.

Gradually, the features of mountain farming in the first few decades of the twentieth century emerged from the older church members' recollections. It was a family-oriented, household mode of production, a subsistence farm economy in which little or no surplus was produced for market. Brother Rastus, born in 1907 and raised on a farm on Long Ridge, remembered that the mountain farm economy differed from the cash-wage way of life:

> [We grew] corn and potatoes and sowed a lot of rye at that time 'cause we was so high up on the mountain that wheat wouldn't grow. And we'd raise a lot of rye and thrash that out and take that to the mill and have it ground to fatten our hogs off of. And we made our living like that. We'd always have three or four right good hogs to butcher every fall, have a bunch of chickens, and, at that time, why, that's about the only way that people had of buying groceries was selling eggs. There weren't no income much, you know, like people's got today. (Lam interview, p. 6)

Brother Allen Dove, born in 1919, remembered his father owning a twenty-acre mountain farm, and like Brother Rastus he emphasized the family's self-sufficiency, adding the qualification that if one family had hard luck, neighbors and kin would help out:

> You take back them days, a person really enjoyed it better than they do now. You take back them days, when a man had him a hog or two, put himself out a little patch of corn, a little patch of buckwheat, have a little rye out, then you'd harvest it, take that off to the mill and have it ground, and get himself a hundred pounds of flour, why he had done his winter's work, back where he was living. You could buy lard for four cents a pound; you could buy sugar for three or four cents a pound. A man who couldn't make a good living back then, why, there wasn't nothing in him. And back them days if a man got sick, went to the hospital, he had just as much

Figure 14. Section of Shenandoah Iron Works District, Page County, Va., showing households along Naked Creek, including Jollett Hollow and Weaver Hollow. Adapted from *Lake Atlas of Page County,* 1885.

when he came out as if he'd be at home all the time. Everybody'd join in, you know, and help. And he had just as much as the other ones. If he got sick or something and his harvest come on, people'd harvest for him. Well, then, when he came back, if you had anything to do, why, he'd work for you, too. People was helpful in that day. (Dove interview, p. 18)

Like Brother Vernie, Brother Allen remembered hunting for food: rabbits and birds, especially pheasants; but the family staple was "a plate of mush. . . . Cornmeal cooked up in a pot and set out in a bowl. You could make a meal of that, breakfast or supper, either one" (ibid., p. 19).

The Folklife of Mountain Farming

As we saw in Chapter 1, homecoming is a powerful sacred ritual for the members of the Fellowship Independent Baptist Church. In their thoughts, *home* is a composite of their heavenly home, their present homes, and their earliest homes, on Appalachian mountain farms. Family, intimately bound up with home, is the most powerful emotional touchstone in their worship services. Apart from their language in religious practice, to me the most striking aspect of this congregation is its members' common descent from mountain farming homes and families.

The mountain farming heritage provides them with a common frame of experiential reference and strengthens feelings of community within the congregation. They *know* each other through shared experience both as sinners-become-Christians and as descendants of a rural agrarian tradition. In fact, many are related through blood or marriage and have known each other all their lives. When Brother Belvin Hurt calls a spiritless sermon dry as a last year's bird's nest everyone knows exactly what he means. Mountain farming traditions are communicated in words and also by example. Sharing them not only enables the church members to understand one another but also relates intimately to the particular style and content of their version of Christianity.

These shared traditions turn the church members into what folklorists call a *folk group*. Barre Toelken's definition of a folk group is "any group of people who share informal communal contacts that become the basis for expressive, culture-based communications." He adds that because folk groups persist over time, "the expressive communications . . . become the educative matrix in which children of the group—or newcomers to it—are brought up" (Toelken 1979:51). A family is an example of a folk group; other folk groups include computer hackers, prison inmates, truck drivers, antique collectors, and so forth. When a folk group embraces a total way of life, understood to be different from other ways of life, the folk group becomes a folk culture. Examples that come to mind are the Amish, migrant farm workers, Mormons. Very often, folk cultures are marked by region,

Brother Vernie sits on his grandfather Ed Meadows' left knee. His father, George W. Meadows, is standing at left. Ca. 1915. Photographer unknown.

religion, or occupations that isolate them to a degree and set them off from the rest of society. It is convenient to call the way of life of people in a folk culture their folklife.

The folklife of mountain farming in the northern Blue Ridge (or anywhere else for that matter) may be regarded as the expression of a mind-set, something like what modern French historians call *mentalité:* ideas and attitudes that form an outlook and a disposition to act in certain ways and not others. This mind-set is not the same thing as behavior; rather, it is the pattern that connects the behavior through its characteristic forms. It therefore occasions the material, social, and ideational expression that comprises folklife within a folk culture. The mountain-farming mind-set in the northern Blue Ridge is thus something very deep—nothing, in these people, is deeper—and, ultimately, it is a view of life arising from an upbringing on the land amidst the lore of generations of people who farmed in a household economy with the family the basic mode of production and unit of consumption. The mountain mind-set defines the well-lived traditional life.

The folklife of mountain farming in the northern Blue Ridge involves three kinds of experience: material culture, or the relation between a person and the surrounding things (house, outbuildings, fields, crops, livestock, tools, furniture, "possessions" in general, things that can be inventoried); social, or the relation between a person and the surrounding people (spouse, children, kinfolk, neighbors, acquaintances, strangers); and ideational, or the relation between a person and the surrounding ideas (ideas about how the world is and how a person ought to behave in it). These will be the focal points of the next three sections of this chapter. I will return to the mountain mind-set again at the close of the chapter after tracing the history of the church members' ancestors and their way of life.

Material Forms: Economy and Ecology of Mountain Farming

The relation between the Blue Ridge mountain farm household and its surroundings was quite literally grounded in the material production and consumption of its inhabitants. An ecological/economic model will help explain this relationship. At the heart of the science of ecology is its controlling metaphor: the cycle. Cycles as understood by ecologists working with the physical world include cycles of precipitation, run-off, and evaporation; of plant photosynthesis involving oxygen and carbon dioxide; of food chains and food webs; of composition and decomposition. Currently, ecological scientists pay most attention to the cycling of nutrients and to the flow of energy within certain physical boundaries, conceived of as whole systems and termed ecosystems. The idea behind the cyclic metaphor is interdependence. The upper portion of Figure 15 shows the Earth conceived as an ecosystem.

Contemporary ecologists view the ecosystem in *eco*nomic terms: organisms are likened to "producers" and "consumers." It is but a small step to recast this metaphor in its economic domain and view the nineteenth-century Blue Ridge mountain farm household as an ecosystem. This is illustrated in the lower portion of Figure 15. Materials involved in farm production include human and animal labor, land, energy, buildings, fertilizer, tools, seed, livestock, and so forth. These are entered at the left side of the diagram. On the right side we see the farm household produce: meats and other animal products (beef, pork, poultry, game, milk, butter, cheese, eggs, wool); crops and other natural materials (corn, wheat, rye, oats, buckwheat, hay, honey, potatoes, flax, flax seed, apples, tan bark, furs, berries, timber); and home manufactures such as clothing, shoes, apple brandy, baskets, barrels, corn whiskey, and so forth. Some of the farm produce was the result of considerable labor and careful nurturing;

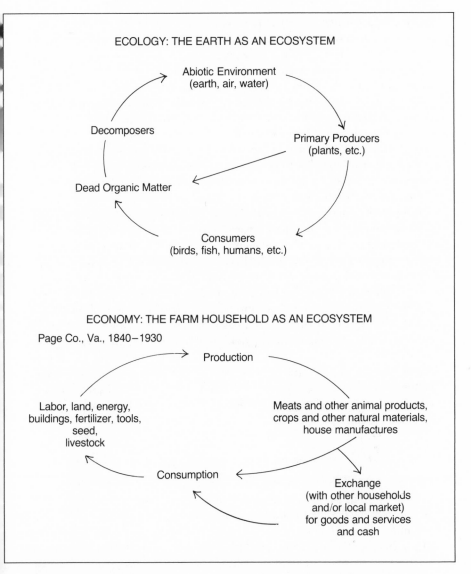

Figure 15. Ecological model of household economy, Page County, Va., 1840–1930.

other produce (pigs, for example, which foraged for their food in the woods) required relatively little attention. The household consumed much of what it produced, while any surplus was stored or exchanged with neighbors or sold to a local market (often a merchant at a nearby flour mill) for cash or bartered for goods. Certain products were aimed especially at the market: wheat, beef, tan bark, furs, berries, home crafts. Other production was aimed first for household consumption, with any excess marketed: cider, brandy, whiskey, pork, corn, wool. Cash thus obtained was used to pay land taxes and to purchase goods, labor, land, or services. It will be useful to bear this ecological/economic model in mind in the discussions of the farm household economy that take up much of the middle of this chapter.

Interdependence is plain in the model: households are dependent upon their members, their livestock, crops, what is available for hunting and gathering, the markets, and the bounty of nature. When upset occurs, the effects are felt in every part of the household economy. In one form or another this model illustrates a farm household pattern centuries old, going back to medieval Britain and Europe, and transported to North America, where as late as 1790 it still accounted for about 90 percent of American households. In the nineteenth century it largely disappeared, but it hung on in some rural areas, including the Blue Ridge Mountains. I will explain the significance of its persistence there as I trace the history of farming in this region among the ancestors of the members of the Fellowship Independent Baptist Church. We pass now from the material culture of mountain farming to social aspects connected intimately to both material culture and religious ideas.

Material and Social Forms: Farming and the Family

The material culture of farming struck me most forcibly in our visit to the Lam house, but I also paid attention to Brother Rastus' authority as the patriarch of his family. I felt a little uncomfortable when Ruth stood serving and waiting on us throughout the meal. I noted Rastus' generosity in giving his sons land to settle on, but along with it went his paternalistic desires to keep them under his watchful care, and his disappointment that he could not control them to his satisfaction. I had already determined that "family" was one of the most important themes running through the rhetoric of the church services: people in the congregation requested prayer for unsaved family members, and all looked forward as children of God and brothers and sisters in Jesus to the heavenly homecoming reunion. For that reason I paid particular attention to family patterns and kinship among the members of the congregation, and noted how they were bound up in memories of mountain farm life when I collected oral histories from the older members of the congregation.

Brother John's memories of farm life center on good times with his family despite the poverty of his early years. He remembers gathering ginseng root with his eleven brothers and sisters, and he recalls Saturday evenings in the kitchen when his mother baked pies and the whole family gathered to listen to the *Grand Old Opry* on the radio. He thinks families were closer and happier then, without "the world's goods," or so much material culture: "Of course we didn't have no bicycles to ride, we didn't have no cars to drive; all we had was a sled, or a little wagon, but we had fun. . . . But anymore it's got so that if they don't have an automobile they can't go nowhere. Or a motorcycle. But we had a good time then, and this went on through life. Of course we was poor; Daddy never did have, as far as the world's goods is concerned, he didn't have it. But he was a fine man" (John Sherfey interview, July 23, 1977, pp. 3–4).

The older generation of church members recall happy times spent with their parents. Brother Allen and Brother Rastus both spoke affectionately about going hunting with their fathers for honeybees. "Back in my earliest memory," said Brother Rastus, "why, I remember well when my daddy was living at that time there. Me and him used to go a-hunting bee trees in the mountains, honey bees" (Lam interview, p. 3).

Times like these stand out because fathers, working in the fields many days, usually were remote and powerful. Sister Goldie spoke matter-of-factly about how as a young woman she worked alongside the men dragging logs behind horses down the mountainsides (Dove interview, pp. 20–21). Brother John's memories of his parents are, characteristically, rich. After talking with him about his childhood, I asked him to search his mind for an image of each of them doing something. He found the image of his mother in the kitchen, preparing food with her hands while rocking the cradle with her foot. He said this of his father:

> I picture him more out in the field working, more than anything, because he and I used to work together a lot. Out in the fields, you know, a-shucking corn. First one thing and then another, but just more so of that than anything. [*Pause.*] Used to see him sit there and shuck corn with the blood a-dripping out of his hands where they'd crack and bust open. He'd never say a word, just shuck on. And there I was complaining about the freezing cold and everything, and him just working on. I tell you. [*Pause.*] But where he's at now he won't have to shuck no corn. (John and Pauline Sherfey interview, December 3, 1979, p. 37)

In this remarkable memory the young man is unable to accomplish the adult task without complaint. The child and father are not quite competing, for the work is familial and collective; yet the overpowering impression is that the young man, failing to endure pain, remains a child, unable to become "a man" like his father, who is pictured as heroic, remote, and bleeding.

Brother John with his son Donny, ca. 1955. Photographer unknown.

It is possible to view this image of Brother John's father in the context of the Crucifixion. That is, the image of his bleeding father must be terribly close to Brother John's image of his Savior in bloody sacrifice. Brother John's father's life was, on one level, a sharecropper's sacrifice for his wife and their dozen children. This image of his father shucking corn with bleeding hands has come up more than once in the numerous conversations I have had with Brother John. Occasionally he talks about it before the congregation; for another of his performances of this story, see Chapter 5, p. 247. He carries the image with him, and it bears heavily on his personality and identity, reminding him of his responsibilities to his father and to Jesus (merged in the blood) and of the difficulty, if not impossibility, of fully meeting them. In becoming a Christian, Brother John became a man. The image of manly endurance, secure in the knowledge of reward in the next world despite being embattled in this one, offers to Brother John and the church members a link with their past and hope for the future. At the same time it is an image that is terribly poignant in its loneliness, bespeaking a need for love and acceptance and the difficulty of attaining it in the face of a patriarchal ideal of heroic, manly stoicism.

The elder members of the Fellowship Independent Baptist Church apprenticed to their parents and other kinfolk to learn what they needed to get on in the world: farming and housewifery. Their instruction came within the family circle and on the family and neighboring farms. Their family supplied the main, sometimes the sole, role-models. The parents ruled them; the children must obey. Tradition dictated their rights and responsibilities. School was endured until the child was old enough to be needed on the farm; then he or she left. Most of the elder members had no more than an eighth-grade education. But when they moved from the mountain farms to the valleys and took "public works" jobs—that is, they worked for wages, in factories or for contractors—and when they bought land near the towns, they began to enter into different kinds of relationships with other people. More and more they—and their children to an even greater extent—dealt with people who were not kinfolk, and they dealt with them on the basis of money and contracts, not on the basis of love and friendship (or, to be sure, dislike, jealousy, and hatred). The personal aspects of daily relationships lessened as they increasingly left the homeplace and entered the marketplace, and this caused strain. One result was an aching for the past, when the family was together (and the lines of authority were clear) and the world was circumscribed. One line of resistance to modernization involves continuing the old family apprenticeship pattern, particularly among the men and boys: when possible, boys follow in their father's trade. Brother John taught his four sons truck driving, and three of them now do it for a living, having more than forty years' experience between them. Other trades among the congregation members—carpentry, stonemasonry, bricklaying—pass from father to son, and keep the family close. Church, obviously, is another means of salving this ache, particularly because it downplays contracts and legality and emphasizes feelings and personal relationships, not only among family (the heavenly homecoming reunion) and friends, but between the believer and Jesus as "personal Savior." Material objects once possessed by dead kinfolk become consecrated; Brother John and Sister Pauline keep their dead son Buddy Wayne's clothes in a cedar chest, and John treasures his brother's gun and his father's watch and cane. He speaks about them on occasion to the church members, and these sacred objects become a public example, tokens signifying the fragility of close personal relationships, and foreshadowing the great reunion day. The cane and gun and watch are kept unused, unsullied, as if to stay the soul on course:

> When Daddy passed away they asked me what I wanted. I said, "I'd like to have Daddy's cane." I've got it. Elsie bought it for him a long time ago. He got so much enjoyment out of that cane. Whenever we'd go round where Daddy was, he'd hook us on the ankle with it or hook us around the neck and pull us up to him and he says, "I can handle it." I can remember those words. But I've got that cane and you ain't got enough money, I don't care if you're a millionaire, to buy that cane. And thanks be to God I'll still have it when I leave this walk of life unless something drastic happens.
>
> My brother, when he passed away, Ester, he had an old rifle. It ain't worth ten cents as far as shooting's concerned. It'll shoot, but the powder'll burn your eyes when you shoot it. He said, "John, I want you to have it." I've got it at the house. You ain't got enough money to buy it. I'm gonna keep it. I've got Daddy's watch at the house, wristwatch, he left that to me. I put it back in the drawer. Here awhile back mine quit. Somebody said, "Why don't you wear it?" I wouldn't wear that watch at all. I'm gonna keep that watch in the drawer. If it's a hundred years from now it'll look just like it is right now.
>
> Thanks be to God. I'll tell you, friends, you that have got parents, you ought to appreciate your parents this morning. After they're dead and gone then you'll know what I'm talking about. . . .
>
> You know I thought I was a pretty big man. I thought I could stand up to anything. But when they shut the casket on my daddy's face [weeping:] I like to went out. But hallelujah thank God I'm going home and I'll see him again. I had one of the best daddies that's ever walked on this earth. I know we got good men here and God bless you I love everyone of you'uns. But I never heard my daddy swear an oath in my life. . . .
>
> Daddy told us about Jesus, thank God. I can see him standing in Howard's Creek Church singing "Sweet Hour of Prayer," and them tears would run down and drop on the floor. I was only six years old but I ain't forgot that. . . . Praise God, there's a great reunion day. (Morning service, July 10, 1977)

Material, Social, and Religious Forms: Husbandry

The mind-set among the members of the Fellowship Independent Baptist Church is a product of tradition and, not surprisingly, venerates tradition. The Appalachian mountain farmers felt the power and the mystery of the natural world even as they experienced the joy of husbandry. They knew there were limits to their powers of intervention and control, and so, like most preindustrial farmers, they hedged their bets by engaging in diversified, rather than specialized, farm production; and what they lost to the efficiency of monoculture they gained in the assurance that a variety of crops and livestock would not all fail in a given year. Such diversity led them to prize the virtue of versatility, the ability to do many things well; and versatility in turn led to self-reliance. Self-reliance did not mean independence but, rather, self-discipline; for it was plain that farmers must rely daily on their immediate families, and at times on other kinfolk and neighbors. This reliance fostered a set of friendships among people for which the term husbandry is especially appropriate.

In the metaphor of husbandry—the word that means both a farmer's loving relationship to the crops and livestock, and a man's loving relationship to his wife—we can see the linking pattern between life in the material world of the farmstead and life in the human, social, familial world (see Berry 1981:213–215). Significantly, the same metaphor connects to the religious world as well. Husbandry is a frequent metaphor in the Judeo-Christian tradition; "husbandman" is regularly used in the King James Version of the Bible to translate what today we would call farmer, herder, or fruit-grower. Here the metaphor means that the farmer stands in relation to his land as a husband to his wife. But in its fullest biblical expression, in John 15, the farmer is the subject of God's husbandry. After they have eaten the fruits of the earth (the Last Supper, the feast of the Passover), Jesus tells his disciples:

> I am the true vine, and my Father is the husbandman. Every branch in me that beareth not fruit he taketh away: and every branch that beareth fruit, he purgeth it, that it may bring forth more fruit. Now ye are clean through the word which I have spoken unto you. Abide in me, and I in you. As the branch cannot bear fruit of itself, except it abide in the vine; no more can ye, except ye abide in me. (John 15:1–4)

In this passage, God is likened to a husbandman, Jesus to a vine, and the disciples and other believers to branches on the vine, "abiding in" (dependent on) Jesus and nurtured by God. In this way the religious relationship between believers and God is expressed through the agricultural metaphor of husbandry. The same metaphor, then, links farmers to their farm and fields; to their spouses (and, by extension, to their family and friends); and to God. As Psalm 23 has it, "The Lord is my shepherd." Language quickens this pattern: "Now ye are clean enough through the word which I have spoken unto you," where "clean" means not only free from sin but awake to the meaning of the metaphor.

To be sure, not all the mountain-farming ancestors of the congregation of the Fellowship Independent Baptist Church were Christian believers, but most were God-fearing, and all grew up within earshot of the most popular book in the region, the Bible. As Jim Garland reports, even the hardest-hearted of sinners were familiar with the oral tradition of Bible stories and scriptural interpretation and argument that provided a framework within or against which the mountain people struggled to establish their identities and make their lives meaningful (Garland 1983:29).

Getting behind "History"

Oral history of mountain farming and family could go back in satisfying detail only to about the turn of the twentieth century, and I wanted to know what went on in the mountain-farming community before that because the traditions were far older. And so I spent the next several years studying the history of food, farming, family, and religion in the mountains of southeastern Page County, Virginia. Monographs on "Appalachia" were useful but too general for my specific purpose. The county historian's book (Strickler 1952) was valuable for the attention it gave to the predominantly German culture in Page Valley, but it had almost no information on the mountain people.

It became clear that I would have to seek out this history from primary source materials as best I could. To do so, I chose four families prominent in the Fellowship Independent Baptist Church congregation today—their surnames are Breeden, Cubbage, Meadows, and Lam—and decided to follow the history of their migration into the region and their fortunes there in the nineteenth century, earlier than oral history could reach. My principal sources were United States population and agricultural census records for Virginia, nineteenth-century county atlases and maps (including Civil War campaign maps), county deed books, tax records, probate inventories, will books, court records, marriage licenses, and vital statistics.

My method was to trace the genealogies of the families back to the Revolutionary War; then, knowing who was who, to follow their movements into Page County in the nineteenth century, and try to determine, from the sources, the broad pattern of their lives: their work and the type of farming they did; their household, family, marriage, and childbirth patterns; their landholding and inheritance and migration patterns; their interactions with the county legal system; and, from probate inventories, the material things they surrounded themselves with. After a while it became necessary to do the same for a representative Page Valley family of German descent for context and comparison. Ultimately I was able to frame my hypotheses regarding the traditions of food, family, farming, and this congregation's religion that underlie this chapter and the next.

In the course of presenting the history of mountain farming in the northern Blue Ridge in the remaining part of this chapter I will argue against the current consensus among historians that Appalachia—"the mountainous backyards of several of our southern states," as William Goodell Frost defined it (Frost 1899)—has been a culture of poverty since initial settlement. That historical consensus runs something like this: Appalachian poverty began when the original mountainfolk made a typical frontier adaptation to their environment, depending on hunting, gathering, and primitive agriculture. As time wore on, the succeeding generations continued this adaptation, concentrating their agricultural efforts on pigs and corn (the familiar "hogs-and-hominy" adaptation of the rural southern poor). While the rest of the nation modernized, the argument goes, the mountain folk became isolated from the cash-wage economy, the marketplace, industrial capitalism, and so forth. The people sank into ignorance and squalor. Historian J. Wayne Flint writes:

> The isolation that helped produce Appalachian poverty dates from its earliest settlement. . . . Isolation aided in the preservation of the customs and traditions of seventeenth-century Britain in the development of a homogeneous culture. . . . Physical access was difficult. . . . The result was a land of subsistence farming and dispersed settlement. Settlers learned to provide for themselves: home remedies, homemade furniture, and homebrew. The first pioneers located in bottom land along streams, with late arrivals moving farther upstream, and finally onto the hillsides. Soil depletion, erosion, and flooding followed, and poverty seemed to be worse the farther one went up the hollow or toward the branch heads. . . . The mountaineers were isolated from both the outside world and from each other. . . . Entire geographical regions were peopled by a family group that had little interest in communicating with surrounding areas. Sometimes the prodigious number of their offspring taxed the resources of their creek or hollow. (Flint 1979:126–128)

The historical base of this "culture-of-poverty" approach is summed up in this 1979 statement from the Appalachian Regional Commission, a federal agency created in 1964 to help eradicate Appalachian poverty:

> The poverty of Appalachia is almost as deeply rooted in American history as the mountains. The first settlers—the frontiersmen—were English and Scotch Irish. They were poor, ill-educated and lacked rudimentary farm skills. Proud, independent, skeptical of organized society, they stayed in the hills, eking out a living. So did their descendants. (Deakin 1979, quoted in Perdue and Martin-Perdue 1979–1980:86)

This historical consensus is based on the Appalachian mountain culture as it was discovered early in the twentieth century by a variety of social workers, educators, and missionaries. When President Hoover vacationed in his camp in the Blue Ridge on the Rapidan, the team of journalists traveling with him found poverty and isolation among the Appalachian hill folk in the Big Meadows area nearby—just a few miles from the ridges and hollows where the ancestors of the members of the Fellowship Independent Baptist Church had lived for several generations—and this resulted in a flurry of public attention, magazine articles, and a sociological monograph, *Hollow Folk* (Sherman and Henry 1973). The historical imagination then projected this culture back into the nineteenth and even the eighteenth centuries, concluding that it represented the survival of an anachronistic frontier adaptation.

But as we shall see, the evidence from the U.S. Census of Agriculture, contemporary newspapers, and probate inventories of the mountain people living in this section of the Blue Ridge during the nineteenth century portrays a much higher standard of living and a diverse farming adaptation—not simply the hogs-and-hominy frontier culture of poverty projected by the historians. In fact, it is possible to divide the history of mountain farming in the region into five periods:

1. Settlement (1830s–1850s)
2. Entrenchment (1850s–1870s)
3. Dependence (1870s–1890s)
4. Subsistence (1890s–1930s)
5. Out-migration (1930s–present)

In each of these periods a different combination of forces affected the husbandman's relationship to his farm and to his family. Being a good husbandman during the first three of these periods meant producing as much as possible of what the household needed on the farm. Corn, rye, wheat, oats, hay, potatoes, milk, butter, pork, beef, wool, flax—the Census of Agriculture reports that each household produced a diverse mix of food products, and many households produced manufactured goods at home as well. In other words, the farm was directed first toward self-sufficiency, with any surplus exchanged or sold to neighbors or at local markets. A few households produced a surplus many times in excess of their needs; yet rather than specializing in a cash crop they maintained diversity to supply their own needs first and accumulated surpluses in several different products.

The Civil War dealt a serious blow to the household economy as lives and livestock were lost. Some households responded with even more vigorous attempts at self-sufficiency, while others saw in the war the incursion of the outside world and the end of self-sufficiency. Moreover, after

1880, the expansion of local tanning and iron industries, the introduction of new industries, particularly tourism, and the coming of the railroad transformed the local economy and linked it irreversibly to the fortunes of distant markets. Talk of money filled the local newspaper. Now a few of the wealthier mountain farmers aimed toward the cash economy, prizing efficiency, specializing in cattle, investing in land and labor. But in the fourth period the local economy crashed and those who had invested lost heavily, while the majority of mountain farmers returned to the household economy of prior years.

Yet in the twentieth century the household economy became difficult and finally impossible to maintain in the face of an expanding population coupled with natural disasters like the chestnut blight, which robbed the mountaineers' hogs of much of their autumn food supply, and the growing attractions of the cash-wage economy and modern town life. Finally, to build the Shenandoah National Park in the early 1930s the government forced many mountain families from their land. The fifth period, from the 1930s to the present, witnessed the out-migration from the mountains into the valley towns and the lower hollows closer to them, along with attempts to maintain as much as possible of the food-producing farmstead on the new lands. The mountain-farming mind-set persisted, as patriarchy, family solidity, and self-sufficiency remained the aim of the household head.

These five historical periods cover approximately 150 years and seven generations of household heads. Not until the third period did community institutions such as schools, stores, and churches enter the mountain hollows, and as the economy faltered after the 1890s, these institutions became precarious. Each time the outside world intruded—in 1860 with the Civil War, in the 1880s with the business boom and bust that followed, and in the early 1930s with the Park—the mountain farmers were victimized. The overriding conclusion is inescapable: mountain history and tradition taught the mountain families that interaction with the outside world was risky and that household and kin-network self-sufficiency was the best strategy. The older members of the Fellowship Independent Baptist Church grew up during the fourth historical period, with parents who had been reduced to subsistence farming and who had learned the hard way to value the household economy. Little wonder that the religion they inherited from these parents emphasized the distance between the church community and the outside world.

The Geographical Context

To understand these events fully it will be necessary, in the discussion that follows, to place the mountain-farming ecosystem within a larger context: namely, the development of the agrarian tradition in the Shenandoah Valley of Virginia, and, specifically, in Page Valley, the portion of the Shenandoah Valley adjacent to the mountain farms. For that reason, it will be useful to review a little Virginia geography.

The traveler who journeys west across Virginia from the coastal Tidewater region through the rolling hills of the Piedmont and then into the Blue Ridge Mountains cannot help being struck by the difference in landscape between the mountains and the Shenandoah Valley beyond. The mountains are not especially high—there is no timberline—but the slopes are precipitous. Virginia's northern Blue Ridge is shaped something like a human spine. A line of high peaks, three to four thousand feet above sea level, runs more or less from north to south, and is punctured by occasional gaps a thousand feet or so lower in elevation. Surrounding this backbone immediately to the east and west lie a series of ridges, highest at the backbone and tapering as they move away. Springs can be found on many of the ridges, while the hollows between the ridges are drained by streams. Ridges and mountaintops occasionally broaden into natural meadows. Further to the south, ridges cluster in whorls like petals in a rose, forming coves at mid-elevations (Wilhelm 1978).

The ancestors of the members of the Fellowship Independent Baptist Church settled in the mountains from Big Meadows atop the Blue Ridge down to the branchwaters of Naked Creek in Jollett and Weaver hollows, and to the north along Long Ridge and Tanner's Ridge, and also to the west in Basin, Cubbage, and Lucas hollows (see Figure 16). This area is part of a political division known as the Shenandoah Iron Works District, the southernmost of four districts comprising Page County. Formed in 1832 from a large section of Shenandoah and a small section of Rockingham County, Page County extends throughout the twelve miles between the spine of the Blue Ridge at its eastern boundary (since 1935 the Shenandoah National Park) and the peak of the Massanutten Mountains (the George Washington National Forest) at its western boundary. These mountain ranges flank the fertile bottomlands of Page Valley, drained by the South Fork of the Shenandoah River. From the west, entrance to this naturally isolated geographical region proceeds over New Market Gap, and from the east, over Thornton Gap. Page Valley is rightly considered part of the Shenandoah Valley, but, as will be shown, it developed somewhat differently owing to its isolation from the chief eighteenth-century Shenandoah Valley migration and trade route.

Pre-Settlement

According to plate-tectonic geological theory, the Appalachian Mountains were created hundreds of millions of years ago when two continents slowly collided and the stresses and strains produced an uplift in the earth's crust (Cook et al. 1983). The continents drifted apart slowly, leaving the Atlantic Ocean between them. Since that time, glaciers have come and gone in

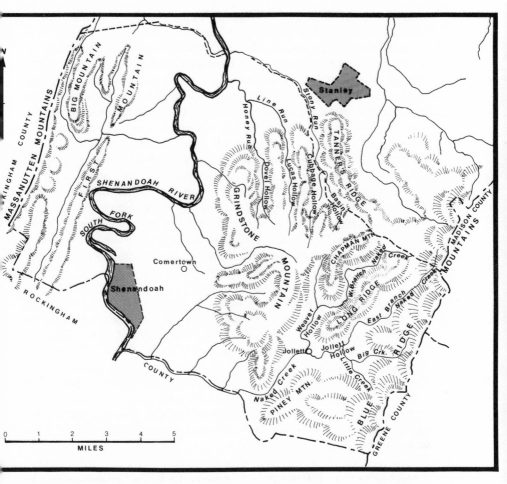

Figure 16. Shenandoah Iron Works District, Page County, Va. Adapted from Potomac Appalachian Trail Club Map No. 10, Shenandoah National Park, Central Section, 1977.

dozens of cycles, changing the climate; while the topography results from a long period of stream erosion (Fenneman 1938; Thornbury 1965). Geologists are divided over whether the glaciers came as far south as the northern Blue Ridge Mountains. But even if they did not quite reach it, glaciation altered the climate, and plants and animals adapted to the cold made their homes in the mountains. As the last glacier retreated and the climate grew gradually warmer, some of the plant and animal species migrated north while others found their niches at suitable mountain altitudes. In southwestern Virginia, for example, at the highest elevations the forest resembles that of northern New England (Watts 1975:5). The significance of this is that because of the glaciation, the migration of species, and the mountain microclimates at various elevations, the Blue Ridge Mountains contained an abundant variety of living things within a relatively small space and served very well for the Indians and, later, the European immigrants who sought their subsistence there.

Mountains, cultural geographers have noted, have had a close connection with religious belief in human history, and it is worth a brief digression to discuss it. Cultural geographers study ideas inscribed on the landscape. "Ideas which express themselves in location and extension of ways of living, or a pattern of life" was how Carl Sauer, the American "father" of cultural geography, put it. "Ideas in the philosophical or psychological sense are not meant here, but ideas expressed in functional form, expressed in ways of doing things" (quoted in Newcomb, ed. 1976:22). The core idea, of course, is the mountain-farming mind-set; but the expression takes specific forms: certain crops and not others, livestock, houses and outbuildings and fences inscribe a pattern on the landscape. Reading the pattern language—understanding it—means understanding the ideas behind the forms.

The mountain-farming mind-set is permeated by the lay of the land. To a person used to life on the flat, time spent in the mountains can be slightly unnerving; it feels askew. On a prairie, or in a broad valley, the landscape impinges horizontally: the sky above, the ground below, with more land beyond. Expansion is regarded horizontally; movement is outward (in America, westward). In the Blue Ridge, the land thrusts vertically; movement is upward or downward.

During the Protestant Reformation and the period of European exploration and discovery, a horizontal conception of the universe gradually replaced the vertical hierarchy represented by the great chain of being. Cultural geographer Yi-Fu Tuan identifies the vertical cosmos with the cyclical view of nature:

"Vertical" here means something more than a dimension in space. It is charged with meaning. It signifies transcendence and has affinity with a particular notion of time. A world model that lays stress on its vertical axis

View from atop Tanner's Ridge, looking southwest toward Naked Creek,
1979.

coincides with a cyclical conception of time; a culture with a sharply articulated calendar of festivals is likely to conceive a highly stratified cosmos
. . . . Corresponding to this geometric bias toward the vertical and temporal
bias toward the cyclical (and eternal) is a special view of human nature—
one which discerns a vertical dimension in the metaphorical sense. Human nature is polarized. Man plays two roles, the social-profane and the
mythical-sacred, the one bound to time and the other transcending it.
(Tuan 1974:129)

The Blue Ridge mountain farmers did not, of course, inhabit a medieval
universe. They were not nearly so isolated as is commonly believed. But
they were, above all, farmers; and it is worth emphasizing that Christianity, with its annual church calendar and emphasis on the Resurrection,
fits well with a rural, agricultural mind-set and its sense of the cyclical
death-rebirth pattern in nature. Farm life was seasonal and climactic.
Growth was followed by harvest, whether of crops or souls. The memory of
mountain farming in the northern Blue Ridge supplies a context in which
a vertical cosmos, if not a chain of being, still points upward from hell to
heaven, while the pattern linking the material, social, and spiritual worlds
is found in the idea of husbandry, replete with its patriarchal implications.

During the early colonial period Tidewater Virginia was occupied by Al-
gonquin Indians, while the Piedmont was home to Siouxan tribes. The Al-
gonquin were farmers (maize, squash, beans) as well as hunters and
gatherers; the Sioux hunted, fished, and gathered food throughout the
Piedmont and the Blue Ridge, but according to contemporary accounts did
not farm. Most of the Virginia Indians were killed or died of disease during
the colony's first fifty years; of those remaining alive, many went west
across the mountains.

At this time, Tidewater Virginians regarded the Blue Ridge as barren
and inhospitable. Writing about his unsuccessful attempts to cross the
mountains in 1669 and 1670, John Lederer advised future travelers that
before reaching the mountains, "You may securely trust to your gun, the
woods [of the Piedmont] being full of fallow, and savanae of red-deer, besides great variety of excellent fowl, as wild turkeys, pigeons, partridges,
pheasants, etc. But you must not forget to dry or barbecue some of these
before you come to the mountains, for upon them you will meet with no
game, except for a few bears" (Lederer 1902:27–28).

As the Tidewater colony grew in the seventeenth century, the Piedmont
became a place for keeping animals, chiefly hogs and cattle, first running wild in the woods and natural meadows, and later driven in herds
(Gray 1933:1:139–151). Population and immigration continued to increase, and in the 1720s some Tidewater land speculators led by Robert
Beverley bought what is now Orange County (on the eastern slope of the
Blue Ridge), subdivided it in large parcels, and sold it to settlers, some of
whom in turn subdivided and sold at a further profit. This pattern of land
colonization was repeated throughout the first half of the eighteenth century, and eventually most of the good land in the Piedmont and along the
eastern side of the Blue Ridge was purchased by westward-migrating
settlers, some coming from the Tidewater, others direct from England
(Hale 1978:13d).

Meanwhile, in 1716 Alexander Spotswood, the colonial governor, had
led a well-provisioned party across the Blue Ridge Mountains to the Shenandoah River. Historical geographers now believe the crossing was made
at Big Meadows, not Swift Run Gap, as had been formerly thought (Hatch
1968:1). If so, the record of one of the members of that group, "The Journal of John Fontaine," is the earliest verbal document describing the precise mountain region where the ancestors of the present Fellowship Independent Baptist Church congregation lived.

Fontaine noted the difficulty of the ascent, owing to steepness, thick un-
derbrush, and rattlesnakes, as they made their way up the windings of the
Rapidan. The mountains were not the barren places Lederer described;
Fontaine reported seeing "the footing of elks and buffaloes, and their beds.
We saw a vine which bore a sort of wild cucumber, and shrub with fruit
like unto a current. We ate very good wild grapes." After reaching the

summit at Big Meadows, they climbed down the western slope only after they "found some trees which had been formerly marked, I suppose, by the Northern Indians, and following these trees, we found a good, safe descent" (ibid.: 47–48).

Evidence is scant concerning eighteenth-century settlements in this section of the northern Blue Ridge. The Fairfax Line survey party, led by Thomas Lewis, crossed at Big Meadows and followed Naked Creek down to the Shenandoah in 1746, but they found no one living in the mountains. In fact, Lewis' journal paints a dreary picture of a difficult journey (Wayland, ed. 1925: 8–9, 16, 69–71). Cultural geographer Eugene Wilhelm, Jr., published a list of thirty-three "squatter" families said to have been living near Big Meadows in 1795 (Wilhelm 1975: 213). Eight of the families have surnames belonging to present-day members of the Fellowship Independent Baptist Church. Charles L. Perdue, Jr., and Nancy Martin-Perdue have challenged Wilhelm's conclusion regarding land ownership, pointing out that because the land in question was claimed by both Lord Fairfax and James Barbour, anyone living on it would have been considered a squatter even if it had been purchased from one claimant or the other (Perdue and Martin-Perdue 1979–1980 and personal communications).

Whatever the status of the settlers, it is clear that by the turn of the nineteenth century a number of families were living within several miles of Big Meadows, and that their surnames were English and Scotch-Irish (Wilhelm 1975: 212). Almost certainly they adapted themselves to their region through hunting, gathering, fishing, and subsistence farming. Blue Ridge mountain land was relatively inexpensive because it was unsuited to commercial farming. It was steep and rocky, the growing season was short and the temperatures cool, and transport was difficult along the mountain paths. But portions of the land, especially near the creek beds in the hollows, could be cultivated, while the forests held oak and American chestnut trees for building sturdy cabins, and the land provided natural meadows for grazing, wild game, nuts, berries, and chestnut mast (for hogs), along with good spring water (Wilhelm 1967: 162–165).

Wilhelm claims that the first pioneers settled at the mouths of the hollows, with later arrivals settling upstream at higher altitudes until at last the headwaters were occupied. Patterns in the Big Meadows region do not bear this claim out. County courthouse and land tax records reveal that the land was held for speculation by absentee landlords who probably never intended to settle on it. It was sold to mountain in-migrants according to its worth, and the hollow settlement patterns reflected the wealth and preferences of the families who purchased it.

Often, three or four households related by blood or marriage migrated into a hollow together or within a year or two of one another. Not all of the household heads bought land; those who did not built their cabins on land belonging to a relative, often farming with the landowner. The result was clusters of families living in close proximity, with such clusters dispersed through the various hollows in the region. Children of neighboring hollows often married, living on land owned by one or the other set of parents until several years had passed and they had accumulated sufficient funds to buy their own farm nearby. As land values increased during the late eighteenth century, many of these young Virginians migrated north along the Blue Ridge or, skipping over the Shenandoah Valley, to the Allegheny Mountains in what is now eastern West Virginia. Instead of selling out for a profit, however, an inheritance pattern of ultimogeniture developed in which the youngest son and his family retained the old homeplace and cared for the parents until death. So powerful was this pattern of ultimogeniture that it endured until mountain farming ceased as a way of life.

This migration and settlement pattern reveals the strength of the patriarchal family and the kinship network in the mountain farm economy. The pattern is evidently far more common than had been thought; it was characteristic of seventeenth-century rural Massachusetts and of the western New York frontier in the late eighteenth and early nineteenth centuries, as case studies have revealed (Greven 1970; Ryan 1981 : 18–59). In this pattern, the patriarch migrates with his unmarried daughters and grown sons, their wives and children if any; he buys a large tract, settling his children on part of it, and lives there until he dies, sometimes arranging the inheritance with his children in exchange for their taking care of the aged parents until death. Mary P. Ryan notes that the patriarch's "personal supervision of an intergenerational family economy and his efforts to settle his family on contiguous landholdings" is an old European agrarian tradition (1981 : 18) whose persistence we have observed in Brother Rastus at the start of this chapter. The families created a "corporate [farm] economy, a domestic system of production that bound family members together, like a single body, in the common enterprise of subsistence" (ibid. : 19). The legal system acknowledged male superiority: beyond the traditional "widow's third" portion, a woman did not inherit her deceased husband's property; it was necessary for her to buy it. Estate sales that followed probate inventories among the mountain families showed widows buying furniture and other items from their own houses (see Appendix B). Women could own property in their own name, of course, and it was not unusual to find enterprising mountain women doing so. Still, the male was the legal head of the household; joint ownership did not obtain.

As I mentioned above, to trace the history of mountain-farming folklife in the Jollett, Weaver, Lucas, Cubbage, and Basin Hollow region (along with Tanner's Ridge and Long Ridge), I chose four families prominent in the church today, traced their genealogies, and then followed the family migration patterns by consulting land records in the county deed books as well as the U.S. Census. In the following section I trace the migrations that brought the Breedens, Cubbages, Lams, and Meadowses into Page

County before the Civil War and I introduce members of the four families who will figure prominently in the story.

Migration and Settlement to 1850

Virginia census records reveal a dozen Breeden households in the 1780s, the name being spelled Breeding, the origin English. Beginning in New Kent County, they migrated, during the next fifty years, west to the Blue Ridge, then north on both sides of the mountains. Two Breeden marriages took place in Page County before 1840: Paschal married Rebecca Nicholson in 1832, and Nicholas (elsewhere called Elias) married Rhoda Nichols in 1835. (The Nichols/Nicholson/Nicholas family settled on the Hughes River in Nicholson Hollow a few miles north of Big Meadows on the eastern slope of the Blue Ridge; see Perdue and Martin-Perdue 1979–1980.) The 1840 census listed seven Breeden households in Page County and eight more just to the south in Rockingham County. Deed books from almost two hundred years ago are vague concerning exact locations, particularly when place names have changed and old boundary markers have long since vanished; but I am reasonably certain most lived along the south branch of Naked Creek. Richard Breeden, for example, is listed in the Page County Land Tax records beginning in 1832 as living on Naked Creek; the 1835 tax records add James and Job Breeding, and the 1836 records add Allison Breeding. Except for Jeremiah (b. 1803), a joiner, and Elias (b. 1811), a shoemaker, all the Breeden household heads were listed by occupation as farmers.

The earliest known Cubbage in the American colonies was John (b. ca. 1730), who migrated from New Kent to Culpeper County, where he died in 1797. County tax records show he owned 100 acres in 1759 (Culpeper County Deed Book C: 200–203). His son Thomas (b. ca. 1765) remained in the eastern Blue Ridge in the section of Culpeper that became Madison County in 1793. Between 1800 and 1843 Thomas conveyed out nearly 250 acres in Madison County, chiefly to his sons William (b. 1791) and Jacob (b. 1795) (Madison County Deed Books 9:84, 434; 10:124–125, 512, 538; 11:66; 15:474–475). In 1836 William owned 136 acres of mountain land in Madison County along the tributaries of the Hughes River, while his younger brother Jacob owned 90. Their land was valued at $1.50 an acre, typical of mountain farmland at that time (Madison County Land Tax Records, 1836).

To follow the fortunes of these families in the next several sections the reader should consult the descent lines and genealogies in Figure 18. Jacob Cubbage, his wife, children, and mother-in-law moved to Page County in 1837, buying 120 acres on Stony Run for $120 (refer to location of James Cubbage in Figure 18). The 1838 Page County Land Tax lists confirm this. The 1840 U.S. Population Census shows him as a farmer with eleven in his household. In 1841 he sold the land on Stony Run to his eldest son, James (b. 1818), a great-grandfather of Brothers Clyde and Rufus Cubbage among present-day church members. The 1842 Land Tax records note a new building on the property, worth $50; probably this was a house for James and his family. Jacob continued to farm the Stony Run land with his son, and after Jacob's death his widow, Nancy, carried the farm on into the 1880s.

Jacob Cubbage's elder brother, William, moved his family to Page County in 1846, purchasing 750 acres of mountain land on Little Line Run from David Dovel (refer to location of Lucy Cubbage in Figure 17). He drove a hard bargain and paid only $300 for land that I estimate was worth three times that (Page County Deed Box F:387). Following the patriarchal pattern of settling his sons on his property, in 1846 he divided his land among his five sons, with Daniel in control, so long as Daniel agreed to care for his parents until their death (Page County Deed Book F:387). Somehow this agreement went sour, possibly because of a legal problem over the original land purchase; in any event William died in 1850, Daniel migrated out of the county, and William's sons Henry (b. 1818) and William, Jr. (b. 1828), repurchased the land from David Dovel for $380 (Page County Deed Book H:352). The U.S. Population Census for 1850 shows William, Sr., as a farmer in Page County with fifteen (including Daniel and William, Jr.) in his household; Henry is listed as a farmer with five in his.

Henry Cubbage was killed during the Civil War, and his estate was probated (see Appendix B). His land was claimed by his younger brother, William, Jr., but Henry's widow, Lucy, sued and in 1875 won the right to buy it for $900, which she did. At the close of the war, James H. Cubbage (b. 1843) came from neighboring Madison County to live in Lucy's household and help on the farm. A grandfather of Brother Clyde, he married in 1867 and again in 1870 after his first wife died, staying on with Lucy and her younger children. James H.'s relationship to the Page County Cubbages remains unclear despite my best efforts, but most likely his mother, Elizabeth (Betsy), or his father, Augustine, or both, were grandchildren of Thomas Cubbage (b. ca. 1765), and Elizabeth probably was a daughter of William Cubbage and sister to Henry Cubbage.

The Meadows family migration pattern into Page County can be presented in greater detail than the others, thanks to the genealogical research of Shirley Seal Breeden (1978). Francis Meadows (b. ca. 1735) sailed to the Virginia colony from Ipswich, England, and settled in Orange County sometime before his second son, James (b. ca. 1760), was born (ibid.: 1–7). After living awhile there, the Meadowses purchased land to the west in the Blue Ridge near Hawksbill Creek in Rockingham County (not to be confused with the Hawksbill Creek in the Marksville District of Page County) (ibid.:6; Wayland 1930:46; Rockingham County Deed Book 000:377). Sometime between 1770 and the start of the Revolution-

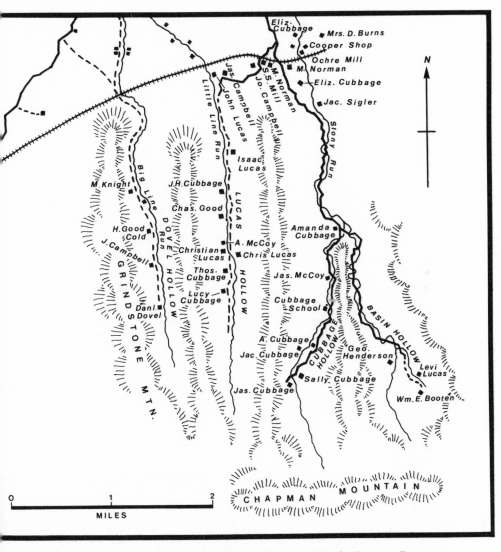

Figure 17. Northeastern section of Shenandoah Iron Works District, Page County, Va., showing households along (*left to right*) Dovel Hollow, Lucas Hollow, and Cubbage Hollow. Adapted from *Lake Atlas of Page County,* 1885.

Figure 18 (overleaf). Genealogies of ancestors of certain members of the Fellowship Independent Baptist Church, showing Breeden, Cubbage, Lam, and Meadows families. (Several offspring have been omitted in each generation.)

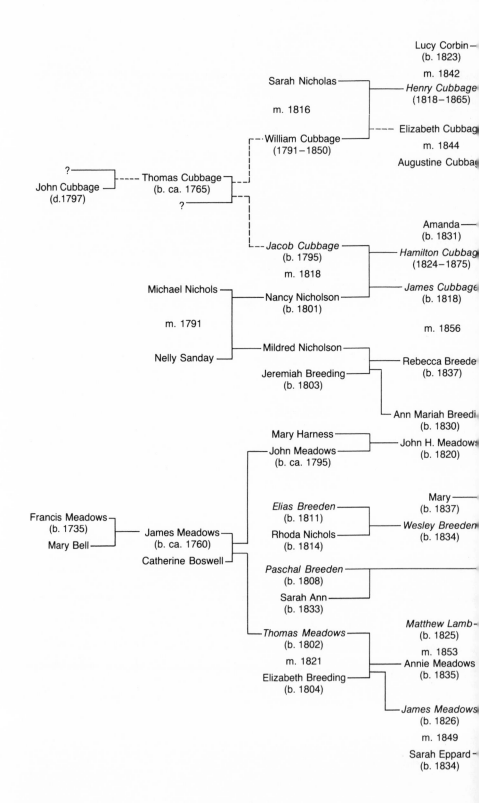

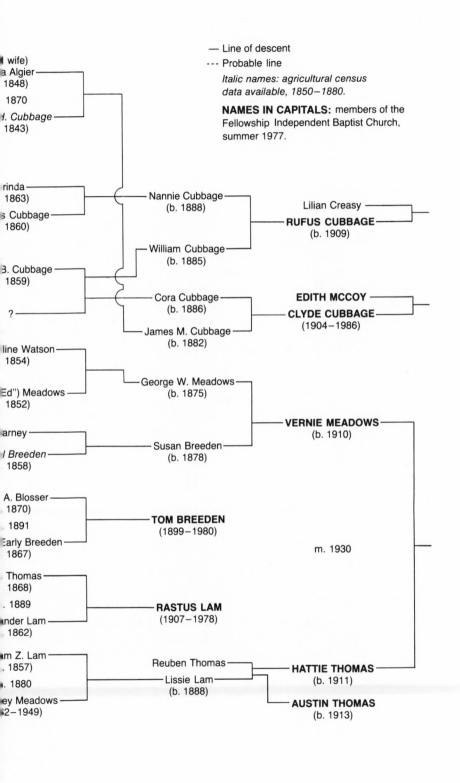

— Line of descent
--- Probable line
*Italic names: agricultural census
data available, 1850–1880.*
NAMES IN CAPITALS: members of the
Fellowship Independent Baptist Church,
summer 1977.

 wife)
 Algier
 1848)
 1870
. Cubbage
 1843)

rinda
 1863)
s Cubbage
 1860)

B. Cubbage
 1859)

?

Nannie Cubbage
(b. 1888)

William Cubbage
(b. 1885)

Cora Cubbage
(b. 1886)

James M. Cubbage
(b. 1882)

Lilian Creasy
RUFUS CUBBAGE
(b. 1909)

EDITH MCCOY
CLYDE CUBBAGE
(1904–1986)

line Watson
 1854)

Ed") Meadows
 1852)

arney
J Breeden
 1858)

George W. Meadows
(b. 1875)

Susan Breeden
(b. 1878)

VERNIE MEADOWS
(b. 1910)

A. Blosser
 1870)
 1891
Early Breeden
 1867)

TOM BREEDEN
(1899–1980)

m. 1930

 Thomas
 1868)
. 1889
nder Lam
 1862)

RASTUS LAM
(1907–1978)

m Z. Lam
. 1857)
. 1880
ey Meadows
2–1949)

Reuben Thomas
Lissie Lam
(b. 1888)

HATTIE THOMAS
(b. 1911)

AUSTIN THOMAS
(b. 1913)

ary War they moved to their land in Rockingham but retained their Orange County property. Francis, Jr., the eldest son, enlisted and served in the company of a Captain Lamm, in the Tenth Virginia Regiment of the Continental Army (Wayland 1930:88–89). This early connection between the Meadows and Lam/Lamb families may have led to their settling near one another in the Swift Run Gap section of Rockingham County (Figure 19). Matthew Lamb (b. 1825), son of Anna Lamb, married Annie Meadows (b. 1835), daughter of Thomas (b. 1802), and was thus the first Lamb to migrate to Page County, coming about 1851.

As the years passed, Francis Meadows' sons and daughters married and started families of their own. In 1780 Francis sold a portion of the land in Orange County, but in 1790 Francis, Jr., with his wife and two children, was living on the remaining portion (Orange County Deed Book 17:380–381; the 1790 Virginia Census lists both Francis and Francis, Jr. in Orange County). By 1810 all the Meadows land in Orange had been sold, and Francis, Jr., with his grown children and their families, had migrated further west to mountain land in Monroe County, now east-central West Virginia (Breeden 1978:10). With the exception of James, who remained on Hawksbill Creek in Rockingham County, all the other Meadowses, including the patriarch, Francis, Sr., followed Francis, Jr., to Monroe County by 1830 (ibid.; Francis, Sr. was reported living in Monroe County as late as 1818).

As James Meadows' children married, some went southwest into the hill country of western Rockingham County (ibid.:13), but others remained in the Blue Ridge. John (b. ca. 1795) bought 112 acres along the north fork of Hawksbill Creek in 1816, while his younger brother Thomas (b. 1802), who had married Elizabeth Breeding in 1821, in 1829 bought 50 acres of mountain land adjacent to his father's near Bear Wallow Spring (Rockingham County Deed Books 3:305–306; 8:468–469).

Thomas was the first Meadows in Page County. In 1833 he bought (for $100) 500 acres of mountain land along the headwaters of Naked Creek in southeastern Page County and northeastern Rockingham County, most of it bordering on land owned by Job and Jacob Breeding, and three years later he sold a small portion to his father; but his father died shortly thereafter and was buried on family land near the northern end of Hawksbill Creek in Rockingham County (Rockingham County Deed Books 11:419–420; Breeden 1978:13). The 1850 U.S. Census of Population listed Thomas as a farmer in Page County with a household of ten. John H. Meadows (b. 1820), son of the John Meadows who remained in Rockingham, moved a

Figure 19. Shenandoah National Park, northern and central sections. Adapted from National Park Service, U.S. Department of the Interior, 1979 auto tourist map.

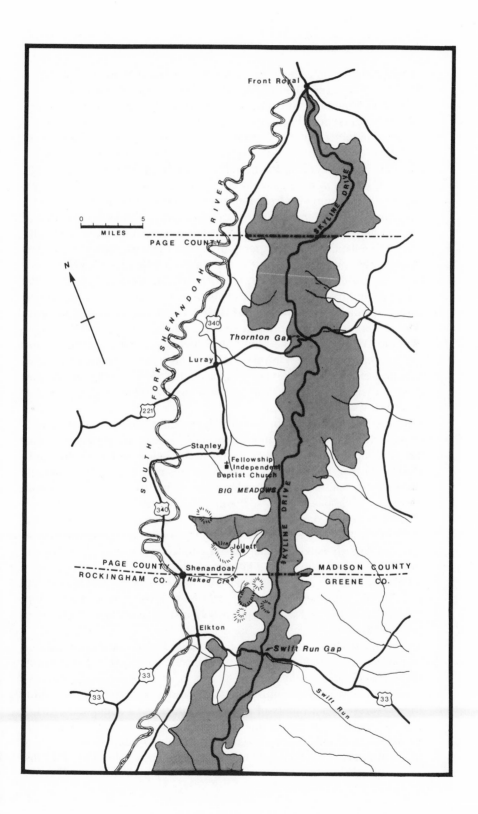

second Meadows household into Page when he bought 186 acres of mountain land in Weaver Hollow along the north branch of Naked Creek in 1858 (Page County Deed Book L:65–66). The 1860 census listed him as a farmer with eight in his household.

These migrations of the Breedens, Cubbages, Lams, and Meadowses fall into an Appalachian highland pattern noted by folklorists Alan Jabbour and Carl Fleischhauer in their landmark study of the Hammons family. These mountain farmers "sought out the upland hollows and woodlands, gaining their sustenance from hunting, gathering, and simple gardening and animal husbandry, entering the cash economy only marginally through the occasional piecemeal sale of logs, pelt, and ginseng. Since [they] cultivated a woodlands lifestyle rather than a settled agricultural style. . . . they tended to be migratory within the general region that fostered the woods life" (*The Hammons Family* 1973:2). The Hammonses moved from Pittsylvania County, Virginia, late in the eighteenth century, into the mountains of Tennessee, Kentucky, and then east-central West Virginia, from 1800 to 1860 (ibid.:4). The Meadowses followed a more northern route, migrating northward in the Blue Ridge, then to the Allegheny ridges and valleys, reaching West Virginia a generation earlier. Meanwhile James Meadows and his sons John and Thomas remained in the Blue Ridge, and most of their offspring grew up nearby along the ridges and valleys near Naked Creek.

It must be understood that some of these migratory mountain farmers entered the cash economy more than others. Jabbour and Fleischhauer describe one end of the spectrum, the largely self-sufficient frontier subsistence farmer. Other families took a greater part in the cash economy through the sale of their labor, livestock, home manufactures, or cash crops. If the various Meadows, Breeden, Lam, and Cubbage households are representative—and there is no reason to believe otherwise—the nineteenth-century spectrum included three types of mountain farmers:

(1) a relatively small number of subsistence farmers with a milk cow, some pigs, a corn patch, and a kitchen garden;

(2) a substantial number of farmers and sharecroppers who kept sheep, pigs, a milk cow, perhaps a steer; who kept forty or so acres in cropland and pasture; and who regularly sold a surplus of their diverse farm produce; and

(3) a relatively small number of mountain-farmer capitalists who invested in land, tools, fertilizer, and hired labor, and who specialized in certain kinds of crops and livestock.

In short, nineteenth-century mountain farmers in the northern Blue Ridge represented a variety of agrarian strategies. To understand why, it will be necessary to spend some time looking at the kind of farming that developed in neighboring Page Valley. Although it is convenient to regard the mountains as a self-contained region and their people as having a distinct culture, to do so is to ignore interactions with neighboring valley ecosystems that helped shape the mountain people's way of life.

The Page Valley Economy to 1860

The Shenandoah Valley of Virginia occupies approximately 6,500 square miles and runs between the Potomac River to just below the Natural Bridge, and lies between the Blue Ridge Mountains and the Alleghenies (see Figure 20). Tens of thousands of Scotch-Irish, English, and German farmers poured into the valley from Pennsylvania during the eighteenth century. Like most farmers of their time, they aimed at producing for home consumption first, with any surplus going to market for cash. Cattle drives, beginning in the 1750s, proceeded north along the Great Wagon Road to Philadelphia. Tobacco, wheat, and hemp were grown for the market during the last half of the eighteenth century. By the time of the Revolutionary War virtually all the good land had been purchased, and by the end of the century half the taxable population of the valley did not own land (Mitchell 1977:232). The continued influx of migrants, from eastern Virginia now as well as from Pennsylvania, coupled with the success of Shenandoah Valley farming, drove land prices higher and fueled land speculation.

Unlike the farmers in the Virginia Tidewater, who had established huge tobacco plantations on vast acreages, the Shenandoah Valley farmers owned smaller parcels, averaging 400 acres; but that was more than sufficient to subdivide, sell a portion at a profit, and leave enough to prosper on. Moreover, inexpensive but good land could be bought in Ohio or further south across the Appalachians in Kentucky. Many of the Shenandoah Valley farmers sold their land and pushed on, Robert O. Mitchell writes, "using the profits of land sales and their previous agricultural experience to better prepare them for occupying new frontiers. In this manner a steadily increasing commercial bias was spread westward, and the American farmer came to view his relationship to the land more as a stewardship than as a lasting covenant" (ibid.:232–233).

Page Valley, however, developed somewhat differently from the rest of the Shenandoah Valley, chiefly owing to the presence of the Massanutten Mountains between it and the Great Wagon Road. Early settlers entered what in 1831 would become Page County either from trails to the north, from the Virginia Piedmont across the Blue Ridge at Thornton Gap, or from the Great Wagon Road across the Massanutten at New Market Gap. This relative inaccessibility of the Page region retarded settlement and also hindered the development of market farming until roads improved in the nineteenth century. Some settlers chose the mountains, but most took up farmlands in the river valley.

Page County historian Harry M. Strickler characterizes the area from

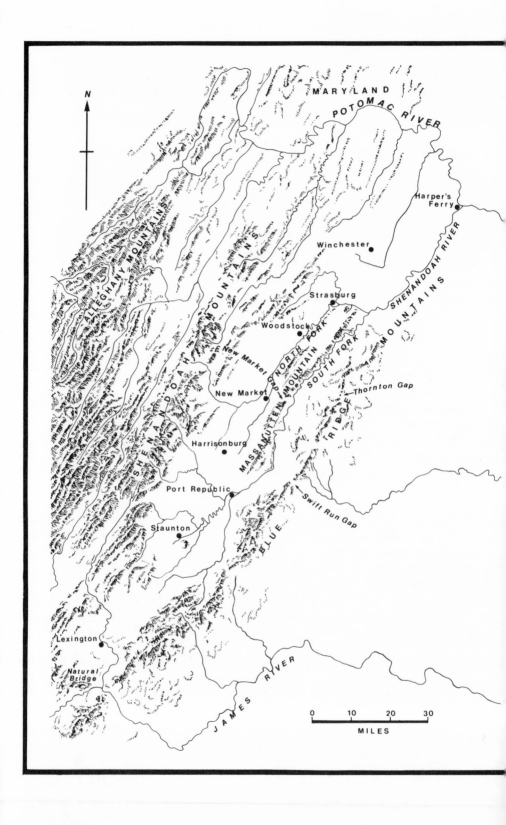

about 1760 to the 1840s as a prosperous agricultural community with small or mid-size valley farms, diverse crops, intensive cultivation, ample livestock, and very little tenant farming, tobacco-growing, or slavery. Butter, cheese, cream, milk, beef, pork, bread, lamb chops, wool, hides, tallow, and chickens and eggs were the main products of the large barns that dominated the landscape. Most of the surplus was sold in local markets. Streams were harnessed for their water power, and sawmills, gristmills, tanneries, forges, foundries, iron furnaces, and carding mills appeared along the river. The Redwell furnace, foundry, and forge just north of Luray was in operation from 1781 until 1860 and furnished most of the stoves, kettles, tools, and iron utensils for the Massanutten Valley. The ore was mined locally and hauled to the furnace; wood was cut and made into charcoal; and limestone was quarried and hauled to fuel the iron works (Strickler 1952).

Tench Coxe's summary of industry in the United States in 1810 shows that Shenandoah County—the county that most of Page was carved from in 1831—led all of Virginia's ninety-nine counties in iron production, fulling mills, and flax seed oil (used in paints and preservatives). It was third in hides tanned, fourth in flaxen goods, and its distilleries were seventh in gallons of spirits produced (Coxe 1814:88–114). This is as much an indication of the general lack of industry in Virginia as it is an indication of a high level of industry in a county whose population was still heavily dominated by farmers.

There was considerable migration into and from Shenandoah County during this period: more than half of the inhabitants in 1780 were gone by 1820, but a greater number took their place (Bauserman 1976:20). Despite an increasing proportion of Scotch-Irish and English, particularly in the iron industry, the Germans who settled on the valley farms remained the dominant agricultural group. As they cleared more land and produced more, they arranged with drovers to have hogs and cattle transported across New Market Gap and Thornton Gap to markets outside the county. The 1830s marked the transition from a barter to a money economy, as the valley farmers began to purchase factory-made clothes and shoes in the local stores and the Germans discarded their German language (ibid.: 15).

In 1836 the Catherine Furnace was built on Cub Run, north of Shenandoah, and the 1840 census noted that the two furnaces and five forges in Page County had a capital investment of $200,000, employed 175 people, and turned out 1,000 tons of iron annually. The 1850 U.S. Census of Industry itemized those manufacturing establishments producing in excess of $500 annually. Those in Page County are shown in Table 1.

Figure 20. The Shenandoah Valley in the eighteenth century. Adapted from *Atlas of American History* (Adams, ed. 1943), plate 58.

TABLE 1. Page County manufacturing establishments, 1850, with
annual production valued in excess of $500

No. and Type of Industry	Raw Material	Product	Value
3 sawmills	175,000 ft. timber	350,000 ft. lumber	$ 2,800
5 tanneries	5,925 hides	5,925 pieces leather, tanned	23,700
1 furnace	2,500 tons ore	1,000 tons pig iron	25,000
2 forges	460 tons pig iron	303 tons iron	30,300
16 flourmills	106,500 bu. wheat	21,300 barrels flour	85,200

SOURCE: U.S. Census of Industry, 1850.

The 1860 U.S. Census lists each household, the name of the head, the occupation of each male over the age of fifteen, and the value of any real estate owned. From this information an overall picture of the work force in the Page County Shenandoah Iron Works District may be drawn (Table 2). The district included the southern third of the county where most of the ancestors of the present-day members of the Fellowship Independent Baptist Church lived: Catherine Furnace, the town of Shenandoah (then Milnes), the smaller towns of Newport and Alma, the farms in the Shenandoah River valley, and the mountain farms in Jollett, Weaver, Dovel, Basin, Lucas, and Cubbage hollows.

Table 2 shows that farming was the chief occupation. The laborers' occupations were not specified, but it can be assumed that most were unskilled and hired themselves out as farm workers, ironworkers, timber cutters, and construction workers. Because in 1860 tenant farmers were listed as farmers without real property they can be distinguished from landowning farmers. Thus, by grouping farm values, we see something of the division of landed wealth in the district at the time (Table 3).

Most of the farmers with real property valued in excess of $2,000 produced considerable surplus for market; in fact, twenty-eight of these fifty-one farmers had property worth more than $5,000 and would have been considered modern farmers for the time and place: they invested in fertilizer, farm machinery, and hired labor, and they must have regarded farming as a business, not just as a way of putting food on the table and selling whatever was left over. Production figures from the U.S. Census of Agriculture in 1850 and 1860 show the fifteen farmers with real estate worth between $1,000 and $1,999 as one of two types: either up-and-coming market farmers (with a high percentage of capital investment) or self-

TABLE 2. Occupations, 1860, Page County, Shenandoah Iron Works District

Occupation	No. of Household Heads Employed in 1860
Farmer	119
Laborer	57
Miller	7
Carpenter, Joiner	4
Shoemaker	5
Blacksmith	7
Wagon maker	4
Collier	6
Stonemason	2
Boatman	4
Tanner	2
Cooper	2
Forgeman	5
Iron master	2
Others	11[a]

SOURCE: U.S. Census of Population, 1860.
[a] Included one each: plasterer, potter, saddler, merchant, machine-builder, tailor, millwright, teacher, distiller, mail-carrier, and brickmaker.

TABLE 3. Division of landed wealth: Farms, 1860, Page County, Shenandoah Iron Works District

No. Farmers Owning	Farms Valued at
28	$5,000 or more
23	$2,000–4,999
15	$1,000–1,999
31	less than $1,000

SOURCE: U.S. Census of Population, 1860.

sufficient farmers with large, undeveloped acreage and production figures not much in excess of the needs of their household. Most of the thirty-one with farms valued below $1,000 were subsistence farmers with very little capital investment. Almost all of the farms valued in excess of $2,000 were in Page Valley, while most of the farms valued below $1,000 were in the Blue Ridge Mountains. Tenant farmers were spread equally in the valley and mountain regions. About half of the tenants were married children farming on their parents' land; another fourth were kin to the landowner in some other way.

The mixed farming pattern of Page Valley had great influence on the mountain-farming culture in the nineteenth century. Indeed, some of the mountain farmers moved to the lowlands and adopted it, while others imitated it as best they could, given the location of their land. It is therefore worth pausing to look at it before examining the mountain-farming patterns in detail.

The German Mixed-Farming Crop-Livestock Pattern in Page Valley

In Page Valley the in-migrants had by and large preserved and extended mixed (i.e., diversified) farming as they had practiced it earlier in southeastern Pennsylvania. The average southeastern Pennsylvania farm late in the eighteenth century, consisting of 125 cultivated acres with a household numbering five, produced small market surpluses, mainly in wheat and beef. From wills, inventories, travelers' accounts, and other sources James Lemon derived the figures for average annual production shown in Table 4.

In this livestock-intensive, diversified farm pattern, most of the grain fed the animals. The farmers ate pork and beef, and sold whatever surplus they had; Lemon calculates that on average they would have sold two hundred pounds of beef and fifty pounds of pork annually. Lemon estimates grain surpluses at twenty bushels of wheat, fifteen of oats, and ten of barley. He does not state what this average household did with three hundred bushels of potatoes, but, given the amount of pork, beef, and flour they consumed, they must have sold most of the potatoes. Among the poorer farmers, fewer livestock were kept, little or no wheat was grown, and they relied more on potatoes, using some corn for flour as well as feed (Lemon 1972:150–167). It must be stressed that these are average figures and that not all farms grew all the crops listed. The crop-livestock diversity shows that the farmers intended to produce for home consumption with any surplus going to market, rather than to specialize primarily for the market and use the cash received to purchase for home consumption.

TABLE 4. Average farm production, late eighteenth century, south-eastern Pennsylvania

Livestock	Food Required Grain	Hay	Average Annual Production
Cattle (3 cows, 1 steer, 3 calves)	100 bu.	20 tons	450 lb. beef + milk, butter, cheese
Swine (8)	30 bu. + mast		550 lb. pork
Sheep (10)	5 bu.	1 ton	30 lb. wool
Horses (3–4)	80 bu.	9 tons	
Poultry			Eggs, meat

Crops	Used for	Average Annual Production
Wheat	Flour, market	80 bu.
Rye	Flour, feed	25 bu.
Oats	Feed, flour	60 bu.
Barley	Feed, flour, beer	30 bu.
Corn	Feed	120 bu.
Buckwheat	Green manure	30 bu.
Hay	Feed	30 tons
Apples	Cider	800 bu.
Potatoes	Food	300 bu.

SOURCE: Lemon 1972: 152–153.

We may briefly compare this mixed farming pattern with others during the period under study. A representative New England farm at the turn of the nineteenth century consisted of about one hundred acres, a third devoted to pasture, a fifth to hay, and only about ten acres to tillage, where the farmer grew corn, rye, potatoes, and a little barley and buckwheat. Oxen served for plowing. Four or five cattle, six to fifteen sheep, two or three pigs, and a dozen or two chickens supplied the household with milk, butter, cheese, pork, beef, mutton, and wool (Zwelling 1977: 2–3). Not only did the average New England farm produce less than the average southeastern Pennsylvania farm, but the crop-livestock mix also differed: New England farmers used oxen instead of horses, could not grow a surplus of wheat, and ate more bread (chiefly corn and rye) and less meat (but including mutton and ox). In the South, the large tobacco and cotton plantations produced enormous amounts of market crops, but they also produced most of the food needed on the plantation; meanwhile, the majority of cotton and tobacco farmers living on small and mid-sized farms produced for home consumption first, and devoted their efforts to the cash crop only after they had taken reasonable care of their household needs (see, e.g., Wright 1978).

In short, apart from the large plantations, the general farm pattern in the early Republic was one of crop-livestock diversity, with subsistence as the basic aim, and profit a goal only after subsistence had been achieved. "Safety-first behavior," writes Gavin Wright, "may not be an indication of restricted vision or a lack of interest in improved standards of living; to the contrary, the last thing an ambitious young farmer would want to do is to place in jeopardy his clear farmownership, his independent decision-making capacity, his room for maneuver. Perhaps the strongest evidence for this interpretation is that we observe a crop-mix continuum, not a sharp division between subsistence farms and staple-growing plantations" (Wright 1978:70–71).

Farmers in the valley portion of the Shenandoah Iron Works District provide an excellent case in point, and the evidence is clear and satisfying. The U.S. Census took a household-by-household inventory of agricultural production in the years 1850, 1860, 1870, and 1880 in Page County. After examining the population and agricultural censuses, I chose a representative family of valley farmers and determined their crop-livestock pattern in 1850 (Appendix C). Three generations of Kites—some quite wealthy, others below the county median—were represented in the seventeen Kite households counted in the Shenandoah Iron Works District.

The average Kite farm in 1850 contained 144 cultivated acres and was valued at $4,967. In livestock it had 4.6 horses, 4.4 milk cows, 6.6 other cattle, 9.5 sheep, 23.2 pounds of wool, and 22.2 pigs. The value of the livestock slaughtered during the previous year was $113. Average farm production figures (for the year ending on June 1, 1850) were 285 bushels of wheat, 277 bushels of corn, 73 bushels of oats, 23 bushels of rye, 138 bushels of apples, 26 bushels of potatoes, 135 pounds of butter, 2 pounds of flax, 7.6 tons of hay, and $35 worth of home manufactures. The crop-livestock mix here was virtually identical to that in late eighteenth-century southeastern Pennsylvania, with surplus production in pork and wheat greater, and in apples and potatoes less. (Actually, this potato figure is quite reasonable; Lemon's figure of 300 bushels per southeastern Pennsylvania farm seems unusually high.) From will books in the Page County courthouse, I have reproduced one Kite probate inventory and one from David M. Dovel to give the reader an idea of the material culture of a mid-nineteenth-century valley farmstead in the Shenandoah Iron Works District (Appendix B). The probate inventories and agricultural production figures for these representative valley farmers will soon be contrasted with similar evidence for the mountain-farming families. But first we must make the food-production calculations more specific. After all, we want to know whether the mountain-farm families were starving, breaking even, or producing a marketable surplus. What will be far harder to determine is whether a household whose production approximately equaled its consumption worked a great deal of the time just to break even, or whether it worked relatively little and cultivated leisure rather than produce a surplus for market. I will take up that question near the end of the chapter.

Calculating Farm Household Food Production and Diet

How well off were the nineteenth-century, mountain-farming ancestors of the members of the Fellowship Independent Baptist Church? How did they compare with the Kites and others in Page Valley? Were they eking out their living in a frontier existence or producing a surplus for market? Their material standard of living can be measured by how well their food production met their needs.

Recall that the U.S. Agricultural Census took a household-by-household farm inventory in 1850, 1860, 1870, and 1880, counting the capital, crops, livestock, home manufactures, and farm produce on every farm. Some of those records were lost, and not every state of the nation was surveyed, but fortunately the figures for Page County, Virginia, are intact; and this means that within the limits of census accuracy for each Breeden, Cubbage, Lam, and Meadows household we know such things as how many bushels of corn, rye, and wheat were produced and how many pigs, cattle, and milk cows were slaughtered and how many were on hand (see Appendix D).

The first thing to determine is how much food a household needed to stay healthy. While today's average American adult needs 2,400 calories per day, food historians say that people ate much more in the nineteenth century; the extra energy was needed for more manual labor and longer work days. National diet estimates made for 1879 by Merrill Bennett and Rosamond H. Pierce (1961:95–119) show that a working adult male consumed 3,741 calories per day, and other historians' estimates do not vary significantly (Cummings 1940:236; Lemon 1967:62; and Battalio and Kagel 1970:30 for slave diets; for a summary see Atack and Bateman 1984:300–302). The annual caloric needs of a working adult male were therefore 3,741 calories × 365 days = 1,365,465 calories. This is a rather large figure. It will be most convenient to express both household needs *and* production in terms of the equivalent amount of caloric energy in a bushel of corn. It takes 1.1 bushels of shelled corn (what the Census of Agriculture measured) to produce a bushel of cornmeal. A bushel of cornmeal contains 78,609 calories, and therefore a bushel of shelled corn contains 71,463 calories (*Agricultural Statistics, 1982*, p. 5; Pennington and

Church 1985:73). Now if we divide the adult male annual energy need of 1,365,465 calories by the amount of energy in a bushel of corn, 71,463, we arrive at a figure of 19.11 corn-bushel equivalents (hereafter CBE) of food energy needed per year by an average adult male farm worker.

Now of course not everyone consumed that amount, only males fourteen and over; to calculate the needs of others, the 19.11 CBE figure should be multiplied by the following factors: females over fourteen and children eleven to fourteen, by .9; children seven to ten, by .75; children four to six, by .4; and children age three and under, by .15 (Atack and Bateman 1984:302). Therefore a nineteenth-century Blue Ridge mountain-farm household's total annual caloric need can be estimated by adding up the adult male equivalent for household size and multiplying by 19.11 CBE. Suppose we have a household with a male head, aged thirty, his wife, aged twenty-seven, and two daughters, aged eight and five. Their adult male equivalent for household size will be 1 + .9 + .75 + .4 = 3.05. Multiplying this by 19.11 CBE yields 58.29 CBE. The household would need the caloric equivalent of 58.29 bushels of corn for a year.

Now, having calculated needs, how may we determine production? Matters are more complicated here, and it may be useful for the reader to refer back to Figure 15 and the ecological/economic cycle of production and consumption to see what was produced and consumed or exchanged. We need to begin with a few assumptions. First, I will assume that a percentage of the crop was saved for seed rather than consumed; Jeremy Atack and Fred Bateman (1984:304) give the following figures: corn, 5 percent saved as seed; rye, 11 percent; wheat, 13 percent; oats, 10 percent; buckwheat, 10 percent; potatoes, 10 percent. These figures may be somewhat high; Atack and Bateman give lower figures in their earlier article (1979), but I will assume the higher proportion of seed saved. Second, I will assume that, given the reported lack of interest in feeding grain to livestock at this time and place, insignificant amounts of grain went to feed. I will come back to this assumption later. Third, I will assume that the average milk cow produced 2,000 pounds of milk, butter, and cheese. Atack and Bateman (1979:115–116) arrive at an average figure of about 3,000 for the North in 1860, but given the butter yields the census indicates in the Blue Ridge (the only clue we have to this production) the lower figure seems more reasonable. One thousand pounds of milk and milk products is the energy equivalent of a bushel of corn (Atack and Bateman 1984:306), so the average mountain farmer's cow gave the annual food equivalent of two corn-bushels.

Next we need to make some assumptions about yields of grain and root crops. I. B. Morrison gives the following equivalents: 1 bushel of corn contains the caloric equivalent of 2 bushels of rye, 2 bushels of oats, 1.3 bushels of wheat, or 4 bushels of potatoes (1940:994–999). Finally, we need to consider meat and fish. Here we run into difficulties. First, the census did not count fish and game, so there is no easy way to estimate the caloric contribution hunting and fishing made to the mountain farm households. I see no alternative but to leave fish and game out of the equation with the understanding that households deficient in food production may have made up the difference by hunting and fishing. Only the 1880 census gives figures on chickens and eggs, but it would appear that their contribution to the diet was negligible, on average only one CBE per household; therefore I will ignore poultry as well.

The annual amount of pork and beef (no mutton was eaten) each household produced is derived from the value of animals slaughtered during the previous year. The 1850, 1860, and 1870 Censuses of Agriculture provide this dollar value. To convert it to CBE we divide by the average price per pound, multiply by the percentage of edible meat per pound (that is, the proportion of dressed to live weight), or about .76; and divide by the number of pounds of pork or beef equivalent in caloric value to a bushel of corn, or 7.6 (Atack and Bateman 1984:302). Newspapers and other reports tell us that pork and beef were sold locally for an average of $.037 per pound in 1849, $.04 in 1859, $.032 in 1869, and $.05 in 1880. Unfortunately, the 1880 census does not indicate the value of animals slaughtered, although like the earlier censuses it gives the total livestock value. To estimate 1880 household values for animals slaughtered, I first figured the ratio of total livestock value to the total value of animals slaughtered for all the mountain households under consideration in 1850, 1860, and 1870 (the result equaled 2.74); I then divided each 1880 household's total livestock value by 2.74. These 1880 estimates are average figures.

Finally, it should be noted (for any researcher going to the references cited) that Bateman and Atack arrive at a figure of 27.84 CBE consumed each year by the average adult male, compared to my figure of 19.11. There are two reasons for this difference. First, Atack and Bateman assume a daily adult male caloric need of 5,000 rather than 3,751, to bias their results opposite their argument. But in the face of reliable evidence for the lower figure I see no reason not to adopt it. Second, they assume grain-fed pork and beef in the diet; in other words, a person who eats corn-fed meat also consumes the corn fed to fatten up the animal, hence the larger consumption figure. My smaller figure, as I mentioned above, assumes no grain fed to the hogs. Why not? Atack and Bateman studied farmers in the northern United States in 1860, and estimated ten bushels corn fed to each pig (1984:303). But in the southern mountains the hogs foraged for their food, fattening themselves before fall slaughter on chestnuts from the woods (McDonald and McWhiney 1980:1106–1108). Most mountain farmers saw no reason to feed them corn before the November roundup and slaughter; and any amounts fed were insignificant. Other livestock subsisted mainly on pasture and forage. Ironically, the "backward" mountain household produced food energy more efficiently than the scientific northern agriculture and did so with less labor and more leisure.

Given these assumptions, we can compute each farm's total production in equivalent bushels of corn as follows:

Production (in CBE) = ($ value of animals slaughtered ÷ [$ market price of meat × 10]) + (no. milk cows × 4) + (bu. corn × .95) + (bu. rye × .89 ÷ 2) + (bu. wheat × .87 ÷ 1.3) + (bu. oats × .90 ÷ 2) + (bu. buckwheat × .90) + (bu. potatoes × .90 ÷ 4).

Again, note that certain foods are omitted from the above formula: fish, game, poultry, eggs, fruits, and garden vegetables. No doubt these contributed to the mountain farmers' diet, and taken together they may have contributed significantly; I just do not see how to make a reliable estimate. For that reason, as we move through the sections that follow, we will evaluate the Breeden, Cubbage, Meadows, and Lam farm household food energy needs and production without taking these foods into account. If anything this will serve to bias the results in the opposite direction of my argument that the mountain farmers were by and large doing well and producing a surplus.

Mountain Farming, 1850–1880: Entrenchment

As we have seen, the mountain families under discussion—Meadows, Breeden, Lam, Cubbage—migrated into the region in the second quarter of the nineteenth century. By the time of the 1850 agricultural census most of the mountain households were engaged in mixed farming practices. Although hogs and corn were the chief farm products, the presence of other crops (especially rye) and livestock (sheep and cattle) indicates that the farmers intended to diversify. Indeed, those families fortunate enough to have purchased the better land at lower altitudes closer to the mouths of the hollows where the streams converged were able to produce more for market. A few families had even purchased several non-adjacent tracts of bottom land and were engaged in commercial farming.

The two Meadows households in 1850 show all the characteristics of a successful subsistence farming operation with surplus production to convert to cash. According to the 1850 U.S. Census of Agriculture, Thomas (b. 1802) owned five hundred acres, only twenty of which were "improved" (i.e., orchard, pasture, and tilled cropland); his household numbered twelve. His eldest son Mitchel (b. 1823) had a household of his own, with a wife and child; he lived and farmed on his father's land, but because he owned livestock and produced crops he is listed separately from his father in the census (see Appendix D). Assuming the two households shared their farm production, the Meadowses for the year ending on June 1,

1850, had two horses, two milk cows, twenty pigs, 21 bushels of wheat, 30 bushels of rye, 175 bushels of corn, and 16 bushels of potatoes, plus whatever food they could hunt and gather, plus whatever cash they could obtain from hiring themselves out as laborers or from bringing timber to sawmills, or pelts or tan bark to the tanneries, or surplus meat or grain to the local market. The value of their slaughtered livestock was $34.

While it is impossible to tell how much food the Meadowses obtained through hunting and gathering, or how much cash they earned through labor, it is possible to determine whether, simply on the basis of their farm production, they had sufficient food. Table 5 shows that they needed 236 CBE and produced 302, giving a surplus of 66 CBE. Most likely they sold their wheat crop, 21 bushels, at the 1850 local market price of $.80 per bushel, giving them $16.80 in cash. In 1850 Page County land was taxed at $.10 per $100; Thomas Meadows' five hundred acres was valued at $400 and he paid $.40 tax on it. In 1850 $16.40 would buy twenty acres of unimproved mountain land, or pay a farm laborer's wages for one month. More likely, with the rest of the cash the Meadowses bought clothing, home furnishings (they had no home manufactures), staple goods, tobacco, and so forth. Thomas Meadows' youngest son, Henry (1840–1920), inherited the homeplace, and his probate inventory (Appendix B) doubtless contains items he inherited with it.

The 1850 Census of Agriculture shows that the Cubbages produced surpluses in beef and wheat (see Appendix D). Even though their production was smaller, the Cubbage crop-livestock mix resembles the Page County German lowlands pattern represented by the Kites (see above and Appendix C). This was especially true of Henry Cubbage, fattening five cattle for market and producing 250 bushels of wheat. His brother William, Jr. (b. 1828), was even more ambitious, as we shall see. But in 1850 Jacob Cubbage and his son James produced a surplus of 124 CBE (worth $148) and Henry produced a surplus of 114 CBE (worth $136; Table 5). At 1850 prices $136 was enough to buy the labor of a farmhand for nine months or to purchase a herd of twenty-five cattle. Henry's probate inventory (Appendix B), taken after he was killed during the Civil War, shows that most of his wealth apart from his land was in livestock and farm produce, not in home furnishings. It is hard to escape the conclusion that Henry Cubbage was an acquisitive, market-minded farmer.

Most of the Breedens lived on high mountain land at the headwaters of Naked Creek, and as a consequence they emphasized herding more than grain production. Of the nine households in 1850 (Table 5), four produced small surpluses, two produced considerable surpluses in the 200 CBE range, and one, Allison Breeden, produced a surplus of 629 CBE, which when converted to 1850 dollars equals $751, a handsome gross income. It is likely that he had to hire some labor to help out, reducing his net in-

TABLE 5. Food energy needs, production,[a] and surplus, selected mountain farm households, Page County, 1850

Surname	Name	Year Born	House- hold AME[b]	Pigs (No.)	Value Animals Slaugh- tered ($)	Milk Cows (No.)	W (
Cubbage	Jacob/ James	1795/ 1818	9.50	14	*	3	
Cubbage	Henry	1819	15.95	5	48	2	
Meadows	Thomas/ Mitchel	1802/ 1823	12.35	20	34	2	
Breeden	James	1767	6.65	4	40	1	
Breeden	Elijah	1792	4.70	4	34	2	
Breeden	Richam/ Sanford	1796/ 1824	3.95	19	40	3	
Breeden	Allison	1797	6.20	21	72	1	
Breeden	Jeremiah	1803	5.90	13	24	2	
Breeden	Paschal	1808	7.95	19	32	2	
Breeden	Elias	1811	6.35	18	40	2	
Breeden	William	1817	3.75	*	4	1	
Breeden	Samuel	1829	2.05	7	*	1	
Average values:			7.11	13.1	37	1.8	

[a] Production does not include wool, flax, or home manufactures, which some families produced. See Appendix D.
[b] Adult male equivalents.
* No information available in this category for this household.

come. But when Allison's production is compared with the average Page Valley farmer's production of 826 CBE[1] it does not look so large. Curiously, two of the Breeden household heads whose farm production was tallied were not listed by occupation as farmers: Jeremiah was listed as a joiner, and Elias as a shoemaker. Doubtless they supplemented their farm income through their trades, and Jeremiah may even have gotten most of his income that way. Jeremiah died in 1851, and his probate inventory (Appendix B) includes shoemaker's tools as well as carpentry tools, and a walnut cupboard that he may have made for himself.

1. The 826 CBE figure is calculated based on the Kite family farms in 1850 (see "The German Mixed-Farming Crop-Livestock Pattern in Page Valley" above).

Corn (Bu.)	Oats (Bu.)	Buck-wheat (Bu.)	Potatoes (Bu.)	CBE Needed	CBE Produced	CBE Surplus
180	0	0	20	181.55	305.62	124.07
75	*	*	30	304.80	418.64	113.83
175	0	0	16	236.01	301.66	65.65
50	0	0	20	127.08	164.11	37.03
15	0	0	12	89.82	163.67	73.85
140	30	0	9	75.48	308.68	233.20
500	0	0	0	118.48	747.11	628.63
50	21	20	0	112.75	154.04	41.29
50	0	6	10	151.92	176.34	24.42
200	40	24	6	121.35	380.43	259.08
*	*	*	*	71.66	—	—
*	*	*	*	39.18	—	—
144	9.1	3.0	12	135.84	312.02	160.11

One of the more interesting facts about the middle generation of Breedens in 1850 was their emphasis on sheep (see Appendix D). In theory, the Blue Ridge was well suited to pasturing sheep, as it was to herding in general; and periodically during the first half of the nineteenth century various agricultural societies promoted the idea of sheep-raising in the southern highlands; but in practice keeping sheep in the Blue Ridge was difficult because of predatory dogs (Gray 1933:2:835). Of course, it could be argued that the Breedens kept sheep to make their clothing, and in so doing carried on an old tradition of self-sufficiency (suggested by the old-fashioned tools in the Breeden probate inventories); but the market for wool was considerable, values fluctuated widely, and in a good year a handsome profit could be made. After the Civil War, however, the price of wool plummeted and remained low, and wool production dropped correspondingly.

TABLE 6.   Food energy needs, production,[a] and surplus, selected mountain farm households, Page County, 1860 and 1870

Surname	Name	Year Born	Census	House-hold AME[b]	Pigs (No.)	Value Animals Slaugh-tered ($)
Cubbage	James	1818	1860	2.05	*	56
Cubbage	Henry	1819	1860	5.45	7	117
Cubbage	Hamilton	1824	1860	2.85	4	10
Cubbage	William	1828	1860	4.65	11	80
Cubbage	James	1818	1870	4.45	1	20
Cubbage	Hamilton	1824	1870	5.85	4	18
Meadows **	Mitchel	1823	1860	4.10	10	90
Breeden	Richam	1796	1860	1.90	12	25
Breeden	Elias	1811	1860	3.95	10	126
Breeden	Sanford	1824	1860	3.60	13	70
Breeden ***	Richam	1796	1870	1.90	1	10
Average values:				3.70	7.3	57

[a] Production does not include wool, flax, or home manufactures, which some families produced Appendix D.
[b] Adult male equivalents.
* No information available in this category for this household.
** Also listed in the 1860 census, but without any household agricultural census:
    Meadows, John H., b. 1820, household AME 5.00, farmer, real estate valued at $400
    Meadows, James, b. 1826, household AME 3.75, farmer, real estate valued at $300
    Meadows, Thomas, b. 1831, household AME 2.25, farmer, real estate valued at $250
*** Also listed in the 1870 census, but without any household agricultural census:
    Breeden, Elias, b. 1811, household AME 1.90, shoemaker, real estate valued at $500
    Breeden, Sanford, b. 1824, household AME 5.15, farmer, real estate valued at $100

Rye (Bu.)	Corn (Bu.)	Oats (Bu.)	Buck-wheat (Bu.)	Potatoes (Bu.)	CBE Needed	CBE Produced	CBE Surplus
110	150	0	0	5	39.18	339.25	300.07
295	200	60	0	80	104.15	683.48	579.33
0	200	0	0	0	54.46	219.00	164.54
30	350	40	0	50	88.86	607.18	518.32
50	50	0	0	15	85.04	143.63	58.59
20	75	0	0	3	111.79	141.08	29.29
100	50	25	6	0	78.35	349.68	271.33
60	60	0	0	10	36.31	152.45	116.14
115	100	10	30	12	75.48	503.38	427.90
20	100	15	0	5	68.80	294.78	225.98
30	40	0	0	0	36.31	86.60	50.29
76	125	13.6	3.3	16	70.79	320.05	249.25

Inflation hit the South generally during the decade prior to the Civil War, and Page County was no exception. In 1860, with secessionist feelings running high, the federal census takers understandably failed to penetrate deeply or remain long enough to take detailed agricultural surveys in the Blue Ridge. As a result, agricultural data from the four families under consideration are incomplete. The statistics, such as they are, are presented in Table 6 and Appendix D. Within the limits of their accuracy, it is nonetheless clear that the 1860 production figures show remarkable increases over 1850. Henry Cubbage and his brother William, Jr., produced five and six times more than their households needed, while James produced nearly nine times his household needs. Even Mitchel Meadows had increased his surplus from 66 CBE in 1850 to 271 CBE in 1860. It is worth noting that both crops and livestock contributed to these increases; in other words, we do not see market specialization in a cash crop but continued attempts at enlarging on several fronts simultaneously. Again the farmers hedged their bets.

Prosperity came to an end quickly with the Civil War. Several mountain farmers enlisted or were conscripted into the Confederate army. Strickler reports that crop and livestock losses in Page Valley were heavy because Union troops under General Sheridan burned all the barns lest they feed the Confederate soldiers (1952:142–160). It is unclear how much was lost from the mountain farms. And in May and June 1862 Stonewall Jackson's Confederate soldiers and James Shields' Union soldiers moved through Page Valley as they positioned themselves for various battles in the Shenandoah Valley. Some of the mountain farmers probably hid to avoid the Confederate draft conscriptors. Hezekiah Lam (b. 1854, a son of Matthew Lamb and an uncle of Brother Rastus), was quoted in the July 3, 1936, *Page News and Courier* as saying, "When the conspiritors [conscriptors] would come I'd run through the mountains and tell everybody and they never got many." Not many, perhaps, but among the four families under study, two first-born sons, Henry Cubbage and Mitchel Meadows, were killed in the war.

Despite the turbulence of this period, or because of it, three of the four families (the Breedens were the exception) made an even firmer commitment to mountain farming as a way of life. Among the Meadowses, for example, a flurry of land-buying along the north branch of Naked Creek took place just prior to the war. In 1854 James' wife, Sarah, bought 193 acres of mountain land for $75 (Page County Deed Book J:210). In 1858, 1859, and 1860 Mitchel Meadows bought 600 and sold 80 acres "lying on the mouth of Aggy's Run and up the meanderings of Jack's prong" (Page County Deed Books K:407; L:84, 246). Another flurry of land-buying took place between 1874 and 1881 and is summarized in Table 7.

It is not hard to interpret what was going on. The sons, grandsons, widows, wives, and married daughters of Thomas and John Meadows deliberately chose to buy land and establish a kin-network settlement. Nine of Thomas' eleven children, for example, determined to remain in the region and farm for a living, carrying on the tradition throughout the nineteenth century. The nine were Mitchel (b. 1823), James (b. 1826), Eliza (b. 1830), Thomas W. (b. 1831), Frances (b. 1833), Annie (b. 1835, m. Matthew Lamb), William Billy (b. 1839), Henry (b. 1842), and Harriet (b. 1844). After Mitchel was killed in the war, his four sons, Hiram F. (b. 1849), James S. (b. 1851), Thomas W. (b. 1854), and Zechariah (b. 1859), farmed on family land and raised families of their own. Of Thomas' children only Lydia (b. 1836) and Mary C. (b. 1838) left the region, both after marrying.

Not only did most of the mountain families deliberately choose to settle here; they purchased their land to do so. Contrary to the pejorative hillbilly stereotype, then, they are best regarded as choosing to remain in the mountains in family settlements rather than as a shiftless people left behind by progress and a westward-migrating civilization. If they had wanted to move to the towns or go west, they surely could have done so

LE 7. Some Meadows family land transactions, Page County, 1874–1881

ear	Buyer/Relation of Buyer to Seller	Seller/Location	No. Acres/ Price
874	Thomas W. Meadows None	Sanford Breeden Mountain land, north branch Naked Creek	120 $40
875	Henry Meadows Brother married a McDaniel	Zechariah McDaniel Naked Mountain	1,000 $150
875	William B. Meadows Sister married an Eppard	Thomas Eppard Near Jollett School	25 $300
878	William B. Meadows Brother-in-law	Virinda McDaniel Meadows (widow of Mitchel Meadows) Naked Mountain	22 $22
878	James Meadows Brother-in-law	Virinda McDaniel Meadows Naked Mountain	85 $50
878	Eliza Meadows Sister-in-law	Virinda McDaniel Meadows Naked Mountain	36 $50
880	William B. Meadows None	Benjamin Merica (from Reuben Eppard) Naked Mountain	30 $30
881	Henry Meadows sells timber rights for seven years to chestnut oak bark on 250 of his 1,000 acres on Naked Mountain to Deford & Co. (a tannery in Luray) for $400.		

JRCE: Page County Deed Books.

with the money they spent instead to buy land in the Blue Ridge.

The Lamb family came into the Naked Creek region during this period. Matthew Lamb (b. 1825), a son of Anna Lamb, migrated the few miles north in the Blue Ridge from the Swift Run Gap area of northeastern Rockingham County, taking the same route as the Meadowses had done a generation earlier (Breeden 1978:29). In Page County in 1853, he married Annie Meadows (b. 1835), a daughter of Thomas, and was farming in the Naked Mountain vicinity about a mile and a half east of Aggy's Run (see Figure 14) in 1859 (Page County Marriage Book I; Page County Deed Book L:84). The 1860 U.S. Census of Population credited him with real property worth fifty dollars. He bought more land on Naked Mountain— forty-seven acres—from his wife's sister-in-law, Virinda McDaniel Meadows (widow of Mitchel Meadows) and the heirs of Mitchel Meadows in 1878 (Page County Deed Book [10 May 1878]). It turns out that Virinda's mother was a Lamb (Breeden 1978).

Thus far we have concentrated on Thomas' branch of the Meadows family. John H. Meadows, son of Thomas' brother John, moved another branch of the family into Page County when he bought 186 acres on the northernmost part of Naked Creek between Long Ridge and Grindstone Mountain in 1858 (Page County Deed Book L:65–66). In 1861 he sold this land and enlisted in the Confederate Army, moving his wife Ann Mariah (Breeding) Meadows and their six children to Mount Crawford, Virginia (ibid.:394; Breeden 1978:21). After the war he took his family back to Naked Creek, and on September 22, 1870, he died of typhoid fever (Page County Vital Statistics, 1870). There is no record of his or his widow's purchasing the land between Grindstone Mountain and Naked Creek where she and her children were living, nor do I know what happened to the money John H. Meadows received for selling his land before the war. It is possible that he never received it, as the sale was contested by the previous owner (Page County Deed Book L:394). Whatever the cause, the result was that this side of the Meadows family was not so well off as the other. Mariah married Benjamin Watson, a collier, but they separated soon afterward. John H. and Mariah Meadows' son John E. ("Ed") Meadows, a grandfather of Brother Vernie, married M. Caroline Watson, niece to Benjamin Watson and daughter of Evan Watson, a thrifty, productive sharecropper (1860 U.S. Census of Population, Page County; 1880 U.S. Census of Agriculture, Page County; Page County Marriage Books I, II).

The 1870 Census of Agriculture counted very few of the mountain farm households, but the effects of the Civil War on those they did count were obvious (Table 6). Hamilton Cubbage, who had produced a surplus of 165 CBE on a 195-acre farm in 1850, was reduced to a surplus of 29 on 40 acres. James Cubbage produced a surplus of only 59 CBE in 1870 compared to 300 in 1860. Most of the Breeden households had migrated from Page County before the Civil War. There was no pattern to the migration;

some older and some younger, some well-off and some not well-off left. The war hurt the remaining Breedens as it hurt everyone in the county.

Elias Breeden died in 1873, and his probate inventory and estate sale bill (Appendix B) give us some useful information about the mountain economy of the period, as most of the items inventoried were shoemaking and farm tools, and many were bought by Henry Meadows (b. 1840), the youngest of the second generation of Meadowses in Page County. The flax wheel (spinning wheel) and wheat fan show up in Henry Meadows' probate inventory from 1920 (Appendix B). Also of interest are the two lots of old books, the small desk and contents (probably used for keeping accounts), and the Bible purchased by Matthew Lamb. Brother Rastus' grandfather's purchase of Brother Vernie's great-great-grandfather's Bible is an event whose meaning is open to conjecture. Had Matthew Lamb become religious at age forty-seven and felt the need for a Bible? Or was this a gift for one of his family? And why was it for sale in the first place? Whatever, the transaction is clear evidence of religious activity among the two families and, in the absence of records of churchgoing (see Chapter 3), takes on greater importance for this study than it might otherwise have.

These probate inventory sale bills are interesting for another reason: they show that some of the mountain farmers continued the old-fashioned agricultural technology at a time when some of the valley farmers were modernizing and investing in farm machinery. When these inventories are coupled with census data on home manufactures, one can cautiously conclude that the household economy, and its mind-set, persisted among the majority of these mountain farmers, at least through the 1870s. Rolla M. Tryon wrote that between 1840 and 1860, Americans generally abandoned home manufacturing for store-bought, factory-made goods. His thesis holds for the industrial Northeast and also for the newer frontiers in the West and Northwest. But in Appalachia the decline was less severe. In Rockingham County, the Shenandoah Valley neighbor west of Page County, the per capita value of home manufactures declined from $3.91 in 1840 to $.60 in 1860, while in Page County the decline was but from $2.23 to $1.21 (Tryon 1966). Nonetheless, Appendix D shows that less than 50 percent of the mountain households under study from 1850 to 1870 manufactured goods at home. In 1880 home manufactures were so insignificant in the nation that the census stopped gathering data on them.

Dependence

The 1880 U.S. Census of Agriculture was comparatively detailed and offers a good look at the economy of mountain farming at this time when the four families had been in the region long enough to establish two and even three generations on the land (Table 8). To simplify matters the following discussion will be confined chiefly to those households that were directly in the ancestral line of present-day members of the Fellowship Independent Baptist Church.

Descendants of Elias Breeden remained in the Naked Creek region of Page County throughout the nineteenth century even though many other Breeden households migrated out. The 1880 U.S. Census of Population lists Elias' son Wesley (b. 1834) as a shoemaker by trade, but the 1880 U.S. Census of Agriculture makes it clear that he and his son Daniel (b. 1858) farmed as well (Appendix D). Most of their land was mountain timber, but between them they cultivated forty-four acres in a diversified crop-livestock pattern that resembled the Page County German lowlands adaptation: four horses, two milk cows, four other cattle, six sheep, twenty-seven pigs, $98.55 worth of animals slaughtered, 25 bushels of wheat, 155 bushels of rye, 200 bushels of corn, 250 bushels of apples, and 255 pounds of butter, for a surplus of 282 CBE plus income from shoemaking (Table 8). It might be thought that the cobbler's trade was anachronistic in the face of the ready availability of cheap factory-made shoes. Yet in the Virginia State Library at Richmond I found a diary kept by John W. Keyser (1847–1917), from 1868 through the 1870s a shoemaker in Page Valley, and it shows that his customers kept him busy making and repairing shoes several days each week. Wesley's son Daniel carried on the family shoemaking trade, but gained most of his living from the land; the 1900 U.S. Census of Population listed him as a farmer. The 1880 production figures and needs of the Breeden households are listed in Table 8. Nathaniel Breeden, a blacksmith, had a corn patch and a milk cow and little other farm production; he probably spent most of his time at his trade. The rest of the Breedens produced moderate farm surpluses—even Richam, alone and a widower at eighty-four.

Like the Breedens, the Meadows households in 1880 appear moderately well off, with surpluses equal to, double, or triple their needs (Table 8). Matthew Lamb, husband of Annie Meadows, lived and farmed on land near Henry and James Meadows, and is properly grouped with them. Figure 14, drawn from an 1885 atlas of Page County, shows that the Meadowses lived in Weaver Hollow, Jollett Hollow, and on Naked Mountain. Hiram F. (b. 1849), James S. (b. 1851), Thomas W. (1854–1941), and Zechariah (b. 1859) were sons of Mitchel (1823–1865); the others were sons of Thomas (b. 1802).

The local newspaper, the *Page County News and Courier,* commenced publication in 1868. Although it seldom published news of the Jollett region, a few items from this period suggest the transitions from hollow to hamlet that were underway. A certain "J. W. J." (whom I have identified as John W. Jollett, a farmer and Methodist local preacher) wrote in the March 15, 1883, issue that "The new store is nearly ready for occupancy and I guess that we can buy goods here nearly as cheap as in Luray. Our schools here are drawing to a close . . ." A school had been built by 1875, and a store and Methodist Church (see Chapter 3, "Religious History in Page County") were erected before 1885 at Jollett, the confluence of Weaver and Jollett hollows (see Figure 14). Clearly the Meadowses and Lambs were the families highest in the Blue Ridge hills, the ones furthest from civilization, the ones whom historians like J. Wayne Flint would expect to be poorest. To be sure, remoteness had its disadvantages. The *Courier* reported on October 5, 1882, that a diphtheria epidemic had struck at the headwaters of upper Naked Creek, and the vital statistics confirm that Thomas W. Meadows and his wife Matilda lost two children and that Henry Meadows (1840–1920) and his wife Ardista (Breeden) Meadows, living highest on the mountain at the old Thomas Meadows homeplace, lost four children aged between four and twelve years within three weeks. But Henry's probate inventory (Appendix B) contains a washing machine, a parlor organ, and a black mare valued at $135—and indicates middle-class aspirations.

The Cubbages demonstrate the entire range from subsistence through market-oriented farming in the 1880s, their nine households producing surpluses ranging from 11.75 to 1,407 CBE (Table 8). Recall that the two brothers, William (b. 1791) and Jacob (b. 1795), migrated from Madison to Page County in 1846 and 1837, respectively. Jacob's eldest son, James, established a household economy in Cubbage Hollow (Figure 18), while William's elder sons, William, Jr., and Henry, were more market-minded. Henry, as has been noted, was killed in the Civil War, but his eldest son, Wesley, carried on the commercial tradition.

The younger sons of the Cubbage brothers did not fare well. Hamilton (b. 1824, second son of Jacob), who had lost land and livestock in the Civil War, died in 1875 at the age of forty-five of "paralysis" (probably a stroke); at the time his occupation was "laborer," suggesting that he no longer owned his farm (Page County Vital Statistics). Thomas (b. 1823, second son of William), a laborer according to the 1860 and 1870 U.S. Censuses, lost his wife Mahala (Nicholson) to "cramps in stomach" in 1868 (Page County Vital Statistics) but by 1880 had 224 acres of farmland with a highly productive orchard and was producing a surplus of 118 CBE. Acre (or Acra; b. 1835, sixth son of William) died of consumption in 1879 (Page County Vital Statistics); his estate was probated and the inventory is reproduced in Appendix B. He had been divorced by his wife Elizabeth "Demphy" (Nicholson) in 1869 (Page County Chancery Book 3:42) and died with a very small estate. The 1870 U.S. Census listed him as a farm laborer; his occupation was "farmer" according to his death record. In one of the odd coincidences that sometimes occurred as I pored over the primary sources, I came upon this entry in John W. Keyser's diary for Friday, September 8, 1876: "Went out to Acre Cubbage's and put a coat of paint on his pump stock and spring house." Shards of a life.

TABLE 8. Food energy needs, production,[a] and surplus, selected mountain farm households, Page County, 1880

Surname	Name	Year Born	House-hold AME[b]	Pigs (No.)	Value Animals Slaugh-tered ($)[c]	Milk Cows (No.)
Cubbage	Nancy	1801	5.45	5	14.60	1
Cubbage	James	1818	7.95	8	63.87	2
Cubbage	Thomas	1823	6.00	2	36.50	1
Cubbage	William	1828	6.10	3	182.48	5
Cubbage	Amanda	1835	6.70	1	27.37	1
Cubbage	Joseph	1839	1.90	2	9.12	1
Cubbage	Early	1843	3.05	2	7.30	1
Cubbage	James H.	1843	4.00	0	7.30	1
Cubbage	Wesley	1845	5.75	2	72.99	2
Meadows	James	1826	6.85	18	51.09	2
Meadows	Thomas	1831	6.25	20	29.20	1
Meadows	William B.	1839	3.70	10	43.80	1
Meadows	Henry	1840	5.00	12	71.17	2
Meadows	Hiram F.	1849	2.20	5	10.95	1
Meadows	James S.	1851	1.90	0	18.25	0
Meadows	Thomas W.	1854	2.85	4	29.20	1
Meadows	Zechariah	1859	1.90	7	23.72	1
Lamb	Matthew	1825	12.35	12	40.15	2
Breeden	Richam	1796	1.00	1	7.30	1
Breeden	Nathaniel	1832	5.25	0	12.77	1
Breeden	Wesley/ Daniel	1834/ 1858	8.45	27	98.55	2
Breeden	Richard	1855	4.95	30	65.69	2
Breeden	Simeon	1859	2.05	18	18.98	1
Average values:			4.85	8.22	40.88	1.4

[a] Production does not include wool or apples, which some families produced. See Appendix D
[b] Adult male equivalents.
[c] Value of animals slaughtered estimated by dividing livestock value by 2.74. See text.

Corn (Bu.)	Oats (Bu.)	Buck-wheat (Bu.)	Pota-toes (Bu.)	Value Live-stock ($)	CBE Needed	CBE Produced	CBE Surplus
80	0	0	10	40	104.15	115.90	11.75
250	0	0	20	175	151.92	404.44	252.52
150	0	0	10	100	114.66	232.87	118.21
1,000	40	0	5	500	116.57	1,523.62	1,407.05
100	0	0	10	75	128.04	164.89	36.85
5	50	0	5	25	36.31	50.62	14.31
60	0	0	0	20	58.29	90.30	32.01
10	0	0	10	20	76.44	98.23	21.79
300	0	0	10	200	109.88	489.34	379.46
100	10	0	14	140	130.90	228.41	97.51
150	18	0	10	80	119.44	233.51	114.07
78	0	0	6	120	70.71	186.20	115.49
50	0	10	20	195	95.55	255.84	160.29
125	10	0	20	30	42.04	189.25	147.21
40	0	0	20	50	36.31	99.94	63.63
50	0	0	20	80	54.46	121.07	66.61
75	30	0	25	65	36.31	150.72	114.41
100	10	10	0	110	236.01	265.85	29.84
50	10	0	5	20	19.11	84.20	65.09
50	0	0	9	35	100.33	79.07	−21.26
200	0	0	0	270	161.48	444.30	282.82
80	0	0	10	180	94.59	272.21	177.62
65	0	0	5	52	39.18	112.84	73.66
138	7.7	0.9	11	112	92.73	256.24	163.51

Simpson Cubbage (b. 1833, fifth son of William) in 1854 married Susan Cubbage (b. 1836, third daughter of Jacob). The 1874 Page County book of vital statistics recorded that her brother James reported her death; the cause listed was "supposed to be murdered." Her husband was arrested three days afterward. Indicted, he pleaded not guilty; in January 1875 he was found guilty of second-degree murder and sentenced to fourteen years in the state penitentiary.

The farm production figures in Table 8 show that the households of Amanda (or Manda, in some of the census records; b. 1835, widow of Hamilton) and Nancy (b. 1801, widow of Jacob) were operating at subsistence levels, as might be expected under the circumstances. Two young men were listed as laborers in each of the households, and they would have contributed some income to purchase staple goods. It is significant that the widows were listed as the household heads; evidently they owned the land. The households of Joseph, James H., and Early Cubbage also produced little surplus. In fact, five out of the nine Cubbage households were operating at a subsistence level.

James, Wesley, and William (Jr.) Cubbage, on the other hand, raised considerably in excess of what they needed for home consumption. James had a surplus of 253 CBE, Wesley 379, and William a whopping 1,407. Several facts suggest their market orientation. Alone among these families, William and Wesley Cubbage spent money for fertilizer and paid wages to hired laborers to work on their farms, according to the agricultural census. Moreover, William and Wesley each owned several tracts of farmland. William, for example, in 1884 was taxed on eight parcels of land (Table 9).

The Page County Land Book, 1884, tells us also that William Cubbage lived in East Liberty, about three miles south of Newport along the Shenandoah, while Wesley Cubbage, who owned five tracts of land on Line Run, lived near Honeyville. Both had moved down from the mountains, closer to the towns, signaling their closer ties to the commercial economy. But bad luck still dogged Henry Cubbage's side of the family; Wesley was drowned in 1885 at the age of thirty-nine, and his estate was divided among his wife and six children.

William had come to specialize in raising beef cattle; the 1880 agricultural census shows him with a herd of sixteen. The *Page News and Courier* for December 14, 1882, reported that "Most of our farmers . . . are turning their attention more to cattle raising, finding it an item of greater profit than anything else produced on the farm." On February 8, 1883, the paper reported that "Buck Brubaker sold seven feed cattle last week [that] averaged a gain of 317 [lbs.]. For one of the seven that brought him $70.25, he paid last winter $23.31." Mr. Brubaker had tripled his investment in one year. And what of William Cubbage? He had already gained local fame: the *Courier* for February 23, 1875, noted that "William Cubbage, living near Honeyville, slaughtered recently a steer 17 months old the

TABLE 9. Land values of property owned by William Cubbage, 1884

No. Acres	Location	Value per Acre ($)
125	Mountain land on Line Run	0.50
7	Line Run	5.00
53	Dovel Hollow	2.00
62	Dovel Hollow	1.00
61	Dovel Hollow	1.00
99	Liberty (on the river)	6.00
61	Kite Hollow	1.00
3	George Glenn's lot	25.00

SOURCE: Page County Land Book, 1884.

weight of which was 509 lbs. We think it will puzzle Rockingham and Shenandoah [counties] to beat it, notwithstanding they can boast of superior stock."

Commercial farming required considerable capital investment and involved risks; and unfortunately for the mountain farmers (and the valley farmers as well), farming for profit in Page County became increasingly difficult in the last two decades of the nineteenth century. The prices of pork, beef, and wheat, the chief cash crops, declined in response to increasing supply. Scientific farming techniques, new agricultural machinery (such as the steel plow that could turn over prairie lands), fertile midwestern soils, and comparatively high rail transportation costs put the Page County farmers at a competitive disadvantage. The price of wheat per bushel, for example, declined, on average, from $1.50 in 1870–1880 to $0.83 in 1880–1890 and $0.65 in 1890–1900 ("Agriculture," *Encyclopaedia Britannica*, 11th ed.). The number of farms in Page County more than doubled, from 462 to 988, between 1870 and 1880, while the average size decreased from 228 to 115 acres; meanwhile, the percentage of tenant farmers increased from 12 percent in 1880 to 24 percent in 1900, according to the U.S. Census of Agriculture. These figures compare favorably with those for many other sections of the South, it should be noted; but the trend is obvious.

What, then, were some of the strategies for mountain farmers without much capital? One strategy, of course, was to get out of the marketplace; but at least some interaction was needed, for as the century progressed the mountain farmers had come increasingly to depend on local markets. The 1850 Census of Agriculture, for example, recorded many households growing flax (for homespun) and much in the way of home manufactures; but by 1880 very few households were making clothes at home, and most people preferred store-bought goods. Another strategy was to try to take advantage of the growing industrial transformation of Page County by supplying raw materials other than the traditional wheat and beef. So, for example, the 1880 agricultural census shows that the Cubbages produced several hundred bushels of apples. There was considerable local production of apple brandy; the U.S. Census of Industry identified eleven commercial apple brandy distilleries in Page County in 1870, and in 1880 the number had grown to thirteen. The actual number was probably well in excess of these because the enumerators counted only those establishments producing more than $500 in goods. How much applejack was made in the mountains is open to conjecture.

The March 1, 1883, issue of the *Page News and Courier* noted that apples were selling at $1.00 per bushel. The 1880 agricultural census placed the value of the orchard run apples from the Cubbages at $.10 per bushel. Still, James Cubbage grossed about $100 from five acres planted with 125 bearing apple trees (the variety most popular in the region at the time was the Milam apple) that yielded 1,000 bushels. Orcharding was profitable.

In 1883 the *Page News and Courier* reported the fortunes of an industry new to Page County: an apple-drying factory in Luray. By the end of the year the factory had shipped fifty tons of dried fruit at $.14 to $.18 per pound; their net profit was $7,500 on $16,000 gross sales and, according to the newspaper, although they were not as successful as everyone had hoped, they "did distribute several thousand dollars in the county" (December 6, 1883).

Another way for the mountain farmer to enter the cash economy was, as noted earlier, to gather chestnut oak bark for the local tanneries. The tanning industry expanded considerably in the 1880s. Many of the mountain farmers stepped up their efforts to supply tan bark, and one enterprising farmer we have been following saw a means of increasing his wealth by signing a piece of paper. In the Page County Deed Books an entry dated July 13, 1881, records that Henry Meadows sold, for the following seven years, to Deford and Company, a Luray tannery, his rights to the chestnut oak bark on 250 acres of his 1,000 on Naked Mountain. For the sale of these rights he received $400. The *Courier* noted on August 3, 1882, an "immense trade in chestnut oak tan bark from Marksville [now Stanley] to the Deford company in Luray." The paper reported on November 30, 1882, that 650 cords of bark on Naked Creek were awaiting transport to the tannery and that the tannery had paid $8,800 since April for bark. On March 8, 1883, readers were informed that 50 more tanning vats were being built; on August 30, 1883, the paper reported that the tannery was in production from dawn to midnight and that the bark mill operated fifteen hours per day; and on October 18, 1883, the paper noted a further enlargement by 130 tanning vats to 350 in all, adding that the Deford Tannery was one of the largest in the South. Aside from the tannery, another traditional Page County industry boomed in the 1880s: ironmaking. The Big Gem Furnace was completed at Milnes (Shenandoah) in 1883 and turned out seventy-five tons of iron per day. The *Courier* proudly told its readers that "These are the enterprises that our Valley needs to build up her waste places and make her people happy and prosperous" (November 30, 1882).

Industrial growth in Page County in the 1880s was greatly facilitated by the construction of the Shenandoah Valley branch of the Norfolk and Western Railroad, which connected Page Valley to the rest of the nation by rail and enabled fast and efficient shipment of its iron products, timber, tanned leather, and farm goods. A large railroad yard was built in Shenandoah to accommodate the new traffic. And yet some of the ironies of the new transportation network and its effect on the county economy were apparent. There is this from the *Courier*'s "Just Think about It" column for January 11, 1883: "Did you ever think of this . . . that hundreds of car loads of cattle shipped through here from the South are taken North and butchered, then the hides are shipped back here and tanned. The leather is then shipped to Boston to be made into soles, which are shipped South and sold back to our merchants here. In other words, the leather of which our shoes are made has traveled North and South about four times." The paper might have added that the fortunes of the county economy were, therefore, linked ever more closely to markets hundreds of miles distant; and that what had been a largely self-sufficient county economy fifty years earlier had become dependent on the outside world.

Almost as if to symbolize this dependence, the Luray Caverns, discovered in 1878, were developed into a grand tourist attraction in the 1880s. Elegant hotels were built to accommodate the visitors who poured in from the North on special excursion trains. The Panic of 1890 put an end to the boom, however. Banks closed. Tourists ceased coming to the caverns. Three of the hotels, empty, burned to the ground. A serious railroad wreck occurred in the northern part of the county in 1891. To make matters worse, discovery of the rich ore deposits in Michigan and Minnesota put the county's ironmaking industry at a competitive disadvantage, and by 1917 the Shenandoah Iron Works had dismantled its Big Gem furnace. Never again would the valley be an industrial center. Resulting unemployment threw a great many workers back on the farms. Young unmarried or newly married mountain men who had been able to add to the family income by working in county industries returned to the land as tenant farmers. Valley employment, which had acted as a safety valve for the pressures of an increasing mountain population, would act that way no longer. For the mountain farmers these were especially difficult times because cash was increasingly hard to come by. Many lost their land for failure to pay taxes, becoming squatters or sharecroppers on land that had been in the family for decades.

Much of the mountain land, too, had been treated harshly. As early as 1884 the *Courier* editorialized that "The destruction of timber in Page County during the past several years has been enormous" (February 28, 1884). During the boom years timber was cut to fire the iron industry and provide bark for the tannery, and after the railroad was in place a great deal of timber was freighted out to supply the housing industry in the industrial eastern corridor. The result was considerable erosion of the steep mountain hillsides after they had been cleared of their trees, and the resulting silt washed into the hollows and wreaked havoc on the mountain farms. Flooding became a serious threat.

Subsistence

The market for farm produce reversed after the turn of the century. Corn prices rose from $.35 per bushel in 1900 to $.52 in 1910 and $.68 in 1915, while wheat went from $.62 per bushel in 1900 to $.91 in 1910 and $.96 in 1915 (Scheiber, Vatter, and Faulkner 1976:213). Between 1900 and 1910 American farmland doubled in value, while real farm income rose considerably (ibid.:217). Agricultural historians refer to this as the golden age of American farming. In Page Valley this meant a return to profits for those market-oriented farm families who had managed to weather the hard times of the previous four decades. Land in the Blue Ridge still was inexpensive, as was labor. As a result, many of the valley farmers bought up mountain land: some, by paying others' delinquent taxes, acquired land which the county had condemned; some sued for land they claimed to occupy; and some simply purchased land outright from mountain farm families. To increase their profits, they began a system of transhumance with the mountain farmers.

Having bought the land, the valley farmer permitted the mountain family to live on it as tenants. The tenant family cleared the land for tillage, making a crop for three years without giving any of it to the absentee landlord. Then the tenant planted grass and turned the field to pasture for the landlord's cattle, and these were kept there from spring through the fall. The tenant watched over the cattle, sometimes for a small salary, and cleared more land, continuing the process. The number of tenants so employed must have been significant because the practice is well remembered even today, not only by the Fellowship Independent Baptist Church members but also by Page County soil conservation officials.

The Great Depression of the 1930s actually hit the American farmer a decade sooner, and once again the result was foreclosures and farm tenancy. The Page County tenancy rate, 8 percent in 1910, rose to 13 percent in 1920 and 20 percent in 1930 when, according to the census, 34 percent of the tenants were related by blood or marriage to their landlords (U.S. Census of Agriculture, Page County, 1910; 1920; 1930). But this time those who returned to their families on the mountain farms found them in a serious state of affairs.

Changes in the economy had driven out most of the mountain industries. Local mills had shut down. A changeover from tan bark to chemical tanning agents had stopped an important source of mountain income (Perdue and Martin-Perdue 1979–1980: 100). In fact, valley businessmen had purchased timber tracts in the mountains to realize profits from tan bark gathering (Sherman and Henry 1973: 13) and now they, too, were shut out. Worse, a bacterial blight killed most of the chestnut trees by 1922. This put an end to another mountain industry, gathering chestnuts for shipment to the eastern cities where they were roasted and eaten. More important, it also deprived the mountain farmers' hogs of an important part of their food supply, making it necessary to grow corn to feed them.

In sum, during the period roughly from about 1885 to 1925, the mountain economy in this section of the Blue Ridge returned to subsistence farming with the household the unit of production and consumption. Population growth, transformations of the landscape and extraction of resources, and natural disasters had greatly altered the mountain ecosystem. It is a testimony to the tenacity of the mountain way of life that the ancestors of the members of the Fellowship Independent Baptist Church chose to continue it throughout these hard times. The land's value had dropped considerably, and those who had cash were able to stay. Brother Vernie's father, George W. Meadows, bought 285 acres of mountain land in Weaver Hollow in 1912 for $700; it was a V-shaped parcel running down from Chapman's Mountain to a narrow point on Naked Creek (Page County Deed Book 65:432). Brother Rastus' father, Alexander Lam, bought and sold several small tracts of mountain land between 1911 and 1920. The 1928 Page County Land Book credited Alexander Lam with 78 acres and one dwelling on Naked Creek, for which he was taxed $130. Brother Clyde Cubbage's father remained a sharecropper on his father's land. All three recall their upbringing on mountain farms during the first two decades of the twentieth century, and none expressed any regret for the household farm economy or the life they had been born into. Quite the opposite, as we will see; they remember their youth on mountain farms with pleasure, pride, and some regret that this way of life had ended.

Nevertheless, mountain subsistence farming as a way of life had been dealt a series of major blows, and it was considerably more difficult for the parents of the elder people in the church than it had been two or three generations earlier. Gathering, whether of pelts, tan bark, or chestnuts, had supplied the mountain people with cash in the past; and now, with the forest canopy letting in a good deal more light, wild berry patches provided a new option. The *Courier* reported on July 1, 1932, that "Huckleberries began coming in at Stanley and other marketing points of the county the first of this week and are arriving in increasing quantities. While this fruit has an opening price of only 25 cents a gallon this year, as contrasted with 60 and 65 cents a gallon in some preceding years, it is likely that never before was the huckleberry crop a greater help to the people in the mountains. In some previous years the sale of this fruit in the county has probably aggregated $50,000—the sum going to persons of little or no means." But apart from gathering huckleberries or picking apples at harvest time there was little to bring in the cash that was needed. And finally the Shenandoah Park put an end to mountain farming by forcing the people from the land.

In 1978 Dorothy Noble Smith interviewed Howard Lam and was told of a vision that his great-grandmother Mary Cathen Thomas (Brother Rastus' grandmother and Sister Hattie's grandmother as well) had about the coming of the Shenandoah National Park. The violence of the vision was a foreshadowing of the park's effect on the mountain people's lives:

> My great grandmother lived at Big Meadow. Mary Cathen Thomas. The most outstanding thing about this is the vision I guess you would call it that she saw long years before the park bought the land. She saw this road being built, and the people thought she had lost her mind. See, she [lived right near the Thomas cemetery] and something happened, she lost one of her eyes. She was blind in one eye. But she got real old, I think she lived to be in her 90s.
>
> And when she got real old, she would look out across the field and tell them that there was somebody digging up the sod. And there was nobody there, and there was nothing there. And she just kept talking about that, seeing the people, said that the Longs that the land belonged to, said they was going to be so mad when they come up there and saw all this sod tore up. See, it was a grazing farm at that time. The cattle were in there and she was worried because they was a-tearing up the sod, and the cattle wouldn't have any grass to eat.
>
> And she would say, "There is great droves of people going through." Well, then, at night, she'd say to us such bright lights shining in her window they'd have to hang something over this window to keep the light from hurting her eyes. I don't remember how many years that was before the park came through.
>
> But then after the park people bought the land, they started putting the road through, there was a shovel a-digging the dirt up, and, see, the people back there had never seen machinery like that work. Well, there'd be a lot of people going through to look at it. And there it was just as plain as could be, what she had told them, and they thought she was losing her mind.
>
> And then at night, they would work there at night, too, and they would have to blast out these rocks with dynamite, and they had to put something over the windows so the rocks from this dynamite wouldn't knock the windows out like that! (My transcription of the taped interview by Dorothy Noble Smith)

George W. Meadows. Photographer unknown.

Mary Cathen Thomas.
Photographer unknown.

Out-Migration and the Shenandoah National Park Removals

The state of Virginia had joined forces with nature and the economy to drive the mountain people from their land. George Pollock, owner of the Skyland resort hotel near Big Meadows, led the drive to convince government officials and conservationists that the Blue Ridge Mountains would make a splendid site for a national park. He pointed out that the land could be taken by the state and the people living on it removed. Because they were backward and deprived, the move might do them good, Pollock reasoned. They would be compensated for their land if they could prove they owned it. Local businessmen and boosters lobbied the federal government, and in 1926 Congress passed a bill marking off 521,000 acres and authorizing the establishment of the Shenandoah National Park, while the state of Virginia began condemnation proceedings against the mountain farmers and against the valley dwellers who owned mountain grazing land. (Reeder and Reeder 1978, Strickler 1952, and Perdue and Martin-Perdue 1979–1980 give accounts of the coming of the park and the removals.)

The landowners were thrown into further confusion when controversy developed over the location of the park boundaries. In 1929 Arno Cammerer, acting director of the Park Service, authorized a survey that cut the boundaries back to 327,000 acres. Sensing that exceptions might be made when the surveyors came around, landowners near the new boundaries pleaded with the Park Service for the right to keep their property. W. E. Carson, chairman of the Virginia State Commission on Conservation and Development, went with the surveyors and made certain they did their best to satisfy the landowners next to the line and, in a letter to Cammerer, explained something of the delicacy of the operation:

> We have been going around the area and have carefully sawtoothed away from your lines where we could in individual instances satisfy some home holder or small farmer. . . .
>
> . . . it would be poor advertisement of the Park to have abandoned farms and homes around the foot of the area. It was [the Secretary of the Interior's] hope that the homes and farms around the Park line should continue in the possession of the people now living there. Added to this we have a hard problem to solve in keeping the people contented, whose land we are taking from them.
>
> It is easy enough to lay down the lines in a whole sale way, but when it is encroaching on thousands of home owners it requires tact, diplomacy, and common sense to keep these land owners from going into frenzy . . . (Reeder and Reeder 1978:73–74)

Frenzied or not, the behavior of Rastus Lam, Clyde Cubbage, Edith McCoy Cubbage, Rufus Cubbage, Vernie Meadows, Hattie Thomas Meadows, Thomas Breeden, and the other young adults who would eventually become members of the Fellowship Independent Baptist Church could not have been equanimous. Their parents stood to lose their land, and they their share in any land inheritance, because the Cammerer Line, as it came to be called, included all the ridges and hollows in the Shenandoah Iron Works District. Brother Clyde had in fact already purchased thirteen acres of mountain land in Cubbage Hollow in 1926, and in 1928 when he married Sister Edith he had increased his property to seventeen acres. He would never build on this land, but its purchase (for back taxes owed by Ambrose Cubbage) shows how important land ownership was.

Not long afterward, the park reduced the boundaries once more, this time leaving out many of the Shenandoah Iron Works District ridges and hollows (Figure 19). Basin, Cubbage, and Lucas hollows would remain outside the park, while only the highest reaches of Weaver and Jollett hollows and Long Ridge and Tanner's Ridge would be included. Many families could keep their lands after all, and they did. But after such upheaval, the young generation could not be blamed for wanting to move closer to the valley towns.

In 1934, before removing the remaining 465 families from park land, the federal government sent enumerators to take an inventory of the culture it was about to destroy. The figures unquestionably reveal a culture of material poverty. The families possessed, on average, two pigs and one cow, and grew forty bushels of grain, chiefly corn, while reporting income from outside labor of less than $100 per year (Reeder and Reeder 1978: 38–45). They must have eaten a great many potatoes. But this was a remnant. More than half were tenant farmers or squatters. Those with the means to do so had already moved away (ibid.: 77). The remainder had already suffered the worsening conditions of mountain farm life. Local newspapers called attention to the current drought, said to be the worst in a hundred years (Perdue and Martin-Perdue 1979–1980: 100). Besides, the nation was in the midst of the Depression. Clearly, the remnant surveyed by the government were not a representative group; they did not represent the families of the church members at that time, nor as they were in the nineteenth century when, as we have seen, documents available in the public archives reveal a living standard several times higher. Unfortunately, this remnant did come to represent mountain farmers to the journalists, sociologists, and historians of the time, and they probed no further. The resulting distortion of the historical record has been considerable.

The Household Economy and the Mountain Mind-set

The household economy, by definition one in which most of the production and consumption takes place in the household and among neighboring kinfolk rather than through market exchange, thus persisted in the

Blue Ridge Mountains until the 1930s, decades after it was abandoned in
the industrial North. Recent studies (e.g., C. Clark 1979; Rothenberg
1981) discuss the growth of markets and decline of the household economy
in the antebellum North. By 1860, for example, innovations in transportation, farming, manufacturing, and commercial markets had transformed
the Connecticut Valley so that its inhabitants had gained a thoroughgoing
dependence upon the marketplace. Local farmers as well as townspeople
bought clothes and flour rather than producing them, and the region became "engaged in the production of cash crops which the south or west
could not yet supply sufficiently" (C. Clark 1979: 171). Home textile manufactures ceased and gave way to cottage industry and then factories. But,
as we have seen, among the ancestors of the members of the Fellowship
Independent Baptist Church the household economy continued for three
generations beyond 1860. What can account for it? Why did they not leave
the mountains sooner and take up a town-based way of life? Why did they
not seek their fortunes elsewhere? We need to examine the nature of the
household economy yet again in light of these questions.

Historians have held a lively debate over the early American household
economy. Some have viewed the household heads as entrepreneurs (e.g.,
Lemon 1972; 1980; Grant 1961; Mitchell 1977). Their evidence comes
from the eighteenth-century pioneers' high mobility rate, the profits they
made when selling their land and pushing on, and the production and
marketing of a farm surplus; and they attribute this entrepreneurial spirit
to the constellation of values we know as eighteenth-century liberalism:
freedom, wealth, and happiness. In other words, the colonies and early republic were peopled with enterprising small capitalists who intended and
realized a profit from farming. When industrial opportunities arose in the
nineteenth century, so the argument runs, the entrepreneurial attitude
had already been formed; and the result was rapid economic growth in the
industrial sector, the exodus of farmers to towns and cities, and the gradual transformation of farming to industry.

This picture of early America as a land of small entrepreneurs has been
criticized by those who view the household mode of production as inher-
ently conservative. According to this counter-argument, the pioneers may
have realized profits from land sales, but their behavior suggests that
profit was not their most important motive. James A. Henretta points out
that clusters of ethnic settlements show communal rather than individualistic values, and argues that providing for their children's futures in the
face of diminishing landowning opportunities was the motive for such acquisitiveness as the farmers had (1978: 3–10). Other historians stress the
small size of markets. Exchange was local and ox-cart transport was expensive; the domestic urban market could easily be supplied by farms in
the immediate vicinity; among foreign markets only the West Indies was
significant (Mutch 1977: 279–281; this view is challenged by Rothenberg

1981). The very use of the word "surplus" to describe production beyond needs argues against a risk-taking mentality. Even southern plantations took care first to raise enough corn and livestock to feed the household and slaves; more corn and pork were produced than the cash crops, tobacco and cotton.

Whatever the outcome of the debate over the preindustrialized farm "mentalité" in the North, its framework is most useful in assessing the persistence of the preindustrial household economy in the northern Blue Ridge, where patterns of landownership and the facts of production argue strongly for what Henretta terms "an intimate relationship between agricultural production and parental values" (1978: 21). He is writing of eighteenth-century New England, but his words are applicable to Page County in the nineteenth century:

> Because the primary economic unit—the family—was also the main social institution, production activities had an immense impact on the entire character of agrarian life. Family relationships could not be divorced from economic considerations; indeed, the basic question of power and authority within the family hinged primarily on legal control over the land and—indirectly—over the labor needed to work it. The parents (principally the husbands) enjoyed legal possession of the property . . . but they were dependent on their children for economic support in their old age. Their aim, as Greven has pointed out, was to control the terms and timing of the transfer of economic resources to the succeeding generation. (Ibid.)

We have seen many illustrations of this "intimate relationship," from William Cubbage, Sr.'s legal agreement with his sons to provide for his old age, to the success of the first generation of Meadowses, Breedens, and Cubbages in settling the succeeding generation as freeholding farmers on land adjacent to their own. Of Thomas Meadows' and Mitchel Meadows' fifteen children, thirteen became local farmers for the rest of their lives; of Jacob Cubbage's and William Cubbage, Sr.'s eleven sons, ten became local farmers for the rest of their lives. The proportion was not so high in the generations who came of age after 1880, for reasons discussed earlier; yet in 1940, for example, fifty-seven Cubbages owned land in Page County.

Although they kept to their household economies, the mountain farmers' mind-set was by no means anticommercial. They were acquisitive and held commercial values and expressed them; but their orientation was largely noncapitalist. They understood trade, and they knew commercialism through their dealings with the marketplace. Commercialism may be regarded as that set of attitudes in which "exchanges between man and land and between man and man are interpreted from a utilitarian, exploitative perspective, and surplus items from productive enterprise are regarded as potential sources of trade and profit within a money-based economic system" (Mitchell 1977:x). The mountain farmers exploited the

natural resources of timber and tan bark and pelts and berries, selling
them in the marketplace; when they could, they produced crop and livestock surpluses and sold these. Skyland, a Blue Ridge resort only a few
miles north of Big Meadows, was a regular buyer of moonshine and apple-
jack, and employed a few mountain people as launderers, maids, seam-
stresses, groundskeepers, and so forth. Household members hired themselves out as farm laborers, and some journeyed for a few months or years
to towns and cities, working in the cash economy, sending back cash and
eventually returning themselves. Visitors to the mountains often remarked
that the people were shrewd traders and prided themselves on it.

Here, however, the mountain-farming mind-set stopped short. Pride in
trading ability, and success at it, led to the notion that more was to be
gained through canny trading than through time spent improving the
goods while growing or making them. In itself, this notion discouraged
capital investment. When coupled with the characteristic mountain view
that resources were finite, that one person's gain was another's loss, mountain commercialism moved toward its characteristic expression: driving
the hard bargain. Meanwhile, outside of a few of the mountain households
under study (the brothers William and Henry Cubbage are the exceptions), the modern concept that value is added and wealth is created
through manufacture, and that economic growth follows from greater productive efficiency, had little chance of gaining a foothold in the mountain
"mentalité."

Finally, the household economy has had a social and religious legacy
that contextualizes today's religious practices of the members of the Fellowship Independent Baptist Church and other like churches. It should be
plain that these families deliberately chose to remain close to each other
on mountain farms rather than go individually elsewhere. In fact, they had
entered the county with family ties that brought kin from elsewhere. In
deciding to stay together, they showed the strength of the cluster of conservative values behind their behavior. Working together, exchanging labor and goods, these families dealt with each other as known individuals
in face-to-face social relationships. Power and authority were vested in the
patriarchal household head. The family was the dominant social as well as
economic unit; outside authority was only grudgingly admitted, and when
in the 1880s institutions like schools entered the mountain hollows they
gave way to the seasonal needs of farm labor. Today, despite the strains of
modernization, the family remains patriarchal and central in the lives of
the church members. Their acquisitiveness is best viewed in the terms
Henretta suggests; that is, in trying to assure (and control) the futures of
their children. Apprenticeship with fathers and uncles is still the most
popular and preferred means for young men to learn a trade, and the most
common trades accommodate apprenticeships: carpenter, stonemason,
electrician, truck driver. The ultimate expression of assurance and control,

the fusion of all themes implied by the metaphor of husbandry, is their stated goal in life: not freedom, not wealth, not happiness, but the family reunion in the heavenly homecoming.

Entering the Cash-Wage Economy

For the young adults who would eventually become members of the church, the 1930s and 1940s were marked by marriage, the beginnings of a family, and a succession of low-paying jobs. Government-funded projects employed a number of mountain husbands in the 1930s; Brother Vernie, for example, worked for the Civilian Conservation Corps, a popular employer in the region. Others sought more traditional work, hiring themselves out as farm laborers or becoming tenant farmers. Brother John, living in northeastern Tennessee, married Sister Pauline in 1940 and tried his luck as a sharecropper, like his father, for a few years, but after World War II he tired of farming and took a succession of blue-collar jobs in the nearby towns of Bristol and Kingsport. (Brother John's life is presented in detail in Chapter 9.) Brother Allen worked as a farm laborer, then after the war took a job pressing cider at a fruit cannery at Timberville, and there he met his future wife, Goldie, a peach-packer. When the cannery closed they found work at a chicken slaughterhouse and got married. Brother Rastus, born in 1907, lost his father in 1921, then stayed on the family farm to help his widowed mother until she died, whereupon he married Ruth Offenbacker in 1939:

> When I was first married I lived back in the mountains here. Rented a little house up there on Tanner's Ridge. I was working on the farm, for a man named Will Graves, making fence and mowing grass and making hay. My first child was born when I was working for ten cents an hour. I started raising a family and I was working for ten cents an hour! And then I moved from Tanner's Ridge to a place down here they call Jollett's. And I went a-working for a man, Gruver Weaver, on a sawmill down there, gave me twenty-five cents an hour. I was in Elkton one day and a plant manager from Merck and Company, he come and ask me if I'd come up and work for them. And I was a tall man [6′ 7″] and he said he wanted one man he could look up to. [*Laughs.*] So I went up there and I went to work for Merck and Company and I worked for them until I took my early retirement at sixty-two. (Lam interview, pp. 3, 27–28)

Eventually, they all left the mountains. Why, with as many as six generations of mountain-farming tradition behind them? We have already seen some of the reasons: the mountain economy had been altered by land speculators, the chestnut blight, transhumance, the elimination of the need for tan bark, elimination of local mills, and the contraction of local markets for surplus meat and grain. (It was still possible to trade eggs with

Brother Allen and Sister Goldie Dove at home, Timberville, Virginia, 1977.

the grocer, however.) The mountain farmers had made themselves increasingly dependent, after the 1850s, on the local economy, while in the
1880s the local economy made itself dependent on the national economy;
after about 1880, the needs of the national economy (chiefly to use the raw
materials the mountains could supply, whether timber or, eventually, the
park) took precedence, local mills closed, local markets dried up, and the
mountain farmers were reduced to poverty. Worse, the transformation of
much of the mountain land into the park had psychological effects extending even to those who owned, rented, or lived as tenants outside the eventual park boundaries. Public attention had been focused on the mountaineers as people who were lazy, ignorant, inbred, illiterate, isolated,
violent, and genetically defective. Of course, the mountain farmers had
endured the epithets hurled at them by the valley residents for many decades, but now newspapers and magazine articles, government surveys,
and even books pointed a finger. Who would not want to escape?

Besides, after the war industrious people could find factory jobs and move into the cash economy and raise their living standard, even in working-class occupations. Some went to the valley eagerly, trading mountain-farm life for the attractions of factory wages and such conveniences as indoor plumbing and electricity in the wood-framed, planked, and weather-boarded houses set on cement foundations near the towns. "After the Second World War come along," Brother Allen said, "people went money-crazy" (Dove interview, p. 18). In the old days, he went on, "if you planted anything around your farm, when you had a dollar you had that dollar." Now money changed hands rapidly. The people had more of it and had to spend more to live. From 1945 until 1972 Sister Goldie worked at the poultry plant on a pinning line, standing up all day, removing from the chicken carcasses the pin feathers that the machines missed. Sister Ella does the same job. She does not mind the smell—you get used to it, she said—but it bothered her that some days she was standing in chicken blood almost up to her ankles.

Brother Allen left the poultry plant in 1953:

BROTHER ALLEN: When I left there I came over and worked for Herman Mason for about three years. He catches chickens. You know, go out and catch chickens, load 'em up and haul 'em to Pennsylvania to those poultry plants.

TITON: I thought all the chickens were already caught from the day they were born.

BROTHER ALLEN: No. You got 'em in the houses, you haul 'em out. You hatch 'em, take 'em into the houses, they raise 'em up in the houses, then you catch 'em, put 'em in the truck and they go to market. I worked for Mason three years, and it got down to where I wasn't making but seventeen, eighteen dollars a week. That was about in '55, I reckon. I went to another poultry plant and I worked up there that winter. And then I come back. Work was pretty scarce at that time. So I went up in the mountains and I cut a bunch of pulpwood and sold that awhile, and drawed my [un]employment for a couple of weeks. And then in February I went to Shen Valley [a meat-packing plant] and I spent nearly fifteen years there.

TITON: What were you doing?

BROTHER ALLEN: Cut the hogs' heads off, and beef heads. I killed hogs, too, long for three years there. Take a knife and stick 'em. But when I was sticking at first, why, they'd snare a chain around their leg, and have a hoist there with a catch on it; it had a hook on the end and they'd slip it over that there catch, run him up on a big pole and just stick him alive, you know. See this mark here? [Points to scar on thumb.] Hog kicked the knife out of my hand, come up and caught me there. Then the boss wouldn't give me the raise I was supposed to have. Made me mad. I told him, said, "Either you give me my raise or get somebody else to do it." He

didn't pay no attention to me. So I said to myself, "Well, fella, I'll fix you." I
started slicing them short. Wasn't too long till I come off of there. [*Laughs.*]

But I worked nearly fifteen years there. Then I went down to Howe
Metals, down here in Shenandoah County, that copper tubing plant. I
worked down there for a little over two years. And I busted myself up here
in my leg. They cut them copper molds about like that, that long, forty-
five, fifty-five, seventy-five, and ninety-five pounds. Well, they put one skid
up here, the other one over here. So I just had a kick back between there.
Get her off of here down on my leg, one come off my leg over on this'n.
And that twisted, and I busted myself up and had to have a hernia operation. So when I went back the boss was going to put me on the same job
that I done it on, you see.

That didn't work for me. I told him, "No." I said, "If you ain't got nothing
else for a couple of weeks at least for me to do, till I get healed up pretty
good," I said, "you ain't going to get nothing from me." I asked him where
was the superintendent. He said, "I reckon he's in the office." I headed for
the office. When I stepped to the door, he made me mad. That's when I got
on him. So when I got on him, he said, "Well, I'll go back and see why
there ain't no job there." And I said, "No, you don't need to." I said, "I've
done quit." [*Laughs.*]

So I started around Harrisonburg to hunt me another job. And I was
crazy enough to stop up here at the hatchery, you know. Rockingham
Hatchery. I stopped in there and I asked the man about a job; and "Yep,"
he said, "I need somebody for the midnight shift." So he told me what he'd
give me, you know, to start out with. So I went back and told her [Goldie]
then. Well, she said that was about the best we could do without further
waiting, so I went on to work up there. I've been up there a little over five
years now. Still on the midnight shift, by myself. I'll sleep a nap before I go
in tonight. I slept this morning a little nap. And if I get caught up in my
work I usually set down and catch a little nap there. (Dove interview,
pp. 26–28)

In 1960 Brother Allen and Sister Goldie bought a prefabricated shell home,
set it on a foundation their neighbors helped them pour, then finished the
inside themselves. Strong and tough, they have given over their adult lives
to backbreaking labor, and they have earned their places among the working poor. Brother Allen's work narratives above are, like Brother John's
story that I analyzed in the Prologue, secular forms of testimony; they
form a temporary communicative community between storyteller and listener, and they confirm the teller's identity as a poor but principled man of
the working class who refuses to be victimized.

Persistence of the Mountain-Farming Mind-set

Page County today is an economically depressed region and has been so for most of the twentieth century (see *Page Co., Va., Overall Economic Development Program* 1977). The Environmental Protection Agency termed Page "One of the ten most healthful spots in the United States" (quoted in the Panorama Realty Advertisement in the August 1977 issue of *Skyline*), but the lack of industry forces most county residents to seek employment outside the county as well as within. The percentage of farm families has declined dramatically since World War II, from 29 percent in 1950 to 13 percent in 1960 to about 5 percent in 1970 and 1980 according to the U.S. Census of Agriculture. The occupational breakdown among county residents in 1972 is shown in Table 10.

Some of the middle-aged and young adult church members work in the Washington, D.C., region, as carpenters, bricklayers, or unskilled laborers. Although it means a daily round-trip commute of four hours, the wages have been sufficient to enable them to buy small, tidy, fully applianced brick ranch houses. Still, the construction industry is sensitive to swings in the economy, and when times are hard they are among the first to be laid off.

Many of the older church members dislike factory work and town life. Joining the cash-wage economy in Page Valley, they obtained a higher standard of living but at a psychological cost. Partly estranged from the earth, sometimes alienated from the fruits of their work, no longer pos-

TABLE 10. Page County occupations, 1972

Type of Employment	No. Employed	% of Total
Manufacturing	2,192	39.2
Self-employed, unpaid family workers, and domestics	852	15.3
Wholesale and retail trade	663	11.9
Government	659	11.8
Services	344	6.2
Agriculture	313	5.6
Contract construction	285	5.1
Transportation and public utilities	161	2.9
Finance, insurance, and real estate	97	1.7
Other	17	.3
Total No. Employed: 5,583		

SOURCE: Page County Planning Commission, Page County Comprehensive Plan, 1974, p. 75.

sessing the vital know-how that their children (now spending their time in the public schools) would need for their futures, they saw the strong family bonds nurtured by cooperative farm labor strain and break, and they felt themselves alone. A transitional generation, they had improved their living standard but not their lives.

But had they really modernized? Unquestionably, experiencing the transition from mountain farming to modern industrial life affected the older church members' beliefs about the world and their place in it, but the result has been a selective rejection of much in the modern way of life and an attempt to hold on to traditions based on a partly real and partly imagined vision of the past, of the mountain-farming folklife as true wisdom, enlightened by memories of their parents and their own early childhoods. Without necessarily having been a time of churchgoing, the mountain past became sacred in a far deeper sense, a golden age. Many recollected promises they had made to their dying parents that they would meet again in heaven. Most had not been saved when they made those sacred vows, but they foresaw that they would be later. And they were; most of the church elders were converted after migrating to the valley, not before.

The older generation's attitude toward the modern world is evidenced not merely in religion, but also in the persistence of the husbandry pattern. After saving money from their factory jobs or inheriting a portion of their parents' estate, they bought lots on the outskirts of town, and next to their houses they built farm outbuildings from sawn planks just as their fathers had done before them. In 1949, for example, Brother Vernie inherited one-third of 271 acres of timber land in Weaver Hollow that had belonged to his father. He and his brother and sister decided to sell this land in 1960. With their share of the proceeds, Brother Vernie and Sister Hattie bought 16 acres in Pine Grove Hollow, about three miles from Stanley. As I noted in describing the visit to Brother Rastus earlier in this chapter, in 1950 he bought 100 acres of timber land on Mill Creek. By 1960 he had sold all but 13 acres, and in 1970 he had 3 acres left. On these small acreages the older generation grew feed corn, kept hogs, and planted a kitchen garden. Brother Allen had a half-dozen hogs in 1977, Brother Belvin had a dozen, and Brother Vernie about four, while Brother Rastus' sons kept several for the family's use, to be butchered, smoked, salted, and kept in their meat house. Ironically, this "subsistence" farming is expensive; labor value counted, it costs more to keep cows, pigs, and chickens on this small scale than it does to buy food at the grocery store. Why, then, does the pattern persist? Partly because of unvoiced fears of another Depression, and partly because the older people's labor is no longer very marketable, their Social Security checks and pensions (if any) are small, and so this represents a continuation of safety-first behavior.

But most important, the mountain-farming pattern persists because the husbandry mind-set persists. It is bound up with the older generation's

Sister Hattie and Brother Vernie Meadows at home, Pine Grove Hollow, near Stanley, Virginia, 1977.

identity. It is both habit and discipline; it affords the pleasure of a job well done, a job they know how to do; and it is an expression of the overriding importance of husbandry. I asked Brother Rastus whether he preferred working at the chemical company to farming. "Well, no," he replied. "I always did want to [farm]. When I'd get out and go in to work [at the chemical plant] I'd see people out in the fields a-plowing, and stuff like that, and that was what I always was raised to do" (Lam interview, p. 28). After seeing his children through school "as far as they would go," Brother Rastus retired on a small pension:

And then at 62 I told my wife that I was just bored to be staying up there. . . . And so I took my retirement when I was 62. And got here and

we raised a few hogs, and got a few chickens, and used to farm a little
back here, raise a lot of corn, wheat. . . .
    I love to go out in the garden, though. . . . My wife does, too. She'd
sooner get a hoe in her hand than anything else in the world. Get out in
the garden and work. There ain't nary a one of us, if we's well and feel
good and got something to work in the garden, we're out in the garden all
the time. (Ibid. : 31)

Land, life, and God. The connection was never more clearly made by
anyone I spoke to than Howard Meadows. One warm and lovely day in the
fall of 1985, Tom Rankin, Barry Dornfeld, and I went up to the fork of
Jollett and Weaver Hollows, where the old Jollett Methodist Church stood,
to do a bit of filming. Afterward we spoke with Howard Meadows about the
mountains. I asked him why mountain people are so religious. "When
you're close to nature," he replied, "you're close to God."

He went on to speak about life in the mountains in the old days, when
people had to depend on each other, when people helped their neighbors.
Church on Sundays was the center of the community, where people visited with each other. In the cities, he said, it was every man for himself; no
one had much time to visit, he thought. But, he wound up, "I always figure the farther up the mountain, the closer I am to God" (Howard Meadows interview, October 4, 1985).

3. Religion

W hen I began my visits to the Fellowship Independent Baptist Church, I found it convenient to view the members' beliefs and practices as a functioning system that, mediated through the language of worship, lent them personal and group identity as Christians, a worldview, and an ethos. By a system I envisioned a set of principles for proper interpretation and conduct that said to them, in effect, given that this is the way the world is, and that you are a Christian, this is how you should behave. My research strategy was, then, synchronic and functionalistic.

But this functionalism could only take me so far. I had noticed certain points of tension in the congregation. For example, it seemed to me that some of the women chafed under the church's patriarchal rules. The deacons and the minister must be male; the songleader was male; prayers always were led by males; outside of participation in Sunday school and in testimony before singing a special or after the sermon, a woman could not speak to the congregation during the worship service. In fact, the men pointed to 1 Timothy 2:11–12 ("Let the woman learn in silence with all subjection. But I suffer a woman not to teach, nor to usurp authority over the man, but to be in silence"), and also to 1 Corinthians 14:34–35 ("Let your women keep silence in the churches: for it is not permitted unto them to speak; but they are commanded to be under obedience, as also saith the law. And if they will learn any thing, let them ask their husbands at home: for it is a shame for women to speak in the church"). Despite these Bible verses, the church allows women to speak; yet there is a residue of uneasiness, and whenever a woman delivered a lengthy testimony, some of the men grew impatient.

At the same time, it was clear that some of the women in the congregation had considerable verbal gifts and, when impressed to do so by the Spirit, did not hesitate to use them. Sister Edith was one such member. When I spoke with her and her husband outside of church, she displayed a strong personality and disputed her husband's view that women could not be called to preach. Sister Lois, who challenged one of the deacons during a Sunday school lesson (the exchange is presented in Chapter 7) when she questioned his right to remain as a deacon when his wife was not a Christian, caused much uneasiness in the congregation and soon stopped attending the church.

Yet other women in the church seemed to accept a non-assertive role. Indeed, during the Sunday school lesson men and women defended the deacon against Sister Lois' challenge, and, from a functionalist standpoint, the whole exchange could be regarded as an example of the way the church's system of beliefs and practices resolved members' disagreements. On another level, though, it did not resolve the tension, for Sister Lois left. Moreover, the history of many of the Baptist congregations in the area is filled with disagreements that were resolved only by certain members splitting off and forming other churches. In fact, as will be shown, that is how the Fellowship Independent Baptist Church began.

A functionalist approach, then, was natural to me as a fieldworker immersed in observation and evocative description (Chapter 1); but despite its laudable holistic orientation, functionalism is misleading because it de-emphasizes conflict and contradiction. Further, by concentrating its descriptive power on the immediate moment, it de-emphasizes history. The fact is that the "system" of church beliefs and practices is an amalgam of elements grafted in at different times and in different places, and not all of these function smoothly. In this chapter, I continue the last chapter's historical perspective but shift the focus to the religion of the Fellowship Independent Baptist Church as a product of history. I find it useful to conceive of the whole system of beliefs and practices as a geologist might look at the earth's crust, and to view it as being layered and fused with elements that came in at certain historical times and were more or less transformed as they were deposited and assimilated.

Take, for example, the church's emphasis on home and family, whether in home devotionals, praying for lost children, or the brothers and sisters of the church who will be one family of Christians in the heavenly homecoming reunion. Home-centering is clearly a Victorian overlay, but it does not fit precisely; that is, the Victorian ideology of domesticity as practiced by middle-class nineteenth-century Americans was an urban revivalism better suited to the regularity of the business world than to the raw, seasonal, spontaneous emotions of the rural camp-meeting or to the work world of mountain farming, in which women's labor produced a considerable portion of the family's livelihood and there was no separate "sphere" in which women and young children could be shielded from assaults of the outside world.

In this chapter I move back and forth from time present to past as the ideas that organize the presentation have guided me, but it will be helpful to understand at the outset that the religious system of the Fellowship Independent Baptist Church is the product of a historical layering that has incorporated a variety of slightly differing Protestant worldviews, and that theirs is an attempt to work out the tensions inherent in the differences. Broadly speaking, this layering may be diagrammed as in Figure 21, starting from time present.

Did each layer add something or were the transitions merely shifts in emphasis? Continuity must be understood, for the cornerstones of experiential religion and the conversion experience that are present throughout derive from the radical wing of the Reformation. Frontier revivalism contributed much that is the subject of Chapter 8, testimony, in terms of the view of one's calling in this world; suffice it here to indicate its theological contribution of open atonement: that salvation was available to all, not a predestined few. The Victorian contribution was also enormous: first, a body of gospel hymnody; second, the emphasis on home and family. But other aspects of Victorian religion were not assimilated—for example, missions and social work. In fact, premillenarian evangelism and the holiness movement emphasized separation between the church and the world. And on close examination, early twentieth-century fundamentalism may be seen as a reaction against the increasing secularization of Victorian religion.

The church's relation to the holiness movement is complex. The church members' ideas about language in religious practice are based in a theory of self and soul that seems to me to be derived from dispensationalist premillenarianism and the holiness movement's doctrine of the Holy Spirit

TIME PERIOD	MOVEMENT
World War II to present	The "New Evangelism" and the movement away from denominationalism
Late 19th and early 20th centuries	Premillenarian evangelism; holiness movement; fundamentalism
Mid to late 19th century	Victorian urban revivalism
18th to early 19th centuries	First and second Great Awakenings; frontier revivalism; evangelism
16th and 17th centuries	Radical wing of the Protestant Reformation (separatistic, pietistic)

Figure 21. The religious system of the Fellowship Independent Baptist Church as a product of historical layering.

(see Marsden 1980:55–80). Today the holiness movement is identified with pentecostalism, but a significant number of churches in the late nineteenth and early twentieth centuries—and the Fellowship Independent Baptist Church today, as a carrier of that tradition—can be characterized as holiness without the popular markings of pentecostalism, such as tongue-speaking. Brother John is characteristically succinct in the matter. "People sometimes called me Pentecostal. Well, that's all right with me; I got what they got on the day of Pentecost." But the fact is that he calls himself a Baptist and his church is a Baptist church; and on balance that is correct, for he rejects perfectionism and does not believe in the "second blessing" (baptism of the Holy Spirit), two key ideas in the holiness movement. All of this will be discussed below; the layering is intricate and needs careful attention.

Let us begin, then, by looking at the place of folk religion in the contemporary United States.

Folk Religion and Official Religion

The mountain farmers, whose traditions were inherited by the members of the Fellowship Independent Baptist Church, prized self-reliance; but when self-reliance failed, they depended on one another and they depended on God. Subsistence farming was strenuous, and a great deal depended on knowledge, proper timing, and the kindness of nature. Misfortune might come, and did, claiming crops, animals, even loved ones. Why was the world as it was? How might one live in harmony with the world, other people, and oneself, without fighting a losing battle to subdue nature? Religion offered answers and some comfort.

Religion is an ideology embodied in a cultural system. It explains the nature of reality and the meaning of life, and it offers directives for human conduct (Smart 1968; Geertz 1973; Wallace 1966). Religion's symbolic forms find expression in ritual, myth, doctrine, ethics, institutions, and the fabric of the believer's daily life. Science explains the nature of reality, but it does not tell people how to act.

A phenomenon of both the Eastern and Western worlds, folk religion is perhaps best understood as religion outside of the "official" or "established" or normative religion. Brother John himself uses the term "formal church" to describe those churches that practice official religion (John Sherfey interviewed by Barbara Schelstrate on NPR's *The Sunday Show*, March 11, 1983). In a heroic attempt to define folk religion, Don Yoder makes use of Ernest Troeltsch's European church/sect distinction to differentiate official religion from folk religion. The official religion (akin to Troeltsch's "church" type) is the established religion of the state or region, identified with the ruling classes, whereas folk religion (akin to Troeltsch's "sect") is religion outside of the establishment (Yoder 1974:3).

What is official religion in America? The United States has no established state church, yet for much of American history the ruling classes have been composed of white Protestants of putative Anglo-Saxon descent (Marty 1976:53). In the colonial South, the Anglican Church was the established religion in fact, but after the Revolution the U.S. Constitution separated church and state. Religious and cultural pluralism in the twentieth century has made it possible for a number of Jews and Catholics to enter the power structure. A highly regarded observer of American religion and public life at mid-century concluded that a man was considered trustworthy so long as he was thought to be religious—that is, a Protestant, Catholic, or Jew (Herberg 1955). American religion moved toward something of an official consensus summed up in the common phrase "the Judeo-Christian ethic."

American official religion also contains a fusion of faith and patriotism, explained in Robert N. Bellah's influential and controversial assessment of America's "civil religion":

> The separation of church and state has not denied the political realm a religious dimension. Although matters of personal religious belief, worship and association are considered to be strictly private affairs, there are, at the same time, certain common elements of religious orientation that the great majority of Americans share. They have played a crucial role in the development of American institutions and still provide a religious dimension for the whole fabric of American life, including the political sphere. This public dimension is expressed in a set of beliefs, symbols, and rituals that I am calling the American civil religion. (Bellah 1984:43)

This civil religion, which unites Americans in patriotic rituals such as Independence Day, Memorial Day, and Thanksgiving, is derived from Judaism and Christianity. It assumes that God is directly involved with history, and that it is the obligation of every American—and the nation as a whole—to carry out God's will on earth. This civil religion has its own rhetoric—one nation, under God—that is solemnly invoked in times of national crisis. When politicians invoke it, many believe it to be empty rhetoric. Members of racial and ethnic minorities take it with more than a touch of cynicism. Yet under conditions of national stress and emergency it appears to motivate the majority.

Civil religion is the religion of the flag, Mom, and apple pie—"what this country stands for." It is the religion of life, liberty, and the pursuit of happiness. It is not specifically Christian, for the rhetoric rarely mentions Jesus. And, as Bellah observes, "The God of the civil religion is not only rather 'unitarian,' he is also on the austere side, much more related to order, law, and right than to salvation and love" (ibid.:47).

In the United States, then, official religion is comprised of two parts: first, one's faith, whether Judaism, Catholicism, or one of the major Protestant denominations; and second, civil religion. By contrast, folk religion is not so much opposed to official religion as apart from it. Members of a religious folk culture may well practice and even believe in civil religion— or they may not—but in any case civil religion is not their chief ideology. For the member of a religious folk culture, folk religion, not official religion, explains the nature of reality and the meaning of life, and offers rules for conduct.

Obviously, one who practices a folk religion need not belong to a church, but many do; and a folk church is provisionally defined as a group practicing folk religion. Some American folk churches deliberately turn their backs on the power structure, viewing it as irredeemably corrupt, while stressing fellowship among their own and waiting for the Lord to come and call a halt to history and gather up the faithful. This behavior is characteristic of Troeltsch's sect-type, but it would be wrong simply to equate the sect with the folk church. William Clements, the folklorist who has written most definitively on the subject of American folk Protestantism, points out that whereas Troeltsch's sect-type stands in opposition to the establishment, in the United States folk churches are not necessarily opposed to the official culture. "Folk religion," writes Clements, "differs from official religion only in its lack of association with the society's power structure" (1974a:21).

Clements finds it unsatisfying to define American folk religion in terms of a negative attribute, so he also lists ten traits that can usually be found in folk Protestant churches in the United States (ibid.:20). These are:

1.   Scriptural literalism
2.   Orientation toward the past
3.   Consciousness of God's providence in man's affairs
4.   Emphasis on evangelism
5.   Informality
6.   Emotionalism
7.   Moral rigor
8.   Sectarianism
9.   Egalitarianism
10. Relative isolation of the church building (i.e., away from "official" institutions—banks, post offices, "downtown")

Clements explains that these traits are to be considered secondary; some folk churches possess none and few all. (Tellingly, the Fellowship Independent Baptist Church has all.)

I would add that many of these ten traits overlap and reinforce one another. Informality, for example, allows for public emotionalism. Moreover, these traits are so redundant that even when a particular church lacks some, the rest are usually sufficient to mark it as a folk church. A helpful analogy might be to a tape recording of the voice of a friend: you recognize it as your friend speaking even though you cannot see her. Her voice is sufficient to identify her.

Aside from these ten traits, two other secondary aspects of American folk churches deserve special attention here because they are directly related to language in religious practice. These are the folk churches' emphases on oral tradition and demonstrative, improvised performance style. By performance style I mean manner of communicating. This includes gesture, tone, mode (speech, chant, or song), dialect, diction, tempo, posture, delivery (improvised, memorized, or read), and so forth. Two congregations identical in doctrine may diverge in performance style, and a believer will feel comfortable in one but not another because of it.

Performance style has become one of the central areas of folklorists' inquiry in recent years (Bauman and Paredes 1972; Bauman 1984; Toelken 1979). Richard M. Dorson, who prided himself on his ability to distinguish folklore from "fakelore" (his term) and who from the 1950s to his death in 1981 was America's most prominent folklorist, wrote almost nothing about folk religion. But in his quick study of black Baptist churches during a survey of city folklore, he contrasted folk and non-folk churches on the basis of social class, normative behavior, and performance style (one must try to forgive his unsympathetic phrase, "catatonic cases"):

> Looking at the Negro church in the United States, I would say that the First Baptist Church which I attended in Gary, Indiana, with its programs of the service, hymn-books, sedate sermon, and decorous congregation, is a middle-class institution, while the Calvary, Trinity, and Primitive Baptist churches, which I also attended, with their chanting preachers, responsive parishioners, spontaneous singing and testifying, and catatonic cases, are folk institutions. (Dorson 1972:32)

Performance style registers the differences between sedate and chanting preachers and, as pointed out in the Introduction, beliefs concerning religious inspiration underlie these differences. The parishioners articulate some of these beliefs. What Dorson mistakenly thought were "catatonic cases" are a type of Spirit-filled behavior that the parishioners term "falling out."

Performance styles have proved especially interesting to folklorists and ethnomusicologists when they involve traditions from an earlier era. Lined-out, heterophonic, congregational hymn-singing, prevalent among numerous black Baptist congregations and also among a small number of white Primitive and Old Regular Baptists in the South, is a survival of a colonial American performance style that derives ultimately from the English parish church (Temperley 1981). Pentecostal congregations continue to sing nineteenth-century camp-meeting choruses; in fact, they continue camp meetings and tent revivals (Titon 1978a). Other examples of older performance styles that have survived include sung and chanted prayers, testimonies, and sermons; holy dancing, falling out, spontaneous group prayer, laying on of hands, and so forth. Most of these are extemporaneous and are said to be led by the Spirit.

Besides performance style, oral tradition plays an important role in the American folk church. By oral tradition I mean knowledge passed along from one person to the next, by word of mouth and imitation rather than by formal instruction, apprenticeship, and schooling. Clements points out that a definition of American folk religion that turns on oral tradition is too narrow, and cites the importance of the written word (e.g., the Bible, religious tracts, Sunday school literature; Clements 1974a: 13–14). This is quite true, and yet a definition that fails to emphasize oral tradition is unsatisfactory, for it has a principal role in the transmission of belief and of performance style.

Worshipers do not learn to pray aloud extemporaneously or to give testimony as a result of formal training or written instructions. Rather, they learn by imitation and inspiration. A young deacon in a black church in Detroit told me about the first time he had to pray aloud from the pulpit. Knowing he could not rely on reading a written prayer, he decided to hedge his bets by memorizing the utterance in advance. But when he stood in front of the congregation he forgot the prayer he had practiced and after a moment of panic improvised one on the spot. I have heard similar narratives from several worshipers in a variety of folk churches. Since these prayers are redundant and formulaic, they are composed quickly once the principles have been absorbed (Titon 1980a). Delivering them in front of a congregation, however, requires the proper frame of mind, intention, and belief.

In fact, much of the manner of worship in the American folk church is passed along orally. Preachers, typically, do not undergo seminary training; nor do they depend greatly on the written traditions of biblical commentary, pastoral literature, or theology. Their "preaching style" is learned, therefore, largely by imitating other preachers. Singing style, too, is an oral tradition, and this is why two congregations will sing the "same" hymn differently. In May 1977 a member of the Little Flock Primitive Baptist Church in Whitehall, Indiana, who had just returned from a visit to a sister church in Kentucky jokingly complained to me that they took "a half-hour, seemed like, for 'Amazing Grace.'" Not only do the Kentuckians take a slower tempo; they also decorate the tune with numerous grace notes, passing tones, catches, and glides. The order of worship is another aspect of the American folk church which is handed down orally and shows the variation over time and space that is typical of the products of oral tradition. Liturgical books and printed programs are unusual in the context of the folk church. Instead, the order of events and the events themselves result from an informal agreement.

So long as the definition of the folk church turns on the "folk" as a group outside the power structure—and with my folklife methodological bias I am certainly happy with that folk-cultural definition—then the character- istics of the "lore," such as the emphasis on oral tradition and demon- strative, spontaneous performance styles must remain secondary. "Out- side the power structure" is admittedly vague, but it suggests differences in wealth, status, education, and most of all economic and political impact among insiders and outsiders. The form that worship takes in the folk church, then, will depend on its traditions, but the traditions themselves cannot define the folk church. It is a characteristic of animals that they have four limbs, two eyes, two ears, a nose, and a mouth, but these charac- teristics do not define "animal."

History: Evangelism, Old and New

In an article on "Old-Time Baptists," Loyal Jones argues that the folk Bap- tists may be understood with reference to earlier American religious be- liefs and practices:

> It is my belief that these Baptists reflect a set of religious beliefs that were typical of a large portion of the people in an earlier age in Appalachia, and elsewhere, and that some of these beliefs persist among other Christian groups in the mountains, including the Southern Baptists, especially in rural areas. It is also my belief that the social values of these sects, which I shall hereafter call Old Baptists, are typical of older Appalachians in general. . . .
>   It seems to me that there is a quality of faith and of life among them that ought to be understood and appreciated. They operate in abstract and in- tellectual realms in discussing their faith, contrary to the claim by some that they lack an ability to think in the abstract. They have a clear sense of the spiritual as opposed to the worldly. They are not led around by fads and styles. They believe in serving one another. In spiritual matters they place trust in no earthly being but in the scriptures and in the Holy Spirit, and they have a respect for traditions. Perhaps they are too religious to suit our modern tastes. (Jones 1977: 121, 129)

The historical roots of contemporary Appalachian folk Baptists lie in Presbyterian, Methodist, and Baptist evangelism from the first Great Awak- ening of the 1740s through the second Great Awakening of the early 1800s. In his recent study, *Religion in the Old South,* Donald G. Mathews affirms that evangelism became the dominant religion, first on the frontier and then generally throughout the South and the Old West. As a religious position that was institutionalized in the Baptist, Methodist, Presbyterian, and Disciples of Christ denominations, as well as numerous other, smaller denominations, evangelism was

> an elaboration of the Protestant perspective that the Christian life is essentially a personal relationship with God in Christ, established through the direct action of the Holy Spirit, an action which elicits in the believer a profoundly emotional conversion experience. This existential crisis, the New Birth as evangelicals called it, ushers the convert into a life of holiness characterized by religious devotion, moral discipline, and missionary zeal. To achieve this remarkable transformation, Evangelical preaching rejects the appeal to reason and restrained sensibilities for a direct, psychological assault upon sin and the equally direct and much more comforting offer of personal salvation. (Mathews 1977:xvi)

In its initial phase, lasting well into the early nineteenth century, evangelism was very much a folk religion outside of the religious establishment, and its adherents formed religious folk cultures. Evangelism opposed the institutionalization of rank and power within the established Anglican Church and created a new mode of social organization in which one's worth was determined not by birth or wealth but by the purity and authenticity of one's religious life. Mathews observes that the evangelical strictures against philandering, gambling, and whiskey were directed against the pleasures of the plantation aristocracy and therefore had revolutionary social implications (ibid.: 34–36, 41–44).

Presbyterianism was overtly the least revolutionary of the evangelical religions in the South, in the sense that its ministers were careful to obey the colonial laws pertaining to dissident churches (see below, "Religious History in Page County"). Nonetheless, their emphasis on the personal conversion experience and the indwelling presence of the Holy Spirit differed considerably in orientation and rhetoric from the Anglican Church's remote formalism.

Baptists did not obey civil laws pertaining to religion; they invoked a higher law. Besides the New Birth and indwelling Spirit, Baptists stressed adult baptism by total immersion, and they emphasized the separation of the church, as a holy community of saints, from the world of sin and corruption. They instituted new kinds of communal rites: anointing the sick, laying on of hands, public testimony meetings, the right hand of fellowship, the kiss of charity, and the washing of one another's feet. These rites, it must be noted, are a distinctive part of the worship service in the Fellowship Independent Baptist Church, where they have persisted in religious tradition even though most non-Appalachian Baptists consider them outmoded.

To the evangelical movement Methodism contributed a democracy of feeling. Accepting the centrality of the New Birth, Methodists tended to ignore the residual Calvinism of Presbyterians and most Baptists. They preached that salvation was open to everyone, even the worst of sinners, and not just to an elect few; and they expected, and witnessed, conversion among the majority of the populations where they preached (ibid.: 19–32).

As the nineteenth century wore on, evangelical religion consolidated its gains. Having become the majority faith of the South, it could scarcely maintain an anti-establishment attitude. It had, in effect, become the Victorian establishment. Evangelicals, once charged with ordaining illiterate ministers who believed themselves qualified because God had "called" them, now stressed organization, discipline, and an educated ministry, and founded colleges and seminaries throughout the nation.

As congregations grew and their members became part of local power structures, it became increasingly difficult to maintain a separation between the church and the world. In an attempt to ensure the continuing purity of the holy community, early evangelicals had made the churches watch over their members' affairs; improper behavior was duly reported, noted, and corrected—or, if not, the churches dismissed the errant member. But during the period of evangelical consolidation in the nineteenth century, this watching, caring, and disciplining was transferred from the church to the family, and gradually the family rather than the church took on the role of ideal community. The family became the most important sphere of religious action and activity. Mothers, especially, were taught to be guardians of religious tradition. More pious by nature than fathers, or so it was believed, mothers were unsullied by the corrupt world and therefore especially fit to nurture the spiritual upbringing of the child. From the outset, evangelism had placed a premium on family devotions. Itinerant ministers made it a practice to stop over with believers' families and guide them in their daily devotions. Before church buildings could be built, people worshiped most often as a family in the home. Now home and family were both traditional and natural repositories of the purest faith and symbolic of the highest ideals in personal relationships (ibid.: 81–135 passim).

As evangelism was transformed during the nineteenth century throughout the South (and, indeed, the nation), it lost its identity as a folk culture. Evangelism had become institutionalized in other denominations—Lutheran, Congregational, Episcopalian. It had become mainstream Victorian Protestantism. It had become official religion. Most of the fervent excesses of its early days had long since vanished. Methodism's insistence that salvation was, in theory at least, open to all seemed an appropriate principle on which to base public religion in a democratic society. Belief now was a matter of individual choice.

But if mainstream evangelism had been transformed, grown respectable, become official, religious folk cultures remained. Quakers, Mennonites, Dunkers (Brethren), the Amish, and other sects set apart from the world had never been swept up in the evangelistic transformations. Black Americans comprised their own religious folk cultures. Hispanic folk Catholicism flourished in the Southwest. American Indian religions preserved much of their ancient heritage as the Indians learned to live in two worlds: the whites' and their own.

Moreover, conservative elements within the evangelistic movement had not gone along with the more worldly trends. Certain Baptist denominations, for example—Old Regulars and Separates—clung to the older Calvinism with its insistence that the church was set apart. Newer Baptist denominations, such as the Primitives (Old School Baptists as they were known in the nineteenth century) were created in response to apostasy (such as Sunday school) within Baptist ranks (ibid.:128). Many Appalachian mountain churches rejected urban, middle-class elements that they perceived in Victorian evangelism. And these purifying movements continued their attempts to return to the beliefs and practices of the early Christians and in so doing create communities set apart from the world.

A recent thoroughgoing analysis of fundamentalism (Marsden 1980) is helpful in understanding the historical basis for certain premillenarian and holiness aspects of the beliefs of the members of the Fellowship Independent Baptist Church. George M. Marsden points out that the main line of nineteenth-century evangelical thought was postmillenarian, in a tradition reaching back to the earliest British Protestants who settled in America. Technically, this refers to the idea that the millennium (a thousand-year reign of peace on earth) will be the last stage of the current historical era, after which the Second Coming will occur and Christ will gather the church into heaven. Practically, it meant that these evangelicals saw signs of progress toward the millennium in the advance of Christianity in America and abroad, as well as in the rise of American civilization as an example to the world. As Marsden writes,

> American evangelical postmillennialists saw signs of the approach of the millennial age not only in the success of revivals and missions, but also in general cultural progress. The golden age would see the culmination of current reform efforts to end slavery, oppression, and war. Moreover, in this wonderful era science, technology, and learning would advance to undreamed of accomplishments. (Ibid.:49)

Premillennialists, a minority among the nineteenth-century evangelicals, saw signs of evil and catastrophe, not progress; and they believed that the Second Coming will antedate the millennium. Brother John's modern-day exposition of this theme is illustrated in a sermon he preached on March 19, 1972:

> Now I realize that we're living in an age and a time when seemingly they've got it to where the world's going to get better. And they're talking a

world-wide evolution saving revival. Well I'm going to tell you something, neighbor. According to the Bible, brother, it'll never happen. According to the word of God, brother, I'd like to see this old world get converted. But, brother, there's more people going to hell today than ever was known in history.

Dividing the eras of time into periods or "dispensations," each dispensation being the result of a new relationship between God and humankind, dispensational premillennialists believed that the current historical era (the era of the Christian church) will soon end, to be followed by a horrendous seven-year "tribulation" period in which the antichrist will rule and humankind will be plagued and tormented. At the close of the tribulation, Jesus will return, lead an army of Christian soldiers, defeat the powers of Satan at Armageddon, and inaugurate a new dispensation, the millennium, ruling the earth from his seat in Jerusalem.

Premillennialists, therefore, anticipating the millennium, looked for signs of the coming of the antichrist, indicating that humankind was about to enter the tribulation period. Meanwhile, the church was to be separate from the world. At the turn of the twentieth century, the dispensationalists were torn apart over whether the church would remain on earth during the tribulation or would ascend to heaven beforehand. (Although this issue may seem obscure to the reader, it is an important question for the Fellowship Independent Baptist Church; their pastor is a pre-tribulationist, believing in a pre-tribulation ascent [rapture] of the church.) Within the conservative evangelical movement at the turn of the century, this controversy lessened the influence of dispensationalist premillenarianism among the conservative evangelicals, who returned to an interest in the workings of the Holy Spirit.

As the premillenarian beliefs were gaining favor with conservative evangelicals during the last decades of the nineteenth century, the holiness movement, with its emphasis on leading a perfect and sinless life, gathered considerable momentum. Premillennialist separatism would best be served if the church were holy, but it was clear to these conservatives that Christendom was tainted by the apostasy of liberal postmillennialism. How could an individual maintain holiness and await the Second Coming? Wesleyan Methodist perfectionism taught that it was indeed possible for a human being to attain a state of perfect sinlessness during this life, and as it was elaborated among the more radical wing of the holiness movement (and, later, pentecostalism), the doctrine involved an act of complete surrender, a "dramatic second blessing attained by an act of consecration described as placing 'all on the altar'" (ibid.:74). In this "second blessing," a stage that followed conversion, the believer would be "filled" with the Holy Spirit. This second blessing was termed the baptism of the Holy Ghost. Once the Holy Spirit took up its abode in the believer, it drove out the forces of sin and evil, whereupon the individual was pure.

Late in the nineteenth century the evangelistic movement split into two camps. The liberals, or modernists, were postmillennialists who wanted to accommodate science with religion and to enlist the church in the battle to improve the lot of humankind on this earth: a social gospel; while the conservatives, or fundamentalists, most of whom were premillenarian, and many of whom accepted holiness principles, resisted and held to the principles of biblical infallibility and the imminent Second Coming of Christ. Uncharacteristically, many of the leading fundamentalists began taking worldly stands on political and economic issues, particularly during World War I. Prior to the war, the thrust of their rhetoric had been separatist and pacifist; but once the United States entered the war they became ardent patriots and urged their followers to fight for their country. In this connection it is interesting to note that when Brother John decided not to fight in World War II (see Chapter 9) he was following the old-fashioned premillenarian pacifist tradition.

Most religious historians (themselves modernists) believe that the modernists prevailed. Certainly they gained control of public life after World War I, and won victory after victory in the newspapers and magazines. The Scopes trial was thought to deliver the deathblow to fundamentalism. Fundamentalism was considered backward and embarrassing. As it moved toward mid-century, mainline Protestantism was liberal, tolerant, enlightened, and even "existential" (Marty 1976:52–79, 84–86). Yet the holiness and premillenarian fundamentalists did not go away; having done battle with the world as fundamentalists, they reasserted the earlier strain of separation from worldly things and temporarily withdrew.

"Mainline" is the term religious historians employ today when describing what folklorists call official or normative religion. A list of churches in the United States generally conceded to be in the mainline includes the following (Kelley 1972:88–90):

Unitarian-Universalist
Reformed Jews
United Church of Christ
United Methodist Church
United Presbyterian Church
American Baptist Convention
Episcopal Church
Reformed Church in America
Southern Presbyterian Church [Presbyterian Church in the U.S.]
Greek Orthodox
Russian Orthodox
Conservative Jews
Roman Catholic Church

American Lutheran Church
Lutheran Church—Missouri Synod
Southern Baptist Convention

The following are outside the mainline:

Church of Christ, Scientist
Church of God
Seventh Day Adventists
Latter-day Saints
Churches of Christ
Orthodox Jews
Evangelicals and Pentecostals
Jehovah's Witnesses
Black Muslims

Although all the mainline churches are a part of official religion, not all the churches outside the mainline are representative of folk religion. The Fellowship Independent Baptist Church is a folk church that falls within the "Evangelicals and Pentecostals" category above, but the category is a catchall and bears explanation. Certain elements within it are better understood as manifestations of popular culture and official religion rather than folklife.

For despite the growing liberalism within twentieth-century Protestantism and its increasing orientation toward a social gospel, conservative Protestants, whether Lutherans in the Midwest or the smaller Baptist denominations scattered throughout the South, clung to their belief in biblical infallibility and their sense of being a people set apart. Elements of evangelism were particularly strong in the South, where even the mainline Presbyterians, Methodists, and Baptists recognized the authenticity of the New Birth, and many congregations made it a *sine qua non* for membership.

In the South the Methodist-Baptist hegemony had given mainline religion a strong evangelical flavor and a personal emphasis. Brush-arbor meetings and yearly revival services continued the tradition of the nineteenth-century camp-meetings, with their emphasis on the community of believers. The role of Jesus as sacrificial Savior and as mediator between man and God took on special importance. The personal relationship to God was maintained in daily prayer "through Christ our Lord." The sinner learned to pray to Jesus for forgiveness. Conversion itself was thought to result from prayer directed at the Savior. With Jesus as a constant friend and comforter, southern religion became exceedingly Christ-centered. The broad consensus in belief was termed "popular southern Protestantism" by Samuel S. Hill, Jr., who noted that beneath the comparative solemnity of Presbyterian worship and demonstrative Pentecostal meeting the faithful had much in common: orthodoxy of belief, natural piety, and biblical dogmatism (Hill 1967:23–26, 34–39, 73–88). For other assessments of southern religion as a regional phenomenon, see Reed 1974; Marsden 1980; Pope 1965; Harrell 1971; Peacock 1971; Boles 1972; and Cash 1941.

Without the persistence of popular southern Protestantism, the New Evangelism of the post–World War II era would not have gained such strength as it has. The original base of this New Evangelism was in the South, and most of its adherents still live there or are recent migrants therefrom. Drawing on a coalition of religious conservatives that included some of the older fundamentalists, as well as newer leaders who were uncomfortable with fundamentalism's anti-intellectual legacy, the movement was led by Carl F. H. Henry, editor of *Christianity Today,* and by evangelistic crusaders, most importantly Billy Graham (Marty 1976:86–87). Today the New Evangelicals cut across the varying Protestant denominations but draw most of their strength from Baptists and Pentecostals. Highly visible, they include the television PTL Club and the ministries of such men as Oral Roberts, a Pentecostal; Jerry Falwell, a Baptist who leads the Moral Majority; and countless other local, regional, and national evangelists. Television is an especially appropriate medium for the New Evangelicals because of their outreach orientation, visible enthusiasm, public testimony, and their ability to demonstrate conversion in mass revivals videotaped on location.

Although it lives outside of mainline religion, much of the New Evangelism is a phenomenon of popular rather than folk culture (Williams 1980). The mass appeal of the television crusaders and their celebrity status make them remote, despite whatever sincerity they project on the air or in person; and the droves of believers who queue up to the outdoor altars to pray the sinner's prayer appear like so many parts on an assembly-line. This is not to deny that conversion at such a revival may be intensely personal; but the spectacle itself cannot possibly evidence the ongoing personal relationships among friends that characterize a folk culture's more intimate way of life. Of course, a person may be converted in a mass revival (with or without media coverage) and then join a folk church. A second reason why much of the New Evangelism cannot be understood as folk religion is that it does not stand outside the political power structure. Billy Graham is a political figure and confidante of presidents. Jerry Falwell's Moral Majority is a political and economic pressure group.

Yet mixing politics with religion is anathema to the more orthodox among the New Evangelicals. It may be recalled that it was on strict Baptist principles of separation of church and state that President Carter, an avowed born-again Christian, reminded Americans that although he was personally opposed to abortion, he thought the government had no right to interfere with a pregnant woman's free choice in the matter.

In short, the New Evangelicals today present a broad spectrum and may well be repeating the history of nineteenth-century American evangelical movements. Consolidation is taking place, educational and economic institutions are being founded and supported, and once again the family, rather than the church, has become the locus of the ideal community. The recent successful battle against passage of the Equal Rights Amendment was viewed as a defense of motherhood and family. Meanwhile, conservative elements go their own way, often constituting religious folk cultures set apart, like the Fellowship Independent Baptist Church, whose members are not particularly interested in the political process. They are far more concerned with God's role in history and the imminent Second Coming.

Religion in Appalachia: Missionaries and Sociologists

Although the Southern Baptist Convention is the dominant religious body in the South, it does not dominate in the southern Appalachians, where the churches are chiefly representative of the smaller Baptist denominations that Loyal Jones termed Old Baptists—Old Regulars, Separates, Freewills, Missionaries, Primitives, and a growing number of Independents—along with numerous holiness and Pentecostal congregations, a diminishing number of Methodist churches, and a fair number of independent nondenominational fundamentalist Christian community churches. Here may be found the most conservative elements in the New Evangelism, and considerable continuity from the old. Indeed, some of the Old Baptists (Old Regulars and Primitives in particular) have preserved traditions such as sung sermons and prayers and lined-out, heterophonic hymnody virtually intact for more than a century, while rejecting the missionary aspects of the evangelical movement right from the start.

There exists a small amount of serious literature on Appalachian religion. It grew from the home missions movement, beginning shortly after the turn of the twentieth century (Campbell 1969; Weller 1965). Viewing the mountain people as culturally impoverished, the educators, social workers, and church missionaries sought to help them, and to help them help themselves; and they spent many decades attempting to bring social, educational, medical, and religious enlightenment to the region. Various Protestant denominations founded colleges throughout Appalachia to help young women and men realize their full potential. The Sunday school was the most widespread institution brought into the mountains; these penetrated even the remotest areas. One was established, for example, in an Episcopalian mission built atop Tanner's Ridge about 1890, but it failed to attract the mountain people, and the Episcopalians abandoned it after a decade.

The failure of this mission only a few miles from the later location of the Fellowship Independent Baptist Church suggests the problem in the early missionaries' analysis of mountain folklife. They failed to comprehend that the mountain peoples' religious heritage gave them a profound distrust of earthly institutions—including the church. Early in the nineteenth century, the Old School Baptists had rejected such innovations as the Sunday school as irrelevant at best and diversionary at worst (Jones 1977: 123–124). The irony was that the missionaries, who were motivated by high social ideals, brought these to a people who had no real sympathy with a church oriented toward a social gospel.

Resulting cultural misperception, therefore, renders much of the missionaries' writing about Appalachian religion unreliable. Viewing the mountaineers as fiercely individualistic, disputatious, stubborn, and unwilling to abandon old beliefs, the missionaries found it difficult to instill in them a sense of social responsibility and to bring them into the modern world. But their mountain stubbornness was as much a response to the missionaries' cultural onslaught as a character trait. These outsiders professed to be Christians, but in the heaven-directed eyes of the mountain folk their emphasis on things of this world rendered them suspect.

Missionaries were the first writers to treat Appalachian religion seriously; sociologists were the first to write about it with some detachment, and indeed they still do. They seem drawn to the more "deviant" or spectacular beliefs and behavior, with the result that most of the description and analysis available in the sociological literature concerns the Pentecostals, particularly the serpent-handling groups, while the more typical churches, like the Old Baptists, are comparatively neglected (e.g., Photiadis, ed. 1978; LaBarre 1969).

In fact, Pentecostals adamantly separate themselves from a world they consider sinful and corrupt. As communities set apart, with their own values and behavior, the Pentecostals comprise religious folk cultures. Derived from the holiness movement of the latter nineteenth century, Pentecostals comprise a diverse group, and it is difficult to generalize beyond certain basic tenets that most hold. It is probably fair to say that most of today's Pentecostals share the New Evangelical beliefs in scriptural literalism, the New Birth, and the coming tribulation period before the millennium, but hold that the conversion process is incomplete without the "second blessing" or "baptism of the Holy Ghost." That is, after repentance and justification, the true believer will attain a state of sinless perfection (sanctification; hence the label "sanctified church" in black parlance) and at that moment the Spirit will enter and fill the "clean vessel." Most, but not all, Pentecostals insist that the attainment of this second blessing is signaled by the convert's speaking in tongues, a language that is audible but incomprehensible to anyone lacking the gift of interpretation. Speaking in tongues is thought by outsiders (and some insiders) to be the distinguishing characteristic of pentecostalism, but for some Pentecostals it is not a benchmark and for others it is not considered especially important. Besides tongues and interpretation of tongues, seven other "spiritual gifts" (including the gift of healing) are said to be available to the Pentecostal convert, but it is rare that any believer comes to possess all. Today the approximately eight million Pentecostals in the United States include many independent congregations, several branches of the Church of God in Christ (chiefly black Americans), and groups of believers, such as the charismatic Catholics, who retain membership in mainline churches while professing pentecostalism (Titon 1978a).

Sociological analysis of Appalachian religion has been influential yet, I believe, is misguided. A typical example is the oft-reprinted article by Nathan L. Gerrard, "Churches of the Stationary Poor in Appalachia." Gerrard defines the stationary poor as those who will never rise above poverty, nor will their children. How Gerrard is able to divine the children's future is not revealed. He mistakenly assumes that all the pious hollow folk belong to holiness churches (some, of course, belong to other denominations) and that they carry religious individualism to an extreme. "Each man is indeed his own Pope," Gerrard proclaims. The stationary poor are described as religious fatalists who extend this fatalism to their material circumstances; hence they feel it is pointless to try to improve them. "These people believe in the reality of the devil, who is hallucinated in various forms," Gerrard continues, distancing himself yet further from his subjects, unable to understand their behavior (Gerrard 1978).

Applied to Appalachian religion, sociological method has involved observing people's behavior and then explaining the "real" reasons for it. These reasons, which I shall examine shortly, include socialization, accommodation, alienation, and deprivation (see Photiadis 1978). The explanations derive from social relationships and goals. Few sociologists are willing to grant that the believers may be temperamentally inclined to a spiritual life, or that such a life satisfies cognitive and emotional needs. Nor are these functional behaviorists inclined to suspend disbelief about the ultimate validity of the people's religious claims. Religion is regarded as superstition. The irony is that social science, supposedly value-free, is committed in advance to denying the worldview it examines. Sociologists could not possibly take seriously a colleague who suggested that God causes religious behavior.

Socialization and accommodation are two reasons for the persistence of Appalachian religion but not otherwise a cause of it. Parents teach children it is proper to lead a Christian life, and the community of believers socializes the newly saved into behaving as they are expected to. Using the born-again analogy, they say that just as a newborn baby is not given all knowledge at birth, neither is a born-again Christian, who needs help from older and wiser people in the church. Accommodation to pressure from close relatives and friends is another reason for the persistence of Appalachian religion. Promises made to dying kin are a characteristic instance. But socialization and accommodation are explanations for all kinds of behavior, not just religion; that is, they carry no specificity for religious behavior itself. If they explain religious behavior for some, why not for all? Why do certain people never accept religion? Why do others delay acceptance despite the pressures of socialization and accommodation? The fact is that religious models of the good life compete with secular models involving wealth, power, and status. If socialization and accommodation are to be understood as causative, it must be that they operate on those otherwise somehow inclined to a spiritual life; and in that inclination or mindset perhaps resides a deeper cause.

Deprivation is a common theory regarding religious belief. People or groups with less than they want, often less than others with whom they compare themselves, enlist the aid of supernatural forces. Appalachian subsistence farmers, so the argument runs, had a hard time of it; they needed all the help they could get; hence they turned to God. When deprivation persisted they cast their eyes on a heavenly reward. Berton H. Kaplan studied three Blue Ridge Mountain congregations and found that members of one, the Freewill Baptists, were economically deprived and sought compensation in religion. Their behavior during worship—which he patronizingly characterized as "rolling in the aisles"—was to be understood as a psychological release from their constant economic worries.

Kaplan asserted that the Freewills' "concept of salvation is different . . . They believe that if you sin in any manner, you must be saved again. As a result, they are frequently in turmoil over whether they're saved or not, which requires frequent revivals to reassure them they are . . ." (Kaplan 1978 : 261–262). Disparaging the Freewill congregation he studied, it is not surprising that the sociologist misunderstood their concept of salvation. Freewills believe a person can be saved but once. Christians will sin (backslide), because it is human nature to do so; they must then ask forgiveness and be restored to a proper relation with God. But this is not the same thing as being saved repeatedly; one cannot be born again and again and again. Kaplan's error leads him to false conclusions about Freewill psychology and behavior. The error could have been avoided if the sociologist had simply asked the members of the congregation what was their concept of salvation.

Appealing as the deprivation argument may be, it fails to explain that when many mountain people did modernize and raise their living standard, their "religiosity," measured by the sociologists in terms of frequency of worship, percentage of people belonging to churches, and so forth, did not diminish; if anything, it increased (Photiadis 1978 : 16–17). If deprivation causes religious behavior, then as deprivation lessens religious behavior should lessen; but apparently it does not. Moreover, such measurements as church membership and attendance are directed more at social behavior than inner religious experience. The argument from deprivation is at best inconclusive.

A group of sociologists associated with West Virginia University under the leadership of John D. Photiadis explains the religious behavior of modernized mountaineers on the grounds of alienation. Analysis of economic changes in Appalachia since the Depression reveals that as the autonomy of the rural system disintegrated and people migrated to the towns and cities they began to judge themselves by the new, urban, consumer-oriented standards and values, and they not only felt deprived but also alienated. They had raised their standard of living, the argument runs, but not enough. "The reason for the persistence of sectarian fundamentalism," writes Photiadis, "is that it performs important functions; in particular, it has helped low-income and rural Appalachians alleviate anxieties produced by social complexity, and in particular the inability to fulfill expectations that the larger society . . . is creating" (Photiadis 1978:14).

People in the Fellowship Independent Baptist Church have told me that as their friends and relatives "get up in society"—earn more money, live in better homes, aspire to more creature comforts—they worship in more sedate churches, if they worship at all. Sectarian fundamentalism no longer has much of an appeal to them. But is this generally true? Not even all sociologists agree that sectarian fundamentalism characterizes chiefly the poor. Kaplan's Baptists were economically deprived, but Gerrard thought that mountain Baptists served the upwardly mobile and Pentecostals the "stationary poor." Yet Luther Gerlach and others have found pentecostalism to be characteristic not of the very poor (who supposedly have no religion) but of the upper-lower and lower-middle classes—that is, I suppose, the working class with middle-class aspirations (Gerlach 1974; *Joy Unspeakable*). Strictures on pleasure-seeking behavior (no smoking, drinking, dancing, makeup, short hair, premarital sex, etc.) among Pentecostals are viewed as a preparation for acceptance into a higher social class. These conflicting sociological observations suggest that religious behavior is often better understood as a local phenomenon rather than as a denominational one.

Explaining religious behavior among Appalachians on the grounds of socialization, accommodation, deprivation, and alienation is an attempt to explain it away; "If it weren't for these things," the sociologists argue, "Appalachian religion would not take the form of sectarian fundamentalism." The chief difficulty with this argument, internal contradictions and faulty evidence aside, is that it ignores the value of mountain religion for its practitioners. In worship, their speech, chant, and songs are eloquent testimony to their human desire to create and perfect form. It is one thing to say, as these scholars do, that mountain religion is a pathological delusion created as compensation for deprivation and alienation. It is quite another to regard it, as I do, as an adaptation to a specific time and place that allows for complex symbolic expression and a fusion of intellect and emotion, mediated through language.

Finally, a good reason for the persistence of religion among Appalachians is the veneration of tradition: the old ways are thought to be the best ways (Bryant 1981; Stephenson 1968; Weatherford and Brewer 1962). New ways may be grafted on if they are in harmony with the old, but one of the most telling characteristics of folklife is the continuity of tradition; that is, of an attitude toward change. The importance of tradition suggests that the literature on Appalachian religion needs a historical framework and a long view, something notably absent from the writings of the missionaries and social scientists.

The Fellowship Independent Baptist Church

One Sunday night a few years ago I was visiting the Fellowship Independent Baptist Church for some follow-up fieldwork. An evangelist friend of Brother John's passed through the region and was invited to preach a guest sermon to the congregation. He began to talk about how the world crises of food and energy, and the wars between nations, particularly in the Holy Land, and the "mark of the beast"—which he identified as the electronic-sensitive, parallel lines printed on consumer packaging in supermarkets—all signaled the imminence of the Second Coming. This was ordinary Pentecostal premillenarian rhetoric, such as I had heard for more than a decade when I surveyed grass-roots Baptist and Pentecostal religion in preparation for my documentation projects. But it had very little effect on the worshipers. There was scarcely an "Amen." Then I realized that references to current international affairs had always been remarkably absent from Brother John's preaching and from the concerns of the members as they discussed them in prayer meetings and adult Sunday school. Oh, Brother John sometimes held forth during his sermons on the wickedness of the world, but the world was always the nearby town of Stanley. Brother John's references, it occurred to me, were either eternal and biblical, or personal and local.

The evangelist continued his harangue, indicting liberal politicians and staking out a position on the far right. This got no response at all. The congregation wanted a message from God that was centered in the Bible, not an assessment of national and international power struggles, complete with conspiracy theories and satanic plots. The Lord would come when he was ready; it might be tomorrow, but there was no sense in trying to calculate when. The Bible said no one knew when it would be. The congregation did not view the Second Coming as revenge. The world was already Satan's domain. As saved Christians, their duty was to live a humble, holy life and do God's will and bring the gospel to the unsaved. They must pray for their unsaved loved ones. God had acted in history and would act again. They knew how it would be. The Bible told them. The evangelist concluded by advocating a buildup in the national defense: more bombs and missiles against the Godless communists. After the service I asked Brother John what he thought about the sermon. "I didn't see much sense in it," he said. "I'm against war."

When considering the beliefs of the members of the Fellowship Independent Baptist Church, it is necessary to realize that they do not all agree on every matter, but they seek a consensus; and if disagreement becomes intolerable, one or more persons leave the congregation. Still, they *do* agree on certain basic principles, many of which are explicitly stated in the church bylaws (Appendix A). As its name implies, the church is independent of any Baptist association or convention, but, as Baptists, they of course hold beliefs consistent with many other Baptist groups. Like other Protestants, they recognize the authority of the Bible, rather than pope, canon law, or church, as the guide to faith in daily life; they affirm a universal priesthood of believers, denying a monopoly to priests in ministering between God and humanity; they hold that Christians are saved by grace through faith, rather than through works and sacraments; and they provide many outlets for lay participation in the worship service, particularly through hymn-singing. Like other fundamentalist Baptists, they believe that the Bible was divinely inspired and therefore is literally true; they hold that the true church consists only of people mature enough to have undergone conversion and baptism; they affirm that each Christian congregation is a true church, with Jesus at its head, and is therefore autonomous and not subject to the rules of an ecclesiastical hierarchy.

In fact, their break with the Freewill Baptist denomination was not over doctrinal differences but, as Brother John explained, because they did not want to conform to the regulations of their district's Freewill Baptist association, send delegates to their conventions, pay a percentage of their offering to support the central administration, or involve themselves in association projects or politics. Baptists are notably independent-minded, and Brother John objected to what was going on in the association:

> When they have their conference you've got to write a letter stating how much money was taken in your church, how many people got saved, how many people got baptized, how many joined the church, how many died. Every year that has to be done. How much money you spent for gasoline, how many miles you traveled, and all this stuff. And then on top of that, you've got to get people out of your church to go as candidates, as many as three up to six. They like for six to come. And then of course they always want the preachers to be there, and to come for this conference and set in, you know. And then your letter is read to the whole body of people. And one thing that burnt me out with it so, [what] some of 'em was writing in

their letters, to me sounded ridiculous. Bragging about what they'd done. And I don't believe people're supposed to brag about what they do. Ought to brag about Jesus. . . . He's the one that done it for us. . . . And their money situation, it was outrageous. Some of 'em, how many miles they drove, way up yonder in miles, and they preached so many sermons, aagh. I'm not knocking it at all, don't get me wrong, but we've been happier, and we're getting along just as good, souls being saved, people joining the church, since we was independent, as when we was in the conference. (John and Pauline Sherfey interview, December 3, 1979, p. 22)

In belief and practice, though, the church feels its closest kinship with the Freewill Baptists, a denomination founded in Maine in 1780 by Benjamin Randall. A group called the Original Freewill Baptists was founded in 1727 in North Carolina and is not to be confused with the denomination that Randall originated. Randall reported that in his conversion experience he had been impressed with God's "universal love, universal atonement, a universal call to mankind, and was confident that none would ever perish but those who refused to obey it" (Buzzell 1827:21). The Freewills struck out against the prevailing Calvinism, with its insistence that atonement was limited to a predestined number of God's elect.

Never a very large denomination, the Freewills had better success in the South than the North during the next two centuries, taking part in the frontier evangelism of the camp meetings and, later, the brush-arbor revivals. In 1911 the churches in the Northeast were absorbed by the American Baptist Convention, for by this time most Baptists had given up the doctrine of limited atonement and agreed with the Freewills' basic tenet. In the South, however, and certain parts of the Midwest, the Freewills retained their identity and joined in the National Association of Freewill Baptists.

In common with the Freewills, then, the Fellowship Independent Baptist Church holds the doctrine of universal atonement, that salvation is open to all, not just an elect few; they practice open communion, offering it to all who are satisfied with their baptism, whether in infancy, or by immersion, or outside the Baptist church; they believe that a Christian, once converted, can (and does) sin and fall from the state of grace, and that to be restored one must sincerely repent of one's sin and ask Jesus for forgiveness; they hold that a person's will is free to yield or not yield to God and accept or not accept the offer of pardon and eternal life through Jesus; they affirm that while every mortal will sin, it is for their own sins and not Adam's transgression that the unsaved will be punished in hell eternally;[1] and on the authority of John 13 they practice foot washing during commu-

---

1. Young children who haven't reached the age of knowing right from wrong— "the age of accountability"—are not condemned to hell.

nion as an ordinance of Christ, a practice abandoned by the New England Freewills in the 1830s (Baxter 1957).

In addition to these doctrines, which they hold in common with other Protestants, other Baptists, and Freewill Baptists, the members of the Fellowship Independent Baptist Church emphasize a small number of additional principles that apply to their congregation and may be understood as rules of their church. They affirm that their ministers must be male (on the authority of 1 Timothy 2:12 and 1 Corinthians 14:34–35) and preach from the King James Version of the Bible; they believe that ministers are called by God and may be ordained through prayer and the laying on of hands; they forbid eating in the church (on the authority of 1 Corinthians 11:22 and 11:34); and they practice river baptism by total immersion, after the example of Jesus and John the Baptist. The foregoing rules are contained in their church bylaws. Moreover, they practice a healing prayer (on the authority of James 5:14–15) during the worship service. Finally, they are premillenarian, believing that the world is in the last days of the present dispensation, that a seven-year tribulation period is soon coming, during which time Satan will rule the world, and that this will be followed by the Second Coming of Christ and his thousand-year rule of peace and happiness on earth.

Millennialism and healing ceremonies are more typical of contemporary Pentecostals than Baptists, but that does not perturb Brother John and his flock, who identify themselves as Christians first and Baptists second. In fact, this church engages in very little denominational wrangling, as Brother John proclaims that a person can be saved as a Baptist, one of the Brethren, a Pentecostal, a Methodist, a Mennonite—and he seldom gets further along the list, but it is clear that in his eyes a person need not be a Baptist to be saved. In the words of Brother Vernie, "The Lord got ahold of me before the Baptists did" (Meadows interview, 1977, p. 19).

The synthesis of beliefs and emphases that comprises the doctrine of the Fellowship Independent Baptist Church is, as I pointed out at the beginning of this chapter, a combination of various strains within evangelical Protestantism. Because the Holy Spirit is so important in their theory of language in religious practice, and because Brother John's views of conversion, the Spirit, the "inner man," and the Christian life mark, in their view, the most important distinction between their beliefs and Pentecostal beliefs, it is necessary to probe the historical antecedents of these ideas. Asked whence they come, Brother John and the church members point out passages in the Bible that bear on these beliefs; but at issue here is the historical tradition within evangelical Protestantism that leads them to this emphasis. I suspect, although I cannot prove, that this emphasis derives from the late-nineteenth-century evangelistic activities of Dwight L. Moody and his associates, particularly those that were influenced by the Keswick movement.

Moody, of course, was the leading American evangelist of the last quarter of the nineteenth century. Moody and his associates, including C. I. Scofield, whose *Reference Bible* is one of the study-Bibles that Brother John consults frequently (the others are *The Thompson Chain Reference Bible* and *The Open Bible*), emphasized the Holy Spirit, but in a less radical form than the Wesleyan Methodist perfectionists, who, it will be recalled, argued that the Christian could achieve a state of sinlessness in this life. The entrance of the Holy Spirit, according to the perfectionists (and most of today's Pentecostals), transforms Christians into holy vessels and makes it impossible for them to sin. Moody and Scofield, following the teachings of H. W. Webb-Peploe, the leading figure in the (British) Keswick movement, rejected the possibility of sinlessness while affirming the importance of the Spirit. "What they [the leaders of the Keswick movement] had in mind," according to George M. Marsden, whose analysis of the varying strands in conservative evangelism at the turn of the twentieth century is the basis for my account,

> is best described by a favored analogy. Our sinful nature is like an uninflated balloon with a cart (the weight of sin) attached. Christ fills the balloon and the resulting buoyancy overcomes the natural gravity of our sin. While Christ fills our lives we do not have a *tendency* to sin, yet we still are *liable* to sin. Were we to let Christ out of our lives, sin would immediately take over. Hence the state of holiness must be constantly maintained and renewed. So rather than using Methodistic-Holiness terms such as "the Baptism of the Holy Spirit" or "second blessing," most Keswick teachers spoke of repeated emptyings by consecration and "fillings" with the Holy Spirit, or the "Spirit of Jesus." (Marsden 1980: 78; italics in original)

This doctrine not only explains how Christians may fall into sin, but provides a reason for their joy in receiving frequent blessings (fillings to the point of bursting forth) of the Holy Spirit during hymnody, prayer, preaching, and testimony. Not only does this equate with Fellowship Independent Baptist Church belief and practice (see Chapter 4), but other emphases besides holiness in the conservative evangelical movement during this period—separation from the world (Moody) and dispensational premillennialism (Scofield) are the most striking—line up as well (see Marsden 1980: 43–101 passim). Brother John speaks of these as the traditional interpretations of Scripture he learned from his father's generation, and it is likely that their currency among the church members today also has something to do with the general reawakening of interest in holiness among a great many Christians in recent years, in Page County as elsewhere. But the similarities among the constellation of beliefs regarding holiness, the millennium, and separation are too great for the relationship between the church members' beliefs and those of Moody and his descendants to be accidental.

For Moody and his associates, as for the members of the Fellowship Independent Baptist Church, separation did not mean total withdrawal from participation in the world—as in refusing to vote, hold office, and so forth—but keeping oneself free from sin and sinful acts. Marsden calls this an inward rather than an outward separation. The church members' emphasis is on purification, a kind of fortification as if for battle. And Brother John frequently uses military terms from the Bible to describe the Christian life—"put on the whole armor of God," for example—to do battle with Satan on behalf of the church. Yet, the church's ultimate triumph is viewed as a "personal victory" (a favorite phrase of Moody's) as well.

Separation from the world must also be understood as qualified by the call to witness and evangelize for God. The world and its institutions, Moody thought, were irredeemable, a "wrecked vessel" (Marsden 1980: 85); efforts at improving it through social action were futile, but it was the Christian's duty to try to bring the gospel to the unconverted. And if the government could not improve the world, at least it could act to limit evil; hence the Christian should work inside as well as outside the political system on such issues as crime, temperance, and so forth.

Having made covenant with one another, the pastor and congregation constituted themselves as a legal body owning their church building and the land it occupies. Their purpose, Brother John said, was to avoid the possibility of future disputes over who "owned" the church and had the right to govern it. Such a safeguard appeared necessary because of the tendencies to factionalism among congregations in the region; indeed, the Fellowship Independent Baptist Church was itself born of a dispute and split among members of the Comertown Freewill Baptist Church (see below, "Religious History in Page County").

The deacon board and pastor make the governing decisions for the church. These include financial disbursements; one of the deacons is treasurer and reports monthly to the congregation during the Sunday morning worship. "If it's anything real big that we feel the deacon board ought to put before the church to have a vote on it, we do it. If it's a smaller thing that we feel the deacon board can take care of without putting it up to vote or something like that, why, we [the deacons and pastor] do it," explained Brother Jesse, himself a deacon (Comer interview, 1977, p. 74).

The treasurer's report for the month of November 1983, read before the congregation by Brother Thurston, shows the ordinary income and expenditure (Table 11). The excess income was deposited in the local bank. The bank balance on December 2, 1983, was $3,245.17.

Majority rules if the deacons disagree. Brother John has no more influence than his single vote and the power of his persuasion. "One thing we don't try to do is tell him how to preach," said Jesse. "We don't get into those spiritual affairs with him. . . . But when it comes down to these other things that have to be done in a church, like work and so forth around the

TABLE 11. Treasurer's report, Fellowship Independent Baptist Church, November 1983

Expenditures		Income	
Pastor's salary	$400.00	Tithes and offerings	
Fares for Sister Pam	18.72	from the weeks of:	
Mortgage on church	155.06	Nov. 4:	$353.37
Guest preacher, one night	20.00	Nov. 11:	368.46
Furniture	5.00	Nov. 18:	270.70
Heating oil for furnace	90.38	Nov. 25:	197.54
Hardware	13.62		
Telephone	18.33		
Expenditures: $721.11		*Income:* $1,190.07	

church, then he's just another vote" (Comer interview, 1977, p. 77).

Deacons are appointed by the pastor and the current deacon board. Women cannot be deacons, nor can they be ministers or lead the adult Sunday school. (They do teach children's Sunday school.) The stated reason for this is the interpretation of the scripture (1 Timothy 2:12) forbidding women to usurp authority over men.

With a male pastor and deacon board, the church is deliberately patriarchal, yet some women make their voices heard, especially during Sunday school and during testimony, when they can command the attention of the others. Sister Edith is one of the stronger female voices in the congregation, and I asked her, "Can a woman be a deacon? Or a deaconess?" She responded warily: "I ain't that well educated to tell you about whether a woman should be a deaconess or not, or a preacher." Her husband, Clyde, commented, "I don't think she ought to be," whereupon Sister Edith shot back: "But if God saved her, God called her to preach, then she got as good a right to preach as a man has" (Cubbage interview, p. 31). Still, she has never been considered for deaconess.

A man cannot nominate himself for deacon, but he is eligible if he has attended regularly and is doing his part in the congregation. Either the pastor or a deacon may initiate the nomination process. After a candidate has been nominated, he must be approved by the congregation; anyone who has reservations about the candidate must speak up publicly at that time.

Once the congregation has voted approval, the deacon is put on trial, under the watchful eye of the church, for a year. "Then at the end of that year if he has lived uprightly and nobody has anything against him, then he is ordained by a committee," said Brother Jesse (Comer interview, 1977, p. 75). The committee often consists of the pastor and some deacons of a nearby Freewill Baptist church as well as the pastor and some deacons here. The committee asks him if he can accept the church rules, visit the sick, help to take care of the problems in the church, and whatever else might come up before the deacon board.

In this fashion, the church conforms to the broad organizational and doctrinal course of southern fundamentalist evangelical Protestantism. But within that Protestantism the various denominations and individual congregations show important distinctions in practice. Some are involved with the regional and national denominational organizations while others are independent. Some take part in the local political process and take responsibility for social work among the poor while others (who frequently comprise the poor) do not. When I called on Brother John early in December 1982, he was being visited by a Methodist minister from Luray who was trying to enlist his aid in the "Page One" clothing drive for the needy at Christmas. Brother John agreed, but this is not the sort of event he would have spent a great deal of time organizing and administering.

A person becomes a member of the church on the basis of his or her testimony. The congregation must vote to accept or reject. To my knowledge, no one who has sought membership has been denied it. A person may also join the church "by letter," that is, transferring membership from another congregation. If a new member wishes baptism, the pastor and congregation will oblige, holding the ceremony in the south fork of the Shenandoah River. Brother John explained the procedure in a service one morning:

> You know what we preach, you know why we preach, you know what we stand for. And I stand for the Word of God, I don't care who knows that . . . And if you'd like to unite with us here as a member of the church to work and to labor and toil with us in the group for the Lord until His coming, why, we certainly would love to have you. The way that we receive membership is if you're coming by letter, from a sister church, the clerk will write and get you a letter of recommendation. If you've never united with a church then of course if you've been saved, you have a testimony that you've been saved by God's grace, and you know that, why then we receive you on that. If you've been baptized, happy with it, we are; and if you're not, then we'll baptize you. (Morning service, April 2, 1978)

What It Means to Be Old-Fashioned

Of the ten folk traits Clements identified above, one has special relevance here: the congregation's orientation toward the past. They are old-fashioned and pride themselves on being so; and in such an atmosphere, tradition and the "old ways" of doing things, the ways their parents and grandparents worshiped, the ways that have come down in oral tradition, are especially prized. Time after time Brother John speaks from the pulpit and stands up for the old ways. One member of the congregation after another said he or she was attracted to the church because it was old-fashioned. They identify the church with a golden age that goes back to their younger days on mountain farms.

If one listens closely to their statements about why they belong to the Fellowship Independent Baptist Church, one finds that they explain what they like about being old-fashioned. Brother John often repeats, during a service, the following (or some slight variation): "I'm old-fashioned and I don't care who knows it. I stand for the Word of God, for the Word will stand when the world's on fire; and I don't cut corners for nobody." Standing for the Word of God means, among other things, that Brother John's sermons are messages based closely on the Bible; that is, he selects a Bible passage for a text and the sermon is taken up with a line-by-line explication, each line being explained first in its biblical context and then given its application to the lives of the members of the congregation. Sometimes, of course, Brother John will conflate two or three lines when the meaning is the same, and he will also point out certain relevant cross-references to other passages from the Bible; like most fundamentalist preachers, he enjoys typology and is fond of pointing out how Old Testament prophecies are fulfilled in the New.

Asked why she chose the Fellowship Independent Baptist Church, Sister Goldie said, "Well, I really believe they preach more Bible over there than any place I know of. They explain it better. . . . They preach the really old-fashioned Bible, like the old preachers used to preach back years ago" (Dove interview, p. 11). Bertha Cave spoke these words to the congregation on the night of April 9, 1978, as she was about to join the church: "Thank the Lord, I'm satisfied. I feel better satisfied at this church than at any church I've ever been in." (Brother John: "Well, praise God.") "I know you preach the Word and I know where the Word's being preached." Brother Clyde said, "Brother John, he preaches like the old-time people. One thing I can say about Brother John, he preaches the Word. That's what I like. If he didn't preach the Word, I wouldn't go over there" (Cubbage interview, p. 18). Preaching the word also means preaching the Word; that is, preaching salvation through Jesus, the Word of God. Sister Edith said, "I first heard [Brother John] on the radio. And I said I'd dearly love to go where that man preaches, and I'd love to see him. Figured him to be an old man, you know what I mean?" (Cubbage interview, p. 19). She meant she thought that, as an old-fashioned preacher, Brother John was much older than he turned out to be. (He was then in his late forties.)

Brother John frequently endorses old-fashioned ways from the pulpit. At the close of a sermon he spoke about baptism, then digressed into one of his favorite topics: comparing old-fashioned churches with modern ones that have strayed from the practices of the true faith:

Now I know in a lot of churches today, and I'm not knocking 'em, brother, they think they're too good, their members thinks they're too good, the pastor thinks he's too good to walk out in a river and baptize 'em. Many of 'em have told me the waters have got so polluted you can't baptize in 'em. Bless God, you know what it is? They've got to have the water warm so they won't get their little legs cold. Amen? Amen, bless the Lord. And it's got to be so nice, and so cozy and all of that, you know, and they've got to build 'em a little pool back here with the heated water. Amen? Praise God, I'm saying we ought to love God enough to go the way Jesus went. You say, "Preacher, it don't matter where it is." Some say, "It don't matter if it's a pond or what it is." It does to me, bless God. Amen? I want it to be running water. I want it to be in a river, praise the Lord. Hallelujah, thank God.

You say, "Preacher, you're old-fashioned." I know it. I know that. I'm not arguing that point. I'm old-fashioned and I believe we ought to stay thataway. Amen? Praise God this morning. A feller said to me the other day, he said, "Why don't you come up and pastor our church?" He talked on for a few minutes and after he talked on awhile he said, "We have our stove and our refrigerator and all these things in the basement." I said, "Uh-unh, Uh-unh. That wouldn't be in there if I was pastoring." Amen? No, that wouldn't be in the basement if I was pastoring. They wouldn't go there and fill their belly and then holler "Hallelujah!" Amen? I believe they ought to start hollering hallelujah before they get their belly filled. They ought to fill their soul, praise God. You say, "Preacher, there ain't no harm in going to the basement and eating." Bless God, that ought to be the prayer rooms. Amen? That's Sunday school rooms down there. But listen, neighbor, we ought to get on our knees and cry out to God. Amen? Not like in a place to fill your belly. The Bible said that many of 'em have made the belly their God. Amen? They can't holler "Amen!" till they fill their belly. We ought to fill our soul. Amen? Let God come in and fill us up. Now you say, "Preacher, you done quit preaching and went to vilifying." Well, you can say whatever you want to but I'm still standing that way. I believe we ought to be old-fashioned for God. I believe in going to the river and being baptized. And I believe, bless God, if you're hungry go home and eat your meal. And if you got it take me with you and I'll help you. Amen? Praise the Lord this morning but don't eat in the house of God. (Spoken by John Sherfey at end of morning sermon, April 2, 1978)

Along with being old-fashioned goes an emphasis on feeling the Spirit's blessing, behavior (such as shouting) that would not be condoned in a modern church (or so they believe), and a recognition that the old-fashioned way of life is often a poor and unfashionable way of life. Sister Goldie was attracted to the church after hearing Brother John's radio broadcasts:

He was on the radio the first time I reckon I listened at him. . . . The more I listened at him, the more I wanted to go where he preached at. And one time he said, bless God, he said, "If you ain't got nothing to wear but your overalls, put 'em on and come on." Said, "We're old-fashioned." I said, "Well, there's where I want to go 'cause I don't have money enough to buy real fancy clothes like they wear in a lot of these churches." So there's where we went, and we've been going there ever since. (Dove interview, p. 1)

Sister Goldie's reasons show class consciousness and indicate a preference for the old-fashioned ways. In fact, I have seen overalls on men in the church, but it is uncommon except on "overalls day," a special Sunday set aside for men to wear them. Very few dress up either; most clothes are inexpensive, ready-to-wear shirts, pants, and dresses of the sort that one can purchase at discount department stores. Brother Belvin, a lay preacher, takes the class distinctions implied by Sister Goldie even further, identifying old-fashioned humility with Jesus, and contrasting it with churches that have "got up in society":

I'm not proud; I'm not high-headed, and boasting. [Now] certain people [think] they're better'n I am. . . . But still, we got to love 'em . . . and then that makes us old-fashioned, to prove that we're not high-headed society over everybody else, and feel humble under the feet of Christ. Society's things are classy; call it "classy." Classy. Well, [but] we just come out flat with it, and that's old-fashioned. Because the Lord Jesus Christ loves the same way. He walked the seashores of Galilee, and down the dusty roads, and anybody he come in contact with he done good with 'em and had good conversations with 'em. And loved 'em. . . . and that's old-fashioned.

I been in some [churches] that been so society that you could hear a pin drop. And this had to be every jot and tittle right so many words, that clock set, so many words said, and you quit. So many songs done picked out before, and everything that right to the very minute of how long it take you to do that, then cut it off. Prayer wrote down exactly how many words to say and cut it off. And [to] stand there like that, and do that, that is not old-fashioned. That is just as dry as a last year's bird nest and just as dry as a Texas wind. And that kind don't do me no good. That don't satisfy me unless I feel the power of the Lord Jesus Christ when I'm preaching and speaking. (Hurt interview, pp. 14–15)

Brother Belvin thus identifies oral, improvisatory performance styles with old-fashioned religion, saying that without the freedom of spontaneous performance he cannot feel the power of the Spirit. Sister Edith makes the same identification:

Some [churches] you get better blessings than others. Seems like the Lord works with you better, and it seems like everything's more easier. In some places you go, you just, I don't know, you can't feel a thing. I don't

Sister Goldie, 1985.

know whether it's you or whether it's the ones there. Now I won't say that 'cause I don't know. But it looks like to me when the Lord's in a thing, it looks like they get blessed better or something. (Cubbage interview, p. 20)

When Brother John conjures up the old-time religion for his congregation, he usually chooses scenes they will recall from their youth, and he never fails to contrast the old days with today's world:

I remember when people used to go to church riding sidesaddle. The ladies would ride the sidesaddles. Men would ride saddles on their horses. Ride the old buggies, the old hacks, T-model Ford cars, and the old open sides out and everything else. But they'd go for miles and miles. They'd walk through the fields and go to church. The houses would be filled. And the old grandmas would shout, brother! They'd just throw them old bonnets across the house. They had them old long strings on them. And I'd see them things a-slinging around over their heads, you know, and directly here'd go one a-sailing a-this way and one going the other way, and the power of God was all over the place! Now it wasn't in the bonnets, see. And it wasn't in their long dresses. But it was in their heart, see.

But now we've got fine automobiles. We got nice pews to sit in. Why, brother, when I started going to church, they had them old pews with slats that wide apart. Cracks in them. You'd sit there, and oh, you'd . . . Oh, it was terrible. But now they got good pews to sit. Got good cars to go to. Got good heat. Back then, you had the old pot-bellied stoves and throw a chunk of wood in. Sometime more smoke would come out in the church than went out the chimney. Back then, they worshiped God. But now, you see . . . (John Sherfey interview, July 28, 1975, pp. 22–23)

Despite the hardships of mountain farming in the old days, people made an effort to attend church, and the Spirit was strong. The old grandmas slinging their bonnets is a vivid image that, significantly, links the old-time religion to family tradition extending back several generations. Nowadays those hardships have vanished, Brother John implies, but the spiritual power is weak. In John's contrast religion is entwined with lifeways, and the meaning is clear: old-fashioned religion was more powerful. The creature comforts of modern times have lulled people into a spiritual sleep.

The golden age of mountain farming, then, nurtured this powerful, old-fashioned religion; and so, despite the poverty, life was spiritually purer. But what was that old-fashioned religion really like? What are their memories of it? How did it affect them when they were young? Are their statements merely expressions of nostalgia for an imagined past? On the contrary, I think their longings express a sense of loss, not just for mountain farming but especially for their years of childhood and youth when they felt secure and close to their families and kin. This fellowship with the family serves for the model of togetherness in the church, where they address one another as brothers and sisters in Jesus.

Family

Family, as noted in Chapter 1, is the central theme of the homecoming service, the highlight of the church year. And so it is not surprising that family is at the heart of the church members' memories of old-time religion, even as it is the focal point of their memories of their lives on mountain farms. The idea of family union is attached to the individual's experience of old-time religion in a most powerful manner, first in early memories of family churchgoing, and next in promises made to dying relatives that they would meet again in heaven. This bears further discussion.

The oral tradition of mountain farming was learned in childhood and youth, to be carried on throughout adulthood; people were in a sense "born into" mountain farming as a way of life. The oral tradition of mountain religion, too, was learned in childhood and youth, but very soon the youngster realized that not all the adults were religious. Some were saved, some not.

And so the youngster's early religious education took place among those family members who were saved. These were frequently not the parents (they would be saved later in life) but grandparents, aunts, and uncles. Everyone, saved or not, agreed that religious instruction was good for children; and if a local church or mission Sunday school was within walking distance, the child was sent there, often accompanied by an adult, sometimes alone.

Reports of early religious education were common among the members of the Fellowship Independent Baptist Church. Brother Rastus said, "My daddy was a good Christian man and I was raised to go to church" (Lam interview, p. 8). Brother Vernie's parents were unsaved when he was a child, so relatives made certain he went to Sunday school. Brother Jesse went to church until he was fourteen, then stopped. When his own children were old enough for church he took them, then was saved himself some years later in a revival. Two churches in the Naked Creek headwaters region offered Sunday school from about 1890 to 1925: a mission atop Tanner's Ridge, near Long Ridge, and a Methodist church at Jollett (see Figure 14).

Despite early religious training, the youngster was not expected as a matter of course to fall under conviction and achieve salvation. It might happen; so much the better if it did, and people prayed hard for it; but the common pattern delayed salvation until a person was settled as an adult with a family of his or her own.

Time after time, in relating their life stories, the church members spoke of promises they made to dying relatives that they would meet them in heaven. The dying relative, a Christian, called the family to the bedside and talked to the members individually, rejoicing with those who were saved and saying that he or she hoped to meet the unsaved once more, in a better life in heaven, but that this would be possible only if the unsaved "got right with God." In these emotional moments, many an unsaved person promised the dying mother, father, sister, brother, aunt, or uncle that he or she would get saved and see them again, and the relief on all sides was considerable. No wonder that these promises were singled out when the church members told their life stories. Certainly these deathbed promises exert a powerful influence, not only in the church members' lives, but also in shaping the content of their language in religious practice, in prayers, Sunday school topics, and so forth.

Examples of these promises abound. Unsaved in his early twenties, Brother John told his dying brother Ester he would meet him in heaven (Sherfey interview, August 14, 1977, p. 7). Brother Rastus' father died when Rastus was thirteen. "My daddy, he told me to meet him in heaven and I'm a-looking forward to that, and I promised him I would," he said

(Lam interview, p. 26). Telling the story of the deathbed promise is itself an example of language in religious practice, as testimony. Sister Edith had an especially compelling narrative that linked her eventual conversion directly to a vision she had while making a promise to her dying mother:

> Well, I'll tell you, here was the starting of me getting saved, and this is the way it was. My mother was sick and she was awful bad off, and she told me that she believed she was going out of her mind, but she wouldn't hurt me 'cause she loved me. And I said, "Mama, I know you do." And she said, "But I'm a-going home," she said, "and I want you to meet me." Now this is the first starting of me getting saved. Well, I told her. I said, "I'll meet you." I said, "If there's any way in the world, I'll meet you, because I know I'm going to be saved and go with you."
>
> .   .   .   .
>
> Well, I just don't know what happened. My mother was gone and I just blanked out. I don't know what happened. I just don't know what happened after that. I just seen it when she was going, and as she was going I blanked out. I never did see nothing more like it.
>
> .   .   .   .
>
> But I, honest, I did see something. This is the truth I'm a-telling y'all. I seen the beautifullest place that I ever seen in my life, the morning that she left home. Now I'm a-telling you this, and this is the truth. And God knows it's the truth, or he wouldn't give me the remembrance of it. And I never could, I never seen a place like that since, nor I never seen it before that, but I seen it then. It was one of the beautifullest-looking places that I ever seen. And I said, "If that place is that beautiful, just for me going by her leaving and a-going, I'm going to accept the Lord as my Savior." And so I just felt like that when she was buried—now this is the truth—when they buried her, I was sorry that I was going to miss her, but I could just rejoice of it, you know, to think that she had gone home. (Cubbage interview, pp. 1–3)

These promises are commonly made to relatives of the same gender: daughter to mother, nephew to uncle, and so forth, an arrangement that echoes the preference for people of the same gender to help pray someone through to conversion. But the overriding purpose is to bring the entire family into the fold. This became more difficult when parents migrated from the mountain farms to the towns and the children moved elsewhere to take employment. Sister Edith reflected, "We should have taken our children to church more than what we did. You know, in the first beginning, when they was little. Of course when we did take 'em they done pretty good, long as we were taking 'em. But then they all scattered out from us and when they scattered out from us they scattered out from theirselves" (Cubbage interview, p. 9). By "scattered out from theirselves" Sister Edith means apart from one another, yet the image points to her belief that an individual is complete only within the family community. She continued, linking three generations as she anticipated her own death:

> That's the way it goes when you're raising a family. You can't look at the parents for what the family does, 'cause after they get out from under you, you ain't got no more control of it. I wish I did have control of mine like I did at one time. But I ain't. But I'm just trusting and praying to the good Lord just to go and save 'em before it's too late.
>
> It might take me, you know, just like it taken my mother—for them to get saved. But if it does, the quicker the better. It don't make no difference to me. (Cubbage interview, pp. 9–10)

Mountain people, of course, were not the only ones dependent on kin in times of need. Traditional farming communities throughout the nation could boast families that had been acquainted and intermarried for generations. Grateful for companionship, cautious to offend, the members of these families maintained a special relationship when they expected "to share line fences and church pews for some generations to come" (Stadtfeld 1972:80). Social historians studying the American family during the early period of industrialism in the Northeast have noted the strength of kin ties in the factory towns and cities (see, e.g., Gordon, ed. 1973; Tufte and Myerhoff 1979). Kinship dependence was especially important in times of stress and in places such as Appalachia where outsiders could not be relied on for aid, let alone understanding.

Religious History in Page County

A history of religion in the Massanutten Valley and the northern Blue Ridge has yet to be written. In the meantime, the little that is available must be gleaned from a variety of sources including oral histories, church and county records, cemeteries, and census documents. Some generalizations regarding religious history on the American frontier and in the Shenandoah Valley are applicable to this region, and some not.

Religion in the Massanutten Valley up to about the Civil War reflected the ethnic mix. The earliest settlers, Pennsylvania Germans in the eighteenth century, were chiefly Mennonites, with a small number of Lutherans and Reformed (Calvinists). The Anglican Church, established in the Virginia Colony, forbade other religious groups to worship unless they registered their places of worship and their ministers obtained government licenses, under the 1689 Toleration Act. This the groups refused to do (Strickler 1952:8–59; Couper 1952:1212–1213). In any case, most frontier settlers did not hold church membership. In his *Letters from an American Farmer* (1782), J. Hector St. Jean de Crèvecoeur attributed this to the lack of social institutions and characterized the people of the frontier as having degenerated to a state of nature, though he excepted Moravians and Quakers because they lived in colonies (Crèvecoeur 1961). Indeed, two Moravian ministers who passed through the Massanutten Valley in 1746 commented on the settlers' having ceased from religious observance: "Many Germans live here. Most of them are Mennonites and are in poor condition. Besides them a few church people live here, partly Luthern [sic], partly reform. Nearly all religious earnestness and zeal is extinguished among them" (quoted by Bauserman 1976:13).

The majority of German settlers were Lutherans, however. In 1733 St. Peter's Lutheran Church had been established on Naked Creek, close to the Shenandoah River and about twelve miles from the headwaters where the Meadows family would settle one hundred years later. This church was moved west of the river in 1747. In the Harrisonburg, Virginia (Rockingham County), public library I found a copy of the parish register from the period 1776–1826, when it was called St. Peter's Evangelical Church. On the chance that some of the ancestors of the members of the Fellowship Independent Baptist Church had worshiped there, I checked the list, but all the surnames were German, as one might expect. Moreover, none of these surnames appeared in the Shenandoah District, Page County, census list for 1860, the year for which I recorded a complete inventory of all names of household heads, occupations, and the values of all real and personal estates. Perhaps the members of St. Peter's Church removed as a group, but I have no evidence to prove this.

Most of the extant early church records from the Massanutten Valley pertain to Pennsylvania German churches. The Hawksbill Church, near Luray, was organized as a Union church (that is, a union of Lutherans and Reformed) in 1765 and later became the Lutheran Mt. Calvary Church. It ceased in 1959, having been the mother church to many Lutheran congregations in the valley. An 1813 confirmation list from this church found in the Harrisonburg public library contained all German surnames. The Stoneberger Lutheran Church was built in 1790, near the river at Alma. Two other important Lutheran churches flourished in Rockingham County just to the south. The Peaked Mountain Church (Peaked Mountain was the old name for Massanutten Mountain) was a Union church that began in 1745 in McGaheysville and lasted until 1935. A search through this church's list of communicants and baptismal records, 1791–1880, turned up no surnames of members of the Fellowship Independent Baptist Church. "The Old Dutch Church," an Evangelical Lutheran Church located several miles north of Keezletown on the mountain road, also showed none of these surnames among its members' records from 1787 until after the Civil War, when the records stop.

The first Great Awakening had a significant impact on religion in the Shenandoah Valley. Presbyterian revivalists were highly successful among the Scotch-Irish settlers during the 1740s and 1750s, but nothing indicates that they visited the Massanutten Valley, where few Scotch-Irish had settled. More significant were the Separatist or New Light Baptists, who reached many of the Shenandoah Valley's poor in the decades before and after the Revolutionary War. The New Lights preached universal atonement; their meetings, often held outdoors, were noisy; and they were persecuted by the middle and upper classes (Gewehr 1930: 106–137). A colorful description of the converts as they appeared about 1790 ran as follows: "There was a company of them in the back part of our town, and an outlandish set of people they certainly were. . . . You could hardly find one among them but was deformed one way or another. Some of them were hare-lipped, others were blear-eyed, or hump-backed, or bow-legged, or club-footed; hardly any of them looked like other people. But they were all strong for plunging and let their poor ignorant children run wild" (quoted in ibid.: 116). The description, though obviously written from an outsider's viewpoint, strongly suggests that the New Lights drew their adherents from among the poorer laborers living on the outskirts of towns and possibly even from the hollow-dwelling mountain farmers.

Baptist and Methodist activity in the Massanutten Valley was underway in earnest in the nineteenth century. A Hawksbill Creek meetinghouse existed as early as 1811, and soon after moved to Luray to become the Mount Carmel Baptist Church (Strickler 1952: 256–257). A black Baptist church (still standing) was built in 1873 on Naked Creek, a mile above Verbena, near the Shenandoah River; it had a congregation of more than one hundred, mostly ex-slaves employed by the Shenandoah Iron Works and by the Shenandoah Railroad. Another church grew up on Naked Creek, the Furnace Methodist Church, built in 1855; it served the community of laborers working at the No. 2 Furnace, about three miles east of the Shenandoah River. The 1866 map of Page County (Figure 22) shows a Mount Hope Church on the New Market to Gordonsville Turnpike, on Hawksbill Creek, about two miles east of Marksville (now Stanley); this church was mentioned in John W. Keyser's diary entries for the 1870s (see below).

The U.S. Census figures show a dramatic increase in the number of churches in Page County during the nineteenth century (Table 12). It is apparent from the figures, also, that most county residents held no church membership. Crèvecoeur had predicted that the European sects that found a religious haven in America would have difficulty maintaining their fervor down through the generations because of cross-ethnic marriages, abundant economic opportunities, and the absence of religious persecution (Crèvecoeur 1961).

Most nineteenth-century Baptist churches in the valley were Calvinist. According to the 1890 U.S. Census only one of the seven Baptist churches in Page County was Freewill and the rest were Old School (i.e., Primitive). None was located in the mountains, and in the absence of the church records it is impossible to know whether any of the mountain farm families worshiped in them. Certainly the Primitive Baptists proved congenial to

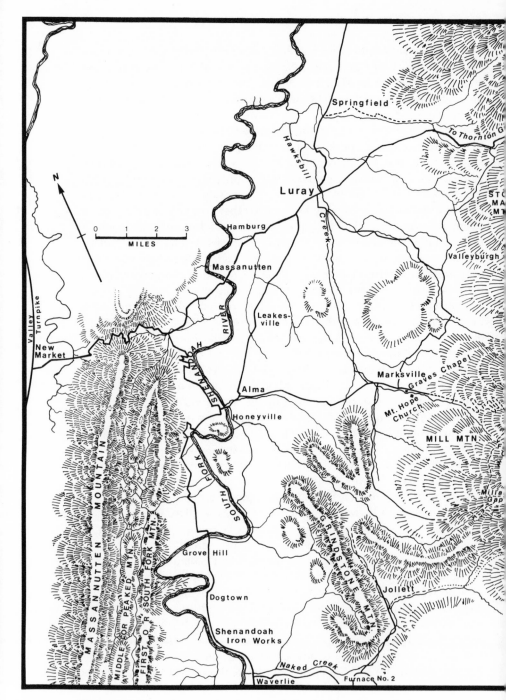

Figure 22. Page County, Va., in 1866. Adapted from map of Office of Chief of Engineers, U.S. Army.

mountain farmers in other areas of Appalachia (*Primitive Baptist Hymns of the Blue Ridge* 1982).

Perhaps the most interesting among documented Baptist activities in the valley was the ministry of a bilingual (German/English) itinerant, John Koontz, who traveled throughout the area beginning about 1770, preaching in people's homes. Koontz was an Old Light (Calvinist) Baptist, but he wore his denominationalism unfussily, and when in 1798 he founded a church, the word *Baptist* was omitted from its name. The Mill Creek Church (later the Mauck Meeting House) near Luray was more of a community church than a denominational one. The list of communicants from 1820 through the Civil War included English and German surnames, one of which (Cave) belongs to the ancestors of the present members of the Fellowship Independent Baptist Church (Strickler 1924:36–41, 156). Koontz preached throughout the Shenandoah Valley from 1770 to 1830, concentrating in the Massanutten portion. It is said he converted hundreds of Mennonites to the Baptist faith and was such a danger that many Mennonite families moved away lest they become Baptists (W.P.A. Virginia 1940:616). He suffered persecution from the wealthy, and a large oral tradition arose about his adventures. Most important, he serves as a prototype of the itinerant revivalist more interested in salvation than denomination. This was the type of minister that succeeded in the northern Blue Ridge Mountains.

The various generalizations about Appalachian mountain religion are insufficient for this study. Information is needed about the specific religious activity in the region of the Blue Ridge where the ancestors of the members of the Fellowship Independent Baptist Church lived. Only then will it be known for certain what religious traditions were passed down the generations. But here, unfortunately, exist serious problems of documentation. Aside from oral history, which takes us back only to about the turn of the twentieth century with much in the way of detail, the evidence is very thin. Still, it is sufficient to conclude that this region *has* a religious history; that is, that the people—some of them—were religious believers, even if they did not attend church regularly; and that certain aspects of the religious character of the Fellowship Independent Baptist Church are specific, local inheritances.

The consensus among the oldest church members was that their parents and grandparents had said that when people first moved into the mountains worship took place in homes because no churches had been built. Itinerant preachers seldom passed through during the first half of the nineteenth century, but if they did, they held meetings outdoors or in people's homes. No one could recall any specific mountain camp meetings in the nineteenth century, but several suggested that Big Meadows had probably been the scene of some.

The *Page County News and Courier* began operation shortly after the Civil War, and I checked the early issues of the newspaper to find notices of camp meetings in the mountains, but it appears that the summer revivals were held close to the valley towns. The July 22, 1875, edition reported a "religious revival" at Alma with a thousand people present; on August 12 of that year a "basket or woods meeting" was to be held "in Mrs. Strickler's woods near the [Shenandoah] River." The newspaper noted that a stand and seats were being prepared and that the event "may continue several days." On September 4 a large revival and baptizing was held at Big Spring Church, four miles north of Luray; on October 14 there was a revival at Rileyville, and on April 13, 1876, there was a protracted meeting at Antioch. It is unclear how many mountain farm families might have attended these revivals. Denomination is not mentioned, but my impression is that most were Methodist.

I was unable to turn up any diaries among the mountain people from the nineteenth century and was told not to look because they were illiterate. The U.S. Census indicates that on the contrary most of the men (and many of the women) of the generations born up until about the Civil War were literate. The Virginia State Library at Richmond houses a single diary from Page County during the nineteenth century but, as luck would have it, it turns out that its author, John W. Keyser (1847–1917), a shoemaker, schoolteacher, and jack-of-all-trades, kept a record of the churches he visited and the ministers who preached.

Keyser came from a Pennsylvania German family and lived on a farm in Mount Hope, in the Blue Ridge foothills about a mile east of Graves (Methodist) Chapel (see Figure 22), where he was a member. He is buried in the chapel cemetery. As a young man he was very pious and went to church two and sometimes three times weekly, visiting different churches (chiefly Methodist and Baptist) throughout the county from Shenandoah to Luray. He attended a revival in 1871 at Dogtown (north of Shenandoah, on the river) and noted it in his diary:

> Sat. Sept. 2nd. Went up to the camp meeting at dogtown today. T. H. Cave was with me. Miller preached at 3 o'clock—went to the forge to stay all night.
>
> Sunday Sept. 3rd. Went down to the camp meeting today. Stayed all day till after night preaching. Rev. Benbush preached at 10—a man by name of Neill from Philadelphia preached at 3 and Quinn preached at night. Went down to Henry Kite's to stay at night. Saw a good many of my acquaintances.
>
> Mon. Sept. 4th. Went up to the camp meeting this morning from Mr. Henry Kite's, stayed all day, heard three sermons, went home with Alan Kite, stayed all night at Wm. Kite's.
>
> Tues. Sept. 5th 1871. Went from Wm. Kite's to camp, stayed all day,

TABLE 12. Churches and membership, Page County, 1850–1890

	1850	1860	1890	Total Member-ship, 1890
Churches				
Lutheran	3	4	10	897
Methodist	1	5	9	720
Baptist	5	5	7	411
Mennonite	1	0	0	
Union	0	4	0	
Dunker (Brethren)	0	1	0	
Christian Connection	1	1	6	335
German Reformed	0	1	0	
Disciples of Christ	0	0	3	160
United Brethren	0	0	2	30
Roman Catholic	0	0	1	20
Total number of churches	11	21	38	
Page County population				
Free	6,643	8,109	13,092	
Slave	646	850	0	

SOURCE: U.S. Census of the Population, 1850; 1860; 1890.

heard three sermons. A blind preacher exhorted after evening services. They had a prayer meeting after night preaching in a tent. Stayed all night in Mr. Davy's boarding house.

Wed. Sept. 6th. Stayed in camp till after the morning services. They all formed a circle and bid farewell. I shook hands with about 2 or 3 hundred persons. Then started for home—came as far as Alma, took dinner at T. W. Phillips', got home about dusk—had a fine trip—formed some acquaintances with the ladies—I wish them all well.

Again, it is impossible to know how many mountain farmers attended revivals such as the one Keyser described, or the ones reported in the Page County newspaper. Certainly they were not designed especially for the backwoods folk. Reading Keyser's diligent record, one feels that he would have mentioned camp meetings in the mountains had there been any, at least from 1868, when the diary begins, through 1875, when he got married and stopped visiting churches so frequently.

Many days of searching in the Page County courthouse finally turned up one piece of satisfyingly concrete evidence: Matthew Lamb (b. 1825), grandfather of Brother Rastus and great-grandfather of Sister Hattie and Brother Austin, bought a Bible (for ten cents) at the February 12, 1873, estate sale of the property of Elias Breeden (b. 1811), deceased. (For the sale inventory, see Appendix B.) Elias Breeden was a great-great-grandfather of Brother Vernie (Figure 17). Unfortunately, out of the dozens of Lams, Breedens, Meadowses, and Cubbages that comprised the mountain farm families in the study area, only five had probate inventories taken, so this type of evidence, satisfying as it is, is not abundant.

If the evidence for camp meetings in the nineteenth century in the section of the Blue Ridge under study is lacking, it is somewhat better for the practice of prayer meetings in the homes. Sundays were chiefly for visiting neighbors and kin, Brother Vernie recalled (Meadows interview, March 16, 1982). Brother Belvin described an old tradition of the "season of prayer" that took place in people's homes. A leader appointed a person to begin the prayer and another to end. Then each person would pray, one at a time after the other. The prayers were extemporaneous and aloud. Anyone refusing to take part (an unsaved person, for example) was omitted from the round (Hurt interview, p. 92). Possibly the currently widespread practice of the Tuesday (or Wednesday) night prayer meeting at Baptist churches (including the Fellowship Independent Baptist Church) is a survival of this practice in a different setting, the distinctive feature being the absence of the sermon. Exhorters could and did encourage any non-Christians to pray through to salvation. Keyser noted a prayer meeting among those assembled at the Dogtown camp meeting in 1871, and the practice was widely reported on the nineteenth-century frontier.

When an itinerant preacher passed through this section of the Blue Ridge prior to the Civil War, a preaching service—that is, with a sermon and altar call—took place in a home or outdoors. Again, Brother Vernie said he had heard the old folks talk about services and prayer meetings in the homes before they had churches in the mountains (Meadows interview, March 16, 1982).

The next stage seems to have been that itinerant preachers held services in schoolhouses. According to the old maps (the most reliable sources here), mountain schoolhouses in the Jollett (Naked Creek) and Cubbage Hollow areas were built sometime between the Civil War and 1885. Many of the elder members of the congregation recall their parents and grandparents talking about worshiping in schoolhouses. Meanwhile, home prayer meetings continued (and they continue to this day). Finally, of course, churches were erected.

In 1885 a church was built on Naked Creek at Jollett, the settlement at the fork of Jollett and Weaver hollows (Strickler 1952:266). The pastor was Reverend John W. Jollett (1828–1916), a Methodist "local preacher"—that is, not a circuit-rider but a local man, expected to earn his living apart from the Methodist Church but licensed by the church to preach in the area where he lived. His name appears thus on the minutes of the regional Methodist Conference (the 110th Session of the Baltimore Conference of the Methodist Episcopal Church, South), held in Fredericksburg, Virginia, in 1894. He probably was active in the study area for several years before his church was built, for the county marriage records show that he was the presiding minister at the 1849 marriage of James Meadows and Sarah Eppard, Sister Hattie's great-grandparents. I would like to think that he preached throughout this section of the Blue Ridge, but the extent of his activity is unknown to me at this time. Despite considerable effort, I have been unable to find out much more about him. That he was a landowning farmer of moderate means is clear from the U.S. Census; how much time he devoted to his ministry remains uncertain.

I had met with no success in my search for the surnames of Fellowship Independent Baptist Church members in the cemeteries and the extant eighteenth- and nineteenth-century records of the other Page County churches, but in the Jollett church graveyard I was at last surrounded by Breedens, Lams, and Meadowses. Most had died in this century, but I noticed a few names that were familiar to me from my genealogical research into the previous century: William Zebedee Lam (1857–1947) and Leurainey Meadows Lam (1862–1949), grandparents of Sister Hattie; Thomas W. Meadows (1854–1941), the son of Mitchel Meadows, and his (Thomas') wife, Matilda Meadows (1859–1953); William Billy Meadows (1839–1903), son of Thomas Meadows, and his (William Billy's) wife, Sarah Weaver Meadows (1842–1919); and Emanuel Hezekiah Lam (1854–1945), who had sat as a "representative mountain man" on the platform with President Roosevelt when he dedicated the Shenandoah National Park in 1936.

This evidence indicates that at least these Lams and Meadowses were Christians at death. Moreover, one suspects that their parents would not have given them biblical names (Hezekiah, Zebedee) unless they too were religiously minded. As to why more of the Lams and Meadowses weren't buried there, it turns out that most were interred in family burial plots on the old homeplace. The Meadows family graveyard is on land that first belonged to Thomas, then to his youngest son, Henry, and now belongs to the park.

The Lams and Meadowses buried in the Jollett cemetery were recalled by Bertha Jenkins Gordon of Luray, who taught at the Pine Grove Hollow School in 1928–1931 and at the Jollett School in 1931–1934. She remembered that in 1929 Hezekiah Lam brought his six or seven children for education at the Pine Grove school. A very tall man, he was followed by his second wife, Lucinda, and then Clara, the sixteen-year-old, and then the rest. "I want you to give my kids some learning," he said to her. None had been to school before. Clara was very intelligent and a hard worker, and in her first year went through the first three grades of school, Mrs. Gordon said.

When she taught at Jollett she took her room and board with Thomas W. and Matilda Meadows. "Uncle Tom," as everyone called him, was an upstanding farmer and citizen who made certain that everyone in the region voted at election time. He didn't tell them whom to vote for, Mrs. Gordon added. He was good, kind, and God-fearing, but he did not attend church regularly. Most of the adults were God-fearing Christians whether they attended church or not. Thomas' wife, "Aunt Matilda," was very pious and active in the Jollett church.

T. Henry Lam (also buried in the Jollett church cemetery) held open dinners every Sunday after church for everyone in the neighborhood; he fed dozens of people weekly. He and Thomas W. Meadows both had parlor organs and asked Mrs. Gordon to play hymns on them. She recalled that after she married (and was forced to stop teaching) she was bitten by a copperhead snake in 1937 and spent a month or so in bed recovering in Luray. William Zebedee Lam walked fifteen miles down from his mountain farm to visit with her for fifteen minutes, and he brought his children that she had taught. Eventually all the children she had taught—and their parents—came to see her at intervals and brought food and other items to help her keep the household running. They didn't always go to church, Mrs. Gordon wound up, "but the backbone of the community was religious" (Gordon interview, June 6, 1983).

When Reverend Jollett died in 1916, his church became a nondenominational community church. Only a few years later Brother Rastus began attending it. He recalls that Methodist and Baptist ministers would hold services on alternating Sundays. In the order of worship these were similar to the current services at the Fellowship Independent Baptist Church, he said. (That is, they were patterned after the revival service.) Some Sundays there was no service. Not many people attended the weekly meetings, but everyone turned out for the week-long revivals held each August (Lam interview, pp. 10–11). Brother Vernie and Brother Clyde also remembered attending services and occasionally a Sunday school class at the Jollett church when they were young boys. But all agreed that the most exciting events were the brush-arbor revivals ("bush meetings") held on grazing lands atop the Blue Ridge in the early twentieth century.

Brother Clyde recalled the brush-arbor revivals with relish. He and his wife, Sister Edith, reminisced about the Reverend Geurdon A. Cave. Brother Clyde had been saved under his preaching, and he called him an old-time preacher. "Well, what he's talking about, the old-time preachers, when they used to preach, Mr. Cave, he talked, and when they first commenced preaching, they would preach in all kinds of buildings, you know, old log buildings and things like that when we was growing up," said Sister Edith. "That's what he's talking about old-time preaching. And they'd go out and preach, or they'd go to people's houses and preach. You know it didn't make no difference. They'd go out somewhere under a big tree and cut logs and they'd all go in, and then he'd set in and preach."

"They used to have tents," said Brother Clyde. "They had poles cut and put brush on top of it for shade. I used to go back there in the mountains a-many a night when Brother Cave would preach. He preached [there] till the park got him and that cut it out, you see." Clyde added that he went to meet and talk with the young girls. "Big crowds'd go back there to it. Set on them logs, holler and shout, praise the Lord and have a big time. I was lost at that time. I still went to hear them. A lot of young girls, you know, went. . . . And a lot'd get saved, too. Them old-time people was always there" (Cubbage interview, pp. 16–18). The brush arbors ceased with the coming of the park in 1936, but the revival-service format continued to shape the weekly worship gatherings in the mountain churches at Jollett and elsewhere, for at about the time of Reverend Jollett's death another itinerant, nominally Methodist, preacher began to exert great influence in this section of the Blue Ridge.

The Reverend Geurdon A. Cave is remembered fondly as "the old-time preacher man" by most of the older members of the Fellowship Independent Baptist Church. He was the brother of Brother Belvin's paternal grandfather, Newman Cave, and a second cousin by marriage to Brother Rastus. He preached, it would seem, in every moment he could spare from farming, traveling up and down the Blue Ridge throughout Page and Madison counties. His home was in Dark Hollow and he built a community church there. Brother Vernie remembered brush-arbor meetings at Dark Hollow in the 1920s (Meadows interview, 1977, pp. 19–20). When the park displaced Reverend Cave, he became a day-laborer, working by day and preaching in the evenings and on weekends wherever his work took him. Brother Belvin's recollection is typical of the other church members':

I could take you to his church over here where he used to come to preach. And he'd come down there—he'd work all day, sometimes he'd work for my daddy, cut corn. That's hard work, like the old people worked then, sunup to sundown, mighty near. And he'd work like that, he'd light his lantern and come to the church and preach, and have to walk. And then he'd go from there back, and get back mighty near halfway, and he'd want to rest, sit down and rest a little. And he'd set his lantern down, and he'd sit down under the old pine tree down there on the turn of the road. And it'd sit so good, them needles, you know, soft and everything. He'd rock back against that tree. Said it was just the same as a chair. He said he'd just rest there real good after preaching hard and working hard all day. And he said he'd just rock back thataway and say, "Well, I'll just rest a few minutes." And when he woke up the sun would be peeping up on him. We ain't got no preachers like that now! They won't walk like that. (Hurt interview, p. 29)

In 1931 the Reverend John Dubosq, a young man from Philadelphia, was looking for home missionary work and decided to try the headwaters of Naked Creek. After an exchange of correspondence, he arrived in 1932 on the train in Shenandoah and was met by a delegation of Lams and Meadowses. The Meadowses provided him with a cabin near the top of the mountain and close to the old Meadows schoolhouse. Interviewed by Dorothy Noble Smith in 1977 for an oral history project involving the park, he recalled that as many as seventy-five people attended his Sunday schools. They were "very attentive" to religion, he remarked. "In other words, this particular area had a very religious group of people?" asked Mrs. Smith. "Yes, some of 'em were," Dubosq replied, adding that others liked to fight. The schoolhouse doubling as a church was packed full for service; the people would come from as far as ten miles away. "Were you Episcopal?" Mrs. Smith asked. "No, nondenominational, independent fundamentalist," he answered. In 1936 when the park took the high mountain land, Reverend Dubosq moved down a few miles and set up a mission on Naked Creek below Jollett where he remained active for three decades, preaching in every hamlet in the valley, sometimes as many as four churches each Sunday.

When the park bought Reverend Cave's home in Dark Hollow, he moved to Comertown and became pastor of two nondenominational churches, one in Comertown and the other in Weaver Hollow a mile up the mountain from Jollett (Strickler 1952:269). He continued to travel and preach through the region's back country until his death in the early 1970s at the age of eighty-five. In 1967 Brother John became pastor of the Comertown church that Reverend Cave had begun.

Before passing to a brief history of the formation and growth of the Fellowship Independent Baptist Church, it would be well to summarize certain highlights of this local religious tradition. First, the community emphasized evangelical fundamentalist revivalism. The week-long revival, the brush-arbor meeting, the preaching service in the home, all were aimed at saving souls and were the highlights of the religious activity. Second, emphasis was on salvation, not denomination. Churches were communitarian and pastors preached a fundamentalist gospel. This is unlike the strict sectarianism often said to characterize Appalachian mountain religion. Third, the itinerant preachers developed a following based not so much on doctrine—they all stood for pretty much the same thing—but on the power of their preaching and the examples of their lives. All of these emphases are prominent in Brother John's ministry, as they were in Rever-

Sister Edith and Brother Clyde Cubbage at home, Stanley, Virginia, 1977.

end Cave's. There is more than a suggestion of these emphases in Reverend Jollett's and considerable evidence of it in Reverend Koontz's. These local traditions therefore in all likelihood extend backward without interruption for three hundred years.

Brother John spent most of his youth and early adult life in eastern Tennessee near Kingsport. He visited the Page County community in 1962, shortly after moving to Falls Church, a Washington, D.C., suburb. (His life history is taken up in detail in Chapter 9.) His evangelical outlook and mountain-farm frame of reference, his powerful, old-fashioned singing and preaching, and his kindness, obvious sincerity, and upright life combined to make a strong impression. He began a monthly preaching appointment at the Stanley Freewill Baptist Church, and in 1967 he was

Left to right: Brother Belvin Hurt, Rev. Geurdon A. Cave, and Mrs. Cave, ca. 1969, Photographer unknown.

elected pastor of the Comertown Freewill Baptist Church. A power struggle among the congregation resulted four years later in the formation of the Fellowship Independent Baptist Church. The story of the conflict cannot be published here, but Brother John led one faction in the struggle. He and nineteen others eventually decided to withdraw and form a separate church. On March 5, 1971, they constituted themselves the Fellowship Independent Baptist Church. On January 14, 1972, they ended affiliation with the Freewills and became an independent Baptist church.

When they made covenant with one another and formed their church in 1971, they rented the old Graves Methodist Chapel in Stanley for their house of worship, a drafty, nineteenth-century building heated by a pot-bellied stove. Soon they set about buying a small plot of land east of Stanley and at the foot of Roundhead Mountain, where they spent the next two years erecting their own building, obtaining a mortgage loan without difficulty to finance it.

Probably the major obstacle to the growth of the congregation was their dependence on a pastor who, living and working eighty miles away, could come into Page County only on weekends. When they broke with the Freewills they gained about a dozen members. From 1972 until 1979 the membership fluctuated between about thirty and forty. Then in April 1979 Brother John gave up his job in Rockville, Maryland, and with his wife, Pauline, moved into a trailer on the church property. The congregation had decided to put him on salary as a full-time pastor. It was not much money—$75 per week at first, then $100, and in 1985 $125—but Brother John believed the Lord would provide. Now the congregation grew, and by 1980 the membership had reached about sixty, by 1985 eighty. Whereas in 1976 when I first visited the church older people comprised the vast majority of the congregation, in 1985 every age group was well represented, both in the congregation at large and in the prominent positions in the church. Of the three preachers, Brother John was in his sixties, Brother Kenny in his late thirties, and Brother James in his early twenties. Of the two teachers, Brother Jesse was in his late fifties and Brother Jimmy was in his late twenties. In addition to the adult Sunday school, the church held two other Sunday schools in the basement, one for about a dozen children up to age ten, the other for another dozen up to age sixteen. It appeared that the church was serving the needs of all age groups, and that it would continue strongly in the 1980s. Some members of the congregation wondered what would happen when Brother John grew too old to preach, and whether the congregation would stay together. Some said they hoped one of his sons would receive the call from God to preach, but thus far none has.

4. Language

By *language* I mean what anthropologists mean: language is "a body of standards for speech behavior, a body of organizing principles for giving order to such behavior" (Goodenough 1981:5). A proper description of a language, therefore, tells what one needs to know to speak and understand the language acceptably. Members of the Fellowship Independent Baptist Church speak a southern dialect of English, comprehensible to virtually all native speakers of English at the levels of sound and syntax. Yet parts of their speech behavior have special meaning to members of their group, meaning which is not apparent to an outsider. Understanding this esoteric meaning, and developing an ethnographic description of their language in religious practice, took up a large portion of the time I spent with them. I listened to their language, recorded it, transcribed it, listened to them talk about their language, and asked them questions about it.

By insisting on the phrase *language in religious practice* rather than the more graceful *religious language* I stress the performance aspects of religious language as it is spoken, chanted, or sung. The fact is that almost all studies of religious language emphasize other aspects: philosophy, poetry, theology—and they center on the written word, not the performed word. In the context of religious ritual, performers say the performed word has the power to alter the course of future events. This is an unusual claim for language because today language is generally regarded as either descriptive (statements which "map" the world as experienced or imagined) or communicative (statements aimed at transferring information about the world from one person to another). Yet this claim for the power of language can be understood if we think of these utterances—prayers and prophetic, chanted passages in sermons are the clearest examples—as poetry; that is, as language of another order, where statements neither map nor transfer but operate in the realm of analogy: metaphor, metonymy, symbol, etc. Quite apart from these claims, I am also interested in the practice of religious language because of the role it plays in people's lives.

As I wrote in the Prologue, I believe religious language defines identities and establishes communities.

Several years ago the sociolinguist Dell Hymes called for "ethnographies of communication" that would "investigate directly the use of language in contexts of situation." By context Hymes meant "a community, or network of persons," and the focus of study was to be "communities organized as systems of communicative events" (1974:3–4, 17). Not only is the Fellowship Independent Baptist Church a community organized as a system of communicative events, it is a community *established by* such a system. This is not to deny other bases for community: many church members are kin to one another, for example. But many are not, and make little effort to socialize with each other outside of church. Many know each other simply by their church names ("Brother ——, Sister ——") —that is, the names the pastor calls them when he asks them to lead the group in prayer or otherwise refers to anyone publicly by name. But that is the point: they are bound in a community as brothers and sisters to Jesus and as children of God.

The "communicative event" that establishes the church is the worship service, and here language in religious practice may be observed and experienced directly. It can be recorded on audio and videotape and then examined later. The worshipers can be overheard discussing the service and may be questioned directly or indirectly about the language and their experience of it. Ultimately one wants to know the answers to a few deceptively simple questions: What is the nature of language in religious practice? Does it differ from ordinary language and if so, how? What is the structure of language in religious practice? How does it function? What does it mean?

When I originally drafted this chapter in 1979 I could (and did) say that no ethnography of communication among an American folk Protestant congregation had been written, but in 1982 Elaine Lawless published a description and analysis of religious speech acts in a Oneness Pentecostal congregation in southern Indiana (Lawless 1982). In it she names and explains many of the esoteric contexts for basic terms, especially active verbs (e.g., singing, praying, witnessing, preaching, healing, baptizing, shouting, prophesying, interpreting, tarrying, getting a blessing, speaking in tongues, getting saved) in use in the church, then discusses the terms as they direct behavior in the activity of worship.

As an aside, it is remarkable that certain of the esoteric terms and their meanings are identical or nearly so in the two contexts—the Indiana Pentecostals Lawless studied and the Virginia Baptists who form the basis of this book, suggesting continuities in American folk Protestant beliefs and language practice that transcend denomination and region. It is not my purpose to do a comparative analysis, but the similarities among the groups

Lawless and I studied are most likely the result of the strains of pietism, holiness, and dispensational premillennialism in both congregations. Congruence of practice—prayers in which everyone prays spontaneously and aloud as he or she is moved by the Spirit, for example—may result from the legacy of revivalism, as well as from borrowings from other church practices. In the 1970s, for example, the Fellowship Independent Baptist Church instituted a healing prayer that many thought smacked of pentecostalism; in the early 1980s they abandoned it. But in the early 1980s each special-hymn was followed by applause from the congregation, a practice that was missing in the 1970s. I had noticed applause after specials among neighboring Pentecostal churches in the 1970s, and I am sure that the practice was borrowed from them. Lawless reports applause after specials in the Pentecostal congregation in Indiana that she studied (ibid.: 15), indicating that it serves to evaluate the success of a performance. Among the members of the Fellowship Independent Baptist Church, however, applause serves more to express warmth and gratitude toward the performers (and thereby indicates their status in the congregation) than it does as an index to a successful performance. Despite these similarities in language and practice, there are many significant differences, as I explained in Chapter 3; unlike the Baptists, Pentecostals believe in a "second blessing," many take tongue-speaking as a sign of this "baptism of the Spirit," and many believe it is possible to attain and keep a perfect, sinless state in this walk of life.

To return to ethnographies of speaking: they are a necessary first step in the study of language in any context, religious or otherwise; yet in this book I have attempted to go beyond them. Most ethnographies of speaking are synchronic, focusing on a particular group for a very short time—often a single conversation among two people is the subject of analysis— whereas this study has a ten-year time depth, with a historical context that goes back well into the eighteenth century. Second, most are analogical rather than dialogical (see the Introduction), and therefore they fall prey to certain methodological problems even when they have resulted from scrupulous dialogue in the field. For in turning field dialogue into the ethnographer's monologue, replacing conversations with several informants by the ethnographer's synthesis of what he or she thinks they said and meant, the ethnographer necessarily distorts and risks misinterpretation, particularly if he or she fails to let the informants speak in detail for themselves. What is more, the ethnographer may not be able to bring out the subtle differences in language and belief among the informants. In this book I let the people speak for themselves, text and interpretation, as much as possible; though of course I do not abandon *my* side of the dialogue.

Finally, most ethnographies of speaking are term-oriented, concentrating on language related directly to action; interpretation of lengthy texts is beyond their scope. Yet it is precisely in the interpretation of lengthy texts—prayers, sermons, testimonies—that we can come to understand the patterns of language and belief—"how they think"—that enable us to know the people we are studying. The members of the Fellowship Independent Baptist Church think in patterns, and their typical method of understanding experience proceeds deductively by analogy, not inductively by observation and experiment. Typology, tropology, and a very high proportion of interpretative language are characteristic of their religious thought and discourse, as we shall see below and especially in Chapters 7–9.

"The Language Itself"

Language in religious practice has certain characteristic attributes, some of which mark it as different from ordinary language. One of the most important is that it is performed and that its utterance constitutes an act or kind of commitment, not merely an observation or a description or a transfer of information. I discuss the implications of this attribute in the last section of this chapter. In addition, the very structure of language in religious practice differentiates it from the ordinary language of, say, conversation.

First, the language in religious practice among the members of the Fellowship Independent Baptist Church has a specialized vocabulary. (It may be noted that this is true of the language of most folk groups; see Toelken 1979:52–56.) Certain seemingly ordinary terms are peculiar in this context: for example, "saved," "lost," "blessing," "Spirit," "conviction," "message," and "power." Each of these words has an ordinary meaning that is different from its meaning in this context. For instance, a message is ordinarily a communication one person or group sends another, but in the worship context, "message" is the word for sermon and it implies the underlying assumption that the sermon is a prophetic message from God spoken by the Spirit through the preacher acting as the mouthpiece. Other words are part of the theological vocabulary of Christianity and, while not different in the context of worship, are nonetheless specialized: "Lord," "grace," "sin," and so forth.

Second, language in religious practice is more redundant and more formulaic than ordinary conversation. To be sure, conversation has its formulaic utterances (e.g., "It seems to me," "I feel like that," etc.) but the proportion of repeated words and phrases is less. The language of prayer (Chapter 6) is especially repetitive, with its formulaic phrases of address ("Our Father") and petition ("Grant, O Lord"), and its standard opening and closing phrases. When prayer is composed at the moment of utterance it exhibits even greater redundancy.

Third, language in religious practice is "marked" or set off from ordinary language by what linguists call "suprasegmental" and "paralinguistic" features. Among the suprasegmental features that are affected are speed, loudness, intonation, and register. Tone of voice is a paralinguistic feature that is altered: language in religious practice among the church members is noticeably hoarser, huskier, and raspier-sounding than their ordinary language. Typically, language in religious practice moves from an ordinary public address mode to a kind of chant, particularly during sermons, prayer, and testimony. When this happens, speed and loudness increase, the intonation range is compressed, the register of the voice is raised, phrase length becomes more regular, and the proportion of formulaic utterances increases. The congregation notices this change, but it is obvious even to an outsider. The voice of the deity in many world cultures is marked or masked by suprasegmental and paralinguistic features and delivers its message in "oracular tones."

These observations about the structure of language in the religious practice of the Fellowship Independent Baptist Church will be made more specific in succeeding chapters when each language genre is taken up in turn. At this point the discussion moves to the theory of language held by the church members themselves.

Language and Conversion

In *The Psychology of Religion,* Walter Houston Clark defines a religious conversion as "that type of spiritual growth or development which involves an appreciable change of direction concerning religious ideas and behavior" (1958: 191). Conversion, in this definition, could refer to abandonment of religious beliefs, but that is not the direction of change commonly understood. Conversion, rather, means a transformation from unbelief to belief. In her spiritual autobiography, *Turning,* Emilie Griffin puts it this way: "By conversion I mean the discovery, made gradually or suddenly, that God is real. It is the perception that this real God loves us personally and acts mercifully and justly towards each of us. As such it is not an event, not an action, not an occurrence. Instead it is a continuing revelation and a transforming force" (1980: 15).

Among mainline Jews and Christians in America, conversion is regarded as a process of gradual growth in spiritual understanding and commitment. Among most folk Christians in America, conversion also involves gradual growth in spiritual strength and understanding, but this is thought to follow from a precise and intensely felt moment when one repents and yields to God and is transformed instantaneously from an unbeliever to a child of God. Prior to that moment of salvation one was "lost"; at that moment one becomes "saved." Becoming saved is likened to a second, new birth; the Christian is "born again" as a child of God and brother or sister to Jesus.

Like many folk Christians in the United States, the members of the Fellowship Independent Baptist Church regard conversion as an intensely felt, instantaneous transformation. Conversion, they think, can only follow after a period of emotional turmoil, called "conviction," during which a person feels condemned or convicted (as in a court of law) for wickedness and sin, and feels sentenced to eternal damnation in hell. (The term *conviction* is used in the King James Version of the Bible and was common until late in the nineteenth century.) "I don't believe a person can get saved anytime they want to. No. I believe the Holy Spirit, the Spirit of God, has got to be convicting 'em, and helping 'em see that they're lost and in need to be saved," explained Brother Jesse (Comer interview, 1977, p. 66).

Conviction is an emotional crisis during which a person feels worthless, alone, rejected. In the term popularized by Erik Erikson, conviction may be regarded as an "identity crisis" that occurs when one feels guilt, shame, and remorse over the things one has done and the person one has become, doubt over one's power to change oneself, and confusion about the future. This is not precisely the same as the normative adolescent "identity crisis" that Erikson conceived, but it is a crisis of identity nevertheless. The classic American spiritual autobiography, Jonathan Edwards' "Personal Narrative," is an account of an identity crisis with periods of conviction and gradual conversion.

The members of the Fellowship Independent Baptist Church agree that prior to conviction and conversion Satan's spirit dwells within the unsaved person. "Either you're saved or you're lost," said Brother John. "Either you belong to the devil or you belong to the Lord" (John and Pauline Sherfey interview, April 2, 1978, p. 6). People are born in sin, "shaped in iniquity and conceived in sin, as David said; and they ain't nothing we can do about that," Brother John continued. Satan's indwelling presence does not determine all, or even most, of the actions of an unsaved person, however. Such a person has an "inward man" that has desires, and some of these may be good. "He wants to be a good moral person. And if that's what he wants, that's what he'll be," said Brother John. "But yet Satan don't care how moral he is just as long as he don't go and give his heart to the Lord" (ibid., pp. 10–11). The church members believe that while Satan's indwelling presence tempts and turns some people to do evil, Satan does not usually bother an unsaved person very much: there is no need to do so, for that person is already bound for hell. Satan is said to strive more with Christians than with the unsaved.

Under conviction, "It's the inward part that desires to be a Christian," Brother John explained. If this "inward part," which Brother John also terms "the desire of man" and "the soul of man," chooses to yield to God, then God's Holy Spirit enters the person and drives Satan out. "The Spirit of God is in a [saved person] at all times. . . . A Christian has the Spirit of God dwelling within him, see. The Bible said, 'If my Spirit be not in you, you're none of mine.' So it's got to be in us to be part of him" (ibid., pp. 6–7).

The indwelling Spirit does not displace the "inward part" of a person, either. Both exist in the saved Christian. "An individual, when he gets saved, [the Spirit] comes into his life, and that's why he knows he's saved: because he can feel the presence of God within himself" (ibid., p. 9). The "he" who knows he is saved and feels the presence of God is the "inward part."

It is important to distinguish between the indwelling Spirit and the inward part because the Spirit is not, in normal circumstances, an agent or actor; it does not "possess" the Christian completely. The indwelling Spirit is said to "speak" to the inward part as a conscience or advisor. Satan, though dwelling outside, also "speaks" as an advisor to the inward part and battles with the Spirit for control. "The Lord will speak to you in a still, small voice," said Brother Belvin, explaining the difference between the voices:

> Now, whether you're in the right direction or not, why, he'll speak to you in a still voice, but if you—a lot of 'em hears a old quick, quickened voice and like-a-that, will throw 'em off sometimes and they'll pay attention to that voice quicker than the other one. . . . There's many spirits in the world but there ain't but one right one. . . . [Those others are] of the devil, reducing spirits, of just the evilness. Got an evilness, and come in a light manner, . . . real nice and soft and tenderly trying to get you, but—it's a different voice, and come all nice in sheep's clothing. And he can change hisself into so many different things. . . . And a quick old hateful . . . tickling voice to tickle you or something thataway to get you to jump for it right quick. (Hurt interview, pp. 122–123)

The voice of the Spirit warns, chastises, and most of all advises, especially in response to questions. "Coming to prayer meeting on a Tuesday night," said Brother Jesse, "I might ask [beforehand], 'Lord, what is the best thing that I could talk about tonight?' And you get to leafing through your Bible and you begin to read and think about certain things. And then all of a sudden one thing seems to stand out to you, and just a small voice says, 'This is it.' Just a small thing that says in your heart, in your mind, 'Well, this is it. This is what I want you to speak on. This is what really stands out to me.'"

I asked Brother Jesse whether it was an audible voice. "No," he replied, "it's just a small voice inside, in your mind, your heart, whatever you want to call it; when you see it, you just know it." "Do you actually hear words?" "No, not really hear the words," he said. "That's where the Bible says 'that still, small voice' a-speaking to you. Not in a great booming voice, but just in a small way. But yet, it's something there that lets you know that that is it" (Comer interview, 1977, p. 69).

One kind of language in religious practice, then, is the voice of the Spirit speaking to the inward part of a person. This is not an audible voice and cannot be overheard. (Some folk Christians, it should be noted, report hearing an audible voice; but no one in this congregation does. Instead, most say they receive an impression in the mind.) This silent language cannot be recorded at the moment it appears, either. Evidence for it comes in reports of its occurrence. During the testimony portion of the worship service, for example, a church member may tell a story about having heeded the voice of the indwelling Spirit. Such testimony is also understood to be given in response to prompting from the same indwelling Spirit. The authority for this comes from New Testament descriptions of the Holy Spirit speaking to and guiding the apostles, especially Paul.

The second type of language in religious practice is the Christian worshiper's audible language of prayer, song, preaching, teaching, and testimony. When the worshiper is in the proper relationship with God, such language is said to be "in the Spirit" or "anointed by the Spirit." At such times the worshiper is understood to be possessed by the Spirit. He or she then becomes a mouthpiece for the Spirit, is "led by the Spirit," and speaks, chants, or sings the words of the Spirit. The church members hold this belief also on the authority of the New Testament, particularly 1 Corinthians 12:1–11 and 1 Corinthians 14, where "prophecy" is understood as preaching and any other Spirit-filled utterance (e.g., Peter, replying in Acts 4:8–13 to the Jewish authorities, is said to be "filled with the Holy Ghost").

There is a third type of language in religious practice, and that is language about language, or metalanguage. This is the language of interpretation, and it occurs in such situations as Brother John's explaining the meaning of a hymn just after the congregation sings it, or Brother Jesse's telling the adult Sunday school what he thinks a Bible verse means. Much of the sermon is interpretative in this sense as well, since it is organized as an explication of a passage from the Bible; yet much of it is also understood as prophetic, and therefore of the second type of language in religious practice; i.e., Spirit-led. In fact, some kinds of interpretation are thought to be led by the Spirit. Interpretative language is usually deductive and operates by analogy.

Closely related to interpretative language is a fourth type of language in religious practice, what we might call directive language, as when Brother Donny asks for prayer requests, or Brother John asks the congregation to shake one another's hands. This comes closest to ordinary language, and yet such directive language is the most concrete in the service, and gets the most immediate results. As I will show below, it forms a class of speech acts termed "perlocutionary."

The members of the Fellowship Independent Baptist Church believe, then, that language of worship differs from ordinary language because it is

Spirit-filled; and it is Spirit-filled because at the moment of conversion the Holy Spirit takes up its abode inside the Christian and henceforth leads, guides, and sometimes directly utters the words of worship.

Language, Power, and the Blessing of the Spirit

Explaining the relationship between the Spirit, language, and power, Brother John declared: "If it's inspired by the Spirit it is the word of God. . . . In other words, as the apostle Paul wrote the Bible the Holy Ghost moved upon him, and that became the power of God. And a man that's saved, and testified, as long as he's in the Spirit of God, then that's the power of God" (John and Pauline Sherfey interview, April 2, 1978, p. 4). Led by the Spirit, the word of God, whether in speech, chant, or song, prayer, hymns, preaching, teaching, or testimony, has the power to alter the course of future events. This belief is the cornerstone of the church members' theory of language.

The most important power granted to Spirit-filled language is the power to convict a sinner and lead him or her through to salvation. "Power is in the word," said Brother John. "The apostle Paul said, 'For I am not ashamed of the gospel of Christ, for it is the power of God unto salvation,' see. So the power is in the word. Whether it be singing or preaching or testifying or what, as long as it's the word of God, it's got power in it" (ibid., p. 3). Here the "word" is the gospel of the Word (Jesus) written in words in the Bible under the inspiration of the Spirit and brought in words spoken, chanted, and sung to the unsaved.

While in the Spirit, the Christian is affected, too. "When [the Lord is] striving with you it's a particular time for you. More of a pleasant time, feel the Spirit more," said Brother Vernie. "You could be a-praying and it would get more greater. . . . You can be a-working and it'll crack in like that sometimes" (Meadows interview, 1977, p. 30).

Other effects of the Spirit upon the Christian during the practice of religious language include weeping tears of joy and "shouting." "I get a good feeling, overjoyed. That's the way he [God] blesses me," said Brother John. "A feeling comes over you that you just don't get any other way. You get to feeling so good inside you can't hold it, you know. . . . But when you get to being blessed real good, you'll shout. . . . And when God shouts you, he just shouts you right then; that's it. . . . When God shouts you he just pours it on you and then you done shouted" (John and Pauline Sherfey interview, April 2, 1978, pp. 26–27). By a "shout" the church members mean a cry of "Amen!" or "Praise the Lord!" or "Hallelujah!" or a similar ejaculation, not a wordless cry or a dance or speaking in a (foreign) tongue. Brother John stresses that it is involuntary, and the emphasis accounts for his syntax: "When God shouts you . . ."

A person praying, singing, teaching, preaching, or testifying in the Spirit is also said to be "under the demonstration of the Spirit": "When [Brother John's] singing and he's preaching . . . I think he's under the demonstration of the Holy Spirit, Holy Ghost. . . . Course there's times it gets greater than it does others," said Brother Vernie (Meadows interview, 1977, p. 18). When the power is greatest, a Christian is said to be "anointed" by the Spirit while exercising a gift of the Spirit.

This "anointment" is signaled, even to an outsider, by the transition, during prayer, preaching, and testimony, in language mode from speech to chant (and sometimes from chant to song). Brother John explained how the anointment moves his body as well:

> When I'm a-preaching, I get anointed by the Spirit. . . . Now I'm a Christian [and I have the Spirit within] all the time. . . . But when I get over there in the church and I start preaching, then God begins to anoint me. And it just, that's when I get carried away, you know, that's when I get to fighting hard when I'm a-preaching. I don't mean fighting, I just mean using my hands, you know. I use my hands, I use my body, use every part about me when I'm preaching. Because I'm anointed, I feel that . . . (John and Pauline Sherfey interview, December 3, 1979, p. 30)

"Anointing" is the activating of the Spirit's power. Brother John continued, explaining how blessing follows from anointment:

> There's a difference in being anointed and being in the Spirit. Now you can be, the Spirit's in you at all times if you're saved. You've got it; you better have. And then if you got in a good service where everybody's praying or everybody's singing or everybody's rejoicing in the love of God, you get anointed by the Spirit of God, and it's just like I guess you would say overcharging a battery. . . . The Christian life, you know, you can get overcharged in the Spirit of the Lord, and you know it's just something different. . . .
>
> Some people are easier to, you could say, get charged than others. When you're preaching they'll throw up their hands, they'll clap their hands together sometimes, some'll holler "Amen!" some, "Praise the Lord!" and some'll just sit there like they was unconcerned. See now, that's the difference. Some are getting anointed. The Spirit's in those Christians but they're just not being anointed by the Holy Ghost. . . . And a lot of times people get anointed while they're singing. They get to singing then and they just get in that anointing Spirit and God begins to bless their soul, they feel so happy they could just—just run! (Ibid., pp. 30–31)

A second and more general use of the power of Spirit-filled language is through prayer to bring about certain events. If the Lord knows what needs are to be met, and will meet them or not when and as he sees fit, one might ask why the Christian should take the trouble to petition through prayer. But just as the Lord requires a sinner to yield through audible prayer ("if thou shalt confess with thy mouth the Lord Jesus," Romans 10:9) in order to be saved, so the Lord requires that the Christian take the initiative to pray for needs to be met.

This requirement is not meant to inform the Lord (he knows all) nor to command him (he cannot be commanded) but rather as an exercise of the primary relationship between the Christian and the Lord through Jesus (in whose name prayer is made). In other words, the healthy relationship between the Christian and God is maintained through communication, through language, whether prayer (as in this case), song, testimony, or the practice of other Spirit-filled utterance.

The most frequent topics of petitionary prayer are for saving the lost and for healing the body. But the church members realize that when they pray they do not command. Their language has power, but only at the pleasure of God's will. Speaking of a preacher she heard on the radio, Sister Edith said:

> I liked his preaching all right until he commanded God what God should do. I don't think we command God; I think God's our command. He commanded God to take the devil out of a woman. And I said, "Well, he commanded God to take it out, but he should have asked him to take it." 'Cause when you command something, that means "Do it," don't it? ["How should you talk to God?"] Pray and ask him to have things done the way he sees fit, the best way to do. And he'll show it to you. . . . If you're saved, and it's something that you think you need, and God shows you that need, and it's God's will, he's going to meet it for you. (Cubbage interview, p. 22)

The church members derive their authority for these beliefs concerning the power of the Spirit from the New Testament. Brother Vernie attributed Brother John's anointment during the healing prayer to a gift of the Spirit: "I mean I ain't got the anointing of the Lord as Brother John's got. I'm not called to [lead the healing prayer]. I think somebody's got to be called to pray for the sick. Anointing, the different anointing of the Lord. You know, there are several different gifts in the Bible" (Meadows interview, 1977, p. 27).

Brother Vernie was referring to 1 Corinthians 12:1–11, Paul's discussion of the gifts of the Spirit. "Preaching and teaching both is a gift of God," said Brother Jesse. "God gives nine great gifts. . . . Preaching is one, teaching is one. Of course there are others, such as prophecy, knowledge, tongues, interpretation of tongues, and all of this. . . . But we're certainly called by the Holy Spirit to do what we do. And it's up to us: how hard we work, how much we apply ourself to it, to how well the Lord is going to bless us to do the job he calls us to do" (Comer interview, 1977, p. 18).

The Meaning of Language in Religious Practice

What is the meaning of language in religious practice, and what is the meaning of language about that language? "Prayer changes things" is a metalinguistic formula that Brother John repeats in the worship service before the healing prayer and the altar prayer. When he does so, he acts (as he frequently does) in the role of interpreter. But what do such statements signify? What is the ontological status of language in religious practice itself?

The classic way to approach this question is to say that the status of religious language depends on the existence of God. If God exists, it is meaningful; if God does not, it is not. The existence of God is an old issue in Western philosophy, but in this century A. J. Ayer took an important new direction in the argument when in his *Language, Truth, and Logic* he argued that meaningful language consists of statements that can be verified (Ayer 1946). A verifiable statement is one which on the basis of evidence can in practice or at least in principle be proved true or false.

True statements and false statements are both meaningful, but, Ayer went on, what about statements such as "The universe is infinite" or "God exists" or, one might add, "Prayer changes things"? Rather than assessing the truth of an argument in favor of the existence of God, as was the normal philosophical practice, Ayer simply claimed that because no set of facts can *disprove* God's existence, the statement "God exists" is not open to the test of verification and hence is meaningless. This method became known as the criterion of falsifiability, and philosophers of science applied it to scientific theories. The test of truth or falsehood was, of course, the controlled experiment.

The issue of whether God exists defies scientific experimentation because God is said to operate in mysterious ways outside of the human understanding of causality. No experiment can determine with certainty whether God answers prayers so long as it is believed that God answers them or not as he sees fit, and that to understand why is beyond human comprehension. Indeed, the difference between scientific and nonscientific (e.g., religious) theories came to turn on the criterion of verification. A good (i.e., scientific) theory was open to being proved true or false. A poor theory was not open to verification.

One difficulty with Ayer's argument is that it assumes the existence of a body of objective "facts" independent of any observer, which "facts" are to be used in applying the criterion of verification. But advances in twentieth-century physics, from Einstein's theory of relativity through Heisenberg's principle of uncertainty and well beyond, have cast grave doubt upon the possibility that anything can be said to exist "objectively" and "in itself" apart from a perceiver and his or her interaction with that "fact." The current climate of opinion in the arts, humanities, and among many thoughtful social scientists emphasizes the relativity of worldview, not the absoluteness of knowledge. Reality is a human, social construction which is "negotiated" between parties to an agreement that "the world is like this." Reality, in this view, is neither objective nor subjective but "intersubjective."

A second objection is directed at Ayer's assumption that knowledge consists of statements corresponding to verifiable facts. Information is passed along not only in statements but also in questions, commands, promises, and other speech acts about which truth and falsehood seem irrelevant. Such acts of speech may be operative or inoperative or, as J. L. Austin put it, "happy" or "unhappy" (Austin 1975:12–14). It turns out that such a class of speech acts, which Austin dubbed "performative," accounts for a great deal of language in religious practice. Because this forms the basis for the next section I will not consider it further now.

The third and, I believe, most serious objection, is addressed to the verification of "facts." If knowledge consists of true, meaningful statements made up of verifiable facts, how do we know that the facts that comprise the statements are themselves meaningful and true? Presumably we can know by attempting to verify them, but in so doing we must rely on yet another set of facts, and these, too, must be verifiable. Applying Ayer's argument lands one in an infinitely regressive series with no possibility of certainty.

Writing about the Pentecostals she observed in Indiana, Lawless points out that "the study of religious language is not the same as an ethnography of religious *speech*. Most of the constructs of Pentecostal belief hinge on active verbs which testify to the traditional nature of the transmission of the faith, and most would not easily lend themselves to debates of verifiability, falsifiability or philosophical reality" (Lawless 1982:11–12). I think, as I have stated elsewhere (Titon 1985), that the philosophical tradition of phenomenology offers the opportunity to explore the social reality of religious language and religious speech as well; moreover, in this book I am making the claim that phenomenological hermeneutics, of the sort practiced by Paul Ricoeur, Peter Berger, Dennis Tedlock, and others, provides a ground for interpretation of language in religious practice. I agree with Lawless that the study of religious language differs from an ethnography of religious speech; but the two are intimately linked, and may be approached from philosophical positions outside of the logical positivism Ayer represents.

Approaching the ontological status of religious language through attempts to prove or disprove God's existence thus appears fruitless. A more promising approach, it would seem, would be to ask what it would mean to "know" God, that is, to have knowledge of God. In fact, the members of the Fellowship Independent Baptist Church do not make statements such as "God exists"; rather, they say things like "God is so real. I feel him in my soul" (Brother John's sermon, August 7, 1977; see "A Representative Sermon," in Chapter 7).

How, then, does one know? What happens to turn belief into knowledge? What is the difference between the two? "Knowledge" cannot be defined as common sense would have it, as true belief for which one has adequate evidence, for this definition is a tautology that turns into an infinite regression. For evidence to be adequate it must rest on other evidence, and this must be adequate, and for it to be adequate it must rest on other evidence, and so on.

When the members of the Fellowship Independent Baptist Church make statements like "God is real" they are claiming knowledge based on experience: I know God is real because I experience God (or, as Brother John simply and eloquently put it, "I feel him in my soul"). The problem with claims to know based on experience is that it is possible to be deluded by experience as, for example, in having a false premonition, or mistaking a person's motivation after observing his or her actions. Experience, it would seem, is ambiguous and multilayered. The trouble with claiming knowledge based on experience is not that it is meaningless but that it is all too meaningful. And yet to the members of the Fellowship Independent Baptist Church it cannot be gainsaid that God is real and that religious language has meaning.

None of these ways of thinking about the relationship between language, belief, knowledge, and meaning is satisfactory for understanding language in religious practice. Fortunately, the folklorist can contribute a different line of thought, one which begins with the idea that knowledge may be regarded as "lore." Knowledge is not defined as true belief but as capability: "A person knows something in virtue of possessing a competence in getting it right. To know, even to know facts, is to know *how* to do something" (Graham 1977:115). Knowledge becomes know-how; and know-how is one of the meanings of the "lore" part of the word *folklore*. Knowledge of God as know-how now becomes the capacity to live one's life in accordance with God's will. To recognize divine will one needs to know how to communicate with God. One communicates through prayer, song, messages (sermons), etc. The convert grows in strength and (literally) knowledge as he or she learns competence in communicating with God and living the Christian life. In short, language in religious practice means experience and knowledge of God.

A few years after working out this line of argument I found that its essentials had been stated several years earlier by a philosopher of religion: "The religious believer must be a participant in a shared language. He must learn the use of religious concepts. What he learns is religious language; a language which he participates in with other believers. What I am suggesting is that to know how to use this language is to know God. This common knowledge of God is religion" (Phillips 1966:51).

The Performed Word

In context, the language of worship exhibits an apparently peculiar feature. Put simply, language in religious practice not only says something but also does something. A worshiper who prays not only says a prayer but performs the act of praying. Singing, preaching, testifying, teaching, and even shouting "Amen!" in response to the sermon are acts or performances, not merely observations or exchanges of information or polite pleasantries.

The British philosopher J. L. Austin first called attention to the sort of statement that not only says something but also does something, and he labeled those statements "performatives" (Austin 1975). He later abandoned the term and the sharp distinction between assertions about the world and "performatives" that act in the world, because every assertion is also an act (the act of asserting) and because every performative is also an assertion (e.g., "I apologize" = "I assert that I apologize"). Austin replaced this concept with another, the idea of "illocutionary acts." He noted that certain statements are chiefly descriptive, "mapping the territory" of the world, and can be shown to correspond or not correspond to facts; these he termed "locutions" and their utterance a "locutionary act." Other statements not only map the territory but do something in saying what they say. These he termed "illocutions." For example, the statement, "I apologize for being so mean," not only maps the territory (I've been mean) but is itself the act of apology. A third class of statements map the territory and cause something to happen as a consequence of saying what they say; these are "perlocutions." A perlocution may also do something in saying something, but its chief attribute is that its utterance brings some future thing about. If I say, "Hadn't you better get your umbrella?" and you get it, I have uttered what Austin would have called a perlocution.

It should be clear that language in religious practice is filled with illocutionary and perlocutionary acts. Austin himself called attention to statements beginning with "I pray" and "I testify" as illocutionary, but in the context of worship such statements are also perlocutionary when they are understood to bring about what they intend to. That is, if God answers a prayer, "I pray" is perlocutionary as well as illocutionary. If a sermon brings a sinner to the altar the sermon is perlocutionary. If performing a hymn brings tears of joy to someone's eyes it is perlocutionary.

Austin's theory of illocutionary acts has had considerable influence among philosophers interested in language and meaning, but they have tended to expand the theory so as to cover almost all "speech acts" (Searle 1969). If all (or almost all) utterances involve doing something as well as saying something, then it makes little sense to claim that language in religious practice is special in this regard.

And yet it seems intuitively obvious that religious utterances *are* special in virtue of committing the speaker to and performing an act that brings something into being which would not have existed without the utterance. I may say, "Last night I ate black bean soup for supper," but whether I ate the soup or not does not depend on my utterance. The very existence of a prayer, on the other hand, depends on its performance. The prayer (sermon, testimony, etc.) *is* the utterance.

Compared with ordinary statements, religious utterances, I believe, are especially context-dependent for meaning. John Searle and others who have attempted to work out a theory of speech acts agree that their meaning is dependent on a mix of intention and convention; that is, upon what the speaker intends and what interpretative conventions obtain among the speaker and listeners. Keith Graham, attempting to redefine Austin's "performative" in a more useful way, concludes that "a statement S is performative if and only if it brings about the truth of the content it expresses as a consequence of people's so regarding it" (1977:76). This characterization surely applies to language in religious practice among a sincere group of worshipers.

Language in religious practice, then, brings into being or activates the relationship between the worshiper and the divine. For the unbeliever, outside of the convention of worship, it brings nothing into being; it is empty, nonsense or a delusion. But, as Brother John explained,

> Life is in the Word, the power is in the Word, when we believe it in the heart. We must believe from the heart before you can be saved. "For with the heart man believeth unto righteousness." And when you believe that, then the power's in it. Now if you don't believe it there's no power in it. In other words, an unbeliever, an infidel, he don't believe the word of God. You can stand there and preach to him all day but because he don't believe it, there's no power in it. . . . [But] when you believe it, and you accept it on those terms, and will take it that way, then there's power in it. (John Sherfey interview, July 23, 1977, pp. 19–20)

The "power" is in the belief; it is the power of faith, and for the believer it makes religious language meaningful and operative.

Poetic and Interpretative Language in Religious Practice

Hermeneutics entered the language as the name for the activity of interpreting the Bible; even though its meaning has expanded to encompass interpretation of all sorts of written texts, it is worth remembering how it got its start; for as the church members spend much of their time in worship, communicating with God, so they also spend much of their time interpreting, puzzling out meaning. The two great texts are, first, the Bible; second, experience, particularly their own lives.

Of course, one need not be religious to be introspective. After a period of soul-searching, many people decide against religion, often on the grounds that it requires a kind of faith or belief that is impossible for them. While it is true that there have been many revivals of religion in the past four or five hundred years since the Reformation, the overall trend in Europe and the United States has been away from the Judeo-Christian worldview and toward the secular, scientific explanation of the universe.

This movement toward secularization has entered language as well; characteristically, the language of science is descriptive, making distinctions between the observing "subject" and the outside "object." Indeed, the subject-verb-object structure of ordinary English reinforces the descriptive character of our language. Scientific explanation, as we have seen, requires that interpretative statements be observationally and experimentally verifiable. Although religious believers move within this explanatory sphere, and make use of it when they make such claims as "God answers prayers," offering evidence of prayers that were answered, they also move within a different explanatory sphere, with its own characteristic language: analogy.

Thus far we have considered language in religious practice, noting that it is special in that it does not so much describe the world as perform acts within it. Singing, praying, preaching, teaching, and testifying are communicative activities designed to change the world, not to depict it. Another kind of language in religious practice is chiefly interpretative; it is designed to explain the world, but its principles are not "scientific"; rather, they operate on the basis of likeness.

Interpretation characterizes much of the language of the sermon, which, after all, is understood as a message from God explaining the Bible passage at hand. Interpretation characterizes Brother John's remarks about the hymns and specials that have been sung, when he talks about the meaning of their texts. Most important, interpretation is the mode of testimony. To say what God has done in one's life is performance, to be sure; God requires public witnessing. But to testify is also to describe and interpret experience.

An example will indicate what I mean. Brother John's conversion to Christianity occurred not long after his five-year-old son Buddy Wayne died. When he speaks about his conversion, Brother John describes these two events and interprets the death of his son as a punishment from God for his having gone back on an earlier (but incomplete) profession of faith. He views his conversion as the subsequent establishment of a covenant.

In his life story (see Chapter 9), he acknowledges that many people will reject his interpretation of his son's death. But to argue his point he turns to analogy: in the Bible, God punished David by killing his son; so God punished Brother John's disobedience. This is the characteristic turn of John's mind to analogy for explanation; in so doing, he typifies the thinking of his church and, by extension, those who take the Bible as literally true.

Analogy, here, is a species of metonymic thought, "a verbal response to God's own verbal revelation," according to Northrop Frye (1982:11). Frye distinguishes three phases in the development of language: metaphorical, metonymic, and descriptive. Metaphoric language is concrete and epigrammatic; subject and object are unified, "linked by a common power or energy" (ibid.:10). An example would be the title of one of the Fellowship Independent Baptist Church's favorite hymns, "When God Dips His Love in My Heart." By metonymic language, Frye means a kind of thinking (and speaking and writing) by analogy, "in which the verbal expression is 'put for' something that by definition transcends adequate verbal expression" (ibid.:15). Language about God, or God's working in the world, is thus metonymic in Frye's sense.

The language of analogy proceeds by deductive reasoning: this is deduced from that on the grounds of likeness. "As Christian theology gained cultural ascendancy," Frye continues, "thought began to take on a deductive shape in which everything followed from the perfection of God, because of the need for irrefutable premises" (ibid.:10). For the Fellowship Independent Baptist Church members, heirs to this traditional mode of thought, everything follows from the perfection of God as revealed in his word, the Bible, when read by a Spirit-led Christian. Two types of analogy, religious allegory and tropology, are, as will be shown in Chapter 7, important to understand in order to realize the church members' mind-set; here, they may be illustrated by returning to the example of Brother John's conversion narrative. To explain how God intervened in his life, he turns to the biblical story of David, viewing it as an allegory with application to his own life: David was wicked, and the Lord punished him, killing his son and putting "a sword in his house forever"; likewise, Buddy Wayne's death is a sword in Brother John's house. Tropology, the view that the events and persons of the Bible transcend their times and places to live today in the Christian's life, not just as symbols but as reality, is illustrated in Brother John's turn to David's example.

A third kind of thinking by analogy, typology, is crucial to the interpretative mode of this religious mind-set. The New Testament is understood as a fulfillment of the prophecies of the Old Testament. In particular, events in the Old Testament are understood as prefigurations of analogous events in the life of Jesus. As Frye points out, such references to the Old Testament abound in the New; the writers of the gospels, Acts, and the epistles intended it thus. "This typological way of reading the Bible is indicated too often and explicitly in the New Testament for us to be in any doubt that this is the 'right' way of reading it—'right' in the only sense that criticism can recognize, as the way that conforms to the intentionality of the book itself and to the conventions it assumes and requires" (ibid.: 79–80). In Chapter 7 I will show how typology operates in Brother John's sermons; in Chapters 8 and 9 I will show how the church members extend thinking by analogy—particularly typology—from the text of the Bible to the "text" of their own experiences, creating life stories that they then interpret in terms of God's intervention in their lives. Thus events in their lives are seen to point to or are put (by God) for later events as a kind of prophetic fulfillment. The meaning of events when they occur is hidden, but upon study events may be revealed as a foreshadowing (type) of a future event, or fulfillment (antitype) of a prior event.

Arranging events in their lives into narrative—telling stories about themselves, in other words—requires them thus to think in analogy in the acts of selection, structuring, narrating, and supplying interpretative comments along the way. Interpreting their lives in this way places them in a line of numerous religious believers, including the Puritans, whose conversion narratives and other writings have been the subject of much recent critical discourse from a similar typological perspective. With the members of the Fellowship Independent Baptist Church we have an opportunity to consider religious narratives and metanarratives in the full context of an accessible, contemporary oral tradition.

Language and the Order of Worship

In Chapters 5, 6, 7, and 8 I discuss the performance genres of language in religious practice: singing, praying, teaching, preaching, and testimony. Before doing so, it will be useful to discuss the order of worship in the Fellowship Independent Baptist Church and fit these language genres into their immediate context. In Chapter 1, I described the homecoming service, which, though it differs somewhat in its order from the ordinary Sunday morning and night services, provides a similar context. The usual order of worship on Sundays is shown in Figure 23. The time should be understood as the years 1976–1979, the ethnographic present for this study. In the Epilogue I discuss some of the changes that occurred over the ten-year period during which I visited the church.

Events begin Sunday morning when the people arrive and talk in fellowship outside the church and inside the sanctuary before ten o'clock. At ten Brother John steps to the pulpit and welcomes everyone, mentioning visitors by name. Then he signals the start of the congregational hymn-singing by saying something like, "All right, let's stand, take out our hymn-books, and turn to page 291." (SINGING:) He leads the congregation in three or four hymns; he chooses some and members of the congregation choose others. (PRAYING:) Next Brother Donny comes to the pulpit to receive prayer requests, and this is followed by the altar prayer. Brother

---

ORDER OF WORSHIP

1. Congregational hymn singing
2. Prayer requests and altar prayer
3. Scripture reading
4. Sunday school
5. Bible count
6. Birthdays
7. Offering, prayer, and hymn
8. Special-hymn singing
9. Healing prayer
10. Sermon
11. Altar call (invitation), prayer, and hymn
12. Prayer
13. Testimony
14. Closing prayer

Figure 23. Normal order of worship, Sunday morning service, Fellowship Independent Baptist Church, Stanley, Va., summer 1977.

John steps back to the pulpit and asks a person designated the previous week to read a passage of Scripture. (TEACHING:) Brother John asks everyone to go to Sunday school; Brother Jesse teaches the adult class in the sanctuary, some of the young adults teach teenagers and young children in the church basement, and John retires to the pastor's study to meditate and pray about his forthcoming sermon.

Sometimes John returns upstairs before the end of the adult Sunday School and takes part in it; otherwise, at about eleven o'clock he returns upstairs with the rest, adult Sunday school concludes, and Brother John steps back to the pulpit, where he asks everyone who brought a Bible to hold it high while he counts them; the number is written on the letterboard for all to see. He then asks for birthdays, and anyone who has had one during the previous week steps to the altar and all sing "Happy Birthday." The offering follows the birthday song: Brother John asks someone (usually Brother Vernie) to pray aloud for the offering, and the deacons pass the collection plates through the congregation while John leads them in a hymn, usually "Amazing Grace." (SINGING:) A period of special-hymn singing is next: soloists, duos, trios, quartets, or quintets sing gospel songs from the pulpit while the congregation listens, seated. (PRAYING:) Brother John steps to the altar and asks if anyone wishes to come forward for prayer to be healed. If someone comes, the deacons anoint the person with oil, and Brother John, standing on the first stair of the altar, places both hands atop the head of the person-prayed-over. He and the deacons then deliver a brief (about 30 seconds) spontaneous healing prayer, each praying a different prayer at the same time. The healing prayer ceremony is usually framed at beginning and end by a quartet—Brother John's sons and their wives (Brothers Donny and Charles, Sisters Pammie and Jeannie)—singing "The Healer" from their hymnal.

(PREACHING:) Following the healing prayer, Brother John steps back to the pulpit, asks the congregation to open their Bibles to the passage God has led him to choose, reads the passage, and then delivers the sermon. At the close of the sermon he asks for a show of hands from those who wish prayer. (PRAYING:) He offers a brief prayer, then invites people to the altar for prayer. (SINGING:) As he gives the altar call, Brother Donny or Sister Bea leads the congregation in an invitational hymn, the words ("Why not tonight?" "Pass me not, O gentle Saviour," etc.) adapted to exhortation. (PRAYING:) If someone steps forward, deacons and ladies of the church come forward to pray with that person; sometimes Brother John prays as well. (TESTIFYING:) The altar call over, Brother John may explain to the church what happened—a soul was saved, someone was restored to the faith, someone drew closer to God—and offer the person a chance to testify to what happened. Brother John steps to the pulpit and asks, "Anybody got a word on your heart?" (TESTIFYING:) Individuals in the congregation stand and testify, one at a time, to what God has done in their lives. The testimony period concluded, Brother John steps to the rear of the sanctuary and asks a member of the congregation to dismiss them in prayer. Following this benediction, Brother John greets all as they pass through the rear door, giving them his blessing as they leave. Some linger awhile outside in fellowship, others leave immediately. It is usually about 12:30 P.M.

The night service differs slightly: Sunday school and the healing prayer are omitted, as are the Bible count and birthday ceremony. More hymns are sung: about five congregational hymns and as many as eight special-hymns. Testimonies are likely to be lengthier. More visitors from the community are likely to appear, as few other churches hold night services, and Brother John welcomes worshipers of other Protestant denominations.

With this order of worship in mind we turn to singing, and to performances that, more than any other, resemble what a visitor would see and hear in a mainline church. The differences, as we shall see, lie below the surface, in intentionality, affect, interpretation and evaluation, and in application of the theory of Spirit-led performance.

5. Singing

"**S**inging," Brother Rastus told me, "is the start of a good service . . . Sing a few pieces, and that kind of gives a man—kind of builds him up in the Lord" (Lam interview, p. 21). As I pointed out in the previous chapter, in the Fellowship Independent Baptist Church the practice of religious language activates the relationship between the worshiper and the divine. In the worship service itself, hymnody marks the beginning of that relationship and opens the channels of communication. A visitor to the Fellowship Independent Baptist Church familiar with mainline Christian practices would not be surprised to see hymn-singing begin the service, but might not be familiar with the theory of language, discussed in Chapter 4, on which it is based.

In this chapter I will explain hymnody as a genre of language in religious practice at the Fellowship Independent Baptist Church, paying most attention to the musical repertory, the social organization of the singing, and the church members' ideas about hymnody. Throughout, I will argue that it is impossible to assess the effect of hymnody without understanding the church members' own interpretation of the act of singing hymns. So, for example, attempts to derive meaning from hymn texts alone must fail. There may be meaning "in the text," but what an outsider to this local religious folklife derives as the meaning "of the text" may well differ from the congregation's understanding.

Characteristically, congregational interpretations of hymnody are themselves performed, as when Brother John tells a story that bears on the meaning of the hymn just sung. Characters and themes in these stories are repeated, as the stories themselves sometimes are, and thus they repose in the collective memory of the congregation. These stories, along with other interpretative remarks from the pulpit, establish the meaning of the hymns. In this congregational context, meaning is personal, local, referential, and memory-based, rather than universal, open, and plain.

Hymnody takes up about one-fourth of the running time of the Sunday morning services, one-third of the Sunday evening services, one-third of the Tuesday night prayer meetings, and three-quarters of the hymn-sings held on Saturday nights once a month. The church members say that they love to worship the Lord in song, and that hymnody, more than any other worship activity, gives them blessings and makes them happy in the Lord.

In the church members' terminology, a religious song is a "hymn" or a "special." A hymn is any sacred song. These statements from Brother John illustrate how the term is used in conversation: "After I got converted, then I went strictly to hymns. I don't sing these old hillbilly songs no more. So we've been singing religious songs now for twenty-five years" (John Sherfey interview, July 17, 1977, pp. 2–3). "Special" is a short form of "special-hymn" and refers to sacred songs that are sung by soloists or small groups in front of a listening congregation or audience. A family gospel duo, trio, or quartet is the most common arrangement for singing specials.

Specials are special in two ways: as a special performance for an audience, and from a special repertory. This repertory consists of two parts: the hymns in the *Church Hymnal* (Hall, ed. 1951), mainly fifty or more years old; and popular gospel songs sung by gospel quartets and professional singing groups. Again, Brother John: "Last night we had the congregational singing, which lasted about thirty minutes, and then after we had prayer, take up the offering and everything, then we had our special singing: in other words, individuals, trios, or what have you, and then go from that into the message [sermon]" (John and Pauline Sherfey interview, December 3, 1979, p. 16).

An overall picture of hymnody in the context of the Sunday morning worship service emerged in Chapter 1. Instead of having a printed program with preselected hymns, the church prefers to let the congregation choose just before singing. Each member selects his or her favorites. I asked Brother Vernie, "Why do you request certain hymns and not others?" He replied, "It just seems like it lifts you up more" (Meadows interview, 1977, p. 16). Brother Allen said, "They really set me off, more or less those few songs it seems like. . . . 'Prayer Bells of Heaven,' and when they get to singing *that,* I mean, it really crawls up my back!" (Dove interview, pp. 16–17). He is describing the affect of a Spiritual blessing.

In 1977 all the music in the Sunday morning service was unaccompanied. A pianist (obligated to a different church on Sunday mornings) accompanied the singing at night. In subsequent years the hymns at both services have been accompanied by piano, folk-style, flat-picked guitar, and, sometimes, banjo played in bluegrass style. The church members prefer to have the hymns accompanied but must depend on whatever musicians are there. They do not maintain a choir or a regular accompanist.

Special-hymn singing by teenagers, 1985.

Social Organization of the Music

Social organization of music is reflected in the divisions among the music-makers, and may be measured by how elaborate and how rigid such distinctions are (Titon, ed. 1984 : 1–9). In Protestant churches, such divisions are reflected in distinctions between choir and congregation, and within the choir between soloists and the rest of the choir. Some churches further divide choirs according to age and gender: the men's choir, the girls' youth choir, and so forth, each choir taking its turn on a different Sunday of the month.

The Fellowship Independent Baptist Church has neither choir nor choir leader. The closest they come during the congregational hymn-singing to separating some singers from the rest occurs in hymns with antiphonal part-singing, and here three or four singers sometimes climb to the pulpit to form a bass section to sing their part. Of course, they have a songleader, Brother John; but otherwise there is no rank ordering among the singers. The social ordering during the congregational singing is, then, comparatively unelaborate—a group undifferentiated as to age and gender, with a leader to guide them. The singers also have the right to select the hymns at the moment of performance, although in practice Brother John chooses about one-third simply by saying, "Let's sing number——," while the rest are requested by number by congregation members. In some ways this social organization suggests the egalitarian society envisioned in heaven: the saints led by their brother, Jesus. The egalitarianism goes further on earth, for the church permits anyone, saved or not, to sing; indeed, they encourage the unsaved to sing along, thinking that the words might help them toward salvation.

The primary social divisions occur as a result of the special-hymns. Not everyone feels able to sing as a soloist or part of a small group before the congregation. Although the church members give anyone who steps forward the chance to sing specials, they do not respond with equal enthusiasm to all comers; and by noting the church members' response to a particular soloist or group an observer can estimate the singer's standing in the church community.

The Saturday-night hymn-sings introduce guest singers, usually professional or semi-professional gospel groups; they are greeted eagerly. These gospel artists sing only after the congregation, led by Brother John, sings about four or five gospel hymns from the *Church Hymnal*. The congregation tries to do its best for the guests, and in so doing puts itself into a happy frame of mind.

The gospel singers, usually with amplified instruments (piano, guitars, bass) and a drum set, as well as a powerful vocal amplifier, make a loud sound in the sanctuary and sing about a dozen of the most popular contemporary gospel hits. Sometimes they sing one or two of the gospel songs that the Sherfeys, Caves, or Hurts regularly sing during the Sunday worship services or on the radio broadcasts, and it is interesting to compare styles; the lyrics usually are identical, but the professional groups use more modern harmonies. They intersperse the songs with testimony from members of their group, usually about their conversion, or the joys of living a Christian life, or the meaning of a particular set of lyrics in the song about to be sung. After they have finished, their leader (or Brother John) makes an altar call to see if anyone will come forward for prayer.

Guest gospel-singers are treated with great respect, but the congregation reserves its most enthusiastic shouts for the pastor and his family when they sing specials. They may not be the most professional of singers, but the congregation loves them best. The congregation lovingly encourages those others such as Sister Hattie or Brother Rastus who are strong, supportive members of the church. They do not sing specials often, but when they do, they get a very positive response. So do the Sherfey grandchildren, Tammy and Denise, in 1977 aged five and eight; and particularly when they sing with their father, Brother Donny. The congregation looks on lovingly and approvingly, knowing that the traditions are being inculcated in the young. By 1985 Denise had begun accompanying the hymns on piano, and she and her sister and father (now playing electric bass) were rehearsing regularly, singing occasionally in neighborhood churches, and contemplating gospel music careers. They are outstanding singers, and if such careers are made on merit they will be successful—if that is what they want.

During the summer of 1977 Brother Belvin and his daughter, Sister Delores, sang in the services and at the radio station on Brother John's program, while Brother John and his family sang on Brother Belvin's program. Brother John and Brother Belvin have been close friends for many years and, like all close friends, have had their differences, but each has respect for the other's strengths and tolerates the other's weaknesses. The congregation responded warmly to Brother Belvin and Sister Delores' specials even though they were not members of the church. But Brother Belvin likes to testify before and after singing and, as a preacher, he might have been led to preach a message right then and there—something which, for a variety of complicated reasons having to do with their friendship, neither Brother John nor Brother Belvin wanted to occur. And so whenever Brother Belvin testified he showed a trace of uneasiness, and the congregation, knowing the situation, did too.

Among the others who sang with some regularity during the summer of 1977 were the Cave Family: Arthur, Welford, Rosalee, and Betty Cave. (Brother Belvin's grandfather was a Cave.) They sang with great feeling and unusual harmonies; but, as they were not well known to most of the people in the congregation, many wondered why they were coming to services. Did they want to join the church? Eventually, they were accepted as friends of Brother Belvin, but they did not join.

Upon occasion still others, apparently known in the community, sang specials, and the congregation seemed a little impatient with them. I guessed that our recording and videotaping might have drawn them out. The response was polite, but not enthusiastic. In this connection I should mention that Brother John eventually prevailed upon Ken and me to sing specials, and that now whenever we return to the church we cannot escape doing it. We refrained at first out of diffidence, thinking that we wanted to maintain our distance and roles as observers, not participants. As we became friends with Brother John, his family, and the members of the congregation, it became impossible to remain apart entirely, and I am

Listening to a professional group sing gospel hymns, 1977. *Left to right:*
Brother Belvin, Brother John, Brother Rastus, Brother Donny.

Singing a special-hymn, 1978. *Left to right:* Missy Owens, Denise Sherfey,
Tammy Sherfey, Brother Donny is partially obscured in background.

sure we caused less interference in the worship service by participating in the singing portion than we would have if we had stood outside the service altogether.

Repertory

A musical repertory is a stock of ready performances, and a music culture's repertory is what most of us think of as "the music itself" (Titon, ed. 1984:5). It consists of six parts: style, genres, texts, composition, transmission, and movement. Style includes everything relating to the way musical sound is organized: scale, melody, harmony, rhythm, meter, voice quality, instrumental tone color, dynamics; and all depend on the music-culture's aesthetics. Together, style and aesthetics create a recognizable sound that a group understands as its own. Genres are the named, standard units of the repertory, such as "song" and its various subdivisions. Each genre has a history. For the members of the Fellowship Independent Baptist Church, important subdivisions include hymn, special-hymn, and altar-call (invitational) hymn. Texts are words, and "the text" refers to the lyrics of any given performance.

Composition concerns the way music enters the repertory: is it composed by individuals or collectively? Is composition the result of human effort, or is it said to be divinely inspired, or even "received" as a gift, passively? Transmission refers to the way the repertory is learned: is there a system of formal instruction, or are songs learned by imitation and example? Is instruction based on books and notation systems or is it given orally? Is music performed from a written score or from memory, or is it improvised? Movement includes the whole range of physical activity accompanying music; that is, music quite literally moves people to sway, shout, weep, and dance; and of course people must move simply to produce music. Material culture of music refers to the tangible, material "things" that a music-culture produces, including musical instruments, devices for reproducing music (stereos, etc.), tune books, method books, even works of documentation, history, and analysis.

The Gospel Hymn

Almost all of the hymns and special-hymns sung at the Fellowship Independent Baptist Church are gospel hymns or gospel songs (the church-members use the terms interchangeably). Gospel hymns, a nineteenth-century development in Protestant hymnody, grew out of the evangelical movement's emphases on emotion, conversion, and the believer's personal relation to Jesus. Gospel hymns represented innovations in both music and lyrics. Whereas the earlier Protestant hymns were written as a succession of verses set to a single melody (e.g., Figure 7, "Sweet Hour of Prayer"), the gospel-hymns exhibit a verse-chorus structure: eight mea-

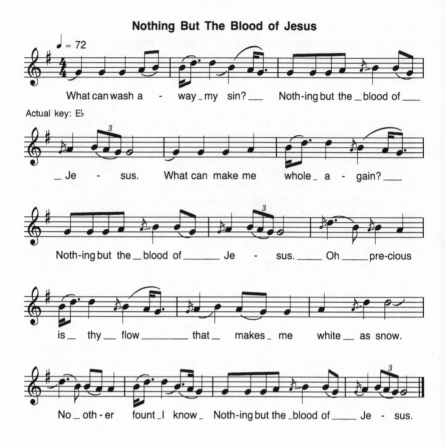

Nothing But The Blood of Jesus

♩ = 72

What can wash a - way _ my sin? ___ Noth-ing but the _ blood of ___

Actual key: E♭

_ Je - sus. What can make me whole _ a - gain? ___

Noth-ing but the _ blood of _____ Je - sus. _____ Oh _____ pre-cious

is _ thy _ flow _____ that _ makes _ me white _ as snow.

No _ oth - er fount _I know _ Noth-ing but the _blood of _____ Je - sus.

sures are given to the verse, followed by eight measures to the chorus, each set to differing melodies. The chorus then alternates with succeeding verses. Figure 24, "Nothing but the Blood," illustrates one typical form of the gospel hymn—including a refrain ("Nothing but the blood of Jesus") after each line of the verse. (It may be heard on the *Powerhouse for God* record album.) The lyrics of most Protestant hymns emphasize God's majesty and mystery, but gospel hymn lyrics are more personal. Usually written to be sung in the first person, they dwell on the felt joys of salvation and emphasize the loving relationship between the Christian and Jesus.

The gospel hymns' immediate forerunners were the folk hymns, camp-meeting songs, and revival songs used mainly in the South during the second Great Awakening (1790–1840), and the hymns associated with professional urban revivalism carried on in the antebellum North (Bruce 1974; Hammond 1974; Foote 1968:168–173). Perhaps even more influential were the midcentury Sunday-school songbooks (Sallee 1978:48).

1. What can wash away my sin?
   Nothing but the blood of Jesus.
   What can make me whole again?
   Nothing but the blood of Jesus.

Cho.   Oh precious is thy flow
   that makes me white as snow;
   no other fount I know,
   nothing but the blood of Jesus.

2. For my pardon this I see:
   nothing but the blood of Jesus.
   For my cleansing this my plea:
Cho.   nothing but the blood of Jesus.

3. Nothing can for sin atone:
   nothing but the blood of Jesus.
   Nought of good that I have done:
   nothing but the blood of Jesus.
Cho.
4. This is all my hope and peace:
   nothing but the blood of Jesus.
   This is all my righteousness:
   nothing but the blood of Jesus.
Cho.

Figure 24. "Nothing but the Blood of Jesus," as sung by John Sherfey, morning service, April 9, 1978, Fellowship Independent Baptist Church, Stanley, Va. Transcribed by author. Lyrics and music by Robert Lowery.

The gospel hymn movement began with Ira Sankey, the songleader, composer, and soloist who joined urban evangelist Dwight L. Moody in 1870. Preaching, exhortation, and prayer had been the chief means of bringing the gospel to the masses in the earlier revivals; Sankey elevated "the gospel song to a position of importance in making converts" (Hammond 1974:56).

Religious conservatives attacked gospel hymnody on the grounds that it was insufficiently solemn for worship. The gospel songwriters answered that evangelism, not worship, was the songs' purpose. As Homer Rodeheaver, one of the more popular gospel songwriters of the early twentieth century argued, "For an atmosphere of decision or action in response to an invitation to accept Christ, we would not be successful with only the great hymns of worship" (Rodeheaver and Ford 1941:21). Rodeheaver continued, quoting John Greenfield on the difference between a hymn and a gospel song: "The hymn is addressed to God. The gospel song is addressed to the people. The hymn is for praise, worship, adoration and prayer. The gospel song, directed to the people, is to warn them of the consequences of sin; give them the promise of liberty, peace, joy and heaven. Through the hymns we may confess our sins to God, claim His mercy and promises, and pledge our loyalty and faithful service. Through the gospel song we can appeal directly to people to do the same thing" (ibid.: 22). Nevertheless, most historians of Protestant hymnody have regarded the gospel song as an inferior product. Henry Wilder Foote, for example, in *Three Centuries of American Hymnody,* declared that gospel songs were excessively sentimental and that they repelled the more "intelligent" Christians. Adequate to the task of soul-winning, gospel songs were inappropriate for worship (1968: 266).

But because the Fellowship Independent Baptist Church's worship service is strongly evangelistic and is modeled upon the revival—the invitation at the close of the sermon is the climax of the meeting—gospel hymns are perfectly appropriate for the unconverted in attendance. And for the converts? Gospel songs are fitting for them as well. Their meaning lies not in the beauty and solemnity of the occasion but in the emotions that their performance engenders in the singers. This is not poetry; it is language performed in religious practice within a community. The performance affects and blesses the converts, and even if the texts suggest otherwise, they understand their act of singing as an act of praise and worship. What is more, they grew up hearing these hymns from their parents and other kinfolk. In other words, these gospel hymns reside in the church members' memories and link the present with the past, calling up the tremendous emotions associated with childhood and family life in the days when they were mountain farmers, and pointing toward the family-based heavenly homecoming. The hymns are thus a case in point of the deliberate use of tradition, and in this setting they are suitable and effective.

Gospel hymn tunes from Sankey's time onward—and there have been thousands of gospel hymn composers, making this one of the most widespread genres of the past century—imitate Anglo-American folk and popular music. (African-American gospel song is a later and different phenomenon.) Gospel hymn tunes almost always use the major scale. Harmonies are simple, confined chiefly to the tonic, the subdominant, and the dominant. (The secondary dominant has been used increasingly in the past fifty years.) Gospel hymn harmonies seldom change except at phrase beginnings and cadences. Tempos are usually lively, rhythms are strong and emphatic, syncopation and antiphony are employed, and a range of metrical schemes, including 6/8 and 9/8, keep the singers' interest. Gospel hymn melodies are relatively easy for most Americans to learn and remember by ear. Congregations ordinarily sing them in unison even when the tunebooks set them in four-part harmony.

The Fellowship Independent Baptist Church's repertory of congregational hymns is contained in their *Church Hymnal,* published in Cleveland, Tennessee, by the Tennessee Music and Printing Company and copyrighted in 1951. It contains texts and shape-note tunes (there is also a round-note version) in simple four-part polyphony, with the main melody given to the uppermost (soprano) part. A majority have antiphonal call-and-response part-singing in the choruses. Despite the polyphonic arrangements in the hymnal, the church members sing chiefly in unison, and when they add harmony they do not follow the hymnal but, as Terry Miller observed, generate "a folk harmony of thirdless chords and non-standard cadences that mark the southern fasola shape-note songbooks rather than the Gospel hymn" (1983:392).

The *Church Hymnal* was edited by Connor Hall, now head of the Church of God Publishing House in Cleveland, Tennessee. Interviewed by Charles Wolfe, Hall said that it was meant to be an interdenominational hymnal featuring the old-time hymns and aimed at rural southern churches. I have seen it in use as far north as Detroit, among out-migrated southerners. When the new Baptist official hymnal was published in 1975, its repertory and high price upset many rural Baptists in the South, and they switched to Hall's *Church Hymnal* (Charles Wolfe, personal communication, February 21, 1983). The *Church Hymnal* contains hymns only. It is a songbook, not a prayer book. If it contained prayers and responsive readings and suggestions for the liturgy it would not have been adopted by the Fellowship Independent Baptist Church and like-minded congregations, for not only do prayer books reek of officialdom, they are considered man-made, and could not yield a Spirit-led liturgy at the moment of performance.

I kept track of all the congregational hymns sung in fifteen worship services and hymn-sings at the church over an eight-week period during the summer of 1977. The congregation sang a total of 104 times in the fifteen services observed, singing forty-nine hymns once only and twenty-one hymns two or more times. Naming those sung more than once gives a survey of their favorites: "Amazing Grace" and "Sweet Hour of Prayer" five times each; "Fill My Way with Love" four times; "An Old Account Settled," "The Great Reaping Day," "I Will Never Turn Back," "When God Dips His Love into My Heart," and "I'll Fly Away" three times; and the following twice each: "I Need the Prayers," "I Must Tell Jesus," "More about Jesus," "Leave It There," "Heaven's Jubilee," "I'm Going That Way," "I'm Going Thru, Jesus," "Prayer-Bells of Heaven," "The Unclouded Day," "We'll Soon Be Done with Troubles and Trials," "When the Redeemed Are Gathering In," "Why Not Tonight," and "The Life-Boat." These twenty-one plus the forty-five sung once each do not exhaust the active repertory of congregational hymns, which I estimated at about one hundred of the four hundred the hymnal contains. The meaning and significance of the texts are discussed below under "Texts." It is worth emphasizing that this active repertory is not coextensive with the hymnal repertory, but is only a portion of it, and that no meaningful study of this church's hymn repertory could be made by a content analysis of the hymnal in its entirety. Field observation was essential.

The special-hymn repertory includes the songs in the *Church Hymnal* but is not confined to it. Specials give soloists and groups an opportunity to sing the recently composed religious songs popular on records or radio. In churches like the Fellowship Independent Baptist Church throughout the South, family groups sing religious songs for both pleasure and worship. Some of these groups have professional aspirations, while others are happy to provide a little professionalism in the church where they worship. These groups are more likely to sing gospel songs outside of the *Church Hymnal* repertory. Many (the Caves and Sherfeys, for example) keep their own repertory of specials in a loose-leaf notebook, and read the words to refresh their memories as they sing. A soloist who performs infrequently is more likely to choose an old favorite from the *Church Hymnal*. The Sherfeys (particularly Brother John) also love to sing these older favorites; and about a third of their specials can be found in the hymnal.

Style

The gospel hymns in the *Church Hymnal* conform, in their printed arrangements, to the above description, but the church members' practice differs from the hymnal in important ways. First, as I mentioned, they do not sing every hymn in the hymnal, but only perhaps one-fourth of them. The main reason is that certain hymns are favorites; in addition, Brother John, the songleader, does not know the tunes for all the hymns and cannot sight-read tunes from the hymnal. The favorite hymns, then, make up the repertory; and it is to them that I will look when I examine the meaning of the texts. Second, the congregation usually sings in unison, but some members try to keep harmony, and when they do, it is not the conventional harmony printed in the hymnal (like Brother John, they cannot sight-read tunes) but the unconventional harmony of the nineteenth-century shape-note tunebooks with its open cadences, parallel fifths, and so forth. This folk hymn harmony has been the subject of considerable musicological attention (see, e.g., Seeger 1977; Horn 1970; Jackson 1965; Tallmadge 1984) and does not require elaboration here. Third, the melodies themselves are not sung as printed in the hymnal but, rather, as they have been passed along in oral tradition. This melodic practice characterizes much of the old-time folksinging in the southern Appalachians, and is traceable to British practice—indeed, it can be found today among folksingers in the British Isles. Brother John's use of it can be seen by comparing transcriptions of the way he sings "I Must Tell Jesus" and "Sweet Hour of Prayer" with the way they appear in the hymnal (Figures 5 and 7).

First, the hymnal melody for "Sweet Hour of Prayer" is diatonic, but the melody Brother John sings is pentatonic. Where the melody as written employs the fourth and seventh degrees (measures 2, 17, and 21 of Figure 7), John repeats the previous pitch (third or octave) and completely avoids the fourth and seventh. Investigating Anglo-American folksingers' twentieth-century recorded versions of nineteenth-century popular music, Norm and Anne Cohen found general tendencies toward pentatonic melodies (Cohen and Cohen 1973). Second, Brother John sings a great many "extra" notes that do not appear in the written version. (Cf. Jackson 1965: 212, who speaks of "the scoop or slide, made use of in negotiating big or little intervals.") These appear both before and after the beat, and sometimes on the beat itself (e.g., in the pickup measure the C is an extra note and comes on the beat). Before the beat they sound like grace notes (e.g., the movement from A to C' in measures 3 and 12, or from G to C' in measures 17 and 21); after the beat they seem to become part of the melody (e.g., measures 4 and 12); and on the beat they actually do become part of the melody.

"Sweet Hour of Prayer" is a rather straightforward example of Brother John's melodic changes. "I Must Tell Jesus" offers greater elaboration and a further principle. Compare the hymnal melody with the transcription of Brother John's singing in measure 2. Borrowing a little time from the end of the first G, he sings a rapid three-note figure that ends on F, the pitch of the next important note. Similarly, in the next measure: he borrows from the C and sings a rapid two-note figure that ends on F, the pitch of the next important note. Not all his melodic elaborations end by anticipating the pitch of the next important note, as these do: the figure that ends measure 3 goes a bit below the note to follow, and so does the figure that ends the first beat of measure 15. Yet the vast majority of his elaborating figures here either descend, ascend, or turn stepwise and end at the same pitch as the note that follows on the downbeat, and this is the further principle of his melodic alterations. While some of those alterations may be understood as grace and double grace notes corresponding to ornaments in European art music tradition, it is arguable whether the correspondence is derived or accidental. In fact, most of the melodic alterations do not so correspond. Instead, it seems as if the operative principle is to break up the large skip by inserting scalar steps along the way. Consider the opening of "Amazing Grace" (Figure 12) for further evidence.

Brother John's wife also sings in this elaborated manner, as do some of the other church members; but most—including Brother John's children—do not elaborate the melody, instead singing the hymnal version or a pentatonic variant of it. It would appear, then, that Brother John's way of singing belongs to an older tradition, and indeed it does. How far back does it go?

The tendency to pentatonicize the melodies goes back at least to the revival hymns and camp-meeting spirituals of the second Great Awakening (1790–1840) where such melody-making was the rule. Melodic alteration typified several earlier hymn traditions, and we may suppose it has come down to Brother John and other singers like him. The earliest eighteenth-century hymns of the Wesleys (1746, *Hymns on the Great Festivals and Other Occasions*) were set to tunes with some melodic embellishments like Brother John's. Gilbert Chase prints one such setting, adding that the florid ornamentation was a concession to the then-current practice (Chase 1955: 48–49). However, this eighteenth-century setting contains trills, appoggiaturas, and other ornaments conspicuously absent from Brother John's singing and, on the whole, represents a cultivated European tradition.

It is more likely that Brother John's way with melody derives from a tradition of psalm singing that survives in the hymns of the Primitive Baptists and the Old Regular Baptists in Eastern Kentucky and western North Carolina (Tallmadge 1975; *Primitive Baptist Hymns of the Blue Ridge* 1982). This tradition, known as the "common way" or the "old way" of singing, may be traced to New England in the seventeenth and eighteenth centuries (Chase 1955:3–40), and prior to that to the sixteenth-century English parish church. As Nicholas Temperley has observed,

> The beginnings of the Old Way of Singing can be traced to the Reformation, when for the first time congregations were invited to sing in worship, in a style derived from the secular folksongs of the time. In those churches of the Reformed [i.e., as opposed to Lutheran] persuasion which banished organs and instruments [that played the role of coordinating the singing] from worship (which means largely, but not exclusively, those of the British Isles and colonies) metrical psalmody gradually diverged from instrumentally accompanied secular song, losing the lively [secular folksong] rhythms of the early psalm tunes and becoming extremely slow. (Temperley 1979a:1)

This "old way" of singing was quite distinctive in its lack of coordination; because of its slowness and the absence of a pulse beat, songleader, or instrumental accompaniment, the singers diverged from one another's melody, and the resulting heterophony sounded as if the singers were out of step, some ahead, others behind. Moreover, because of the length of time (two or more seconds) for each note, additional notes were inserted. Temperley describes the result:

> The principal notes of the tune always begin where they are supposed to begin—on the beat; any additional notes occur between beats, and they consist largely of stepwise connecting notes. Often they form a simple scale linking one note of the tune to the next; but sometimes they go beyond the next note and return to it. Conspicuously absent are the . . . ornaments characteristic of eighteenth-century art music, which begin on the

upper note and delay the main note until after the beat. (Temperley 1979b:94)

This is a good description of the principles of Brother John's melodic alterations. Temperley believes that this singing style was not the result of deliberate artistic embellishment but, rather, the effect of "less-confident singers following the leaders from note to note" (Temperley 1979a:1).

The tunes were ordinarily transmitted by ear alone. This must mean that in any congregation some singers knew the tunes well, while others younger or less confident had to follow as best they could. At any point in the tune the next note would be sung first by the experienced singers; the rest would then copy them, but would vary in the amount of time they took to reach the new note. Some of the less musical would raise or lower their voices gradually towards the new note, stopping only when they were aware of being in tune with it; occasionally they might even overshoot it. By the time the laggards had got there, the leaders might already have moved on. . . . As long as reasonable order was preserved, however, the principal effect would be of people sliding gradually, and in their own times, from one note of the tune to the next. (Temperley 1979b:94–95)

If this accounts for the origin of Brother John's melodic alterations, what accounts for their transmission to him and for their persistence in gospel hymnody? As these are not deliberate embellishments—Brother John does not employ them consciously—it is most likely that he inherited the style from earlier generations, particularly from his father (see below under "Transmission"). No doubt the old way of singing was much more prevalent in the rural South in the nineteenth century, when the Old School (today Primitive) Baptists were more numerous and influential. Why the style persists in gospel hymnody in those regions of the South where the old way antedated it may be explained easily enough by inheritance through oral tradition. At the same time, the style has been invigorated by commercial bluegrass singing, including bluegrass gospel songs, where these practices of melodic embellishments and some harmonies that date back to the practices of the nineteenth-century Southern shapenote tradition have kept the music in the air and on the media where it continues to influence Appalachian singers.

Composition

The church members believe that all authentic hymns originate from God. Hymns, like all other sacred language, are God-given, and the human "composer" of a hymn is but a mouthpiece for the Lord. All of the hymns in the church's active repertory for worship services (including congregational hymns from the *Church Hymnal* and special-hymns) during the summer of 1977 were composed by songwriters outside the congregation.

The church members acknowledge that some of the human composers have testified to being in the Spirit when writing them, but the blessings received when singing them are taken as the proof that the words are indeed inspired.

One member of the congregation, Brother Belvin, received a hymn from the Lord while driving a schoolbus (see Titon 1980b). His account of this event deserves close attention. It shows how the process of musical inspiration is understood to operate. His description of the song and how it came to him, as well as the text and tune of the song itself, is transcribed here verbatim from my field tapes:

HURT: Made it going along on the bus, on the schoolbus.

TITON: How did that come to you?

HURT: I was just riding along and I was just so glad and happy that the Lord saved me, and knowed I was saved and wholly acceptable unto the Lord Jesus Christ. Just the song came to me, said, "Sing it," and I just started to humming and a-going on. Some of the big boys and girls on there said, "I heard you hum and sing. Heard your singing." I said, "Well, I just sing when I get happy." So I just pulled off beside the road and just jotted her down the best I could, which I couldn't spell my words exactly right and everything, but the girl [Brother Belvin's daughter] knows what was meant, and she went ahead and wrote it down.

TITON: Were there kids on the bus?

HURT: Mm-hmm.

TITON: So you pulled right over to the side of the road?

HURT: No, no, no [laughs]. When I was coming home. I just had it in my mind, and I didn't want to forget it, and I didn't want it to get away from me. And I just got down some of it, and then when I got home, why, I just let her start writing it, as I give it to her, and then after I had her copy once. She went ahead and put it down. Fell right in its place.

TITON: Did that work any differently from the way a sermon works, or was it—

HURT: A little bit, yeah, yeah, a little bit, it worked a little different, but anyhow it was the Spirit leading.

TITON: How was it different?

HURT: It was just, well, I can't hardly explain it, how good that it was to me. And it just filled my heart with melody from the Lord Jesus Christ. And just sing and felt the good power of the Lord through the song, and without anointment to preach—and so that's, that was just a little different there. But it's just about the same thing, anointment of the Spirit. It's just, just happiness.

TITON: What about the words?

HURT: I just, I just, well they just came to me, just come out to me, just

Brother Belvin at home, 1977.

like preaching from the Bible, just speaking. Just reading the Bible. And the good word come to me.

TITON: You mean like after reading the Bible, or like reading it?

HURT: Just reading, just like reading it. Just fell right in place, each word, just as plain as it could be.

I got that somewhere. I see it laying here, I thought, somewhere. I don't know. [*Pause.*] Here it lays.

TITON: Could you sing it?

HURT: [*Shows Titon the paper with the song's words typed on it.*] That's what come to me. [*Calls to his daughter in the next room:*] Delores? Come here. [*Speaks to Titon:*] She's my leader, she leads my singing. [*Delores enters and both sing, reading the words from the paper:*]

"He Brightened My Soul and He Made Me Whole"

1.   Since I found Jesus and he showed me the way.
2.   Now I am so glad that I can say so,
     That Jesus brightened my soul and he made me whole.
     We're tempted and tried in this world below,
     Since he brightened my soul and he made me whole.
     Now I can see the smile of the angel,
     Since he brightened my soul and he made me whole.
3.   Now I know that there's no use for sinners to say so,
     For he'll brighten their soul and he'll make them whole.
     Now I will see Jesus on the great judgment morning,
     Since he brightened my soul and he made me whole.
     Now Jesus will carry my burdens on through the portal,
     For he brightened my soul and he'll make you whole.
4.   And I found Jesus and he showed me the way.

A few comments on the structure of the song (Figure 25) are in order. It is unusual in that it is built on two-line textual units which together occupy five measures. The first lines of these two-line units introduce new words, while the second lines comprise a refrain containing the words, "He brightened my soul and he made me whole" or some close variant of it. In addition, this song exhibits a brief, one-line, three-measure introduction and a similar conclusion which, taken together, act as a framing device for the text and tune and which, again, is an unusual structure in Anglo-American gospel hymnody.

Figure 25. "He Brightened My Soul and He Made Me Whole," as sung (in octaves) by Belvin and Delores Hurt, at the author's request, in their home, Etlan, Madison County, Va., August 11, 1977. Transcribed by author. Lyrics and music © Belvin Hurt, reprinted by permission.

The theme of the text, on the other hand, with its emphasis upon the felt joy of salvation, is typical. The special attention to "soul-brightening" (or "cleaning," as Brother Belvin later interpreted it for me) is noteworthy in the context of Brother Belvin's personal beliefs for, unlike most of the church members, he is a "perfectionist"; that is, he believes it is possible for the Christian to become perfect and sinless in this walk of life. While perfectionism is a sine qua non of Pentecostal belief, Brother Belvin's is derived from Methodism, which traditionally had this strain within it.

The awkwardness of Brother Belvin's song (the odd structure, shifts of musical meter to accommodate the metrical eccentricity of the lyrics, the occasional absence of rhyme) suggests an amateur composition, but it is also consistent with the composition process as Brother Belvin described it: namely, that it was felt to be a message from the Lord, and that it was written down without revision.

Throughout the composition process, Brother Belvin played a passive role, he believes. "Just the song came to me, said, 'Sing it,'" he recalls, feeling that he had been commanded to sing by the force which "said" he should sing it, a force that he separates from the "I" that "just started to humming and a-going on." He was separated from the world, "out of it," but he was not embarrassed when the older children asked him about it; in fact he was proud: "I just sing when I get happy," he told them. We have a further clue to Brother Belvin's view of the composition process in his reiteration of the idea that the words of the song "just fell right in place." He did not have the sensation of active composition, of working his way by trial and error, thought and revision, toward the final product. Instead, he received it whole. At once, he felt, it was "just as plain as could be," having about it the same kind of authority as the Holy Scriptures.

I would like to be able to say that this song took its place in the musical repertory of the Fellowship Independent Baptist Church but, for reasons not known to me, I never heard Brother Belvin and his daughter sing it outside of that one performance in their living room. That performance, too, was hesitant, and suggests that they did not have the song in their own active repertory at the time.

In the fall of 1985 Brother John and other church members performed a small number of songs of their own composition, and one woman read a few religious poems that she had received.

Transmission

The church members learn the repertory of gospel hymns by imitation and example. Most are literate but none can sight-read music well, though Brother John and Brother Rastus understand the notation. The few who are illiterate memorize the texts; the others sing the texts from the hymnal and make no effort to memorize them, though some texts become memorized through frequent performance. Brother John, for example, likes to have the congregation sing a hymn that most people have memorized when it comes time to take up the collection. Hymns like "Amazing Grace," which most know by heart, allow them to reach into their pockets while they continue singing. Learning a new hymn consists chiefly of learning the tune and how to fit the lyrics to it. New church members catch the tunes from Brother John and the rest. Occasionally a member of the congregation requests a hymn that Brother John doesn't know, and he asks the person who requested it to lead it. I have never seen anyone agree and come to the front to lead the hymn on such an occasion, but I am sure the opportunity is genuine.

Some of the church members, particularly those who sing specials, have backgrounds that include amateur secular singing of some sort; a few others attended the singing schools that once flourished in the mountains (see Stanley 1982; Wolfe 1982). Brother Rastus recalled attending a singing school at Jollett in the late 1920s or early 1930s. Henry Garrison, from Charlottesville, was the schoolmaster; he taught using the four-shape shape-note system (notes shaped as diamonds, triangles, circles, and squares to indicate pitch), an alternative system of notation developed in New England late in the eighteenth century that passed into tradition and was widely used by itinerant music masters in the South in the nineteenth and early twentieth centuries (see Chase 1955). Garrison was able to keep this school in operation for a few weeks in each of two or three successive years. "A lot of us joined [Mr. Garrison] and got so we could sing notes," said Brother Rastus. "See a new piece, we could just go right ahead and sing over the notes and then sing the words. We'd gather there, maybe a couple of times through the week and practice singing" (Lam interview, p. 12).

Brother Rastus was unconverted at the time, but he enjoyed singing gospel songs and with about fifteen other scholars who learned to sing the new gospel songs (special-hymns) printed in the dozens of songbooks that were issued every year for rural hymnodists and singing conventions, he formed a gospel group that was paid expenses to travel (in the back of a pickup truck) to Harrisonburg, Waynesboro, and other neighboring towns to sing in churches. "But you know something: [if] you don't practice along thataway, it kind of gets away from you," Rastus continued. "And after I got married and moved away from all my people around over there [near Jollett] we didn't get together to practice on it much. And of course I know the notes yet but I can't read music good like I did at that time" (ibid., pp. 12–13).

As a young boy Brother Rastus learned to play the guitar, fiddle, and banjo. His older brothers bought instruments with money they received for picking apples, and he learned from them and from his father, who played fiddle left-handed. (Brother Rastus learned to play right-handed, however.) He learned fiddle tunes like "Soldier's Joy" and "Liza Jane" and played for dances near Elkton in the 1920s and 1930s; his best instrument, however, was guitar, and in 1977 he kept an old Gibson guitar at the church even though he seldom played it, and then only to accompany gospel hymns. Brother Rastus abandoned secular music for social and religious reasons:

> I got rid of my fiddle and banjo. . . . I don't know why that I laid it down, as good as I loved to play. I just, after I got older I didn't take the interest in it that I did when I was young. . . . I don't take no interest at all in it, since I started out to live for the Lord. . . . They ain't no good much goes on at a dance, you know. The Bible tells you to withdraw yourself from all appearance of evil, and that's mostly the kind of people what's got a bottle with 'em, you know, or something like that at a dance, which I used to [have]. Like I tell you, things I used to enjoy, why, I don't got no desire to do it no more. (Ibid., pp. 11–13, 32–35)

Like Brother Rastus, Brother John showed musical ability and had an amateur interest in singing before he was converted.

> I started singing when I was a boy, and I think really I picked up a lot of it from my daddy. He was a songleader at Howard's Creek Baptist Church, in North Carolina, and he took me to church when I was small. I'd set and watch him lead the singing, you know. And of course as time grew on and I got older, why, I began to pick up the tunes of the gospel songs. And then in later years when I got to be about fourteen years old I wanted to pick a guitar. So my brother had one, and I'd slip his guitar, beat on it. And the first song I ever learned to play was "Going Down the Road Feeling Bad."
>
> Well, of course I wasn't too good of a singer at that time. It was hard for me to carry the tune, but I kept practicing, kept playing. And then me and my wife, we got to singing together [after getting married at age seventeen]. And of course me picking the guitar and singing them old hillbilly songs, country music, boys would come in from all around, and we'd just set up a lot of times till way after midnight and sing and play music. And we had a good time. And of course we weren't singing religious songs, because I wasn't saved at that time. And yet, through this, we just learned to do it, I guess. (John Sherfey interview, July 17, 1977, pp. 1–2)

Brother John learned songs from hearing others sing them in person and on records and radio when he was a young man.

> Back when I was a boy we couldn't afford cars or bicycles or anything to go [out on Saturday nights], so my daddy and my oldest brother went to Bristol and they bought one of these old-timey radios. Course then it was new. . . .
> And of course the *Grand Old Opry* was our pride and joy. Mother would bake a cake and we'd lay there and listen to the *Grand Old Opry* and it

didn't go off till one o'clock in the morning. So we'd lay on the floor, and kick our heels and listen to Uncle Dave Macon and all of them fellows, the Fruit Jar Drinkers, and all of it, you know. And it was just a lot of fun. We was there, just the family. Of course a great big family of us, and we just had a great time together. (Sherfey interview, August 4, 1977, p. 1)

Brother John remembers his father's singing from this period the best, however. Among his favorite hymns were "Rock of Ages," "When the Roll Is Called Up Yonder," "Sweet Hour of Prayer," "The Unclouded Day," "Amazing Grace," "What a Friend We Have in Jesus," and "Nearer, My God, to Thee." Brother John noted, also, that his father played the banjo in frailing or clawhammer style. "And he was a good singer, and he used to pick a banjo, and he'd set on the porch, you know, when he wasn't in church, of the nighttimes, he'd get that old banjo down, and he'd play and sing gospel tunes, and of course we learned of lot of that from him" (John Sherfey interview, July 17, 1977, p. 4).

Shortly after John and Pauline were married they bought a wind-up, spring-motorized record player and learned country songs from the records. They learned some hymns as well.

Then of course as years went by, why, we started singing hymns, and, you know, just pick up a hymn and sing it. Of course we used the book to sing that by, and you notice I have to use a book yet. Now "Amazing Grace," I know that by heart . . . but [for] most of 'em I depend on the hymnbook. I went to church and I'd sing hymns, but yet when we'd get to singing I'd sing anything. Because I wasn't converted. But after twenty-five years ago, after I got converted, then I went strictly to hymns. I don't sing these old hillbilly songs no more. (Ibid., pp. 2–3)

When Brother John was about fourteen years old he attended a shape-note singing school like the one Brother Rastus attended. He went for a total of three nights and in that period learned to read music, but did not learn to sight-sing.

I learned the notes: alto, soprano, and the tenor, and the bass. I know them. I know which part is to come in, and—. But you see, like some men do, do so re mi fa sa lo do, I can't do that, you know. They can take a book and go over the notes and then sing any song they want to. But I can't do that. Now after I hear it sung, then I grasp the tune and I go from there, see. It's not hard once you learn it. (Ibid., p. 3)

Brother John knows the tunes to perhaps two-thirds of the hymns in the *Church Hymnal*. His personal repertory includes a great many of the older gospel hymns popular since the nineteenth century as well as several of the more modern ones introduced for the singing schools, singing conventions, gospel quartets, and church services during the twentieth century, all learned from various sources: oral tradition, radio, and recordings. "Preaching by the Roadside" (Figure 25; it may be heard on the *Powerhouse for God* album) is one of the special-hymns he and his wife learned orally. They heard it from the singing of a man named Henry Barker and his wife in Morrison City, Virginia, near Kingsport, Tennessee.

> I used to go, back when I first started preaching, and him and his wife would sing this song at the State Line Mission, right where Kingsport, Tennessee, and the Virginia line met. They had a church there and they called it the State Line Mission. And I had an appointment there every fourth Sunday in each month. Him and his wife would come there, and they were two of the sweetest people I ever saw. And they sung that song so much, "Preaching by the Roadside," and I learned it by heart. (Ibid., pp. 12–13)

When he sings special-hymns with his wife and children, however, he prefers to choose the more modern pieces, particularly from among recently popular gospel hits on radio or record. Once one of them decides to learn a hymn, he or she picks up the tune orally; then Brother John tries to get the published sheet music for the lyrics, or they buy the record and Sister Jeannie copies down the lyrics. "I guess there must be some reasons why you choose certain songs and not others?" I asked.

> Well, it's more or less what we like, I think, and what I think the public would like . . . I mean a lot of times maybe I like a song but my children, they don't care about it. Well, if they don't care about it, then I try to leave that one off, because if they don't like a song [they] can't sing it too good. You've got to have that feeling for it, you know, and then you can sing it. And that's the way we've sung. Of course the children and myself, we just sung at home, and at church, and that's how we got together the way we did. (Ibid., p. 4)

Texts

The church members say that the texts (words) are the most important aspect of the hymns they sing. The meaning of the lyrics registers in the mind, resonates in memory, and "lifts up" (activates) the indwelling Spirit. Singing, the church community generates the power to experience the Spirit. Brother Vernie explained:

> BROTHER VERNIE: Well, I think singing really revives you up, you know. . . . It just seems like it lifts you up more [than other forms of worship].
> TITON: What is it that lifts you up?
> BROTHER VERNIE: Well, it's just the Spirit in it, that it's sung in.
> TITON: Could you be lifted up by a song without any words?

Sister Pauline and Brother John Sherfey singing "Preaching by the Road-side," 1977.

Preaching by the Roadside

Figure 26. "Preaching by the Roadside," as sung by John and Pauline Sherfey, July 3, 1977, Fellowship Independent Baptist Church, Stanley, Va. Transcribed by author.

youʼll find _____ me, ___ yes, youʼll _ find _____ me.

Some-where _ in ___ glo - ry youʼll find ____ me _____

sing - ing and _ shout ___ ing in e - ter - ni - ty.

1. Preaching by the roadside, under a tree,
    folks come along and make a mock of me.
    They say weʼre crazy, soon weʼll meet our fate;
    but now weʼve churches in every state.

Cho.   Somewhere in glory youʼll find me,
        youʼll find me, yes, youʼll find me.
        Somewhere in glory youʼll find me,
        singing and shouting in eternity.

2. Some folks wonʼt own us, turn us away
    Weʼd give all this world just to hear Jesus say,
    "You have been good and faithful, too;
    so come right on in, thereʼs a mansion for you."

Cho.

3. While I am resting beneath the sod,
    my home is ready at the right hand of God.
    The angels are holding my robe and crown,
    while Gabriel is ready, trumpet to sound.

Cho.

4. If you donʼt see me [when] you enter the door,
    just keep right on searching, over the shore.
    Iʼll be there watching, waiting for you,
    so come right on in shouting, praising God too.

Cho.

BROTHER VERNIE: . . . You mean a song with just the music? No, it don't do me no good. (Meadows interview, 1977, p. 16)

In performance, some hymns have more power to affect the members of the congregation than others; these become their favorites. "Some I like better than I do others," Brother Vernie added (ibid.). Affective potential is stored in the texts.

Emphasis on affect orients interpretation toward listener response. In a series of cross-cultural studies of folksong, Alan Lomax maintained that compared with other communicative forms, music is especially redundant; that is, folk music presents information familiar to the group. The folk musician is not interested in the new, the untried, and the untested; rather, by presenting and re-presenting what is known, folksong is a form of cultural validation (Lomax 1968). A more recent study affirms that "A song, hedged by the demands of unity and clarity, must say things that are simplifications, and generally familiar simplifications" (Booth 1981:13). If song texts are simple, it would seem to follow that their meaning is accessible to relatively unsophisticated kinds of thematic analysis. Certainly, writers intend hymn texts to be plain.

In a pioneering work on the meaning of Victorian hymn texts, *Gospel Hymns and Social Religion,* Sandra S. Sizer developed a method of textual content analysis and applied it to Ira Sankey's *Gospel Hymns Nos. 1–6 Complete* (1895), the most important nineteenth-century gospel hymn collection. It will be useful to apply the same content analysis to the Fellowship Independent Baptist Church's favorite congregational hymns, to show similarities (there is an overlay of Victorian religious sentiment) and important differences (we are dealing with a twentieth-century rural, working-class, southern phenomenon, not a nineteenth-century urban, middle-class, northern one). The differences are interesting because the congregation's repertoire is an emphasis selected from the limited range of textual possibilities afforded by the total gospel hymn repertoire. Simply put, the texts in Sizer's sample emphasize safety and control of the emotions; those in the sample under consideration here emphasize joy, emotional release, and rapture.

Sizer examines the content of more than six hundred lyrics from Ira Sankey's *Gospel Hymns.* She observes that the texts are built on a dualistic opposition between sin and salvation. This dualism characterizes the hymns in the Fellowship Independent Baptist Church's *Church Hymnal* and in the selected repertoire that they sing from that hymnal as well. On one side are the world, the flesh, and the devil; on the other are the church, the Christian soul, and God. She writes:

Generally, dualism between "the world" and heaven or Jesus is articulated primarily by means of seven sets of contrasts: (1) negative versus positive emotions, as in joy/sorrow, love/fear; (2) turmoil versus rest, as in a stormy

sea versus a safe harbor, or wandering in the wilderness versus arriving
home; (3) weakness versus strength, as in the sick being healed or burdens
being lifted; (4) darkness versus light, as in night/day, shadows/sunshine;
(5) battle versus victory; (6) purity versus impurity, as when the sinner is
"washed white as snow"; and (7) guilt versus atonement, as when the
debtor's debt is paid by Jesus, the rebel is forgiven. (Sizer 1978:25)

Sizer also examines the themes in the hymn texts. "Theme is under-
stood simply as the answer to the question, 'What is this hymn about?'
The answers might be, 'Christ's sacrifice,' 'God's kingship,' 'the beauty of
Jesus,' 'the glories of heaven,' or 'the pilgrimage of the Christian'" (ibid.).
In an Appendix, she lists the themes and compares their frequency in certain representative hymnals, including Isaac Watts' *Hymns and Spiritual
Songs* (1707–1709, representative of hymns), John Wesley's *Collection* of
1780, and, of course, Sankey's *Gospel Hymns Nos. 1–6 Complete*. Looking
at the gospel hymns in the Fellowship Independent Baptist Church's
Church Hymnal as a whole, I found their thematic frequencies to correspond rather closely to those in the Sankey collection. But when I tabulated
the themes from the portion of the hymnal the church members sang more
than once—their favorites—I found a different emphasis. To Sizer's figures
I added a final column with the themes of their favorites (Table 13).

Looking at Table 13, one might conclude that the church members
choose to sing more often about the Christian pilgrimage and about heaven,
and less about Jesus, than those indicated in Sizer's sample. In fact, however, they sing about Jesus often, but usually in one of a hymn's subsidiary
themes, not its main theme. This led me to consider subsidiary as well as
main themes among the Fellowship Independent Baptist Church congregation's favorites, and to move somewhat outside Sizer's categories to
create others. Counting main and subsidiary themes—three or four in
each hymn text—I prepared Table 14.

The church members' emphasis on heaven is even clearer in the themes
of the special-hymns. Whereas the *Church Hymnal* repertory is bounded
between the covers of the book, the special-hymn repertory is far larger,
potentially consisting of tens of thousands of gospel songs penned by untrained and professional songwriters over the past hundred years. The radio, recording, and sheet music industries make these available as popular
songs. Family groups that sing specials choose from this wider repertory,
and it is particularly significant that almost all of the songs the church
members choose have heaven as their major theme. Heaven is often called
"home," forging the familiar link:

I'm going home some day to a city far away,
Friends and loved ones will be waiting on the shore . . .

                                          ("Some Day I'm Going Home")

TABLE 13. Relative frequency of hymn themes, various hymnals and
Fellowship Independent Baptist Church favorite hymns, summer 1977

Theme	Watts (%)	Wesley (%)	Sankey (%)	FIBC (%)
God: creator, holy, powerful	20	9.1	0.5	4
God/Jesus: conqueror-king	6	3.6	1	0
Repentance, atonement, damnation; Jesus a mediator	38	16.3	3.8	8
Grace; salvation	4	18.2	15.8	16
Jesus: refuge, guide, helper	8	9.1	14.8	4
Jesus: healer	0	3.6	1.1	8
Jesus: loving and beloved	8	14.5	17.4	0
Heaven	4	1.8	15.6	32
Christian pilgrimage	0	1.8	4.2	16
Mission, service	2	1.8	6.7	0
Christian fellowship and joy	2	1.8	0.2	4
Battle, storm	2	1.8	5.7	0
Jesus: suffering	2	1.8	2.0	0
Jesus: light and beauty	0	1.8	0.3	0
Holy Spirit, revival	0	1.8	1.5	4
Vanity of world	2	0	0	0
Purity	0	5.5	2.1	0
Miscellaneous	2	0	2.1	0
Unclassified	0	5.5	5.5	4[a]

[a] Theme is prayer; this is not one of Sizer's theme categories.

'T will be goodbye to friends that I've met on the way,
But I'll meet them again on that homecoming day.

.   .   .   .

Then I want to see mother, she's been gone so long,
She said she'd be waiting just to welcome me home.

("Homesick for Heaven")

I've never met one man without sorrow,
Never looked into eyes with no pain;
But there's a land where grief is a stranger,
And joy is the only song they sing.

("Tears Will Never Stain the Streets of That City")

I want at least a million years to view the throne;
So many friends I want to see when I get home.

("When I Get Home")

TABLE 14. Frequency of all themes in congregational hymns sung more than once, Fellowship Independent Baptist Church, summer 1977

Theme	Fre-quency[a]	Percen-tage[b]
Heaven	20	95
(May be subdivided as follows)		
Heaven as home, as port in a storm, as place of rest and peace	3	14
Heaven as place where friends and family will meet	4	19
Rapture of the church; resurrection day; homecoming	6	29
Relief from trials and tribulations	7	33
Ephemerality of this life	3	14
Safety and security within the Christian faith	5	24
Christian pilgrimage	6	29
Jesus as friend, companion, brother	9	43
Exhortation to be saved	5	24
Sinlessness and perfection	2	10
Prayer	6	29

[a] Number of times theme appeared, either as major or subsidiary theme.
[b] Percentage of the 21 hymns in which theme appears.
Note: As many as four themes may appear in each hymn; thus percentages add up to more than 100%.

After examining the metaphors and themes and their frequency Sizer concluded that twin ideas of passivity and control characterize the texts of the gospel hymns in her sample. The lyrics "portray the human condition as that of a passive victim. The solution to the difficulty is equally passive: to rest in some safe place" (1978:30). The ultimate refuge, of course, is heaven. In that safe place, the Christian comes into intimacy with the Savior and into control of his or her emotions. "In that realm," writes Sizer, "the individual by relying on Jesus achieves inward control to counter the turbulent world and his own evil passions" (ibid.:33).

One text from among the Fellowship Independent Baptist Church favorite congregational gospel hymns perfectly exemplifies the idea of passivity: "The Life-Boat." Humans are said to be "floating down the stream of time" when they hear the "Master" call them to enter the life-boat that is coming "to rescue" them and land them "safely" in the "home" port. God's life-boat saves the victims and brings them home to heaven. "Floating down the stream of time" suggests aimlessness and, certainly, passivity. But control is not an important idea in the Fellowship Independent Baptist Church's repertoire; quite the opposite. To be sure, heaven is sometimes portrayed as a place of relief from trials and tribulations, and as a place of rest: "And I'm gonna sit down beside my Jesus, / Lord I'm gonna sit down and rest a little while" ("We'll Soon Be Done with Troubles and Trials"). But for these Baptists heaven is not portrayed as a place of emotional control. Many of the hymns describe the rapture of the church and the celebration of homecoming, with singing, shouting, a great deal of noise, and, significantly, an outpouring of the emotions. For example:

Oh what singing, oh what shouting,
On that happy morning when we all shall rise;
Oh what glory, glory hallelujah!
When we meet our blessed Saviour in the skies.

("Heaven's Jubilee")

When the redeemed are gathering in,
Washed like snow, and free from all sin.
How we will shout, and how we will sing,
When the redeemed are gathering in.

("When the Redeemed Are Gathering In")

Sizer notes that nineteenth-century revivalist religion was intense and passionate, and claims that "the issue of *control* of intense emotion became central in the attempt to make social religion a workable source of order" (1978:52). Ultimately women and clergy "developed an ideology of . . . 'evangelical domesticity': of home and woman as primary vehicles of redemptive power, as embodiments of a pure community of feeling" (ibid.: 87) in opposition to the aggressive, emotional, impulsive, and evil world of business and society. Home became the ideal "community whose purpose is the ordering of the passions" (ibid.: 89). Most scholars of nineteenth-century urban revivalism agree with this analysis. Some argue that with the dissolution of the older, patriarchal forms of social control in the workplace—as family farms and craft apprenticeships were replaced by factories—the newer, voluntary, contractual relationships between worker and boss required self-restraint, an inner control that the converted Christian was eager to provide (Johnson 1978). Thus revivalism provided industrial capitalists with an honest, clean-living, cooperative workforce.

Whatever its validity for nineteenth-century, urban, northern families, this analysis does not fit the social behavior of the Fellowship Independent Baptist Church congregation, who recognize, accept, and value emotional outpourings in church and elsewhere—even in the workplace—as blessings from God. Moreover, one of their favorite hymns underscores this theme of Spiritual blessing as emotional release:

When God dips His pen of love in my heart
And writes my soul a message he wants me to know,
His Spirit all divine fills this sinful soul of mine,
Hallelujah! When God dips his love in my heart.
Chorus. Well I said I wouldn't tell it to a living soul
How He bro't salvation when He made me whole,
But I found I couldn't hide such love as Jesus did impart;
'Cause it makes me laugh and it makes me cry,
Then it sets my sinful soul on fire,
Hallelujah! When God dips His love in my heart.

The church members' thematic emphases on joy and the outpouring of emotion, on heaven and the rapture of the church, fit somewhat better with Dickson Bruce's analysis of antebellum southern camp-meeting choruses (Bruce 1974). It would appear that the church members have selected, from the gospel hymn repertory that Sizer analyzed, those hymns that embody the camp-meeting themes: assurance, conversion, rejection of the world, heaven as "home," the Christian pilgrimage, Jesus as Lord and Savior, and the community of saints (ibid.:96–122); and to these have added an emphasis on those that portray singing, shouting, and the blessings of the Spirit.

Yet Bruce and Sizer were interpreting historical texts of an uncommon religion from their own vantage point, no matter how much they tried to enter into the interpretative framework of the nineteenth-century worshipers and, as Bruce put it, "understand the plain-folk's religious activities and expressions on their own terms. Doing so involves . . . explicating plain-folk religious symbolism as the plain-folk themselves might have done, rather than simply taking the religious terms they used to mean about the same as those terms have always meant" (ibid.:9). It was left to Bruce and Sizer to do the explicating, with no means to verify that their interpretations of the meaning of the hymn texts were the same as those of their otherwise silent informants. Bruce claimed that the hymn choruses encapsulated frontier revivalist theology as understood by the converted masses (ibid.:95) and then assumed that since the meaning in the texts was plain he could understand them as the frontier men and women must have done. But in my experience the folk hermeneutic is not so easily caught.

Having read Bruce's book with considerable enthusiasm just prior to beginning my field studies with the Fellowship Independent Baptist Church, I found it disquieting to learn that I could not read a hymn text, or look at my transcription of a prayer or sermon, and interpret it from a church member's viewpoint. What seemed plainly in the words of a text to me was not necessarily the meaning the church members derived from it. The meaning was contexted by their lives, not mine. Early on, I realized I must rely on the church members' own remarks about their language in religious practice. I got some interpretations by asking for them in conversation, perhaps forcing them to interpret at times when they would not need to articulate, and occasionally (I am sure) getting an explanation that, although coherent, was shallow or simply wrong. Still, the church members' interpretations in response to my questions were essential: they provided information, context, explication, and they corrected me when I had guessed wrong about what they believed. This is not to say I accepted everything they said at face value, but to underscore that I had to know what they thought they believed and how they thought it motivated their actions before I could understand their language in religious practice in terms of its affective power when performed in the church community.

I was especially fortunate with hymns because Brother John habitually interprets the hymns by speaking about them just before and after performance in the service. That way I did not have to ask. In fact, as I have remarked before, the pastor's role when he steps into the pulpit is both prophetic (as when he preaches) and interpretative (as when he explains the meaning of a ritual they are about to perform). The pastor's interpretation of a hymn performance is a performance in itself, a performance about a performance, and often comprises a story. A simple example will illustrate how unreliable my outside, "objective" reading of a text can be.

On June 26, 1977, Brother John asked the congregation to sing "Sweet Hour of Prayer" (see Figure 7 for the text). The chief theme of this text is, obviously, prayer. An important subsidiary theme that I, a teacher of literature with the training and authority of my profession, derive from the text is the relation between the praying Christian and God, who is personified as "Father." The hour of prayer is quiet and peaceful; the Christian prays tenderly to a loving God. There is no question in my mind that this is "in" the text and that in some contexts it is an acceptable interpretation of it. But it was not Brother John's interpretation. Here is what he said to introduce it:

> Let's sing Number 71, "Sweet Hour of Prayer." This is one of my favorite songs I love so much. "Sweet Hour of Prayer." Prayer changes things, prayer is the keys to the kingdom, prayer unlocks heaven's door.

Brother John's interpretation has to do with the efficacy of prayer, not the relationship between the human and divine. In fact, his three assertions about prayer ("Prayer changes things," etc.) are personal formulas. (His son, Brother Donny, repeats them as well when asking for prayer requests before the altar prayer.) Here I suspect they were triggered by the theme of prayer, not by the words of the hymn. *After* the performance of the hymn, after the text has registered, is the time for interpretation of the text; but here again, Brother John's is a personal interpretation, and we may ask *why* this hymn is such a favorite. For one thing, Brother John associates it with his father—it was one of his father's favorites. Here is what he said about it after another performance (audible responses from members of the congregation are in brackets):

Daddy left us five years ago tomorrow. But thank God he just moved out of this old house and went on to get a new one. Left this old world of sin and sorrow and heartaches and went on to be with the Lord. I'm looking forward for the day when I can see him again. [Amen.]

I've told you before, I've seen him sit in a cornfield. I'm the worst grumbler I guess in the world. I complain about every little ache, every little pain that I have. And I've seen Daddy—I've shucked corn on one side of the pile and him on the other—you that used to shuck corn in the field you know what I'm talking about [Amen.]—frost all over it and everything, I've seen his hands crack open [Huh! Bless the Lord], blood would run down on the corn. I never one time heard Daddy say "My hands is a-hurting." If it'd been me I'd have been setting there, and probably a-crying. But thank God he's gone to a place where hands won't crack anymore. [Amen.] Where labor and pain will never come. A place of rest. My Bible tells me in Hebrews, Chapter 4, "There remaineth therefore a rest unto the children of God." [Praise the good Lord.]

I'm glad I'm saved tonight. [Amen.] If I wasn't saved tonight I'd be afraid to walk out those doors. [That's right.] I would. I'd be afraid to go out those doors if I wasn't saved. [That's the truth.] But thank God I know Jesus tonight. [Amen.]

And that song I sung, the last one we sung, "Sweet Hour of Prayer," that was one of Daddy's favorite songs that he always liked to sing. [Bless the Lord.] I've seen the tears run down his eyes so many of a time when he'd sing "Sweet Hour of Prayer." Thanks be to God I believe we can sing it again in glory one day. [Bless the Lord.] He won't shed no tears [Amen.] when he sings it over there. (Church service, July 9, 1977)

We might guess Brother John chose "Sweet Hour of Prayer" to commemorate his father's death on the day following. The story about his father's bleeding hands in the cornfield is, as I wrote in Chapter 2, an extremely powerful image in John's memory and probably bears a relationship to his image of Jesus crucified. Yet, aside from "Amazing Grace," usually sung during the offering, "Sweet Hour of Prayer" was the gospel hymn most often sung during the fieldwork period in the summer of 1977. Knowing the importance of family and the heavenly homecoming, I am sure that John's father is often on his mind, and for that reason he loves this hymn and chooses to sing it.

In a sense, Brother John's commentary on the hymn is highly personal:

it was one of his father's favorites; tomorrow marks the anniversary of his father's death, and so on. How, then, can he interpret its meaning for the congregation? He does so by telling a story that many, drawing on their mountain-farming heritage, can identify with: they, too, have shucked corn. They, too, get caught up in the image of John's father's stoicism and his bleeding hands. John's father becomes a figure of endurance, perseverance, just as the saints are thought, as part of church doctrine, to persevere to the end. And just as John's father will have relief and reward in heaven, so (it is clearly implied) will the others who are saved.

My point is this: through the story Brother John turns his father into a heroic figure, a symbol whose meaning can be shared by the entire congregational community. This kind of interpretative performance is characteristic, linking personal experience (John's own, or something he observed, or was told) to a meaning that all can share, often (though not always) through narrative. The congregation feels itself a community when its members think about the shared mountain-farming heritage, brought to mind by John's corn-shucking image. More important, most have heard this story of his father before. This heroic, suffering figure resides in their memories. Knowing the story, they share, in a sense, in its re-creation; they, too, bring it out by anticipation as it moves along, and answer with "Amen" and "Praise the Lord." In this way performance quickens community.

Moreover, congregational hymn-singing, unlike other forms of language in religious practice, is performed in unison by the entire congregation. In preaching, teaching, testimony, and special-singing, individuals perform for a group. In group prayers, such as the altar prayer and the healing prayer, it is true that the group performs; but they are performing individually, not to be heard by each other (though, to be sure, they pray for one another). In congregational hymnody, however, the singers are performers and audience simultaneously. This double role acts to join the individual to the group (Booth 1981 : 128).

None of this is to deny that individuals in the congregation may have their own interpretations of the text in addition to the one they receive from Brother John. When they request hymns they have their reasons, and these are not necessarily the same as what Brother John might say before or after the hymn. Brother Allen, for example, told me he chose certain hymns because they gave him good blessings while singing them (see below); Brother Vernie said essentially the same (see above). But when Brother John performs an interpretation as he did for "Sweet Hour of Prayer," he provides a communally meaningful explanation.

Consider, now, some more of Brother John's interpretative remarks prior to singing each of the following congregational hymns:

"An Old Account Settled." I'm glad I had mine settled long ago. Just get it settled, get it under the blood. Amen. (July 3, 1977)

103, "More About Jesus." You know, I think this would be the desire of
every Christian, just to know more about the Lord. I've never gotten to know
all I'd like to know about him. I know enough about him to live for him, I
know enough about him to serve him, but I'd like to know more about him.
Wouldn't you? But thanks be to God, one day after awhile I'm going home,
and then I'll know it all. Amen, "More About Jesus." (July 31, 1977)

These are direct comments on the themes of the hymns as suggested by
the titles. The remarks are purely conventional. On occasion, however,
particularly when Brother John selects a hymn himself, he will elucidate
its personal meaning and extend that to the congregational community, as
he did after "Sweet Hour of Prayer." I pointed out above the importance of
"When God Dips His Love in My Heart" as a hymn that gives sanction for
loss of emotional control when God blesses. Here is what he said before
the congregation sang it on July 3, 1977:

> As I've said so many times, I'd rather wear my throat out for God than to
> let it rust out for the devil. . . . Anyway, we went to the hospital on the way
> to the broadcast, and they had him doped up and knocked out, and he
> couldn't talk to us, and they told us not to wake him. So we didn't. I try to
> obey the orders when they ask us to, that's why I can go in anytime I want
> to. Don't have to have a pass or anything; I can just walk through. And I
> try to obey their orders because I think we should.
>   A long time ago in Kingsport we had to get cards to even get in the
> hospital because some went there and, well, they just caused the people to
> almost have a nervous breakdown, a-carrying on, and they told us we'd
> have to get cards to get into the hospital. But over there I don't have to
> have a thing. All I need to do is walk in through the door and keep on
> walking. They'll ask me no questions . . .
>   But we went back after the broadcast, and Sister Edith was there, and
> one of her boys, and we did talk to him, and he said he'd made peace with
> God in his heart, and that he was ready to go. And when we was praying
> with him, why, he was crying, weeping, and thank God for the testimony
> that he's ready to go. That should be every man's testimony today: "I'm
> ready to go." Ready to meet Jesus, thank God. Paul said, "For I am now
> ready," not gonna be but *now* ready, and that should be every man's
> testimony.

Again, Brother John tells a story; here the issue is how a Christian should
behave in the face of society's rules about emotional control. John presents
himself as a man willing to obey orders, and it might appear at first that he
is making light of those people in Kingsport who prayed so fervently at the
hospital bedside that it caused a disturbance. In fact, though, it is the hospital officials, not the sick person, who come near to having a "nervous
breakdown," and they issue pass cards as a result. If anything, John di-

rects his irony at the situation itself, the disparity between the social rules and Christian behavior. He affirms the priority of Christian behavior when he ends the story by saying how he and a group from the congregation prayed by the sick person's bedside at the Harrisonburg hospital, and how the patient was "crying" and "weeping," as they were being blessed.

In Chapter 1 before "The Uncloudy Day" (Figure 6) I left out part of John's introductory remarks. The county was in the grip of a year-long drought, and there had been a storm the previous day:

> Amen, how true that is. Thank God one day we're going someplace where the clouds will never hover. Yesterday afternoon we were here at the church making a tape. We noticed the clouds got dark, awful cloudy, and after awhile the rains started pouring. Thank God for the rain. Thank God that he answers prayers. God will hear and answer prayers when we believe him. We had a wonderful rain here yesterday evening while Jeff and them were taping the broadcast for us for today, due to being here in the homecoming. But one day after awhile if we hold on to the Lord and are faithful to God we can go to a city where the clouds'll never hover over. Won't be a cloudy day.
>
> This is an old song, one Daddy used to sing a lot when he was a-living, "The Uncloudy Day." You don't hear this song sung too much anymore. I heard it this past week but they kind of jazzed it up. To me, take these old songs and jazz them up, you lose the true meaning of the song. Same way with the gospel: if you jazz it up and change it around, you lose the meaning of the word of God. So I believe we ought to take it just like it is. "The Uncloudy Day," let's sing that from our hearts, just like we mean it. (August 7, 1977)

After commenting on the rain, and explaining the occasion (Ken and I were tape-recording Brother John's half-hour radio broadcast for WRAA because the next day would be homecoming and he could not make the broadcast live as he usually did), Brother John brought up one of his favorite ideas: that the old-fashioned way was best; here, singing. As I pointed out in Chapter 4, the chief reason most people joined this church was their love for the old-fashioned way of worship: Spirit-led sermons and prayers, and a preacher who took the gospel "just like it is" and preached by explicating the Bible, verse by verse.

Brother John is not the only one to perform interpretations of hymns. During the period of special-hymn singing, others will sing and offer comments, often as testimonies, before and after they sing. On July 10, 1977, Brother Belvin and his daughter, Sister Delores, had just sung a popular, contemporary gospel song, "I Saw the Face of My Jesus," that describes a vision. Brother Belvin commented, in his typically plain fashion, on the difference between true and false visions; note his comment on the performance ("I often said that . . . ") shortly after he begins:

> I had a vision one night but wa'n't no mess of
> old green cabbage and fat meat.

> I often said that and I made the smile come on their faces when I
> tell that.
> Why, some of 'em'll take and
> say they seen Jesus on the bedpost and everything else.
> And they take and, bless your heart, they'll take and eat a great big old
> mess of green cabbage and fat meat and stuff of that,
> and lay right down on it in the bed,
> and, bless your heart, then they, they, they dream and kick all night, half
> the night,
> and then they'll get up and tell somebody they seen a vision!
> That's wrong, neighbor, if it don't come up with the word of God, it's
> wrong, it's of the devil.
> And so,
> bless your heart, a vision is something other,
> that is beautiful, and it's of the Bible.
> God's good word.   (Morning service, July 10, 1977)

But the most powerful and affecting interpretations are those spoken by
Brother John concerning the heavenly homecoming reunion. For example:

> Amen, you know my father's gone on five years ago. Singing that song
> about the glad reunion day, no doubt you have loved ones done gone on,
> you're looking forward to that reunion day. Here we have a homecoming
> every year, the first Sunday in August, people come together of all de-
> nominations, families get together, have a good time, but that's nothing to
> be compared with that reunion in heaven. You know how it is when one
> goes off from home, when they stay a long time. When they come back,
> everybody greets you so, they love you, they'll hug you. Those that's been
> gone for years—what a reunion that's going to be. We'll meet in the air
> and, thank God, I believe there'll be some rumbling. I believe there'll be
> some shouting in the air, when all of God's people gather in the air to meet
> the Lord. Praise the Lord. (After "That Will Be a Glad Reunion Day,"
> special-hymn, July 10, 1977)

> Singing this for Sister Cave, and this is one her husband always liked so
> well. When he was a-coming to the services . . . course, he's passed on . . .
> every time he'd come to church, just about, he'd request to sing "Rock of
> Ages." And when we'd come to the last verse, "while I draw this fleeting
> breath," I've seen him so many times raise them hands toward heaven and
> praise God. He's gone on, but thank God for the reunion day. (Before
> "Rock of Ages," special-hymn, July 10, 1977)

Amen, won't that be a hallelujah time? Everybody that's sowed the right kinds of seeds, thank God, will reap the crown that's waiting for them. (After "The Great Reaping Day," July 3, 1977)

Looking at the texts of the hymns and the interpretations given them from the pulpit by Brother John and other church members, it is clear that the most important major theme is heaven. But heaven is pictured not so much as a passive, resting place (though there will be relief from pain) as a joyous, happy, noisy, shouting place where people will "have a new body," perfect and glorified; where they will enjoy eternal life with those among their family and friends who have been saved. The second most important theme is leading the Christian life. The Christian life on earth is depicted as difficult, as a life of forbearance and denial, as a life of refusal to be tempted by the devil, as a life that appears "crazy" to many people outside the church, as a life that is separated from the world. Yet there is joy in the Christian life as well: the joy of fellowship with other Christians, the satisfaction of living a principled life, and (very important) the joys of the blessings of the Spirit and the anticipation of eternal life in heaven. Finally, the third important theme is conversion. Songs and pastor exhort any unsaved in the congregation to convert, and the invitation after the sermon gives them the opportunity to pray through to conversion if it is God's will. In fact, after the sermon, Brother Donny leads the congregation in the "altar-call hymn," an invitational hymn whose words beseech the sinner to come forward to pray for conversion.

Ideas about Music

Members of the Fellowship Independent Baptist Church do not sing unreflectively. As we saw, Brother John usually speaks from the pulpit and interprets the theme or most important idea of the hymn text just before and after the congregation performs it. Singers frequently testify before or after singing a special, and their testimony usually includes something about the words of the song. Often they dedicate a special to someone by name. Additionally, they talk among themselves about the relative merits of various professional gospel songs, and make observations about others' performances of special-hymns. Indeed, visitors who want recognition in the church usually demonstrate their sincerity by singing a special-hymn, and the performance gives the church members a means of talking about the visitor. Finally, the church members were forthcoming in response to my own indirect and direct questions about music.

Ideas about music include the place of music in the group's basic ideas about the nature of the universe and humankind's role in history, aesthetic judgments as to what music is proper and beautiful, and opinions regarding the contexts or musical occasions for musical performance (Titon, ed. 1984).

In one sense, of course, the church members worship in song because singing is traditional in Christian worship. But they also know why they do so: because the Lord requires it of them. "You pray and sing and make a joyful noise unto the Lord and I'm sure that everything'll turn out all right," said Brother John to the congregation just before the hymn singing on Sunday morning, June 26, 1977. He is not as explicit in his remarks during the worship service about the purposes of singing as he is about prayer; for the most part, he confines his remarks to interpreting the meaning of the lyrics. But of course "make a joyful noise" echoes the Psalms (81:1; 95:1; 100:1–2), and their injunctions to praise God in song (Psalms 9:11; 33:2), acknowledging that according to God's word this is a duty as well as a pleasure.

I directed my questions concerning the church members' ideas about music into four areas: affect, intention, interpretation, and evaluation. That is, I asked them how they felt when singing, what they intended by singing, how they interpreted the meaning of a song, and how they judged the worth of a performance. Not all had precisely the same ideas, but I found a wide range of agreement.

I usually phrased my questions on affect quite simply, as "How do you feel when you're singing hymns?" Here are some representative responses. From Brother Rastus: "Well, you know, with the good spiritual songs you feel good. I get blessed up here singing in the church [so much that] sometime I got to quit. I just get filled up with the Spirit of the Lord so and sometimes I just got to quit for awhile. Tears begin to run down my cheeks" (Lam interview, p. 22). I asked Brother John about that:

> TITON: Do you ever get a blessing during a song?
> BROTHER JOHN: Oh yes! Yeah, I get happy and the tears'll start running, I can't see the words.
> TITON: What is it about the song that does it?
> BROTHER JOHN: Well, it's just the words in it sometimes, and the way they fit. There's just something in there that God'll just bless you all over the place. (John Sherfey interview, July 17, 1977, p. 11)

Nine months later Brother John returned to the same idea:

> BROTHER JOHN: I know [the Lord] blessed me while we were singing the song that you sung. . . . I got blessed again. . . . That's when I got to feeling real good.
> TITON: Yeah, it looked like all of a sudden you were near to weeping.
> BROTHER JOHN: I was just happy. I weep a lot when I get happy. I can't help that. And I don't want to help it either, praise the Lord. When I get overjoyed, why, I cry.

TITON: It comes suddenly?

BROTHER JOHN: Yes, it just hits you all at once. It sure will. . . . Like I
said, the Spirit's in you, and it'll do this. (John and Pauline Sherfey interview, April 2, 1978, pp. 18–19)

The church members agree that the indwelling Holy Spirit, touched by
the truth in the lyrics of the hymn, generates a sudden feeling of joy and a
sensation of overflow, or fullness, producing well-being, tears, or, in some
people, shouts of "Hallelujah!" "Glory!" and the like.

It is a short step from the hymns' affect to the intent behind them, for
one of the purposes of hymnody is to produce in the Christian this feeling
of joy. I asked Brother Vernie, "What is it that singing does?" He said,
"Well, I think singing really revives you up" (Meadows interview, 1977,
p. 16). I asked Brother Rastus, "What is the purpose of singing?" He said,
"Singing is the start of a good service. . . . Sing a few pieces, and that kind
of gives a man, kind of builds him up in the Lord" (Lam interview, p. 21).
This buildup or renewal is a second purpose of hymnody. Brother Jesse
said, "Singing . . . lifts you up in the Spirit, gets you in a good frame of
mind and spirit to enjoy the Word, when it's preached. Singing'll lift you
up. When the Word comes along it might cut you down" (Comer interview, 1977, p. 35). Preaching can cut down when it highlights a Christian's shortcomings, imperfections, and sins, whereas singing gospel
hymns, with their lyrics focused on the joys of heavenly reward, is up-
lifting. Brother John contrasted preaching with singing the same way:
"Singing is good to get people moving, you know, to get 'em revived. . . .
Singing will lift you up, but the Word cuts down. That's a true difference. . . . And that's why you can hear more shouting in the singing than
you do in the preaching" (John Sherfey interview, July 23, 1977, p. 22). In
sum, the church members think that hymnody produces joy in the Spirit,
revives a Christian and builds up his or her power and the collective power
of the church for the act of worship. But, observed Brother John, "Not
every time that you sing a song does the—that you're in the Spirit. Course
a lot of 'em, we do get in the Spirit, but not all the time" (John and Pauline
Sherfey interview, April 2, 1978, p. 26). The Spirit dwells within but does
not automatically dominate. When it does not, it is usually because of an
unforgiven sin bothering one's conscience.

Evaluation and interpretation of hymns turn upon authenticity. Brother
Rastus said, "Now, singing good hymns, most of the songs is wrote out of
the Psalms, you know . . . and they got good words in there, Spiritual
words out of the Book, out of the Bible" (Lam interview, p. 21). Authentic words are sacred words, religious words, inspired, Spiritual, or Spirit-
filled words. Brother Allen emphasized that "the more [you sing], the more
the Spirit gets to working in your life" (Dove interview, p. 16).

Authenticity in singing involves not only the texts but also the performance. Brother John, who leads the congregational singing from the pulpit, favors a slow and measured tempo, "because to me [if] it's a slow song, the way the words are in it, it gives you the full meaning" (John Sherfey interview, July 17, 1977, p. 13). Recall Brother John's remarks to the congregation that if you "take these old songs and jazz them up, you lose the true meaning of the song."

Authenticity follows from sincere, heartfelt effort, and is not to be measured by conventional standards of musical beauty. Brother Jesse explained:

> We give everybody a chance to sing that wants to. As you know . . . some people maybe wouldn't even stop to listen to us, but we give that person a chance to do what they can for the Lord. . . . We know that we have no great singers in our church altogether. Our pastor is probably the best singer that we have, and he leads the singing. And he's had a little musical training, not very much. Nobody else to my knowledge has any. But we do give everybody a chance to sing that wants to, because they can't go out of the door of the church and say, "Well, he gave someone a chance to sing there today and didn't give me any." We believe in giving everybody the same equal chance to sing, pray, or whatever that's done in a church. . . . It doesn't make any difference how well you do it; it's how much effort you put forth that really counts. (Comer interview, 1977, pp. 5–6)

Brother John is a fine singer in the Appalachian folk tradition and, despite his diffidence, he is an effective songleader. "They want me to lead the singing. They say they can follow me better than they can anybody else that's a-leading singing here. . . . And I don't know whether it's 'cause I'm loud, or what; I don't think I'm that good a singer" (John Sherfey interview, July 17, 1977, p. 7).

It is noteworthy that both Brother Jesse and Brother John distinguish between the congregation's singing and "good" singing, by which they mean a smooth blend of sweet voices on pitch and in correct time, the qualities of school-trained singers that may be heard, for example, in the Mormon Tabernacle Choir or in the singers who accompany Billy Graham. I asked Brother John whether he preferred harmony to monophonic singing. In his answer he noted that harmony was an innovation in this regional style of congregational singing. "Back in [the old-fashioned days] they didn't try to keep harmony like they do now," he said.

> Not near as much. Now I believe you ought to keep harmony if possible, but like the brother said here this morning, that somebody because they couldn't carry a tune just exactly like some others, they wanted to throw him out of the choir, and all that. And you can't do that. Lots of people can't carry the tune just like maybe I will, but yet you got to let 'em do their parts, you know. So that's the way they sung back in them days:

they'd pick up a hymnbook and sing it. Bless the Lord, if somebody was
out of tune, he *stayed* out of tune. But they'd sing! (Ibid., p. 5)

Although the church members recognize conventional aesthetic standards, they subordinate them to heartfelt sincerity, using "good" primarily
to describe authentic singing. Just after the last congregational hymn during the Sunday night service on July 10, 1977, for example, Brother Donny
addressed the following evaluative remarks to the group: "I thought the
singing sounded pretty good tonight. It sounded like everybody was putting their heart into it. You know you can put your throat into it but until
you put your heart into it, you ain't going to get nothing out of it. You get
your heart into it and things seem to work out pretty good." I asked Brother
John, "What makes a good song good?" He summed it up this way:

To me, it's the words and Spirit. If you've got the good words in the song,
and you've got a good Spirit in the song. And I think it ought to be a
religious song. Now I don't think you ought to sing a song about grandma
or grandpa or something like that in church, which it has been done. And
another one I don't particularly like is "Give Me the Roses While I Live."
The reason why I don't is it's not praising God, it's praising man. And I
think if we're going to sing a song, it should be praising the Lord. The
Bible says, "Let everything that hath breath praise ye the Lord." And if it's
got praise to God in the song, the song's good. Now that's what I like.
That's what I like. Amen! (John Sherfey interview, July 17, 1977, p. 17)

6. Prayer

P rayer is the way that we talk and communicate with our Lord," said Brother Jesse. "Now we can praise the Lord through many other ways: through song, and lifting up the Lord by word of mouth and in various ways and working for him and showing others that he has blessed us. There's many ways I guess we could do that, but prayer is the key to the kingdom" (Comer interview, 1977, p. 14). In their definition of prayer, members of the Fellowship Independent Baptist Church agree with most Christian theologians, clergy, and laity, who understand prayer as communication between humankind and God. "Prayer," writes Friedrich Heiler, is "a living communion of the religious man with God, conceived as personal and present in experience. . . . *To pray means to speak and have intercourse with God,* as suppliant with judge, servant with master, child with father, bride with bridegroom" (Heiler 1958:305, 362; italics in original). For Thomas Merton, prayer "means yearning for the simple presence of God, for a personal understanding of his word, for knowledge of his will and for capacity to hear and obey him. It is thus something much more than uttering petitions for good things external to our own deepest concerns" (Merton 1971:67). For Brother John, being a Christian is being committed to a life of prayer. Since his conversion, he has "always been a praying man." In a sermon on April 2, 1978, he told the Fellowship Independent Baptist Church congregation, "I believe when God says pray I believe we ought to pray. Whether we're in the woodshed or at the smokehouse, at the barn or in the farm or in the house or wherever we might be, when God says pray we ought to pray. And the Bible says, 'Pray without ceasing.'"

Brother John's life of prayer involves communicating with God several times daily. But private prayer, by its nature, is outside the scope of this study because the texts of the church members' private prayers were inaccessible to me. It was left to examine public prayer in worship, and that will be the focus of this chapter. Even so, many of the texts of public prayer in worship were impossible to transcribe, particularly in the altar prayers and healing prayers when everyone prayed simultaneously. Yet by expedient microphone placement I was able to record clearly and tran-scribe enough individual altar and healing prayers to feel confident that I had workable and representative texts. Moreover, as with the other genres of language in religious practice, I was able to ascertain the church mem-bers' interpretative ideas about prayer from what was said about it in inter-views and informal conversations, and from their direct statements in the worship services about prayer.

The church members pray because they believe God requires it of them. Their remarks about prayer during services help us understand these be-liefs. "Seek the Lord and his strength, seek his face continually" (1 Chron. 16:11) is one of Brother John's favorite verses. As we have seen, they pray for the sick, the unconverted, for themselves, and for each other. Before taking prayer requests, Brother Donny interprets the act of prayer:

> I think at this time we should go before the Lord in prayer. Prayer is the keys to heaven, prayer unlocks heaven's door. And when you're feeling low and when you're feeling troubled, if you go to the Lord in prayer, he'll take you out of them troubles if you'll just believe in him. Anyone have a re-quest they'd like to make known at this time? (Donny Sherfey, spoken before prayer requests, July 10, 1977)

As witnesses for God, the church members are required to bring the gos-pel to the unconverted people they meet daily, but most find it difficult to proselytize openly. Prayer is a more characteristic means of effecting change. Brother Jesse's altar prayers (see below) are filled with petitions for God to convict sinners. Brother John speaks at times to the entire con-gregation, exhorting them to pray for the unsaved in the nearby town and countryside:

> And church, I want you to help me pray. Truthfully I want you to help me pray tonight that God will begin to deal right here in this community. Not away off from here somewhere but I'm talking about right around here. We've got people in hollering distance of the church and you couldn't get 'em in church, and we need to get 'em saved, amen? If we work hard enough and pray hard enough to God, I'll tell you what he'll do. He'll make the lumps in that old bed just about as big as a pillow, and that old bed'll lay so rough, amen? And brother every time they start to put their feet under the cover, the cover'll fly off of them, and they'll have the awfullest time you ever seen. So let's pray. I want you to pray, I really do. I want you to help pray that God'll break 'em down. They's people here that need to be saved, praise God. And they's some here that call themselves Christians that need to be back in church working for God. So let's pray. If you'll take 'em on your heart and help me pray for 'em, next week we'll see the re-sults. Amen? I believe that, I believe that, and if you'll believe that, we'll see the work done. (Concluding remarks at night service, June 26, 1977)

Prayers that were answered form the basis for some of Brother John's interpretative stories told from the pulpit. This, too, is a kind of witnessing. Here Brother John speaks about an effective healing prayer:

Y'all have heard me talk about Brother Holt Harrell so much. And he's gone on to be with the Lord. And I thank God for that day that I went to Holt Harrell's bedside. I'll never forget that as long as I live. That was a great testimony to me. It's been a great witness in my life just to continue on working for the Lord. Just to go there and see a man that was dying—the doctors had told him not to come back to the hospital—but yet through the power of God, by the laying on of hands, and praying for him, Holt Harrell came out of the bed and preached the gospel of Jesus Christ. That goes to prove to me there is a higher power. I know there's a higher power. Thank God for the higher power. (Concluding remarks, morning service, July 3, 1977)

The church members distinguish by name several types of prayer in worship according to occasion. In order of occurrence in the service, they are: the altar prayer, the prayer for the offering, the healing prayer, the radio broadcast prayer, the prayer at the close of the sermon, prayers at the altar for people who accept the altar call (invitation), and the closing prayer (benediction). Yet another type of public prayer is ejaculatory: individual cries of "Amen," "Bless the Lord," "Praise God," and "Hallelujah" in response to a blessing during a hymn, sermon, or other worship activity.

Public prayers may be distinguished by function as well as occasion. The most common is the petitionary prayer, a request to God for oneself or others. Another is the prayer of thanksgiving, expressing gratitude to God. A third is the prayer of glorification and praise to God; a fourth is the prayer of surrender and confession, seeking God's forgiveness. Sometimes more than one function is combined in a single utterance.

The Altar Prayer

As we saw in Chapter 1, the altar prayer is preceded by public requests for prayer for oneself and others.

The prayer request is to give everybody a chance to speak what's on their hearts. In other words, if you was sitting here in the congregation and there was something pressing on your heart that you wanted to say, like you had a wife or a child or somebody that was real sick, in your mind, that you wanted to pray for, and by you speaking out you let the whole congregation know that you wanted them to help you pray for that matter, see. Then when people begin to pray, when the whole group begins to pray, things begin to be done. (John Sherfey interview, July 23, 1977, p. 22)

People do not speak their requests hurriedly. Brother Donny (or whoever calls for the requests) asks for them, and several seconds elapse before a person responds. "Anyone else?" says Brother Donny, and again a few seconds pass before someone makes a request. It is all polite and orderly. Occasionally someone will say, "I have an unspoken request," whereupon Brother Donny responds, "The Lord knows what it is." An unspoken request is for a need that the person requesting prayer wants to keep private, knowing that people will pray to God to grant the unspoken requests as well as those that have been specified.

Once all requests are taken, most of the people come forward and kneel at the altar to pray. Why not pray in their pews, as some congregations do? Brother John explained,

> Well, [the altar prayer is] just something that I was raised up with. As far as I guess praying is concerned, why, you can pray just as good back in your seat as up in the altar, but the altar was given to the church and people used to do it in the olden times and we still do it and I just feel that people will pray more and pray better if they come to an altar in prayer. . . . Lots of your Freewill Baptist churches [have an altar prayer] until they start getting up in society, and then they quit doing it. And I don't understand that. If they're going to do it while they was humble, why, they ought to keep being humble. So we've always done it here. (John and Pauline Sherfey interview, December 3, 1979, p. 29)

In the altar prayers, as in the healing prayer, the people pray aloud and spontaneously, each person praying whatever comes to him or her to say. Brother Rastus explained the reason for praying all at once:

> When there's a bunch of Christian people together, maybe you'll just call on one certain one to pray. Well maybe there's a somebody else there that really wants to pray, really feels like praying. Well if you call a church together, you don't all the time know which one to call on that's really got the prayer maybe would help somebody. Well if you call the church together and ask anybody that feels like praying to go ahead and pray, why that gives everybody a chance, you see. Of course you can't understand all what they're saying, but the Lord knows all about it. He understands. And that's why that we just ask anybody that feels like praying to go ahead and pray, and that's why we all pray at once. (Lam interview, p. 20)

Spontaneous prayer is an evangelical Protestant tradition. Many evangelical Protestants believe that prayers with texts fixed by others cannot possibly express the feelings of the person praying. I asked Brother John if he felt it would be wrong for him to speak a non-spontaneous prayer. Brother John explained, "Now if I wanted to stand up and read one of these [prayers from a prayerbook] to a congregation, then it wouldn't be nothing [wrong]. But now if I took this and got down to pray out of it and read that off, see, that wouldn't be the Spirit praying me. I'd be praying out of a book" (John and Pauline Sherfey interview, April 2, 1978, p. 22).

TITON: Do you ever do the Lord's Prayer in church?

BROTHER JOHN: Hardly ever, hardly ever do we do the Lord's Prayer. Now normally when I start off to praying I say, "Our Father, which art in heaven, thank you Lord," but of course sometimes I really don't understand what I do say. [*Laughs.*]

[There is nothing wrong with praying the Lord's Prayer] because Jesus told his disciples [to do it]. But on the other hand, if a man, that's the only prayer he ever prays, then he'll get in the habit of it, and it'll just come natural for him to say it and that's all, see. So there's a lot of times there's other things to be prayed for . . . And they get to the place to where they're just saying the Lord's Prayer and they wouldn't say it with any meaning to it, see. (Ibid.)

This congregation's tradition of spontaneous group prayer probably derives from a frontier, camp-meeting practice. In his autobiography, Peter Cartwright describes people at a frontier revival praying aloud simultaneously and mentions a "praying circle"—that is, a group gathering in a ring (Cartwright 1856:56–57). He does not mention the date, but I guess from the context it was about 1801. Certainly Christians must have prayed aloud simultaneously as they exhorted would-be converts in the mourners' section of a camp meeting (ibid.:222). Cartwright also recounts a trip through the Alleghenies (most likely what is now West Virginia) a few decades later. He attended a mountain church but found that this comparatively sedate sermon was ineffective. Then the mountain preacher "rose and began to sing a mountain song, and pat his foot, and clap his hands, and ever and anon would shout at the top of his speech, 'Pray, brethren.' In a few minutes the whole house was in an uproarious shout" (ibid.:200).

Spontaneous group prayer can be found among Pentecostals and some Baptists today. Praying thus at the altar may be more specific to Baptists, but I am uncertain how widespread the tradition is. Folklorists, historians, and ethnomusicologists have observed it in other parts of Appalachia, but to my knowledge no one has surveyed its extent. Brother John learned the practice in eastern Tennessee in the 1930s:

Now the altar prayer is another old tradition, I guess you would say. But it's a good one. I like it. And I have continued with it. Now when I was a young man, going to church . . . the old people used to have an altar prayer. They called anybody that wanted to and would to come to the altar and pray. And everybody prayed as you felt led to pray. You could pray out loud if you wanted to, or you could pray in silence. . . . But I feel this way: that the more you get on an altar, on their knees, the more power you're going to get from God, because when a man or a woman comes to that altar to pray, they mean business, see. (John Sherfey interview, July 23, 1977, pp. 22–23)

Listening to an altar prayer, a visitor to the church would hear a cacophony of voices, some speaking, some weeping, some chanting. What, in fact, do they say? Here is a representative altar prayer from Brother Jesse, who knelt down next to one of the recording microphones on the morning of July 17, 1977 (Transcription 6-1):

Our Lord and our heavenly Father, we thank you again this morning, Lord, for this privilege we have to gather together once more this side of eternity this beautiful Sabbath morning. And, Lord Father, we thank you, Father, for looking over us down through another week for the blessings of
5   life, but most of all for your goodness, your mercy, and your wonderful love. But above that for Jesus the one that came down into this old sinful world and died upon an old rugged cross at Calvary. You gave your precious blood and your life there hanging upon the old tree, Lord, for the sins of the world. And I'm so thankful this morning, dear Lord, that a drop of
10   that blood was shed for me and everyone, Lord, that knows Jesus this morning. And, Lord Father, this morning we pray, Lord Father, that you've heard the spoken requests here in the little church house this morning, Lord Father, most of all for those that are walking in sin, our loved ones, Father, our children, our parents and, Lord Father, brothers and sisters.
15   Lord Father, we pray that you'd reach down wherever they might be this morning, Lord, that you would convict 'em up hard and help 'em that they might see the light before it's eternally too late. And, Lord, we pray also for the sick and afflicted, Lord Father, that you would reach down, Lord, and touch them this morning wherever they might be upon the bed of afflic-
20   tion, in the homes, the hospital, and some here in the little church house, Lord, this morning that're not feeling well, we pray that, Lord, you'd reach down and touch 'em with your mighty healing hand this morning, Lord, that you would remember and set free everyone that would have faith in Christ. That you would make 'em whole in the name of Jesus, Lord, and
25   we'll thank you and we'll praise you for it. And, Lord, now, Father, we pray as we go into the Sunday school this morning. Open up the word of God that we might be blessed and lifted up, be made strong and, Lord Father, that we might be the kind of a Christian that you can be proud of that, Lord, might go out and tell the story of Jesus and witness to the lost souls
30   along the way in this pathway of life. We promise, Lord Father, to be mindful, Lord, of what you put us here for and what you saved us for, and that's, Lord, to get up off the stool of do-nothing and go to work for Jesus and tell the story to those that are lost and walking in sin this morning. And, Lord Father, this morning we pray that you'd help us to let our light
35   shine on someone else. For in your word you said hide not your light under a bushel but, Lord Father, set it up on a high place that the world might

Brother Jesse praying during the altar prayer, 1977.

see it. This morning let that light shine to the world and to the children of
darkness but, Lord Father, on those we're concerned about that shows
we're concerned and that might somehow get 'em saved by the power of
40   God. Bless the pastor here too this morning, Lord, as he breaks the bread
of life behind the sacred desk. Lord, that you might bless him through the
word and that you might bless him and bless us alike that, Lord Father,
they might be the very words that we need to hear. But most of all if
there's a lost or an unsaved here under the sound of his voice, Lord, this
45   might be the morning they might step out and accept Jesus as their own
personal savior. Lord Father, help this little church to grow, help us, Lord,
to be an inspiration and a light in this community for the lost and unsaved
that, Lord Father, we might do our share and we know, Jesus, that you will
do yours, that you'll meet us halfway if, Lord Father, we'll meet you. And,
50   Lord Father, this morning we put all things in your hands. We thank you
for everything that you've done. Forgive each one of us this week where

we've failed you and come short of the glory of God. Forgive us, Lord,
where we've failed to speak out and tell the story of Jesus. Forgive us,
Father, for the things we've done against you and forgive us, Lord Father,
55   for all the things of this life for, Lord Father, you said you'd forgive for all
sin to those, Lord, that come to repentance. And, Lord, this morning we
thank you for the promises in your word. We believe 'em from the beginning of the book of Genesis to the last word of Revelation. Help us this
morning not only to believe it but also to be producers of the word of God.
60   And all these blessings we ask in Jesus' wonderful name, amen.

I have numbered the lines in the transcription for the reader's convenience. Lines 1–11 involve thanksgiving, and the rest is a petition.
The requests are several, and of a general nature rather than in specific
response to specific requests made just before the altar prayer. Brother
Jesse's requests concern the following subjects:

1. That God would convict sinners, particularly the church members'
kinfolk (lines 11–17).
2. That God would heal the sick (lines 17–25).
3. That God would bless the Sunday school so that the people would
understand the Bible so they can witness for God (tell the story of Jesus) to
the unconverted (lines 25–40).
4. That God would bless the pastor as he preaches a sermon that will
meet the needs of the congregation (lines 40–43).
5. That God would convict sinners (lines 43–46).
6. That God would help their church to be an example and to witness in
the community (lines 46–49).
7. Surrender, thanksgiving, and a petition for forgiveness (lines 49–56).
8. Thanksgiving, and a petition to help the congregation witness for God
("be producers of the word of God"; lines 56–60).

Brother Jesse covers a good deal of ground in the prayer, but he concen-
trates on asking God to come to the unconverted. His chief theme is evangelism. Compare Brother Jesse's altar prayer with the following altar
prayer from Brother John in the morning service on April 2, 1978. About
twenty seconds of unintelligible speech is indicated by four ellipses. About
halfway through this comparatively brief altar prayer, Brother John begins
to chant, and he punctuates the ends of his lines with a loud exhalation,
"+hah+" (Transcription 6-2):

Precious Father, we thank you, Lord, for the privilege of prayer this
morning. We thank you, Lord . . . Father, we're here tonight to glorify your
ways, to glorify Jesus Christ the Son of God. Father, we pray for all that's in
the hospital, our Father, Brother Caney, Lord, in the hospital tonight, we
5   pray, Lord, that you'll bless his soul. Touch him, Lord, and make him

whole, dear Lord, that he'll be able, Lord, to get back home. And for Sister
Elsie, Lord, we pray for her. And we pray for every sick one tonight. Lord,
we pray that you'll bless them tonight. Father, now we pray that you'll
bless this service tonight, bless these two preachers tonight, Lord, have
o   them preach the holy divine word . . . let the power of God and the Holy
Ghost . . . and, O God, tonight, Lord, you know . . . our Father, we come
willing and obedient, God, to . . .

    and that we know dear Lord that you'll take us home +hah+
    our Father when this race is over +hah+
5   if we'll put our hand in the nail-scarred hand +hah+
    and let you lead us Lord through +hah+
    +hah+ this unfriendly world +hah+
    Lord have your way tonight +hah+
    +hah+ save some precious soul tonight. +hah+
o   God send 'em to the house of God +hah+
    that they can hear the word of God +hah+
    +hah+ and be made whole. +hah+
    Our Father tonight +hah+
    Ohhh God tonight +hah+
5   +hah+ move in this community Lord tonight +hah+
    and shake the people Lord +hah+
    that show up to church about your work +hah+
    and about your business tonight. +hah+
    Have your way bless these preachers Lord
o   have your way in every heart, every soul, every mind.
    Open the windows of heaven and pour out a blessing,
    our Father we'll not fail to bow,
    give you the honor and the praise and the glory,
    and we ask it in Jesus' name,
5   amen.

Brother John's subjects are thanksgiving (1–2), praise (2–3), and petition: for the sick (3–8), for the service (8–11), for the unconverted
(18–22), and for blessings on the congregation (23–30). The prayer is
more specific than Brother Jesse's altar prayer naming two sick people
(Brother Caney and Sister Elsie), and is not so clearly organized. Except
for a brief section in which the subject is assurance (lines 11–17), the
subjects are the same as in Brother Jesse's prayer, but there is a concentration of energy, fueled by the chanting. Brother John's language is
simpler and more formulaic during the chanted portion. (I will discuss formulas in these oral prayers below.) Still, both prayers are similar in subject
matter, and they well represent the content of most individuals' altar
prayers in this congregation.

The Offering Prayer

Brother Vernie usually is asked to deliver the prayer for the offering. A man of few words, Brother Vernie delivers a brief prayer such as the following (Transcription 6-3):

> Lord, we thank you for this another opportunity, Lord, to grant, O heavenly Father, Lord, another beautiful day to gather together, Lord. We thank you and praise you, dear heavenly Father, for thy presence. We thank you, Lord, for everything that you've been sending down. We pray, heavenly Father, Lord, that you'll lead for the remaining part of the service. We pray, Lord, that you'll bless the giver and the one who don't have to give and remember all the blessed holy names for Jesus' sake, amen. (Vernie Meadows, offering prayer, April 2, 1978, morning service)

The offering prayer, 1977.

Brother John wipes his face when finished with his altar prayer, 1977.

Again, thanksgiving and praise are offered before a short petition that God will lead by the Spirit in the service and bless those who contribute and those who cannot. It may be noted that Brother Vernie does not ask God to bless those who can afford to give but do not. The average contribution is a few dollars per person. Brother Vernie speaks the prayer rapidly and so softly it is impossible to hear it outside of a distance of ten feet. Most of the congregation cannot make it out. Comparing Brother Vernie's offering prayers over a series of weeks revealed that many of the phrases were repeated more or less verbatim.

The Healing Prayer

I described the context of the healing prayer in Chapter 1, and offered a transcription of Brother John's healing prayer from the homecoming worship service on August 7, 1977. Again, it is not easy to pick out one prayer from among the many being uttered at the same time, but as there are fewer people praying—Brother John and the deacons—and as Brother John is the loudest by far, transcription is somewhat easier here than in the altar prayer.

The biblical authority for the healing prayer is in James 5:14–15. The congregation follows the biblical instructions literally. Sometimes the people prayed over are healed at that moment, sometimes later, sometimes not at all. The necessary conditions for God to heal comprise the believer's faith and purity, the praying community, and God's mysterious will. Sister Edith said God sometimes delayed healing to try a person's faith:

> If God says he'll heal, he'll heal. If he don't heal it that minute, he'll heal it sometime when he sees fit. Now that's what I believe about the healing. There's some people that can go up and maybe get healed right at that time, and that's good. But I believe when you ask the Lord if it's his will to do it, and it's to be done, it can be done right then; but then sometimes we got to wait on him. I believe it's got to be showed to us then in our faith. I believe then our faith's tried. (Cubbage interview, p. 28)

Brother John echoed that belief, saying that "God lets us be sick to make us more humble":

> So we anoint 'em with oil, and then we pray the prayer of healing. "Touch 'em, Lord, and heal, if it's your will." Now I don't say that every time somebody comes up here they're going to get healed. And of course maybe it'll run through your mind or somebody's mind, will say, "Why? Don't you believe that the Lord can do it?" Sure. Sure I do. But I believe that they's times that God lets us be sick to make us more humble. And until he gets done with us, you just as well not pray. But the Lord can heal. When he gets done, then he'll heal you anyway, see. I'm a firm believer that when

you're sick you'll do more praying than you will any other time. That's why
I say that. But I have—and I'm not bragging, don't get me wrong, I'm
giving God the praise . . . they's been people walked right here, in front of
this little desk, and we anointed 'em with oil and healed 'em. They shake
hands when they went out the door and said "I haven't had another pain.
It's all gone." Others has went out and didn't get healed. So I can't blame it
on the Lord, see. So that's the way these things happen. (John Sherfey
interview, July 23, 1977, pp. 24–25)

When prayers for healing have been successful, the believer has a testimony to that effect; and this feedback reinforces the belief in the process:

I told you all last Sunday that I had this sickness of the night spells, you
know. Somebody must've prayed for me. I didn't have one all week long. I
slept of the nights just like a baby, so somebody has been praying and God
has answered your prayer. So thank the Lord for that. God is so good and
so loving and so kind, so merciful . . . And again, I want to thank you for
your prayers that you prayed, for I know beyond a shadow of a doubt somebody was praying for old John. And I thank you for it; most of all I thank
the Lord for doing the job. Amen? And thank you for asking him to. So I
just wanted to let you know that your prayers have been answered. I slept
all week just like a baby, I couldn't hardly—I usually try to go to bed about
ten o'clock of the nights, and you know it's awful hard for me to stay up
till ten o'clock. I just got so sleepy, I'd go to bed. And so thank the Lord,
he's certainly been good to us. So if you'd like for us to pray for you, why,
we'll certainly do that the best we know how. (John Sherfey, before healing
prayer, April 2, 1978)

A healing prayer is unusual in Baptist churches; it is more typically Pentecostal. I asked Brother John whether this, too, was a religious tradition
that he had learned as a young boy. His answer, that the church adopted it
on Brother Jesse's suggestion, shows the congregation's openness to new
rituals so long as they have biblical authority:

Brother Jesse Comer brought it up one Sunday, said he thought it would
be nice if we'd have a healing prayer, and I said, "Why, sure, ain't a thing
wrong with that." So we started doing it. . . . Like we do it over here,
[before the sermon], I've never seen it done before in any church. Except,
you know, I saw it on [Rex Humbard's television ministry]. He calls everybody down to the altar if they want to be prayed for, and they anoint 'em
with oil. I guess maybe that's where Brother Jesse saw it. I don't know. But
anyway, he's the one that brought it up one Sunday morning over there, to
me, you know, he told me. He said, "John," he said, "I think it'd be great to
have that." He said, "The Lord can heal." I said, "Sure the Lord can heal. I
know that." And so we got oil and put the oil right there on the front seat,
underneath. We anoint 'em with oil and we pray for 'em. They's been

people healed there, too. At least they testified to it when they shook hands with me back at the door and said, "The pain that I had has left and gone. I don't have it no more." Course it's been times they weren't healed. So we just got to let the Lord work it out. If it's his will to do it, he'll do it, and if it's not, he won't. You can't force the Lord to do anything. (John and Pauline Sherfey interview, December 3, 1979, pp. 17–18)

It would be easy for an outsider to view the introduction of the healing prayer as an instance of the "corrupting" influence of popular culture through television on the church rituals. My view is that it represents an appropriation of a fitting ritual into a meaningful context. Yet the healing prayer is not considered a highlight of the service. People do not come to church primarily to be healed. The healing prayer is given in only about half of the services, and then only when someone asks Brother John beforehand. Even so, he sometimes forgets and is reminded during the testimony period, whereupon he and the deacons perform it. By 1983, as I noted in Chapter 4, the healing prayer had been abandoned as a regular feature of the order of worship. Brother John performed it only on request.

Consider the text of the healing prayer given in Chapter 1 (Figure 11). Brother John begins with the idea of surrender, then affirms belief in the Lord's power to heal. Then he begins to chant and petitions God and Jesus to heal the ones prayed over. Moreover, he asks that they be healed so they can "lift up holy hands and shout the praises of God"—in other words, for the glory of God, not themselves. On April 2, 1978, Brother John and the deacons performed a healing prayer for Brother Allen Dove. Here is Brother John's text (Transcription 6-4):

Brother Dove has come to be prayed for, so let us pray that God'll touch him and heal him.

Our Father in heaven, Lord, we thank you for this hour. We thank you, Lord, for the grace of God and for your power. Lord, that you said that
5   you're going away but you said "I'll imbue you with power from on high." Lord, we thank you for the power of God, so, Father, this morning, Lord, as we come with this our brother, Lord, has been anointed with the oil, our Father, as you said in your blessed Word. "Is there any sick among you? Let him call +hah+ for the elders of the church and let them pray over
10   him, anoint him with oil, in the name of the Lord, and the prayer of faith shall save the sick"; so, Father, we come, Lord, boldly before the throne of grace, and as humble, God, as we know how this morning, asking you, Father, right now in the name of Jesus, rebuke this infirmity in his body, +hah+ drive it from him, Lord, this morning, and, Father, heal him and
15   make him whole, let him go free in the Spirit of God, and we'll praise you for it in Jesus' name, hallelujah. Amen, amen. Amen.

Brother John seldom fails to chant in the healing prayer, but this was one time he did not chant. The prayer is slightly different from the prior text. It begins with thanks, omitting surrender. Brother John repeats the biblical authority for the prayer from James 5, then petitions God to heal the person prayed over "in the name of Jesus" to "go free in the Spirit of God." Belief is more implicit than explicit in this text, and the prayer as a whole has less specificity and less energy.

The Radio Broadcast Prayer

The radio broadcast prayer is the first item on the radio program after the theme song. In the summer of 1977 Brother John and his family broadcast from the WRAA studios in Luray at 1:30 P.M., driving there directly after the close of the Sunday morning service, and Brother Donny regularly said the prayer. In 1979, to conserve his energy, Brother John decided to tape-record a portion of the morning worship service for the broadcast, then deliver the tape to the station after the service. The result was a slight alteration of the order of the worship service. The healing prayer was placed before the broadcast; the congregation sang a hymn ("Precious Lord") as the theme to open the broadcast; this was followed by the broadcast prayer, given now by Brother Jesse, the announcements of upcoming services and events at the church, and an invitation to the public to worship there, then the special-hymns, and then the sermon. Usually the half-hour broadcast time elapsed a few moments into the sermon and the cassette ran out. In 1983 Brother John decided to give up the broadcast. It will be useful to give the text of one of Brother Jesse's radio broadcast prayers; as far as I can tell, it is very much like the texts of his altar prayers. Here is what he said on December 2, 1979. He spoke very rapidly, saying 736 words in 213 seconds, or 3.5 words per second; he did not chant, but spoke loudly and clearly (Transcription 6-5):

> Our Lord and our heavenly Father, we thank you once again for this privilege that we have to come out, Lord, for no other purpose, Lord, but to worship you in Spirit and truth. We thank you, Father, that you've spared our lives down through another week, given us the God-given privilege that so many people in the world don't have today. We pray, Father, that you would look down upon us and that you would pour thy Spirit out upon us, Lord, that we might feel the good Spirit of God down in our hearts today. And Lord, Father, forgive each one of us where we've sinned and come short of the glory of God. Lift us this day, Lord, and plant our feet on the solid rock. Lord Father, help us to get our mind off the worldly things about us this morning and get our mind upon Jesus Christ our Lord and Savior. Lord, this morning, Father, we pray that you would reach down in

this church this morning into this world that we're living in and touch the
sick and afflicted. Lord, remember each one that Brother John has men-
15 tioned here this morning, as, Lord, he brought the names forth, I can't
remember 'em, but, Lord, you know where they are and you know their
condition today. We pray that you'd reach down and that you'd touch them
in body, Lord, raise them up and make them whole in the name of Jesus of
Nazareth, and we'll thank you and praise you, Lord, for what you're about
20 to do. And, Lord, most of all we pray for those, Lord, that are our loved
ones, Father, that are walking in sin today, our wives, our husbands, our
children, Lord, our uncles and grandmothers and grandfathers today, and
the unsaved over the world, Lord, reach down we pray this day into the
home of every home and, Lord, wherever people might be. Convict them of
25 sin, help 'em, Lord, that they might come to the saving knowledge of Jesus
before it's eternally too late. Lord, we pray for those people, Lord, on the
other side of the waters today in the war-torn lands of the world, for the
hostages held, Lord, in the country of Iran that, Lord, Father, you might
intervene and, Lord Father, that strife might not be brought about. Lord
30 Father, we make a mess of things down here sometime in our own way
but, Lord, we put all of these things in your hands today. Lord, to feed
those and clothe those in the war lands that, Lord, have not. Lord, to free
those, Father, and bring about peace, Lord, among nations today. Lord Father, we know you said in your word you didn't come to bring peace among
35 people, that, Lord, you know the hearts of people, but, Lord, put peace in
the hearts of people, Lord, as know you as Lord and Savior. Lord, we thank
you today, Lord, as this word today is preached, and we pray that you
would anoint it as it goes out there into radio-land today, Lord, that it
might speak to the hearts of those, maybe they're riding down the road,
40 that woman there washing the dishes or whatever they might be doing,
that they might stop for just a moment, if they're lost and in sin, and look
up to you, Lord, and say, "Forgive me, Lord, for my sins, come into my
heart and save my soul." And, Lord Father, we believe if they're saved
they'll be found in a church somewhere worshiping you. Lord, this morn-
45 ing, Father, bless now our pastor, Lord, as he breaks the bread of life.
Anoint the message and anoint our pastor from on high with the Spirit of
God that, Lord, it might be as a two-edged sword, cuttin' and a-comin',
Lord, that if we're found come short of the glory of God that we might
draw our feet back up under the benches and say, "Lord, it's me this morn-
50 ing that's in the need of prayer." Lord Father, bless each one of us through
the word, save the lost, heal the sick, and meet the need in every heart
that's present this morning and those in radio-land today. And we give you
the praise, honor and glory for it because we ask it in Jesus' wonderful
name, amen and amen.

Brother Jesse's subjects are similar to those in his altar prayer (Transcription 6-1), but the order differs and he includes a petition for the American hostages in Iran. He begins with thanksgiving (lines 1–5), petitions for blessings of the Spirit (5–8), for forgiveness (8–9), for strength to worship (9–12), for healing the sick (12–20), for conversion of sinners, particularly kinfolk (20–26), for international peace and to free the hostages in Iran (26–36), to anoint the pastor as he preaches a sermon that will convict sinners (36–44), to anoint the pastor as he preaches so that those in the congregation who need to confess sin will do so (44–50), and concludes with a summary, asking that it be done in Jesus' name (50–54). It is more of a public prayer, and it dwells more on those in "radio-land" who might hear the sermon and be convicted of sin. Brother Jesse does not ask for blessings on the Sunday school, for it has already taken place. Nor does he ask for blessings on the special-hymn singing, which will follow shortly. Brother Jesse in this and his altar prayer (Transcription 6-1) is mainly evangelistic in his concerns, but here he extends them to international relations, a theme that seldom arises in this church. (I have never heard Brother John preach on it, for example, even in passing. His references to "the world" are invariably local; the world is represented by the nearby town of Stanley.) In this sense, then, Brother Jesse is expressing his special concerns in the radio broadcast prayer. Other radio broadcast prayers are similarly oriented to the listeners and the wider world.

The Altar-Call Prayer

Brother John offers a prayer at the close of each sermon, then gives the altar call, asking those who wish to come forward for prayer to do so. On these occasions, Brother John asks the deacons (if a man has come forward) or his wife and the ladies of the church (if a woman has come forward) to join him at the altar, and all (including the person who stepped forward) pray. Sometimes, however, the person coming forward signals members of the congregation to come along and help. Sister Pauline spoke about such an incident during the summer of 1977: "She punched me on the arm, and wanted me to come up there with her. So that's when me and Jeannie went up and prayed there [at the altar] along with her" (John and Pauline Sherfey interview, August 14, 1977, p. 26).

I have seen three kinds of positive responses to the altar call. First, an unconverted person comes for prayer and hopes for salvation. I did not record these prayers, but I have been told the sort of prayer that an unconverted person ought to say. Here are some examples of these "sinner's prayers" as reported by Brother Belvin:

> Lord Jesus, I am a sinner. I'm a guilty sinner. I'm lost without you. And, Lord, save me, for mercy's sake. I want to be saved. And I will serve you from here on out till you call me home. (Hurt interview, p. 10)

Women praying at the altar following an altar call, 1977.

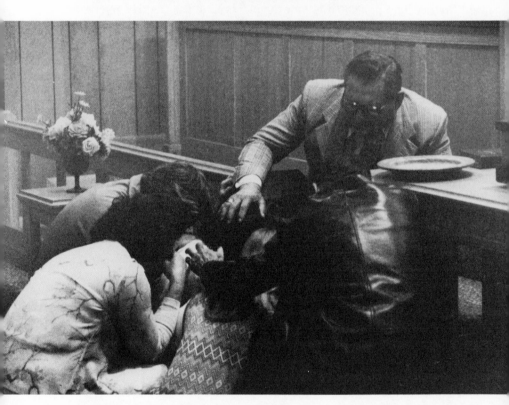

Brother John and church members pray for Sister Virginia Cubbage following an altar call, 1978.

Brother James Moomaw (*top*) prays with Brother Todd Stroupe after an altar call, 1985.

> Lord, be merciful to me, a sinner. I am a guilty sinner and I'm so tired of sin, and I'm ashamed of sin, and I want to be saved. Lord, save me, for mercy's sakes. I know you died on the cross, for my sins you shed your blood. And, Lord, be merciful to me, a sinner, and save me. I'll live for you from here on out. And I mean that from my heart, my whole heart, not half a heart; a whole heart. (Hurt interview, p. 40)

The church members affirm that a "sinner's prayer" is the only prayer from an unconverted person that may be effective. I will say more about conversion in Chapter 8.

A second response to the altar call is from one who "once knew the Lord but then strayed away," someone who was converted but fell into sin and for a period of time has been estranged from God. On the night of April 9, 1978, Sister Virginia Cubbage came forward to the altar for prayer to be reunited with God. My recording microphone caught the following dialogue between Brother John and Sister Virginia, followed by Brother John's prayer (Transcription 6-6):

BROTHER JOHN: Have you ever been saved?

SISTER VIRGINIA: Yes.

BROTHER JOHN: You have been?

SISTER VIRGINIA: Yes, I have.

5 BROTHER JOHN: You disobeyed? All right, now we're going to have to get
you back. All right, we'll pray, and you pray and ask God to forgive you.
[*Holds up Bible.*] Do you believe this is the word of God?

SISTER VIRGINIA: Yes.

BROTHER JOHN: Our Father in heaven tonight, Lord, we thank you for
10 this precious soul, Father, that's walked down this aisle tonight, God, and
I believe, Lord, just as honest in her heart, Lord, as she knows how. Lord,
tonight she come weeping her way to this altar tonight and said, Lord, that
you'd saved me. Our Father, tonight we're so glad that you'd saved her and
that she cast her cares upon him
15 +hah+ for he cared for you,
  he said, "I lay down my life +hah+
  so that they might have life and have it +hah+
  +hah+ more abundantly," Father tonight +hah+
  +hah+ here's a precious soul +hah+
20 +hah+ that O God that's come forward +hah+
  +hah+ that's failed Lord tonight +hah+
  +hah+ and O God tonight +hah+
  her heart is broken tonight +hah+
  and Father her heart is crushed tonight +hah+
25 underneath the load of sin +hah+
  and God in heaven right now +hah+
  let the Holy Ghost come down +hah+
  and move this burden +hah+
  away from her tonight +hah+
30 +hah+ take it off her heart +hah+
  and let her go free +hah+
  in the Spirit of God
  saved to the uttermost
  right now Lord Jesus, hallelujah, hallelujah.
35 Amen, amen.

Sister Virginia and other members of the church who had come forward
prayed also, but their prayers were unintelligible. Virginia wept freely.
Brother John's chanted, petitionary prayer asks God to lift the burden from
Sister Virginia's wounded heart that she may be "saved to the uttermost."
Burdening, conviction, and the crushed and repentant heart are also part
of the psychology of conversion and will be considered in Chapter 8.
"Saved to the uttermost" suggests the possibility of comparative degrees of
salvation and will be considered in Chapter 8 as well. The prayer is related
structurally to the healing prayer.

The third kind of response to the altar call is from one who has been converted but wants to draw closer to God. Brother John strongly endorses the altar for this purpose. Brother Jesse explained:

> We give the altar call because a lot of times it's good for the Christians to go to the altar and use it for various reasons. Maybe not because they've done anything wrong, but just for the simple cause they want others to pray with 'em, like we did two Sunday nights ago when Brother Rastus came to the altar and asked the people to pray for him. Not that he had done anything wrong, but that he wanted to grow stronger in the Lord and get closer to the Lord. (Comer interview, 1977, p. 3)

Altar calls bring out the most demonstrative emotion in the congregation. Weeping, testifying, and shouting, the members of the congregation embrace and shake hands with one another in what Brother John terms "an old-fashioned handshake." On the occasion Brother Jesse mentioned above, Brother Rastus came forward for prayer, and the rest of the deacons came forward and all including Brother John prayed very loudly, touching Brother Rastus on the head and shoulders as if he were being prayed over in a healing prayer. Directly afterward, Sister Janice Turner came forward for prayer to get closer to God, and a similarly intense prayer occurred.

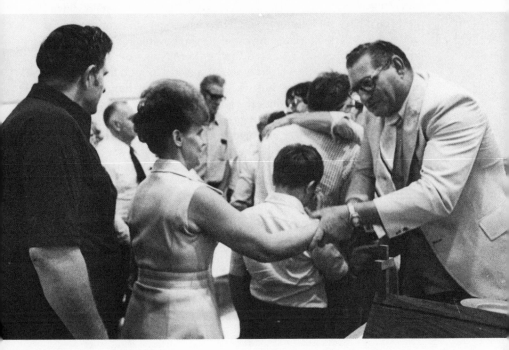

"Old-fashioned handshake," 1977.

There was so much emotion in the church that Brother John invited the entire congregation to the altar; they all came and prayed fervently, and after it was over Brother John instructed them to do the old-fashioned handshake as he cried, "Love one another." Under such conditions men embrace men, taboo under most other circumstances.

The close of the service is the last occasion for prayer. Here Brother John asks a church member to say a "closing prayer," to end the service with God's blessing. One time during the summer of 1977 he deliberately omitted this ritual, saying he was leaving the congregation "in the fear of God." Perhaps one of the churchgoers was under conviction and Brother John thought this would bring him or her to the altar.

Composition at the Moment of Performance

The church members believe that a true Christian's spontaneous prayer, like all sacred language, is led by the Holy Spirit. Their biblical authority for the belief is Romans 8:26–27. "Jesus is speaking to him [Brother John] when he's a-praying," said Sister Goldie. "That's Jesus putting the words in his mouth that come out. He's led by the Holy Spirit" (Dove interview, p. 15). Brother Vernie affirmed, "You know, it says in the Bible if you open up [your mouth] he'll fill it, so when it comes time to pray, you can pray." I asked, "Is that what happens to you?" "Yes sir. Just get down there and you'll have something to say. Then when you ain't got nothing to say, you quit. . . . The Spirit teaches, it leads you how to pray" (Meadows interview, 1977, pp. 21–22). I asked Brother Vernie whether he heard a voice. "The Lord imparts the words for you to speak. Through the Spirit. I mean, he don't speak it to you, but it's just the gift that he gives you" (ibid., p. 22). Brother John describes the gift as an "impression" on the mind (see "Ideas about Preaching," in Chapter 7). Of all the people in the congregation, only Brother Belvin affirmed that he heard a voice when the Spirit communicated with him. Brother Jesse, the Sunday school teacher and the most analytical among the congregation, pointed out that the Spirit did not always lead a person in prayer.

> But then there's a spiritual prayer that you can get on the altar some-
> times—it doesn't happen every time that you pray—but sometimes you
> can get on the altar and the Lord'll really bless you. He'll give you the
> words to say as fast as you can say them. And you feel so good about it
> because you're doing what the Lord wants you to do, what he wants you to
> say. And they are the needs that need to be met. And the Lord is blessing
> you in that prayer. He's leading you, in other words, by the Spirit. The
> Spirit of God that's in you. And he's helping you in that prayer. (Comer
> interview, 1977, p. 12)

Sister Edith was characteristically blunt: "Well, you're just kneeling there in the face of the Lord, and believing the Lord is going to answer your prayers, is all that is to it. . . . He'll really bless you afterward. And he'll give you what to do or what to say. If he don't give you nothing you better not say nothing. And so if he blesses you, tell it" (Cubbage interview, p. 29).

It is obvious from their texts that these prayers, though spontaneous, are purposeful, and that their diction is highly specialized. Certain words and phrases are repeated from one prayer to the next, either verbatim or with variation, especially at the beginnings and endings of the prayers. Such phrases as "we ask it in Jesus' name" or, as Brother Jesse prefers to utter it, "we ask it in Jesus' wonderful name," or "Bless the giver and the one who don't have to give" seem memorized and retrieved whole. But the other phrases, the ones that vary, are not exactly memorized. There is no effort to memorize even the repeated phrases; yet comparison of prayer texts reveals that Brother John and Brother Jesse each favor certain phrases and constructions that express recurrent ideas. If the prayers are not memorized, how do we account for the seemingly high proportion of repeated phrases? How, in fact, does the person praying compose the prayer at the moment of performance? Or, to put it as a church member might, how is it that the Spirit leads in patterns?

A great deal of scholarly attention has been paid to composition in oral literature. Most of the attempts to understand composition at the moment of performance have applied, often with some modifications, the oral-formulaic theory of Milman Parry and Albert B. Lord (see Lord 1968) to the oral (or written, but suspected to have resulted from oral) literature at hand, whether stories, poems, songs, psalms, or sermons. Their theory was derived originally from the study of Homer and of a then-living tradition of Yugoslavian epic singers. More than a thousand books and articles in the short space of a few decades were spawned by Parry and Lord's enormously influential work. Briefly, they maintain that singers of oral epic songs ("narrative poetry composed in a manner evolved over many generations by singers of tales who did not know how to write") compose at the moment of performance with the aid of formulas and themes. The composition "consists of the building of metrical lines and half lines by means of formulas and formulaic expressions and of the building of songs by the use of themes." Lord went on to define "formula" with Parry as "a group of words which is regularly employed under the same metrical conditions to express a given essential idea." A "formulaic expression" is "a line or half line constructed on the pattern of the formulas." A "theme" is any of "the repeated incidents and descriptive passages in the songs" (Lord 1968:4). More recently, folklorist Bruce Rosenberg applied the Parry-Lord theories to folk sermons. Arguing that the preachers' sermons were metrical when chanted, Rosenberg found many repeated, formulaic words and phrases, and concluded that the Parry-Lord theories successfully described composition in a living oral tradition (Rosenberg 1970). If we consider Brother John's healing prayers we will certainly find repeated words and phrases that appear to function as formulas and formulaic expressions. Thus far we have looked at two texts, one chanted in part and one not chanted. Here is another, partly chanted (Transcription 6-7):

Our Father in Heaven, this morning, Lord, as we come with these two, Lord, and we come to the throne of grace, Father, as humble, God, as we know how, Father, you said in your blessed Holy Word that by your stripes we are healed. Father, we believe that gospel this morning to be the truth, to be the infallible word of God, and we believe, Lord, that when we come, Father, in faith-believing, Lord, that you're able to heal, you're able to make whole. Father, you said in your blessed Word you was able to kill and you was able to make alive. And, God, we know, Lord, that you raised the dead, you gave sight to the blind, you cleansed the lepers. You healed those that were lame and, our Father, those who were sick. And, O Father, you even touched the ones that had the fever. Lord, we have the same Jesus this morning +hah+ that we had in the old days, had back in the old days +hah+
we still have the same Jesus this morning +hah+
because you said in your blessed Word +hah+
you're the same yesterday and today
and tomorrow unchanging Lord. +hah+
O Lord we bring these two this morning +hah+
and present 'em to you +hah+
and in the name of Jesus Christ of Nazareth +hah+
we [unintelligible] now Jesus +hah+
+hah+ touch 'em and make 'em whole +hah+
and let 'em go free +hah+
in the name of Jesus +hah+
and we'll praise you for it,
hallelujah hallelujah.
Amen, amen.   (John Sherfey, healing prayer, March 5, 1978)

5

10

15

20

25

The following phrases are repeated verbatim or with slight variation at or near the opening of each of the three prayers:

(1a) . . . as we come before the throne of grace . . . (Fig. 11:1)

(1b) . . . Father, we come, Lord, boldly before the throne of grace . . . (Trans. 6-4:11–12)

(1c) . . . we come to the throne of grace . . . (Trans. 6-7:2)

· · · · · · · · · · · · · · · ·

(2a) . . . Father, we come, Lord, this morning as humble, God, as we know how. (Fig. 11:2)

(2b) . . . as humble, God, as we know how this morning . . . (Trans. 6-4:12)

(2c) . . . Father, as humble, God, as we know how . . . (Trans. 6-7:2–3)

The following phrases are repeated verbatim or with some slight variation at or near the close of the prayers:

(3a) . . . in the name of Jesus we make this prayer. (Fig. 11:27–28)

(3b) . . . we'll praise you for it in Jesus' name, hallelujah. (Trans. 6-4:15–16)

(3c) . . . and we'll praise you for it, hallelujah hallelujah. (Trans. 6-7: 25–26)

Moreover, the climactic moment of the prayer—the moment when Brother John petitions directly for the healing—is expressed in very similar language from one prayer to the next.

(4a)

and in the name of Jesus Christ of Nazareth +hah+
we [unintelligible] now Jesus +hah+
+hah+ touch 'em and make 'em whole +hah+
and let 'em go free +hah+
in the name of Jesus +hah+   (Trans. 6-7:20–24)

(4b)

. . . Father, heal him and make him whole, let him go free in the spirit of God . . . (Trans. 6-4:14–15)

(4c)

+hah+ Lord that right now thou would heal +hah+
+hah+ would heal and touch O Jesus +hah+
upon their bodies Lord right now +hah+
in the name of Jesus Christ Father
+hah+ Lord touch 'em and make 'em whole +hah+   (Fig. 11:12–16)

(4d)

Ohhh God O God +hah+
send down your power +hah+
+hah+ through the Holy Ghost right now +hah+
and make 'em whole +hah+
in the name of Jesus Christ +hah+
let 'em go rejoicing +hah+
in the Spirit of God +hah+   (Transcription 6-8, excerpt from healing
                  prayer by John Sherfey, April 9, 1978)

(4e)
Our Father, dear Lord, we don't know
+hah+ what the infirmity might be but, Jesus,
we know that you know.
Dear God, today
how we pray, Lord, that you'll touch him
+hah+ make him whole from this very hour
(Transcription 6-9, excerpt from healing prayer for
Rev. G. A. Cave, radio broadcast, April 16, 1972)

Yet despite these formulaic phrases (to say nothing of formulaic words such as "Lord," "Father," and "Lord Father"), I do not think we have oral-formulaic composition in these prayers in the sense that Lord and Parry describe it. Their theory was meant for a special kind of oral composition at the moment of performance: narrative, metrical verse. The church members' prayers are composed in performance and are oral, but they are neither metrical verse nor narrative. Lacking a story, they lack the repeated incidents and descriptive passages that comprise the themes of oral epic. Moreover, their form is not influenced by an audience's attentiveness, an important additional claim Lord made (1968:16).

Nevertheless, the prayers are formulaic, and more so than ordinary language. We may still ask why, and whether the method of composition, even if it is not oral-formulaic in the Parry-Lord sense, gives rise to the high proportion of formulas. It is tempting to say that these prayers are intermediate between the looseness of ordinary conversation and the highly constrained forms of metrical verse. If the prayers are not metrical in the sense of having a fixed number of syllables or accents per line, neither are they so variable in length, syllabification, or accent as the phrases spoken in ordinary conversation. The chanted lines, especially, approach regularity of length, intonation, and accent. Moreover, the rapid pace and the need to keep the prayer going—one does not, cannot, stop, gather one's thoughts, and proceed when the Spirit leads—tends to keep the phrase and sentence structure simple and regular, and to encourage the expression of ideas in familiar phrases. Lord makes a similar point about oral epic (ibid.: 17, 21–22).

A more general theory of oral composition is needed, one that would account for everything from conversations to Maltese song-duels and view the Parry-Lord theory as a particular case. Lord himself suggests this: "[In oral epic song] we find a special grammar within the grammar of the language, necessitated by the versification. The formulas are the phrases and clauses and sentences of the specialized poetic grammar. The speaker of this language, once he has mastered it, does not move any more mechanically within it than we do in ordinary speech. When we speak a language, our native language, we do not repeat words and phrases that we have memorized consciously, but the words and sentences emerge from habitual usage" (ibid.:36). Among the variables to be considered by a general theory should be the constraints of form, intonation, syntax, diction, mode of speech (speech, chant, or song), theme and subject, and time, upon all purposeful oral utterance (Titon 1975; 1976a). This is not the place for the construction of such a theory, but I would make some few observations on it in the case of these prayers.

First, regarding speech mode: while the chanted portions of these prayers have a higher proportion of formulas and formulaic expressions than the non-chanted portions, the non-chanted portions are still far more formulaic than ordinary conversational discourse. Ordinary discourse has its repetitive phrases, its clichés, but it is freer to range in subject matter. Brother Jesse's altar prayers, though spoken rather than chanted, are dense with formulas. Brother John's, partly chanted, are only slightly denser. Consider the formulas and formulaic phrases that appear in three of Brother Jesse's altar prayers and one of Brother John's, as shown in Table 15.

It is remarkable that between 12 and 15 percent of all the words in these prayers consist of these five formulas. If we were to subtract personal pronouns, auxiliary verbs, articles, and other such words, we would find that the proportion was much greater. Another aspect of this prayer language is that it has comparatively more nouns and verbs, and fewer adverbs and adjectives than ordinary conversation. Furthermore, when adjectives appear, they are more likely to come inside than outside of formulas (e.g., "this sinful world").

Second, in an article several years ago treating musical improvisation and more recently in a textbook chapter treating improvisation in blues lyrics, I suggested that it would be useful to consider the whole range of improvised behavior—not just speech or song, but mundane sequences of improvised activity like mowing a lawn or eating a meal—and fashion a general theory of improvisation (Titon 1978b; Titon, ed. 1984:140–148). It is beyond the scope of this book to do so, but I would mention one concept that was useful to me in writing about repetitive yet varied utterances: the "preform." A preform (the term comes from clothing patterns) is something roughly sized and shaped, then stored, to be retrieved and finished when needed.

The "preform" concept is able to account for the variety of phrases in the prayers that express similar thoughts. Consider:

+hah+ Lord touch 'em and make 'em whole (Fig. 11:16)

+hah+ touch 'em and make 'em whole +hah+ (Trans. 6-7:22)

. . . Father, heal him and make him whole . . . (Trans. 6-4:14–15)

TABLE 15. Frequency of certain formulaic words and phrases in four altar prayers

	No. of Times Uttered as % of All Words					
Prayer	"Lord"	"Father"	"God"	"Jesus"	"this morning"	Total
Comer no. 1	6	2	1	1	2	12
Comer no. 2	7	2	1	1	1	12
Comer no. 3	5	3	0.5	1	2	11.5
Sherfey	5	4	2	1	3	15

Comer no. 1: Altar prayer, December 2, 1979, Transcription 6-10.
Comer no. 2: Radio broadcast prayer, December 2, 1979, Transcription 6-5.
Comer no. 3: Altar prayer, July 17, 1977, Transcription 6-1.
Sherfey: Altar prayer, April 2, 1978, Transcription 6-2.

The preforms here are "touch," "heal," and "make whole." When retrieved, these preforms are given their final shape by the context: whether there is one person being prayed for ("make him whole") or several ("make 'em whole"); whether God is to be called "Lord" ("Lord, touch 'em") or "Father" ("Father, heal him"); and so forth. Albert Lord distinguished between formulas (specific word groups) and formulaic phrases (similar phrases, often with one word substituted for another). "Father, heal him" and "Lord, touch 'em" are, in the terminology I am suggesting, formulaic phrases constructed on the pattern of the preform.

I was fortunate to get two clear recordings of prayers by Brother Jesse on the same day, December 2, 1979: his altar prayer (Transcription 6-10) and his radio broadcast prayer (Transcription 6-5). We would expect to find more of the same formulaic expressions in two prayers on the same day than, say, in two of his prayers uttered years apart (such as Transcriptions 6-10 and 6-1, for example). And we do. Here is Brother Jesse's altar prayer from December 2, 1979 (Transcription 6-10):

> Thank you, Lord, for this privilege, Lord, as we gather together once more this morning. We give thanks, Father, that you've given us a chance once more to come before you. We thank you, Father, this morning. Lord, we just pray that you would forgive each one of us, Lord, for coming short, but
> 5 O God, we pray that you would lift us up this morning and plant our feet on the solid rock. Lord, we pray that you would guide us and help us to walk in the light of day as our spirit is sanctified. O God today we pray for those that have spoken requests this morning, Lord, that you would reach down and touch each one, Lord, Father, that's out in sin today. Many more
> 10 families are lost, Lord Father, that we're concerned about today. And we're

concerned that you would convict each one of 'em of sin, oh but, Lord, to see the light before it's eternally too late. Lord, remember those today that are sick and afflicted in body. Father, we pray that you would touch them and lift them up and make them whole. Lord Father, reach down and touch Brother Will McAllester this morning, Sister Cubbage, Lord, that's wanting to get back in your house, Lord, Brother Tom Breeden that's not able to be here; Lord, we pray that you would lift us up and plant our feet on the solid rock, and make us whole in the name of Jesus, and, Lord, today, Father, we pray that you would watch over the teachers of the Sunday school this morning, Lord, that you would bless and give us all something to say about your precious Word, enlighten our hearts and our minds in the word of God. Lord, keep us on that straight and narrow path, Lord, that leads to heaven this morning. Lord Father, bless the word, with the Spirit from on high, and anoint our pastor this morning, as he breaks the bread of life, and, Lord, everything that's said and done, and we'll give you the praise and the glory because we ask it in Jesus' name. Amen.

Brother Jesse (*bottom*) praying during the altar prayer, 1977.

Some formulas and formulaic expressions are common to all three prayers. For example:

(5a) Our Lord and our heavenly Father, we thank you again this morning, Lord, for this privilege we have to gather together . . . (Trans. 6-1 : 1–2)

(5b) Our Lord and our heavenly Father, we thank you once again for this privilege that we have to come out, Lord . . . (Trans. 6-5 : 1–2)

(5c) Thank you, Lord, for this privilege, Lord, as we gather together once more this morning. (Trans. 6-10 : 1–2)

(6a) Bless the pastor here too this morning, Lord, as he breaks the bread of life . . . (Trans. 6-1 : 40–41)

(6b) Lord, this morning, Father, bless now our pastor, Lord, as he breaks the bread of life. Anoint the message and anoint our pastor . . . (Trans. 6-5 : 44–45)

(6c) . . . anoint our pastor this morning, as he breaks the bread of life . . . (Trans. 6-10 : 24–25)

(7a) Forgive each one of us this week where we've failed you and come short of the glory of God. (Trans. 6-1 : 51–52)

(7b) And Lord, Father, forgive each one of us where we've sinned and come short of the glory of God. Lift us this day, Lord, and plant our feet on the solid rock. (Trans. 6-5 : 8–10)

(7c) . . . forgive each one of us, Lord, for coming short, but O God, we pray that you would lift us up this morning and plant our feet on the solid rock. (Trans. 6-10 : 4–6)

(8a) . . . that you would reach down, Lord, and touch them this morning . . . (Trans. 6-1 : 18–19)

(8b) . . . we pray that, Lord, you'd reach down and touch 'em . . . (Trans. 6-1 : 21–22)

(8c) We pray that you'd reach down and that you'd touch them . . . (Trans. 6-5 : 17)

(8d) . . . Lord, that you would reach down and touch each one, Lord . . . (Trans. 6-10 : 8–9)

(8e) . . . we pray that you would touch them . . . (Trans. 6-10 : 13)

(8f) Lord Father, reach down and touch . . . (Trans. 6-10 : 14–15)

The variations in these formulaic expressions come about because parts of them are stored as preforms, such as (in 8a–f) "reach down and touch."

(I cannot help thinking of the telephone advertising campaign slogan, "Reach out and touch someone." I wonder if the phone company was aware of the slogan's resonance with prayer.) "Reach down and touch" is also a preform for Brother John, as a look back at his healing prayers reveals.

In use, the preform is retrieved and then the pattern is adjusted to fit the context: "each one," "them," etc., often filled out with other formulas ("Lord," "Father," etc.) beforehand, in the midst, or after the preform, possibly as filler while awaiting the retrieval of the next preform. For example, the preform "reach down and touch" is transformed for utterance to "reach down, Lord, and touch them" in 8a as the formula "Lord" is inserted in the midst and "them" at the end. In 8f the same preform is transformed for utterance into "Lord Father, reach down and touch," as the formulas "Lord" and "Father" are inserted at the beginning. The other variations can be accounted for in a like manner.

The formulas and formulaic expressions in Brother Jesse's two prayers on the same day have more in common with each other than with those uttered two years earlier. Consider these:

(9a) Convict them of sin, help 'em, Lord, that they might come to the saving knowledge of Jesus before it's eternally too late. (Trans. 6-5:24–26)

(9b) . . . convict each one of 'em of sin, oh but, Lord, to see the light before it's eternally too late. (Trans. 6-10:11–12)

(10a) We pray that you'd reach down and that you'd touch them in body, Lord, raise them up and make them whole . . . (Trans. 6-5:17–18)

(10b) . . . we pray that you would touch them and lift them up and make them whole . . . (Trans. 6-10:13–14)

This is what we would expect. Yet it is remarkable how stable the preforms in Brother Jesse's altar prayer were over the two-year period. Or, for that matter, Brother John's over a six-year period, 1972–1978 (Transcriptions 6-4, 6-7, 6-8, 6-9, and Figure 11). Finally, some of his preforms are personal; that is, he favors certain ones, while others ("reach down and touch") are part of the common stock. Some are phrases taken directly from the King James Version of the Bible; these especially are available to all who pray.

How, then, should one describe this composition at the moment of performance? Spontaneous fabrication by means of formulas and formulaic expressions would seem to characterize it. Indeed, the process of learning to pray lends evidence to that theory. The church members affirm that newly converted Christians do not "just know" how to pray but must learn as they grow in grace. It is important to realize that the church members reject the idea that they learn to pray by imitating others. Brother John, speaking before his sermon on June 25, 1972, said:

There used to be a preacher in Johnson City that I thought could pray the prettiest prayer that I ever heard in my life and I would have give anything if I could have prayed a prayer like that man, but I, you know, beloved, I never did try to get up there and mock him and try to pray like he did because God never did pray me like that. Brother I have to pray the way God wants me to pray, I've got to preach the way God wants me to preach, I've got to sing the way God wants me to sing, and that's all I can do.

The newly converted seldom pray as volubly or with as much authority as those who have practiced prayer for a long time. As Lord pointed out that the singer of tales learns formulas and formulaic systems from listening to other singers, and gradually becomes adept, so, I believe, the newly converted learn formulas and formulaic expressions unconsciously by overhearing such prayers as are given solo. But in the church members' view, they are most certainly not improvising language in religious practice. Rather, they are being led by the Spirit when performing sacred language. During sermons, prayer, and testimony, the Spirit leads by giving the words to speak or chant. In hymnody, the Spirit leads them by guiding their singing and their understanding (as well as their choice of hymns), but it does not give them words to sing. The Spirit leads the understanding during Bible reading also, whether in church or at home.

The common factor in all instances of language in religious practice is that the performance, rather than the composition, is ideally always Spirit-led; and to understand language in religious practice from the church members' viewpoint, the emphasis should be upon the passive process of the Christian's being led rather than any active process of improvisation. The outsider may conclude that improvisation or something very like it takes place during preaching, praying, and testifying. In some ways it is useful to conceive it thus; but, as I have just attempted to show, it may also prevent understanding and lead one to see logical inconsistencies in the church members' theory of language where such inconsistencies exist only in the observer's theory. The outstanding aspect of these performances is that the performers, saying they are "led," experience a loss of control, and this has a significance beyond language; the believer merges with the divine and identifies with the indwelling Spirit. The memory of these moments quickens the believer's identity as a Christian (see Chapter 8).

Affect, Performance, and the Praying Community

As affect plays a central role in the performance of religious language, I was careful to find out from several church members how they felt when praying. Brother Allen is ecstatic during prayer:

Kneel down to pray [and] you can feel all kinds of things coming through your system. Just like you want to go home! . . . When I kneel down to pray I feel like I'm just ready to float off. And that's when I'd like to go. [*Laughs.*] Praise the Lord. I'll tell you, you can't find nothing wonderfuller than that. (Dove interview, p. 14)

Brother John, too, speaks of the "thrill" of prayer:

I feel great [when I pray]. There's something about praying that really enlightens you, gives you a chance to tell everything to the Lord, talk to him about what you need, and what you stand in need of. And most of the time I find it good to just thank him, and pray. Thank the Lord, praise him for what he has done. I feel like a lot of times we ask for too much. And so it's good just to get on your knees and thank him. Many of a time I've gotten down and said, "Lord I'm not here to ask you for a thing. I just want to thank you for what you've done: for saving my children, for blessing us and giving us a home, giving us air to breathe, food to eat, clothes to wear," and just thank him for saving your soul, and thank God for his son Jesus, and come into the world and died on the cross to save a wretch like me. And it's just a thrill, I feel like, to me inside, there's a thrill when you're praying that you don't get any other way. (John Sherfey interview, July 23, 1977, p. 25)

It is interesting to hear how he reaches for the formulaic expressions even when illustrating prayer in conversation; they must be deeply ingrained. The other side is how it feels to be prayed *for*. Brother Vernie said being prayed for increases the indwelling Spirit's intensity: "I just, you know, feel the presence of the Lord more better. When somebody's a-praying for you, why, it really helps you" (Meadows interview, 1977, p. 13). Brother Austin Thomas (Sister Hattie's brother and granddaughter to Mary Cathen Thomas, who had the vision of the coming of the park—see Chapter 2) testified at a prayer meeting on the importance of group prayer:

You know when,
    when you got a prayer list and you pray daily it's good to have a little
help along with people. You know I believe
    that Christian people should pray for one another, see, because the Bible
says they—.
So it's kind of like a
    burning a brushfire. If you set a brush pile afire it burns utterly, burns
down pretty long. And stuff gets scattered out, why, it don't burn
    much more then. But you come along and you pile it back up and then
she begins to burn again.
So that's kind of the trouble with a lot of the Christian people. We let the
fire get too low sometimes. We
    we need to be kindled up a little. So prayer's a good way to get kindled

Brother Austin Thomas, 1977.

up, is to trust in the Lord and pray to the Lord and ask the Lord about things.

> And then I believe
> the Lord is ready to help.
> (Testimony, prayer meeting, June 28, 1977)

The extended metaphor of the brushfire is typical of the church members' habitual use of homely analogy to interpret the world. I asked Brother Jesse, "How do you feel when you're there with the hands on you and they're praying the healing prayer for you?" He replied,

> It makes you feel good to know that you have asked somebody to pray for you, and you go forth in faith, believing that the Lord'll meet those needs. And it just makes you feel good to know that the other people *are* praying for you. And you *know* it when they're doing it orally, in public. You know then that they *are* praying for you. In other words I can sit in the congregation and if anybody asks me if I have a request I can speak out and say, "I've been sick this past week and I wish that y'all would pray for me." Then when they all gather 'round the altar I *take* it that they are praying for me, but I don't know it to be a fact. But then I feel like I'm showing more faith when I get up out of my seat and go forth and be anointed with oil, as it is in James 5:14, then I feel like I am acknowledging my faith by stepping out more and asking 'em to pray for me, whether they lay hands on me or whether they don't lay hands on me. (Comer interview, 1977, p. 27)

Here Brother Jesse brings up one of the most important aspects of prayer in the Fellowship Independent Baptist Church: the relationship between affect, performance, and the community of church members. A church united in prayer is acknowledged to have great power, to be a powerhouse for God. "You get everybody around the altar, and get 'em to praying, then things will happen," said Brother John. "And to get something to happen, we got to be in one mind. And that's the best way I know to get in one mind and one accord, is everybody praying. As they were in the upper room. Jesus told 'em to go back in the upper room and tarry and wait, and, he said, 'You'll be imbued with power on high'" (John Sherfey interview, July 23, 1977, pp. 23–24). In one mind and one accord, the congregation becomes a community.

Touching physically becomes a figure for touching spiritually, and it resonates from "Reach down and touch," so common in the texts of prayers, to the biblical promise that communal prayer will be answered: "Again I say unto you, that if two of you shall agree on earth as touching anything that they shall ask, it shall be done for them of my Father which is in heaven. For where two or three are gathered together in my name, there am I in the midst of them" (Matthew 18:19–20).

In this community, distinctions drop, strangers become brothers and
embrace. "Have you ever prayed for strangers?" I asked Brother Jesse.
"Oh yes, I've prayed for people that I didn't even know. . . . They were a
stranger in one respect: that I didn't know their name or where they lived
or who they actually was, but when they come up off of that altar and said,
'I'm saved, I know I'm saved, I'm satisfied with what I got,' then I know
that they're a brother or sister with me in the Lord, regardless of what
their name was. I can rejoice with that person" (Comer interview, 1977,
p. 41). At moments like this, affective performance of language in religious practice establishes an intensely felt, egalitarian community. Especially when, through prayer, someone is converted, "born again," changed
in identity, and merged into the group, the community feels itself as one,
and prayer has become the key to the kingdom of God on earth here in the
church sanctuary.

"Old-fashioned handshake" after altar call, 1985.

7. Teaching and Preaching

T eaching and preaching, two of the genres of language in religious practice, are related because both are hermeneutical; that is, at the Fellowship Independent Baptist Church, both interpret the Bible. The church members understand the Bible to be literally true and infallible, but also to have a hidden meaning that the Spirit can reveal to the born-again Christian. The chapter begins with a discussion of Sunday school teaching that emphasizes the relationship between performance and community. The relationship is foregrounded in an incident that occurred when a new member of the congregation, unfamiliar with or willfully disregarding the church's tacitly agreed-upon rules of performance, violated those rules and lost her place in the community. A discussion of preaching follows, highlighting the church members' ideas about preaching as a specially anointed language with the power to convict sinners, and presenting some examples of the "call to preach" personal narrative. The rest of the chapter is given over to analyzing the themes, subjects, and interpretative method Brother John employs in his sermons. After printing a representative sermon text in full, I discuss its meaning in the context of about forty more of his sermons, bringing in excerpted texts from these sermons where necessary. The chapter concludes with a discussion of Brother John's habitual interpretative cast of mind, noting that its methods—parallelism, analogy, metaphor, typology, and tropology— drive toward an analogical comprehension of the Bible. In Chapters 8 and 9 I will point out how analogy shapes the church members' perceptions of their own experience, as evidenced in the last language genre under examination—testimony.

Teaching

Under the right circumstances the language of prayer in worship integrates the individual church members into "one mind." In Sunday school teaching, which proceeds through the Bible verse by verse, and gives everyone an opportunity to interpret each verse, that "mind" is cyclically separated into its constituent parts and re-formed when they agree on meaning.

Members of the Fellowship Independent Baptist Church believe that teaching and preaching are gifts of God (Comer interview, 1977, pp. 17–18). Brother Jesse, who leads the Sunday school, counts teaching as one of the nine "gifts of the Spirit," as the "word of wisdom" (1 Corinthians 12:8; the *New English Bible* translates this as "the gift of wise speech"). Every Christian is obliged to teach, but Brother Jesse is recognized by the church members as especially apt at interpretation, and he himself feels gifted at it: "I love to do the job that the Lord has called me, and I believe the Lord has called me to teach" (ibid., p. 8).

In conversation with Brother Jesse I was struck by his analytical cast of mind, and when Ken and I interviewed him, I asked him to interpret various aspects of the service. Applying himself enthusiastically to the task, he spent several minutes identifying the various stages of the service, then took a few hours to tell us the meaning of each activity. By the end of the session—actually, not far from the start—it was apparent to me that he had a scholar's curiosity, and I was very pleased to have his thoughtful and articulate explanations.

Many Protestant churches assign denominational literature—Bible study aids—for the Sunday school lessons, but Brother Jesse prefers not to. "I feel like adults ought to be able to take the word of God as it comes along. In other words, get off of the bottle, off of the milk and onto the meat of the word, regardless of how deep you get into it" (ibid., p. 14). Another reason he dislikes denominational literature is that it emphasizes certain parts of the Bible at the expense of others. Prior to teaching at the Fellowship Independent Baptist Church he was a member of (and led Sunday school at) a United Brethren church, where "in a two-year period, we would use some of the same literature over again. [But] using the Bible you can go straight through it, and you get it all; where they leave so many things out using literature . . . Now I don't mean as a teacher you can always explain all of it. We do get a lot out of it, and that's why I say again, if a teacher does not understand a verse of Scripture, maybe there's someone in the class that does" (ibid., p. 15).

Brother Jesse believes strongly in a participatory Sunday school. This is sound Baptist theory—to let no authority come between the individual believer and God's revealed word. In practice, it allows people to teach each other:

> I believe in a Sunday school that it is a part of the service that every person can participate in, take a part in if they want to. They *should* take a part in it. . . . I feel like that in Sunday school we ought to be able to learn one from another. If I get a half-dozen people's view on a certain verse of Scripture, then I feel like I can come to a better conclusion of what that verse means than I can just from one person.

And this is why that I think Sunday school is so important. It's different from preaching in this respect: that I, if I'm sitting in the pew and the Sunday school teacher's standing up there teaching, I have the right to stop him or her, and ask them what a certain comment or a certain verse means . . . I can ask 'em, "Well, you better explain that verse," or whatever you were talking about, that I, too, might be able to understand.

And this is how I think Sunday school should be run that we might grow in the grace of God, that we might know more about God's word, that in doing this we might study it a little more, and share our views with a broader group of people. (Ibid., pp. 7–8)

The church members' purpose in Sunday school, then, is to teach and learn from each other the meaning of the word of God. When Brother Jesse began leading the Sunday school, he decided they would begin at the start of the New Testament. When Ken and I arrived during the summer of 1977 they had progressed to the Epistle to the Philippians, taking about one-third of a chapter per week. Each person studies the chapter at home beforehand, sometimes with Bible aids: reference Bibles, concordances, dictionaries, and so forth; but they bring only their Bibles to the Sunday school, relying on memory, occasional penciled notes on the pages, and the Holy Spirit to guide their understanding. Many read in the Bible on their own for pleasure and instruction; they find Sunday school illuminating. Some in the adult Sunday school are illiterate, but their ears are keen and they participate as the Spirit leads them.

Performance and Community in Sunday School

On one level, then, teaching and learning take place in the Sunday school; this is quite straightforward in principle, and it is very much like a school classroom. But to an outsider interested in the use of language in religious practice, the most fascinating aspect of Sunday school is the rhetorical strategy involved in performance, and its effect on dissolving and reforming the community. Specifically, the language of teaching creates and resolves tension over interpretations of the Bible. Occasionally these disputes ride on social tension as well, and by looking closely at one of them I will bring out the way of performance and community in Sunday school.

I mentioned earlier that Sunday school provides one of the few opportunities for women to speak authoritatively in the church. Most of the women speak briefly and to the point during the Sunday school lesson. Normally, the lessons proceed without incident. Occasionally, however, a newcomer to the church makes him- or herself felt at this time. Sister Lois, a strong-minded participant who, prior to my visit in April 1978, had been coming to the church for only about a month, challenged Brother Jesse's right to be a deacon on the basis of the contents of the lesson in 1 Timothy

Chapter 3 that morning. I have reconstructed the following argument and its resolution from my tape recording and notes, presenting it as close to the original as possible; all dialogue is, of course, verbatim, but the running analysis is my own.

Brother Jesse, standing at the altar, facing the pews, Bible in hand, read verse 11: "'Even so must their wives be grave, not slanderers, sober, faithful in all things.' Now how do you see that one?"

"I think the wife should have the same quality as the husbands as deacons," said Sister Lois, sitting in the second pew. Tall and slender, entering middle age, Sister Lois was not well known by the congregation, and her forthrightness was a little startling.

Brother Jesse modified her statement. "Well," he said, "they don't have all the qualifications but they do have some of them. We see that they must be honest, and must also be boldly to speak out for the Lord."

Brother Clyde, reminded of an earlier discussion of tithing, spoke up next. "If you're honest, though, brother, you'll pay your tithes."

Brother Jesse tried to steer them back to the subject. "Well, yes, speaking on the tithes, I'd say you would do your best to. I'm like Brother John; and now sometimes it takes a lot of faith to start into that. I'm not making any excuses. But it says here on the wives, 'not slanderous, sober'—we know that even all of us must be this if it's talking about sober as far as drinking is concerned—and 'faithful in all things.'"

Sister Lois demurred. "I believe it means pure and godly, is what that *sober* means," she said.

"Could be," said Brother Jesse. I felt the tension rise in the room; Sister Lois had been too direct in contradicting Brother Jesse.

Brother John dispelled some of it, saying *sober* could have more than one meaning. "I think what they mean there too is sober minded. In other words, you know, have a clear mind and not be drawn away with every enticement. That'd be sober minded."

"Could be both," Brother Jesse admitted, but he stuck to his train of thought. "Did you know you got more, if I'm not mistaken, women alcoholics in the world today, really, than you've got men? But a lot of them are at home, and you don't know about it." By disparaging women he may have been striking back at Sister Lois. In so doing, he baited her. "Is there anybody else maybe would have something on that?" he added.

Now Sister Ella took up Sister Lois' point: "I believe the wife it says of the deacon and I just believe they's supposed to be as perfect as a deacon is, and go along with him, agreeing with him, and help him, and talk things over to go with people that, bring people to the Lord. 'Cause if not—."

Brother Jesse interrupted: "I believe they ought to go along with their husbands—." His mind was on a single track.

"That's right," Sister Ella replied. Temporary accord had been reached,

Brother Jesse teaching Sunday school, 1978.

but now Brother Jesse introduced a delicate example.

"—if they can get 'em to. I have to use my own case in this; I can't say anything about anyone else. My wife has laid out of church until I don't know whether she has a desire to come back anymore. She's been sick for a long time, but there's been times that she could come with me and didn't do it. Now you look at it from this standpoint: I cannot make her come."

Sister Ella said, "That's right, you can't count—."

"Now what are we to do about something like this?" said Brother Jesse.

"You can't help that," replied Sister Ella, still wanting to agree.

Sister Lois was sympathetic: "Well, if she's sick you shouldn't expect her to come."

Brother Jesse was pleased. "I don't believe in bringing up someone else on this, but I'll just use myself."

Sister Lois had a sudden thought. "Well, but first of all, really I wonder if you should have been voted in as having the deacon's office. I mean by

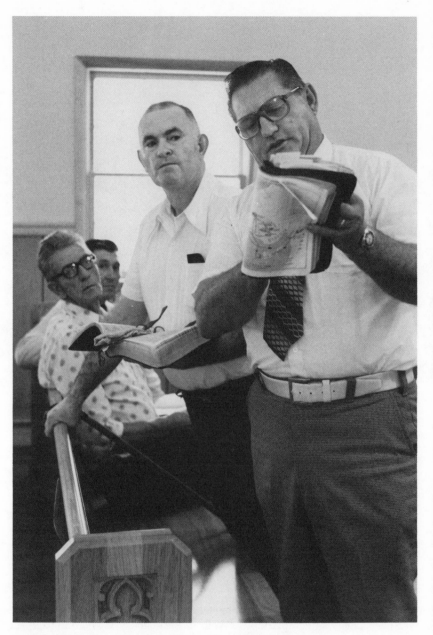

Brother John offers his opinion during Sunday school, 1977.

your wife not having desire to be in church and everything. I mean I don't know what your wife is, but if she's slanderous, somebody that meddles into the affairs of people and everything or whether she says anything or not, but really this qualification is supposed to be met by anyone who is voted in as deacon."

There were a few seconds of embarrassed silence, then Brother Jesse laughed nervously. "Well, that's a hard thing to say. I believe I don't remember whether my wife was coming or not when I took the deaconship here at the church. But certainly I have no power over making the other one do what I want 'em to do. As long as she treats me right and I'm the head of the household—and I still am—at home, not to brag, but I believe the man ought to be. And still, I don't mean that I'm a boss, or something like that. We talk things over and try and do things in the right way. But as far as coming to church and living a Christian life, you can't force this upon anyone."

Brother Jesse was caught in a dilemma. If the verse meant that deacons' wives should lead Christian lives, then he was not presently qualified to be a deacon. But if "faithful in all things" meant a deacon's wife should be obedient to her husband, then he was qualified, for his wife was obedient at home; and, after all, it would be wrong to try to force her to come to church. Brother Jesse was appealing to the group's knowledge of the Pauline epistles on the subjection of wives to their husbands; but Sister Lois would not be stopped.

"No," she said, "but I believe that faith can move mountains, and if we'd step out and exercise faith and do what God wants us to, we'd see God do blessings for us. We can have those things which we desire to have."

The rhetoric fascinated me. Brother Jesse and Sister Lois each made pronouncements whose literal meaning the congregation must agree with, yet whose implications suggested female or male incompetence. Brother Jesse indicted women as secret alcoholics, then reiterated male superiority, while maintaining that he is not a "boss" and would not force his wife to come to church. Sister Lois, in a masterful rhetorical move, agreed with Brother Jesse that he cannot and should not force his wife to attend church, but she went on to suggest that if he prayed harder his wife would decide to come. In saying so, Sister Lois cast suspicion on the strength of Brother Jesse's faith.

It was too much for Brother Jesse; he could only assent: "Well, I'm hoping so." Again, there was silence for a few seconds, whereupon Brother Rastus spoke up, not so much to defend Brother Jesse, as to show sympathy by admitting that he, a deacon himself, was in the same situation.

"Brother Jesse," he said, "my wife's the same way. Claims she has neuritis and stays out of church a lot, and I never come not unless I ask her to come. But I'm like you; I think she could come a lot of times when she don't come."

"Mmm-hmm," agreed Brother Jesse.

"Just as well be honest about it," said Brother Rastus, "'cause the Lord knows all about it."

At last several people murmured "Amen."

"No excuses for it," Brother Jesse continued.

"Well, I don't think the Lord would hold you responsible for it because you do as you was talking, and they just want to stay theirselves," said Sister Ella.

"I know the Lord's not holding me responsible for what she's doing," said Brother Jesse, still chipping away at the doubt cast by Sister Lois. He wasn't satisfied, and went on to try to puzzle it out. *Was* he doing everything he could? "Every person has to answer for their own self. But this is something that we can, that we think about when you take something like this, whether it would keep you from taking office in the church. Certainly I wouldn't want my wife to be a slanderer. I know Brother Rastus wouldn't. And I'd want her to be sober minded, and certainly sober, not drinking. And I wouldn't allow that in my house." Brother Jesse needed to regain control. He would do so by telling a story and making the congregation laugh. The content of the story, too, would show him the master of a situation.

"I've had one drink poured in my house since I've been a Christian, as I know of, and that was my brother. I was gone at the time. He walked in and he was drinking and he was about half—." He paused, and everyone chortled. "I walked in the front door, and there he was sitting at the bar and had a beer in his hand. I didn't have to say anything but I just gave him a real hard look and he got up and walked out, and he's never brought one back over to the place since then. He's respected me. But while he's got something in him, sometimes people forget. But he knows where I stand and he knows how I feel."

The story—on a topic relevant to Brother Jesse's interpretation of *sober*—showed how he could lead someone close to him—his brother—to do what he wished, not by forcing him, but by having him respect his wishes in his house. Again, Brother Jesse presented himself as the ruler of his home. But equally, perhaps more, important, he recovered the rhetorical control that as Sunday school leader he may have felt he needed.

Sister Lois would not be denied. "But you brought it up that you didn't leave your tithes, and I believe really if you'd step out on faith and give to God what is his, you can expect God to bring your wife and your children into the church where you've been praying about," she said. Now Sister Lois' argument was out in the open where it could be debated at face value. In fact, Brother Jesse did tithe most weeks; he could have corrected her at this point. But she had overstepped her bounds. She had reopened the wound. She had become too personal. Brother Jesse—and the rest of the congregation—was beyond this kind of debate. He simply agreed. "I'm still believing in that," he said.

She backed off a little. "I mean we have to exercise faith, though, for the Lord to move. I mean we just don't get it. You start stepping out and taking the promises of God and believe in him for it and do what he says and then expect him to give blessings in place of it."

"I'm still hoping that, I'm still praying on that," Brother Jesse said. He did not contradict her. It was time to resolve the argument, not to prolong it. She had gone on to say something all could agree with again.

Another member of the congregation wound it up, relating her argument and Brother Jesse's and Brother Rastus' problems to the larger picture: all of them have problems, and all must pray about them, and eventually God will answer their prayers. "Well, Brother Jesse," he said, "we've all got stumbling blocks, but we've got to just pray about the things, and sometimes that stumbling block will move in a year or two years. And I feel like that a person should pray about these things."

"Right," said Brother Jesse. He paused. "All right, look at the twelfth verse there . . ." The lesson continued.

Sister Lois stopped coming regularly to the Fellowship Independent Baptist Church not long afterward. Unfamiliar with the performance context, she had spoken out of turn, been too aggressive, and prolonged the argument after it had been resolved. In short, she had violated the church's rules for performance. She may have won the argument, but she lost the community.

Preaching

Both preaching and teaching at the Fellowship Independent Baptist Church center on interpreting the Bible. Teaching offers us an opportunity to notice rhetorical strategy in the give-and-take of community performance. Sermons reveal doctrine primarily, but also have a style and method and show Brother John's interpretative cast of mind and its drive toward analogy.

Brother John's sermons begin with a passage from the Bible: the passage anchors the sermon, as the preacher explains it, verse by verse. Sometimes he makes parallel reference to other verses bearing on the chosen Scripture. When the last verse has been explained, the sermon is over. As I indicated in Chapter 1, Brother John's sermons are characterized by alternating periods of repose—that is, a normal, public-speaking voice—and chant. Typically, he begins in repose by reading the Scripture chosen for the sermon; then, he continues in repose for up to a minute or so, explaining the meaning of the first verse, whereupon his voice changes. His intonation compresses toward a monotone; the duration of some of his syllables lengthens; he speaks more rapidly, with few pauses; his lines—that is, what he says between taking in breaths of air—become shorter and more regular in length; and his voice becomes louder. When all of this occurs, he is chanting: his lines are punctuated by exhalations that sound like vehement grunts—"+hah+"—prior to taking air into his mouth for the next line. Occasionally he seems to sing his sermon: he has a definite "reciting pitch" and a high pitch for emphasis, and no others. These changes are obvious performance markings that set these parts of the sermon off from others. After thirty seconds or so of chant, Brother John stops abruptly and returns to repose, almost always changing the immediate subject of his discourse, sometimes going on to the next verse. He remains in repose for a moment or so, then moves to chant, remains there for another half-minute or so, then stops abruptly and the cycle begins again. As the sermon progresses, the periods of repose grow longer, and after about fifteen minutes the periods of chant grow shorter, to perhaps ten seconds each. It appears that his body tires, though he says he feels wonderful when he preaches, and I have no reason to doubt it. Sermons last for anywhere from about twenty minutes to about forty-five; most are in the thirty-five-to-forty-minute range.

I calculated the line length in syllables between breaths in three modes of discourse by Brother John: ordinary conversation, sermon repose, and sermon chant. I then drew a graph of the number of occurrences of lines of given numbers of syllables (Figure 27). From this graph it is evident that line length compresses dramatically during sermon chant, and that most lines of chant contain from five to ten syllables, whereas in conversation Brother John's lines are likely to be any length from one to twenty syllables. Through the kindness of Robert Port and the Phonetics Laboratory at Indiana University, in 1977 I was able to make representative sound spectrograms of Brother John's chant and ordinary conversation as well (Figures 28 and 29).

Ideas about Preaching

As I pointed out in Chapter 4, to comprehend the church members' ideas about language in religious practice, it is crucial to bear in mind that they understand it to be led by the Holy Spirit; and this applies to preaching as it does to praying, teaching, singing, and testifying. First, when, prior to the sermon—it might be the day before, or a few minutes before the sermon—Brother John prays, the Spirit leads him to choose the Scripture passage that will be the basis for the sermon. In other words, he opens himself up and lets God direct him to a passage. Shortly before the closing prayer in the Sunday morning service on July 3, 1977, Brother John invited everyone back for the night service, saying he would be preaching

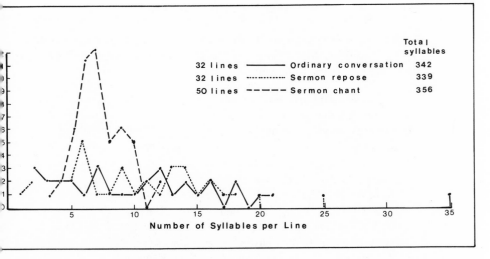

Figure 27. Line length in Brother John's sermons.

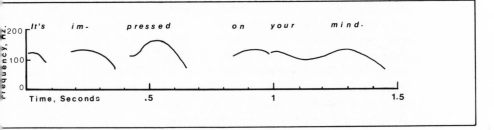

Figure 28. Tracing of sound spectrogram of tonal range of Brother John's conversation.

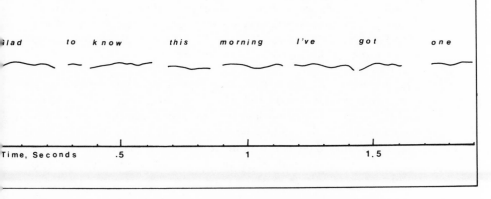

Figure 29. Tracing of sound spectrogram of tonal range of Brother John's chanted preaching. Note near-monotone and compare with Figure 28.

from the book of Revelation. Then he went on to describe a revival service he had preached for the previous night, illustrating how and why the Spirit led him to the Scripture passages:

We're going on through the book of Revelation, or just as long as the Lord leads. Don't know just how long that'll be, but we never know how the Lord's going to lead. I went to church last night, I had my Scripture already marked in the Bible, where I was going to preach. And to show you how the Lord leads, I was setting on the front seat, singers was up singing, and God said, "Don't preach from that." You know how he speaks, I, uh, some of you may not know how God speaks, but God don't speak to me in a big voice, it's just an impression on my mind. "Don't use that." And so I said, "Well, what do you want me to use?" So I was thumbing through the Bible and I got up to the fourth chapter of Revelation. And something just said, "That's it." And so I preached from that by the help of God.

People had a wonderful time; they enjoyed it so much when I got back in the aisle, the lady that was here and played the piano for the quartet the other night hit me on the arm and said, "Preacher," she said, "you don't know how proud I am you preached that." I said, "Why?" She said, "Me and these four ladies," and she pointed to the ladies standing there, "were talking about that today and couldn't understand it. And through you by the help of God we know now." And I said, "Why, thank God, I know now why he changed me." Now I'd have been in a terrible mess if I'd had my sermon wrote down, wouldn't I? But I don't write 'em down, I get 'em down. [*Laughs.*] That's what I told somebody one time, on a job a-working, and he said, "How in the world do you ever get time to write your sermons the way you work?" I said, "I don't write 'em." "You don't write 'em?" I said, "No, I don't." I said, "I pray mine down." [*Chuckles.*] So I can be a-working and praying at the same time and get the sermon. I got one sermon one time, I don't know if you remember it or not, when I was coming back from over in Israel. As we flew across the Atlantic Ocean I had my testament out reading and God give me a sermon while we was flying in the air, 38,000 feet up. And I delivered it after I got back here. So God does work wonders for us if we'll just trust him. Amen.

The subject of choosing Scripture was on Brother John's mind that day— certainly, Ken George and I had asked him about it between the morning and night services—and not long after the start of the night service he told the congregation about a time he disobeyed the Spirit and tried to preach what he wanted to preach. Wanting to preach a sermon that would cause people to be blessed and shout, he chose his own text with disastrous results.

God will lead us to what he wants us to preach. God will give us [the message]. I told you before, I was up one time preaching and of course I

used to, every time I preached, I wanted somebody to shout. [*Laughs.*] I still
like for people to shout. But if God don't give me a shouting message, and if
you have to draw your feet up under the bench and holler "Oh me," praise
God, then I want to do that, too.

But I wanted somebody to shout, you know. God gave me a message [but]
I went over to Corinthians to where I was preaching on the Resurrection.
And I tried my best to preach and I couldn't do it. I was there and I just
hammered away, beloved, but it just hit me right back in the face.

And so after awhile I walked around from behind the desk and I told 'em, I
said, "Children, I'm going to tell you something. I've not been preaching
what God wanted me to."

And I told 'em what God wanted me to preach from, and I took the text,
and brother, let me tell you the Holy Ghost hit me, and praise God, the power
was all over me,

and then, brother, we had a service. +hah+
But as long as you try to do it within yourself +hah+
you won't have any service
and God won't bless us +hah+
until we get right with him. Get where God can use us.

Interestingly, as Brother John narrated the incident he began chanting just
after the spot in the story where the "power" hit him then. This means of
choosing Scripture is common to all members of the congregation, not just
the pastor. For the Tuesday night prayer meeting, each person brings a
Bible and reads a passage he or she has been led to select, then offers a brief
interpretation.

The Spirit not only leads Brother John to the Scripture passages that form
the basis of his sermons; it is understood to give him the words to preach. I
asked Brother John how the Spirit led him as he preached. He replied,

You read the Scripture out of the Bible, and then you start preaching
from those verses, you know, just like I preached from this morning. And
as you preach, why, God just begins to pour it on you and words'll come
that you never even dreamed. Why, Lord, there's been a-many of a time
I've been in the pulpit preaching and the Lord just showed me things in
the Scriptures that I'd never seen before in my life—while I was preaching. And that just makes you get so happy, you just want to run! (John and
Pauline Sherfey interview, April 2, 1978, p. 27)

On another occasion Brother John likened the process to words that
simply appeared in his mind and were uttered:

When I'm in the pulpit preaching, God just seemingly—. Now God don't
talk to me like I've heard some people say he does. To me, when God is
speaking to me, it's through the impression on my mind. In other words it
seems like it's said, but you—there's no voice. And of course when I'm

preaching, it goes the same way. It just comes in my mind and it's said. I don't have to stand and wait, or meditate what I'm going to say. Because I depend upon God, and it just comes thataway. It always has. (John Sherfey interview, July 23, 1977, p. 14)

I then asked Brother John whether the words he uttered were his words or the Lord's words. "The Lord is putting it in my heart what to say," he replied.

Because I couldn't think of, you know, preaching like that, I mean, read the Scripture, I, many of a time I've read Scripture and the Lord'd say use it, and I didn't know what to say from it, what to preach from it. But when I'd get started, it just unrolled, just like a book, just like a scroll. Unrolled: just unraveled. And I'd tell the congregation: "Well, Lord, I've never seen that before. Never thought of that before." It's just something that hits you. (Ibid., p. 15)

"Can you remember what your sermons were about after you get through with them?" I asked, thinking that if he were led passively he would have difficulty recalling them. He confirmed what I had guessed: "Hardly ever. Hardly ever. I couldn't even tell you what I said. Now when I hear 'em played back lot of times on tape, then I remember it. But until they do, I don't't" (ibid.).

The church members take the rapidity, loudness, and other marked features of Brother John's chanted sections as an indication that he is being led by the Spirit. "A teacher's not as fast as a preacher," Brother Vernie said. "It don't come as fast as it does from a preacher. A teacher . . . don't get the rate that a preacher does when he gets under the power of the Lord." "Does a teacher ever get under the power of the Lord?" I asked. "Yes, sir. Jesse does. Yes, sir. He can really come down in that Bible" (Meadows interview, 1977, p. 15). Brother Rastus agreed, adding that when the Spirit leads so quickly that a person cannot talk, he hollers:

I reckon when he gets to preaching the Book, if he preaches the word like it's in there, that's when the Spirit of the Lord comes down on him. You can tell it. I can. When the Lord just anoints him with his word, and that's when he gets to preaching hard. That's when you just feel the presence of the Lord so that you, he just puts it in your mouth sometimes so fast you just can't hardly talk it out. . . . And that's when he hollers sometimes, you know. He can't help that. I know exactly what it is; I've felt it myself. (Lam interview, p. 18)

Brother Belvin, who, like Brother John, has the gift of preaching, described the alternating periods of chant and repose, saying the chant was anointed and likening repose to "talking":

You see [preaching is] anointed. You see it's a little different from just talking, me and you, talking. And just like after you were, come down a little
and get back to your self and go to talking. And then when you go to
talking, then the power of the Lord hits you again, and you go on, right
along with it, it's out. It's just like a shout. . . . You've done preached! It's
gone. It's done preached. The power of the Lord hits you [and] it's done
preached. . . . The Lord uses you. That's the reason why he anoints the
preacher. That's the reason why preachers can't hardly teach. . . . When I
get to teaching I, well now, quite a few times you'd have seen that I had to
stop . . . it'd get me to preaching. (Hurt interview, pp. 125–127)

Brother Belvin emphasizes the passive role of the preacher when he
chants: he is a vessel for the Spirit of the Lord; he has no control over what
is said. But then "you [a preacher] come down a little and get back to your
self and go to talking." Chanting, a preacher is not located in his "self" but
elsewhere, anointed by the Spirit, used by the Lord. In repose, he is back
to himself.

I asked Brother Belvin, "How do you feel when you're preaching?" A
farmer, he turned to some of his favorite images to describe the freshness
he felt:

Just a real light feeling and just as happy as can be . . . And when you're
anointed, well, with the power, why, then you are light, and it feels like
that you could move on for miles, and outrun everything that's on the
ground. [I can be tired but I'll] get ready and go to service and the power of
the Lord'll hit me and send down a good message upon me, and I get in
the Spirit and go to preaching, why, I feel like a little young ewe that just
turned out. I feel so good and super. And after, after the Spirit dies down,
you've preached your message, then you feel like a old mule that's been
turned out for ages and ages and so old it can't hardly get about, been
worked all day and pulled through a mudhole. (Ibid., p. 94)

Brother John agrees, frequently saying that when he preaches whatever
pains he may have felt just beforehand vanish during the sermon, despite
the obvious energy he uses when he preaches:

Not everyone that gets up to preach is under the inspiration of the Holy
Ghost. Amen? He's under man's service, and he can read off a paper and
he never cracks a sweat, he never gets tired. Now that don't hurt that one.
But when you get up and preach under the demonstration and the power
of God, as the apostle Paul told the church at Corinth, he said, "when I
came to you," he said, "I came not with the excellency of man's speech, or
man's wisdom and man's knowledge but I came with the demonstration
and the power of the Holy Ghost." And so, beloved, tonight, when you
preach thirty minutes under the demonstration and the power of the Holy
Ghost, brother, it's equal to eight hours of manual labor. Statistics says it

takes as much out of a man's body, out of this Adam-nature body, it takes as much strength out of it as eight hours' manual labor. Now I don't know about it this week. Statistics must be wrong this week. 'Cause I put in about a eight or ten hours and, brother, I was ready to fall over. But I can preach thirty minutes and I want to go another thirty. [*Laughs.*] (Spoken before sermon, July 10, 1977; the reference is to 1 Corinthians 2 : 1 – 5.)

I mentioned earlier that sometimes Brother John's chant turns to song. These periods of song are brief—lasting perhaps for ten seconds at most— and were rare during the summer of 1977 (and rarer still afterward). Still, intrigued by this, and knowing that singing the sermon was a normal aspect of the Old Regular Baptist preaching in eastern Kentucky, I asked Brother John if he had ever sung his sermons. He confirmed that he had done so when he was much younger:

> I used to, when I'd get in the [Spirit while preaching], when the Lord was really blessing me, I had a habit, I'd reach up and get my ear, like that [*cups hand in front of right ear*], and I was more or less, in preaching I'd be singing. Just singing it off. Well, it wasn't—I guess it was a little different to singing, of course, but a lot of 'em told me I used to do it. And, well, that come from the old Primitive Baptists. That's the way they used to do. And I don't know why I done it. It was just something, when the Lord was blessing me, that's what I'd do. When I first started preaching, I preached so fast, you know, that I could just keep on going like that. . . . It's kind of hard to explain to you really how it, how I did do it, but you would go high with it, and then you come low, you know, just like you would if you was in a song. (John and Pauline Sherfey interview, April 2, 1978, pp. 13 – 14)

Brother John's reference to cupping his hand over his ear is particularly interesting to me because I have seen the Old Regular Baptists do the same when they sing their sermons. I have not seen Primitive Baptists sing their sermons, nor do I know of any reports of that in the scholarly literature; but I do not doubt that Brother John has seen them do it.

Brother Belvin spoke excitedly about singing the sermons, saying it was a "special" kind of anointment, one which had the greatest power to save souls:

> I've sang the preaching. . . . You just sing it off, it comes so fast to you. I've heard Brother John do it . . . It's just anointed, a good anointment, I mean it's the power. . . . I mean not like a song like you sing, you know [with the words written down or memorized]. Just like preaching the Scriptures, you just get so fast, and just get all to singing. You're going on down the line. . . . Maybe one of these days if the Lord anoints him [Brother John] real good he'll sing. . . . Boys, I'm telling you one thing, when the Lord anoints you that way it's something going on. Neighbor, souls a-coming, souls going to come to saving. They'll come, come to your altar of prayer.

Gonna get there to be saved. Well, that's a special anointment. . . . I mean, that's really anointment. The old cup is full then. . . . A colored man is quick for that. . . . They go to singing quicker. (Hurt interview, pp. 132–136)

Chanted and sung preaching is a tradition among black American Protestants, particularly Baptists. Its origins are unknown. Reports of evangelistic preaching during the first Great Awakening called attention to the "holy whine" of such ministers as George Whitefield, and it is possible that Baptist chanted preaching among white Americans today—by no means confined to Brother John or to Appalachia, though it is more common there—derives from this "holy whine." Yet it seems to me that if Whitefield and the others had sung their sermons, observers would have said so. It may be that the sung sermon is the result of black Americans' African-based transformation of the chanted Baptist prayers and exhortations. This would clearly seem to be the case as regards the black Baptist tradition of sung and chanted prayers and sermons. But how can one account for the sung sermon among the white Primitive Baptists and Old Regulars? Have they preserved a tradition their ancestors had learned from blacks at frontier revivals and camp meetings during the second Great Awakening? The question awaits further research.

The members of the Fellowship Independent Baptist Church believe that a Spiritually anointed sermon will convict sinners, understood as the chief purpose of sermons. Brother John said:

I feel that when the word of God is preached, and in the demonstration and the power of the Holy Spirit, that it will convict the heart, if he's sinned. We are all sinners at one time, and when the word is preached, about the crucifixion of Christ, his death, his burial, his resurrection and his coming again, that will convict a man of his sins. And he has a desire to repent. (John and Pauline Sherfey interview, April 2, 1978, p. 31)

Brother Jesse explained that a Christian's indwelling Spirit can discern when a preacher is anointed, and that same Spirit will come into a sinner's heart and convict him:

That soul-salvation inside, you can feel this when a man's preaching in the Spirit. In other words his Spirit and your Spirit will link together and will let you know that he's preaching the word of God. And he's preaching it in the Spirit. And when he's a-doing this, it will convict, many times it will convict that lost sinner that's sitting in that congregation. That same Spirit that saved me is convicting him of his sins. And when the preacher quits preaching then and gives that altar call while that Spirit is still working in that person's heart, that's the time to give that altar call, that that person might move out of that seat when that small voice that we talk about that speaks to the man on the inside says, "This is the time." Then he might get up out of his seat and go to the altar and confess his sins before the Lord and ask him to come into his heart and save him. That's the purpose of preaching: to get that lost man saved. Also, a purpose of preaching is to lift up those that are Christians. It's like coming to the table and eating. (Comer interview, 1977, p. 16)

Aside from bringing the gospel to the unconverted, preaching blesses, uplifts, and instructs the converted. Tempted by the devil, a convert may yet sin. "Why does Brother John preach to the converted?" I asked Brother Vernie. "Maybe they ain't! They might confess it but maybe they ain't," he said. He went on to speak about the sermons that, as the church members put it, cause them to pull their feet up under the bench.

[Brother John] is led by the Spirit. So if the Lord lays it on him to preach that, why, then he's got to preach it. Maybe there's somebody in there that ain't a-doing what they ought to do. You could be saved and still do things that you shouldn't do. And the pastor's supposed to get up and preach and explain it to you, show you where it's wrong, and then you're supposed to quit it. (Meadows interview, 1977, pp. 36–37)

Stepping on toes, not cutting corners for anyone, Brother John teaches the converted how to live, what the Christian life is like, and what the believer can expect now and in the future, as the Spirit reveals it to him. Brother Allen seeks this from the sermons: "What I'm listening for [in the sermon] is to learn everything the gospel is about, and to learn more about the Lord. The more you learn, the more you want to walk toward his way" (Dove interview, p. 13). Brother John sums up both functions of the sermon—convicting sinners and teaching converts—as helping people live close to the Lord:

The purpose of a sermon is to, to me, is to win the lost people and to help those that don't understand to see more clearly how to live close to the Lord, how to do the Lord's work. In other words, it's what Paul taught; the gospel is the power of God, and if it's preached and people believe it, then it will lead 'em closer to God if they'll accept it. And that's the whole purpose of a sermon: to keep people close to God. (John Sherfey interview, July 23, 1977, p. 16)

The Preacher and the Congregation

A Spirit-led preacher's effectiveness depends on how receptive the congregation is. If members of a congregation are in the Spirit, they will be led to shout. Brother John encourages shouting, saying it helps him preach:

And I certainly do thank God for those amens. You know, it was kind of weak last Sunday but we had 'em coming today. So I, I appreciate that. I wish I could get the whole church to hollering amen. You say, "Preacher, that's too much like Pentecostal." Now, bless God, Baptists ought to do it, too. He said, "Let everything that has breath praise the Lord." And if it's the truth, holler amen to it. It won't hurt you. And if you know it's the truth, holler amen. Even when Brother Jesse's teaching, he teaches the truth, holler amen. Signify it and he might teach a little harder. He might get carried away. I'll tell you how I am, and I guess most of you know. When you start hollering amen at me it's just like a-sicking a dog after a fox. I go "yap yap yap yip" and just keep on going. (John Sherfey, morning service, just before closing prayer, April 2, 1978)

In his homely and effective fashion Belvin told me that some people in a congregation make it difficult for the preacher, but that when all are in "one mind" the Spirit leads better:

You can preach anywheres, but there is thisaway—some that will hindrance and tie, draw the service. And when it's hindrancing and drawing the service, well then, you ain't got his deliverance, as you would for everything to be one mind and one accord. . . . After coming of one mind and one accord, then that's when it seems like opening up the bucket of honey, just eat right fresh. But there is times of refreshments of the Spirit. There's time that you're more Spiritual than you are at others. There is time that the Spirit is more fresher, pours out, showers the blessings [more] than others. (Hurt interview, p. 39)

The activity of the Spirit, then, depends not only upon the preacher but also upon the receptiveness of the congregation. Insofar as the congregation forms a community of a single mind, in one accord, responding to the "message," the preacher's anointment becomes stronger and the message more powerful and effective. At the same time, though, the preacher himself must be properly trained and prepared.

The Call to Preach

Neither Brother John nor Brother Belvin has had seminary training. Once Ken George innocently asked Brother Vernie where he thought Brother John learned to preach. "Learned to preach!" Brother Vernie scolded. "Did he learn how to preach?" Ken put forward tentatively. "No, sir. He was called to preach. The Lord called him to preach." "And he could preach [snaps fingers] like that as soon as he got that call?" asked Ken. "Yes, he could," said Brother Vernie. "Of course, now, he had to, a young preacher that's just been called to preach, he can't get up there and preach just like a preacher that's been in there a couple of years. . . ." In fact, Brother John's first sermon was a disaster, as described in his life story in Chapter 9. "You've seen that little baby awhile ago. He ain't as big as we are. He's got to grow. So it's the same thing . . . After you're saved you grow in the Spirit," Vernie wound up, likening the newly called preacher to the newly converted Christian, born again as a baby, having to learn (Meadows interview, 1977, pp. 23–24).

Brother John explained that he felt himself called to preach the gospel: "Then he [Paul, in Romans 10] went on to say, 'But how can they hear without a preacher? And how can they preach except they be sent?' In other words except God sends 'em they can't preach nohow" (John Sherfey interview, July 23, 1977, p. 16). "God called me to preach, and if God called me, God can preach me" (ibid., p. 11). Most of the church members—including Brother John—feel there is nothing wrong with seminary training per se, but Brother Belvin indicts it for killing the Spirit:

> I just don't believe in [seminary training]. I don't believe God is that little. It's good to have a education, don't get me wrong, I don't kick education or nothing of that. But to stand, what kind of position to stand in, what shape to stand in to preach, and when to cry, when to make the motion as and all such stuff as that. And to have it wrote out, a notebook with their sermons from time to time on that out of the Bible, and their Bible laying there and then just read a little verse, and then lay that little ol' piece of paper up in there and go on with that. I'll tell you what it does do: it makes a awful dry, dead, whole meeting. It'll wear the people out and they will not come back. . . .
>
> Just ain't no Spirit in [a sermon preached by a man with seminary training]. It's just dry, that's all, just standing there just the same as reading out of a newspaper. And it don't mean nothing to people and that won't get people saved. I mean it won't get them under conviction. . . . You go to the cemetery, they're all dead. And the same way with the seminary, that's dead too. . . . And I don't like it that way, whenever I can't feel the power of the Lord Jesus Christ and find where my power is coming from, know where it's coming from, why it ain't no good to me. His power's real. (Hurt interview, pp. 78, 83–84)

Written and read sermons—whether or not produced by seminary-trained ministers—are understood to violate the rules of Spirit-leading and to be powerless and ineffective. "There's no trouble to tell if the Holy Ghost is leading a preacher or's not leading him," Brother Vernie said. "How do you tell?" I asked. "You can tell it in his action, you can tell it in the power that he preaches in. You take a man that has a wrote-down sermon, there ain't no power to it. Be just the same as you setting there reading off what you wrote." As a folklorist, my field being oral performance, I was pleased to find that the people I was studying favored oral performance themselves; but as a writer I was not prepared for their categorical rejection of written-down sermons. As I pursued this theme, I came to believe that the rejection is directed at a whole style of service, including language, behavior, and social class. Brother Belvin told a lengthy story about how uncomfortable he was trying to sing in such a church:

> I got in a church like that and they asked me to come sing, wanted me to sing a couple of songs for them, me and the girls, so I told 'em I would. . . . So [the pastor] read his text off, what he said he was going to preach. I noticed it, and I kept watching him a little bit, I seen that and I turned around and I said, "Well, what kind of a funny way is this? I've never been in a service like this, just a hard one. I'll do my best."
>
> And he read it off, and so then he said, "We're going to have prayer." He read that off, and I didn't know [that he had read it] right at the time, but I could feel something or other that was, ah, wedging . . . [Then he called me up to sing.] So I hit the pulpit, and I got there, and there it laid. One of these here old translations that denies the deity of Christ and all of that, had it laying there, and then besides had notes on that thing. Had them notes a-laying there, old big piece of paper laying there, and then had his prayer written down below it. Wrote out on it what he had just prayed— made out he'd prayed—he just read it off, see?

When Brother Belvin saw that the preacher's sermon Scripture was different from what he knew it to be in the King James Version, "God just hit me like a firecracker," he said, and he preached on the text as he knew it right then and there. It must have been quite a surprise to the pastor, who was expecting Brother Belvin to sing, not to preach ahead of him on the same Scripture passage. Each was operating by different rules for performance. The pastor had violated the rules of the Holy Spirit as Brother Belvin understood them, and Brother Belvin had violated the performance rules in that church's community.

> And when I got done with it we singed and I tell you one thing, they never did ask me to come back anymore, uh-uh, never no more I had the opportunity, but I got a good one in that time. And I can mighty near tell and if they're going to let me come back again or not when I get where they're at and talk to them . . . I get in once and a while, but that's all. When you get in them kind, see, well, they just got their little group the way they want it. . . . (Hurt interview, pp. 78–81)

Brother Belvin and Brother John both tell such stories about their infrequent visits to churches that Brother John calls "up in society" and Brother Belvin calls "classy." Usually they feel very uncomfortable, notice some things they don't believe in—baptismal pools behind the pulpit, for example, or a kitchen in the basement, or written prayers and sermons— and if they are asked to give a performance, they succeed in their own terms but fail to conform to the rules of the church and are not invited to return. Such churches are "modernistic," according to Brother John; they fail to realize that God calls preachers:

Then God called him [Paul] to preach the gospel. I know a lot of you folks out there don't believe God calls men to preach. You ought to study your Bible, bless the Lord. Amen, God's still calling men to preach just like he did back in the Bible days. Brother, the Bible hasn't changed nary a bit. The only thing that's changed has been this modernistic age, brother, that's whitewashed, galvanized, shined up. And brother, they push God off in a small corner and say, "We're going to run it like we want to." But you won't go to heaven running it like that. You'll go to hell, neighbor. (Sermon, March 27, 1972)

The Bible, according to Brother John, has changed "nary a bit"; it is alive, and God is alive, just as it was "back in the Bible days." God calls men to preach now just as he did then; the Bible lives in the present. Brother John's tropological allegorizing will be examined later in the chapter. Here, however, it serves to distinguish true Christians from those apostate, "modernistic" Christians who in caring so much for appearances ("whitewashed, galvanized, shined up") disobey God's will and fail to acknowledge that preachers are called.

A preacher must not write his sermon out beforehand, but he should study the meaning of the verses God has led him to preach. Brother John, anointed by the Spirit, preached briefly on this subject in the morning service on July 17, 1977:

I like what this brother said
about God saving him, God calling him to preach.
So many of 'em have to write their sermons down
on a little piece of paper beloved +hah+
and I'll tell you bless God, +hah+
I believe when God calls men +hah+
+hah+ brother into the gospel field, +hah+
I believe he'll give him the message +hah+
if they'll do what he says, study the word +hah+
+hah+ to show thyself approved, +hah+
a workman rightly dividing the word of truth +hah+
and not be ashamed of it, thank God.

Brother John was referring here to 2 Timothy 2:15: "Study to shew thyself approved unto God, a workman that needeth not to be ashamed, rightly dividing the word of truth." In the Scofield tradition, he interprets "the word of truth" as the Bible. His own practice is to pray for a Scripture during the week, and when it comes, to study its meaning in the *Scofield Reference Bible* (Scofield, ed. 1945), *The Open Bible* (1975), and the *Thompson Chain Reference Bible* (Thompson, ed. 1964). The Scofield is particularly useful for interpretation, while the Thompson is good for interpretation and for "chains" of parallel reference (by analogy) to thousands of topics throughout both the Old and New Testaments. Brother John explained that to use the chain of reference one must link verses from various parts of the Bible:

> Brother Jesse told you here in the Sunday school we run reference, go back in the old Bible, pick up some, link it together, and it becomes a great chain. This Bible is a great chain. Brother, I'll tell you, bless God, it's such a strong chain that everybody in the world can climb on it and never break it . . . And brother—but listen. If you go over there in Saint John, take one verse, come back to Revelation and grab another verse, and never link 'em together, never put 'em where they belong, never rightly divide the word, never know where it is, you've broke the link. You've broke the chain. And it's got no meaning, it's got no power. (Sermon, night service, July 17, 1977)

Brother John does not automatically follow the interpretations in these reference Bibles; he disagrees with them sometimes on the basis of the way the Spirit leads him, and sometimes on the basis of an oral tradition of interpretation of certain key verses—a tradition that comes from the preachers and teachers he himself has heard. But by and large he agrees with Scofield. When Brother John gets to the service, the Spirit will sometimes lead him to another Scripture; but ordinarily he will preach on the Scripture he studied during the week.

Brother John's unintentional preaching when trying to teach Sunday school is thought to be an additional evidence that his gift is in preaching and that he was called to preach. After preaching in Sunday school one morning when he substituted as leader for the absent Brother Jesse, he spoke to the congregation about it:

> I said awhile ago I'd preached last night and at the morning service but I preached in the Sunday school, too. I got started—Brother Jesse wasn't here to teach, and it's the hardest thing for me to try to teach without preaching. I don't know why, I just can't hardly. A young man asked me today why was it so difficult. Well, I told him, I tried to explain to him the difference between teaching and preaching. God calls teachers and God calls preachers. And when a teacher's called, why, he can stand there and teach all day and just love it. He loves it. But when I get started teaching, I get off onto preaching. And I can't help that. And of course I don't care, anyway [*laughs*], amen? I believe we ought to be willing to take a little preaching in the Sunday School. . . . I'll tell you, I got happy last night preaching, and I just been happy all day. I don't know a better way to be than to be happy in the Lord. (Night service, July 3, 1977)

Faced with the task of explicating the Bible, the indwelling Spirit anoints the preacher, whether in Sunday school or from the pulpit during the sermon. At lunch I had asked Brother John to tell me why he preached in

Sunday school that morning, and he spoke of the difference between preaching and teaching:

> It's hard for me to teach. In teaching you just stand and talk. In preaching you get carried away. I'm one of them hellfire and brimstone preachers. . . . The Spirit works different in the preachers than it does in the teachers. See, now, there's diversities of gifts. In other words many different kinds. One's teaching, one's preaching, one's prophecy, and speaking in tongues. All these different gifts; there's nine. That's why I disagree with a lot of 'em [Pentecostals]. I don't knock tongues but according to the Bible they have to have an interpreter. [See 1 Corinthians 12:1–11 and especially 14:1–19.] So you see the Spirit don't work in every person the same way. It works different. In other words a teacher can get up there and stand and teach all day and never raise his voice. But a preacher in the Spirit and he gets up, he don't say but a few words and something's done hit him and he's—I guess I busted your eardrums last Sunday night, didn't I? I can't help that.

"Call-to-Preach" Narratives

Like the conversion narrative—a person's story of how he or she was saved—the story of how a person came to accept being called by God to preach the gospel is a common narrative type in the repertory of preachers who feel themselves called to the ministry. I have heard several narratives from preachers who described how they experienced the call to preach. They tell the story as a testimony, and do so often, to strangers, to congregations, and to other preachers.

My ethnopoetic transcription of Brother John's call-to-preach narrative, as he told it to me on July 9, 1976, in his home, with his wife present, follows. To read it silently and hear it as he spoke it, observe the following conventions of the spacing and typography on the page:

Standard (roman) type: ordinary conversational volume and intonation.
Boldface type: increased volume and expanded intonation range.
Italic type: decreased volume and compressed intonation range.
New line, not indented: continue without pause.
New line, indented: pause about 1/2 second.
Double-space, new line, indented: pause about 1 second.

> When God called me to preach which has been twenty soon be twenty-four years ago
> I was working at the Mead Corporation in Kingsport, Tennessee.
> . . .
> And uh
> so

I was working there the on the three-to-eleven shift, well
before this the Lord had been dealing with me
uh
to go I—I felt to go preach.
See it kept **dawn**ing on me.
But I kept saying, "No, that can't be it"
and uh
every time I'd testify or something in church *why*
somebody'd walk up and say, "I believe God's calling you to preach," *see.*
I said, "Well if he does, I'll go."
So I—I kept fighting it off and going you know with this
I don't know, it was a burden seemed like or a heavy feeling on me, a
load upon me
and uh
so one evening I was working the three-to-eleven shift and I was coming
home from work and
and uh it just got so heavy upon me I just couldn't stand it.
And I pulled an old '42 Studebaker car I had
oh it was about eleven-thirty in the night
and uh I was about a half a mile from home and
I pulled that old car over to the side of the road and stopped
and of course I'd 'a-been I was praying and a-crying, you know the tears
got so big in my eyes I couldn't see the road.
I just fell down over the steering wheel.

And I said, "Lord, if it's preach, I'll go.
If you'll lift this burden."
And, believe me, it left.

Just like that
it was gone.
I felt like I could fly away.
So I went on home and I was just as happy as a little lark, you know.
And because the
the burden had been **lifted,** see.
It'd **gone.**
. . .
It was just
I don't uh
actually it's hard to explain.
Uh to describe
the uh **pressure**
that was on me.
. . .
It was just,

it just, just felt,
you just felt like you know that you were just
in a cage or something and you couldn't go nowhere.
. . .
I just felt like I was
pressed down.

And uh I kept praying and trying to get out from under it until I said,
"Lord, if it's preach, I'll go."

And when I said that it just [*snaps fingers*], just gone.
Just **vanished.**
Just like if you'd have lift a big rock right off the top of me.

Brother John's call-to-preach narrative is familiar to the church members from their conversations with him and also from his sermons, where
he offers portions of the larger story to illustrate his belief that God calls
preachers and to assert his identity as one of those whom God has called.
The wording of the key lines during the climactic moment when he talks
to God and accepts the call to preach is virtually identical whenever he
tells it, indicating that Brother John has memorized that part of the story.
For example:

I was saved a good while, brother, before God called me, and then
when he did call me I tried every way in the world +hah+ to get
out of it.
I run, I did everything I could do +hah+
to keep from preaching +hah+
but brother God was still calling me +hah+
and until I said, "Yes, Lord," brother,
I'll tell you that burden was still there. +hah+
But the moment I said, "Yes Lord, if it's preach, I'll go," God lifted that
burden. And brother, praise God, I'm still in the field, hallelujah. (Sermon,
March 19, 1972)

The fact that a kernel of the narrative (here, the immediate circumstances
surrounding his acceptance of the call to preach) and its language is the
same in each version, while the language that surrounds it and the points
it illustrates may differ on different occasions, is another example of what I
have called the "preform" technique of oral composition. Earlier, in Chapter 6, I showed how the preform theory accounts for phrases and lines
generated in prayer. In narrative, a kernel or important episode can be
treated as a stored preform, similar to the stored phrase but at a larger
order of magnitude, that when remembered is given its final shaping to fit
the current context. In this case the context involved an associational
transition from Brother John's previous point—that a man must be saved

before he is called to preach—and a related point, that John was saved a good long while before he accepted the call; in fact he ran from it. Sometimes (but not this time) he likens himself to Jonah in disobeying God's will.

Brother Belvin's story of how he received and eventually accepted the call to preach is similar to Brother John's but more detailed. The period of misery is fleshed out with great care, and the story parallels his conversion narrative (see Chapter 8), even to the extent that a preacher (then Geurdon A. Cave; this time Brother John) looms as the wise, all-knowing, accusatory prophet who makes it clear what God wants him to do. Brother John, who has worked with machinery all his life, and whose twin ambitions were to be a truck driver and preacher, was overcome and gave in to the call while driving a car; Brother Belvin, a man of the soil, accepted the call in the field above his chicken house and his meat house. Brother Belvin's call-to-preach narrative came in the midst of a seven-hour near-monologue in his home when Ken George and I visited him:

I'd been going around putting on prayer meetings and singing, praying. That wasn't what the Lord wanted me to do. I was old Jonah. [*Light laugh.*] I was running, I was putting on something else, just like Jonah was doing. Got his ticket to go some other direction, and the Lord wanted him to go in Sodom.[1] And so, I put it on praying, and testifying, and singing. And so, Brother John he come down on it that night. I was sitting on the third bench. And I never will forget it as long as I live, sitting at the third bench.

And I done ran a long time. I'd ran a long time from preaching. And Brother G. A. Cave told me about it. He was telling me that, "I know that you're a preacher, I know you're a preacher." He wanted me to preach. [*Light laugh.*] And his wife got all over me, and I had different ones, "I want to hear you preach." I said, "Well, maybe one of these days I will."

So Brother John that night, the Lord give it to him, the Lord just poured it on him, so that he could give it to me. I knew exactly, I knew it afterwards then, what it was. I thought somebody had certainly been telling stuff on me, but they hadn't. Yes they had, it was the Lord that told him. [*Laughs.*] I set there and he got in the pulpit and I'm telling you he come down on it. And he said, "You're sitting right in here," and he was pointing his finger right down at me. He says, "You're sitting right in here," he says, "you're just as guilty as the one out yonder if you don't do what the Lord Jesus Christ tells you to do, and you're supposed to do it. And you're not a-doing it, you're guilty, and you know you are."

And he pointed his finger right down where I was at, too, mighty near it, just right down. Had to be of the Lord, and I done drawed my old toes back

1. Actually Nineveh.

under the bench thataway; he was getting on them you know. And he said, "I'm going to tell you what I'm going to do." He said, "I hope that the Lord will beat the britches off of you, and I'm gonna pray that he will, before you get home. And I hope," he said, "that you don't get nary a nap of sleep." He said, "I hope that bed gets so rolly and hill-sidey that you can't stay on it, and that old cover'll get so short you can't pull it up on you. . . ."

I was guilty. I come all the way home from there, and I cried all the way across the mountain. I'd cry, wouldn't let them see me crying. The Lord was really whipping me. Oh, he was pouring it on me. I got home . . . I got into bed. That just got so rolly that I couldn't, oh I just couldn't, well it just felt like, well it was just so lumpy and hateful, I couldn't lay there. Cover got so short I couldn't pull it up on me, just exactly like he said.

Way in the night I just did nap off, I don't know if it was a dream or a vision, I don't know what it was, I don't know why it was. But anyhow I was tripped up some way or another, I don't know how I done it—my wife can tell you the same. And [in my dream] the Lord [was] just preaching me, and I was to preach, that's what it was, and I just give out a war-whoop, thataway. And man when I done that from the pulpit, I done that way from the pulpit, and when I done that I was right on her back! When I done that I mighty near taken her out on the floor, might near getting rowdy. And she jumped over and she grabbed the pillow and says, "What's the matter here?"

I turned on over and I didn't get much sleep, that was around three o'clock, and I just couldn't sleep hardly. And just every time it was preach, preach, a sermon, a sermon, and it just went that way. And oh my, I couldn't hardly wait for daylight to break a little bit so I could get out of there. I wanted to get out of there. And I knowed I was worrying her. . . .

And oh, thank the good Lord, I seen the breaking of day and I hit the floor, I got out. And I said, "Lord, I'm going to get out of here." [*Laughs.*] "I'm going away from it." I got out, and I got out to the door, and when I got to the door, I made my way up there to that chicken house, above, right there, and the meat house here, and I got up above the house, and I said, "Lord, if it's preach, I'm willing, I'll go."

My burden it was just as real to me as it could be. "That's what I want you to do." [*Laughs.*]

I come back in and I set down to the table, she had breakfast ready. And I told my children, and all of them, I said, "Before we bow our heads to say the grace this morning I've got something to tell you." I said, "I want you to recognize Daddy in the home this morning, and from now on, as one of God's preachers." [*Light laugh.*] They bowed their little heads and commenced a-crying. And I said grace and they had breakfast, recognized me as a preacher in the home. Yes, I thank the Lord for that.

Then it hit my heart, I had to get on the road then. See, I had to go make them paths straight. I had to get on the road then. I done fooled Brother

John, thought I had, but I hadn't. I had to get on the road now and I went out and got in the car and we hit the road and I went down to his home. Got down to his home—he wasn't there. He was out, hadn't come in yet. So we sat down with his wife and we talked it over, and talked it over to her, and she sat there crying, and I cried, wife [cried], and how beautiful it was, how the Lord used me.

And so, when he come in he hadn't gotten through the door good but she said, "John," says, "gonna lose him." Says, "Why? Lose who?" Said, "Lose Belvin." "No." Said, "Yep." Said, "He's got to go into the field," she said, "he's been called to preach, he's announced his calling."

And John got in the kitchen there, and I was standing there crying, talking over it. [*Light laugh.*] John commenced a-crying, I commenced a-crying. So good, so real to us. And he asked, he commenced asking me a question. He said, "Let me tell you something." He said, "I'm glad of this. I'm going to tell you something now. I could have told you that two years ago, that you were God's preacher." [*Laughs.*] He said, "I could have told you that but I didn't want to butt in on you. That was between you and the Lord."

But Brother John, he waited until I went down to his home, after he preached on it and laid it down to me what he hoped the Lord would do, and the Lord done that, and I come back and got a good rest. Same bed, same bed. I slept good, slept same as a baby in it. You do the will of the Lord, sleep same as a baby. I have taken and been many miles, and Brother John he's been a blessing to me, him and his family. (Hurt interview, pp. 61–65)

Both these narratives, and the other narratives of the call to preach that I have heard from a few dozen Baptist and Pentecostal ministers over the past fifteen years or so, conform to a general pattern. People notice that the future preacher is gifted with words, particularly when he gives testimony. Someone tells him, "I believe God is calling you to preach." Usually he has already realized it himself. He resists the call, sometimes for months or even years, not wanting to give up his way of life; but ultimately he becomes miserable and the burden becomes too great to bear. At that point he gives in and promises God that he will preach the gospel. The parallel with the conversion-narrative pattern is striking. First there is a period of conviction-like misery and resistance to God's will (in one case resisting the call to preach, in the other reluctance to repent and abandon one's former way of life). When the burden becomes overwhelming the sinner or future preacher yields and does God's bidding.

The fact that these narratives conform to a pattern suggests the possibility that they are learned. Certainly they are heard and could be learned. Brother Belvin must have heard such narratives from G. A. Cave and Brother John, for example. His acceptance statement—"Lord, if it's preach,

I'm willing, I'll go"—is virtually identical with Brother John's "Lord, if it's preach, I'll go." Jonah is the biblical prototype for the call-to-preach narrative just as the apostle Paul is the prototype for the conversion narrative. Preachers use them as examples; I have heard Brother John refer to Jonah this way in sermons several times (e.g., in the morning service on July 17, 1977). More likely, though, the body of call-to-preach narratives serves to guide the future preacher's interpretation of his experience. They shape his *perception* of his experiences, and thus, for practical purposes, the experiences themselves, as they come to live in memory and to be shaped and reshaped in narrative. The same is likely the case with conversion narratives. In the church members' view, the consistency of the pattern confirms that the call is real, and is taken as evidence of God's direct and consistent dealings with humankind.

But what happens when experience does not fit the narrative pattern? We shall see in Chapter 9 when considering Brother John's life story. He narrates an instantaneous conversion, conforming to the basic doctrine of "popular southern Protestantism" (Hill 1967: 23–31, 137). And it is this conversion narrative that he relates in his sermons and testimonies (see below). But the facts of his life, as he talks about them in the give-and-take of conversation (rather than in the one-voice shaping of an extended narrative), indicate that he experienced a gradual conversion, one that proceeded by stages over a number of cycles and a period of several years. The differences, I will suggest, are due to the constraints of public performance and his need to resolve ambiguity when in a narrative mode.

Sermons

In keeping with Brother John's aims, his sermons are designed to help people live closer to God. He conceives of three kinds of audiences: the unconverted, those who "once knew the Lord but strayed away," and the born-again Christians. He began as an evangelist, not a pastor; he preached in revivals and over radio stations, and he conceived of his task as bringing the gospel to the unconverted. For most of the twenty-plus years that he has preached in Page County he has been a pastor, but he also retained a ministry on local radio; and these radio sermons are heavily evangelistic. The sermons he preaches at the Fellowship Independent Baptist Church are different because the audiences are different. Because there may be some unconverted persons in the congregation, he always includes an evangelistic message and a plea for the unsaved to repent and let God in their lives; indeed, shortly before the invitation, he asks those who are unsaved to raise their hands if they wish for prayer. Yet the sermons delivered at the church are addressed primarily to the converted. This is especially true of the sermon at the night service, which attracts a more interdenominational congregation than the morning service, where the church members predominate. When Ken George and I began documenting the church services, Brother John's morning services did emphasize evangelism; God, he thought, might have led us there for purposes other than folklife documentation. As professor and graduate student, we heard a good deal in Brother John's sermons about Nicodemus, the intellectual to whom Jesus explained how it was that a person could be born more than once. But after a few weeks the morning sermons returned to their normal emphasis.

The sermons on which I will base the analysis in the rest of this chapter, all preached by Brother John, cover the period from late 1971 until late 1983. (I am omitting the fourteen sermons I recorded in the fall of 1985; they were not significantly different.) In all, they comprise twenty-five recorded in worship services at the Fellowship Independent Baptist Church, two recorded at a revival in North Carolina, and eighteen more recorded from Brother John's radio ministry on WRAA in Luray, Virginia. Among the radio sermons are the ten kindly recorded by Cameron Nickels in 1971 and 1972, when he monitored the station's religious broadcasts for me, and another eight that Ken George and I recorded in 1977 from inside the radio studio.

In "The Rhetoric of the Radio Ministry," William Clements, basing his studies on fieldwork with Pentecostal churches in 1972 and 1973 in northeast Arkansas, concluded that "a radio preacher's broadcast can be comprehended most clearly by viewing it as a folklore event similar to occurrences in the context of the preacher's church" (1974b:318–319). Clements, who to my knowledge is the only folklorist to publish on the subject of radio ministers, wrote that the Pentecostal preachers attempted, over the radio, to create a church-like atmosphere "in which spiritual emotionalism can be manifested overtly and in which the affairs of the world are allowed to intrude only rarely" (ibid.:322). Their sermons over the airwaves, like their church sermons, all had the same evangelistic theme: "sinners must convert and saints must help them" (ibid.). Interestingly, these radio ministers created the church-like atmosphere with their rhetoric alone, for they made their recordings in advance of the broadcasts, in the confines of their homes or elsewhere, without the presence of live congregations. In so doing, they were "exploiting the mass media as fully as possible" (ibid.:318).

Brother John's radio ministry is, in certain ways, an even more faithful transfer of the church onto the airwaves. The radio station WRAA has a small studio where Brother John, his family, and a few members of the congregation broadcast the program live on Sunday afternoons. The program begins with a prayer by Brother Donny; special-hymns and church announcements follow; and the program concludes with about fifteen minutes of Brother John's evangelistic preaching. In 1971 and 1972 he ended the programs with an invitation to sinners to accept Christ and a prayer to help them do so; in 1977 and 1978 he allowed himself to be cut off in mid-sermon, concluding with an exhortation for sinners to "get right with God," and telling Christians that "if we don't meet you next Sunday on the air, we'll meet you in the air," a reference to the rapture of the true church that he believes is coming soon.

The presence of his family and members of the church as radio audience creates a church-like studio atmosphere, for they are blessed and shout during the broadcast. This community widens to include the sick whose names are mentioned over the air as needing prayers, and those who have sent in money to help sponsor the broadcast. (The cost in 1977 was $20 for a half-hour.) Yet, as I pointed out above, the radio sermons emphasize evangelism more than the church sermons do. Brother John addresses the audience as "you," saying he knows many disagree with this or that among his beliefs. In other words, although the studio audience provides a church-like atmosphere in which the Spirit leads, blesses, and anoints, Brother John conceives of his audience as the unconverted in the local broadcast area and aims the broadcast at them. At times, crammed into the tiny 10×10 studio with a half-dozen extended families from the church, setting up and operating our video and audio equipment, dripping in the 100-degree heat while keeping the windows shut to prohibit traffic noise, I thought of the group as a beleaguered community sending out a message from inside a fortress under siege.

A Representative Sermon

The sermon, as the focal and most time-consuming event in the worship service, deserves great attention. It would be uneconomical to print the texts of several sermons; interested readers may look at many transcriptions of these in the Library of Congress Archive of Folk Culture in the materials housed with this project (see Appendix E). I have decided, therefore, to print a single sermon in its entirety, and then, in discussing its subjects and themes, to bring in excerpts from other sermons as they bear on the discussion.

The following sermon was preached on Sunday, August 7, 1977, at the homecoming service, and may be heard in its entirety on the *Powerhouse for God* record album. It is characteristic of Brother John's sermons in many ways. It is addressed primarily to the converted even though it contains exhortations to the unsaved. It is concerned with the future. It pits the church against the world. It is characteristically autobiographical. It involves the explication of a biblical text: here, 1 Thessalonians 4:13–18, on the post-millennium rapture of the church. It proceeds, as Brother John's sermons always do, from the assumption that the Bible not only is true at face-value, but also has hidden meaning that can best be gotten out by typology, tropology, parallel textual reference, and analogy to personal experience, rather than by simple logic, scholarly tradition, or historical evidence. Throughout the sermon, Brother John develops its main theme: the heavenly homecoming reunion of the church; but the references are local and familial. The raptured church is not conceived as a worldwide gathering of saints, but as one's kinfolk and friends. Concerned as many are with the aches of old age, Brother John stresses the change during the rapture to a perfect and "glorified" body free from pain. He tells his audience what the saved must do before the church is "caught up" to heaven and assures them that the church will triumph. In one respect the sermon is unrepresentative: it is a trifle short, lasting only about twenty-five minutes. In all other respects it is typical. The text follows; I have numbered the lines for later reference.

    I'd like to read this morning by the help of God from the fourth chapter of the First Thessalonians, reading a few verses there, about five verses, to be exact. Said, "But I would not have you be ignorant, brethren, concerning them which are asleep, that you sorrow not, even as others which have no
5   hope. For if we believe that Jesus died and rose again, even so them also which sleep in Jesus will God bring with him. For this we say unto you by the word of the Lord, that we which are alive and remain unto the coming of the Lord shall not prevent them which are asleep. For the Lord himself shall descend from heaven with a shout, with the voice of the archangel
10   and with the trump of God; and the dead in Christ shall rise first: Then we—ones is a-living—which are alive and remain shall be caught up together with them in the clouds to meet the Lord in the air: and so shall we ever be with the Lord. Wherefore comfort one another with these words." I don't know of anything, beloved, in my life that's any more comforting
15   this morning than to know, praise God, that there is a homecoming day for God's people. Now, beloved, we call this a homecoming day; we have our homecoming here at this church on the first Sunday in August each year. And, beloved, this *is* a homecoming. But, my brother and sister, I'm looking forward on to the great final homecoming of God's people. Beloved,
20   that's the one when we'll meet in the air with the Lord Jesus Christ, my beloved friends. Now if you'll notice beloved in +hah+ in the verse 17, he said, "Then we which are alive and remain shall be caught up." Now, beloved, caught up means to be picked up and carried away. My friend, now this morning it's going to do away with this old thing, beloved, that a lot
25   of people believe that when +hah+ they get saved, beloved, then +hah+ when people are lost they're all going together, but the Bible don't teach that and I can't preach that. If I did I'd be preaching you a false doctrine this morning, and God forbid that I'd ever do something like that. My friend, the Bible said, "Then we which are alive and remain," talking of
30   Christian people, +hah+ the Apostle Paul was writing +hah+ to the church of the Thessalony, and, brother, he was saying, beloved, that those

that are dead and gone on to be with the Lord. +hah+
He said "We will not prevent them
which are asleep for the dead in Christ +hah+
35   +hah+ shall rise first. +hah+
Then we which are alive and remain +hah+
+hah+ shall be changed in a moment, +hah+
my friends or be caught up together
+hah+ to meet them in the clouds +hah+
40   +hah+ with the Lord and so shall we +hah+
ever be with the Lord." +hah+
Wherefore comfort one another +hah+
with these words neighbor, +hah+
if you've got a loved one +hah+
45   that outstripped you in this walk of life +hah+
and gone on to be with God +hah+
don't weep for 'em here +hah+
but look for the homecoming day +hah+
that's on the other side.
50   That's what I'm looking for this morning. Oh, it's a homecoming here, yes.
And I'm proud of it this morning. But I'm looking forward to that day when
every child of God can meet Jesus in the cloud. Oh, you say, "Preacher,
what about those that died a long time ago?" Thank God, brother, the old,
this old tabernacle, brother, the Bible said will dissolve and go back
55   +hah+ to the dust of the earth, +hah+
my friends but hallelujah,
we've got a building eternal in the heavens, +hah+
my friend not made with hands, +hah+
that we're looking for after awhile +hah+
60   and brother praise God, +hah+
old John's gonna move +hah+
after awhile. +hah+
I'm gonna leave this old robe of flesh, +hah+
I'll drop this robe of flesh +hah+
65   and seize the everlasting prize, +hah+
life eternal +hah+
in the Lord Jesus Christ.
Can't help but think as I asked you to come forward huh this morning to
pray, you that are sick, brother, let me tell you something. One day after
70   awhile, sisters, you're going to drop off that old robe. That old flesh is going
back to the dust from which it came.
Praise God this mortal put on immortality.
This corruptible put on the incorruption.
My friend then shall be brought to pass.
75   O death where is your sting?

O grave where's your victory?
Thanks be to God who giveth us
+hah+ the victory through Jesus Christ our Lord. +hah+
Brother I'm saying to you today +hah+
80 the victory's in Jesus this morning. +hah+
It's not because you're Baptist. +hah+
It's not because you're Pentecostal.
It's not because you're Methodist. +hah+
But it's [*claps hands*] because you're saved +hah+
85 by the power of God +hah+
and filled with the Holy Ghost, +hah+
brother that you're in his care today.
Oh, caught up. [*Light laugh.*] That's one of the greatest words I ever—.
That hit me like a wedge. Caught up. Brother, caught up, thank God.
90 Brother, I'll tell you every time I think of that I remember a sermon I
preached a long time ago. A man that God caught up by the locks of his
hair and took on a sightseeing tour. Amen, it's in the Bible, praise God.
Brother, God's gonna catch every one of us up. Saved people that are here
this morning. God's gonna catch you up, neighbor. He'll take you right
95 through the clouds. You say, "Preacher, how am I going? I don't have any
force." If you've got the Spirit of God in you, you're going. Amen, brother,
praise God, you won't have to have a Sputnik +hah+
+hah+ to put to your feet and +hah+
+hah+ go down to Cape Canaveral and be set off to go up +hah+
100 but thanks be to God, you can go from the [*claps hands*] church house,
+hah+
you can go from the kitchen, +hah+
you can go from the living room, +hah+
if your heart's right with God.
But if it's not right with God, you're not going nohow. Amen. So brother,
105 this morning we'll be caught up. Caught up. That's what he said here.
Together. Caught up together. Now it's not, my friend, some are going
ahead of the others. You say, "Well, preacher, I thought the dead already
been there." Yes, they have, they're basking in the sunlight of God right
now. Amen, I know this morning, my daddy and my son, Pauline's people
110 and my brother, and others that's outstripped me and your loved ones that
were saved, they're basking in the sunlight of God. Amen. My friend, but
I'm going to tell you something according to this blessed holy Bible. And I
believe this to be the infallible word of God. I believe it'll stand when this
world's on fire. Praise God this morning, the Bible says that the Lord him-
115 self shall come. At the trump, brother, he'll come with a shout. Brother and
listen, the spirit of those, or the soul of those men, women, boys, and girls
+hah+ that's done gone on to be with God, he'll bring 'em back with him,
they'll go to the dust of the earth, brother, where they were put down, and

praise God, they'll come forth with a glorified body huh fashioned like the
120 Lord's. "All right, preacher, then after they do that what else is going to
happen?" When they get up even with us—brother, you're talking about a
quick change. Amen? Sometimes it takes me a long time to get dressed.
Sometimes I just can't hardly get one foot in the leg, pants leg. Amen, it
takes me awhile to get dressed. But brother, that day I'm gonna change so
125 quick nobody'll see me. Amen?
      Hallelujah thank God this morning.
      You say, "Preacher, you sure have some wild ideas."
      Brother I'm just telling you the Bible says +hah+
      we'll be changed in a moment,
130   in the twinkling of an eye. +hah+
      Brother as fast as you can twinkle your eye +hah+
      you'll get out of this old house and get in the new one. +hah+
      Glory to God you won't have to pack. +hah+
      Some say I'm gon' pack and get me ready; honey, I've done packed.
      +hah+
135   Amen, I'm not packing, praise God, +hah+
      I'm packed and ready right now. +hah+
      If God wants me, here I am.
      You say, "Preacher I'd be afraid to do that." You better get on this altar
      then. If there's something in your life that's a-bothering you,
140   there's something that's hindering you,
      you better get on this altar and repent of your sins [claps hands] +hah+,
      get your name in the Lamb's book of life +hah+
      because, praise God this morning,
      if God wants me, I'm not afraid to die.
145 Hallelujah hallelujah. Told a boy the other day. We was talking about driv-
      ing a gasoline truck. I know this don't have nothing to do with the mes-
      sage. But I've drove 'em and I think nothing about it. "I'd be going down
      the road," he said, "well, Lord, I'd be scared to death." He said, "I'm afraid
      that thing'll blow up and kill me." I said, "You're forgetting while you're
150 driving that dump truck. You've got a hundred gallons of gas a-swinging
      on each side of you." I said, "That's enough right there to blow you to
      kingdom come." And I said, "If your heart was right with God you wouldn't
      worry whether it blowed up or whether it didn't." Amen? If you're ready to
      go, you're not worried. Praise God this morning. You say, "Well, I don't
155 believe in rushing it." You ain't rushing it. You ain't rushing it a bit. That's
      not rushing it. We've got to work to make a living, praise God. Amen,
      you're not rushing it. If you watch what you're doing, there's no danger.
      But they're just scared to death. Amen, you know why he was? I'll tell you
      why. He likes to grab the old bottle and nip it a little bit. Amen? Every time
160 he comes around. I run him out of my shop one day because he had a can
      of beer in his hand. I said, "Get out of here and don't bring it back. I don't

Brother John preaching, 1977.

want to see it." Amen? Praise God this morning. I believe children of God
ought to stand up like a lion. Amen, brother. Praise God, he don't like me
now because I told him that. Praise God, but that's all right, I still stand the
65   same way. Amen brother praise God this morning, because when Jesus
comes I'm a-going with him. I mean that this morning. I'm a-going with
him. Praise God. All right. Brother, let me tell you, the church, I said the
church, is going up, and the gates of hell can't stop it. Amen. The church
is going up and the gates of hell cannot prevail against it. Jesus told 'em in
70   Matthew, he said, "Peter, I say unto thee that thou art Peter, and upon this
rock I'll build my church, and the gates of hell shall not prevail against it."
You say, "Well, preacher, what in the world has happened? What's wrong
with the churches today?" Brother, let me tell you it ain't the church of
Jesus Christ; it's the devil's crowd. Amen. Praise God, that's exactly what's
75   wrong. People yield to the lust of the flesh more than they yield to God
Almighty. My Bible said to be ye leaders of the Spirit. Let the Spirit of God

lead you where God wants you to, and brother, then it'll be all right. My
friend I want you to notice. Brother, there's a lot to do in the church.
Brother, there's a lot to do in this church. Nowhere did God ever tell you:
180   saved, set down, do nothing. Brother, the first of all, there's a war to be
fought. Amen. There's a war to be fought in the church. I'm talking about
believers now, not unsaved. I'm talking about saved people. Look in Ephesians, Chapter 6, verse 10 and through 18. Brother, there's a war to fight.
Jesus told 'em, he said, "Put on the warfare.
185   Put on the whole armor of God +hah+
         That you be able to stand against the wiles of the devil."
         Church if you don't put 'em on this morning +hah+
         the devil's gonna tear you down.
You've got to put 'em on. The whole armor of God. Brother, then there's a
190   race to run. Some say, "Well, preacher, all I've got to do is just get saved.
I'm all right." Honey, I disagree with that. Amen, I disagree with that.
Bless God, there's a race to run. My brother, you don't win a race a-setting
down, do you? Amen. I've never seen nobody win a race a-setting down.
Brother, to win the race they've got to run.
195   If it's in an automobile they've got to set there and steer the thing
+hah+
         and keep it a-going to stay ahead. +hah+
         Same way in the Christian life [*claps hands*], brother.
         You've got to stay on the mark, toe it, +hah+, and God'll bless your soul.
That's what's the matter with the world today, brother. They got saved and
200   somebody sugar-coated 'em a sermon and they went to sleep. Amen, let
somebody come along and wake 'em up and they get so mad at him they
could kill him. Amen. Praise God this morning I'm saying to you there's a
race to run. If you want to win the race, brother, you're going to have to
stay in there and fight it, brother. Praise God this morning I used to run in
205   the sack race. You ever run in the sack race? That's pretty hard to do, get
your feet down in a sack and run. Amen, but I've done it and I've won
the race.
         Amen, I'm in a race this morning +hah+
         and if you're going to run with me, let's go, bless the Lord, +hah+
210   Let's win it for Jesus.
He'll bless our souls. Amen. Brother, there's a race to be run. Brother, Paul
said, "I run the race with patience." Amen, brother I'm saying look in Hebrews Chapter 12, verse 1 and 2. My brother, the Bible says, brother,
"These have run the race before us." He said, "We're laid under such a
215   great cloud of witnesses, let us," he said, "run the race with patience.
Looking on the author and the finisher of our faith which is in Christ Jesus
our Lord." Brother, you run the race and the finishing line's on out yonder
somewhere, you'll cross it after awhile. Amen, all right. Then there's something else. Look in First Corinthians Chapter 3, verse 9: the labor of love.

20   Brother, let me tell you there's love in God's people. Brother Belvin mentioned it this morning. If we're saved by God's grace there's love in our
hearts. Amen, if you've got hate in your heart this morning you ain't right
with God. I don't care who you are or what you say you are,
     where you stand or how high you are,
25   whether you're president of the United States +hah+
     or of Congress or of whatever it is, +hah+
     if the heart ain't right with God +hah+
     there's no love there
     and you're on your road to hell.
30   Brother, let me tell you. First Corinthians Chapter 3, verse 9, will tell you.[2]
Paul said, "If I give my body to be burned and have not love, charity, it
profit me nothing." Brother, you could give a man everything in the world,
but if you don't have love, church, you ain't got nothing. Amen, and I'm
proud to tell you this statement this morning. And I'm not bragging, but I
35   feel like I should brag. I've had people to come here to this church praise
God, and say they felt the freedom and the liberty of God right here.
Honey, I'd hate for these singers or these people to come here, these
preachers, and these people to come, walk into this church, and say, "Lord,
I never felt so out of place in my life." [*Weeping:*] Honey, if you'd go ahead
40   and tell that on me, I'd have to sit down and cry. I would. I want you to feel
at home when you come here. Why, if you don't feel at home this morning
there's something wrong with you. It ain't me; I've tried. I've done my best.
I want everybody huh to feel like they're God's children this morning. The
house was built for God's people.
45   The house was built for the unsaved +hah+
     to come in and get right with God.
     Brother, that's the love of God this morning.
We've got to have that love, before we'll ever get anywhere with God.
Brother, we've got to have that love. Praise God this morning. Brother, I
50   want you to know the church of Christ will triumph after awhile. Amen,
did you know this morning the church has been kicked from pillar to post.
Brother, they've suffered the persecution. They've had lies told on 'em and
everything else. Amen, I'm talking about the church. Of the living God.
Brother, every time you do something good the old devil'll run down the
55   road and make a lie on you. Amen. But I'll tell you, bless God, we're going
to triumph over it, all of it. Amen, brother, Jesus went down in Jerusalem
one time. If you remember he set down right on the hill and looked over in
Jerusalem. And he said, "O Jerusalem, Jerusalem, how oft have I prayed
for you and prayed that you would do what you're supposed to do but you
60   didn't do it. You've killed my prophets; you've stoned 'em to death." And he

2. After listening to this performance on tape, Brother John corrected the reference to Chapter 13, verse 3.

said, "Now," he said, "I weep for you." He set there and wept as he looked
over it. My friend, but I want you to know one thing. Brother, when he told
'em to go down there and get the foal of an ass and bring it up to him, he
said, "If they ask you any questions just say, 'My Savior has need of it.'"
265 Amen, thank God, went down and got this little donkey and brought it up
to Jesus,
    and he got on that little donkey.
    I can just see him this morning, my Savior,
    as he got up on that little old donkey,
270 and brother they even put their coats on him,
    +hah+ they spread their coats down for the donkey to step on.
    Brother he triumphed over Jerusalem.
    I want you to know this morning the church is gonna triumph +hah+
    over this world, praise God, +hah+
275 and it's soon coming +hah+
    whether you believe it or not. +hah+
    The church is [claps hands] gonna triumph +hah+
    over this world, thank God. +hah+
    I'm glad to tell you +hah+
280 that Jesus is the head of it.
So many people say, "Well, he's the head of our church." Honey, Jesus is
the head of this church. Amen, I try to pastor here by the help of God. And
I'm not very well thought of, I know that, by a lot of people, but I try to do
my best. Amen. But praise God this morning, we're going to triumph after
285 awhile. Amen, we're going to come forth with the victory. Amen, listen,
honey. The future of the church is in the air. Amen, brother. Praise God,
we'll be caught up with him in the air. That's the most blessed thought
this morning, of being caught up. And just think. That daddy or that
mother of yours, that brother or that sister of yours or that baby that you
290 once loved so dearly, loving him or her so much, that you wept and you
cried, you've cried. One day after awhile when Jesus steps off of the throne
of [unintelligible] God's gonna look over at the Son and say, "Son, it's time
to go get 'em." I believe it's close. I believe it's close. "It's time, Son, to go
down and bring 'em home." Thank God, he'll come through the clouds,
295 Brother Jesse, with a shout when he comes. That soul a-going back wherever that loved one of yours was praying, that soul's going right down to it.
Thank God it'll get up. You talking about a reunion, this is a reunion here.
I have a lot of my, some of my folks here this morning. Praise God and this
is a reunion. Not only a reunion is it just because they're here, but because
300 all of you are here. It's a reunion. But I'm looking forward to that reunion
in heaven. Some'll say, "Preacher, preacher, it's gonna be awful quiet." No
it won't. I believe it'll be noisy. I sure do. I believe this is the quietest world
you'll ever live in. I sure do. I believe when God's people, when those that
have been gone so long, as I've told you before, I'm a pretty big man, I

5 thought I was bigger than what I really was the day they closed the casket
in my daddy's face, [*weeping*] put the lid down, I couldn't stand it no
longer. But I'm telling you this morning, praise God, the next time I see
Daddy he'll have a new body. Next time I see Buddy he'll have a new body.
Praise God walking with Jesus, hallelujah. I'm looking forward to that day.
10 I've told you before about my little, my brother that died. Died with TB. He
called us brothers around his bed, said, "Boys, I want you to meet me in
heaven." I said, "Ester, I'll meet you." I wasn't a Christian at that time. I
wasn't saved, but praise God this morning, I can look into the portal of
glory and say, "Ester, I'm on my way." I'm not there yet, but I'm coming
15 praise God +hah+. Some say, "Preacher, I wouldn't make a statement like
that." Why not? +hah+ If you've got God on your side you can make it,
neighbor. 'Cause God'll help us. I want to tell you something. When that
day comes, brother, there'll be some shouting in the air. Amen. These Baptists so dead they can't shout will shout then, praise God. Amen, some say,
20 "Preacher, I don't believe in shouting in the church and I don't want to
shout in heaven, then." I believe in it here and I'll believe in it when I
meet Jesus. I'll believe in it when I meet all of God's people on the other
side. And when I start marching down through heaven singing that song,
"Raise the bloodstained banner," I'll march through, have on the most
25 beautiful robe. [*Weeping:*] Elsie, I love the suit—her and James give me
this suit—but, praise God, I'll get my robe on without a spot, without a
wrinkle. You talk about an old boy a-marching, honey.
   Whooo! Glory to God.
   I'll march brother right down through the portal of glory. +hah+
30 I don't worry about being saved in it. +hah+
   I can't say much here, +hah+
   have a throat saved over there. Thank God +hah+
   I'll have a new throat then, +hah+
   one that'll never tear up, Sister Bea,
35 Praise God this morning. Hallelujah, hallelujah. Hallelujah praise God this
morning. If you're not saved get right with God. You need to be a child of
the King this morning. There's coming a reunion day, brother, when all of
God's people will get together, brother, praise God, 'round the throne eternal. I'll tell you when I get there I'll be one of the happiest men in the
40 world. Brother, I'm happy now; I'm happy in my soul. I don't know
whether you are or not. I don't know whether you're happy this morning or
not, but I'm happy in my soul. Brother, I feel a wheel in a wheel, as
Ezekiel said. Ezekiel said there was a wheel in a wheel. Brother, I used to
run the old mowing machine. I don't know whether you ever drove one or
45 not, the old horse-powered mowing machine. It run by a lot of cogs.
Brother, there's a great big old cog on that thing about this big around that
does the work, and then they have a little bitty one there. Brother, I want
you to know when that old big one starts to begin to rolling, brother, that

little one really gets up and going. That's the way it is. Jesus is the big on
350   I'm the little one. Brother, when he gets started in me, sometimes he kee
me moving. Amen, thank God, thank God. Brother, it's so real this morning. Hallelujah, hallelujah. Amen, so beloved, I'm looking forward to that
great reunion day. And then we, you right here, sitting right here this
morning, then we which are alive and remain shall be caught up togethe
355   with them who, those that've outstripped us in this walk of life, gone on t
be with the Lord, and so shall we ever be with the Lord. We'll meet the
Lord in the air. It don't say a word about him setting his feet on the Mou
of Olives. But brother, I'll tell you, you will find it in there where he will s
his feet on the Mount of Olives, but when he does, you'll find the armies
360   heaven'll be following him upon white horses clothed in linen white and
clean. He'll set his feet right on the Mount of Olives. I stood on the Mou
of Olives one day, and looked over into Jerusalem. Standing on the Moun
of Olives, you look in this direction and the eastern gate is there. They
have double gates and the Bi— our God told us when Jesus, when Jesus
365   comes back and sets his feet on the Mount of Olives, he'll march right
straight across through the eastern gate, into the city of Jerusalem.
That's when he'll set up with his father David's throne and rear it again.
The Bible says it and I believe it. Thank God this morning. I believe it. I
believe the word of God. I believe it'll stand when the world's on fire. Oh
370   hallelujah. The Mount of Olives is a beautiful place. It's a beautiful place
But neighbor, I'm saying to you this morning, the new Jerusalem is gonr
be more beautiful than that. Amen, thank God for that homecoming day
the city of God. I think I told you this before, a long time ago. Pauline
remembers very well. I, some of you's maybe never heard me tell this. I
375   just feel like telling you this morning. I was laying flat on my back in the
bed. I don't know what happened. I can't tell you. I'm like Paul; I was
caught up into the third heaven. But I seen something I can tell you abo
I can see you about. I can see something I can tell you about. Whether ir
the flesh or out of the flesh I don't know, in the Spirit or out of the Spirit
380   don't know. I can't tell you. But I was laying flat on my back. Brother and
thought I was dead. I thought I was gonna die that time. And I was layir
there that day and something happened to me, I don't know what happened. But I do know one thing. I got up in about twenty feet. I was clim
ing this narrow path. Somebody said it was a vision. I don't know whethe
385   it was or not, but I was going this narrow path and just room for me to
walk on it. And somebody caught me around the shoulders and tried to
throw me off, and I remember very well I did thisaway [rolls shoulders to
left] and they went down into the pit a-hollering. They went out of soune
out of—they just kept on a-going. Hollering and screaming. And I kept o
390   walking. And when I got in twenty feet of that door, the beautiful gate, a
I got in twenty feet of it, Jesus and Buddy Wayne walked by. Buddy Way
was on and he walked this way. The most beautiful hill I ever seen in my

life. I haven't got there yet—I'm still trying to make that twenty feet—but bless God, I'll soon make that twenty feet, amen? Praise God this morning. And when Buddy Wayne spoke to me, that's when I come out of whatever I was in. I come out of it, and thanks be to God this morning, I'm still traveling that narrow path. And I'm gonna keep on traveling it. Praise God this morning. God is so real. I feel him in my soul. Elsie, just look up to the Lord; he's able to heal your body. Praise God, you won't have to stay over there in the hospital. You can be back home with James. I know what God can do this morning. Hallelujah, Sister Bea, would you come to the piano for us, please. Glad to have her come at this time. Ask her to kindly play "Just as I Am." Donny, get you a song ready. That's my message to you this morning. I hope you've enjoyed it by the help of God. [John's prayer and the altar call follow.]

Sermons: Themes and Subjects

In Chapter 5 I stressed the problems in any outsider's attempt to interpret hymn texts on the assumption that the meaning would be plain to any intelligent observer. While this hermeneutical principle may operate effectively in some literary realms, it is problematical here; for outsiders to this—or any—church lack the ability to look at a text, be it a sermon, hymn, or testimony, and report confidently that what it plainly means to them is what it plainly means to the church members. In the case of hymn texts, I was fortunate to be able to rely on Brother John's interpretations made in the natural context of the service. In the case of Sunday school, my explanation of the text at the beginning of this chapter seeks to point out what I saw, from my vantage point as an outsider, that was not plain to the participants. In the instance of the sermon text, I am dealing with language that is itself exegetical: Brother John is attempting to make the Bible text plain to Christians and non-Christians alike. Yet to an outsider unfamiliar with this church's version of Christianity, a single sermon's representativeness will become clear only in the context of the larger body of Brother John's sermons. My interpretative method, therefore, is to give special attention and weight to those themes and subjects that recur in his sermons.

The themes of Brother John's homecoming sermon—indeed, the doctrine in all his sermons—may be grasped most easily by referring to Figure 30. The structure turns on the polar opposition between the true CHURCH, on the left side of the diagram, and the WORLD, on the right side. The church is ruled by the Holy Spirit; the world is ruled by Satan. A person passes from the world to the church by CONVERSION, becoming born again, getting saved. A person passes from the church to the world by BACKSLIDING, straying away from the Lord. At the end of history the church (those who died converted as well as those converted still alive)

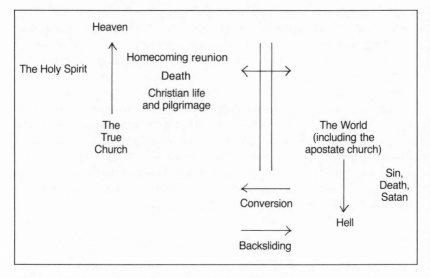

Figure 30. Doctrine and themes in Brother John's sermons.

will ascend to heaven for the homecoming reunion, while the world (the unconverted, dead and alive) will descend to eternal torment in hell. This structure is familiar to anyone who understands conservative evangelical Protestant doctrine.

The subjects that Brother John returns to—the ideas that he expresses most often—may be understood as occupying certain points along the lines and comprise the thematic structure. These include the following:

1. Representations of the WORLD
   a. Wickedness in Page County
   b. The apostate church
   c. Examples of sinners' behavior
   d. Satan and how he tempts people
2. CONVERSION
   a. Exhortations to accept Christ
   b. Salvation is open to all
   c. Examples of conversion, from the Bible and from personal experience, including Brother John's conversion narrative
3. The true CHURCH and the Christian Life
   a. The war against Satan
   b. Persecution of believers (not well-liked, called "crazy")
   c. Unimportance of money, fashionable clothes, and food
4. The RAPTURE of the church: HOMECOMING and TRIUMPH
   a. Promises made to dying relatives
   b. The tribulation period and the rapture of the church

c. Homecoming as a family reunion
d. What heaven will be like
e. The final victory of the church

Representations of the World

Brother John refers from time to time to the local community, saying that Stanley is a wicked town ruled by Satan, and that the people have become "gospel-hardened" (morning sermon, July 10, 1977). Interestingly, Stanley does have a regional reputation, deserved or not, as a place of criminal activity, and one can read in the local paper about people burning their pickup trucks to collect insurance, violent crime resulting from family quarrels, and various scams and swindles. Bogus auto accidents were one of the more imaginative scams. People crashed their cars, then bloodied themselves and climbed inside, later filing injury claims with the insurance companies. But criminal activity in the area is no more frequent or vigorous than in other regions of rural poverty in the United States. Brother John does not preach against crime, but against sin: he singles out drinking, adultery, smoking, and drug-taking as sinful behavior, saying that when a person is saved God takes away the desire to sin. Interestingly, these sins are not crimes directed against others but activities that for the most part endanger the self and lead to loss of self-control.

False prophets, false preachers, and false Christians—apostasy within the Christian church—is one of Brother John's favorite topics: "You say, 'Well, preacher, what in the world has happened? What's wrong with the churches today?' Brother, let me tell you it ain't the church of Jesus Christ; it's the devil's crowd" (homecoming sermon, lines 172–174). Preaching on the parable of the sower (Matthew 13:3–23), he likened the seeds that fell on stony places that sprung up but withered away in the sun because they lacked deep roots to Christians who were saved by someone who "sugar-coated 'em a sermon" (homecoming sermon, line 200) and then when a "called preacher preached a message and got on their toes, amen and they just trimmed the bark off and the knots off, and then they pouted, they got mad. Well, that's because the root didn't get down deep enough" (morning sermon, July 17, 1976).

Some false Christians, prophets, and preachers may fool people by appearing to be led by the Spirit; but Satan can animate persons also. Those preachers "hop up and down and make a lot of noise," but they are preaching for the devil (morning sermon, December 11, 1983). The same with the congregation:

Not everything that jumps up and down +hah+
and runs up and down the road +hah+
and my friends can holler real loud +hah+

is God's people tonight. +hah+

The devil's got 'em out also tonight.   (Night sermon, June 26, 1977)

In a radio sermon preached on February 27, 1972, Brother John used 2 Peter 2:1–18 as a text for an entire message on false prophets. In the course of the sermon he offered a personal narrative about such a preacher who "cut corners" by apologizing after the sermon:

> Heard a preacher one time preach a good message. Walked around by the side of his desk and leaned upon it. He said, "If I've said anything to hurt your feelings I'm sorry." I was setting in the congregation; I said, "O my God." Brother, let me tell you, when God gives me a message I have no apologies. Brother, I've always said this, I'm gonna repeat it today. +hah+
> You take a pack of dogs out here and throw a rock at 'em, +hah+
> the very one that you hit, he'll bark every time. +hah+
> Boys, we've heard a lot of barking. +hah+
> You ought to get right with God, +hah+
> then you'd quit barking so much.

The old-fashioned churches had more Spirit. "Now listen, today we have good seats to set in, but if you don't have a lot of 'em padded you still can't get people to go to church" (morning sermon, July 17, 1976). Brother John enjoys contrasting the old with the new:

> If we could get our Christian people hungry for the word of God today as they do for their bellies, brother, the house of God would run over. Amen, back in the olden times I could remember a few years ago
> brother they'd walk to church. +hah+
> If they didn't have no way to go they'd walk to church. +hah+
> They'd carry the old lanterns in their hand. +hah+
> My friends they'd walk down the muddy road, +hah+
> they'd go through the fields, thank God. +hah+
> My friend but listen, +hah+
> this day and time it's altogether different.
> I'd like to know why; it's the same Lord, same God; there's no changing him. Hebrews tells us he's the same yesterday, today, and forever. Why I can remember when the old-timey people used to go to church, they didn't have good pews like we got to sit on, they didn't have nice rostrums like we got, they had just a little stand that the preacher laid his Bible on, my friend, but praise God, they didn't have intercoms and all those things. Oh we ought to be happy people this morning, praise God this morning, because
> God has blessed us +hah+
> and let us go forward +hah+
> but instead of doing what we ought to do for God we're going the other way. Amen, we've turned around like the children of Israel . . . when they

hung their harps upon the willow. (Morning sermon, July 10, 1977; transcribed by Ken George)

Brother John thus distinguishes the "true church" of born-again believers from the apostate church, those self-professed but false Christians who have fallen away from the faith or never possessed it. Such energy spent in preaching against other preachers and members of other Christian churches, said to characterize Appalachian religion, has often been interpreted as an example of mountain people's narrow-mindedness and gossip. But it must be remembered that in preaching against apostasy Brother John has a great deal of New Testament precedent, particularly in 1 Timothy, 2 Timothy, and 2 Peter, where apostasy was prophesied to occur shortly before the tribulation period. Indeed, Brother John's preaching here falls in a tradition of biblical exegesis that is emphasized by Scofield in his *Reference Bible* and extends back to the early Christian church.

The most affecting representations of the world derive from Brother John's personal experience with sinners. The image of fire provides him with an especially good opportunity to preach on sin and hell. On July 3, 1977, in the morning sermon Brother John told of a coworker who thrust a can of beer under the preacher's nose:

> Brother, there was this young man come into the shop where I work; he had a bottle of beer in his hand. I said something to him about it and he stuck it under my nose, said, "Smell." I said, "Get it away from here. Get it away from here. I don't want to smell the rotten stuff." I used to drink it, but thank God, when he saved me he [*unintelligible*] me from that old rotten rotgut stuff. I don't want nothing to do with it. And so, brother, he left the shop. Boss man said something the other night about putting him in there to work with me. I said, "I don't want him in there, just leave him out. +hah+ Let him keep his cursing and his beer on the outside. I don't want him in the shop!" He said, "I get the message, I get the message."
> (Transcribed by George)

Brother John drew on another experience with this same coworker in the homecoming sermon: he was the one who was afraid he would be blown up and die in a fire driving a gasoline truck (lines 145–164). At that time both Brother John and his son Brother Donny worked for oil companies near Washington, D.C. It happened that shortly before Ken George and I began our fieldwork with the church in the summer of 1977, one of Brother Donny's coworkers was horribly burned in an accident. Both Brother Donny and Brother John used the incident to prefigure the fires of hell. Brother John's descriptions were startlingly graphic, and his two narratives may be compared to see how much of the story became a memorized preform:

As we told you this morning, the fire in Fairfax, my friend, this past week. Some of you'uns weren't here this morning; I'll tell you now. The Amoco plant where they load the tractors and trailers caught on fire. Donny was [with]in twenty feet, about twenty feet of it when it went up. Into flames. My friends and of course it scared him. I don't blame him, I'd have been scared too.

Amen, one boy was in the flame. And it burned his clothes off of him; burned his hair off and his skin. Donny said he was standing in the bathroom and his skin just fell down around his ankles! My friend, where he burned. Then he went into the state of shock when they got him in the ambulance. My friend tonight, and I said, "My God, that's reason enough not to want to go to hell." Praise the Lord tonight,
I'm not going to hell, thank the Lord. +hah+
I'm going to heaven. +hah+
My friend tonight God said I could, +hah+
and by the grace and the power of God
I will go. My friend, but listen, the power of that fire +hah+ was so fierce that it just melted those big steel beams. +hah+ Why I've been there many of a time, worked out of the plant, and it just melted those things and they crumbled to the ground.
My friend the trailers burnt up. +hah+
The trucks burnt up. +hah+
My friend listen, +hah+
+hah+ beloved tonight there's no power
like God's power. That fire was terrible, but listen, my Bible tells me one day God's going to rain fire from heaven, neighbor. You talking about stuff a-melting and burning up! (Night sermon, June 26, 1977)

Two weeks later he reminded the congregation of the same incident. He gave his sermon a title: "On the Way to the Death Chamber," and had this to say near the close:

Well, I can imagine the other day when Lee Park got on fire, when the gasoline was on his clothes and he was a-burning. Burning just like you know the blazes all over him. I can just imagine how he felt. Then Donny told me, I think I told you this last Sunday, the way he was standing in the bathroom. He'd burnt all of his clothes and his hair, everything off him. Said his skin just slipped right down around his ankles. My God, my God. Just think of hell this morning. When you get in hell you just burn, burn and burn. (Morning sermon, July 3, 1977; transcribed by George)

No wonder Brother John acknowledges that he is a fire-and-brimstone preacher. Another time he told me with a grin that Sister Bea had come to him after church and called him "Fireball, Fireball Sherfey. I laughed when she told me. She said, 'I'm gonna call you "Fireball!"'" (John and

Pauline Sherfey interview, December 3, 1979). Yet despite Brother John's effectiveness in preaching about the world, he does not dwell on the subject; he spends more time preaching on conversion and the Christian life.

Conversion

Brother John's stories about the burning young man and about his coworker who was afraid of being blown up driving a gasoline truck led him to plead that any unconverted in the congregation be saved before it was too late. His sermons are sprinkled with exhortations to accept Christ, and they conclude with an invitation and prayer. As a consequence of his Freewill Baptist beliefs he emphasizes that salvation is open to all. Heaven will be populated with Baptists, Pentecostals, Methodists, Presbyterians—all who have been born again in Christ (homecoming sermon, lines 81–87). He humorously identifies himself as a Pentecostal or an Old Regular Baptist:

> Sister Janice told me today +hah+ that a woman came to her this evening when I was on the radio, and said, "Well, he preaches like a Pentecostal." I said, praise God, "I've got what they did on the day of Pentecost" [i.e., the Spirit]. +hah+
> Amen, I'm Pentecostal. +hah+
> I'm praise God I'm a child of God. (Night sermon, June 26, 1977)

> My, you say, "Preacher, you talk like a Holiness." Yeah, I been called that, too, amen. +hah+ I been called everything in the book. +hah+ Fellow, I told him where a while back, +hah+ [I'll] tell this to my brother-in-law and my sister
> a-setting here this morning. +hah+
> I was in a revival meeting not long ago +hah+
> and one lady said, "You
> sing like the Old Regular Baptists." I said, "I am, +hah+
> I go to church every time the door is open, +hah+
> I go to church regular." +hah+
> Hallelujah I believe people ought to be regular in God's house. Amen.
> One said one time, said, "You sing like a Pentecostal."
> I said, "I am," +hah+
> said, "I got what they got on the day of Pentecost." +hah+
> Amen, "What'd they get, preacher?" They got the Holy Ghost. +hah+
> Amen, without the Holy Ghost +hah+
> you're none of his this morning. +hah+
> Brethren, it's got to be in you, +hah+
> praise God it'll move you. (Morning sermon, July 10, 1977)

He makes it a point to say all races will be in heaven:

I don't want to see nobody +hah+ going to hell. I don't want to see nobody, whether it's your people, my people, or brother whether it's a black
man, a red man +hah+ or a yellow man, I don't want to see nobody a-
plunging off into hell, neighbor . . . (Morning sermon, July 3, 1977; transcribed by George)

I don't care if he's a black man, a red man, a white man, or a yellow
man, if his heart's right with God, God will save him. (Morning sermon,
July 17, 1977)

Brother John has preached effectively as an evangelist to congregations
containing black Americans, and he would welcome any black person to
the congregation and any saved black person to church membership;
however, the church never has had a black member. Blacks comprise
about 10 percent of the Page County population and have churches where
some worship. Integrated congregations are more typical of Pentecostal
than Baptist churches. Revivals, traditionally nondenominational, attract
integrated congregations, in a tradition that reaches back to the second
Great Awakening.

Preaching on conversion, Brother John retells the story of Paul on the
road to Damascus, or Nicodemus coming to Jesus:

Old Nicodemus was a great man, he was a wealthy man, yes he was; but
praise God, he didn't understand how to get to Jesus. He came to Jesus by
night and he said, "Rabbi,
   we know that thou art a teacher come from God
   and for no man +hah+
   that can do these miracles that thou doeth except God be with him."
+hah+
   And then he said, "Now,"
   +hah+ Jesus said, "Nicodemus,
   ye must be borned again." +hah+
   And Nicodemus said, "How can I?
   Seeing that I'm old, +hah+
   how can I enter the second time +hah+
   into my mother's womb +hah+
   and be borned again?" +hah+
   My friend but Jesus said, +hah+
   "Marvel not, Nicodemus, +hah+
   as I said unto thee you must be borned again. +hah+
   That which is borned to the flesh +hah+
   is flesh and that which is borned to the Spirit +hah+
   is Spirit." Praise God, +hah+
   I want you to know today +hah+
   when you get borned to the Spirit of God +hah+

you know praise God +hah+
you're saved by the power of God +hah+
and you don't care for the world beloved. +hah+
You know you've been redeemed out of the blood of the lamb. (Morning
    sermon, July 3, 1977; transcribed by George)

In this retelling of the biblical narrative, Nicodemus is as alive to Brother
John as anyone of his acquaintance; Nicodemus and Jesus are timeless.

To aid in his evangelizing, Brother John tells stories of other people's
conversions. He knew a certain Brother Mullins in Kingsport who had a
difficult conversion:

Many of you heard me tell about Brother Mullins. My friend, he went to
the altar, he went to the altar, he goed back again, and he prayed and he
prayed and he prayed, but he never got right with God. He went home and
so he kept going and kept going. Finally at last one night God woke him up
at two o'clock in the morning, and he said he felt his need to pray. He said
something was telling him to pray. He said, "I got out of my bed and shook
my wife, told her to get down and pray with me but," said, "she didn't."
    But he said, "I got down beside of my bed." +hah+
And he said, "I started praying." +hah+
And he said, "That time +hah+
I let everything go."
And he said, "God saved me by my bedside." +hah+
Honey, God will save any man +hah+
when we let everything go
by the glory of God. +hah+
Turn loose the wife, children, home, +hah+
farmhouses, whatever it might be,
and turn it all in the hands of God +hah+
and God will save your soul.
    (Morning sermon, July 3, 1977; transcribed by George)

Through such conversion narratives, heard and overheard, the unconverted obtain a blueprint for the experience they will undergo if they are
saved. Brother John's most powerful and affecting conversion narrative is,
of course, his own; yet he seldom offers it in detail before the congregation, most of whom know it well and could tell it to someone else (as, indeed, Brother John told of Brother Mullins' conversion). In a masterful
study of Brother John's conversion narratives in nine separate contexts,
Ken George showed that the fullest versions—with many episodes, from
the beginning of conviction through assurance—were given in interviews,
when the audience was expected to be the least familiar with the story.
Brief versions occurred in sermons in the Fellowship Independent Baptist
Church, referring only to a few aspects or episodes in a story most in the

congregation knew well (George 1978). Here is the conversion narrative as spoken and chanted in the morning sermon on July 27, 1975, recorded and originally transcribed by George. I have amended his ethnopoetic typography slightly so as to fit the conventions of the sermon excerpts in this book:

> Brother, praise God, the night I got saved there was a little span in there I don't remember what happened. Amen; the only thing I know is I got on my knees in the gravel and I started praying, brother.
>   Now I remember saying, "Lord, +hah+
>   here I come, swim sink or drown, I'm coming home" +hah+
> And brother then something happened, I don't really remember +hah+
>   but when I came to myself I was standing up +hah+
>   hugging people and a-crying +hah+
>   and praising God because I was saved.
>   (Adapted from George 1978:57)

Other brief conversion narratives occurred in the radio sermons. Again, they usually fastened on one aspect of the conversion process as, for example, conviction. Here Brother John's text, from Hebrews 4:6–16, emphasized that "the word of God is quick, and powerful, and sharper than any two-edged sword, piercing . . . of the joints and marrow." Applying these verses to his own experience of conviction, he recounted an episode in which he went to a doctor to find out what was wrong with him:

> It got me to where I used to, I couldn't do anything. I'll tell you I set down on the sidewalk one time. I bowed my head between my knees to die, brother, because I wasn't in the center of God's will, +hah+.
>   My friend I went to the doctor, thought I was having a heart attack. +hah+
>   The old doctor put that thing on me, +hah+
>   he checked me from head to toe. +hah+
>   He said, "I can't find a thing wrong with you." +hah+
>   Brother it was God dealing with me all the time. +hah+
>   When I repented, thank God, +hah+
>   then brother I got all right. +hah+
>   And I'm still living, going strong, hallelujah. +hah+
>   Praise God, God +hah+
>   can make a difference in us +hah+
>   if we'll put God first in our life, +hah+ get rid of everything else.
>   (Radio sermon, July 17, 1977, transcribed by George)

Mid-length conversion narratives were more likely to occur in a revival context where the audience was familiar with the *type* of narrative, yet did not know Brother John's own story, and could be expected to benefit from a detailed recounting of aspects appropriate to the context of the sermon.

This version comes from a revival sermon Brother John preached in Piney Creek, North Carolina, in September 1977:

I told some of 'em here a while back, Brother Jimmy, when God saved me,
Everybody around me looked so sweet, +hah+
everybody looked so good. +hah+
Brother, God changed my eyesight, +hah+
God changed everything. +hah+
When I came off of that altar, brother,
the man that used to look so bad, +hah+
praise God, he looked good. +hah+
God will take you all over, thank the Lord,
if we will trust him as our Savior. The night God saved my soul I stood up and when I got off of that altar I started hugging people and crying. A pile of tears running down my cheek. I tell you I had a ball.

But before I got home, Satan said, "Now look at you. Look at you. You stood up over there, you cried and you told them people you was saved, but now look at you." O my God. I got home. I lived in a little three-room house behind my wife's daddy and mother. We lived there in, in that little house. Put 'em in the house and I started toward the barn. I got about halfway out to that old barn and I got on my knees. I said, "Lord, if that was real I felt over there tonight, I want to feel it again." Thank God, I felt it right there in the road.

Hallelujah, I still got it tonight. +hah+
He's just as real tonight +hah+
as he was that night +hah+
Twenty-five years ago. Thank God hallelujah and he'll be just as real to-morrow as he is tonight, thank God. +hah+ (Adapted from George 1978:61)

Here, Brother John used his conversion story not so much to illustrate the process of conversion, but to show how wonderful it felt, alluding to the experience that Victor Turner has called *communitas* (see Clements 1976a for a discussion of conversion and *communitas* in American folk Protestant churches; see also the discussion of conversion in Chapter 8). Moreover, he emphasized another aspect of conversion: a person who is truly saved can *know* that he or she is saved; one need not give in to doubt.

Assurance that one is saved is a final subject that Brother John preaches on in the context of evangelism. Seldom does he tell his conversion narrative without concluding, "I still got it," or "It's just as real today as it was then." His phrase to describe assurance is "a know-so salvation." The church members agree that the person who doubts whether he or she is saved is not saved.

The Church and the Christian Life

In Chapter 5 I wrote that while the rhetoric of some of the gospel hymns emphasizes passivity, rescue, and heavenly peace for the Christian, life on earth is viewed as a battle between the saints of the true church and Satan. Although the lifeboat image occurs in one of their favorite hymns, the Fellowship Independent Baptist Church members do not generally regard the Christian pilgrim as a being huddled in a lifeboat, tossed this way and that by the storms of life, awaiting calm waters and the safe port of heaven. As Brother John put it in the homecoming sermon, "Nowhere did God ever tell you: saved, set down, do nothing" (lines 179–180). Rather, the Christian is viewed as a warrior in God's army, whose missions are to combat the devil and to witness and evangelize among the unsaved. Activity, not passivity, characterizes this religion. The fact that the church members sing about passivity, control, and heavenly peace does not preclude them from acting as if they are soldiers engaged in war, despite the fact that they do not sing "Onward, Christian Soldiers." The hymns dwell on the joys of heaven; teaching and preaching, concerned with this life, prepare the believers for the fight against Satan. Studies of folk and popular religious thought based primarily on one kind of evidence—hymn texts, for example—may thus be fatally flawed. The holistic folklike approach attempts to guard against such a mistake.

Brother John references a single text again and again in building an allegory of the Christian life: Ephesians 6:11–17. Among the sermons under consideration (see Appendix E), one was devoted exclusively to this text (morning sermon, July 27, 1975; transcribed by George and published as "Dressed in the Armor of God" in Titon and George 1977). Related to this text are three others: Hebrews 12:1–2, Matthew 21:1–11, and Revelation 7:9–12. The allegory is controlled by the idea of conflict and eventual victory. Christians wear "the armor of God" to protect them against the temptations of Satan; life is likened to running a race, and at the close the Christian receives the "palms of victory." Examples abound; the two most extensive occurred during the summer of 1977. One may be seen in the homecoming sermon, with repeated references to victory (lines 78, 80, 285), and a full and straightforward exposition (179–218, 265–280). The other was inserted into a sermon on Revelation 7:9–12:

Amen, "and palms in their hands" [verse 9]. What's palms mean? It's victory. Victory. In this walk of life you and I, we have a fight with the devil. As I told you I believe the other Sunday morning, people tell you you can get saved and just live on; that's all there is to it, just get saved, you've got a bed of ease—that's a lie. Amen, brother, that's not true. My friends, when you get right with God, start living for God, then the old devil begins to flog you on every side. He'll climb all over you, he'll flog you every way you turn, just like an old mad wet setting hen. +hah+

Brother they'll flog you. +hah+
Thanks be to God tonight. +hah+
But brother, God will give us the victory +hah+
if we'll stand for God. He'll give us the victory; you remember if you recall
when Jesus went down into Jerusalem, riding on the foal of an ass. Amen,
what did they do? Brother, the children of Israel got out in front of him;
they spread their coats down in the way, my friends, and let that mule
walk on 'em. Amen; Jesus was sitting upon the, upon that little old donkey
where never a man had sat. And brother, they had palms in their hands,
+hah+ waving the victory sign. Hallelujah, thank God tonight. Brother,
listen, we're on, we're winning the battle.
Christians, we're winning the battle. +hah+
The devil's mad and I'm glad.
The devil hates me tonight. +hah+
He's tried his best, +hah+
trying to tear us down, but God
is going to give us the victory. +hah+
Let's raise our hands +hah+
and wave the palms of victory +hah+
because we've got the devil on the run. +hah+
He can't stand it tonight. +hah+
God said, "I'll give you the victory. +hah+
You stand and I'll stand with you." +hah+
Hallelujah. +hah+
They'll wave it, hallelujah. We'll wave it when we march down through
heaven. Whew; you say, "Preacher do you actually believe that?" If I didn't
I'd quit preaching tonight. Amen, brother, I'll tell you: palms of victory,
then palms of victory. Shouts of glory, hallelujah, why? Because we've won
the race, amen. I was reading Hebrews, Chapter 12, tells us there,
"Wherefore see we're compassed about with so great a cloud of witness, let
us lay aside every weight and the sin which dost so easily beset us, and let
us run with patience the race that is set before us. Looking unto the author and finisher of our faith which is in Christ Jesus our Lord." Amen;
brother, we're on a foot race tonight, hallelujah. Satan's trying every way
he can to tear it down. Thank God, God'll give us the victory. (Night sermon, June 26, 1977)

Of course, there are other aspects of the Christian life apart from the
war against Satan. In his sermons Brother John exhorts the converts to
serve God, to love others (e.g., the homecoming sermon, lines 220–249),
to abstain from sin ("I believe we ought to squeal a little bit but we ought
to walk right when we hit the ground"—night sermon, June 26, 1977), to
obey God as a child should obey its parents ("You expect your children to
listen to you; God expects his to listen to him. Amen. Take orders from the

Lord +hah+ and be led by the Spirit of God"—morning sermon, July 11, 1976), and to be ready for the secret rapture, when the true church will be taken out of the world before the tribulation period. But the most telling sermonizing on the Christian life concerns the subject of poverty, usually contrasted with the riches of heaven. Here Brother John often draws on his own childhood experiences, and his narratives speak for the experiences of many others in the congregation. I have already pointed out the importance of the mountain farming heritage, in Chapter 2; the economy did not turn on money, yet money was valuable because the church members' ancestors needed to pay taxes to retain their land, and in the latter part of the nineteenth century some of the mountain families entered the cash economy as market-oriented farmers and lost heavily. Money thus has a particular relevance as a worldly temptation grounded in local and family history.

> Many a man has stretched out his hand for the almighty dollar and left God out. Amen, brother, a-many of a preacher's stretched his hand out for the almighty dollar and left God out. God will not bless in that category. No, he won't. . . . I've had brick homes offered to me. I've had salaries offered to me. But I haven't accepted that. I'm still here. I'm still here. Amen. I really am; I'm here. (Morning sermon, July 11, 1976)

Sometimes Brother John injects a bit of humor in his personal narratives concerning money, but he is always serious underneath:

> I never have set a price. I've never in my life since I been preaching for twenty-four years, I have never taken up an offering for myself. And I never will. Praise God tonight, I believe if God wants me to have it and God's got it and you've got it, I believe God'll tell you to give it to me. Amen; I don't believe I'll have to take it up; I believe you'll give it.
>
> I've been in revival meetings, and God knows my heart tonight, I've been in revival meetings where I'd have to borrow money or go in debt for the gas that I put in my car. Amen, I drive just about all week and one little feller, he'd finally at last he'd say, "Well, the preacher's been here all week. Now we ought to take him up a little offering." Amen. I've had that said: "We ought to take him up a little offering." And it *was* little. I'm not complaining about that. But God has always seen that I got exactly what I needed. Amen; I got by. I got by and God'll fix it so you can, if you live for him. (Night sermon, June 26, 1977)

The idea that God will provide for a person's material needs—not wealth, just enough to "get by"—relates to the church members' belief that "God blesses people that's humble people":

> The material things of life we didn't have. Amen, many of a time +hah+ I wore a shirt made out of a feed sack. You say, "Preacher, I wouldn't tell it."

I'm telling you. Bless God, but we were a happy family.
   Amen, we didn't have plenty of things +hah+
   as other people had, +hah+
   my friend but thanks be to God +hah+
   we had a glorious time together.
                    (Morning sermon, July 10, 1977, transcribed by George)

"I wouldn't tell it" is a voice that comes to shame Brother John and the other church members who have known poverty; perhaps it is the voice of someone, a relative, who has "gotten up in society" and is ashamed of the past. But Brother John wears the poverty of his past as a badge of humility:

I can remember back a few years ago when I ate cornbread three times a day, and I was glad to get it, thank the Lord. Brother, I'll tell you, I ate bean soup. I didn't see the beans; I just got the soup. But praise God, I was glad to get that. My friends, I got one pair of shoes a year. And if the soles wore out of 'em Daddy done the best he could. He'd take a carcass or some old rubber thing and nail soles on the bottom. I was glad to wear 'em, praise the Lord. Brother, I wore patched overalls; I'm not ashamed of it. I know a lot of you smart-alecks out there today, you're gonna make fun of that, but praise God listen to me +hah+ if you don't get right with God you're gonna be worse off than that! (Radio sermon, June 25, 1972)

Food and clothing (not shelter) are the most frequent of Brother John's poverty referents. Clothing is particularly pertinent when one realizes that, dressed in the spiritual armor of God, Brother John does not trouble himself about fashionable clothes. In fact, most of his clothing consists of gifts and castoffs. Recall how in the homecoming sermon he mentions the suit that his sister and her husband gave him (lines 325–326). From a sermon five years earlier:

Just about every piece of garment I've got's been give to me,
   I'm not ashamed to admit that, +hah+
   praise God brother let me tell you something. +hah+
   Lot of our preachers say oh well, +hah+
   "I wouldn't wear it if they give it to me, I'll buy my own."
   Brother if you've got a suit you can't wear, give it to me and if I can
wear it,
   I'll put her on and wear it, bless God.
   My friend today +hah+
   that's what's the matter with the world. +hah+
   They're too high-minded +hah+
   and forgot God.   (Radio sermon, February 27, 1972)

"Salvation's not in clothes, +hah+ / it's in the heart, bless the Lord" (morning sermon, July 10, 1977) is the way Brother John sums up this subject. Still, he points the church forward to the riches of heaven, even when described as material wealth. In life he may be poor, but in heaven Brother John will "walk on gold" (night sermon, June 26, 1977).

The Rapture of the Church; Homecoming and Triumph

The rapture, homecoming, and triumph of the true church is a subject that occurs throughout Brother John's sermons. Whether preaching about conversion or the Christian life, he holds out the promised reward of heaven for the saints. In the homecoming sermon, heaven is pictured as a family reunion (lines 288–301), full of noise, shouting, and praise to God (301–302, 317–322) where the saints will have new clothes (324–327), new, perfect, and "glorified" bodies (332–334), and where all will live in joy and happiness (339–356). Newness, perfection, eternal life, eternal day, blessings, shouting, noise—this is not the Victorian heaven of control and propriety Sizer derived from her study of gospel hymns (Sizer 1978). Rather, it appears as a place of great freedom and release.

Family is the most pervasive theme. The homecoming is prefigured in deathbed scenes in which the converted, dying person asks unsaved kinfolk to gather around and asks them to promise they will meet him or her in heaven. Following the promises, the person dies, sometimes indicating a glimpse of heaven at the dying moment. The unsaved may have a vision as well—as Sister Edith did (see Chapter 8). Brother John's brother Ester was dying from tuberculosis, and when the family gathered around him Brother John promised he would meet him in heaven. One version of Brother John's narrative of this event appears in the homecoming sermon (310–315); he preached a fuller version of the story three weeks earlier:

My little brother had TB. His little bony arms got so skinny he had nothing but the bone. That's all he had. And when he got ready to leave this walk of life—he'd been saved for about three or four years before he left this walk of life. And I've seen him many of a time—I wasn't a Christian then, I was lost—but many of a time he'd get to trying to shout while he was laying down. He couldn't get his breath and they'd hold him up in the bed while he'd shout the praises of God. He'd raise them little old bony, skinny arms, he'd raise them up toward heaven and shout the praises of God. He'd sing that song, "I've been waiting, Lord, to go."

. . . Then, beloved, when he left this walk of life he called all of us boys around his bedside and said, "I want you to meet me in heaven." I made him a promise that day that I would meet him. I wasn't saved but later on I got right with God. . . .

But beloved, when he left this walk of life he raised them little old bony arms up and said, "I see Jesus coming," and folded 'em and went to sleep. That was the last of it. He never grunted, he didn't kick. He went out to meet God. Amen. One day after awhile I'll get to see him again . . . I'm looking forward for our reunion day. (Morning sermon, July 17, 1977)

"He never grunted, he didn't kick"—Ester's stoicism is very like Brother John's father's shucking corn uncomplainingly with bloody hands (see the two versions of that narrative, in Chapters 2 and 5). The importance of family was underscored further in Brother John's interpretation of Revelation 8:1–5 in the night sermon on July 10, 1977. He preached that the Spirit had led him to believe that every prayer that the church members had prayed for their unsaved loved ones had been and would continue to be "bottled up" in heaven, and that during the tribulation period they would be "poured out" back on the land as fire from the angel's golden censer. When those prayers fell on the unsaved kinfolk and friends, many would accept Jesus and be saved. This interpretation gave comfort to those who were worried that if the secret rapture occurred very soon many of their loved ones would be lost forever and that there was nothing they could do to help them. It was, Brother John admitted during the sermon, an unusual interpretation—not one he had read in a book, not one that Scofield or Thompson propounded—but it is what the Spirit showed him when he prayed about it. Validity of interpretation aside, it shows just how critical the theme of family is in this church; we have already seen in Chapter 2 how important it is as a theme in their history.

The homecoming sermon itself explains the process of the rapture of the church (lines 1–144 and passim). From other sermons it is clear that this is the "secret rapture" that takes the true church from the world prior to the tribulation period:

> But the church is raptured in the fourth chapter [of Revelation in] which John said he saw a vision in heaven typifying to the catching away of the bride of Jesus Christ. (Night sermon, July 3, 1977)

> If you'll go back into the fourth chapter, where he said, "John, come up hither, I want to show you a few things," beloved, that's typifying to being caught away. And brother, the church is going to be gone, brother, before that all hell breaks loose. (Radio sermon, June 25, 1972)

Brother John's use of typology here operates on analogy: just as the apostle John was lifted in the Spirit to heaven and shown the vision of the tribulation period, so the true Christians will be caught up to heaven and remain there during the tribulation. I will comment on Brother John's typological cast of mind in the next section; suffice it to say here that in interpreting these verses Brother John follows the *Scofield Reference Bible* (see its notes to Revelation 4:1 and also to 1 Thessalonians 4:17, the text chosen for the all-important homecoming sermon).

Indeed, 1 Thessalonians 4:13–18 is one of Brother John's frequent textual referents in his sermons, as well it might be. After quoting those verses in the night sermon on June 26, 1977, he went on to picture the rapture of the church as a family reunion:

And I know you all have seen me do this many times. I've stood right here behind this desk and I've wept because of my daddy, my children, my loved one, my wife's parents. I've wept. Many times. I've done that. But thanks be to God, when they all come forth from that grave. Brother, they're going on. They've gone on to be with God. But when they all come forth, then there'll be reunion in heaven. There'll be a shouting time. I believe people'll shout then, brother, that's never been known to shout in this walk of life.

Homecoming is portrayed as a family reunion most fully in the homecoming sermon itself: "That daddy or that mother of yours, that brother or that sister of yours or that baby that you once loved so dearly, loving him or her so much, that you wept and you cried, you've cried. One day after awhile when Jesus steps off the throne of [*unintelligible*] God's gonna look over at the Son and say, 'Son, it's time to go get 'em'" (lines 288–293). Brother John includes the story of his dying brother Ester, and concludes the homecoming sermon with a lengthy narrative of a vision he had of his child Buddy Wayne, whom he looks forward to meeting in heaven. From the familial level Brother John has progressed to the most intense, highly personal, autobiographical mode of testimony. He weeps as he is blessed in telling the concluding vision, obviously an allegory of his own Christian pilgrimage (lines 373–397), the lengthiest narrative inside a sermon I have heard him preach.

The final victory of the church is typified in Brother John's mind by the figure of Jesus triumphantly entering Jerusalem (Matthew 21:1–11), a Scripture passage he refers to often in connection with the victory. In Matthew, Jesus enters meekly, on the foal of an ass. The writer of Matthew declares that the entrance was a fulfillment of a prophecy in Zechariah 9:9: "Rejoice greatly, O daughter of Zion; shout, O daughter of Jerusalem: behold, thy King cometh unto thee: he is just, and having salvation; lowly, and riding upon an ass, and upon a colt the foal of an ass." The palms of victory (specified in the apostle John's account of Jesus' entry into Jerusalem, John 12:13) have considerable force as an image for Brother John; recall their association with the triumphant entry of Jesus into Jerusalem and the triumph of the church in the excerpt printed earlier (p. 347) and the passage in the homecoming sermon where the analogy is plain:

> I can just see him this morning, my Savior,
> as he got up on that little old donkey,
> and brother they even put their coats on him,
> +hah+ they spread their coats down for the donkey to step on.
> Brother he triumphed over Jerusalem.
> I want you to know this morning the church is gonna triumph +hah+
> over this world, praise God, +hah+
> and it's soon coming +hah+

whether you believe it or not. +hah+
The church is [*claps hands*] gonna triumph +hah+
over this world, thank God. +hah+
(Lines 268–278)

To my knowledge, this entrance is not a commonly recognized biblical
type; Scofield, for example, is mute on the subject, and so even is Walter
Lewis Wilson's *Dictionary of Bible Types* (Wilson 1957). Yet it is perfectly
in keeping with the analogic method of typology, and, however Brother
John was led to it, it illustrates the powerful hold typological analogy has
on his mind.

Sermon Narratives and the Analogical Cast of Mind

Brother John's narratives pervade his public speaking in the church,
whether in sermons, interpreting hymn texts (see Chapter 5), or offering
remarks in transitions from one part of the service to the next. In sermons,
his narratives are most often from personal experience; less frequently, he
retells biblical stories. But when he does the latter, he assumes a famil-
iarity with the biblical characters that suggests they are very much alive
today:

You remember when old Moses walked yonder to the Red Sea. Moses was
standing there at the brink of the water. Here come Pharaoh's army on
behind him. The children of Israel started grumbling and complaining.
"Moses, if you'd have left us down in Egypt, we was down there where we
had the onions and the garlic and the melons and all, and the water to
drink. Now look, Moses, where you've got us. You got us in a mess, Moses.
You've led us up here; there's the Dead Sea, ah, Red Sea in front of us;
here comes the army behind us. We've got no place to go." My friend but
thanks be to God, that angel came down to old Moses there in the water.
He stood there and he said, "Moses," he said, "tell the children to stand
still and see the salvation of God."
   Old Moses turned around +hah+
   and he said, "Children, +hah+
   children stand still +hah+
   and see the salvation of God." +hah+
   "What happened, preacher?" +hah+
   +hah+ God rolled the water back +hah+
   and the angels held it there +hah+
   until they crossed on the dry ground.
   God'll do it for you and me. He's the same God.

(Night sermon, June 26, 1977)

This means of biblical interpretation, in which the events and personages
of the Bible are viewed as timeless, is called tropology. In a recent article,

Frances Malpezzi and William Clements wrote that medieval and Renaissance Christians viewed the Bible tropologically: "Thus an action reported in the Old Testament might serve as a spiritual 'type' of an action in the New Testament and might become a potential happening in the spiritual life of Everyman" (1985:32). Malpezzi and Clements found that tropology occurred frequently in the mid-1970s sermons of a Pentecostal preacher, William Ouzts, from northeast Arkansas. The likely reason, they assert, is that Pentecostals such as Ouzts emphasize "the contemporaneity and vitality of the Bible. . . . As the spiritual powers of the New Testament are assigned contemporary valence by Pentecostal theology, so the events of the Old and New Testaments become contemporary through tropology. Tropology asserts the immediacy of the mythic experience of the Bible, an important concern for Pentecostals, who believe strongly that God's miracles did not cease in biblical times" (ibid.:36–37). No doubt this is one of the reasons Brother John, a Baptist who likewise believes that God's miracles continue as God's revelation does also, employs tropology in his sermons:

> Amen, that man stood out on the deck of that ship when the waves were
> boisterous high—oh how they were beating on the old ship—while he
> [Jesus] was down in the hindward part asleep. They went down, said,
> "Master, carest not thou that we perish?" He got up and he walked out on
> the deck of that old ship and he stretched forth his hands and said, "Peace,
> be still. Peace, be still." That's the man that we have tonight. He puts
> peace in your soul, gives you joy, satisfaction beyond, my friend, that the
> mortal tongue cannot tell. (Night sermon, June 26, 1977)

In Brother John's case, there are, I believe, numerous additional reasons why he turns to tropology; but the basic reason is that analogy is his characteristic mode of interpreting the world. Why that should be so is the subject of much of the next chapter and of the Epilogue.

Analogically framed narratives from Brother John's own life are, I believe, habitual; that is, they are characteristic of his turn of mind and, indeed, of the turn of mind of many other church members. This is so much so that a period during the service is given over completely to the church members for the delivery of narrative testimonies from their personal experience. Autobiography, then, as a style of language in religious practice, is characteristic, frequent, and recognized by the church members as singularly important. After all, a person is admitted to church membership on the basis of his or her conversion narrative. In a paper read at the 1980 annual meeting of the American Folklore Society, Ken George discussed the autobiographical style, pointing out that when one of these church members spoke autobiographically, he (or she) was understood to speak from his heart, from the very center of his being (George 1980).

Speaking thus, Brother John is understood to have great authority, for in their "heart-religion" the heart is the seat of the Spirit. Personal experience is one seat of knowledge; the Bible is the other. They are viewed as mutually validating. Thus the personal events of daily life gain meaning and significance within the matrix of the teachings of the Bible. But the other side is true as well: the Bible is illuminated by personal experience. Brother John alludes to his own experience to make the Bible plain for others; that is, he assumes that others who have lived as he has lived and felt as he has felt will be able to put themselves in his place and understand the Bible as he does.

Now, there is a broad range of personal experience that Brother John might choose to draw upon. When I consider the variety of stories I tell others about my life or things that I notice or hear about others' lives, the range is quite broad. But in the church context, Brother John's is narrow: he returns to a small number of topics. These are work (especially farming), family, and stories of God's intervention in people's lives—healing, for example, or conversion, or the advent of an unexpected but needed gift. Farming is perhaps his favorite topic. Recall how in the homecoming sermon he likened his religious zeal to the rapid spinning of the small cog on the mowing machine: Jesus was the big cog, revolving slowly, while he was the small one, set in motion by Jesus. This is especially interesting because he was not explaining something in the Bible at this juncture; he was explaining himself, and in doing so he characteristically operated by a farming analogy. This is what I mean by a habit of mind. Brother John's is autobiographical, favors farming, and proceeds by analogy; that is, by likeness.

There is, of course, precedent for farming analogies in the Scriptures. The parables involving husbandry, and the passage from John 15 on the true vine are perhaps the most famous examples, and so it is not surprising that Brother John preaches on these texts. In fact, he chose John 15 for his very first sermon (see Chapter 9). Preaching on the parable of the sower (Matthew 13:3–23), Brother John recalled his own farming days:

> Now, beloved, I'll tell you I used to be a farmer boy and many times we've sowed the grain. If I didn't get that field +hah+ worked up into the seed bed like it ought to be, when you went through with the old drill, brother, you could go back
> and it cut out a little trench +hah+
> and the seed would be laying on top. +hah+
> And then brother here come the birds. +hah+
> They'd follow you through the fields +hah+
> and they'd gather it up.
> (Morning sermon, July 11, 1976)

Later in the same sermon Brother John spoke about planting corn in new ground:

You couldn't plow, there's so many roots in it. And you know what [my father'd] do? He'd give us boys mattocks and hoes, and "All right boys, get out there and chop them bushes down. Grub what you can and what you can't grub, chop her off." Amen. Then he come through there with an old plow or something and jiggle out a little ditch and we'd plant the corn in there. And then we'd have to go back before the corn ever got up and cut the weeds out from the bushes. And then when the corn got through you could see where the row was and we just had to keep on working all summer long to keep the weeds and the bushes chopped down. And I hated that. But I'll tell you some places, beloved, the weeds'd get ahead of us. When it'd start raining or something, we couldn't get to it, and the first thing you know, they'd outgrown the corn and that corn would get down underneath there and it'd be the sickest-looking thing you ever seen. Brother, because it was choked down and didn't have the light

it didn't have what it needed. +hah+

Brother, we got to have the sunlight. +hah+

And praise God if you're in Jesus this morning +hah+

you're in the light, praise God.

You'll stay in it +hah+

if you'll be led by the Spirit of God.

In another sermon Brother John spoke of the time his father was sold the wrong seed:

I used to be a farmer boy, and when we sowed the wheat, beloved, we'd sow it in the ground, in the fall of the year, and in the summertime when we reaped it we reaped wheat off it. That's what we sowed: we sowed wheat, we reaped wheat.

Ah, but one time I remember a long time ago, my father raised tobacco years ago, and beloved, we sowed a tobacco bed. Now, beloved, somebody had sold us some seed which was supposed to be tobacco seed but when it came up it was all wheat. My friend, he sold us the wrong kind of seed. And so, beloved, we sowed the wrong seed. And so, beloved, if you sow the wrong thing you'll reap the wrong thing, but if you sow the right thing you'll reap the right thing.

(Radio sermon, Sunday between Christmas and New Year's, 1971)

Brother John always interprets these stories, draws the moral, and makes the analogy plain. Recall that Jesus also interpreted the parable of the sower (Matthew 13:18–23).

The parable of the sower is an extended analogy: each object and event stands for something else, and what they signify fits together, revealing the hidden, true meaning behind the literal sense of the parable. In other words, the parable is an allegory. Brother John's characteristic modes of biblical interpretation involve analogy, typology, and parallelism; and they drive toward allegory, as, for example, in the battle of the true church against Satan (see above), where Brother John puts the armor of God, the race, the labor of love, the rapture, and the final victory into a coherent, revealing whole.

I discussed the relation between typology and analogy in the previous section. As a method of biblical interpretation, typology is grounded in the assumption that the word of God is a continually evolving revelation. Scofield's definition, "A type is a divinely purposed illustration of some truth" (Scofield, ed. 1945:4), is not particularly helpful. The type—an object, event, person, etc., in the Bible—is viewed as an earlier revelation of some later truth. The later truth—again, an object, event, person, etc.—is "typified" by the type, and almost always stands in some sort of analogous relation to it. Thus the apostle John's ascent to heaven to view in a vision the tribulation period is said to typify the future "secret rapture" of the church; or Moses is thought to be a type of Christ in that he was a divinely chosen leader, prophet, and deliverer. The later truth that is typified by the type is called the antitype. Scofield lists forty-eight Old Testament types of Christ in his Index (1945:1356) and the number is potentially greater; clearly, typology is a matter of interpretation.

Typology can be found in the New Testament writers who seek to show how Jesus fulfilled Old Testament prophecies. Paul calls Adam a type or "figure" of Christ in Romans 5:14; this, to my knowledge, is the closest any New Testament writer comes to naming the method. As a method, then, it has biblical sanction; by the time it reached Brother John, it had the sanction of a Protestant evangelical scholarly tradition as well. Here is another of Brother John's uses of typology:

> This same chapter I read to you [John 3] he said, "As Moses lifted up the serpent in the wilderness even so must the Son of Man be lifted up." You say, "Preacher, what are you talking about?" Brother, back yonder in Exodus, beloved, when, my friend, the children of Israel begin to grumble, begin to complain, begin to murmur amongst themselves, my friend, God sent fiery serpents right in among 'em. Brother, the serpents would bite them. They were poison. And they would die. People were dying like flies. And God spoke to Moses; he said, "Moses," he said, "make a brass serpent and put it upon the pole. And all who look unto the serpent shall live." What was that typifying? Jesus Christ being lifted up. And between the heavens and the earth, all who look to that serpent shall live. (Morning sermon, July 3, 1977)

As far as I can determine, the suggestion of the Resurrection here is Brother John's own interpretation. Scofield believes that this serpent (which comes, incidentally, from Numbers 21:9) is a type of Christ in sacrifice, bearing the sins of mankind; Wilson adds that the serpent on the pole is a type of Christ on his Cross (Scofield, ed. 1945:195; Wilson

1957:400). But Brother John was led to expand upon the traditional interpretation.

Besides typology, tropology, and plain analogy, which flower in narratives, Brother John habitually employs parallelism to interpret the Bible. That is, he frequently "runs reference" through the various biblical verses in other parts of the Bible that bear on the Scripture he happens to be explicating in the sermon. As a "great chain," the Bible is understood to be fundamentally coherent and unified. In the homecoming sermon, for example, explicating the rapture of the church (from 1 Thessalonians 4:13–18), he references—at one point not even mentioning that he is doing so, by the way—1 Corinthians 15:51–55. The passage reads: "Behold, I shew you a mystery; We shall not all sleep, but we shall all be changed, In a moment, in the twinkling of an eye . . . For this corruptible must put on incorruption, and this mortal must put on immortality . . . O death, where is thy sting? O grave, where is thy victory?" The relevant sermon lines are 72–76 ("Praise God, this mortal put on immortality. This corruptible put on the incorruption. . . . O death where is your sting? O grave where's your victory?") and 128–130 ("Brother I'm just telling you the Bible says +hah+ we'll be changed in a moment, in the twinkling of an eye. +hah+"). Parallel reference is Brother John's most frequent method of biblical exegesis. To those in the congregation familiar with their Bible—for many, the only book they read, and they do so for pleasure—there is no need to mention the referenced verses. Brother John quotes or paraphrases them as his mind associates them with the topic at hand.

For Brother John and the members of the Fellowship Independent Baptist Church, parallel reference, analogy, tropology, and typology all assume the unity of Scripture, and an allegorical correspondence between Bible events and persons, on the one hand, and present-day life, on the other. Throughout this chapter I have emphasized how personal experience, often in the form of sermonic narrative, serves as a guide to understanding Scripture. In the next chapter the subject is testimony—that is, narratives of what God has done in one's life. There, Scripture serves as a guide to experience. Mediated by the Holy Spirit, and very little else, personal experience and the word of God illuminate each other in the minds and lives of the church members.

8. Testimony and the Conversion Narrative

Testimony is the final genre of language in religious practice to be considered in this book. In every worship service after the altar call, Brother John steps up to the rostrum and asks, "Anybody got a word on your heart?" A period of testimony follows, during which individuals tell what God has done in their lives or speak as they are moved. One by one, members of the congregation rise at their pews and are recognized by Brother John. Facing the altar and Brother John, each delivers a monologue for anywhere between fifteen seconds and five minutes, punctuated by responses from the pastor (indicated in brackets in some of the following transcribed texts). Often five or ten seconds elapse after the end of one person's testimony before the next person rises. Not everyone testifies; at any given service three to eight people do so. More testimonies are given during the night service than the morning service; I am not certain why, but the night services tend to be more enthusiastic, and the enthusiasm carries into the testimonies.

Looking at testimonies offers an opportunity to see what is on the church members' minds. William Clements points out that "Much of the research dealing with religious events undertaken by folklorists and other investigators of oral art in the United States has focused on the role of the preacher or on the performance of a particularly talented singer. While this research emphasis accords with the centrality of these figures in public worship and the esteem granted them by their coreligionists, exclusive concentration on preachers and singers ignores the contribution of the average worshiper to a religious event" (Clements 1980b: 22). Indeed, upon reflection their testimonies turn out not to be ordinary but revealing about the parishioners' inner lives, belief, and feelings. Moreover, as I pointed out earlier, testimony affords women one of the few avenues of attention for solo verbal performance in the church. Denied the right to preach, or to hold office, yoked by the Pauline admonition that women must keep silence in church, some of the women, particularly Sister Edith, take full advantage of the opportunity to testify.

Another word the church members use for testimony is *witnessing*, and this stresses the personal aspect of testimony, the eye-witness account. It also throws into relief the extended metaphor of trial and judgment, the legal language that runs through these people's mouths as they describe the salvation process: guilt, conviction, condemnation, testimony, witnessing, evidence, judgment, and so forth. A testament is, of course, a covenant; and to testify is to declare solemnly and publicly.

"[Testifying is] just telling what the Lord's done for you," said Brother Vernie (Meadows interview, 1977, p. 27). It would, of course, take too long to tell all; most people who testify confine themselves to expressing their feelings and beliefs as Christians. Chiefly, what the Lord has done for them is that he has saved them; hence their testimonies are filled with expressions of joy and thanks and even pride that they are children of God and destined for heaven. Some testimonies are relatively brief expressions of faith. Based on fieldwork with Pentecostals in northeast Arkansas, William Clements identified the type as a "straight testimony," defined as "a short impersonal statement" (1980b: 28–29). Clements found these to characterize 90 percent of the testimonies he observed. The percentage is high at the Fellowship Independent Baptist Church as well, where roughly two-thirds were straight testimonies. Here are two examples, first from Brother Oscar:

> Brother John, I'm glad that I can be here tonight again to worship the Lord. I want you all to pray for me that I can grow stronger, and I want to grow stronger in the name of the Lord Jesus Christ. Thank God for his blessings and what he's done for me. It means the world and all. (Night service, July 31, 1977)

Straight testimonies, like all testimonies, are personal in the sense that the testifier says "I" frequently and speaks to and from his or her own experience; but the straight testimony is highly conventional. Many phrases in any straight testimony appear in other testimonies; thus, Clements conceives of them as impersonal. Brother Vernie attributed his short, infrequent testimonies to a lack of talent: "Some people's got more talent than others. . . . I don't testify so often. I just ain't got the talent to do it" (Meadows interview, 1977, pp. 38–39). Indeed, his testimonies are brief and "straight":

> Brother John, I'm glad that he saved me, and he told me I could go all the way with him, and I'm counting on it, and y'all pray for me. (Night service, July 31, 1977)

Identity and Madness in Personal Reminiscence Testimonies

A second type of testimony Clements identified among his Pentecostal churchgoers in northeast Arkansas was "the personal reminiscence testimony," in which the testifiers "recall the experiences of their childhood and youth as exempla. Much longer than the straight testimony, the personal reminiscence testimony involves more than praise for God, for the performer usually tries to develop an ethical point or to provide a moral admonition" (1980b:29). Personal reminiscence plays a role in about one-third of the testimonies given at the Fellowship Independent Baptist Church. Certain people seem given to personal reminiscence just as others almost always deliver "straight" testimonies. And although they sometimes recall the experiences of their youth, they tend to draw their exempla from more recent experiences; nonetheless, they invariably draw a lesson from these experiences. These personal reminiscences sometimes rise to the level of artfully told stories; at other times the reminiscence is offered briefly to make a point. Even so, the largest part of any testimony involving personal reminiscence is taken up with expressions of praise, thanksgiving, and professions of faith; reminiscence and storytelling are embedded.

On the night of April 9, 1978, Sister Virginia came forward at the altar call and prayed with Brother John, Sister Pauline, and other church members (see Chapter 6 for her dialogue with Brother John and his prayer). When through, she felt she had come back to the Lord after backsliding. She had already been saved but had strayed from God. As Brother Belvin explained:

> You're born twice, once in the flesh and once in the Spirit. And then if you're backsliding and go back out on the Lord and go back out into the worldly crowd doing the worldly things, well then you're backsliding on the Lord. And if they die in that shape they go to hell. Then if they can't be borned again [again], all they can do is to come back and renew their cove-nant and take up where they left off. (Hurt interview, pp. 11–12)

Sister Virginia offered testimony on why she went to the altar that night. (Bracketed expressions are responses from Brother John.)

> The Lord saved me down at Al Kling's one Saturday night. [Bless your heart.] Called me to the altar, the Lord did. And I said, "Lord, take me and guide me, lead me, strengthen me." And he did. But he's told me things and I disobeyed him. [Bless your heart. Confession is good for the soul.] And this week he's held me all week, and tonight he's dealt with me again and I've given my full heart and my full soul to him. And I thank him for that. And I'm gonna live for him for the rest of my days. No matter how short or how long, I'm gonna live for him. 'Cause he is the only way. If you don't let him into your life you don't have nothing and you're not nothing. You're not. And I thank him for that. I thank him for all the love he's put in my heart towards everybody. And I have feelings for more people now than I've ever had in my life. And I'm thankful for that. And he has given me

strength for my work everywhere and I thank him for that and I praise him for it. [Praise the Lord.]

This concise reminiscence testimony describes how Sister Virginia fell out of God's grace by disobeying his will, then how God "held her" all week—that is, God kept her from dying as a sinner—and how that night God convicted her and she made up her mind to yield fully once more. She concludes with a profession of faith and the assertion that she has "feelings for more people now than I've ever had in my life," an expression of the sisterly love she feels as a result of coming to the altar and being restored to the faith. I will have more to say on this subject in the section "Conversion: Performance and Community."

Sister Edith testified more often than anyone else in the Fellowship Independent Baptist Church during the summer of 1977. She was known as someone who always had a testimony and, indeed, no service that she attended went by without her giving one. In most she mixed personal reminiscence with professions of faith and words of wisdom. In the following testimony, the centerpiece is a reminiscence of a visit made the day before to a black woman in the hospital in nearby Harrisonburg:

Brother John, you know I got to thank the Lord for being here this morning. I just thank him for just sparing me another week. You know I just thank him for everything. And I know God can heal. And I know he's healed my body a-many times, which is just about gone, you know it's about ready to go home. What's in there. But you know I just thank the Lord that he's kept it as good as he has and give me the strength to go as I have went. And you know I need every, all prayers, to pray for my body. But it's like I told a woman yesterday at the hospital: whenever God calls us away, we're just a-going home to live, and she said, "I don't mind going." She said, "Don't nobody worry about me 'cause I'm just a-getting ready to live, I'm a-going home." And I said, "Praise the Lord for that." And I said, "When you get there I'm going to be there with you." And you know it just done me good to go into the room. It was a Negro woman, they call her Viola, I believe, and you know she really did have a good spirit when I talked to her. It really done me good to go in and talk to her, but which I hadn't seen the woman about once or twice in my life, but I still enjoyed it. You know after all I'm glad that I'm saved. I'm glad that the Lord thought enough of me to save me. Do you know I know that I'm saved and I know when I got saved. If I didn't know when I got saved I wouldn't know I was saved. But you know I know that I'm saved. I can't say who else is saved and who's lost. But I do know that I'm saved 'cause God promised me a place in heaven and he said he would prepare that place for me. And you know I believe he's just about got it finished and I believe I'm soon going on. You know that's what makes me feel so good. People say about dying. No, I'm not going to die. My body's going to die just like I said in Sunday school this morning. But you know my soul's just a-getting ready to live. And I'm getting so close to home. You know it just makes me feel good, days when I sit by myself and I just think that I'm so close to home. I just feel like sometimes I'm almost home. And you know I've not got but just a little ways to go and I feel like that I'll be there. And I'm so proud of that you know. I'll stay here as long as the Lord keeps me here and if I got work, if there's work for me to do, I'm willing to do it, but I'm proud when the time comes that he'll say "Come home." And y'all pray for me. (Morning service, July 24, 1977)

The reminiscence about her talk with Viola at the hospital is brief but revealing. Trying to help Viola, apparently a patient near death, Sister Edith tells her that dying is just the beginning of a new life. Viola, obviously sharing the same belief, says she does not fear death; she is just "a-getting ready to live" and "going home." These performances establish a rapport between these two elderly women, one black, the other white. Although Sister Edith until now has scarcely known Viola, she feels a bond with her and asserts, "When you get there I'm going to be with you." Edith concludes that she (Edith) benefited from the encounter; she "enjoyed" it. The joy of fellowship, of communal sisterhood, even with a stranger, gave her a blessing. And this is what she reports to the church in her testimony.

Her testimony, though it may seem rambling, centers on her impending death. She begins by thanking God for giving her the strength to live another week and come to church. She acknowledges that God can heal and asks for the others to pray that he would heal her body. She is reminded of her encounter with Viola at the hospital and tells that story. After the story she thanks God for saving her, then expresses her belief that she will soon die and go to heaven. Underlying the testimony is a paradox: Sister Edith is old and often in pain; she wonders why God has let her linger on. God has "healed my body a-many times," she says, but it's "just about gone." *Why* is God keeping her here, week after week? The question itself lingers, surfacing daily. At the close of her testimony she hints at the answer: "If I got work, if there's work for me to do, I'm willing to do it . . ." She will remain to witness and bring others to the Lord through her testimony.

Pain and healing were the subject of another of Sister Edith's testimonies that contained a comparatively lengthy personal reminiscence. She had been given some pain-killing pills, possibly codeine, for her legs, and the pills made her dizzy. Rather than continue taking the pills, she asked the Lord to heal her. (Bracketed expressions are responses from Brother John.)

You know, Brother John, I just thank the Lord for giving me another week to be back again in the house of the Lord. [Yes.] You know I enjoy coming to the house of the Lord, and I love to see people get saved. You know nothing fills my heart no better than to see people confess and come up and get saved. 'Cause you know if they could just see what was going on in this old world and see these worldly things. It's like the one said, "Give up to God." You know we got to give up these things, too. [That's right.] And if we don't give 'em up and if we hold on to 'em, we're not pleasing God. You know that I'm glad that I'm saved, and I know that God thought enough of me that he saved me. And I know just like in Esther it says here awhile ago: the Lord answers prayers every day and night. [Yes, he does.] Anytime that you call on him in need, you know that he's right there. And more people's out and gone and they never know how to get in touch with him. But all you got to do is call up to the telephone to the Lord [laughter] and he's right there for you to hear. 'Cause you know [amen] I've spent many a night that I thought I was going to be by myself. But you know I wasn't. The Lord was with me, and he kept me just like I was meant to be. [Amen.] And I'm so proud of that. It's awful plain that we got a God today big enough to take care of just a little thing as we are. [That's right.]

You know I studied that the other night and got to praying about it, this, and I've got to tell this for the glory of the Lord. You know I was a-praying about this t'other night. I've had such a misery in my legs that I just couldn't stand on my feet to walk around the bed. I still thanked the Lord for it; I didn't get worried nor get upset about it. I just thanked the Lord. And I said, "If it's my time to go, I'm ready to go, Lord. You know what's the best. But if it ain't, to give me some ease." You know it eased off. And you know I said, "Lord, you're a bigger thing than what these medicines that I've been taking, and God and (if I) trust that and can't trust you?" These pills I take and the doctor gave me—I have to tell this because it's for the glory of God. [Might be (for) somebody else.] It's not for me. He give me some pills, and I'm going to tell you that night I went to bed if I would have died I wouldn't have known where I was at 'cause I just felt like I was numb all over. The next morning, I didn't have no feelings until the next morning in my legs and arms. Now this is the truth and God knows it is [bless your heart] and I said, "Lord I don't have to take things like this. Trust things and such a little old thing as that little old pill [bless your heart] to make me feel like that. And as great a God as you are and as big as your heart you can't take care of a little old thing like this?" You know I just got a real good blessing out of that. And you know my legs has not bothered [amen, amen] me too much since. And them pills is a-setting there in that drawer in that cabinet this morning, and I've not touched a one, but God's healed that leg that it don't hurt like it did. [Amen.] And I don't say it's going to be well, 'cause it might not be. But what stripes and what pains we carry is nothing to what he's carried for us. [That's right.] If we would just think one time, our little suffering here is nothing to what he has done for us. [Amen, amen.] And you know I think that sometime, and when I feel bad I just still thank the Lord, and you know when I do that, I feel better than I do if I was to get this stuff, Lord have mercy.

You know [praise the Lord] I'm so proud of that and I know that I've got a God that saved me and I know he's big enough to keep me. [Amen.] And you know I'm so proud of that. People might think I'm crazy, but if I could stand up here and tell you that everything that I have prayed and asked to the Lord myself that he's answered, you know I—it would take me till next week this time for you all to get home. 'Cause I couldn't tell you all of it. But I do know God has saved me, and I know God's big enough to keep me. [Amen.] And I know he's heaped promises upon his promises he can do and I know you all know that. And I want you all to pray for me 'cause I got children that's lost. But I'm a-praying for 'em that they'll come in before it's too late. [Keep praying.] And bless the Lord, I know that the Lord's bigger than the people on earth. And oh I'm so proud that I've got somebody that's so much greater than the devil. Oh, I'm so proud of that this morning. [Amen.] I'm so thankful that I've got a Lord that keeps me day and night. [Amen, bless the Lord.] Ohh, there ain't nobody knows that until he comes down with some—. When we come down let's don't wait till we come down to die before we ask God to save us. You know we don't know what we might have to go through with for God to save us. But you know when he says he'll save us we're going to bear it, and he don't put no more on us than we can bear. You know I'm so proud of that. And I'm so proud that we've got a Lord that will tell us the truth. [Amen.] And you all pray for me 'cause I want to be just what the Lord wants me to be. And there ain't nobody knows how I'm filled with the Lord this morning but myself. I couldn't tell you all. [But I imagine how you feel.] You might think I'm crazy. But the Lord has really blessed me, I mean through all this time that I've been through here God has really blessed me. I'm still thanking him, and he's going to bless me more. And if we don't, I'll soon go on home to see the Lord. [*Weeping:*] Ohh, I'm so proud that the time has come for me to go home. Ohhh, hallelujah, Jesus, thank you Lord, he's answered prayers so many times. Oh, hallelujah, thank you, Jesus. Thank you, Lord. Thank you, Jesus. (Morning service, April 9, 1978. The testimony may be heard on the *Powerhouse for God* album.)

Here, Sister Edith has offered a faith healing narrative within her testimony. She says she tells it "for the glory of God" but, as Brother John responds, it serves also as an example for others.

Sister Edith does not always bring narrative into the core of her testimonies. Some are simply expressions of her gratitude, beliefs, and hopes, with acknowledgment of the trials she has endured. Dwelling on the trials too long produces impatience among the congregation, most of whom think a testimony should be an expression of joy (see below). In a sense, though, she speaks for all of the church members; she articulates their feelings and their beliefs; and the responses from Brother John (in brackets) and from her husband, Brother Clyde (in brackets, preceded by *), speak their assenting replies:

You know, Brother John, I'm glad to be here this morning [*amen] [yes, thank the Lord]. You know I just thank the Lord for everything. I thank the Lord for saving me, [unintelligible] and God can reach down that deep canyon [yes, he can]. And you know there ain't nothing, no trials that ever come too great that he can't overcome [that's right] [*praise God]. And he can help you with it if you can trust him [amen]. You know when we ask God for something we want and we never doubt it [unintelligible] [yes, amen] and when we ask God for something we should pray to God 'cause he'll give it to us if it's a need [*yes, he will]. And if he don't give it to us when we first ask, just hold on 'cause he's a just God, he answers [*thank you, Jesus] prayers. You know sometimes things gets terrible and the devil brings things that you can't [*yes, that's right] [that's right] take if you try but you know if you do look up to the Lord, the Lord can lighten all these burdens and make you feel better. And you can be blessed and not even know it in the time that you feel that you're so down that you're no good that you can't do nothing. And you know we got a good Lord that can come along and give us a good blessing [yes] and cheer us up that we can feel better every way [amen]. The Lord blesses [thank God] us every day [yes, he does]. You know, a sinner ought to thank the Lord [amen]. 'Cause you know the breath that's in the body of a sinner is God's [it's God's, that's right]. And he can take it that quick, it can be gone [amen]. And if people could only look, if they ever could see. I'm going to tell you when I got saved I seen it. I seen it before me [bless your heart]. I ain't saying I seen it, but I seen it [getting close to it]—yeah, it looked like that almost I could see what it looked like, I knew what it looked like then and I thought God revealed it to me that it was like it was. And do you know I know that I got borned again 'cause God said he'd [slaps hand on pew] save me and saved me [*glory to God]. And I'm just standing on that today until the day I leave here and when I leave I know that's where I'm a-going [amen, amen, hallelujah]. Don't make no difference if everything's [unintelligible] [praise God] here or whenever it may come, come to get me, God's for me and there ain't nothing else [unintelligible] [amen]. You know that's what I'm proud of, that I can overcome these things of the devil [that's right]. And I just pray every day to God to give me faith and give me power to overcome things that comes up [yes, praise God] that I think I can't stand. There's some things come against me sometime that I think I cannot go through with [God'll give you the victory]. And I said, "Lord, I can't without your help," and I couldn't. But you know God's helping me. And I'm a-living for God and I'm living just as close as I know [bless your heart] what's best. I can't read the Bible, but I can pray to myself just as good as I can to somebody else [*amen]. And I've prayed for people that I know they don't like me [bless your heart; you're supposed to]. I know they don't [unintelligible], but you know God loves me and God's going to fix it up. It don't make no difference. When they cut that boy's head off he still lived for

Sister Edith Cubbage testifying, 1977.

God. They can kill this body but there's one thing there God's got, nobody
can take it out, and I'm so proud of that, don't make no difference [*glory!]
nor what's said or what's done. God saved my soul [hallelujah] and I
[*amen, hallelujah] know I'm saved because God knows that. I might not
have the [bless your heart], this ability to go around and do things that
some people do, but I do know that God's in my heart [amen] and I know
[amen] that I'm saved. And I know the Lord has answered my prayers. I
have prayed for my children [*crying:*] and they're lost. I have prayed for
people that has talked about me, I know it. And God's blessed me for it.
And I'm going to stand for the right. I can't help it to get mad [amen] when
they bring something up of the devil and I don't agree with it and God
don't approve of it, I'm not going to take it in and go on smoothing it over.
I'm going to say just what God gives me to say about it [amen]. And I'll

pray for God to give me the knowledge and what to say to people [yes, amen] not to hurt 'em but to tell the truth [tell 'em the truth]. And I'm going to tell the truth, [that's right] don't make no difference what [amen]. And if something happens today that causes this whole place to be blowed up [unintelligible] in a lie I'd say cannot do it 'cause God saved me [that's right]. And I know that I'm saved and I want you all to pray for 'em. And I've got children that I've talked to and I've told 'em and I've been good to 'em, I do everything I know and I've been just as good to people as I can be and I don't know what to do to get them saved [bless your heart, just keep praying]. But God knows. And I pray for 'em. And if they talk hateful to me I used to would get mad. You know the devil'll push it into you [mm-hmm] for it to make you mad, but you know with the good help of the good Lord that I can stand it [amen] and go through with it. 'Cause this thing that's in here is God's. This body's weak but God's got something there that's greater than the whole world [light laugh]. And you know I'm so proud of that. I don't know what I did. People might think sometimes that I've just [bless you, sis] gone out of my mind, but I am not, 'cause I'm saved and I know it [amen, amen]. 'Cause God told me he'd save me I give him everything, whatever belongs to me now [praise the Lord] but I'd turn over everything, even if it's my life, so I don't care. To die, to me, it's a gain [mm-hmm]. But I hate to see the one that's lost [yes]. And I grieve about the one that's lost [amen]. I lay down at night and I pray for the one that's lost and I cry about it. But still I say, God, it's up to you, I can't do no more [amen]. And I can go to sleep and sleep like I want until daylight. And you know I do, if you do [praise God] the will of God you can live. And people say about good times, good times, yes it's good times for people to live to what we used to live in, in eating and lying and living places, but Lord it's one of the worstest times that's on this earth that ever was, 'cause the devil is just a-going [yes, he is] and doing everything and the world is living for him. But you know the best thing in the world, if you ain't got a thing, if I didn't have a dress on my back this morning, I'd rather come here and live for God than I would to go out there and be dressed in the finest silk [yes, amen] and the finest ever [amen] was than to be living for the devil [that's right]. 'Cause I got a home when I leave here; I know where I'm a-going [amen]. 'Cause I know that that's a better place than what it is here. (Morning service, July 3, 1977. Incomplete; unfortunately the recording tape ran out just before she ended.)

Again, Sister Edith begins by thanking God for saving her and giving her strength to be in church, and for helping her to overcome evil. These opening expressions of gratitude are conventional, but in this testimony Sister Edith dwells on her earthly trials. The controlling idea is that she has faith and that she will persevere despite the work of the devil.

How she presents her trials reveals an important clue to her inner life and her struggle over her identity and self-worth. She mentions periods when "you feel that you're so down that you're no good that you can't do nothing." Identity—one's sense of who one is—is, as I will argue throughout this chapter, the key issue in the language genre of testimony. Here, Sister Edith feels her self-worth threatened: she is "no good." Later she says, defensively, "I can't read the Bible, but I can pray to myself just as good as I can to somebody else. And I've prayed for people that I know they don't like me. I know they don't [*unintelligible*], but you know God loves me and God's going to fix it up." Again: "I might not have the, this ability to go around and do things that some people do, but I know that God's in my heart and I know that I'm saved."

In these statements she overcomes her doubts and feelings of inferiority by assertions that God loves her and has saved her. Apparently sometime in the recent past she confronted some people—we are not told exactly what the issue was, because that is not the point—and they got angry: "I can't help it to get mad when they bring something up of the devil and I don't agree with it and God don't approve of it, I'm not going to take it in and go on smoothing it over." Perhaps it was a confrontation with one of her unsaved children: "I've got children that I've talked to and I've told 'em and I've been good to 'em, I do everything I know and I've been just as good to people as I can be and I don't know what to do to get them saved. But God knows. And I pray for 'em." Each of these arguments challenges the validity of Sister Edith's worldview and threatens her feelings of self-worth.

In this context it is useful to consider Erik Erikson's definition of "ego identity" as "the accrued confidence that one's ability to maintain inner sameness and continuity . . . is matched by the sameness and continuity of one's meaning for others" (1967:202). This confidence—and therefore, ego identity—is impaired whenever people do not believe her or accept her at face value, writing her off as a religious fanatic. "People might think sometimes that I've just gone out of my mind, but I am not, 'cause I'm saved and I know it," she states. She is often concerned that others think she is crazy; this fear surfaces in several of her testimonies. Another example, from a different testimony: "Don't make no difference when they call us crazy. We might be wise. You know, [the three] wise men, they wasn't crazy, they was wise men, wasn't they?" (night service, July 10, 1977). In Erikson's terms, when Sister Edith is called crazy, she feels the sharp discontinuity between her meaning for herself and her meaning for others.

It may clarify the discussion to introduce another term here to name the "meaning for others" that Erikson writes about. "Stance" is the meaning or role that others assign a person (Titon 1985:18). The argument can now be summarized as: under ideal circumstances, stance (meaning for others) and identity (meaning for oneself) are the same. Discrepancies threaten identity. Overcoming the devil and withstanding a trial involves a reassertion of identity, sometimes by attempting to alter one's stance but never, for the born-again Christian, altering identity. If identity changes, one has backslid. Speaking of her children, Sister Edith said, "And if they talk hateful to me I used to would get mad. You know the devil'll push it into you for it to make you mad, but you know with the good help of the good Lord that I can stand it and go through with it. 'Cause this thing that's in here is God's." The "thing that's in here" is Sister Edith's identity: her sense of herself.

In this testimony, Sister Edith makes reference to her conversion, saying she had a glimpse of heaven and the glory of God: "I seen it before me. I ain't saying I seen it, but I seen it [getting close to it]—yeah, it looked like that almost I could see what it looked like, I knew what it looked like then and I thought God revealed it to me that it was like it was." This personal reminiscence of her conversion was offered in greater detail in other testimonies (Brother John's responses are omitted here):

You know, Brother John, I'm so proud that I'm saved and that I'm not going through that tribulation period. I don't think I'm going to be here 'cause God said he's going to take his children and I believe he's going to take me. When Noah built his ark the ones that was saved was taken out of there, out of the drowning in the water, and that's the way he's going to take us out of hell, out of the fire when the time comes to go. You know I'm proud that I'm saved and I know that I'm saved. And if anybody don't know that they're saved I'm going to tell you [unintelligible] the way things is a-going and you know just like the book that he's a-reading in tonight, it's a-coming right on up there. It might not be there yet, but it's a-coming, 'cause it's in there and I believe it. I believe it's a-coming, and I believe it's going to be worse than we can imagine it's going to be, too. We imagine it's going to be bad, and it's going to be worse than that.

You know I'm proud that I'm saved. I don't think I'm going to see that 'cause the good Lord has made a place for me and I'm a-going there before the time comes. You know because he showed me places that he had prepared for me and I know I'm a-going there 'cause and I got friends that I know's there. 'Cause I got some people that's gone. My mother's went and I believe firmly from my heart that she's in heaven today, tonight. And she's rejoicing to think that we're saved, 'cause she rejoiced when she went out, when she went to sleep. She didn't go like some people do, she didn't suffer, but she just asked the Lord to have mercy on her. And I went so far with her and I believe that I was caught up. I can't tell it myself but I really seen a real place when she went to go. But I wasn't fit to go. I just felt like if I would have been I could have went with her but I couldn't. But you know after ever since then I've always thought about these things and I've always prayed about it and I think that she's there. I *know* that she's

there 'cause she said she was a-going and I went so far with her but I
wasn't able to go the rest of the way because I wasn't, I wasn't fit to go
there. That's what it was. But you know I been a-looking all the time.
Every time I hear a song sung about Mother gone home I think about her.
She talked to me so much about things you know like that when she got so
bad, I—. She told me she loved me and she wouldn't hurt me for nothing,
and I don't believe she would. And but when she left this world I hated to
see her go, but you know I wouldn't bring her back if I could because she's
resting. When we got all those trials and troubles to go through with—. I
got to tell this every once in a while 'cause God puts it on my heart to tell
it, but I'm so proud and thankful that I know that that's where she's gone.
I've got others that's gone but I can't say where they've gone because I
don't know. But I do believe and firmly from my heart what God showed it
to me that she's in heaven, she's a-resting.

[*Crying:*] You know that's enough to make you rejoice in things. If
you've got one that's done so much for you and when you get there that
you're going to see her. I believe she's a-waiting to see me come home, yes
I do. And you know I'm just so proud that I can get there and see her. I'll
be proud to see Jesus. I'm going to see him. But I'll be proud to see her too,
and I believe she's going to know me 'cause she done so much for me
when she was here, and I believe she's going to still [*unintelligible*] for me.
And y'all pray for me 'cause you know I'm saved. I'm not afraid of being
lost. I can go through a whole lot of things that's in this world. We're all
going to have trials and have to face 'em, we're going to have to stand 'em,
or else we'll be like what's his name and have our head cut off. But I'd
rather go to heaven without a head or a body. It's one thing they can kill
the body but they can't kill that soul. God's got his hand on it and it can't
be killed. You know that's what I'm proud of. We got somebody that can
take care of the inside of you now [*unintelligible*]. You know this sure ain't
nothing but corruption nohow 'cause it's going back to what it come from.
But [*crying*] you know I'm so proud of what's in there, that God's going to
take and we're going to have a good place [*unintelligible phrase*] one of
these days. And I'm so proud of that. I couldn't tell you how many blessings that God has given me and blessed me with. I got children, and I
think he blessed me when he give me eleven children, and they're all
grown. And all of 'em's smart, and all of 'em's got children. You know I
think God was great to me and good to me and blessed me just to [*unintelligible word*]. But you know that ain't half of what he done when he prepared a place for us, and I'm so proud that I know that I'm going there.
And y'all pray for me. (Night service, July 17, 1977. A portion appeared
as "A Vision of Heaven" in Titon and George 1978:78–79.)

Sister Edith begins her testimony with a response to Brother John's sermon from Revelation about the tribulation period. The centerpiece of the

testimony is a personal reminiscence of a vision she had when her mother was dying. This is the vision she referred to in the previous testimony, a vision of heaven. Bound up with it is Sister Edith's love for her mother and her sorrow to have lost her, buoyed by her faith that she will be with her again in heaven.

Given such frequent, intense professions of faith, one can only speculate concerning the internal doubts that these professions apparently resolved. The church members admit to doubts, saying they are temptations of the devil; Satan, they say, works hard to tempt converts and estrange them from God. With sinnerfolk the devil can relax. Whatever the source, the professions of faith assert Christian identity and strike at doubt. When these professions are made publicly as performances in the church community, the testifier feels no discrepancy between stance and identity, and ego identity in Erikson's sense is strengthened because the community reinforces it. Still, there is more to identity in these circumstances than community reinforcement: there is the assurance that comes from experiencing blessings from God while performing.

Sister Edith's mother's death must have been especially difficult. "She talked to me so much about things you know like that when she got so bad, I—. She told me she loved me and she wouldn't hurt me for nothing, and I don't believe she would." Why would the mother have told the child she would not *hurt* her? What threat did she represent? When Ken George and I interviewed Sister Edith and her husband in her home, I started by asking, "Is there anything that either of you would like to say to begin this tape for the folks at the Library of Congress?" Sister Edith immediately recounted her vision at her mother's death. She repeated what she had said but, in the interview context where, presumably, we were less familiar with the circumstances than the congregation that has heard it several times before, she filled in greater detail. I have transcribed her words ethnopoetically; reading directions are the same as for Brother John's call-to-preach narrative in Chapter 7.

> Well, I'll tell you for the starting of me getting saved and this is the way it was.
>
> My mother was sick and she was bad, she was awful bad off and she told me that she believed she was a-going out of her mind, but I wouldn't be— you know, that she wouldn't hurt me 'cause she—
>
> she loved me. *And I said, "Mama, I know you do."*
>
> *And she said,* "But I'm a-going home," *she said, "and I* want you to meet me."
>
> Now this is the first starting of me getting saved.
>
> Well I told her, I said, "Well, I'll meet you."
>
> I said, "If there's any way in the world I'll meet you because I know that I'm going to be saved and go with you."

So when she left **out of this world**—I believe sometimes, I always
thought maybe
    the good Lord seen fit to take her maybe to save **me.**
You know I always felt like that.
    And so Brother [Guerdon] *Cave* was the one that baptized me, I never
will forget it.
    I told him, I said, "Brother Cave," I said, "Mother went on and I felt like
that I could have went to heaven if I would have been ready but I wasn't
ready."
    But I, honest, I did   see something, this is the truth I'm a-telling y'all.
I seen the beautifullest place that I ever seen in my life the
morning that she left home.
    Now I'm a-telling you this and this is the truth and God knows it's the
truth or he wouldn't give me the remembrance of it.
    And I never could—I never seen a place like that   since, nor I
never seen it before that, but I seen it then.
    It was one of the beautifullest-looking places that I ever seen.
    Well, I said, "If that place is that beautiful just for me going by her
leaving
    and a-**going,** I'm going to accept the Lord as my Savior."
    And so I just felt like when she was buried—now this is the **truth**—
when they buried her I was **sorry** that I was going to **miss** her and all like
that but I could just rejoice of it you know to think that she had gone home.
    Now that's a **long story** on that, but you know I'm just proud that I'm
saved and I'm proud that I know the Lord did save me.
    I say I've made mistakes along the road and we all have.
    But you know God's children   he forgives.

Thus Sister Edith promised her mother that she would meet her in heaven.
Her account is remarkably similar to Brother John's account of his brother
Ester Sherfey's death (see Chapter 7). Sister Edith's mother dies peace-
fully, but she must have been delirious prior to death. Her mother asks her
to promise to meet her in heaven, and she agrees. Thus far the narrative is
conventional, but it also contains one of Sister Edith's thematic touch-
stones: madness. Her mother is aware that she is going mad: "She told me
that she believed she was a-going out of her mind." Still, she would not
hurt her daughter because she loved her. How, we may ask again, could
she hurt her? By dying and leaving her daughter lonely, for one thing; by
lying about where she was going, for another. Insane, she is not to be
trusted; her faith is not to be trusted. But she asks Sister Edith to trust her
because she loves her. Sister Edith assents, whereupon her mother says
she is "going home" and wants her to meet her there.
    If that was not enough to convince her that her mother was sane, Sister
Edith had a vision of heaven when her mother died, and this confirmed

her worldview. As Sister Edith tells it, her mother, threatened by madness, asserts her Christian identity. Her daughter finds verification in her own vision of heaven, and vows that she will accept the Lord. Even more poignant, she wonders whether "the good Lord seen fit to take her maybe to save me." In other testimonies not printed here she mentions her willingness to die if it would help save her own children. She thinks that may be the reason God has let her linger on in pain: not until they are ready to accept Jesus will she die; before she goes they will vow to meet her in heaven. That will be her work and her Christ-like sacrifice, and the cyclic bond will continue.

The Church Members' Ideas about Testimony

Testimony is understood to be Spirit-led right down to the spoken words. Sister Edith, characteristically, affirms so in the midst of a church-delivered testimony:

> Don't make no difference what kind of clothes I got on or what I got on, he [God] knows what's in my heart. And why do I care about man? And they say you're going crazy when you do like that, but I don't care. If the Lord gives it to me to go through here and to holler I got to holler, and if he says, "Keep talking," I've got to keep talking. (Morning service, July 31, 1977)

She explained how the Lord put the words in her mind:

> When I testify I give just exactly what the Lord gives me to say. He tells me to get up and tell it, I get up and tell just what he gives me that time to say. And after that maybe I couldn't repeat it over again. But I just say exactly what he puts in my mind and what he gives me to say. Just what God gives me as testimony, that's what I testify to. I don't make that testimony up and get up there. . . . I don't wait, I don't make it up or sit and wonder what I'm going to say. Just whatever he puts in my mouth to say, when I get up there, that's what I say. (Cubbage interview, p. 34)

Testifying, for Sister Edith, operates in a fashion similar to preaching for Brother John: the words come as an impression on the mind and are uttered at once; they need not wait. And like Brother John's sermons, Sister Edith's testimonies move through speech to chant. (This may be heard in her testimony on the *Powerhouse for God* record album.) One difference, however, is that whereas the sermon is expected—that is, Brother John or someone else is expected to preach at every Sunday worship service—testimonies are not expected from all members of the congregation. Sister Edith said she testifies when God gives her a testimony. It is so immediate that if she must wait for someone else to testify she might "lose" it:

If God gives [you] a testimony to testify in the church, I believe [you] should testify. And the next time you might have none. 'Cause I've had the Lord give me a testimony, and somebody else get up and take that away from me 'cause I was waiting on somebody else. [TITON: How do you know when to go?] When the Lord calls you and tells you it's right to get up. Now if somebody else gets up and you don't take your turn, you might not have none. [TITON: I see, the blessing might—] —go to somebody else. That's right. I believe that, I believe if you're told to do something and you don't do it, he'll give it to somebody else. . . . You're doing wrong to what the Lord's will is for you to do. . . . You feel pretty bad [afterward] if you don't obey. (Cubbage interview, p. 32)

Occasionally, it seemed to me, some people in the congregation became impatient with hearing Sister Edith testify so often and at such length. Not so Brother John; he welcomed her testimony and provided a continuously supportive atmosphere. Her favorite subjects—healing, madness, salvation, gratitude—provide a certain weight to the testimony portion of the service, which Brother John affirms is an important characteristic of their church. After the testimony period on July 24, 1977, he remarked:

Thank God for these testimonies. You know, not many places you go do you get a chance to testify. Preacher'll preach and he'll dismiss right quick, 'fore you will testify. But I feel like that every child of God would have a word to speak for Jesus. After what the Lord's done for us? I guess, I don't know, maybe you all weren't as vile a sinner as I was. My goodness alive, I can't help but thank him for what he done for me. Hmmh. Thank the Lord.

According to Brother John, a testimony should give evidence of the Lord's blessing. He emphasizes that the testifier wants to "share" the blessing with somebody else.

I feel that in any service, and every service, for that matter, a lot of people have a testimony on their heart that they want to share with somebody else. And what I mean by testimony is something that's happened to them that they feel like that God's blessed them in a certain special way and they want to share it with somebody else. . . . And of course most of the testimonies you hear is telling about how the Lord's blessed 'em and even while they was washing dishes or while they was cleaning the house or the men while they was in the field or while they was on the job. Now that's a testimony that the Lord's inside of them, blessed them, and they want to share it. (John Sherfey interview, July 23, 1977, p. 26)

Brother John points out how people can be and are blessed during mundane activities like dishwashing. Brother Belvin accepted the call to preach, as we have seen, in his upper garden; we will soon see that he was converted while plowing new ground for corn. Brother Jesse agreed completely with Brother John, that a testimony was something that a person wanted to "share" and ought to be based on a particular blessing:

> A testimony is not focused on any one certain thing [only], but it's on the blessings that the Lord has given you. Maybe it might be something in God's word that you might want to testify to that the Lord has blessed same as the Lord did somebody in the Bible. . . . Or something in the word of God that the Lord has showed you that you want to share with somebody. (Comer interview, 1977, p. 43)

This sharing, of course, occurs when the testimony is performed in the church community; the desire to share is an urge for communal validation of the testifier's identity as a Christian, on the one hand, and for the experience of community on the other. "It strengthens a person when they [testify]," said Brother Jesse (ibid., p. 44). It strengthens the community as well. I asked Sister Edith, "Do you ever get a blessing from somebody else's testimony?" "Indeed I do," she replied. "It just makes you feel good to think that they're living for the Lord" (Cubbage interview, p. 37).

I asked Brother Jesse why Brother John asks for testimonies by saying, "Anybody got a word on your heart?" He replied:

> Because a testimony comes from the heart, of what the Lord has blessed you with. Some people even tell their troubles, and all of this that they've been through, but the main thing is, in a case like this, any testimony ought to be from the heart and from the true feelings that a person has. . . . That's from the center of man, the Spirit that God puts in man, and the center of him that man believes with. It's hard to explain, but it's that part of man that God has come in, and it's the indwelling of the Holy Spirit. (Comer interview, 1977, p. 41)

But not all testimonies are delivered in the proper frame of mind. Brother Jesse criticized testimonies that dwelled on trials and tribulations, saying that the purpose of a testimony is to help others by sharing one's joy in the Lord's blessings, adding that it helps the testifier as well, and summarizing most of the ideas that the church members expressed to me concerning testimony:

> Some people testify the fact of the troubles and so forth that they've had, and how the Lord has helped 'em over these troubles to overcome them. Say there's a sinner in there and is listening to these things that a person is testified that they've had such a hard time with, the sinner may begin to feel in his own heart that, well, if they're having such troubles as that as Christians, I want no part of it. But then the person testifying might say, "Well, I know that I've had troubles; we all have troubles. But the joy that the Lord has put in my heart has fought by far greater than the troubles

that I've had, and he's helped me overcome every one of them." You see, that's what lifts, that you're praising the Lord. . . . [The purpose of a testimony is that] it helps others. . . . And then you tell how the Lord has blessed you. And you share things like that with other people, helps them too, as well as yourself. And a lot of times you can tell when a person is testifying and it's a real Spiritual testimony. . . . And sometimes I have heard people stand up in church, and again I don't like to see people do this. They have the same old testimony every time. There's no Spirit to it. It's like listening to a record over and over. . . . [A testimony] can be short, it can be long. As long as the Lord gives you something good to say, say it. When he's through with you, sit down. (Ibid., pp. 41–42)

The short, "straight" testimonies conform more closely to these rules of performance than do Sister Edith's lengthy mixtures of personal reminiscence and professions of faith. Perhaps that is why some of the church members were impatient with her testimonies week after week. Nevertheless, her testimonies comprise revealing personal documents: she says what is on her mind, and in so doing she allows access to her deepest concerns.

The Homiletic Testimony

Clements identifies a third type of testimony as "homiletic." It is a sort of miniature sermon that "affords the performer an opportunity to develop an idea, but does not necessarily involve personal recollection" (Clements 1980b: 29). Although Sister Edith developed ideas in her testimonies, she was not really addressing the congregation as a teacher might. She did not seek to instruct them; she sought confirmation of her ideas from them. Only two people in the congregation delivered homiletic testimonies with any regularity: Brother Belvin, himself a preacher; and Brother Rufus, who faithfully attended all the night services by himself after accompanying his family to morning services at a United Brethren church where they held membership. For his testimonies, Brother Rufus rose from his pew and often stood at the altar, facing the congregation. Very animated, with his voice full of enthusiastic anticipation, his testimonies developed sermonic exhortations amidst expressions of praise and gratitude. For example (Brother John's responses are in brackets):

Well I want to thank and praise the Lord to be here tonight [bless you, Brother Rufus], Brother John. I want to thank him for the wonderful message that the Lord had give you tonight. [Amen.] We need that message tonight. [Amen.] I want to thank and praise the Lord for what he means to me, how he keeps me [hallelujah] tonight, saved. I was glad when they all accept him by his word [praise God] praise God to keep 'em from sinning and they keep him in his hands [yes, amen]. I tell you right now there's nothing better than serving the Lord [amen]. The blessings are worth serving him [amen]. My God, people don't know what they're missing when they don't serve the Lord [mm-hmm]. I'm glad tonight I know my redeemer [amen]. I'm glad that I accepted him when I did [praise God]. I'm glad I accepted him when I did [praise God]. I'm glad I accepted the call [hallelujah]. I'm on the firing line tonight, praise God. I'll end up, the devil'll cheat me out of nothing. But through the grace of God I'm going to make it through to that city [amen, amen]. I tell you right now the Lord promised a new heaven and a new earth [That's what he said, amen] and I'm looking for that [I believe that] one of these days. And you said tonight. Oh, that book of Revelation's a deep book; I read it through and through here just awhile back, and a lot of things going to happen to this old world before [yes, sir] the Lord comes, but praise God the church'll be gone, Brother John [yes, it will]. We'll be in heaven; beyond sin is where we'll be. I'll walk down the streets of pure gold. Ain't that be wonderful? [(*Joyful tone:*) Amen.] Ain't going to be no more sorrow, ain't going to be no more pain. All things have passed away. Won't be no more hospitals, no more doctors [that's right, thank God], no more nurses. We'll live with Jesus for ever and ever [amen, amen]. Ain't that wonderful? He did that for us and it's free [yes, it is]. It don't cost a nickel [that's right]. [*Unintelligible sentence.*] I'm glad I'm a servant of the living God. Oh so many of 'em, talk about the [*unintelligible*] and all these things. My God is a real God; he's alive. I tell you right now a lot of people don't know Jesus Christ as their savior [bless him, Lord]. You don't know anything about God. Tossing a pitcher out on a stream. I tell you we ought to fight against a thing like that [bless him, Lord]. I tell you right now the devil would like to stir our young children's minds [yes, they would] and get 'em blind to the word of God [amen], to the gospel, that Jesus Christ is not a son of God, Jesus Christ is something else. But he's heaven-born [yes, he was], filled with the Holy Ghost, certainly he is, praise God [amen], and he's alive in heaven tonight and he's alive for evermore. [(*Enjoying Brother Rufus' performance:*) Amen.] I'm glad he lifted me, I know he done. And somebody talked about [*unintelligible phrase*] [bless you, brother]; wish I had a way to tell some of 'em, I tell you right now, when we stand for Jesus Christ, we the God's people [that's right], Brother John; a lot of 'em go along with a little sin here and a little sin there [yeah], but in the eyes of Jesus that ain't going to work [no, it ain't]. You know you either be clean or you be holy or you ain't going there [amen]. I'll tell you right now I want to be ready, I want to be holy. I want to accept him, I want to do all I can to make it through. By the grace of God [amen] we can make it through [thank God, bless your heart]. Praise God, I tell you right now I'm in the gloryland way. As the brother said, "Keep on the firing line" [(*laughter of enjoyment*)]; I'm on the firing line tonight, brother. Praise God. You all remember me in prayer and I'll remember you all. [Amen, bless you, Brother Rufus.] (Night service, June 26, 1977)

In this homiletic testimony, Brother Rufus begins with conventional statements thanking and praising God, and adds other formulaic statements affirming that he is saved and on his way to heaven. Next, he affirms Brother John's interpretation of the secret rapture of the church prior to the tribulation period, and talks about heaven. Ultimately he delivers his sermonette on those people who deny the divinity of Jesus, dwelling more on that divinity than on the unbelievers, thereby lifting the congregation's spirits more. He returns to unbelievers briefly, referring to those who call themselves Christians but who have deliberately retained what they consider trivial sins, saying they cannot matter much. (An example of a "trivial sin" would be smoking cigarettes. Properly, the church members feel, a Christian should pray for God's help in breaking the habit, and then make a genuine effort to quit. In this connection I recall a conversation with Brother John in which he said that it took him several months after he was converted to stop habitual sins like this.)

Still, although this testimony develops ideas, it remains focused on the testifier, who repeats the personal pronoun throughout. Far more like a mini-sermon is the following testimony, also from Brother Rufus (responses from Brother John omitted):

Brother John, I got something to say. I want to thank and praise the Lord tonight to be here and feel his presence and his power. I want to thank the Lord for saving my soul. I was lost one day, but praise God, then I got the victory through Jesus Christ. I'm glad tonight because he give me the strength to be here tonight. I wasn't able to be here a week or so ago. I was very sick. But I thank God, I'm here tonight to hear the gospel, the word of God, to be fed off the words of God. I thank God for that tonight. And I thank God for what it stands for. It stands for the truth and the word of God. And that's what will stand. That's what it's going to take to stand: take the truth, take the word of God, and the spirit of prayer'll be with the word of God. It'll bear witness. If you don't agree there's something wrong with your Spirit. I'll tell you right now when your Spirit don't believe the word of God it's something wrong somewhere. And I'm saying right now, you cut off those little bulbs up there, those bulbs shut, ain't got no current there, and ain't no light. But brother, if you got the bulb burning, you got the current there, you're going to get light. Jesus said, "I am the light of the world, I am he." Praise God, I'm glad one day Jesus said God said Jesus cleanses us from all sins. You mentioned that I want to see power. Some people can live like the devil and they cuss and they drink and do all ungodly things [and say], "I'm a Christian." Brother that's what Paul said, they would have a forum to deny, that the power was their own. But he said such eternal [*unintelligible word*]. But I want to tell you he said we would walk in the light, we would have fellowship one with another, and above Jesus Christ, God's son, will do what? Cleanse us from all sins.

Brother Rufus Cubbage testifying, 1977.

Brother, we don't have to have confusion. We don't have to have all these things in churches. But it's the devil that's getting, that'd like to see the churches tore down. He'd like to see them won over. Say, "I got that bunch right now. I got that little bunch of them now." Now I want to tell you as long as the Holy Ghost is in that church and the people keep praying, the devil got to stay away. I'm thanking God that I'm here tonight. I don't know, I just feel good in my soul tonight. Hallelujah, I'm sixty-four years old but I feel like fifteen tonight. Even been sick. Praise the Lord, it'll make you feel good, brother! Hallelujah. I was going to keep quiet. I'm telling you [*unintelligible phrase*]. You know it's good to love everybody, Brother John. Especially a houseful of God's. But I can't love that sin. That sin out there in the world, I can't love that, but I love their souls. I was talking with an old man the other week over in town. He's eighty-seven years old. I was talking with him there and poor fellow was smoking a great big cigar, and talking with him there. I said, "D'you accept the Lord?" "No," he says, "I don't want to hear it." Just think now. The man was in—his time, according to God's word, was over. Said you may reach threescore and ten by reasonable health and strength. But he was 87 years old. No time much longer, time is running out on him. "I don't want to hear it." Hardened his heart. Lord, he that hardeneth his heart and a stiff neck shall surely be destroyed and cut off without remedy. But I want to tell you something: you don't play around with God. I want to tell you, you come on God's side or no side. You can come on God's terms, brother! I'm glad tonight I'm on God's side. God's going to be the winner. Hallelujah. I was very sick, I had a temperature of 103. Who did I look to? I looked to the Lord. I thank God I'm here tonight, brother. Hallelujah, he'll keep me here a little longer. If he don't, nevertheless die and be gone. Just beyond the river. Hallelujah, a beautiful star will—. There'll be no more pain, for the former things will have passed away. I'm glad to meet these brothers here. I learned to love 'em. I think they're going away 'fore long. Some of these boys, brothers, I'll call you brothers, I never will meet you again this side of heaven. Some day I want to walk down that street of pure gold. Brother John, that goes for you all. I'm going to walk down one of these days a street of pure—just think while you're going through the world— pure gold. Here we might have a little pocket change made out of copper, but there there'll be streets of pure gold. Won't that be wonderful, sister? Ain't that going to be wonderful? We won't need no doctors, won't need no ambulances, won't need no rescue squad, we won't need no judges, no lawyers; all we're going to have is Jesus. And that's all we're going to [*claps hands*] need! Ah, that lamb with just the river water flowing to everlasting to everlasting. But then think of that back, oh those in hell. I heard one say you go, oh, you know where, go to hell. Think of the way he said there a one time. I heard a fellow say [*unintelligible phrase*]. Just for an illustration [*unintelligible*], I said, "Brother—buddy,"—I said, "you go stick your finger on the end of a gas stove just one second and you'll change your mind about going to hell." I often bring that up. Anyhow, I thank the Lord for being here tonight. You all pray for me and I'll be praying for you all. Let's pray for Brother John. He needs help. He needs the strength. Pray to the Lord to give him the body to preach the gospel. We need these kind of preachers, brother. We don't want people with a running around with a hung-down head and a chew of tobacco in his mouth, and going to the theater and going to all sorts of worrisome places. We need somebody to preach Jesus Christ, that's filled with the Holy Ghost. People now are going down the assembly line and send you out there, "Preach," and "I got my D.D. here, and so-and-so," but brother, when it's missing the Holy Ghost, don't think one thing about it. Unless he's borned again in the Spirit of God he don't know one thing about it. Jesus told 'em plainly. One day he was with a very high educated man; he was a ruler. He looked at Jesus. Man cannot believe things except they be of God. But Jesus took and said, "Except that man be what? be born again, he cannot see the—." Not out of the will of man, not out of the flesh, but of what? of the Spirit. Born of the Spirit. [*Unintelligible phrase.*] That's what it takes, brother and sister, I better keep quiet. I went on too long. (Night service, August 14, 1977)

Here is the sort of homiletic testimony that leads one to think that God is calling the testifier to preach (Clements 1980b:29). Certainly, Brother Rufus shows a command of language, an ease with the audience, and an ability to develop ideas that would make him an effective preacher. He begins again with thanksgiving, the conventional opening of most testimonies. But soon he is off on a metaphor of light and power that extends from the bulbs in the ceiling to Jesus as the light of the world. He demonstrates his desire to teach by asking rhetorical questions of the congregation: "Christ . . . will do what? Cleanse us from all sins," and "Who did I look to? I looked to the Lord." By addressing them as "you," by saying "let's pray for Brother John," "won't that be wonderful, sister?" and so forth he shows that he intends to lead them. He embeds two personal reminiscences in his testimony: the story about the eighty-seven-year-old cigar smoker who didn't want to hear about God, and the reference to the man he told to stick his hand on a hot stove to realize what hell would be like. Each of these reminiscences serves as an exemplum.

Brother Rufus is not a member of the Fellowship Independent Baptist Church, but he comes often, and as a member of the congregation he feels the bond of fellowship with the church community. "I'm glad to meet these brothers here. I learned to love 'em. I think they're going away 'fore long. Some of these boys, brothers, I'll call you brothers, I never will meet you again this side of heaven," he says. He does not know many of these people socially, outside of church. Yet in the midst of performance-created community—indeed, as one of the creators of that community—he is secure in his identity as a born-again Christian. Testimony confirms it as well as any other language in religious practice save, perhaps, prayer; for only testimony proceeds to social validation of identity: the community's acceptance of one's stance as one's identity.

Conversion and Testimony: The Conversion Narrative

In the section entitled "Language and Conversion" in Chapter 4 I pointed out that the church members regard conversion as an intensely-felt, instantaneous transformation from sinner to saint that follows conviction, repentance, and spoken confession. The confession—language in religious practice—does not, of course, bring about salvation; God is the agent. Nonetheless, "confession by mouth" is the sign that a person has yielded his or her will to God, and immediately precedes salvation, so much so that it almost seems that the confessed words, the "sinner's prayer," the last requirement prior to being born again, effect the transformation. Brother John is fond of quoting Romans 10:8–10 on the subject:

" . . . For with the heart man believeth unto righteousness; and with the mouth confession is made unto salvation."

Conviction—the feeling that one is wicked, sinful, and condemned to hell—is thought to occur at any time after a person reaches the "age of accountability" when he or she "knows right from wrong." No one who dies before reaching that age is condemned to hell. Probably Brother John places more emphasis on that aspect of doctrine than he might otherwise because of the death of his five-year-old son, Buddy Wayne. Conviction does not always lead to conversion:

> Some people will be under conviction and you really can't tell it. And then some gets under conviction and it's no trouble to tell it. They're weeping. And some of 'em will weep and still won't come. They'll wear it off, and then it's harder to ever get 'em in that state again. If the devil can get you back one time, can make you a blunder one time and not step up when the Lord is convicting you, why, it's harder the next time. He's got more control of you. (Meadows interview, 1977, p. 29)

Brother Jesse maintained that a person cannot be saved simply by willing it. A person must be undergoing conviction to be able to yield to God:

> I don't believe a person can get saved anytime they want to. No. I believe the Holy Spirit, the Spirit of God, has got to be convicting 'em, and helping 'em see that they're lost and in need to be saved. I believe the Bible teaches that we can't just get saved anytime that we want to. The Bible even teaches that the Spirit of God will not always dwell with man. In other words, the Lord can speak to you and speak to you and speak to you, till you turn him aside so much that he'll speak to you no more. Then you're on dangerous ground. (Comer interview, 1977, p. 66)

A person need not come to the church altar to be saved. A person can be saved at home, at work, in an automobile, anywhere he or she casts off the burden of conviction and accepts God's will. Brother Belvin told Ken George and me how he helped two neighbors to convert in his home:

> If the Spirit is dealing with them and God speaks to their heart, why then the Lord can save them anywhere. He don't have to be [in church]; can be out in the fields, boy, right out here. There's a dear lady that got saved right over where you're setting. Her husband, he come to me, he hunted all day long trying to find me. And I was right out down in the field there, and he found me. And I seen him a-coming, and when he got pretty close to me he just broke down, and he was crying. And he come throwed his arms around me, and commenced hugging me. And he said, "You're the very one I been, wanted to look for." He said, "I've been hunting for you all day." He said, "I want to be saved." He said, "I want to be a Christian, I want to be saved." "Why," I said, "why, repent. If the Lord is speaking to

your heart," I said, "son, don't go no farther." I said, "Repent, right now."
And [he said] "I want to be saved." I said, "Well, just fall here beside this
apple box, make your altar right here." And that's the altar, see. Right beside this apple box. And I said, "Do you know how to be saved?" "No sir,"
he said, "I don't." And I told him how to be saved and he repeated it
over. . . . And then I said, "Now when you say that and the Lord speaks to
your heart and saves you, and you know you've passed from death to life,
then you start praying. Praying, right along with me; I'm going to pray."
And he commenced to going on. And after he'd prayed he jumped up and
lifted his hands. He said, "Praise God, I know I'm saved." And so I said,
"That's all it takes. The Lord hears and answers a sinner's prayer that
way." And he said, "I got something to ask you," and he cried all the way to
his house. He said, "If I bring my wife over here, will you tell her and talk
to her like that?" I said, "I certainly will." And she give her heart to the
Lord right over there, that night. (Hurt interview, pp. 39–41)

Most of the church members experienced conversion at a church altar,
however. That is to say they yielded themselves to God fully in the powerful language context of the church. It would be interesting to discover a
relationship between context and the convert's temperament and personality. I do not think it is accidental that some accept the Lord in the midst
of the church community while others—Brother Belvin is the most prominent example in this congregation—yield in the midst of nature, completely apart from human company. I asked Brother Jesse to explain how
he and the church members help someone get saved at the church altar.
He emphasized prayer: the sinner's, and the church community's:

The preacher prays with 'em, and the deacons, or whoever might. If it's
ladies come forward, we ask the Christian ladies of the church to come
forward and pray with 'em. The preacher will also pray with 'em. If it's
men comes forward, we ask the deacons and men to come forward and
pray with 'em and help the preacher out. And then after we've prayed with
'em we ask 'em if they're satisfied. Do they feel like they're saved? And do
they know they're saved? And if they get up and stand up and say, "Yes, I
know, I'm satisfied," well, that's the biggest difference that's in the world
there. . . . [We're] praying that the Lord will show 'em the right way or
help 'em to be a Christian once they've accepted the Lord, will give them
strength to live for him. . . . And many lay their hands on 'em and pray for
'em. . . . [And if they're not satisfied the preacher says] "Stay and we'll
pray with you longer. We'll take the word of God and show you what it says
about it." And especially in Romans 10, verses 9 and 10. I like to see those
couple of verses showed where if you confess your sins by word of mouth
the Lord is just to forgive you. . . . A lot of 'em come to the altar, some'll
pray out loud, some won't, some will come to the altar and they'll cry just
like a little baby. You know they're sincere. Everybody doesn't get saved

the same way. It's no one set pattern for anyone to get saved. A man could get saved out in the field cutting his corn. Getting up hay. But when he does get saved, I believe he'll want to go to church, and when he gets to the house of the Lord, he'll want to make an open confession that he has been saved. And I believe he'll do it openly. . . . He'll confess it to the whole congregation and be glad to do it. (Comer interview, 1977, pp. 37–39)

Brother Jesse distinguishes between the first confession, or "sinner's prayer" (for examples see "The Altar-Call Prayer," in Chapter 6), and a second, "open confession" or public testimony that one has been converted. Such a public testimony may be merely a series of statements expressing gratitude to God for being born again, or it may take the form of a conversion narrative.

Many of the church members, particularly those who have been Christians for some years and who are at ease speaking publicly, have a story that they tell about how they got saved. Just as preachers' stories about receiving the call to preach form a narrative type within the story repertoires of folk Baptists and Pentecostals, so these conversion narratives form another type. A conversion narrative is taken as evidence that one is saved and acceptable as a member of the church. Yet not everyone in the congregation seems capable of a conversion narrative except, perhaps, under the most favorable circumstances; and mere assertion that one is saved, without a narrative, is acceptable also. God, not the church, will judge whether a person is saved, says Brother John.

I heard conversion narratives in testimony and sermons given in church, and in conversations and interviews with the church members outside of church. As a genre, these conversion narratives fell into a pattern; that is, they had a similarity of setting, plot, and character. At its most basic, the plot is problem, struggle, and victory—or lack and lack liquidated—the structure that Vladimir Propp delineated in the Russian fairy tale and that folklorists have found in heroic narratives the world over (Propp 1968). An outsider might conclude that these conversion narratives portray the narrator's struggle and triumph. But from the church members' point of view, the conversion story cannot not be understood as a struggle in which the "I" is heroic and triumphant. The "I" is the battleground between God and Satan. God is the hero; the "I" is rescued and transformed.

Clements reports that many of the Pentecostal conversion narratives he heard in northeast Arkansas dwelled on the preconviction period, detailing the sinner's wickedness, with the implication (sometimes directly stated) that if God could save someone that wicked, he can save anyone—including the person to whom the narrative is told (Clements 1984). The members of the Fellowship Independent Baptist Church who tell conversion narratives allude to but do not dwell on their preconversion sinfulness.

Typically, they begin with the events that led to their falling under conviction, then detail the misery of conviction. They refer to their sinful past when they progress to the repentance stage of the stories. The "sinner's prayer" and conversion immediately following are the climax of the narrative. The narrative ends fairly abruptly, with some evidence of the person's transformation: other people recognize it, or the person feels inwardly transformed and expresses joy by embracing others, or states that "I've still got it," referring to the indwelling Spirit.

Even though conversion narratives fall into a basic pattern, there exist significant variations. Pentecostal narratives progress further to the "second blessing," the "baptism of the Holy Ghost" that often leads to speaking in tongues. Mainline narratives may include a period of searching, and another period of inward intellectual debate. In *Turning*, an impressive, contemporary spiritual autobiography of a well-educated woman from an old Southern family, Emilie Griffin divides conversion into four stages: "First, there is Desire or longing; second, the Dialectic, or argumentative, reasoning phase; third, the Struggle or crisis; finally, the Surrender" (1980:29). Desire involves the recognition that "things as they are, even the heights of worldly pleasure, are not enough. They do not satisfy" (ibid.:31). Dialectic is the stage of intellectual inquiry into the meaning and purpose of the universe and humankind's place in it; it is an intellectual search for a philosophy of life. This stage was lengthy, difficult, and necessary for Griffin, but she recognizes that "it seems possible to leap over it or pass it by (as in some instantaneous conversions)" (ibid.:51). Struggle follows from a willed choice in the direction of faith, and involves an overcoming of doubt, the acknowledgment of sin, and repentance. Surrender is the resolution of the struggle, a total commitment to God's will, and a recognition that the love of God is a mutual love. "Looking back on that moment," Griffin writes, "it still seems to me charged with meaning, as though it represented the most fundamental choice I had ever made. Not just to believe in God. Not just to acknowledge him. Not just to live a good life in the best way I knew how. But to accept the idea that in my encounter with the Lord, there would be definite things that he would ask me to do, and that they would not always be easy. And to know that once I knew who was asking, I would answer yes" (ibid.:148).

Griffin finds an identical pattern in those intellectuals whose spiritual autobiographies most seemed to speak to her ongoing experience: C. S. Lewis, Thomas Merton, Bede Griffiths, Avery Dulles, and Dorothy Day. But there are important differences between these accounts of conversion and the conversion narratives of folk Baptists and Pentecostals in the United States.

First and most obvious, Griffin's account of conversion does not involve a period of conviction. Her would-be convert undergoes an intense struggle, to be sure, but the struggle results from an intellectual reluctance to make that step into the darkness, that leap of faith that leaves reason behind. The members of the Fellowship Independent Baptist Church do not feel that intellectual reluctance—or, at least, their narratives do not say so. They do not experience the philosophical debate that Griffin calls Dialectic. Their dialectic revolves around an unwillingness to give up certain pleasures of their former life; and their narratives suggest that their most intense struggle results from conviction: a knowledge of sinfulness, a resultant feeling of self-hatred, and a certainty that if they do not accept God they will be punished eternally in hell. Griffin writes, on the contrary, "I think that for converts—indeed, for all Christians—the acknowledgment of sin is not self-hatred at all, but the beginning of self-acceptance and (in the healthy sense) of self-love" (ibid.: 111). Members of the Fellowship Independent Baptist Church do learn to come to terms with the self, accepting it for what it is. They accept that the self can be led astray by Satan or led to do God's will by the indwelling Spirit. But their acceptance does not include love or trust for the unaided self, or "inward part" as Brother John puts it (see "Language and Conversion" in Chapter 4). Finally, whereas concern for the afterlife motivates folk Baptists and Pentecostals prior to their conversion, Griffin does not even mention heaven or hell; for her, and the others whose experience she represents, it is enough that conversion culminates in a transformed earthly life.

Second, the members of the Fellowship Independent Baptist Church are mainly silent in their conversion narratives about any stage of desire or longing antecedent to falling under conviction. This is not to say that they fail to recognize it—some, like Brother Rastus, say they were searching, while others, like Brother John, admit to being dissatisfied. And, as I pointed out in Chapter 2, this desire involves a nostalgia for a less-complicated, more secure past, usually located in childhood on mountain farms. But the search, per se, does not enter into their conversion narratives. I think this is because they do not view conversion as something that can be sought or willed, but rather because they understand it as something that falls upon a person. It is more appropriate to say that God searches, not the sinner.

As an admissions test for church membership, the conversion narrative may be traced at least as far back as the early seventeenth-century English Puritans, though other Protestants (notably Presbyterians) vigorously opposed the criterion (Caldwell 1983). Indeed, many Puritan conversion narratives and spiritual autobiographies have survived, and they (and the literature devoted to them) reveal that conversion was an immensely complex and doubt-ridden process, particularly when one believes (as the Puritans did) that one cannot be perfectly certain that one is a child of God and destined for heaven. And even though I see numerous parallels between Puritan conversion narratives and those of the members of the Fellowship Independent Baptist Church, including, most importantly, the analogical habit of mind that looks for signs of God's hand everywhere in the universe, it would be wrong to consider these church members latter-day Puritans, for they believe they have perfect assurance. They do not admit to the possibility that they are not saved. If they enjoy a personal relationship with the Lord, and do his bidding, and know they are saved, they are saved. And anyone who is truly saved, they believe, can tell when and how it happened. Indeed, the conversion narrative is regarded as the centerpiece of testimony, for (and here Griffin most heartily agrees) in showing how God intervened in their lives, these narratives show the un-converted how God might operate in theirs. In so doing, they help the un-converted to perceive what they might not have recognized as God's hand in their lives, and then to adopt the taleteller's worldview, leading even-tually to the ability to see their own lives in terms of the conversion pattern and, if they experience conversion, to fashion and perform their own narratives.

In conversation I asked the church members to tell me about their con-versions. Not all responded with narratives as well formed as Sister Edith's above. Brother Vernie, characteristically taciturn, offered a bare summary. Sister Ella's account was brief and matter-of-fact:

> Well, when I first got saved I went to the church there on Mill Creek. They was having revival down there. And [unintelligible] was having revival, it was on a Sunday night. Well, Earl [Sister Ella's husband] hadn't went to church then, but I mean me and the children had went to church some. And of course the children wasn't with me that night, and that's when I got saved down on Mill Creek at a revival. And I mean I really got a good blessing, and I know the Lord forgive me and saved me, because I know when he saved me. That's been, that was about ten years ago, I guess, when I first got, when I got saved when I went to the revival. (Earl and Ella Turner interview, pp. 3–4)

Brother Rastus' conversion narrative offered more detail:

> I was up at Comertown one night. And Brother John was a-preaching up there. He was a pastor at Comertown. And there was a preacher come in by the name of Robertson. He's an evangelist. You know, he just goes all over the country and preaches, you know. And this fellow, when I got saved, he come up there one night and one day and Brother John asked him to preach. And he got to preaching and he preached so good that after he quit preaching, why, Brother John give a altar call. Well, I went to the altar.
>
> Well, I really, really didn't get—I didn't feel like I wanted to feel, and there was service up there that night. And I went back. And before I left here that day, I just asked the Lord to really save me, you know. And I asked the Lord to help me that night when I went back. And I went back

up there that night and I really, the Lord really blessed me. I never felt so much like flying in my life. It's the truth; I just, well, I got so happy I hugged everything I got in reach of. The Lord just blessed me thataway, and I ain't never got tired of the way. I get sometimes, as the old saying is, I ain't on the mountain all the time, I get down in the valley sometimes. But I never have got tired of the way. I never have forgot what the Lord done for me. And he really blesses me yet today. I go to church up here sometimes, I just feel so good I don't know what to do sometimes. And I wouldn't be without him for nothing. (Lam interview, p. 14)

Although this is more fully a narrative than Sister Ella's, it, too, omits the conviction stage, possibly because I asked a question ("Can you tell me when you got saved?") that directed him to the time and place (the revival) rather than to the events that led up to his coming to the revival. Later in the interview I asked, "What brought you to the revival in the first place?" He replied, "I'd got to the place that I wanted to get saved. I really did. I'd got to that place and I just—looked like the Lord led me there that day for some reason or other." "How were you feeling just before?" I asked. "Well, I just weren't a-feeling like I should, wanted to feel. I didn't feel like that if I'd have, well if I'd have passed away I wouldn't have been saved. That's what it was, and I'd heard people talk about being lost, and what a awful place hell is to go, and I didn't want to go there. I really didn't. . . . And I just wanted to get saved. And I just thank the Lord that he did save me" (Lam interview, p. 16).

It is hard for me to tell whether Brother Rastus would have delivered a fuller narrative had I been less directive in my questions. In 1977 I was still learning how best to elicit such narratives within the artificial context of the interview, and, apart from Brother John, Brother Rastus was the first church member to be interviewed. The model for the interview—what the church members expected—was direct questions followed by direct answers. Asking vague, nondirective questions—an alternative form of interviewing recommended as a means of obtaining more trustworthy information—was unsatisfactory and confusing; it upset the expectations of the church members, and they floundered. Certainly the response is tailored to the setting, and to who the church member thinks the audience is. But practice and narrative skill are involved also. On one occasion I spoke with a recent convert who wanted to tell me his conversion narrative, and in fact he launched right into it at the beginning of the interview; but he had not yet gotten his story together. Though he elaborated on the before and after, he left out the climactic moment of conversion. He emphasized certain moments of particular, individual intensity and omitted what must have seemed to him the more conventional aspects of conversion—particularly the moment of conversion itself. The more practiced teller is distanced from the tale to the extent that he or she can view it, unconsciously, of course, as artifice, as a construction, and so can form it whole. And the more practiced member of this Christian community has had more experience reading allegorical significance into the events of daily life. Practice in interpreting the events of the unfolding drama of one's life leads him or her to see connections in events, and toward narrative as the fitting expression of the connectedness and the drama.

Beyond that, there is what Dell Hymes has called a "narrative view of life"—that is, a tendency among certain people to view life "as a potential source of narrative. Incidents, even apparently slight incidents, may have an interest that is worth retelling. This is to be distinguished from the idle gossip or even torrential flow of people who have nothing but themselves to talk about—their illnesses, their marriages, their children, etc. Not that the difference is in the topics. The difference is in the silences. There is a certain focussing, a certain weighting" (Hymes 1978:138). Of all the church members, Brother Belvin paid the most attention to focus, weight, and silence, though I think he was only imperfectly conscious of so doing. Listening to him was difficult. He spoke haltingly, giving the impression that words were hard for him. His language contained unfamiliar expressions, some of which he may have coined. The thread of his discourse was hard to follow. Ken George and I sat through a seven-hour near-monologue in his home; Ken told me later that he "tuned out" about halfway through. It would have been hard for most people to last that long. But Brother Belvin—and this is the point—spoke intensely and, I can say now from having transcribed and analyzed what he said, coherently, weaving a complicated narrative of various incidents that had significance to him in his life as a Christian.

Unlike most of the church members, Brother Belvin lives on the eastern slope of the Blue Ridge, in Madison County, near the town of Etlan. He lived in Stanley a decade earlier and got to know Brother John then, was a member of the congregation at the Comertown Freewill Baptist Church, and when that church split he followed Brother John. A grand-nephew of the old community preacher, Brother Geurdon A. Cave (see Chapter 3), Brother Belvin had ties to the Fellowship Independent Baptist Church congregation that continued after he moved to Etlan, and every Sunday in the summer of 1977, he and his family traveled an hour over the mountain to come to church. Technically they were visitors, having withdrawn membership when they started a church in Etlan, turning their carport into a small chapel. I attended a service there on April 4, 1978.

Etlan, on Route 231 about ten miles north of Madison, consists of the Etlan General Store and Post Office, and its competitor, Weakley's Store. Identical in function, they differ in appearance: the Etlan General Store is framed in wood with white weatherboard siding on a concrete foundation, while Weakley's is constructed entirely of concrete blocks, overpainted chartreuse, and has four cupolas on the upper story. Each has gas pumps in front: Shell at Weakley's, Amoco at the General Store, both 61.9 cents per gallon of regular gas in April 1978. Maybe there is no competition after all. Route 231 itself cuts through the valley. On either side mountains are visible at a distance of about two or three miles. In early April they are light brown; the darker pine trees are few and far between, but their green stands out. The cleared fields rise on hillsides to the forest-covered mountains: green stubble, dried old tan growth from last year mixed with the red clay of newly plowed ground. Brother Belvin's daughter shops at Weakley's.

Whereas Brother John keeps his peace outside the pulpit, Brother Belvin seems compelled by some inner drive to talk, testify, or preach all the time, no matter where he is. He would say it is the indwelling Spirit that compels. But the compulsion seems constant. Psychologists might see in this a sign of mental unbalance; sociologists might say he is highly selective in the signals he picks up from the people he meets; polite society might say he is a fanatic. When Ken George and I visited him in the summer of 1977, we were treated most cordially and carefully, given a tour of the farm that lasted forty-five minutes (Brother Belvin knew I was interested in mountain farming), and then invited to a delicious dinner after spending hours listening to him in his living room.

More than anyone else in the congregation, Brother Belvin retains the older farm ways, even though in 1977 he was only entering middle age. Born and raised on mountain farms, he has not given up farming, though he supplements his income by driving a schoolbus. He raises small numbers of pigs, cows, and steers; he keeps chickens for meat and eggs; he uses horses and tractors; he raises corn, hay, and apples. Most of his farm production is for his family's use; he sells a small surplus. He works hard and enjoys it; he loves working with animals and is good with them. He likes machines, too; he tinkers with them, and he experiments with various inventions to improve fences, gates, pens, and so forth. His farm is well used and well kept. The few years he spent working near Stanley—he was not farming—were unhappy; he became ill, and he was cured when he went back to farming.

His conversion narrative was remarkable. It was quite long, but perhaps most notable is the web of cross-reference and complex handling of themes that unifies it beneath a seemingly meandering surface. We did not elicit it. It just seemed to come to its own accord. His constant talking had lulled us into listening. He was telling us what he wanted to say, and for the most part I was delighted to have it that way. We would find out what was on his mind.

Directions for reading this ethnopoetic transcription:

Brother Belvin spoke softly and slowly, pausing longer between phrases and sentences than most people. To hear it in your mind's ear as he spoke it, observe the following conventions:

Brother Belvin on his farm, 1977.

New lines are indented. Each new line is assigned a number. After each line, pause for about one second.

If a line is skipped (left blank, though it will be counted in the numbering scheme), pause for about two seconds.

Anything flush left is a continuation of the previous line. It does not receive a new number. Therefore do *not* pause when continuing a line by dropping and moving to the flush left margin.

Pause about one-half second within a line for each extra space between words.

Normal (roman) type: normal loudness and intonation.

Italicized type: softer than normal, nearly a monotone.

Bold type: loud, emphatic, with expanded intonation range.

And this dear heart [Brother G. A. Cave] here was leading me to the Lord,
and what he told me.
And   that one little word now, people thinks, well, it just takes a whole
Bible
    to get me saved.

5
    But that's not so.

    One word is just as good as the whole Bible.
    Something or other change your mind and heart
10 [*snaps fingers*]
    and look to the Lord.
    Now I went for a week
    under conviction. [K. G.: A week under conviction?]
    That's right. [J. T. T.: Mmm.]
15 Now I   I couldn't hardly work, I'd,
    I'd start working and,
    and the more I'd work the faster and harder I wanted to go after it.
    And the tears would fill my eyes so, and
    the Lord was talking to me,
20 and   I was, I would work and pull, and work and pull on   cutting them
bushes and grape vines, and the more I done that the faster I tried to go.
    Well,   that was the devil trying to work it out of me
    to keep me from accepting the Lord.
    But the Lord filled my eyes with tears so I'd stop.
    And my little boy was with me.
25 He'd sit there, he'd—   sometimes I'd notice he'd be a-watching me, *you
know, he didn't know what's the matter with me.*
    Well,
    when I first got saved I,
    when I first was saved, accepted the Lord, I was

(I'm ahead of my story)
30   my mother was having services over at their home, in a home just
        like this.
        So
        I was sitting out on the bench, and
        my truck sitting there.
        And see I, I was a mean man,
35   and that's why I say when I stand in the pulpit,
        and I say, "If God
        could save a man like me,
        and which he did,

40   there is none that's too toughy for him."
        Now that's the way I feel, now that's the kind of man I was. I was, I was
        a hard rock
        and, ah, I don't like to give the devil the praise, I give the Lord the praise
        for it all.
        I was, ahh,
        I was a drunkard;
45   I drinked hard,
        made the liquor,
        sold it,
        and drinked it,
        drinked it   by the gallons.
50   Now I was mighty near alcoholic, man.
        And when I,   I got down there,
        why I don't know why I was there;
        well I just happened to be a-sitting there when the preacher come, the
        preacher there. [K. G.: George Cave?]
55   Brother Geurd Cave.
        And   he looked at me and he,
        he said, "Why don't you
        come on in?"

60   I said, "No, it ain't no need of me a-coming in."
        I said, "Listen."
        I said, "I've done told people—"
        (*and I had*)
        "—that it wasn't no show for me,
65   that I was hell bound."
        And   so   I taken and   said that,   and he said, "Listen."

        I said, ah, anyway, I just made remarks, you know, I said, "Listen," I

said, "the Lord is too good,
 turn me down."

70

And that was the word he wanted me to say.

He said, "Remember."

75   He said, "Son, you're already turned down."

And that was the word hung with me.
 "You're already turned down."
 And the Bible says it,   you're already condemned,[1] already, right now,
don't have to wait till tomorrow, next hour.
80   Right now.
 You're condemned already.
 Well,

he just turned around. He never argued with me, hunh-unh.
85   He just turned around with his,
 with his little book satchel, something like that one yonder with them
handles on it, just exactly like that,
 with songbooks in it and his Bible in his hand. Turned around and went
on up towards the house.
 He made three trips.
 He made three trips over here after me.
90   He said he seen something good in me.

 [*Laughs.*]
 And, ah, that's the kind of preacher he was.
 He said, "I seen something good in you" and he made three trips from
Shenandoah.
95   And, ah,
 so, ah,   I went all that week, a-working like that,
 and that Monday morning,
 ah, let's see if it was Monday morning; I believe it was a Monday
morning or a Tuesday morning,
 anyway I always get up and get out, *I had cows* and
100   mule and
 things like that to feed up.
 So

---

1. The reference is to John 3 : 18.

it was   right smart cold yet, was in, in March,
ah, feeding weather yet   and it was cold   in March, right cool weather
yet [*laughs*],   some snow.
105   So anyway
I   went out and
I got into the little hay house, a-   studying on that, I was studying it all
the time.
And I got out there in the little feed house, and
I done stayed, I
110   went to the barn and
give the grain to the mule and things.
So then I,   I was talking all along, and just—
and the Lord speaking to me,   dealing with my heart,
and I crying   and went on, and so I
115   got into the little hay-house and so I, ah,
I sat down, I, ah,
I didn't sit down, I was standing up right there and pulled my bales of
hay down and was cutting it to get some hay.
And my wife she said, ah,
she figured I was taking a little longer than usual, you know.
120   She come see about me.
And I lied to her.
Yeah, I lied to her
in a hurry.
I didn't want her to see me a-crying.
125   [*Laughs.*]
I,   I was cutting the hay, and I couldn't hardly see how to cut it for the
tears filling my eyes.
And she said, "What's the matter?" Somebody said it right in the door
and I   peeped around and it was her. I said, "Nothing."
See, I lied to her.

130   So she said, "Come on
to, ah, breakfast." Said, "It's ready." I said, "I'll be there in a minute. Be
there in a little bit."
She went on and left me.   That's what I wanted her to do.
So I got the haying through and go on   back to the house and   eat
breakfast, and
so
135   at the end of the week I, well, I went on up yonder to work, and   working
and just the Lord dealing with me, and that, still that, that word just
a-hanging in there:

"You're already condemned.

You're already condemned."
And that's just, I was just,
140   well, I was just
well, I was just, ahh,
just under conviction so that I just couldn't hardly
do nothing.
And before that, now, I tried to live it, four years
145   of goodness and righteousness
and treat my neighbor right and all of that,
but you know

that's just a trick of the devil.
150   And then I'd
I'd take and
go ahead on in   self-righteousness,
trying to do it myself.
Go on for a good while:
155   "I'm a Christian."
That's what the devil'll say:
you're a Christian.
And good works, just what I was telling you out there a while ago, turn
a leaf over, turn it around in the road, that's, the devil'll push it right back
in your face.
And   so I,   I taken and
160   just as soon   then that something would fly into me,
something would fly into me real,   real
raw, you know, the old devil would
just wrinkle my feathers right up,
ah, so to speak.
165   And, ah,
just as soon as he'd do that I'd fly right into it,
and wheel right off, and the nastiest words and everything that could
come out of a human's mouth could be, come.
And   then,   then you see I'd go on.
And all this and I'd have to get out, I go out to myself,
170   be out to myself and all of it would repeat right back to me:
what I had said
rolled right back around.
Every word what I'd said.
The nastiest words,   the nastiest things would come back to me
175   and   I'd have to cry over it. It hurt me so bad I'd cry over it. I'd sit there
and cry,   for I wasn't saved.
But, ah, that was before that I got under conviction.
And ah

then when I got saved I,   I, ah,
I was back up in the upper end of my garden
180   in March,
plowing my ground up with a   little old mule and plow, and that little
old thing, you'd plow with him, and   you could stop him,
you could turn around to do something else or just leave him just a few
minutes,
he'd back up out of the traces, he'd back up out the harness, and he'd
turn around, and he'd muck up everything.
And so I, ah,
185   that morning, my wife she was going up to the neighbor's house, and   I
just had to saw these stumps off, you know, to   clean the land.
And cleaned that land all up good and I was plowing it to put corn in it,
so it—you work it with corn, you know, in new ground—
and them stumps there,
and my wife was going up through the field,
just, oh, she hadn't gone too far, she was mighty near up to the upper
end of the orchard over there.
190   And I was plowing there and that little old mule just acting just as nice
as he could be.
And I still, I couldn't hardly plow, I was humming a song
and I   couldn't hardly see where I was hardly going for the   tears
filling my eyes.
And, ah,   more I'd study the more I'd cry.
195   And just kept on, just more I'd cry, more and more I'd cry, the   more I'd
want to cry.
And just,   the Lord was just   so   oh, so good to me.
So pushed the impression up on me so much until   then I
right there, just a,   just a second,
just in a second
it, ah,   just stopped the   old mule in a stump there, it was leveled off,
and I just got right up on that.
200   And I said, "Lord Jesus,   here I am.
If you can take something,   take nothing and make something out of it,
I'm willing.
I want to live a Christian life.
I want to be born again; I'm sorry I've sinned
and I'm tired of living in sin,   and I want to live for you.
205   Lord, save me, and if you do I'll go right and make a confession to all the
people."
And that moment the Lord saved me. [*Light laugh.*]
God saved me and even down that little old mule knowed it, you know?
Hunh, he stood just as still, he never go out of a trace, he never moved a
bit.   Just propped his foot up there and rested, and set right, stood right

there and   till I got done praising the Lord for saving me.

And I was the same as a little old bird out of a cage, hunh, flew out.

210   God lifted the **burden** and, ah,   that's what I tell you that

by this,   no man, I don't care who he is, he can't say that the Lord Jesus Christ,

that,   I got to wean off this, I got to do a little of, just to wean a little bit at a time.

It's no such thing. Now I was a cusser,   I was a mean man,   I drinked, I made the liquor and drinked it and sold it and everything and,   and I smoked 'em by the packs,   two and three packs a day, cigars, an old pipe and, and box tobacco and chewing tobacco, kept my jaw full of it.

But, neighbor, I want you to know when God saved me he taken that out of me.

215   He taken me away from all of it, had taken, just cleaned it.

I didn't want no more of it.

The want-to was gone. God taken the want-to and I said, "Lord, here I am.

I'll furnish the man,

220   You furnish the grace." [*Light laugh.*]

And   he, he done just what he said.

And then that,   that weekend,

that was in,

that was back in March about the twenty-seventh day

225   of March,

about nine o'clock

was when I got borned again.

In about in the twenty,   in the sixty,   in 'sixty-three

230   and God wonderfully saved me,

and just as that song we sing,

"I never shall forget the day."

Ah,   and that's why I know   that, them   them dates

of twenty-seventh day of March,

235   about nine o'clock

that sixty and 'sixty-three, nineteen and sixty-three,

God saved me

and, ah,   that'll soon be, it's going into the fifteenth—.

And so

240   by the help of the Lord that's what I said. Some of 'em said, after I got saved I,

I went back yonder,   went back to the little church where I was, to where he was having preaching and I,   I had to hug him.

And   I knelt down, surrendered,

for 'em to pray with me.

I wanted 'em to pray with me, I was a convert.

245   "**Pray** with me," and I wanted to prove to the eyes of people

that God had saved me.

And after he saved me

and after they prayed with me, I told 'em that.

And   that one little word,

250   that's why I say it don't take the whole Bible to save a person.

And then from there on I,

I come back and

and I, I don't believe,

well, I just made trips every direction.

255   I went up to the hollow to the people that had been so friends to me,

but what they was friends to was this, was the bottle on the table.

To set and drink and smoke

and say great big blasting words

and   blast the Lord's name.

260   Well, now, that was my friends then,

but after I'd taken this man called the Lord Jesus Christ   in my

heart   and accepted him   and cleansed me from the sins of the world and

old filthiness and things that I was doing,

then them people turned their head on me.

But it wasn't long before they was in the hospitals before they went back

and called on Belvin. [*Laughs.*]

They wanted help then, you see,

265   needed something or another that they didn't have,

and   and so they come back to me then afterward.

they wanted some of it, they wanted something of it, they wanted

something or other but they couldn't.

You can't go, the   the Lord says you can not.

You cannot take him,   you cannot accept him

270   just any time you want to.

Just any time they want to they can't do it.

He said, "Without my Spirit drawing you,

you cannot come to the Father except my Spirit draweth."

275   And when the Spirit draweth, then they can come to him.

And it's nowheres in God's word they can find

and, ah, that,   that God

will ever strive but one time with them.

No place in God's word you can find where he has to take 'em back after

backsliding.

280   But it's through and by the mercies that he does it.

People, people is so wrong as I've often said it, they're wrong as,   as two
left shoes.
And they say, "Well, what do you mean by that?"
I say, "Well, by this," I say, "you try to put two on that same foot, same
shoe, left one."
I says, "You can't get one on there but just one at a time.
285   So try to put both of 'em on now. Of course you can put one over the top
of the other'n,
but let's see you can get 'em on the same, on that foot
at the same time,
two left shoes."
And I,   I went up
290   to their homes
of them that were called my friends
and
set down to eat,
and like always they'd just go to eating, you know,
295   and   bowed my head and give thanks over the food
and, ah, they seen then it was something wrong, that they didn't have
that and something wrong, something different.
And
then we, then we, then we got to, they got to asking me questions.
And the first thing you know then, ah, they had the news out,
300   old Belvin Hurt had gone crazy.
He was losing his mind. Give him two weeks, give him three months.
"Give him three months, he'll be over 'cross the mountain.
He'll be in Staunton. He's going off fast.
Three months and he'll be gone."

Brother Belvin's conversion narrative is unified by theme and by chro-
nology. Except for the digression on trying to live righteously without God
(lines 144–176), the story progresses from conviction through repentance, confession, conversion, and assurance. No important detail seems
omitted. Like other gifted narrators in the church, Brother Belvin employs
dialogue and typological foreshadowing to dramatize the story. The pathetic fallacy involving the mule who behaves himself when he senses
Brother Belvin's transformation (207–208) is prepared (181–183) by the
description of his usual misbehavior. The conversion scene itself (185–
208) is foreshadowed by a parallel scene of conviction in the hay house
(95–128) which brings Brother Belvin equally to tears. Foreshadowing
here is particularly apt, for like Brother John's, his mind is characteristically typological and analogical; the first scene typifies the second, and
the second fulfills the prophecy of the first. The phrase "You are already
condemned" is a unifying leitmotif (75–81, 135–143, 249–250); and

when the conversion narrative is reread, it is plain that those are the same words under discussion at the outset (1–11), even though they are not revealed at the time, thereby heightening the mystery and drama. Brother Belvin unifies his narrative thematically as well, as he returns to the ideas of work, tears, and madness. Tellingly, he is aware of his performance: "I'm ahead of my story" (29) is a metanarrative recognition that he is actively shaping and controlling the tale.

Two rhetorical strategies enable Brother Belvin to affirm his identity by means of his conversion narrative (Titon 1982). First, the story contains an abundance of its own interpretative material; as an out-of-church testimony (witnessing), it is a sermonette. Second, by relying on the conventional pattern of the conversion narrative, he incorporates the approving community of believers into the story and confirms his identity as a member of that group. By doing so he controls his audience.

Conventions of plot and character in the conversion narrative offer Brother Belvin an opportunity for controlling his sense of self while projecting it into several roles: carefree sinner, newly re-born Christian, tempted Christian, assured Christian. In other words, his identity as a convert is secured by the knowledge that he, like others in the community of believers, passed through the same stages on the road to salvation.

Of the 304 lines in the transcription, roughly two-thirds can be understood as event, and the other third as interpretation. Sometimes the interpretation is clearly apparent, as in lines 21–22: "But that was the devil trying to work it out of me to keep me from accepting the Lord." Sometimes the interpretation is woven more directly into the narrative, as in lines 207 ("God saved me and even down that little old mule knowed it, you know?") and 209 ("And I was the same as a little old bird out of a cage, hunh, flew out"). Interpreting the narrative as he proceeds, Brother Belvin makes certain that his meaning is clear. A listener, of course, might well draw a different meaning. When later in his monologue he denied that the astronauts had landed on the moon because God had not meant for man to enter the heavens, I understood his meaning but did not share his belief. The storyteller's interpretative remarks, then, help clarify his meaning, and function as much for the storyteller's own benefit as for the listener—in this case, more. In so doing, they affirm the storyteller's sense of who he or she is.

Consider the identity Brother Belvin presents. He refers to his sinful, preconversion self; he was "a hard rock," a moonshiner, nearly an alcoholic (34–51, 213), and unable to control his anger (150–175); he contrasts that with his postconversion self, obedient to God and cleansed from sin. Most interesting, though, is the recognition of the discrepancy between his identity and his stance, a problem similar to Sister Edith's: they know certain others think they are crazy. In Brother Belvin's conversion narrative the theme is foreshadowed early. Working with him in the field, his young son saw the tears of conviction in Brother Belvin's eyes and "you know, he didn't know what's the matter with me" (25). It comes back full force at the end when he returns to his former friends, tells them of his conversion, and witnesses for God. They conclude that "old Belvin Hurt had gone crazy. He was losing his mind. . . . Give him three months, he'll be over 'cross the mountain. He'll be in Staunton [in the insane asylum there]. He's going off fast. Three months and he'll be gone" (300–304). And there the narrative ends. He doesn't say—he doesn't need to say— that three months passed, three years passed, and he did not go to the insane asylum. He is here, in his home, speaking his narrative—proof that, despite what his former friends thought, he is all right; they are the ones who are all wrong. In this way he conjures the doubt engendered by the discrepancy between his stance (who his friends think he is) and his identity (who he thinks he is), and overcomes it (as Sister Edith did) by asserting his identity to the listener and denying his stance; indeed, he does so by bringing his identity to life through narrative language in religious practice. By now it should be evident that repetition through testimony and conversion narrative sustains the church members' identities in the face of their nonconformity and self-doubts.

As the teller controls the tale, so he or she controls the identity of the "I" in it. It is worth emphasizing that each telling of the conversion narrative offers the teller a chance to refashion his or her identity in the act of reasserting it. The conversion narrative thus becomes a continual reassertion, reinforcement, and remaking—in the same mold—of the teller's identity in the act of telling. Language in religious practice literally forms and presents the self, to the teller as much (more, surely) as the audience.

What accounts for this urge to reassert Christian identity? For one thing, the Bible tells Christians to witness to the unsaved. Brother Belvin drew out his conversion in great detail, probably to explain to Ken and me how we, too, ought to go about preparing for conversion, and to learn how to pray a sinner's prayer. Here, obviously, context and audience strongly influenced the narrative. It might be argued that the presence of sinners was a challenge to Brother Belvin's identity, and that this is what called forth the conversion narrative in the first place. But whatever the external challenges to his identity, it seems to me they are insignificant compared to the internal ones. Outsiders may think he is crazy; he knows he is not. And yet, and yet—he hears internal voices, sees visions, gets impressions on his mind, and sometimes it is hard to distinguish the voice of God from that of Satan (see "Language and Conversion" in Chapter 4). For the members of the Fellowship Independent Baptist Church, the issue of possession and control is fundamental because they believe they *are* possessed—by the Holy Spirit. Hence identity is truly all, and testimony is their personal affirmation that they are and remain counted among God's people. The various strategies—personal reminiscence, conventional narrative patterns, interpretative remarks and sermonettes, professions of faith, thanksgiving, and praise, and direct assertions of identity ("I'm glad I'm a child of God") protect the testifiers from external challenges while quieting internal doubts and reassuring them of their religious identity. But I am convinced that there is one more important reason for these testimonies, particularly the conversion narrative: the conversion experience itself. What is so powerful about the conversion experience that it leads to such self-assertion, and to continual reaffirmation? The answer may be found in the relation between individual performance and community during the conversion period.

Conversion: Performance and Community

Folklorists William Clements and Patrick B. Mullen have convincingly applied concepts of "liminality" and "antistructure" to the conversion experience and to conversion narratives. Clements argues that the conversion that follows from conviction, repentance, and confession "should be viewed as ritual" (1976a:39) and that it is a classic example of a rite of passage in the sense meant by Arnold van Gennep (1960). Ritualized conversion behavior involves "standardized vocalization (shouting, sobbing) and conventionalized movement (the jerks, hand clapping) and visions" (Clements 1976a:39). Victor Turner introduces examples of Christian ritual as he draws out van Gennep's idea of the liminal stage: the time when the convert is "betwixt and between the positions assigned and arrayed by law, custom, convention, and ceremonial" (Turner 1969:95). That is, as the convert moves from sinner to born-again Christian, he or she experiences "liminality" (from Latin *limen*, threshold).

In cultures the world over, persons in the liminal stage of passage rites tend to break ordinary social conventions. Clements points out that the folk Baptist and Pentecostal churches condone converts' public displays of weeping (1976a:42); trance, including loss of control of one's speech and body, is not only condoned in some churches, it is expected. Moreover, Turner asserts that with the breakdown of ordinary social conventions and social structure in the liminal stage, persons experience a feeling of "human interrelatedness" that he calls *communitas*—an egalitarian community subject only to supernatural control.

Clements contends that "the crisis conversion involves the subject [convert] in existential *communitas*" (ibid.:41). The conversion experience thus introduces a powerful utopian social ideal, and traces of it remain in the church community itself: the church members address one another as "brother" and "sister" (ibid.:43), each believer has direct access to God, the church is governed democratically, and heaven is understood as the realization of the egalitarian social ideal.

Admittedly, evidence for the experience of *communitas* during conversion is difficult to come by; in the liminal stage the convert cannot explain what is going on. And postconversion explanations—that is, conversion narratives—do not stress the experience of *communitas*. Yet I think they do offer powerful evidence that suggests it. Consider the following conversion narrative excerpts:

(a)

And brother then something happened, I don't really remember +hah+
> but when I came to myself I was standing up +hah+
> hugging people and a-crying +hah+
> and praising God because I was saved.

> (Brother John; see p. 344)

(b)

The night God saved my soul I stood up and when I got off of that altar I started hugging people and crying. A pile of tears running down my cheek. I tell you I had a ball.

> (Brother John; see p. 345)

(c)

I thank him for all the love he's put in my heart towards everybody. And I have feelings for more people now than I've ever had in my life.

> (Sister Virginia; see p. 361)

(d)

I never felt so much like flying in my life. It's the truth; I just, well, I got so happy I hugged everything I got in reach of.

> (Brother Rastus; see p. 389)

(e)

. . . After I got saved I,
> I went back yonder, went back to the little church where I was, to where
> he [G. A. Cave] was having preaching and I, I had to hug him.

> (Brother Belvin; see p. 399)

The common element in these passages is joy and "human interrelatedness"; it leads the converts to express their love for their fellow saints by embracing them directly after conversion. This hugging violates ordinary social rules and seems to me to be both an expression of and evidence for the experience of *communitas* during conversion.

Clements writes, further, that encouraging religious emotionalism in folk Baptist and Pentecostal churches "rejuvenates" the feeling of *communitas*. That is another way of saying that the blessings of the Spirit are a powerful reminder that one is a child of God, and that such blessings are actively sought during worship. The members of the Fellowship Independent Baptist Church would agree with this latter formulation, and the fact that they are uncomfortable in churches that are "classy" or "up in so-

Embracing after prayer at the altar in response to an altar call, 1985. *Left:* Sister Virginia and Sister Sharon; *right:* Sister Tammy and Sister Pauline.

ciety" where social rules discourage weeping and shouting lends further credence to this argument. Moreover, the entire worship service drives toward the invitation at the sermon's close, and the church members show their greatest joy after someone is saved, returned to the faith, or moved closer to God at the altar. After powerful communal prayer is successful, the "old-fashioned handshake" not only seals the event but expresses *communitas* in the wholesale embracing that takes place in the sanctuary.

Writing about sacred narratives in the Blue Ridge Mountains, Mullen argues that the act of narration—the performance as testimony—functions as a means of "reincorporating the *communitas* ideal into social structure: the oral narrative form structures an unstructured mystical ideal in order to communicate it meaningfully to the world" (Mullen 1983:36). Testimonies involving healing and conversion are cases in point. Throughout the Fellowship Independent Baptist Church service, language in religious practice enables the believers to traverse the boundary between the ordinary social structure of their daily lives outside the church and the extraordinary social utopian community embodied in the idea of the heavenly homecoming reunion.

One of Brother John's sacred narratives shows him traversing that boundary quite literally: his vision of his son, Buddy Wayne, and Jesus in heaven (homecoming sermon, Chapter 7, lines 373–397; also in Chapter 1). This vision narrative, which I have heard him tell on several occasions, has about it the mystery of liminality, for in the beginning, ego and the sense of self disappear: he cannot be certain whether he was flesh or spirit, and he makes reference to Paul's narrative of a journey to "the third heaven" (2 Corinthians 12:1–4). Plainly, it is an allegory of his Christian pilgrimage: climbing the "narrow path," being buffeted and tempted by sin (personified as the being who tries to throw him off the mountain), overcoming sin, and, finally, seeing Jesus and Buddy Wayne walking by the gate of heaven, a short distance ahead. Experiencing the vision, John feels "caught up" from earth to heaven. Narrating the vision, giving it form and substance, he and the listener are "caught up" in a different, but related sense: from the uninterrupted world of daily life to the world of pure meaning; here an allegory of the purpose of his life. This critical insight comes to John not through reason but in a vision, and his performance to the church community takes the form of an allegorical narrative presenting a divine and personal revelation concerning the heavenly homecoming reunion. In this community, then, Brother John's life must be exemplary; and that life is the full subject of the next chapter.

9. The Life Story

The Life Story, the Self-Made Man, and the God-Made Man

Brother John's life stands open as a public example in the Fellowship Independent Baptist Church. His are the most prominent and powerful performances in the church; his narratives about his personal experience exemplify how God has worked in his life and, by extension, how God works in other people's lives. The broad outlines of his life—the rural poverty of mountain farming and blue-collar town work, the early days of sin and rebellion, the conversion to Christianity, and the trials of living the Christian life—these resemble his parishioners' lives. By telling and interpreting life stories, he means to persuade and instruct. At the same time, because he has told his stories so often, the story of his life resides in the church members' minds as well as in his own as a model of God's providence. In prior chapters I printed several of his personal experience stories; some he gave to me in conversation, and others were performed in worship services, as testimonies or while interpreting hymns or during the course of sermons. It is time to consider his life story as a whole and what it represents.

Life stories are one of my chief interests. My first published work in folklore comprised life stories I was told by blues singers (Titon 1969a; 1969b; Titon, ed. 1974), so it was natural that I asked for life stories in conversation with Brother John and other church members. Further, there is in the church service a natural context for the performance of life stories, namely, the testimony period. Many of the church members were skilled storytellers, having had the opportunity in church to practice this public witnessing, and most had at the least a conversion narrative to tell when asked when and how they were saved. In the midst of the fieldwork in the summer of 1977, I asked John if I could videotape him telling the story of his life. He agreed, and a week later Ken and I set up the camera in church. John's wife, Pauline, was present during the session. John spoke without interruption for a half-hour until the tape ran out, and this life story is printed in the following section of this chapter. It comprises incidents from his life, tied together by the themes of poverty, family, and God's providence as exemplified by John's conversion, his call to preach, and his first sermon. Each of the stories in the life story is a narrative I have heard from John on other occasions; here, he strung them together more or less in chronological order, interpreting as he went along.

Folklorists have increasingly turned their attention to life stories in the past decade, with most work done on *memorates* and *personal experience stories*. Sandra K. D. Stahl, the first to argue at length that the personal experience story is a legitimate folklore genre, defines it as a secular, first-person narrative that expresses a traditional attitude (Stahl 1977:21–26). By contrast, a *memorate* is a "personal narrative about supernatural experience" and "contains at its core a belief that is in nearly all cases collective" (ibid.:20). Belvin Hurt's conversion narrative (Chapter 8)—indeed, any of the conversion narratives of the members of the Fellowship Independent Baptist Church—fall into the category of memorate, for they are told in the first person, involve a supernatural experience of God, and have at their center a shared belief in the common process by which God convicts sinners, brings them to repentance, and saves them. Patrick B. Mullen has challenged Stahl's distinction between memorates and personal experience stories, arguing that such stories as conversion narratives should be called "sacred [personal] narratives":

> Stories based on personal religious events are difficult to classify generically. One definition [Stahl's] limits personal narrative to discussions of secular experiences in order to distinguish the genre from memorates, which are defined as dealing with the supernatural. Sacred personal stories do resemble memorates since they have a supernatural quality; but unlike the memorate, the core belief in the sacred narrative is part of a system of folk religion [as opposed to superstition]. This crucial connection between sacred narrative and folk religion is significant not just in terms of the classification of these narratives but also in terms of our understanding of their function. Sacred narratives must be considered in the context of the folk religion from which they have emerged. (1983:17–18)

Mullen's point certainly is well taken as regards the narratives under consideration here, for as I have argued throughout this book, all of the language in religious practice, including narrative, is the consequence of the folk religious belief system. Moreover, inasmuch as I have emphasized a hermeneutic dialogue as well, I would stress that in a personal religious narrative the folk hermeneutic—that is, the storyteller's interpretation—turns the story sacred. Events narrated in a memorate have a mysterious or supernatural quality in themselves quite apart from the collective beliefs that explain them. A memorate involving a person's encounter with a ghost is a fair example. In a sacred personal narrative, however, the events in themselves need not have a supernatural quality at all. Instead, it is the

teller's *interpretation* of the events, based on shared, traditional beliefs
and attitudes, often (but not always) systematized into a folk religion, that
makes the personal narrative sacred. Even when the events are mysterious or supernatural they are not sacred until they are interpreted.

I would not want to give the impression that every story Brother John
tells is a sacred narrative. He is a gifted storyteller, and he exercises that
gift often; but he does not always turn personal experience sacred, nor
does he always tell about personal experience. He enjoys making people
laugh, for example, and loves to tell jokes. Yet so strong is his habit of interpretation that he never tells or hears a joke without explaining the
punch line a few seconds after the laughter dies down. This drive toward
explanation, this need to resolve ambiguity, this urge to interpret and clarify, is striking and characteristic of his analogical cast of mind.

Viewed thus, Brother John's life story is an extended sacred personal
narrative, comprising numerous smaller sacred narratives. Certainly, his
life story illustrates his traditional, shared, folk beliefs and attitudes toward
experience. But, as I have argued throughout this book, it also reveals his
beliefs and attitudes about himself: his identity. In an article that appeared
in the *Journal of American Folklore* in 1980, I attempted to make a contribution to the discussion of personal narrative, defining the *life story* as
any purportedly true personal experience story, sacred or secular, that has
significance in the storyteller's repertoire (Titon 1980c:276). The mark of
significance is repetition: if a story is told once or twice and forgotten, it is
too trivial to be a life story; if it is told and retold, becoming a part of the
storyteller's fund of narratives, regularly served up under the proper circumstances, then it is a life story. Stahl, as I noted above, limits personal
experience narratives to secular stories, but I extend the life story category
to cover supernatural, sacred, and secular narratives. Some people have
mistakenly assumed that by life story I mean an oral autobiography: a
rather complete rendering of a life; the real equivalent, perhaps, of the anthropological *life history*, an artificial composite garnered from conversations and interviews, and put in chronological order by an editor. My view,
however, is that a life story is simply a significant, first-person narrative
from life. Thus life stories may be long or short; they may involve one incident or several; they may be an attempt to offer a whole life or just a small
part of a life.

My major claim in that article was that the life story is best understood
not as history but as a fiction: a making, rendering, and interpretation of
the remembered life:

> The naïve listener might assume a life story to be a truthful, factual ac-
> count of the storyteller's life. The assumption is that the storyteller has
> only to penetrate the fog of the past, and that once a life is honestly re-
> membered it can be sincerely recounted. But the more sophisticated lis-

tener understands that no matter how sincere the attempt, remembering the past cannot render it as it was, not only because memory is selective, but because the life storyteller is a different person now than he was ten or thirty years ago. . . . So life storytelling is a fiction, a making, an ordered past imposed by a present personality upon a disordered life. (Ibid.: 290)

Even if the life story is not factually true, I wrote, it is always true evidence of the storyteller's personality and identity, for it explains and affirms the storyteller's identity in the act of the telling. Most folklorists were willing to agree about the fictive nature of life storytelling, but Roger Abrahams rightly protested my presentation of personality and identity in that article as insufficiently malleable to suit different performance contexts (Abrahams, personal communication). Certainly, people present different aspects of themselves under different circumstances. Abrahams' conception of personality and identity in storytelling derives mainly from his work in Afro-American culture, where storytellers and rappers act out various roles that often mask inner identity. In other words, if the storyteller is always "on," always performing, always acting, he or she has many identities, not a single "core" identity that is projected in each situation. Yet it seems to me an inner identity in the Eriksonian sense remains (see Chapter 8), assuming the personality is stable. Even Brother John, who resolutely projects his Christian identity at all times, and narrates incidents where strangers recognized immediately that he was a Christian, plays a role in doing so: that is, he acts as the indwelling Spirit moves him to act.

What, then, does the life story reveal? I think the first thing to recognize is that it reveals itself. By that I mean that the life story subordinates experience to the demands of its special conventions. The personality and identity projected in the life story are just as much "makings" as the story itself. Abrahams, I think, would agree with this formulation. Nonetheless, I would still claim that the "fictive" identity and personality presented by the life storyteller has motivating power in his or her own life: that is, the life story presents who the storyteller *thinks he is* (his identity) and how he *thinks he came to be that way*. That, of course, is the storyteller's interpretation, his part of the dialogue, and it explains to him why he persists in being as he is—for Brother John, why he remains a Christian.

When Brother John told his extended life story in 1977—the thirty-minute narrative that follows—I was aware that it was an artful rendering. But at the time I did not have enough additional information about his life to see how the life story would stack up against the "facts" of his life or against other people's interpretations of that life. It took many years before I was able to gather and sort the information that allowed me to place this life story in this perspective. This is not to say that his life story is false, but it is to underscore that it is an artistic product. His selection of incident and interpretation here not only reveals what his life means to him, but when viewed in light of the additional incidents and interpretations of his life that I will present later, his life story reveals how his mind fashions from a welter of possibilities a coherent narrative pattern and Christian identity.

Brother John casts his life story in the form of a conversion narrative, and the conventions of that genre among contemporary, born-again Christian witnesses force an interpretation of crucial events in his life, eliminating ambiguities and resolving uncertainties. Most assuredly, they transform a cyclical pattern of movement, into and away from the will of God, into a linear progression of sin, salvation, and assurance. But this will be our topic after we look at the life story that follows. (It may also be heard in its entirety on the *Powerhouse for God* record album.)

Brother John's Life Story

I was borned in Boone, North Carolina, Watauga County, in a little place called Howard's Creek. At that time Daddy was hard up and I had a granny woman, if you know what that is: no doctor, just an old woman. In that community a lot of women used her, and so she's the one that delivered
5   me. So my mother told me [*laughs*]. I don't remember all about that. My mother told me that this lady, I forgot what her name was, was what they call a granny woman. So she delivered me and she's the one that named me. And she's gave me the name I've always went by: John Claymon Sherfey.
10   We stayed in North Carolina while I can recall I started at school. Howard's Creek School. I was six years old. And going to church in the Howard's Creek Baptist Church. And I can remember very well seeing my daddy lead singing in that old Baptist church. When I was about six and a half years old we moved from there, and he moved to Virginia, and stayed
15   in Virginia one year. Course I didn't learn too much during that length of time. I went to school at the Three Springs School but I wasn't satisfied. And moving into the community new and all, it took awhile to get used to the people in that area. So in about another year's time we moved to Tennessee, down around Blountville. And the most of my life was reared up in
20   Tennessee, from around Johnson City, Kingsport, and Blountville, Bristol.
And so then as time grew on, why, naturally I grew to be a young man. And all young men I guess are probably so much alike. And I got to courting. I thought I was a bigger man than I really was. I fell in love with a little girl, Pauline Doran. I met her at church. I never have been against
25   going to church. I was raised that way, to go to church, and my father would take us to church when I was young, and when I was older I still wanted to go. Anyway, when I got there and saw this black-headed, beautiful girl, why, naturally I fell for her. And you've heard the old saying, "Love at first sight." Well, she lived about two or three miles from this

30 church. So I made eyes at her of course and, well, the way she looked at
me I felt she fell for me, too. So I asked her for a date when she come out
of the church that night. She didn't give me a date the first night, but later
on, why, I got to taking her home, and dating her. And at that time I couldn't
afford an automobile. My daddy had an old '28 Chevrolet and times was
35 hard. People didn't have the money back then that we have today. So I had
to walk to do my courting, which was about three miles. But I enjoyed it.
I enjoyed going to see her. So I guess really and truly she was the only girl
that I ever dated. And then we went together for about eight months. And
I got tired of walking, so I proposed to her to marry. And we first set the
40 date for a later date, to get married at Christmas in 1940. So then I grew a
little tireder of walking, you might say, and I moved that date up. I asked
her if it'd be all right if we got married on the twenty-third day of November, 1940. Times was hard. I guess you people're going to laugh when I tell
you this, but after I paid for the license, paid the preacher (and I only give
45 him a dollar at that time), and paid a boy a dollar to take me to get married
(in his car), and after I got through, I didn't have one penny left in my
pocket. Not one penny did I have left. And I sold a wheat crop that I had
sowed and had growing. I sold that to my brother-in-law to get the money
to marry my wife with. Now that's how poor I started out. But God has
50 blessed us through these years. I'm not rich. I mean naturally speaking,
as far as the wealth of this world's concerned, I'm not rich. But I do have
a wonderful family, and God's blessed us. We have a place to stay.
    But we started out poor. We stayed in the house with her parents until
six months or longer. And then we got a little stuff together by her father
55 and mother helping us. And of course my parents helped, too. And we
moved up on the hill above her parents, in a little house that belonged to
her brother. And he didn't charge me any rent or anything. He just let me
live there. So we got started and by working in 1941 I got me a job in
Kingsport, Tennessee, at the Mead Corporation. And from then on of
60 course, well, I worked there for a long time and then changed jobs around.
    But going back a little here before I get into that, I come from rather a
large family. My daddy was the daddy of eighteen children. He was married twice. His first wife died when she had two children, and then sixteen
by my mother. Not all of them lived, but they had twelve that lived up till a
65 few years ago; then one of my brothers died with TB. Course the rest of us
are still living, and sort of scattered all over the country. We've been poor
all our life. I don't have a rich brother nor a rich sister, but I have some
that's got nice homes, living well, doing well. Thank God for that.
    But that led us into this poor race, I guess you would call it, but we were
70 a happy family. We used to have the best times together when we were all
home. All of us children would get out to playing. In the wintertime, even.
And of course we didn't have no bicycles to ride, we didn't have no cars to
drive. All we had was a sled or a little wagon, but we had fun. And usually

on Sundays, why, we'd all get together and we'd go ginseng hunting if we
75   weren't in church, or if we were in church, when we come back home that
evening, we'd get out and go ginseng hunting, and just have a good time.
And play ball and all that. We just had a wonderful time. But anymore it's
got so that if they don't have an automobile they can't go nowhere. Or a
motorcycle. [*Laughs.*] But we had a good time then, and this went on
80   through life.

Of course, we was poor. Daddy never did have, as far as the world's
goods is concerned, he didn't have it. But he was a fine man, one of the
finest men. Not saying it because he's my daddy, but he was one of the
finest men that I ever knew. And I've told here at the church and every-
85   where I've been, I can truthfully say I've never heard my daddy swear an
oath in my life. And I never saw my daddy take a drink of liquor. I never
saw my daddy drink a can of beer. He did chew tobacco up till he got sick,
and then he quit chewing tobacco. But outside of that, that's all I've seen
my daddy do. My mother, I never saw her take a drink of liquor, never
90   heard her swear an oath in my life. And I just had wonderful parents. I
thank God for that tonight. I praise God that my parents were that way.

Then after we got married we went on our own, and Mother cried when
I told her I was going to get married. She hated to see us leave home.
Course Pauline's mother and father hated to see her go, too, but still, that
95   goes along through life. People, when they meet together, and they fall in
love with one another, next thing they think about is getting married, and
which is a great step. Now the Bible teaches us that marriage is honorable,
and the bed is undefiled, so God honors a marriage, but he wants it to be
done through the Lord. Now I admire anybody when they get married in
100   the Lord, in other words, both of 'em be Christians, living for the Lord, and
things will work out great. Now when me and my wife got married neither
one of us was Christian. We were going to church, we went to church, but
when we got married we didn't start off going to church right then.

Went on a few years, and as I said, I got a job in Kingsport in 1941. I left
105   that job and just jumped from place to place. I never seemed like could be
satisfied. Nowhere I went to work I was satisfied. I don't know why, but I
guess I was just a country boy. [*Laughs.*] So I just jumped from place to
place, and it seemed like I never could get ahead till finally at last I got old
enough to realize and understand that I was going to have to settle down.
110   Well, I was living at the Tri-City Airport. God blessed us with four children: my oldest son, J. C., then Wanda, my daughter, and then Buddy
Wayne, and then Donny. We was living at the Tri-City Airport at the
Holston Institute. And Buddy Wayne took sick. Well, I wasn't living for the
Lord. I had made a profession in earlier life but I had failed. I didn't mea-
115   sure up to what I had professed to be.

And so I took the boy to the doctor, and the doctor said he had a little bit
of pneumonia, and give him medicine, said he'll be all right. I took him

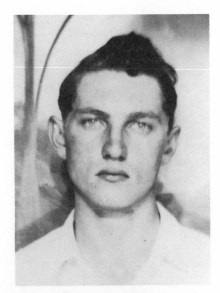

Brother John, aged about sixteen, ca.
1939. Photo booth picture, prob.
Blountville, Tennessee.

Brother John's parents, John Henry Sherfey and Josie Coffey Sherfey,
ca. 1955. Photographer unknown.

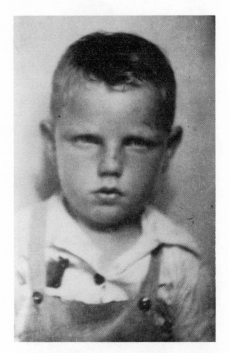

Buddy Wayne Sherfey, ca. 1951. Photographer unknown.

back home and started giving him the medicine and it went against him,
seemed like. So I called another doctor in Blountville, Tennessee, Dr.
120   McDowell, and he came down and just as he walked in the door he started
shaking his head, and said, "There's no hope." And he told me what to do:
just give him a little sweetened toddy and try to keep his buds stimulated
and all. He wasn't hardly five years old.
       And to make me realize and understand that I had been rebellioned
125   against God, in not doing the will of God, I lived in this house that had a
hallway from the living room all the way back to the kitchen and then each
[room] was offset from the other. And I had that boy in my arms. Pauline,
my wife, was in the kitchen and she couldn't possibly see me. Or him. And
I had him up in my arms when he was dying. And she screamed just as
130   loud as she could scream, "Pray!" But children, I couldn't pray. There was
no way I could pray because there was sin in my life between me and God
that I had not repented of. And that began to haunt me later. I didn't repent at that time. And it went on. Course the boy went on to meet the
Lord, and I know beyond a shadow of a doubt that one day soon I can see
135   him again. But I feel that that was the Lord dealing with me.

Now some will say, "I don't believe that. I don't believe God works like that." But David, if you recall, studying in the word of God, David said that he had committed adultery with this woman. And God took the child from David. He wouldn't let David keep that child because he'd committed adul-
40 tery. And he had this woman's husband killed. He told Joab to put Uriah in the hottest part of the battle, put him out in the front line: "I want him killed." And he had Uriah killed trying to cover up David's mistake, David's meanness. And of course I hadn't done anything like that, but yet I feel that because I had made a profession and I had let down on God, I hadn't
45 done what God wanted me to, I feel that God was bringing me to my knees.

So after the boy was buried and everything and I went on, that was always on my mind. The Bible said, David said, there'd be a sword in his house forever. Well, there's a sword in my house forever that keeps me
50 thinking about this, because Buddy Wayne, seemed like, we loved him better than ary child we had. And I don't know why. I never have been able to figure that out. But we really did love Buddy Wayne.

So that would haunt me. By the night times it would haunt me. And so in time, to come through this terrible time I tried drinking. I'd go and get
55 whiskey and drink it. I'd drink beer. And I done a little bit of everything that I can think of, trying to get rid of that trouble that was in my heart. But it didn't help.

So we were living down next to Fordtown. Brother Milburn Morlock, a Jewish preacher,[1] conducted a revival meeting at the Gray's Station, a little
60 town over there called Gray's Station. He was in a tent revival on the school grounds. So we heard about it and went over there.

And the first night we set out in the car, me and Pauline and the children, and wouldn't go inside the tent, but I could hear him. And, Lord, how that dealt with me that night when he made that altar call. I smoked
65 cigarettes, I bit my fingernails, I twisted and squirmed because God was dealing with my heart. Well, I didn't go to the altar that night. I went home and I tried to sleep, but my sleep was gone. I was just in trouble. So I went to work the next day. I'd promised God that night, though, if he would let me go to sleep, I made him a vow that I would go back to the tent the next
70 night and get right. So the next day I went to work and I still had that burden. It was a burden: that's all it was, just a burden. I went back home that evening when I get off from work. I went home and got dressed and we went to the tent. And Brother Milburn Morlock preached that night.

I'll never forget this as long as I live. I was sitting on the fifth row of
75 seats back. He had chairs, folding chairs. And I set in the fifth row back from the front, from the preacher, looking back on the left-hand side. And seemed like everything that preacher said, he looked right at me and

1. John believes he was Jewish before converting to the Primitive Baptist faith.

pointed the finger. Pointed at me. And of course I thought somebody's told
him something. "Lord, who's he been talking to?"

180   But when he got the message over, I couldn't hardly wait for him to
make that altar call. I wanted to get out of there and go to that altar so bad.
And I'd already made a vow to God that I would fix things up with him. So I
did. I went to the altar that night and when I went, I meant business. I got
on my knees and I prayed and I confessed. Everything I could think of was

185   in my heart, I told it to the Lord. And I said, "Well, Lord, I've done all I
know to do. Here I come, swim, sink, or drown, I'm a-coming to you. And
Lord, if I go down, I'm going down for you." And don't you know the Lord
saved me that night. And I've been saved ever since.

         We was living down there then next to Fordtown, Route 11, and I was
190   working in Kingsport at that time, at the Mead Corporation again, which
was years later. And when I got the job there that time and this happened
to me, why, coming home one night from work—.

         Now a lot of people—and God knows I say this as lovingly as I know
how to say it tonight—God calls men to preach the gospel. And I in times
195   past had been rebellioned against God, but when God saved me, then he
started dealing with my heart to preach.

         Well, I'll never forget, though, after I got saved, I went back to the Mead
Corporation the next morning. Old Brother Fred Weston, he sung bass in
the Moving On Quartet, I was sitting up on skids and he came in the door
200   and when he looked at me he said, "John, something's happened to you."
And of course when he said that I said, "Yes, Brother Fred, praise God, the
Lord saved me." And we just had a good time. I come off of the skids and
we was just having a ball. Course he had prayed so much for me.

         And after that then, every time I'd start talking or testifying or anything,
205   they'd say, "John, I believe God's calling you to preach." And of course, you
know, I didn't want to preach.

         Now since I said that, it takes me back to when I was in school. Teacher
asked us one time, when I was about nine years old, "When you children
grow up, what do you want to be?" And I told that teacher I wanted to be a
210   truck driver and a preacher. Now to show you that you'll get your heart's
desire, you can have it if you want it, I've been both of them. [Laughs.] I
got saved, and of course I drove the truck before I got saved. I drove a
tractor and trailer. The first tractor-trailer I ever drove was hauling milk
out of Abingdon to Big Stone Gap, Virginia. I was hauling for the King
215   Brothers. They taught me how to drive. And I drove that tractor-trailer.
That was my heart's desire. Then of course I wanted to drive tankers,
which that was a tanker also, but that was hauling milk. I wanted to haul
gas, because when I was just a young boy, my daddy lived on a farm, they
called it Nalph Barnes's. The old man that owned it was Nalph Barnes, and
220   daddy lived on this place. Well, when old Mr. Barnes would take off somewhere and go somewhere he'd want us, me and my brothers, to come and

watch his place. So we would sleep in the old wagon, in the crib shed. And of a night times those big red Texaco tractor and trailer gasoline tankers'd go through there, and them tires a-crying, and that's what I wanted to do, of course. But I told the teacher I wanted to be a tractor and trailer driver and a preacher. Well, I got to be both of them. So I drove the truck first, and then after God saved me, he started dealing with my heart, like I said a moment ago, and everybody, every time I'd testify in church or anything, they'd say, "John, I believe the Lord's calling you to preach." I said, "Well now, if he does, I will." And me knowing all the time that he was.

Well, I went on for a long time like that. And one night I was coming in home from work at the Mead. I was working the three-to-eleven shift. And when I got to within about a half a mile of home, why, I was praying, and talking to the Lord, crying, tears running down my cheeks. So I decided to pull over to the side of the road. I had an old '42 Studebaker car. Pulled over to the side of the road and I just laid down over the wheel and I said, "Lord, if it's preach, I'll go." And when I said that, brother, it was just like if he'd have lifted that piano off the top of me. I mean that's how heavy I was burdened down so. But when I said that, the load left.

Brother John, ca. 1953. To his right is the car he was driving when he accepted the call to preach. Photographer unknown.

240   And then I went to church on prayer-meeting night, and I announced
       my calling to preach the gospel. I told them that the Lord had called me.
       "Brother Milburn Morlock," I said, "the Lord's called me to preach." So he
       said, "Well, John, I want you to go with me Sunday, down in Goshen Val-
       ley." He said, "I have a Sunday appointment down there and you can go
245   down there and preach for me." I said, "All right, Brother Morlock, I'll go."
           Well, I went back home and I got my Bible. We lived in a little old house
       behind her [Pauline's] mother and daddy, three-room house, and I got my
       Bible down and started studying. And I never will forget this, either. I was
       studying about John, Chapter 15, where it says, "I am the true vine, my
250   father's the husband, and every branch that beareth not fruit, he purgeth
       it," and all, cast 'em into the fire and all. I took the whole chapter and I
       was going to, I just about had it memorized and I was going down to show
       'em what a great preacher John Sherfey was.
           Well, honey, believe you me, I did. I showed 'em what a great preacher I
255   was. 'Cause when I got down there, and I'd studied so hard, you know,
       thinking surely that I can preach a great sermon, you know, and that being
       my first time ever getting up to preach.
           Brother Milburn Morlock and I, we went out in this old sagegrass field.
       Sagegrass up to our belt. And after he opened up service and singing and
260   prayer, he said, "Now I have a young preacher here with me today," and he
       said, "I'm very happy to have him." He said, "He was converted under our
       preaching not long ago, and God's called him to preach." And he said, "We
       have Brother John Sherfey here," and he said, "I want him to come and
       bring the message."
265   Well, you know, I guess I just felt important. But I got up there to
       preach, and when I got up there I couldn't remember one verse in that
       whole chapter. I was in the awfulest shape you ever seen. And of course I
       started crying and testifying, telling 'em how I got saved and all of that,
       you know, but as far as preaching is concerned, I didn't do no preaching.
270   And so then after I got through what little bit I had to say, I set down and
       turned it back to Brother Morlock and he preached. And he was a good
       preacher. I still love him, bless his heart.
           Anyway, he was coming back up the road that evening and he just
       looked over at me and said, "John, pray. It'll be all right." Oh, I wish he'd
275   have shut up his fist and hit me. It wouldn't have hurt any worse, you
       know? Me already in misery, and him telling me, "Just pray, it'll be all
       right." [Laughs.]
           But that learnt me one of the greatest lessons that I've ever indulged in
       in my life: not to depend on myself for nothing when I'm behind the
280   pulpit. Trust the Lord, put him in it. Because God's the one that called me
       to preach, and if God called me, God can preach me. Of course now I
       realize the Bible says, "Study the word to show thyself approved, a work-
       man rightly dividing the word of truth and not being ashamed." So I study

the word, but I depend on the Lord when I get up here. When I get up to
285   preach, I depend on the Lord, not John Sherfey. And not what little bit I
know, because I don't know much. I didn't even get to the eighth-grade
education. But the Lord has blessed me in my ministry, and I thank God
for that. God blessed me to have a job, during all this time I been preaching, except in one time in Kingsport.

290   I'd got out of a job. I couldn't get a job nowhere. I'd held a revival meeting in North Bristol, in the Shiloh Freewill Baptist Church, a few months
prior to this. And after our table was bare, we didn't have anything to put
out to eat, and the children was home, and of course I got up and I prayed
after midnight. And of course I was all the time talking to the Lord after
295   midnight about what to do, because we didn't have anything to cook. And
something spoke to me about two o'clock in the morning and said, "Everything's all right."

Well, the next morning we got up and she fixed what we had. That was
it. Old Brother in Bristol, a deacon in the church there in Bristol where I'd
300   held the revival, Shiloh Freewill Baptist Church, and a good man, he came
down by my house and he stopped down in the road and blowed his horn.
And of course I went out to see what he wanted. I tried to get him to come
in and he says, "I can't." He says, "John, I'm here and I don't know why
I'm here." So I kept talking to him, you know, got in the car and set down
305   with him, and we set there and talked, just about church, and church
working, and his job. And of course we talked on awhile. And he said,
"Well, John, I've got to go. I've got a job in Kingsport. I've just got to get
down there." And so he handed me a ten-dollar bill. Well, I started rejoicing when he gave me that ten-dollar bill. And I said, "Brother Ike [Blalock],
310   you don't understand." I said, "We don't have anything in the house to fix,
to cook." And I said, "This will put some food on my table." And I was
rejoicing, you know. And he said, "Give me that back." And so I handed it
back to him, and he wrote me a check for twenty-five dollars. And he went
down the road rejoicing, and I went back in the house rejoicing. And that
315   just proves that God will take care of you. And of course as I've said we've
been poor all our lives, and we're still poor. But I'm happy in the Lord.

Allegoresis and the Folk Hermeneutic

John narrates his life chronologically, save for a few digressions he makes
to provide background and emphasize ideas. His life story can be divided
into sections as follows:

1. Birth and early childhood (lines 1–20)
2. Courtship and marriage (21–52)
3. Work after marriage (53–60)
4. Digression on John's parents, brothers, and sisters (61–91)
5. Digression on marriage (92–103)

6. The death of Buddy Wayne Sherfey (104–157)

7. John's conversion in the tent revival (158–188)

8. John's call to preach (189–196)

9. Digression on incident at work when Fred Weston recognized John had been saved (197–203)

10. John's call to preach, continued (204–239)

11. John's first sermon (240–288)

12. Story of gift of $25 when the Sherfeys had nothing to eat (288–316)

Tellingly, most of these sections of the life story come to a point. John narrates with a purpose, and interprets the events of his life as he tells them. Repeated points turn into themes and unify the life story. Poverty, for example, recurs often: John's family was poor when he was a child (66–82); he had no money after he got married (43–54); he was unemployed for a time in Kingsport and without the means to feed his family (288–316). John's interpretation, however, is that no matter how poor they were, they were rich in God's blessings, and that God took care of them. "We've been poor all our lives, and we're still poor. But I'm happy in the Lord," John says at the close of his narrative, tying up one of his major ideas. Family is another recurrent theme. He reminisces about his family when he was a child, and carries it through with his marriage and departure from his immediate family to start another family with Pauline. The family they begin is broken by the death of Buddy Wayne, but John is sure the family will be reunited in heaven at the homecoming reunion. Certainly, these emphases on poverty and family in John's life story are consistent with his emphases in his sermons.

John takes great pains to interpret his life story as he proceeds, thereby providing what I have called a folk hermeneutic, the narrator's explicit interpretation of his narrative. He tells the listener how he feels, what he believes, and what the events in his life mean. He may be poor but he is happy. His father was an illiterate sharecropper but a good Christian who never drank or cursed. John and Pauline were unsaved when they married but he wishes they had been saved. God will bless a Christian marriage. God will supply John's needs, whether spiritual (the words to preach) or material (food for the table). God punished John by causing Buddy Wayne to die. Buddy Wayne's death brought John to salvation. And so on. In fact, as I have written earlier, John engages in interpretation and explanation so frequently during the worship service and even during conversation that one must conclude he feels compelled to explain: he is a man who cannot abide a mystery.

I commented earlier on John's habit of explaining joke punch lines. A punch line involves a figure of speech; that is, it says two (and only two) things at once. Like an allegory, a joke turns on a double meaning; to "get" or understand the joke, the listener must make a mental analogy that reveals the hidden meaning in the punch line. John's compulsion to explain jokes, I feel sure, derives from what I called in the last two chapters his analogical habit of mind. It is an unusually strong habit, exercised interpreting his two great texts: the Bible and his life.

But the meaning of the events in a person's life is not so clear as the meaning of a joke. Analogy, allegory, tropology, typology, parallelism—these are the characteristic methods of John's mind. It is useful to understand these methods as *allegoresis*. Maureen Quilligan distinguishes allegory as a literary mode from allegoresis, which is "textual commentary or discursive interpretation." Allegoresis is "that critical procedure . . . which can, in fact, make *any* text . . . whatever its literal meaning, appear to be about . . . any other (latent) subject" (Quilligan 1981 : 163–164). Considering John's life as his text, its literal meaning is plain enough, but through allegoresis its meaning becomes evidence of God's actions, and the key to interpretation is to understand how God works his purposes in the world. The Bible, thus, as a record of God in history, is a repository of how God has acted in the past; to understand the Bible is to understand how God works in history and in the lives of individuals, then and now.

Allegoresis serves well to interpret signs whose meaning is obscure. In typology, of course, which operates by analogy and parallelism, the "type" is unknown as a type until it is fulfilled by the "antitype"; in other words, foreshadowing is only revealed as foreshadowing after the foreshadowed event occurs. "What seems specific to allegory," writes J. Hillis Miller, "is a larger degree of incompatibility between the tenor and vehicle than we tend to expect in symbol, where the 'material' base and the 'spiritual' meaning are thrown together . . . with some implication of overlapping, consubstantiality, or participation. In allegory the one does not directly suggest the other" (1981 : 357). In other words, allegorical meaning is not derived from the immediate or literal context, nor from a symbolic relationship in which the meaning is grounded in the literal context, but from a pattern that links a series of events in an unambiguous chain of cause and effect, whereby the mysterious event is explained by the pattern it fits. Such an interpretation is implicit in John's story of his conversion, explicit in his story of his call to preach, and insistent in his explanation of Buddy Wayne's death, an event I will discuss at some length below.

The heart of John's life story is his conversion to Christianity and his call to preach the gospel. He gives these central events in his life the most attention in his life story, and thus the life story becomes an extended conversion narrative. Asked why he tells the story of his conversion, John replied that he felt it could bring others to God; that is, they would see how their lives were similar to his, and how they might let God into their lives as he did. The narrative serves as a "model *of* and a model *for* religious action and belief" (George 1978:93). As a model for religious action and belief, it leads the unconverted toward God, and to the converted it reaffirms the presence of God in the world. Though readers who come to conversion narratives for literary merit may find their conventions dull, those very conventions illustrate God's consistency in dealing with men's and women's souls. To the convert and potential convert, it is important that God is "the same yesterday, today, and tomorrow." The very conventionality of the narratives, in other words, offers assurance to the teller and listener alike. As a model of religious belief, the conversion narrative reaffirms the teller's identity as a Christian and a child of God. In fact, it reconstitutes that identity in the act of the telling: every time John tells the story of how he was saved, it is as if he is saved once more.

Interestingly, besides the conversion narrative, John's life story contains another, related pattern: the success story, with its particular cast as the fulfillment of the dream, something that occurs so often in American autobiographical writing that it is referred to as the American Dream. The dream is the dream of success, and the underlying idea (or American Myth) is that no matter how poor one is, genuine effort will be rewarded by success because America is a land of opportunity and abundance. Benjamin Franklin's autobiography is the earliest American version of these secular success stories. Wealth is not always the end; Abraham Lincoln, for example, whose biographers use the pattern, became a great and good man. Some writers in this category emphasize virtue, some emphasize shrewdness, some admit that luck plays a role; but all stress that they are "self-made"—that is, their efforts made them successful. One need only think of Lincoln reading by firelight in his log cabin home.

Both the conversion narrative and the success story show the transformation from deprivation to fulfillment, even though one is sacred and the other secular. But, significantly, in the success story the "I" is self-made, whereas in the conversion narrative the "I" yields to the will of God. In one, the "I" is active, while in the other the "I" lets God come into his life and direct him. In his life story, John emphasizes his humble beginnings, and illustrates how God has rewarded him. Moreover, he mentions the fulfillment of twin dreams: being a truck driver and being a preacher. His elementary school teacher had asked him what he wanted to be when he grew up, and he was both. "You'll get your heart's desire," he concludes (lines 210–211).

In the life story narrative, the tension between the sacred and secular patterns is resolved: God rewards with money (not wealth, but enough to provide) as well as salvation, and the result is happiness. In John's life, however, as we shall see, money and work were (and remain) serious issues, not so easily or permanently resolved. As a child he and his family knew grinding poverty; as an adult he was better off, but still poor. His children recall sleeping two and three to a bed, even in Falls Church, where John held his highest-paying jobs. John often says that "God doesn't want his children to be poor," yet John has been poor all his life. He also says that God sometimes keeps his children poor so they will remain humble. In so saying, he rids himself of envy, and justifies his status. Thus he reconciles his life through the combination of the conversion narrative and American myth, finding identity as a child of God, a metaphor that suggests that God will take care of him like a father, chastising him when he does wrong, rewarding him when he does right, but all the while providing for his needs.

Biography and the Life Story

As an extended conversion narrative, John's life story follows a pattern found in Christian spiritual autobiography. Broadly speaking, the pattern involves a progression from sin to salvation to assurance. In some versions assurance is certain or "perfect," in others hoped for and believed in, but not certain (no one knows God's will) and imperfect. More specifically, among contemporary evangelical fundamentalist Protestants, the stages proceed through sin, conviction, repentance, confession, salvation, and assurance. The prototype is Paul (Saul) in the book of Acts, particularly for the vileness of his sin and the simplicity and swiftness of his conversion. To some extent, these stages formed the conventional pattern in spiritual autobiographies from Saint Augustine's *Confessions* through John Bunyan's *Grace Abounding,* and their later North American counterparts. Among the Puritans in colonial America, for example, in order to be admitted to church membership, it was necessary that one's conversion narrative be read publicly, and similar testimonies are requisite even today among certain evangelicals. Brother John's life story fits the conventional pattern. After a young manhood of restless drifting, after the death of his five-year-old son, and after a period of drinking and gambling, he falls under conviction upon hearing the word of God preached; he repents and confesses after the first night of the tent revival at Gray's Station; he attains salvation at the altar on the second night; and he receives perfect assurance as he feels the call to preach and learns to depend on God to take care of him, whether giving him words to preach or putting food on his table when he is unemployed.

For some years I taught Jonathan Edwards' *Personal Narrative*—a spiritual autobiography written by the eighteenth-century New England divine perhaps best known for his Calvinist sermon, "Sinners in the Hands of an Angry God"—to my American literature students, and marveled how this account of conversion differed from the conventional pattern in emphasizing the periodic struggles of Edwards' mind or soul, and the gradual deepening of his faith and understanding of God. It is impossible to point to a time and place in the narrative when Edwards (like Saul) is saved; rather, conversion for Edwards proceeded in a series of encounters with God, of steps toward God (and some fewer steps away), through partial conversions to a fuller conversion. For many years I wondered whether

Edwards' spiritual autobiography was an aberration. Did Edwards' unusual temperament result in an unusual conversion, or was his conversion typical, the report being unusual because his superior intellect was equipped to deal with its complexity? If his conversion was typical, how then account for the conventions of most other spiritual autobiographies, other than saying that the prestructured mold proved irresistible, both as a guide to understanding experience and to writing about it? And as I came to learn more about Brother John's life, I began to wonder why his life story emphasized a Saul-like conversion whereas in fact he, too, was converted in a series of encounters with God, and once in conversation with me made the distinction between his being partially and fully converted.

In *The Puritan Conversion Narrative,* Patricia Caldwell challenges the majority view that "the [American] Puritans had not only devised a linear scheme that they thought workable but had held to it with relative ease" (1983: 163). Careful analysis of Puritan spiritual autobiographies revealed that in the British colonies these conventions served only imperfectly "as the basis of a literary structure" and that the writers needed "to depart from established literary structures in order to accommodate a set of experiences that [were] unprecedented just by virtue of their taking place in the new land and that must find expression within an imaginative framework only partially defined by the magistrates and ministers" (ibid.: 164, 166). Disoriented and distracted in pioneer America, the Puritans found the structure they were looking for in the Bible, Caldwell concludes; and their autobiographical writings give "the reader an impression not so much of being marched through a morphology as of being led through the Bible" (ibid.: 168–169). Reality, on the American frontier, was not so well grounded as in England; events and personages in the Bible seemed more real, and so the American Puritans compared their experience to that chronicled in the Bible, internalizing biblical personalities, and bringing "real life into the closest possible touch with Scripture" (ibid.: 174).

Caldwell's reading of Puritan spiritual autobiography fits well with my claims concerning Brother John's analogical mentality, for he turns to Scripture at points when he needs to prove something, and deduces the truth from the first principle of God's existence and the Bible as his revealed word, relating to the characters in the Bible as if they were his acquaintances (which in a sense of course they are), and relying on the events of the Bible rather than, say, modern history, for a usable past. This is most evident when he compares himself to David in explaining that God took away his five-year-old son to punish him.

We have reached a crucial juncture with respect to the telling and interpreting of life story narratives: the difference between the public performance and the private memory, the narrative and the conversation. Why does Brother John's public conversion narrative remain a set-piece, stable and conventional, whereas his memories of conversion, elicited in conversation (as we shall see), point to something far more complicated? Why does his conversion narrative present an instantaneous new birth, preceded by conviction and followed by assurance, whereas conversation reveals two prior trips to the altar, two professions of faith, and, as far as he must have known then, two conversions ten and twenty years before the conversion in the tent revival? Why do the two prior encounters with God disappear from the narrative? Why does he have difficulty recalling them, even at the prodding of his wife and other relatives who remember him as he went through the events surrounding them?

Certainly, narrative demands coherence; and the mysteries of the prior encounters with God resist the shaping needed for narrative. But not totally; a complex narrative might emerge in writing, if not orally. More likely, in his public role as preacher and leader of the church, as an evangelist whose personal experience teaches by example, John is constrained by the conventions of the narrative genre: the audience expects a type of Saul's conversion, and that is what they get. This is so much so that the narrative comes to stand for the experience; and when, in the presence of his family, John discusses his earlier professions, he is in somewhat the same position as anyone who is puzzled and slightly embarrassed by stories about his former self. He has changed his mind; his wife and family remind him of earlier professions, but they do not understand what happened then in the way that John does now, in the light of his subsequent experiences. To follow this out we must look closely at a fuller picture of his life, based on what I learned from conversations with him, his friends, and members of his family over a ten-year period.

Childhood

Brother John was born on April 6, 1923, at Howard's Creek, North Carolina, near Boone, in Watauga County. The midwife who delivered him named him: John Claymon Sherfey. Claymon was originally spelled Clamian, but it is Claymon on his birth certificate. No one else in his family is named Claymon or Clamian. As a child John went by the name Claymon to avoid confusion with his father, also named John. "I never did like Claymon," John said. "I never have. Children used to aggravate me and they'd call me 'Claymud' at school" (John and Pauline Sherfey interview, November 7, 1985, p. 1). Sherfey is a German name, possibly derived from Sherffig, and related to Sheffey, another common name in central Appalachia. A well-known preacher in eastern Tennessee and southwestern Virginia during the late nineteenth century was named Sheffey; he was an itinerant Methodist and a throwback to an earlier nineteenth-century tradition. A large oral tradition grew up about him. Brother John had heard of Preacher Sheffey but does not know whether he is related to him. The Sherfey family migrated from Germany to Pennsylvania and then down through the Shenandoah Valley with the waves of other Pennsylvania

Dutch immigrants beginning in the eighteenth century. Exactly when they came is uncertain. Sherfey is a common name today in northeastern Tennessee.

John's mother, Josie Eleanor Coffey Sherfey (1899–1983), his father's second wife, bore sixteen children. Twelve lived; from the eldest they were Earl (b. 1917), Ester (1919–1949), Bertie (f.), John, Henry, James Ellis, Howard, Charles, Elsie, Raymond, Reena Sue, and Willa Jo. Josie was an orphan, living in an orphanage in Watauga County when John's father courted and married her. His first wife had died in her twenties after giving birth to two children.

John's memories of his mother center in the home. He remembers her in the kitchen, cooking up a big, plain cake for the family on Saturday night, when they listened to country music on the *Grand Old Opry:*

> We couldn't afford cars or bicycles or anything to go on, so on Saturday nights now everybody's out going everywhere but we couldn't do that, so my daddy and my oldest brother went to Bristol and they bought one of these old-timey radios. Course then it was new. . . . And the *Grand Old Opry* was our pride and joy. Mother would bake a cake and we'd lay there and listen to the *Grand Old Opry,* and it didn't go off until one o'clock in the morning. So we'd lay on the floor, and kick our heels, and listen to Uncle Dave Macon, and all them fellows, the Fruit Jar Drinkers, and all of it, you know. And it was just a lot of fun. We was there, just the family. Of course a great big family of us, and we just had a great time together. (Ibid., August 14, 1977, p. 1)

He remembers his mother in the kitchen sewing:

> Lord, she worked all the time, you know . . . Now I picture her more than anything, in my mind now, as she used to sit and make our shirts, and take her foot and rock the cradle. She'd keep the cradle a-rocking with a baby a-laying in it while she was making clothes for us boys. And the girls, too. She made the girls' dresses, and all of the shirts that we wore. (Ibid., December 4, 1979, p. 36)

John's paternal grandfather was John Henry "Jim" Sherfey, a farmer who lived in southwestern Virginia near Benhams and Three Springs. A grandmother, known to the family as "Grandma Beechboard," lived nearby. "Jim" Sherfey died when John was in his twenties. John was very close to his father, John Henry Sherfey (1890–1971). An illiterate share-cropper, his father knew no other work. He never spoke of a desire to own a farm, but John guessed he would have been happier with his own land. Unlike John and most of his brothers, his father genuinely enjoyed farming. "He'd go out there, you know, in them old new grounds and use that hoe all day long and just whistle all the time he was a-doing it, and there I was out there gritting my teeth and so aggravated. . . . But Daddy always acted like he loved it. He never complained about the work" (ibid., p. 8). As a young boy, John learned farming as his brothers did by following his father:

> Everybody had to work. I mean, the girls had to help Mother, and us boys had to help Daddy. Of course, a lot of time the girls would go in the field with us, and we'd just use hoes when we was too small to do anything else, why, we had to use a hoe, you know, and chop out the corn and take the weeds out of it. . . . Back then you plowed your corn about four or five times, and used that hoe; you went through and cut the weeds out, you thinned it, and it was just hard work. Everybody'd go, and so we was in the field, and of course when we got big enough to plow, why, he'd let us take a time about, you know. One would want to plow, and naturally I guess a boy [thinks] it looks so big to follow the plow, drive a horse, you know. And oh, we'd have some big arguments a lot of times about who was gonna do the plowing, who was gonna do the hoeing. And so Daddy'd let one plow awhile, then he'd let the other'n plow awhile. And you had to walk behind that plow. You didn't ride, you know. And so you just keep on gradually coming into it as you grow up, you know, and then you learn all these things as you come into it. That's the way I learned. I didn't have to go to school to learn to be a farmer. I just was raised in it. (Ibid., p. 6)

John went part way through the eighth grade in school, but he values the education he received from his father most highly. John did not like farming, and did not spend much of his life as a farmer; the apprenticeship to his father, in the communal family context, was what he loved, not the work itself. Later, he saw to it that his sons went through high school, and then he taught them his trade, truck driving. "You send a man off to school to learn to be a truck driver and he comes back, he still can't drive a truck. But you take him out and give him self-experience, teach him to drive it and let him learn it on his own, and he knows it. That's the way I've always found it works better, for you to learn these things as you go along" (ibid.). Three of his four sons (Donny, Charles, and Dana) have been truck drivers ever since they began working after high school, and now have about forty years' experience among them.

John's parents, like most parents of that time and place, were strict rather than indulgent with their children. They taught the children to control their desires, not to assert themselves overmuch, and never to lie or steal. They instructed them in the Golden Rule. John's father often told the family, "I believe in living and letting live" (ibid., p. 3). Punishment was by instruction, scolding, and whipping:

> But they would certainly give us our lessons if we did do something wrong. Which we did; I mean there ain't no use in saying we were perfect children, because we done a lot of things that they didn't approve of. And

Brother John and his father, ca. 1965. Photographer unknown.

they'd set us down, talk to us, and go over it with us, and say, "You shouldn't
do this." Of course, Daddy, a lot of times when I was small, growing up,
you know, instead of sitting you down and talking to you, boy, he'd bust
your hide! (Ibid., p. 4)

Spanking, beating, and whipping (with a belt or rope or branches) were
not uncommon in Appalachia at this time, nor elsewhere in the rural
United States. Sister Minnie, Brother Vernie's sister, spoke of the whip-
pings she received from her father, whom she considered wicked. The
mark of wickedness was that he beat her when he felt like it, not when she
had done something wrong. I asked John if he felt the same way about his
father, and John insisted he was punished only when there was a reason.
In other words, he thought whipping was a fair punishment when punishment was deserved, and he did not hesitate to strike his own children
when they were young. Still, as a boy he went to his mother, hoping she
would intercede for mercy with his father; and his own children followed
suit. Sometimes his mother would take care of the punishment herself.
John remembered that when his mother caught him chewing tobacco she
made him continue until he got sick:

She called us in the house, me and my brother, and set us at the windows,
open windows at the end of the house, and she gave us a great big cud of
tobacco, cut it off, and said, "Now chew this. And I mean chew." So we
started chewing and spitting, chewing and a-spitting. So after awhile we
both got sick. I mean it made us so sick we like to die. She said, "Now
maybe you won't go back and bum no more tobacco." (Ibid., p. 5)

Unquestionably, with fourteen in their household to feed, a sharecropper's living during the Depression years numbered the Sherfeys among
the working poor. Sharecropping in northeastern Tennessee in the 1930s
was little different from sharecropping in the Blue Ridge. Yet for John
Henry Sherfey, a man of uncommon energy, it provided:

He understood that [farming was] what he had to do, I guess. And . . .
during the Depression times was hard and you had to make everything you
could. And he'd go out and rent these old new grounds and clear 'em up,
clean the brush off of 'em and just cut the trees off and work around the
stumps, go in there and take a hoe and plant corn. . . . And then cut it all
down, he'd get two-thirds of that. Where the other way he just got a third.
They'd give him two-thirds because he was cleaning up their ground. And
so he'd plant him some black-eyed peas. I was telling somebody . . . that
we used to eat off black-eyed peas. They had these old three-bushel meal
sacks, and we'd raise them black-eyed peas in these new grounds and
then haul 'em out, you know, and put 'em in them sacks. We'd have two
or three of those three-bushel sacks full, black-eyed peas, and when the

winter's come, snow started flying, well, we had black-eyed peas and corn-bread. (Ibid., p. 7)

While the Sherfey men and boys worked in the fields, the women and girls worked in the house, washing, cleaning, sewing, cooking, and putting food by for the winter. They canned beans, tomatoes, and cucumbers, and pickled beets. They stuffed wooden barrels with sauerkraut, and cellared cabbage, potatoes, and apples. The Sherfeys raised three or four pigs each year, butchered them, salted them down, and kept the pork in the smokehouse. John often had no shoes, wore shirts made from feed sacks, and ate cornbread and beans. "Of course we were poor people, growed up poor, which I'm not knocking poor people at all, I'm still poor," John re-called. "But Daddy and Mother done the best they could do. . . . Daddy worked for seventy-five cents a day. And then he didn't get the money for that. All he got was potatoes or beans or beets. The landlord would pay him off in meat or something to eat. But anyway we ate. We didn't go hungry. Sometimes it was cornbread and bean soup or cornbread and milk" (ibid., p. 2). "So that's the way we used to have to live," he said. "I'm not ashamed of it, because that was the survival way" (ibid., p. 10). And they did survive, as subsistence farmers; but how different, how much more work it was sharecropping in the 1930s to make a living compared to farming fifty years earlier when the pigs could feed in the forest and when mountain farmers owned their land.

John reiterates that the family enjoyed themselves together; the children formed their own play community and did not need to find friends outside the family.

We were a happy family. We used to have the best times together when we were all home. All of us children would get out to playing. In the winter-time, even; and of course we didn't have no bicycles to ride, we didn't have no cars to drive. All we had was a sled or a little wagon, but we had fun. And usually on Sundays, why, we'd all get together and we'd go ginseng hunting if we weren't in church, or if we were in church, when we came back home that evening, we'd get out and go ginseng hunting, and just have a good time. (John Sherfey interview, July 23, 1977, p. 3)

The twelve young children had only "a few scuffles, like any children will do, but other than that we got along good" (ibid., p. 1). Actually it seems they fought and wrestled quite a bit, even though their parents discouraged it. The family made a bit of money selling ginseng gathered in the mountains, but again John stresses the communal aspects of the work, and the enjoyment of working with his family. More than anyone else, he enjoyed working with his father. "Me and my daddy were so close," he said. "He and I worked together more than any of the rest of them. . . . I like Brother Joe Stallard [a member of the congregation]; he puts me in

Brother John talks to Brother Joe Stallard, who reminds him of his father, 1985.

the mind of my daddy a whole lot. And of course I act the fool with him and take him places where I go when I can. It's not easy . . ." (John and Pauline Sherfey interview, October 7, 1985).

John began attending church quite early in life. He remembers seeing his father lead the hymn-singing at the Howard's Creek Union Baptist Church when John was six years old. He had started school at the Howard's Creek School, but the family moved from North Carolina to another farm near Three Springs, Virginia, where John Henry had relatives, although by this time John Henry's father had moved to eastern Tennessee, about halfway between Blountville and Kingsport. John went to school at Three Springs, but had difficulty because people were new and strange and John was bashful. "I didn't take to people too much when I was little. I would just shun them," he said (ibid., November 7, 1985, p. 3). He was not shy toward his family, however. When they first moved to Virginia they settled on a farm owned by a widow named Leffert, and the following year they moved to a neighboring farm owned by a railroad engineer, Lewis Pitts. The family sought to live in the homes of such part-time farmers, more or less running the farm and taking care of the young children with their own. The arrangement required almost no cash from the Sherfeys. They stayed in Virginia for about three years, attending the Three Springs Church, where Methodists and Baptists held services on alternate Sundays. The Sherfeys, like most people in the area, showed no preference and attended both sets of services. "You couldn't tell which was which," John said (ibid., p. 2). This kind of community church, where salvation is more important than denomination, has been a feature of all the churches John has pastored.

John's parents were both born-again Christians and raised their children in the ways of the church, taking them along as little children. John's father no longer led hymn-singing once they moved to Virginia, but he sat on the porch at home when he could spare a moment and sang hymns, sometimes accompanying himself on the banjo in clawhammer style. In his later years he sang hymns as he walked around the house, praying and talking to God.

John's parents and kinfolk took John to church and, at the age of nine, he went to the altar at Three Springs Church to be saved. It was a week-long revival, and he was sitting next to his father's sister, Ellar Bolling. At the time he felt he was saved, and he made a profession of faith; but in retrospect, he doubts he was saved then, for he did not fall under conviction, and his memory of the events is hazy:

When I went to the altar at nine years of age I had never been under conviction. Just the night that preacher preached, and of course my aunt was setting there, and she looked at me and she said, "Well, don't you feel like you ought to go to the altar?" Well, naturally, I said, "I do," and I went up and they prayed with me, and I felt pretty good. Of course now whether I got saved or not, I don't—I was just nine years old and I don't remember it too good. (Ibid., April 2, 1978, pp. 28–29)

But really and truly I didn't know any more when I got off the altar than when I went. Because I didn't make the commitment, I just done what they told me. (Ibid., November 7, 1985, p. 4)

At that time, in the early years of the Depression, many poor families chose to live as subsistence farmers rather than be unemployed in the town and cities, and the rural areas in the South gained in population, reversing a trend that had begun in the nineteenth century. In other words, the Sherfeys' way of life, though traditional and even old-fashioned, appeared to be a sound and successful adaptation to the crisis of the Depression; and John Henry Sherfey most likely took comfort in that.

In the early 1930s the family moved into the hills between Blountville and Kingsport, where John's paternal grandfather lived, and they repeated the pattern of moving onto a part-time farmer's land. More successful here, and with several kinfolk in the area, the Sherfeys remained in this section of Tennessee throughout the next few decades.

What are we to make of John's childhood? Certainly the classic ingredients for unhappiness and rebellion were there: a large, poor family; an illiterate father who knew only sharecropping as a way of life and could barely provide for his family; a strict upbringing, with the children forced to work from an early age, forced to attend church, and given little incentive to learn anything but farming as a way of life. Yet John remained obedient and was happy as a child. He took his cues from others. Safe among his family, he was shy with strangers.

John was unusually close to his father. He loved him and wished he could be strong like him, working the animals, plowing the ground, leading the household. He must also have feared his punishments. His childhood picture of his father as a stern, loving, powerful judge is of course the same as his adult picture of God. He had a longing for his father, perhaps best shown in his story of his father's shucking corn with bleeding hands (Chapters 2 and 5). As he grew older, he had to come to terms with the fact that his father was neither all-wise nor all-powerful, and that he was poor and that sharecroppers were given low status in the community. Perhaps this accounted for his withdrawal from the church—he did not attend much as a teenager—and for his eagerness to enter the adult world. He rebelled. His mother said of her children, "I tried to bring them all up to follow the Lord. Course then some of 'em strayed off. It's like John said. He did stray off but he come back. . . . He never was a wild person. . . . He was a good boy. He obeyed his daddy" (Josie Coffey Sherfey interview). Today he understands his father as a good man, practically a saint, enduring the hardships of his life, raising a family of twelve children, holding to Christian beliefs and ethics. He is nostalgic for his childhood. Certainly, this nostalgia fuels his desire to be with his parents and brothers and sisters once more at the heavenly homecoming.

Courtship, Marriage, and John's Second Experience at the Altar

Brother John met his future wife, Pauline Doran, in church. Pauline came from a large family, with four sisters and five brothers; and, like the Sherfeys, the Dorans were close. Her father had seen how to enter the cash economy: he and his sons cut pulpwood, and it was not long before he owned a farm and banked the surplus income from woodcutting. John remembers him as "a tight feller. He didn't mind spending a dollar if he could see where it was going. He's not like people are today. When he got hold of a dollar he held it till he—if he had to spend it he'd spend it, but if he didn't have to, he held it" (John and Pauline Sherfey interview, December 3, 1979, p. 33). By the time he and his wife grew old he had accumulated some money that they spent on doctor bills at the end of his life, and on support for Pauline's mother in the nursing home before she died. Pauline agreed that her father was stingy. "We didn't get the clothes that some people would get, and I thought, well, he could pay me the money and I could go buy something new" (ibid.). He paid her for working in the fields and around the house. Unlike John and his brothers and sisters, who moved out of northeastern Tennessee to find lives elsewhere, the Dorans stayed in the area, and remain there today. In courting and marrying Pauline, John was marrying above his station.

Sister Pauline's family and friends, ca. 1937. Her parents are seated in front. Pauline is the tall teenager with long dark hair standing in the spotted dress in the second row at the center-right. Photographer unknown.

Brother John and Sister Pauline, ca. 1939. Photo booth photo.

They courted awhile, broke it off, then got back together again and were married on November 23, 1940. An attractive photograph John and Pauline made in a photo booth, probably in Kingsport, at about this time shows them earnest and well-scrubbed. John has a sensitive look, slightly like the late actor James Dean. Neither was attending church regularly at the time, although Pauline, like John, had been taken to church as a child. Both were estranged from God, but it was not a matter of urgency to them. At seventeen (John) and eighteen (Pauline) they were anxious to enter adulthood and get on with their lives. Another photo from this period shows John standing next to Pauline with a cigarette dangling rakishly from his mouth and with his hand thrown possessively over her shoulder. John remembers his mother weeping when he told her he was going to marry, for she did not want him to leave home. Pauline's parents liked John, but they were reluctant to see her move out, because it would have left only one of their children, a brother older than Pauline, at home to help with the household. John recalled a joke his father-in-law told: "He always had a slogan, though: 'When my daughters gets married I'm gonna give 'em a thousand dollars apiece.' Then he'd wait a long time and he'd say, 'But they'll have to take a dog for five hundred and a cat for five hundred.' But to beat it all I didn't even get a dog and cat!" (ibid., November 7, 1985, p. 9). John sold a wheat crop he had growing in the field to buy the marriage license, and after he paid the preacher and the driver who took them to the church he had no money left. Without a honeymoon, they moved in with Pauline's parents, who had an extra room.

Brother John and Sister Pauline, ca. 1941. Photographer unknown.

John farmed for Pauline's father for about a year, then after both families gave them some household furnishings they moved up the mountain into a house owned by one of Pauline's brothers, and John went to work for him. But after John had gotten in a good wheat crop his restlessness got the better of him and he left the crop in the field for someone else to harvest. He was anxious to get away; he wanted the cash that a job in town could bring. In 1941 he took a job with the Mead Corporation, a papermaking company, in Kingsport, Tennessee, where two of Pauline's brothers, who worked there, had recommended him.

This was a period of stress in John's life; his sense of identity was changing. Now an adult, he had married and left farming to work at a factory in town. To make things more unsettling, the Mead Corporation changed his name. "So after I went to work in Kingsport in 1941 I told 'em that I went by my middle name. They said, 'You don't here. You go by your first name here.' Said, 'We call everybody by their first name.' So it started with John. Everybody there got to calling me John, so it's been from that time on as John. Pauline still calls me Claymon," he said (ibid., p. 2). The job itself was a challenge. To test him, they had him carry wood:

> I went down there and the first thing they put me to doing was carrying pulpwood. . . . Believe me, that'll kill you. You got to be a mule to do that. And I went out there and got some of that wood. You'd have to pick it on your shoulder, out of the boxcar, and carry it about ten ricks back, and then rick it up, and then go back and get you another one, do that all day long. (John and Pauline Sherfey interview, August 14, 1977, p. 4)

Eventually John told his boss he wanted to work inside, and said he would quit unless they gave him another job. He left for two days, then received a letter saying he could work indoors rewinding paper; the new job was hot but not difficult.

Pauline did not want children right away, but in January 1942 their first child, a son, J. C., was born. Now John experienced renewed religious feelings. Simon Moudy, John's uncle (brother to his father's first wife), held services in the farmhouses where the Sherfeys and other families lived near Blountville, and he asked John to accompany him. Simon called on John to sing, testify, and pray aloud at these home meetings. For John to do so, he must have felt then that he had been saved. Yet his life story and briefer versions of his conversion narrative (Chapter 7) indicate that he was saved several years later in a tent revival under the preaching of Brother Milburn Morlock. The puzzling incident is the "profession in earlier life" that he refers to in his life story (line 114).

It turns out that, aged about nineteen, John went to an altar in one of his uncle's services, repented, prayed for forgiveness, felt satisfied that he was saved, and dedicated his life to God (John and Pauline Sherfey interview, November 7, 1985, p. 14). John, Pauline, and I discussed this period in

their lives one Sunday afternoon in April 1978 as they sat in their house
trailer next to the church. At that time I did not know John had felt satisfied at the age of nineteen that he was saved. We were talking about John
accompanying his uncle Simon. "He'd call on you to pray and things,"
Pauline said to John, "and I know I sat there and thought, 'He's not living
right to do these things.'"

"I don't think that back then that I was totally—how do I want to say
this?—fully converted," John said. "I think I just more or less took it upon
my own self."

"He'd tell you you was all right, then," Pauline continued.

"A man can't tell you, though, that you're all right," said John, with
thirty-five years of hindsight. "They might say you are, but just because
you got a, you can handle words good or sing or something like that, it
don't make a man all right."

Pauline looked at me. "He had John believing it," she said.

The explanation, as I found out some years after this conversation, was
that Simon Moudy believed that once a person was saved he or she was
heaven-bound no matter what. He did not believe that backsliding would
take a person to hell if he or she died estranged from God. John characterizes this doctrine as "eternal security" and sometimes describes the belief as "once in grace, always in grace." It is an interpretation of the doctrine of the "perseverance of the saints," that the children of God will
persevere until the Judgment Day. In other words, although at the time
John knew he had sin in his life that he had not repented and been forgiven of, he believed he had been saved and enjoyed eternal security.

Who in John's place at the age of nineteen would not have thought that
his verbal gifts were a sign from God? In fact, John fell under conviction
and "felt my calling then to preach, but I wouldn't do it," he said (ibid.,
April 2, 1978, pp. 29–32). "I felt like the Lord was calling me to preach,
and then a lot of other folks, when you testify, they said, 'The Lord's calling
you to preach.' And naturally, that'll get you to believing it, see" (ibid., November 7, 1985, p. 14). Still taking direction from others, he spoke to his
family about what was happening to him. His mother recalled:

> When he first started out, the Lord called him, we all talked to him, and he
> said the Lord wanted him to work for the Lord. Well, we got him to go
> around homes, you see, and he was conducting services in homes, and he
> kept that up for a long time, and he finally said, well, he didn't see no need
> of that. (Josie Coffey Sherfey interview)

John recalls that he helped conduct services in homes for about a year. "So
then I strayed away, or I guess you'd call it backslid," he said (John and
Pauline Sherfey interview, April 2, 1978, p. 29). During those two years he
and Pauline moved their household numerous times. "Me and her moved I
think it was eighteen times in two or three years. How many times was it

Brother John and Sister Pauline with their first child, J. C., ca. 1942. Photographer unknown.

we moved?" John asked Pauline. "It was so many times I don't know," she said. "It was a bunch of times. . . . We just kept moving around. And I don't know why. I mean really, I don't know why; I have no explanation for it. Wasn't no use in it," he said (ibid., August 14, 1977, pp. 4–5). Moving signified John's restless mind and his continuing search for an adult identity. Under conviction, believing that God had called him to preach, not wanting to preach, his movements reflected his attempts to escape.

Looking back on this episode, Brother John's memory is unusually hazy. In his maturity he realizes that not everyone with verbal gifts belongs to the true church. He has seen too many false prophets to believe that verbal gifts alone are a sign of God's grace. Yet his recognition of his own immense abilities and their limitations came in conversation at a moment of considerable self-insight, for he now realizes that when he held services in homes with his uncle he was not "fully converted." That would not occur until several years later, after the death of his son Buddy Wayne and his experience in the tent revival under Brother Milburn Morlock—the centerpiece of his conversion narrative.

Conversion, for Brother John, was a more complex process than the conventions of his community's conversion narrative allow for. Those conventions demand that salvation be a single, instantaneous event, that it lead to perfect assurance, and that it be engraved in the memory in detail, so that it may be recalled at any moment. John was saved at the age of nineteen, or so he thought at the time, but subsequently he drifted away, and lost from memory the circumstances of that trip to the altar. "I had been saved, you see," he told me in 1985. "I just wasn't living as close as I should, but I'd been saved, and knew it."

"And was this at the age of nine, or—" I asked.

"No, this was at the next, it was running around with Simon Moudy. See, I'd been back to an altar again," John said. "And then I got to going around with him, see, and started singing, and testifying, and but there again I fully hadn't dedicated my all to God. And until you do, you just ain't, you're not all there, you see, you're not in the will of God. But when I went over to Milburn's—"

I pressed the point. "So then would it be truer to say that you were saved in the tent revival with Milburn Morlock, and you hadn't been saved before then, or that you were saved when you went to the altar with Simon and then backslid—"

"Backslid. Backslid is what happened," he said. "Strayed away and then came back, see. Yep. The story of it is that I was truly saved but, you know, it's like the Bible says: For joy they spring up for awhile, like the seed, you know. But the cares of the world choked it out. Things that I let get into my heart, my life, you see, and that killed the power of God. Because God cannot live in a dirty vessel" (John and Pauline Sherfey interview, November 7, 1985, p. 15). This is clear enough. He "knew" he had been saved then, so he must have backslid, and his experience in the tent revival was a rededication. Or was it? He had been saved, but not "fully converted." The conversion narrative does not allow room for such complexity. We will learn more as we pursue the events that led to John's return to the altar in the tent revival about ten years later.

When the United States entered World War II John had no desire to fight. "I didn't want to leave my wife and baby," he said. "So they put it out on radio that anybody that wanted to stay out of the army could go to farming. So they could raise crops [and aid in the war effort]" (ibid., August 14, 1977, p. 11). John returned to sharecropping and renting in 1944, again in the hills between Blountville and Kingsport. Like his father, he usually moved into a farmer's house, often an older farmer whose wife was ill or had died. Pauline took over the household duties while John helped in the fields. He farmed for a man named Vanderhawk for a year, and then moved into a schoolteacher/farmer's home:

> We've had to work hard all our lives. She [Pauline] used to go with me when I lived on Jim Freeman's place. Course Jim's dead. He was a schoolteacher. And she'd take the babies and lay 'em on a blanket, and she'd get her hoe and help me chop out corn, tobacco, and stuff like that. (Ibid., p. 5)

They were on the Freeman farm when the war was over, but instead of moving back to town they decided to continue farming, staying with Jim Freeman another two years. In 1948 John was contracted to sow a wheat crop for a farmer, Wesley Garland, who lived close to Blountville. He told a story of how he thought the world was coming to an end:

> And that's the time I got scared to death. I don't know whether I told you that one or not, but Wesley wanted me to come up and fix the ground for a wheat crop. Now wheat crop's what you sow in the fall of the year, and then in the summer, why, you'd reap it. So I went up there, and I left down next to the river and I had to walk. I didn't have a car and no way to go, so I was hitchhiking. And it's a good distance from down there in Blountville, probably about fifteen or twenty miles. So I started up through there walking, and in the meantime somebody in Knoxville, Tennessee, said that at that day, it was on a Wednesday, he said that at that day, at ten o'clock the Lord was coming. (Ibid., p. 6)

John was impressionable and believed what he heard on the radio: that the end of the world was at hand. Today he attributes his panic not to naïveté but to unfamiliarity with the Bible:

> Well, believe me, I hadn't studied the Bible enough to realize and understand, you know, and I thought he was. I was scared to death! I wasn't saved; I was on my road to hell if he'd have come. I'd have went to hell, see. And it had me scared to death. And I was going up that road, you

know, and I was afraid to take a step. I ain't kidding you. I was afraid to take a step. But after the time passed by and he didn't come, I said, "Well, thank God." And after I got to studying the Bible, you see, I found where that man was a liar. Because no man knows the coming of the Lord, not even to the angels which are in heaven. And then a man get up and say stuff like that on the radio! [*Laughs.*] (Ibid., p. 6)

It must have been a terrifying moment for him. He had not been living a Christian life. Estranged from God, he was convinced that if he died he would go to hell. By this time John and Pauline's second and third children, Wanda and Buddy Wayne, had been born, and John was tiring of farming again. A good hand on a farm, knowing with animals, skilled with tools, John had plenty of ability but little desire for farm work. They moved onto Wesley Garland's farm, but soon John's brother Ester became seriously ill with tuberculosis, and they visited him frequently in Kingsport. To be closer to his brother John took a job in Kingsport, driving a truck and hauling milk in the Tri-State region for the Roy King Company.

In 1949 Ester died, but before doing so he called his family to his bedside. "Many a time while he was real bad off he'd start singing, 'I'll Be a Friend to Jesus,' or some of the old songs he liked, like the one 'Lord, I've Been Waiting to Go.' And they'd have to hold him up in the bed while he shouted. And when he was dying he asked us all to meet him in heaven. And I made him a promise that I would" (ibid.). At that time John still had not repented, and no longer knew that he was saved. He could not accept the idea that he would go to heaven simply because he had dedicated his life to God at an altar six years earlier. He had not been attending church; he had not been praying; he had been outside the will of God. He drank; he took the Lord's name in vain; he gambled. In so doing he was no different from most of his coworkers in Kingsport. But he knew he was restless and would have to settle down someday.

The Death of Buddy Wayne Sherfey

In 1950 John and Pauline moved to Holston Institute near the Tri-City Airport in Kingsport. He returned to work at the Mead Corporation, and that year their son Donny was born. In 1951 their son Buddy Wayne became ill. "For some reason or other it didn't dawn on me that he was as sick as he was, and so finally at last [Pauline] said we ought to take him to the doctor" (John and Pauline Sherfey interview, October 7, 1985). Their regular doctor, a man named McDowell, was unavailable, so they drove to Bluff City and saw an unfamiliar doctor. She prescribed some medicine, but it did not help. Taking him back home, they reached Dr. McDowell, who paid a visit that afternoon. "He just walked in and looked at Buddy and started shaking his head," John said (ibid.). The doctor asked if John had any whiskey—he did not keep any in the house at the time, even though he was drinking—so John borrowed some from a neighbor, fashioned a "toddy" and gave it to the boy as Dr. McDowell instructed.

But the toddy did not help either. At about 7:30 in the evening Buddy Wayne died. In their living room, John picked him up in his arms when his "fingernails turned blue and his lips turned blue and his eyes rolled back in his head" (ibid.). Pauline, who was in the kitchen, sensed that the child was dying, and she screamed out to John, "Pray!" "Well, I couldn't pray," said John. "I had sin in my life, and I'd lived for the devil" (ibid., April 2, 1978, p. 29). "There was something between me and God," he said. "I hadn't confessed it, and so I had to fix things up with the Lord" (ibid., August 14, 1977, p. 8).

John believes that God's hand was in Buddy Wayne's death. "God had to impress her [Pauline] to scream or she never would have hollered out, 'Pray!' because she hadn't been going to church either" (ibid., October 7, 1985). Further, John now believes that God took Buddy Wayne to punish John for having backslid:

> I had been under conviction, and the fact of the matter is I had been con-
> verted [i.e., under Simon Moudy's preaching about nine years] before
> Buddy Wayne's death, but I hadn't surrendered. I had strayed away from
> the Lord, and therefore I think this was the whole thing: that God showed
> me that I wasn't going to do as I pleased, that I was bought with a price,
> see. And then he brought me back, or, well, he showed me that I'd better
> come back. And that was the whole thing, and then of course I fought it off
> for a long time. It went on anyway, after God took Buddy Wayne from me.
> But still, God was dealing with my heart. (Ibid., April 2, 1978, p. 28)
>
> I run from the Lord. And so then [I] gave up a five-year-old boy, and I
> believe it with all my heart that the reason God took him was to bring me
> into the fold of God. Because he had a job for me to do and he wanted me
> to preach. . . . (Ibid., October 7, 1985)

John's family agrees with John's interpretation of this turning point in his life. His sister Elsie told me God took Buddy Wayne because John had disobeyed a call to preach (Elsie Sherfey McNally interview). His mother said, "And that's when the Lord got ahold of him and come to bring him back. He said that he was on the wrong road and he had to come back, and he did. . . . He kindly dropped aside and dropped loose, and that's when the Lord took his boy away from him. He died in his arms" (Josie Coffey Sherfey interview).

John realizes that others might derive a different meaning from Buddy Wayne's death. I said to him, "You know, some people would interpret the death of a child, like Buddy Wayne, as a sign that there is no God." "No," he said. "If anything, it helped me to believe more that there was a God" (John and Pauline Sherfey interview, November 7, 1985, pp. 22–23). John yields to faith, because denying God would be intolerable. Denying God would mean that Buddy Wayne's death was meaningless. John must have a reason to believe in; his faith in God is unshakable.

The question remains, why did God not permit Buddy Wayne to live? John's explanation is, characteristically, based on analogy: God took away David's son (2 Samuel 12:15–18) because David had committed adultery. John points out in his life story that he himself had not committed adultery, but the nature of the sin is not the issue; the Bible shows that God chastises his children in this fashion (lines 136–146).

Buddy Wayne was John and Pauline's favorite among their children, and his death sent John into depression. For the next several months he drank heavily and gambled, betting on "just about anything" with his coworkers at the Mead Corporation. The gambling must have been an effort to convince himself he could control his chaotic life. One night he came home and Pauline told him he smelled like Beaver Creek, the waterway behind their house that carried sewage from the town. Trying to cover up his drinking, he lied and said he had fallen into the creek (John and Pauline Sherfey interview, October 7, 1985). In the midst of his despondency— he must have felt even guiltier for not having recognized how serious Buddy Wayne's illness was—he received a letter from his mother's brother, Charles Ristin Coffey. "He told me that this was the hand of God, that it was to chastise me. And not to blame God with it, but that I needed to get saved" (ibid.). I asked John if this was the first time he felt Buddy Wayne's death was a punishment from God. "No," he said. "I felt that even when she hollered out, 'Pray!', see, and I couldn't. Because I knew where I stood" (ibid., November 7, 1985, p. 23).

Fully Converted

In August 1952, not long after receiving the letter, John and Pauline decided to attend a nearby tent revival that was being held on school property in Gray's Station, Tennessee. They sat in their car, listening to the sermon over loudspeakers, and John fell under conviction. Never going into the tent, they drove back home. Unable to sleep, John vowed to God that he would repent at the altar the following night. After the vow John fell asleep. John had made up his mind to rededicate his life to God.

After work the next day, John, Pauline, and the children drove to the school grounds and entered the tent. Sitting close to Brother Milburn Morlock, the evangelist, it seemed to John that every word of the sermon was meant for him. When the sermon closed and Brother Milburn extended the invitation, John went to the altar, prayed, repented, and felt he was forgiven. "I just asked him to move everything out of my life and forgive me of what I'd done, see. And he did. And therefore he blessed me that night, and he's blessed me ever since" (John and Pauline Sherfey interview, April 2, 1978). Afterward, the same night, John felt the tempta-

Brother John and Sister Pauline at home, 1979.

tion of Satan and asked God to give him assurance:

> But before I got home, Satan said, "Now look at you. Look at you. You
> stood up over there, you cried and you told them people you was saved, but
> now look at you." O my God. I got home. I lived in a little three-room house
> behind my wife's daddy and mother. We lived there in, in that little house.
> Put 'em in the house and I started toward the barn. I got about halfway out
> to that old barn and I got on my knees. I said, "Lord, if that was real I felt
> over there tonight, I want to feel it again." Thank God, I felt it right there
> in the road. (Excerpted from a sermon at a revival meeting, September 6,
> 1977, at the New Home Baptist Church, Piney Creek, N.C. Transcription
> adapted from George 1978:61.)

The voluntary aspects of John's full conversion are worth attention. His movements were deliberate, from the time he decided to attend the meeting, to his vow in his bed, his covenant at the altar, and his request for assurance. Knowing what was expected of him, worried what else might happen if he failed to return to God, he went through conversion self-consciously, burning each step into his memory. Certainly, the emotional turmoil of the two days left an indelible mark on John; his memory of these experiences is strong, and from them he fashioned the conversion narrative that he tells in sermons, testimony, and conversation, and that provided texts for George's penetrating analysis (ibid.). I do not mean he deliberately chose to go to the revival in order to come out with a correct conversion and a proper narrative, finally to "do it right." Instead, I think, he yielded to the experiences in full knowledge of their meaning and significance, in so doing was fully converted, and then, with his verbal gifts, was able to fashion a conversion narrative that met his and his community's criteria and that also could serve him in his quest for a stable identity. Previously he had been converted but had not surrendered; this time he surrendered completely. A few days later Pauline went to the altar in the same revival:

> I waited to see what John was going to do, because we had made a start before then and seemed like it just didn't work, because John was, like he said, he was out doing some things that shouldn't have went on. And so I just kindly waited to see what he was going to do. So I think it was just about a week; the revival was still going on about a week in the gospel tent, and that's when, before any preaching—they had just started singing—I made my way to the altar, and that's when I accepted Christ as my blessed Savior. (John and Pauline Sherfey interview, November 7, 1985, p. 11)

Soon afterward John and Pauline were baptized together.

John and Pauline memorialized the death of their son. Numerous photos show them and the rest of the family making pilgrimages to his grave, pilgrimages that continue even today. A small photograph of Buddy Wayne was enlarged and hand-colored, and today it rests in their bedroom, atop a small cedar chest containing Buddy Wayne's clothes. I asked John if his parents had grieved much when they had lost children early on—six did not live to adulthood. Yes, he said, they had grieved heavily. Memorializing the dead child was a family tradition; here, coupled with the belief that the death was a punishment for John's sinfulness, it is no wonder that in his life story John declares, "There's a sword in my house forever" (line 149). The material evidence is in his bedroom, where he keeps it.

I have argued throughout this book that religion at the Fellowship Independent Baptist Church is not a compensation for powerlessness and poverty, but that it involves the deliberate use of inherited traditions to make life meaningful. John's life story is a case in point. Without the biblical tra-

Brother John at Buddy Wayne's grave, ca. 1952. Photographer unknown.

dition of God punishing sinfulness, without John's uncle pointing out God's chastisement in the death of Buddy Wayne, without the fundamentalist Christian traditions available to him, John most likely would have interpreted the death otherwise, or would not have felt compelled to interpret it at all. And even with those religious traditions at hand, some might have rejected the interpretation John accepted. Secure in the knowledge that he will meet Buddy Wayne again in heaven, bolstered by his vision of his Christian pilgrimage, climbing the narrow path toward Jesus and Buddy Wayne (Chapter 7), looking forward to seeing his mother and father again, he is reconciled. Does he think about them constantly, I asked? "It's hard," he said. "If you let your mind concentrate on them it would drive you nuts. Well, the same way with Buddy, you see. Because that's a part of you" (John and Pauline Sherfey interview, October 7, 1985).

Strengthened by these experiences, John was able to overcome the temptations that he had given in to beforehand:

> Well, back on the job, when I went back to work, you know, the ones I had been running to the beer joints with, you know—you see, we got a fifteen-minute break and when we'd get this break all of us boys would—er, men—would pile into our cars and run over to the beer joint, up to the beer joint. We'd sit there and drink down two or three mugs, you know, as fast as we could drink it. And then we'd go back to the plant with our eyes all blurred and everything. . . . And after the Lord saved me, why, we started a prayer meeting at the end of the building where you go out, which was a fire escape. . . . And quite a few of us—sometimes we'd have fifteen or twenty of us up there for prayer service. But some of the men that I'd drank with said, "We'll give him two weeks and he'll be back with us." Well, it's been twenty-three years, honey, and I ain't been back yet! [*Laughs.*] (Adapted from George 1978:23. The interview, by George, took place July 28, 1975.)

Fred Weston, a coworker at the Mead Corporation, who sang bass in the Moving On Quartet, heard John's testifying and praying and, impressed with his facility with words, told him he thought God was calling him to preach. John felt the same call—he had felt it earlier, after he was saved under Simon Moudy's preaching—but struggled against it. He knew that a preacher's life was a difficult life, and he wondered if he had the strength for it. In retrospect, he believed Satan put these doubts in his mind, and told him he could not preach because he lacked education. But John was convinced that God calls men into the ministry, and that education is secondary. Eventually (see John's call-to-preach narrative in Chapter 7) he gave in and accepted a call to the ministry. He announced his call to Brother Milburn Morlock, who asked him to accompany him when he evangelized.

Rise and Decline of Brother John's Early Ministry

A Primitive Baptist, Brother Morlock's tent evangelism was unusual for that denomination, but not for that time and place. (Due to the changing nature of his beliefs, he became a Missionary Baptist in 1954. Evidently he had been a Jew before becoming a Christian.) John attempted to deliver his first sermon in 1953. He and Brother Morlock had gone down to an open field in Goshen Valley for a revival—John remembers that the sage-grass was so tall it came up to their waists—and John, wanting to impress everyone, had practically memorized John 15 and the sermon he hoped to deliver. But when it came time to preach, he forgot everything. He cried, testified, told them his conversion narrative, but did not preach. Next time, however, he let God lead him instead of trying to memorize a sermon, and he was able to preach. On November 14, 1953, John was ordained as a preacher by Brother Morlock and his congregation, the Greenvale Primitive Baptist Church, in Gray's Station.

In 1954 John began a Sunday morning radio ministry on WKIN in Kingsport, preaching and singing for a half-hour. He was preceded by another preacher, Lester Smith, who had a half-hour program as well:

> He come on first. Because he'd get in the Spirit, you know, when he'd get preaching, he'd get caught away in the Spirit, and he went out the door one morning, after he went off the air, he was still preaching when he went out the door. And he kept on preaching, and when he got outside and got in the car, they said he left preaching. So the next Sunday, when he came back, I was setting on the piano stool—they had a piano in there. I called him up there and I said, "Lester?" I said, "If you ever in your life do again what you did last Sunday I'm going to kick you just as hard as I can kick you."
>
> He said, "What's that, Brother John?"
>
> I said, "You went out of here preaching, got in your car preaching, and left preaching." I said, "Now the time's paid for, it's God's time, use it. Don't never leave when God's preaching you like that."
>
> So that same day, that same Sunday, he got caught away again. [*Laughs.*] He said, "Brother John, can I have a few minutes?"
>
> I said, "Help yourself, brother." The announcer didn't even cut us off, see. He just went right on. And you know there was a man met me at the door when I went out that morning, out of the radio station, and he said, "I'm going to pay for your time. Any man that will let somebody else go over on his time like that, I'm going to pay for your whole broadcast." He gave me a check to pay for the whole broadcast. (John and Pauline Sherfey interview, August 14, 1977, p. 19)

John stayed on WKIN for the next three-and-a-half years, following Lester Smith and no doubt absorbing some of his preaching style. His son Charles

Brother John reading the Bible, ca. 1954. Photographer unknown.

was born in 1953, and his son Dana Joe in 1956. It was difficult for Pauline and the children at home while John traveled to preach in revivals in the Tri-State area, but John felt he must obey the Lord. He pastored a community church at Fordtown, the area near Blountville where he lived. Increasingly he thought of himself as an evangelist, and in the mid-1950s he left his job at the Mead Corporation to travel and preach on a full-time basis. But he gradually realized he was not going to be able to support his family from the offerings he received. In the late 1950s he took a job in Kingsport as a house carpenter; but the company he worked for went bankrupt. After a period of unemployment, he took the job of night jailer at the Bristol jail.

At this time his religious feelings declined once more. He virtually ceased his ministry and stopped regular churchgoing. Looking back on this period, he attributes the slackening of his religious zeal to the people he associated with at the jail. "With people a-cussing and drunks and every kind of [evil] thing in the world that you can think of, it was there [in

Sister Pauline with Donny, ca. 1953. Photographer unknown.

the jail]" (ibid., November 7, 1985). "They cuss you and everything. It's terrible, what you have to go through. . . . Well, you've got drunk women; you've got drunk men. You've got people wants to fight. And all that kind of stuff, you know. And foul language. It's terrible. . . . [So] I had got cold and indifferent [to God because] of hearing all that stuff, and everything. Didn't preach [anymore]. . . . But I'll never [be a jailer] again. I know they holler we ought to have preachers and Christians in law enforcements, and we ought to do it. But that's nothing for me. I can't cope with it. My Bible says, 'Shun the very appearance of evil.' And they're cussing you and spitting at you and everything else. It's just too much for me" (ibid., August 14, 1977, pp. 13–14). John could not show charity to these people; it was impossible to act as if they were redeemable.

As we have seen, John had always been impressionable, following and joining in the activities of those around him, finding it difficult to resist on principle, doubtless because he wanted to be liked and accepted. Working as a jailer in Kingsport took a strong internal constitution, something John had for periods in his life when he lived close to God; that is, when he felt the presence of the indwelling Spirit. But now, despite having been fully converted only a few years earlier, and having gone into the ministry, he must again have had his doubts: why was God not providing? Some of the stories he tells about this period in his life (e.g., "I'm Here and I Don't Know Why I'm Here" [Titon and George 1977:30–31]) illustrate divine providence in the form of food or money, but the fact is that on his salary of $250 per month he could not pay his bills and eventually realized he must look for work elsewhere.

One of his brothers—Ray—told him good-paying jobs were to be had in the Washington, D.C., area, so he came up there late in 1960 to scout around. Soon he got a job with a moving company, Kneeland Transfer, but after a few weeks he quit; hauling furniture around was not to his liking. Next he found a job delivering oil for Robert Shreve Fuel in Falls Church; it was a good job, and he rented an apartment there and brought the family up on New Year's Day, 1961. "Snowed all the way up here," he said. "Had a wreck coming up!" (John and Pauline Sherfey interview, August 14, 1977). But it was not serious, nor an omen; for the next nineteen years he worked as a truck driver and mechanic in the Falls Church area, earning enough money to provide for his family while his sons and daughters grew to maturity.

Brother John's Rededication to God and the Ministry

With his economic crisis over, John was ready to renew his religious commitment once more. His life shows a pattern of ebb and flow: he came to the altar and dedicated himself to God at the age of nine, then strayed away; he rededicated himself to God and was saved under his uncle's preaching at the age of nineteen and felt his call to preach but fought it and after a year or so strayed away once more; he was fully converted and baptized at the age of twenty-nine, accepted the call to preach and evangelized for six or seven years, but then lost his religious fervor yet again. At thirty-nine, in Falls Church, working for the Irwin Concrete Company, he was sought out by a Baptist minister, Lester Horton:

> Lester came over and talked to me. Somebody told him I was up here. . . .
> He asked me to come down to the church. He said, told me where it was,
> and, why, I didn't know a bit more how to get down there than nothing. So
> he just kind of dismissed it and left, and it wasn't long, maybe a few weeks
> or a week or two went by, and he came back, with a feller named Shotgun
> Johnson. And Shotgun said, he started talking to me, he said, "You re-
> member me, don't you?" I said, "Yessir, I sure do." And then of course
> Lester told me he was having service Sunday morning at ten, said, "Why
> don't you come on down?" I said, "I'll do that." And I did. (John and Pauline
> Sherfey interview, November 7, 1985, p. 18)

Horton, a stranger, was unable to convince John to make the effort to find the church, but an old friend from home, Shotgun Johnson, persuaded him. John went back to the altar that Sunday morning: "I'd made up my mind that I was going to get in it and stay in it, and I promised God that morning that I would, and I have" (ibid.). This was the fourth, last, and most deliberate of John's covenants with God. Each time he had made such a covenant, except for the first (about which we have almost no information), he resolved a deepening crisis in his life. By nineteen he had left his home and family, had married, and had changed from farm to factory work; his first son had been born. Needing stability in his life in the face of all this change, he was led to the altar. At twenty-nine the crisis was, of course, the death of Buddy Wayne. At thirty-nine it was poverty, debt, and a job that caused him pain. His life, therefore, shows a cyclical pattern of movement into and away from the will of God, rather than the linear, instantaneous conversion required by the conventions of the Saul-modeled conversion narrative, and that is how his biography is at odds with his life story. The why of it, as I have written earlier, concerns the demands of public performance coupled with private needs for coherence of the presented self during life storytelling, along with John's analogical cast of mind and his urge to resolve ambiguity.

Soon afterward, John began traveling with Lester Horton, helping him evangelize in the Washington, D.C., area. Horton was a Freewill Baptist, and John was ordained a preacher in that denomination. He preached in homes in Maryland, and regularly in a home in West Virginia on Saturday nights. Again, John repeated the pattern of traveling and evangelizing under the wing of the older man whose altar he had used to rededicate himself to God: first Simon Moudy, then Milburn Morlock, then Lester Horton. Some visitors from Page County heard John preach in Horton's home church, and in 1964 they invited him to preach in a revival at their church, the Stanley Freewill Baptist Church. That took John into Page County. After preaching in the revival, he accepted an invitation to preach regularly there every fourth Saturday night. In 1967 John accepted an invitation to become pastor of the Comertown Freewill Baptist Church, in the southern part of Page County near Shenandoah.

Under John's leadership the Comertown congregation grew until it was larger than the church building could accommodate. They built another structure, and paid for it, but rivalry within the church led to dissension, and eventually John and nineteen others left to form another congregation (Chapter 3). Calling themselves the Fellowship Freewill Baptist Church, they rented the old Graves (Methodist) Chapel in Stanley, standing unused at the time, in 1971, then bought two acres of land at the base of Roundhead Mountain just southeast of Stanley and two years later had built a brick church on the site. Withdrawing from the Freewill denomination (for their reasons, see Chapter 3), they declared themselves the Fellowship Independent Baptist Church. John remained pastor, commuting from the Falls Church area until 1979, when the church voted to pay him a salary, and he and Pauline moved into a house trailer next to the church, where they have lived ever since. John took a job as a bagger at a local supermarket to supplement his $75 per week church salary, but in 1983 the supermarket closed and he has worked at odd jobs ever since. His salary in 1985 was $125 per week, and it was supplemented by Social Security income.

Living in Page County next to the church he pastors, John is near two of his sons and their families. Donny and Charles live a few miles away, and Dana Joe and his family come down from West Virginia for church on Sundays. With three generations of Sherfeys in the congregation, and John as patriarch, there are often as many as sixteen Sherfeys present at any given service, and they comprise nearly one-fourth of the congregation. Steadfast in his faith, happy that the church is growing slowly but surely, John continues in his path close to God.

From Husbandry through Performance to Community

In Chapter 2 I wrote that we could understand the mountain-farming mind-set best through the metaphor of husbandry: a man's loving relationship to the land, to his wife and family, and to God. Not all mountain farmers had this worldview, of course; but those of a religious bent did, and many were religious in spirit even though they did not attend church. This mountain-farming mind-set passed into the older people in the Fellowship Independent Baptist Church congregation, men and women who spent their childhoods and young adult lives on mountain farms, chiefly through their parents. Brother John's father, for example, is a case in point; his devotion to the land, to his family, and to God was exemplary.

But John's is a generation in transition, from mountain farming to town life and blue-collar wage work in factories, driving trucks, and so forth. John could not follow his father, could not be a sharecropper; he was restless and wanted more of what the world could bring him. Husbandry was not easy for him. At nineteen he had a new name, a new job, and a new baby. At twenty-nine a favorite child died. At thirty-nine he could not provide for his family. Again excepting his trip to the altar at age nine, his covenants with God resolved crises involving stress in husbandry as well as identity. John is a loving patriarch now, but it was not always so. In his twenties he was rough and had a mean temper. His son Donny told me he thought one reason J. C. (b. 1942, John and Pauline's oldest child) is unsaved is that as a boy he experienced too much of his father's anger (Donny and Jeannie Sherfey interview, November 17, 1985). Both J. C. and Wanda (the next oldest child) live in the Washington, D.C., area, both have much higher family incomes than the other Sherfey children, and, though they visit, they seldom go to his church. They have moved outside their parents' social and religious sphere. Donny, Charles, and Dana and their families are inside it; they take up roles in the church and live close by, visiting often. Still, they are in the modern world. As truck drivers, they commute from Page County and work in the Washington, D.C., area. Donny's passion as a teenager was drag racing; today he is a truck driver and a fine mechanic. John preaches that woman's place is in the home, but Donny's wife, Jeannie, works forty hours a week at the local Tastee-Freeze, and outside the pulpit John is perfectly well reconciled to it. Asked why she works, she told me she started in order to buy a car for herself, continued to help Donny pay for a new pickup, and continues still to help meet payments on their new house. Charles' wife, Pammie, works too, now that her youngest child is in school. Charles was an outstanding athlete in school, and still can pass or kick a football sixty yards. He enjoys

Reminiscing over old family photos, 1985. *Left to right:* Jeff Titon, Brother Dana Sherfey (holding microphone), Sister Pauline, Kim (Dana and Sharon's baby daughter), Sister Sharon, Brother John. Photo by Barry Dornfeld.

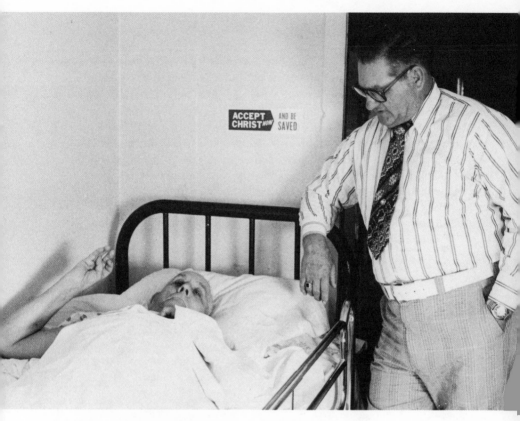

Brother John visits Brother Tom Breeden, 1978.

watching *Sesame Street* with his kids and loves *The Muppets*. He wants his children to go to college. Pammie is thinking of going to college so she can get a better job. Dana hopes to go to college himself someday.

Husbanding his congregation is difficult for John. His greater gift is for evangelizing and witnessing. He was a pastor at the Fordtown (Tennessee) Community Church for a brief period in the 1950s, but until he was appointed at Comertown in 1967 he had been chiefly an evangelist. Moreover, pastoral counseling was difficult for him when from 1967 until 1979 he lived two hours' drive from the community of his church. Only after he moved to Stanley in 1979 did he have time to concentrate on pastoral duties. Without years of experience in it, and without a great deal of natural talent for it, he nevertheless tries as best he can. He visits the sick, and counsels people in difficulty. But despite his conversational gifts, he struggles to find the patience necessary to spend day after day with members of his congregation. Besides, kin networks remain strong, people are close, and there is much he does not know about his flock. He can and does counsel them about the Lord; social work is beyond him, perhaps even irrelevant. Troubles are Satan's doing; their resolution involves listening to the still, small voice of the indwelling Spirit. People are weak; they have not fully surrendered; there comes a point when as pastor he can do no more. The weak and wounded must take the initiative and yield to God and be healed and whole.

Husbandry integrates the initiative of performance with the empathy of friendship. In this culture, men are the chief public performers; too much from women is suspect. Women gifted in performance sing or testify; they do not preach or teach. Brother John, of course, is a superb performer. Performance gives the lie to the Victorian themes of passivity and control. "There'll be some shouting in the air" when the church rises to heaven, John often says. Passivity and self-control are social virtues "up in society," but John does not encourage them in worship. "I believe in shouting; if you want to shout, shout, and I'll shout with you. If you want to cry, I'll cry with you," John says—and he does.

There is more to performance than shouting and crying, needless to say, and John's gifts to sing, preach, and interpret should be well known by now. Language in religious practice—whether in song, prayer, sermons, Sunday school, or testimony—is performed. Having affective power, language establishes and maintains, and reestablishes, and alters, individual identity and social relationships. Religious language does so by establishing and maintaining the believer's identity (as a particular sort of Christian) and social relationships, both among believers and between the believer(s) and the divine. The church is a community of believers established by language.

So, too, in the church members' families, the language of husbandry establishes and maintains bonds. Clothing, shelter, and food, particularly food, with its associations in the heavenly homecoming, provide the metaphors for performance. John's life story portrays him as a family man and a child of God. Children are thought to be antitypes of their parents; they fulfill their desires, are later revelations of their parents' characters. Identity is maintained through community-approved performance, passed down through the generations, through history, as religious folklife. Why is it so necessary to maintain identity? Is it so fragile? Does the world tempt continuously? Or is it, rather, to experience the force of language in organizing one's experience and others', to order it through analogy, and thus to comprehend it? John's urge toward the mastery of interpretation cannot be denied. In a passage from a sermon delivered on the morning of July 7, 1977, he united the various themes of husbandry—the land, family, food, and the church—in a prophecy of the heavenly homecoming reunion banquet. When he begins, he is talking about the church as God's children:

Brother Donny holds Denise while they sing a special-hymn. Brother Charles holds Cameron in background. WRAA (Luray, Virginia) radio studio, 1977.

I'm listening for that cry:
Come home, children, come home.
I've told you many of a time,
used to, we lived in the old houses,
the snow'd blow through the cracks in your face;
I'm not complaining about that,
but thanks be to God, many times we'd be cold, we'd be out sleighriding,
riding a sleigh in the snow;
Mother'd walk out on the porch and holler,
"Children, come on in; it's suppertime.
Come on in." We'd go in the house. A lot of times it was bean soup and
cornbread.
But oh, how good it was to come in out of the cold,
and hear that sweet voice of Mama as she walked on the porch,
said, "Come home, come on in, children; it's suppertime."
Thanks be to God, I'm listening to that voice from heaven this morning.
One day he'll cry out and say, "Come on home, children; it's suppertime."
Thank God, the call for suppertime.
Thank God, the call for suppertime.

A splendid performance, this, drawing on personal reminiscence and a
scene that all of his generation in the church can identify with, rural poverty and the call to the dinner table, the reward not the food but the fellowship and the "sweet voice" of mother, and then, typically, the leap that
makes the scene a metaphor of heaven, with the voice of Jesus and the
homecoming reunion. This is Brother John at his performing best, weld-
ing the church members into one through personal narrative, passing tradition through individual experience to forge communal truth.

Epilogue

 t was a warm October night in 1985. I was back in Page County for
three months to shoot the *Powerhouse for God* documentary film.
Barry Dornfeld and I lugged our sound, camera, and lighting equip-
ment into Brother John and Sister Pauline's house trailer next to the
church. We had visited some after supper, and now we wanted to film
some of John's stories. I would ask him to tell about his life with God.

As we sat there talking, I thought about the ten years that had passed
since I became acquainted with John. How much had the church changed?
Had he changed? Had I changed? What perceptible changes had been
worked over nine years into a book, three months (or would it be twelve
years?) into a film? The ground of the "ethnographic present" was shift-
ing under me, for I had noticed changes. I had changed in ways I had not
anticipated. Initially fascinated by John as a preacher, and thrilled to hear
such a fine traditional Appalachian singer, I had become his friend. Although I was still thinking and writing about language in religious practice, I had taken him and his family into my consciousness. We had
adopted each other, and now that the film was underway, Tom and Barry
were being adopted as well. When Jeannie showed up one Sunday looking
very pale, telling me she was having migraine headaches, I was surprised
at how upset and concerned I was. I sought for signs that the Sherfey
grandchildren wanted to go to college. I remembered Denise and Tammy
singing in Donny's arms when they were five and eight; now they were in
high school. Tom and Barry felt especially close to John's son Charles, an
easy-going fellow and a great athlete; athletics meant a lot to them. We
had become concerned about one another. What would happen to them?
We had planned to come back next August to film the homecoming; now
we thought we would return for the homecoming and hire someone else to
film it.

There had been changes in the church, too. As the congregation grew,
late in the 1970s, I wondered if it would move away from its folk-cultural
traditions and become more of an establishment church. When I visited in
1981 I learned that Brother John had been attending seminars on minis-

terial work, driving to Maryland to do so. No doubt his community responsibilities presented him with new problems now that he was a full-time
pastor and, typically, he recognized his need to become a better counselor.
But in 1982 he stopped; he had learned what they could teach him,
he said.

There were other changes. In the early 1980s Brother John no longer
drove directly from the Sunday morning service to do the radio broadcast
at WRAA in Luray; instead, he recorded a tape at the morning service that
included a prayer, the special-hymns, and as much of the message as fit in
the half-hour's allotted time; and he or one of the church members living
in Luray took the tape over in time for broadcast that afternoon. By 1983
he had abandoned the radio ministry altogether, saying he felt it was ineffective. Preaching only two sermons on Sundays instead of three helps
conserve Brother John's voice and energy. His zeal has not diminished, he
says; it's just his aging body letting him down. Yet in 1985 he was talking
about resuming the radio broadcast and had gone to the studio to see
when he could get back on. Television, he thinks, would be even better.

A change occurred in the hymnody, in that with more members in the
congregation, they now have musicians to accompany the singing in all
the services. John has returned to the guitar, Donny plays electric bass, his
daughter Denise plays piano—all by ear—and other musicians contribute
on guitars, harmonicas, and a banjo. So long as this accompaniment
makes the singing stronger and livelier, they are happy to have it and glad
to let the musicians do what they can for the Lord. Two of the younger
church members, Sister Sharon and Sister Virginia, took over the role of
songleader in 1983 to allow Brother John to concentrate more on preaching. They, rather than the congregation, now select the congregational
hymns to be sung at the start of each service. In 1985 Sister Virginia told
me this was because they did not know how to lead most of the hymns in
the book. If this is a loss for Spirit-led performance, it is a gain for women
in the church. Their strong voices ring out during the hymnody. Sister
Denise (Brother Donny's daughter and Brother John's granddaughter) has
an unbelievably powerful voice, louder by far than anyone else in the
church, including her grandfather; when she learns to add subtlety, she
will be an outstanding singer, with a professional career open to her. So
will her sister, Tammy. "This is what the young Dolly Parton must have
sounded like," Cameron Nickels, himself a country singer of no little ac-
complishment, told me.

In the early 1980s the elders decided not to offer the healing prayer at
every service. Brother John will hold one if asked, and did so once during
the three months of the fall of 1985 when I was there. The altar call brings
more to the altar now, as people come forward to be prayed for, either for
healing (this apart from the separate healing prayer), to draw closer to
God, to be saved, or to be restored to the faith after having moved away

from God. Finally, the testimony period just before the close of the service appears to have fallen by the wayside. People continue to testify before and after special-hymns, and on occasion a congregation member will answer Brother John's "All hearts and minds clear?" with a testimony before the benediction, but most services close without them. Brother John attributed the lack of testimonies to the absence of Sister Edith, now too old and infirm to attend. One powerful and moving testimony by Brother Jesse in October 1985 drew three people to the altar for prayer directly afterward, however. The healing prayers and testimonies have not been abandoned, then; there is space for them in the service, and when the Spirit moves, they occur. The Spirit simply moves in that direction less frequently, and many of the church members told me it was a sign of the falling off of the Spirit in the final days.

Some of these changes reflect modernization. Brother John said it was getting harder and harder to find a place to baptize in the Shenandoah River. In the spring of 1985 they held a baptism and had to remove dead chickens from the waters. He is reluctantly considering a baptismal pool in the church. The church bought seat cushions for the pews.

What is one to make of such changes? One explanation is that the church *is* becoming more modern, as a younger generation is being heard. Other voices than Brother John's are asserting themselves in the running of the church. Brother John still preaches from the King James Version and stands for his beliefs, but in 1983 the congregation had a second preacher, Ed Cave (since gone to pastor the Stanley Freewill Baptist Church), and in 1985 they had two other preachers, Kenny Stroupe and James Moomaw, though they preached only when Brother John asked if they wanted to. John calls them teachers, not preachers; they are not prophets, and they do not get carried away when anointed by the Spirit as he does. An assistant Sunday school teacher, Brother James Bailey, represents the younger generation; his reliance on interpretative aids to the Bible is a far cry from Sister Edith's illiteracy and dependence on the Spirit for guidance, but his sincerity is unquestioned, his doctrine does not differ from that of the older church members, and he is an effective and impressive teacher. Many of these changes in practice suggest flexibility in ideology, and their consequences for Spirit-led language have had a certain effect. Fewer people "amen" during the sermons, for example. With few testimonies there is less of an emphasis on Spirit-led performances from the congregation. Yet the church has grown. No longer drawing most of its membership from the middle-aged and elder members of the community—as it did in the mid-1970s—the congregation now has many young people—teenagers, young adults, people in their twenties and thirties; and the younger preachers and assistant Sunday school teacher appeal to them. Brother John is old-fashioned, and he knows it, and everyone knows it; and he knows, also, that for the continued strength of the church community, he must allow other, younger people to become prominently involved as performers and in church governance.

If in 1985 Brother John was singing and preaching as powerfully as ever—and he was—fewer people in the congregation were hanging on his every word. Some were restless. To an extent, Brother John has adapted himself. In his sermons he spends more time elaborating his ideas. He has become a teacher as well as a prophet. Always a master storyteller, he now makes his pulpit narratives more elaborate. He makes the congregation laugh. At sixty-two he seems happier now, more at peace with himself. Yet he still becomes fiercely anointed by the Spirit and preaches hard, chanting and fighting the devil, running in place and dancing behind the pulpit. He just does not do it as often.

These thoughts about the passage of time went through my mind as I began to ask John for life stories. I wanted to hear them exactly as I knew them, years ago; but we had changed, and the stories came out subtly different and somehow unsatisfying. So I decided to bring up incidents I knew of from others, but that he hadn't told me about.

I knew John had preached once in the Stanley homecoming parade, but we had never discussed it. I thought there must be a good story in it. The Stanley homecoming is a secular, town version of the church homecoming. Instead of affirming a reunion after death, it celebrates the community as it presently stands. It lasts a week, and features various kinds of entertainment in the evening, climaxing on the weekend with the parade. People who grew up and lived in or near Stanley return every year for it. No other town in Page County has a homecoming.

When I came to Page County in the summer of 1977 I wanted to see the local attractions, so I visited the Luray Caverns and went to the Stanley homecoming. The caverns were astonishing and monstrous, and I did not wonder that many stalactite and stalagmite formations had been given the harmless and domestic names (e.g., "Bacon and Eggs") that their shapes somehow suggested. The homecoming parade, domestic by design as well, was meant above all as an entertaining diversion from ordinary life that nevertheless celebrated and reaffirmed what was outstanding in ordinary life. Although different in kind from a church homecoming, with different performance principles, intentions, and interpretation, different affecting power, a different community, and a different history, it was no less a ritual than a worship service, and as I took up my post on the sidewalk of Stanley's Main Street, I knew I wanted to remember what I saw.

I saw actors playing roles, some more clearly defined than others, all artful. Here was the grand marshal, like all the others specially dressed for the occasion, standing on the back seat of a convertible. Here came the clowns, tossing candy to the children lining the streets. Here were the baton twirlers—hundreds of them. It turned out there were three categories of these majorettes: seniors, juniors, and tiny tots, with various groups representing different schools and civic groups and voluntary associations. And the bands! Elementary school bands, junior high school bands, high school bands, and crack outfits from neighboring counties, not to mention bands that formed around lodges and associations. Each passed by, marching, some playing college fight songs, others giving out with pop hits, current and not so current. One band played "Eleanor Rigby" and did a creditable job of it. Color guards came through, and the police, and the honorary police, and the firemen, and the honorary fire chief, and the antique cars, and the funny cars, and the horses, and the rescue squads. Meanwhile, local and state politicians worked the crowds along the streetsides. The mayor was there, and other county officials hoping to be reelected, and their opponents were there too, saying hello and mixing it up with the people. The governor of Virginia walked through too, shaking hands, and so did his opponent, working the other side of the street. They met and shook hands, exchanging pleasantries.

Mixed in with it all were the floats, clearly the major audience attraction. The homecoming queen and her court rode on the "official" homecoming float, decorated each year and stored at all other times where all could see, just off the main highway near Shenandoah. But there were many other queens. Miss Virginia was in the parade, in a convertible; and Virginia's Junior Miss showed up as well. Miss Teenage America paraded by on a float of her own, and they told me next year Miss National Teenager was scheduled to come. (In 1985 the Pre-Teen Miss Virginia lived in Stanley, and the parade then boasted two hometown queens.) And there were other floats: comic floats, depicting cartoons; commercial floats, from sportsman clubs, lodges, and local businesses; and even a few church buses and church floats. I wondered why Brother John and the Fellowship Independent Baptist Church did not have a float for the parade. I thought they just did not want to mix in such a worldly affair. But I learned later that they had had a float a few years earlier, had won first prize, and that John had preached so hard he never knew when they passed by the judges' stand. I asked him about it.

"I hear that once you preached in the Stanley homecoming parade," I said.

"Yes, oh yes," John replied, his voice becoming reflective. He looked over at Pauline. "That's been—how many years ago? Ten?"

"Eight or ten."

"Eight or ten years ago, Stanley homecoming, we built a float. We took the seats, those eight-foot pews out of the church, and put it on a wagon, and we took the amplifier and put loudspeakers on and used the microphones. And Donny and the girls sung as we was going out the town. But when we passed the judges' stand over in Stanley, I was a-preaching!" John became animated, and his voice became light and happy. "Man, the Lord had blessed me and the power of God was on me and I just, I mean

Tiny tot baton-twirlers, Stanley homecoming parade, 1977.

the Lord really preached me going right through Stanley. People just, I seen 'em hide their beer cans, some of 'em throwed 'em away." He laughed. "I mean that's one time they got rid of 'em! We had a time."

He described the float. "Of course we built the wagon up, we fixed the wagon just like if it was a church, you know. Had the rafters up there and the roof on it and all draped in. It was beautiful. And we won first prize in that category, which I thought was pretty good."

I reminded him about the judges' stand. "I understand when you went by the judges' stand you didn't even know that you passed it."

"I didn't. I didn't know I passed it. We went by it and some of 'em said, 'Well, you went by the judges' stand,' and I said, 'Where was it at?'" He laughed again, and shook his head.

"I didn't see it either," said Pauline.

I asked what Pauline was doing at the time. "She was sitting in the seat, wasn't you?" said John.

"Mmmm, I was in there singing," she said, laughing and enjoying the memory.

I never said to myself, "I wish I had been there to see it." I saw it through John's eyes, and that was pleasure enough. Going through the homecoming parade on their float, they had confronted the fallen, secular world of Stanley, but on their terms, not Stanley's. It may have been Stanley's homecoming, but John preached within the paradigm of the church homecoming. The crowd was embarrassed; some hid their beer cans. Others, perhaps more profoundly touched, threw them away. The town establishment judged them the best in the "commercial float" category, but John was carried away, anointed by the Spirit, and never noticed the judges' stand. Neither did Pauline.

Now, he thinks it is fitting that they won first prize; but they were not looking for a reward at the time. Their performance must have been so uncompromisingly authentic that the townspeople were caught off guard. Making use of family and community traditions, the church members had adopted a worldview and had sought and found an answer to the problem of meaning in life. The townspeople knew these traditions, and even if they had rejected them, they still had power over their lives. For a ritual moment, different worldviews confronted one another through performance. Uneasy with their appearance, some threw away beer cans, props of identity. Did they want to be in the church community? Did they expect to be some day? Or was it enough simply to enjoy the day, the warmth of the weather, the gathering of friends and acquaintances and loved ones, the pageant of the parade, the tiny tot majorettes barely able to walk straight, their mothers striding off to the side and ready to put them back on course? For this, too, was a tradition, and for many in the parade and alongside the road it served well enough to mark the movement of the seasons into the summer of the year.

Appendix A

Bylaws of the Fellowship
Independent Baptist Church

THE GOSPEL CALL

The call of the gospel[1] is co-extensive with atonement to all men,[2] both by the word and strivings of the spirit,[3] so that salvation is rendered equally possible to all;[4] and, if any fail of eternal life, the fault is wholly his own.

---

1. Matt. 28:19, Go ye, therefore, and teach all nations, baptizing them in the name of the Father, and of the Son, and of the Holy Ghost. 2 Cor. 13:14, the grace of the Lord Jesus Christ, and the love of God, and the communion of the Holy Ghost, be with you all. 1 Peter 1:2.
2. Mark 16:15, Go ye into all the world, and preach the gospel to every creature. Isa. 45:22, Look unto me, and be ye saved, all the ends of the earth. Prov. 8:4; Isa. 55:11; Rev. 22:17.
3. Joel 2:28, I will pour out my spirit upon all flesh. John 16:8; John 1:9; Isa. 55:11; Luke 2:10.
4. 1 Tim. 2:4, Who will have all men to be saved, and come unto the knowledge of the truth. Acts 10:34, God is no respector of persons. Ezek. 33:11; 2 Peter 3:9.

REPENTANCE

The repentance[1] which the Gospel requires includes a deep conviction, a penitential sorrow, an open confession, a decided hatred and an entire forsaking of all sin.[2] This repentance God has enjoined on all men; and without it in this life the sinner must perish eternally.[3]

---

1. Acts 3:19, Repent ye, therefore, and be converted, that your sins may be blotted out. Heb. 4:2; 11:6; Rom. 9:31, 32; Acts 13:38, 39.
2. 2 Cor. 7:10, For godly sorrow worketh repentance to salvation not to be repented of. Psa. 51:17; Prov. 28:13, He that covereth his sins shall not prosper; but whoso confesseth and forsaketh them, shall have mercy. Isa. 32:3, 5; Ezek. 36:31, Then shall ye remember your own evil ways, and your doings that were not good, and shall loathe yourselves in your own sight for your iniquities and for your abominations. Psa. 51:3, 4; Ezek. 18:30, Repent, and turn yourself from all your transgressions so iniquity shall not be your ruin.
3. Acts 17:30, But now commandeth all men everywhere to repent. Luke 13:5, But, except ye repent, ye shall all likewise perish. Acts 3:19.

FAITH

Saving faith is an assent of the mind to the fundamental truths of revelations,[1] an acceptance of the Gospel, through the influence of the Holy Ghost;[2] and a firm confidence and trust in Christ.[3] The fruit of faith is obedience to the Gospel.[4] The power to believe is the gift of God,[5] but believing is an act of the creature, which is required as a condition of pardon, and without which the sinner cannot obtain salvation.[6] All men are required to believe in Christ; and those who yield obedience to this requirement become the children of God by faith.

---

1. Heb. 11:6, He that cometh to God must believe that he is, and that he is a rewarder of them that diligently seek him. Heb. 11:1, Faith is the substance of things hoped for, the evidence of things not seen. John 5:46, 47; Rom. 10:9.

2. Rom. 10:10, With the heart man believeth unto righteousness. Gal. 5:22, But the fruit of the Spirit is . . . faith. 1 Cor. 12:8, 9.

3. Acts 16:31, Believe on the Lord Jesus Christ, and thou shalt be saved. John 3:16; Rom. 4:20–25; Eph. 3:12.

4. Jas. 2:17, Faith, if it hath not works, is dead, being alone. Gal. 5:6; 1 Tim. 1:5.

5. Phil. 1:29, Unto you it is given in the behalf of Christ, to believe on him. 2 Peter 1:1; Eph. 2:8.

6. John 3:36, He that believeth on the Son hath everlasting life; and he that believeth not the Son shall not see life; but the wrath of God abideth on him. Mark 16:16; John 8:21, 24; Heb. 11:6.

REGENERATION

As man is a fallen and sinful being, he must be regenerated,[1] in order to obtain salvation.[2] This change is an instantaneous renewal of the heart by the Holy Spirit,[3] whereby the penitent sinner receives new life, becomes a child of God,[4] and is disposed to serve Him.[5] This is called in Scriptures being born-again, born of the Spirit,[6] being quickened,[7] passing from death unto life,[8] and partaking of the divine nature.[9]

---

1. John 1:7, That all men through him might believe. Gal. 3:26, Ye are all the children of God by faith in Christ Jesus. Acts 10:43; Rom. 5:1; John 3:15.

2. John 3:3, Except a man be born again, he cannot see the kingdom of God. Heb. 12:14; Rev. 21:27; Gal. 5:19–21.

3. John 3:5, Except a man be born . . . of the Spirit, he cannot enter into the kingdom of God. John 1:13; Ezek. 36:26, 27; Titus 3:5; Eph. 2:10.

4. Rom. 8:16, The Spirit itself beareth witness with our Spirit, that we are the children of God. John 1:12; 5:25; James 1:18; 2 Cor. 5:17.

5. Ezek. 11:19, 20, And I will give them one heart, and I will put a new spirit within you; and I will take the stony heart out of their flesh, and will give them a heart of flesh: that they may walk in my statutes, and keep mine ordinances, and do them. 1 Peter 2:5.

6. John 3:6, That which is born of the Spirit is spirit. John 3:5–8; 1 John 4:7; 5:1.

7. Eph. 2:1, You hath he quickened, who were dead in trespasses and sins. Psa. 119:50, 93; Eph. 2:5; Col. 2:13.

8. John 5:24, He that heareth my word, and believeth on him that sent me . . . is passed from death unto life. 1 John 3:14.

9. 2 Peter 1:4, That by these ye might be partakers of the divine nature. Heb. 3:14.

JUSTIFICATION AND SANCTIFICATION

1. Justification. Personal justification implies that the person justified has been guilty before God; and, in consideration of the atonement of Christ, accepted by faith, the sinner is pardoned and absolved from the guilt of sin and restored to the divine favor.[1]

2. Sanctification. Sanctification is the continuing of God's grace by which

the Christian may constantly grow in grace and in the knowledge of the Lord Jesus Christ.[2]

---

1. Rom. 5:1, Therefore, being justified by faith, we have peace with God through our Lord Jesus Christ. Rom. 5:16, The free gift is of many offences unto justification. Acts 13:39; Isa. 53:11.

2. 1 Thess. 5:23, And the very God of peace sanctify you wholly: and I pray God that your whole spirit and soul and body be preserved blameless unto the coming of our Lord Jesus Christ. 2 Cor. 7:1; 2 Peter 3:18, Grow in grace, and in the knowledge of our Lord Jesus Christ. Heb. 6:1; 1 John 5:4; Col. 4:12; Prov. 4:18; 1 John 1:7, 9; 1 Peter 1:16.

PERSEVERANCE OF THE SAINTS

There are strong grounds to hope that the truly regenerate will persevere unto the end, and be saved, through the power of divine grace which is pledged for their support;[1] but their future obedience and final salvation are neither determined nor certain, since through infirmity and manifold temptations they are in danger of falling; and they ought therefore to watch and pray, lest they make a shipwreck of their faith and be lost.[2]

---

1. Rom. 8:38, 39, For I am persuaded, that neither death, nor height, nor life, nor angels, nor principalities, nor powers, nor depth, nor things present, nor things to come, nor any other creature, shall be able to separate us from the love of God, which is in Christ Jesus our Lord. 1 Cor. 10:13, God is faithful who will not suffer you to be tempted above that ye are able: but will with the temptation also make a way to escape, that ye may be able to bear it. 2 Cor. 12:9, My grace is sufficient for thee. Job. 17:9; Matt. 16:18; John 10:27, 28; Phil. 1:6.

2. 2 Chron. 15:2, The Lord is with you, while ye be with him . . . but if ye forsake him, he will forsake you. 2 Peter 1:10, Wherefore the rather, brethren, give diligence to make your calling and election sure; for if you do these things, ye shall never fall. Ezek. 33:18, When the righteous turneth from his righteousness, and committeth iniquity, he shall even die. John 15:6; 1 Cor. 10:12; Heb. 6:4–6; 12:15; 1 Chron. 28:9; Rev. 2:4; 1 Tim. 1:19; 2 Peter 2:20, 21; 1 Cor. 9:27; Matt. 24:13; Acts 1:25; Rev. 22:19.

THE SABBATH

This is one day in seven, which from the creation of the world God has set apart for sacred rest and holy service.[1] Under the former dispensation, the seventh day of the week was commemorative for the sabbath.[2] Under the Gospel, the first day of the week, in commemoration of the resurrection of Christ, and by authority of Christ and the apostles, is observed as the Christian Sabbath.[3]

On this day all men are required to refrain from secular labor and devote themselves to the worship and service of God.[4]

---

1. Gen. 2:3, God blessed the seventh day, and sanctified it. Mark 2:27, the Sabbath was made for man. Neh. 9:14.

2. Ex. 20:8–11, Remember the Sabbath day, to keep it holy. Six days shalt thou labor, and do all thy work: but the seventh day is the sabbath of the Lord thy God; in it thou shalt not do any work, thou, nor thy son, nor thy daughter, nor thy maid-servant, nor thy man-servant, nor thy cattle, nor thy stranger that is within thy gates. For in six days the Lord made heaven and earth, the sea, and all that is within, and rested the seventh day: wherefore the Lord blessed the Sabbath day, and hallowed it.

3. Luke 24:1–7, Now upon the first day of the week, very early in the morning, they came unto the sepulchre. . . . He is not here, but is risen. . . . Luke 24:33–36; John 20:19, 26; Acts 2:1, 20:7, and upon the first day of the week, when the disciples came together to break bread, Paul preached unto them. 1 Cor. 16:2, Rev. 1:10; Psa. 118:22–24.

4. Isa. 58:13, If thou turn away thy foot from the sabbath, from doing thy pleasure on my holy day; and call the sabbath a delight, the holy of the Lord, honorable; and shalt honor him, not doing thine own ways, nor finding thine own pleasure, nor speaking thine own words; then shalt thou delight thyself in the Lord. Isa. 56:2; Ex. 20:8–11.

THE CHURCH

A Christian Church is an organized body of believers in Christ, who statedly assemble to worship God, and who sustain the ordinances of the Gospel according to the Scriptures.[1] Believers in Christ are admitted to this church on giving evidence of faith in Christ, obtaining consent of the body, being baptized, and receiving the right hand of fellowship.[2] The church of God, or members of the body of Christ, is the whole body of Christians throughout the whole world, and none but the regenerate are its members.

---

1. 1 Cor. 1:2, Unto the Church of God which is at Corinth, to them that are sanctified in Christ Jesus, called to be saints. Acts 2:41, 47; 20:7; 1 Cor. 16:1, 2; Rev. 1:4.

2. Eph. 5:25, 27, Christ also loved the Church and gave himself for it . . . that he might present it to himself a glorious church. Eph. 1:22, 23; 1 Cor. 12:27, 28; Col. 1:18, 24; 1 Peter 2:5; John 18:36; 15:2, 6.

TITHING

Both the Old and New Scriptures teach tithing as God's financial plan for the support of his work.[1]

---

1. Gen. 14:20, And he gave him tithes of all. Gen. 28:22, Thou shalt truly tithe. Mal. 3:8–10, Will a man rob God? Yet you have robbed me. But ye say wherein have we robbed thee? In your tithes and offerings. Ye are cursed with a curse for ye have robbed me, even this whole nation. Bring ye all your tithes into the storehouse of God, that there may be meat in mine house. 1 Cor. 16:2, Upon the first day of the week let every one of you lay by him in store, as God hath prospered him. Matt. 23:23; 1 Cor. 9:9–14; Heb. 7:9–17; 2 Cor. 9:6–8.

THE GOSPEL MINISTRY

Qualifications of Ministers. They must possess good, natural and acquired abilities, deep and ardent piety, be especially called of God to the work, and ordained by prayer and the laying on of hands.[1]

Duties of Ministers. These are to preach the Word, administer the ordinances of the Gospel, visit their people, and otherwise perform the work of faithful Ministers.[2]

We affirm that preachers must preach the old King James Version Bible.

The minister must be a male. Because the Bible forbids women to usurp the authority over the man.[3]

---

1. 1 Tim. 4:14, With the laying on of the hands of the presbytery. 2 Tim. 1:6; Acts 13:3.

2. 2 Tim. 2:15, Study to show thyself approved unto God, a workman that needeth not to be ashamed, rightly dividing the word of truth. 1 Tim. 4:13–16, Till I come give attendance to reading, to exhortation, to doctrine. Neglect not the gift that is in thee. . . . Meditate upon these things, give thyself wholly to them; that thy profiting may appear to all. Titus 1:9; 2:7, 8; 2 Tim. 1:7; 2:2; 1 Tim. 3:2–7. Acts 20:28, Take heed therefore unto yourselves, and to all the flock, over which the Holy Ghost hath made you over-seers. Heb. 5:4; 1 Cor. 9:16; Acts 13:2. Mark 16:15, Go ye unto all the world and preach the gospel to every creature. 2 Tim. 4:2; 2 Cor. 4:5; Ezek. 33:7.

3. 1 Tim. 2:12, But I suffer not a woman to teach, nor to usurp authority over the man, but to be in silence.

EATING IN THE CHURCH

The Lord was against eating in church, as taught in the Bible.[1]

---

1. 1 Cor. 11:22, What have ye not houses to eat and drink in? 1 Cor. 11:34, And if any man hunger let him eat at home, that ye come not together unto condemnation. And the rest will I set in order when I come.

BAPTIZING IN THE CHURCH

John the Baptist was baptized in the river of Jordan. Jesus was baptized in the river of Jordan by John the Baptist.[1]

---

1. Mark 1:9, And it came to pass in those days that Jesus came from Nazareth of Galilee. And was baptized of John in Jordan. John 1:28, 29, These things were done in Bethabara, beyond Jordan where John was baptizing. Matt. 3:13.

ORDINANCES OF THE GOSPEL

1. Christian Baptism. This is the immersion of the Father, the Son, and the Holy Spirit, in which are represented the burial and resurrection of Christ, the death of Christians to the world, the washing of their souls from the pollution of sin, their rising to newness of life, their engagements to serve God, and their resurrection at the last day.[1]

2. The Lord's Supper. This is a commemoration of the death of Christ for our sins, in the use of the bread which He made the emblem of His broken body, and the cup, the emblem of his shed blood, and by it the believer expresses his love for Christ, his faith and hope in him, and pledges to him perpetual fidelity. It is the privilege and duty of all who have spiritual union with Christ to com-memorate his death; and no man has a right to forbid those tokens to the least of his disciples.[2]

3. Washing the Saints' Feet. This is a sacred ordinance, which teaches hu-mility, and reminds the believers of the necessity of a daily cleaning from all sins. It was instituted by the Lord Jesus Christ, and called an example of the night of His betrayal, and in connection with the institution of the Lord's Sup-per. It is the duty and the happy prerogative of every believer to observe this sacred ordinance.

1. Matt. 28:19, Baptizing them in the name of the Father, and of the Son, and of the Holy Ghost. Col. 2:12, Buried with him in baptism, wherein also ye are risen with him. Acts 8:36–39; Matt. 3:16; Mark 1:15; John 3:23; Acts 16:32–34; 2:41. Rom. 6:4, Wherefore we are buried with him by baptism into death: that like as Christ was raised up from the dead by the glory of the Father, even so we also should walk in newness of life. Col. 3:3; 2:12; Titus 3:5; Gal. 3:27; 1 Cor. 15:29.

2. 1 Cor. 11:23–26, For I have received of the Lord that which also I delivered unto you. That the Lord Jesus Christ, the same night in which he was betrayed, took bread; and when he had given thanks, he broke it, and said, Take, eat; this is my body, which is broken for you; this do in remembrance of me. After the same manner also he took the cup, when he had supped, saying, this cup is the New Testament in my blood; This do ye, as oft as ye drink it, in remembrance of me. For as oft as ye eat this bread, and drink this cup, ye do show the Lord's death till he come. Matt. 26:26–28. 1 Cor. 10:16, The cup of blessing which we bless, is it not the communion of the body of Christ? 1 Cor. 10:21; 11:27–29.

DEATH

As a result of sin, all mankind is subject to the death of the body.[1] The soul does not die with the body; but immediately after death enters into a conscious state of happiness or misery, according to the character here possessed.

---

1. Rom. 5:12, As by one man sin entered into the world, and death by sin; and so death passed upon all men, for that all have sinned. Heb. 9:27, It is appointed unto men once to die. 1 Cor. 15:22; Psa. 89:48; Eccl. 8:8.

SECOND COMING OF CHRIST

The Lord Jesus, who ascended on high, and sits at the right hand of God, will come again, to close the Gospel dispensation, glorify His saints, and judge the world.[1]

---

1. Acts 1:11, This same Jesus, which is taken up from you into heaven, shall so come in like manner as ye have seen him go into heaven. Matt. 25:31; 1 Cor. 15:24–28; 1 Thess. 4:15–17; 2 Thess. 1:7–10; 2 Peter 3:3–13; Matt. 24:42–44.

THE RESURRECTION

The Scriptures teach the resurrection of the bodies of all men each in its own order; they that have done good will come forth to the resurrection of life, and they that have done evil to the resurrection of damnation.[1]

---

1. John 5:28, 29, The hour is coming in which all that are in the graves shall hear his voice, and shall come forth; they that have done good, unto the resurrection of life; and they that have done evil, unto the resurrection of damnation. Acts 24:15; 1 Cor. 15:22, 23; 2 Tim. 2:18; Phil. 3:21; 1 Cor. 15:35–44; Dan. 12:2.

THE FINAL JUDGMENT AND FINAL RETRIBUTION

The Final Judgment. There will be a final judgment, when time and man's probation will be closed forever.[1] Then all men will be judged according to their works.[2]

Final Retribution. Immediately after the final judgment, the righteous will enter into eternal life, and the wicked will go into a state of endless punishment.[3]

---

1. Acts 17:31, Because he hath appointed a day, in which he will judge the world in righteousness. 1 Cor. 15:24; Rev. 10:6; 22:11; 2 Peter 3:11, 12; Eccl. 9:10.

2. 2 Cor. 5:10, For we must all appear before the judgment seat of Christ; that every one may receive the things done in his body, according to that he hath done, whether it be good or bad. Eccl. 12:14, For God shall bring every work into judgment, with every secret thing, whether it be good, or it be bad. Matt. 12:36; Rev. 20:12; Rom. 2:16.

3. Matt. 25:46, And these shall go away into everlasting punishment; but the righteous into life eternal. 2 Thess. 1:8–10, Taking vengeance on them that know not God, and they that obey not the gospel of our Lord Jesus Christ; who shall be punished with everlasting destruction from the presence of the Lord, and from the glory of his power; when he shall come to be glorified in his saints. Rom. 6:23; 2 Peter 1:11; Mark 3:29; 9:43, 44; Jude 7; Rev. 14:11; 21:7, 8, 27; Matt. 13:41–43; Rom. 2:6–10.

CHURCH COVENANT

Having given ourselves to God, by faith in Christ, and adopted the Word of God as our rule of faith and practice, we now give ourselves to one another by the will of God in this solemn covenant.

We promise by His grace to love and obey Him in all things, to avoid all appearance of evil, to abstain from all sinful amusements and unholy conformity to the world, from sanction or the use and sale of intoxicating beverages, and to "provide things honest in the sight of all men."

We agree faithfully to discharge our obligations in reference to the study of the Scriptures, secret prayer, family devotions, and public worship; and by self-denial, faith, and good works endeavor to "grow in grace and in the knowledge of our Lord and Savior Jesus Christ."

We will not forsake the assembling of ourselves together for church conferences, public worship, and the observation of the ordinances of the Gospel; nor fail to give according to our ability for the support of the church and all its benevolent work. We agree to accept Christian admonition and reproof with meekness, and to watch over one another in love, endeavoring to keep the unity of the Spirit in the bond of peace, to be careful of one another's happiness and reputation, and seek to strengthen the weak, encourage the afflicted, admonish the erring, and as far as we are able promote the success of the church and of the Gospel.

We will everywhere hold Christian principles and obligations supreme, esteem it our chief business to make Christ known to the world, and constantly pray and toil that the kingdom of God may come, and His will be done on earth as it is in heaven.

To this end we agree to cooperate in the promotions of denominational institutions and enterprises, the support of the work of the local church, and the evangelization of the world.

May the God of peace sanctify us wholly, and preserve us blameless unto the coming of our Lord Jesus Christ.

A NOTE ON THE SOURCES OF THE BYLAWS

Brother John told me that the above bylaws are the same as those of the Free-will Baptists, that the church accepted them when they began as the Fellow-ship Freewill Baptist Church, and kept them when they dissociated them-selves from the Freewill denomination.

Sources for most of the bylaws can be found in the "Revision of the Treatise and the Faith and Practices of the Free Will Baptists," adopted at the annual session of the National Association of Free Will Baptists in July 1948, at Poca-hontas, Arkansas. It is reprinted in Lumpkin 1959: 369–376.

The following bylaws do not appear in the "Revision": "Eating in the Church"; "Baptizing in the Church"; "Church Covenant"; and the portions of "The Gospel Ministry" that state that ministers must be male and preach from the King James Version of the Bible. The bylaw on "Baptizing in the Church" encourages, but does not seem to require, river baptism. It can safely be as-sumed that these additional bylaws pertain to this particular congregation.

Oddly, certain chapters of the "Revision" do not appear in the bylaws; these are chapters 1–7 and concern basic doctrinal matters: the infallibility of the Old and New Testaments; the perfect being and attributes of God; divine gov-ernment and providence; the creation and the fall of man; Jesus Christ; the atonement and Christ as mediator; and the Holy Spirit. These chapters must have been omitted through oversight, as nothing in them is contrary to the church's doctrine.

That doctrinal statements, amounting to a confession of faith, should, along with the church covenant, be made bylaws of the congregation, indicates that the group seeks unity in belief as well as practice.

How important are these bylaws? As rules of doctrine, they are exceedingly important, but they live in oral tradition, not in the booklet they are written in. In ten years I have not heard anyone mention them, and I discovered them by accident. To be sure, the booklet containing them is given to any new member on admission. But certain other things about them convince me that they be-long to oral tradition: the missing first seven chapters; and the requirements to support the Freewill denomination—which, of course, they decided to cease. Apparently, no one thought to excise the offending passages when they left the Freewills; it was unnecessary. Nor, I suspect, does anyone miss the first seven chapters. In character with this church, then, except for the Bible, what the members *know* takes precedence over what is written down.

Appendix B

Probate Inventories and Sale Bills
(Page County, Virginia, Shenandoah Iron Works District, Mountain and Valley Farmers)

(SOURCE: *Will books, Page County Courthouse, Luray, Virginia.
Discrepancies in totals are the result of items not tallied by the appraisers
and sellers, items tallied after totals were done, or copyists' errors.*)

I. Mountain Farmers, Heads of Household

1. JEREMIAH BREEDEN (D. 1851)

INVENTORY OF PERSONAL ESTATE OF JEREMIAH BREEDEN, NOV. 7, 1851

[Note: *At the estate sale most items were sold to Mildred Breeden, wife of the decedent.*]

Item	Value	Item	Value
white heifer	$5.00	walnut cupboard	$5.00
lot shoes	.75	book case	.50
template shoes	5.00	5 head sheep	7.50
shoemaker's tools, bench	3.00	lot cups & saucers	.25
6 shoe lasts	.06	1 gallon jug	.12
foot stand	.10	chest	.75
lot irons, bridle	.50	bedstead and bedding	2.00
broad axe	1.41	looking glass	.25
hand axe	.50	scythe and cradle	4.00
wood axe	.50	lot cabbage heads	1.50
corn cutter	.12	jointer plane	.50
1/2 bu. corn	.12	tongue and groove plane	2.50
set flooring dogs	.75	jack plane	.25
iron square, auger	.50	hand saw	.50
box brace and bits	1.00	foot adze	1.00
box trowels	.50	gauge, screw, compass	.75
lot chisels	1.00	6 head hogs @ $4.00	24.00
2 gauges	.37	4 barrels corn @ $1.75	7.00
2 smoothing planes & bit	.75	bedstead and bedding	5.00
set grand planes	3.00	crout tub	.16
lot of hay fodder	2.80	3 weeding hoes	.40
large distillery pot	1.00	4 chisels	.82
flour barrel	.12	froe	.12
tub	.50	stove	4.02
pr. hooks	.25	lot spoons	.26
churn	.37	shovel	.50

Total appraised value of estate: $75.06

2. Henry Cubbage (d. 1865)

Sale Bill of Personal Property of Henry Cubbage, 29 Dec. 1865

Item	Sold to	Value
2 old chairs	Lucy Cubbage (Lucy)	$ .50
1 corner cupboard	"	.50
1 looking glass	"	2.00
1 linen sheet	Simpson Cubbage	1.00
2 linen sheets	Lucy	2.00
1 rifle	Wesley Cubbage	10.00
2 wooden counterpanes	Lucy	8.50
2 " "	Martha Cubbage	7.50
1 bedstead, bed, bedding	Lucy	20.50
1 " " "	"	30.50
5 bu. rye, @ $1.25	David Dovel	6.25
45 bu. rye, @ $1.25	9 people	56.25
1 axe	Saylon Murray	.28
1 grindstone	Lucy	2.75
1 "	Saylon Murray	.20
5 bu. corn	David Dovel	3.42
1 cow bell	Pleasant Housden	2.05
1 wagon	Lucy	42.25
3 sows and 6 shoats	"	38.00
2 shoats @ $3.30	Dr. Keyser	6.60
2 shoats @ $2.50	"	5.00
2 shoats @ $2.40	Thomson Burner	4.80
2 shovel plows	Lucy	1.50
10 sheep @ $3.00	"	30.00
4 sheep @ $5.00	Henry Sours	20.00
4 sheep @ $5.45	"	21.80
4 sheep @ $4.25	David M. Dovel	17.00
4 sheep @ $4.25	Reuben Sours	17.00
1 red calf	William Corbin	8.25
1 " "	"	11.30
1 white face calf	"	7.55
1 bull	David M. Dovel	17.00
1 spotted steer	Reuben Nauman	21.00
1 white heifer	Lucy	18.00
1 cow	Wesley Cubbage	35.00
1 gray mare	Lucy	140.00
1 white mare (old)	"	75.00
1 cutting bin	"	2.00
3 bundles rye and straw	David M. Dovel	1.35
3 " " " "	"	1.35
1 set of shingles	Henry Sours	14.25
1 kitchen table	Lucy	.50

1 pot oven skillet	"	2.25
200 lb. pork @ 12 cents	"	24.00
100 lb. pork @ 12 cents	"	12.00
[plus a few other items, illegible]		

Total: $780.18

3. ELIAS BREEDEN (D. 1873)

Inventory and Appraisement of Personal Property Belonging to Elias
Breeden, Feb. 12, 1873

Item	Value	Item	Value
set shoemaker's tools	$2.00	watch and pistol	3.00
shoemaker's bench	.25	2 shotguns	4.00
set shoemaker's lasts	.50	shot powder	.25
old books	.10	cups & saucers	.50
grindstone	.50	bucket, noggin, & iron pot	.50
barrel and vinegar	3.00	shovel and tongs	.25
candle stand	.10	candle molds	.05
3 sheepskins	1.50	4 chairs	1.00
3 old barrels	.30	small basket	.10
flax wheel	1.00	lot old books	.10
2 planes	.50	old wheat fan	1.00
set tongue & groove planes	2.00	cutting box	.10
set old tools	.25	meat tub	.25
crosscut saw	2.00	kraut tub	.25
lot old irons	.50	2 augers & handsaw	.50
hatchet	.25	horse stretcher	.75
small desk and contents	1.50		

Total: $28.35

Sale Bill of Personal Property of Elias Breeden, dec'd., Feb. 12, 1873

Sold to	Item	Value
Alexander Hensley	brace & bits	$ .03
Henry Meadows	lot old irons	.05
—do—	—do—	.25
Alexander Hensley	—do—	.03
—do—	chisel	.12
Kelly Eppard	2 squares	.06
James Eppard	wood saw	.20
Thomas Breeden	hand axe	.11
Jewel Hensley	froe	.10

Stacy McDaniel	cooper's adz	.25
Henry Meadows	small hand saw	.50
James Hensley	auger	.31
Wesley Eppard	—do—	.25
Newton McDaniel	sheepskin	.75
Thomas S. Breeden	—do—	.50
S. M. Biedler	—do—	.80
Alexander Hensley	claw hammer	.07
Henry Meadows	awls	.31
Samuel Eppard	shoemaker's hammer	.30
Robert Hensley	lot old lasts	.19
Henry Meadows	clamp & knife	.14
—do—	peg & awls	.16
S. M. Biedler	chisel	.07
Henry Meadows	leather apron and tools	.07
—do—	pincers	.41
Alexander Hensley	shoemaker's rasp	.07
S. M. Biedler	awls	.18
Henry Meadows	shoemaker's bench	.05
—do—	grindstone	.85
—do—	flax wheel	2.00
Robert Hensley	grain scythe	.26
Henry Meadows	4 flour barrels	.20
—do—	candle stand & stretchers	.26
—do—	crosscut saw	5.95
—do—	barrel and vinegar	1.30
S. M. Biedler	shotgun	6.10
Alexander Hensley	shotgun	.50
William Marshall	shot pouch	.85
Thomas Hensley	pistol	2.90
Alexander Hensley	pistol moulds	.25
Samuel Eppard	watch	5.75
Thomas Breeden	cups & saucers	.24
Henry Meadows	glass tumblers	.18
George Bailey	box & contents	.02
Alexander Hensley	3 vials	.03
—do—	lot old books	.05
Stacy McDaniel	funnel	.15
James McDaniel	2 books	.12
Alexander Hensley	razor	.05
Thomas Breeden	small mirror	.30
Henry Meadows	gimblet	.11
James McDaniel	lot chisels	.18
Henry Meadows	tin pan basin	.70
Kelly Eppard	bottle	.01
Matthew Lamb	stone jug	.05
William A. Marshall	stone crocks	.10
Kelly Eppard	tin bucket	.16

Henry Meadows	coffee pot	.12
Kelly Eppard	noggin	.05
Thomas S. Breeden	shovel & tongs	1.00
Kelly Eppard	candle moulds	.10
Matthew Lamb	oven	.45
Stacy McDaniel	chair	.20
Henry Meadows	chair	1.10
—do—	chair	.95
—do—	chair	.75
George Bailey	lot old books	.02
Matthew Lamb	bible	.10
Henry Meadows	small basket	.55
—do—	small desk and contents	3.00
—do—	set tongue and groove planes	2.00
William Meadows	kraut tub	.05
Henry Meadows	meat tub	1.00
Thomas S. Breeden	cutting box	.06
Henry Meadows	wheat fan	3.10

Total: $51.19

4. Acra Cubbage (d. 1879)

Inventory and Appraise Bill of Personal Property of Acra Cubbage, 10 June 1879

Item	Value	Item	Value
10 flour barrels	$ .50	2 hammers	6.00
2 washing tubs @ 10 cents	.20	1 shovel plow	.75
1 firkin	.25	1 blind bridle	1.00
1 half bushel basket	.25	1 2-year-old colt	40.00
2 axes	.25	1 bedstead and bedding	15.00
2 bells	.20	1 set chairs	2.40
1 bucket and chain	.10	2 pillows and bolster	.75
2 plowplates	.13	1 bed curtain	.50
1 oil can	.10	1 sheet	.40
1 post auger and hatchet	.75	4 pillow slips	.40
1 saddle	6.00	2 feather ticks	4.00
1 riding bridle and halter	.75	1 linen tick	1.50
1 collar and saddle	1.25	6 goblets	.30
1 well bucket	.25	2 preserve dishes	.20
1 grain cradle	.25	1 preserve stand	.20
1 mowing scythe	1.00	2 pickle dishes	.30
1 wheel barrow	2.00	1 sow and 2 shoats	2.00

Total: $94.60

5. Henry Meadows (d. 1920)

Sale Bill of Personal Property of Henry Meadows, deceased,
made at Public Auction, 30 June 1920

Item	Value	Item	Value
1 sack dried fruit	$ .20	2 sacks beans	$ .30
1 small wheel	.20	1 spinning wheel	.50
1 table	.05	1 quilting frame set	.50
1 basket old irons	.45	1 corn planter & basket	.40
1 rasp and tools	.60	1 adze	.65
1 saddle	6.50	1 barrel and onions	.25
1 halter	.50	1 box onions	1.05
1 brace & bits	.75	2 boxes irons	.30
1 monkey wrench & auger	.75	2 bells	.25
2 dishes	.20	1 dish	.20
1 dish and cup	.15	3 dishes	.30
1 dish	.25	1 lot cups	.05
1 lot glass dishes	.50	1 bowl and glass	.10
1 dish	.50	6 glasses	.50
4 glasses	.25	1 lot tinware	.20
10 rods wire	3.75	1 lot forks	.12
1 stove	1.50	1 table	1.50
2 benches	.50	10 jars	.70
1 2-gal. jar	.25	2 jugs	1.00
1 jug	.25	1 tub	.80
3 jugs and 1 tub	.60	1 blacksmith's forge	3.80
1 grindstone	.50	1 harness and collar	15.50
2 barrels	.15	1 water cooler	2.25
1 grain cradle	2.10	1 scythe and snath	.40
1 scythe	.30	1 kraut cutter	.20
3 pans	1.15	1 bread pan	.30
1 jug	.15	1 cake pan and lid	.15
1 pan	.10	1 sausage mill	3.25
1 coffee mill	.10	1 pan	.40
19 fruit jars	.80	3 jars	.15
1 bowl	.20	1 washing machine	3.00
1 kettle	.85	26 lbs. ham	5.46
57 lbs. side meat	10.93	1 cider mill	1.90
bee stands	.80	2 garden hoes	1.00
1 saw	.50	1 plow	1.00
1 plow	1.30	1 buggy	7.25
1 black mare	135.00	1 horse	16.00
1 set harness	4.50	1 desk	.85
1 iron last	.40	1 basket	.80
1 can and seed	.80	1 shotgun	1.55
1 mirror	.50	1 bed and clothing	4.25

1 corn sheller	.35	1 keg	3.85
1 set scales	.50	1 lantern	.25
1 tea kettle and coffeepot	.30	1 kettle	1.75
1 strainer	.40	1 buggy harness	3.10
1 side saddle	12.00	1 cutting box	2.30
1 wheat fan	11.10	1 cow	63.00
1 square	1.05	1 hand saw	1.00
2 riding bridles	1.95	1 sheep shears	.25
1 lamp	.40	2 beds and bedding	21.00
1 rocker	2.00	1 bureau	5.00
1 parlor organ	10.00	1 dining table	2.50
1 safe	3.00	1 cook stove	15.00
1 feather tick	3.00	1 wagon	8.00

Total: $442.00

II. Two Representative Nineteenth-Century Page Valley Farmers, Heads of Household

1. JOHN KITE (D. 1850)

Sale Bill of Property of John Kite (of Henry), 7 June, 1850

Item	Price	Item	Price
ladle and skimmers	$ .62	2 shoats	1.00
set cup and saucers	.25	2″ auger	.40
set table spoons	.50	1″ auger	.14
set plates	.25	3/4″ auger	.13
9 plates	.25	small auger	.16
2 dishes	.25	half bushel manure	.41
6 bowls	.40	basket	.31
8 bowls	.30	crosscut saw	1.61
set cups & saucers	.25	2 meal bags	.25
—do—	.25	5 meal bags	.64
coffee pot & pitcher	.75	axe	.50
coffee mill	1.00	3 hoes	.50
2 wash pans	.25	shovel	.37
oven —— [?]	1.00	spreading hoe	.25
—do—	.75	5 middlings [?] bacon	9.40
—do—	.50	6 1/2 middlings [?] bacon	9.90
iron pot	.75	meat tub	1.00
—do—	.80	meat tub	.25
tea kettle	.75	stand of bees	3.40
2 pr. pot hooks	.25	bay horse	10.00
2 water buckets	.50	bay mare	20.00
water bucket	.25	2 roan mares	48.50

barrel	.84	sorrel mare	74.00
2 small tubs	.50	red cow & calf	12.00
wash tub	.62	red & white calf	3.00
chair	.25	white & black cow	11.63
light [?] barrel	.52	—do—	9.25
firkin	.31	white cow	9.12
6 milk crocks	.30	bull calf	3.50
iron kettle	3.51	black cow & calf	13.00
—do—	2.75	small white heifer	3.77
breading oven	4.00	rifle gun	8.37
4 shoats (1st choice)	7.00	6 square bottles	.28
5 shoats (2nd choice)	3.00	bottle & oil	.25
2 hogs	2.00	razor, strop & paste	.26
shovel plow & single tree	.75	bible	.13
plow	.34	lot of books	.51
shovel plow & tree	.39	set windsor chairs	3.00
lot old irons	.21	3 windsor chairs	2.00
plow	1.75	bed, bedding, bedstead	12.00
scythe & cradle	2.95	clock	3.00
2 plows & trees	12.00	bureau	5.00
harrow	3.00	2 slates	.15
old wagon	6.00	dining table	2.00
good wagon	30.00	bed	12.00
log chain	.52	bureau	4.50
lot chains	.33	loom	5.00
mattock	.20	[loom equipment]	2.80
lot irons	.05	17 lbs. wool	3.50
small hatchet	.15	spools	.50
2 shovel plates	1.00	7 1/4 lb. spun cotton	1.00
cutting box & knife	.31	oil cloth	1.49
axe	.31	walnut chair	1.50
man's saddle	1.80	3 coverlets	9.25
riding bridle	.50	2 cotton bedspreads	3.40
3 riding bridles	.97	chiff tick	.81
square & saw	.50	cotton sheet	.33
4 wood forks	.63	3 bedsteads, beds, bedding	25.00
manure fork	.19	pr. saddlebags	.80
hay fork	.26	flax wheel	4.00
mowing scythe	.19	—do—	1.00
claw hammer	.18	brass kettle	.52
manure fork	.26	wool —— [?]	1.75
horse collars	.13	3 flour barrels	.50
blind bridle	.25	29 lbs. soap	1.81
4 horse collars	2.75	10 lbs. soap	.62
pr. hand gears [?]	11.00	8 bars of iron, 4–5 lb. ea.	22.60
wheat fan	11.00	8 sheep	8.75
leather line	.53	bedstead & crib	.15
tin bucket	.12	slate	.08

mowing scythe	.50	120 bu. wheat @ 63 cents	75.60
mowing scythe	.52		

Total: $625.44

2. David M. Dovel (d. 1871)

Inventory and Appraise Bill of Personal Property of David M. Dovel, dec'd., 9 May 1871

Item	Value	Item	Value
1 wash kettle	$4.00	2 stills and caps	$80.00
25 still tubs	18.75	1 apple mill	10.00
1 oven	.50	blacksmith tools	.30
1 old irons	.50	3 double shovel plows	4.00
3 shovel plows	1.50	2 guns	1.50
2 flax wheels and reel	2.50	1 jackscrew	2.00
2 plows	2.50	2 shovels, spade, mattock	1.50
chairs	1.50	cider mill	20.00
2 grain cradles	2.50	1 crosscut saw	4.00
1 wagon	25.00	1 cow	15.00
5 head cattle	65.00	4 calves	26.00
1 speckled cow	18.00	1 gray horse	75.00
1 sorrel horse	75.00	1 wheat fan	15.00
1 lot of forks	1.00	1 harnesses	2.00
1 lead gear	7.00	1 safe and dishes	5.00
1 blind bridle	2.00	1 dung hook	.10
2 horse collars	1.00	6 hogs @ $5.50	33.00
7 hogs @ $5.50	38.50	7 shoats @ $2.50	17.50
2 sheep	3.00	8 lambs @ $1.25	10.00
18 sheep @ $2.00	36.00	3 old axes	1.00
3 barrels vinegar	9.00	1 grindstone	2.00
1 bee stand	1.00	1 cane mill	.50
1 lot of brick	1.50	1 bedstead and bedding	5.00
1 bedstead and bedding	4.00	1 bureau and bookcase	8.00
1 clock	1.50	1 small table	1.00
1 lounge	.50	1 looking glass	.50
1 lot of books	1.00	2 augers	1.00
1 chest	.75	1 sausage cutter	2.00
2 tables	.25	1 small table	.50
14 chairs	8.75	1 steel trap	.10
1 desk	8.00	1 small table	.50
2 candlesticks	.25	1 safe and dishes	5.00
1 table	1.50	1 lot of old barrels	.10
40 lb. wool @ 30 cents	12.00	1 sheep shears	.50
6 linen tablecloths	6.00	4 linen towels	3.00

1 tea set and tea spoons	1.00	1 doz. knives and forks	1.20
1 doz. plates (set)	.90	10 goblets	1.00
1 blue-edged dish	.05	5 prs. andirons	1.00
1 large churn	1.50	6 large tubs	3.75
1 molasses can, cake and candle molds, pitchers	.90	1 shaving box	.10

Total: $789.72

[*Note:* Various moneys owed to the estate totaled nearly $2,000.]

Appendix C

Household Agricultural Inventories, Valley Farmers
(Page County, Virginia, Shenandoah Iron Works District,
Kite Family, 1850)

TABLE C-1.

ACREAGE, LIVESTOCK, ETC.

Name	Surname	Unimproved Acres	Improved Acres	Value Farm ($)	Value Tools ($)	Value Livestock ($)	Horses (No.)
Abraham	Kite	39	50	1,600	120	254	2
Daniel	Kite	75	25	1,000	10	110	1
Daniel	Kite	101	135	4,500	200	530	6
David	Kite	60	100	5,000	345	455	
Elizabeth	Kite	64	50	1,500	0	42	0
Henry+Adam	Kite	35	275	10,000	300	733	6
Isaac (of H)	Kite	48	110	2,000	50	200	2
Jacob	Kite	452	300	12,000	990	937	9
James	Kite	153	200	7,500	250	543	5
James A.	Kite	30	195	5,500	100	554	6
John	Kite	100	200	7,160	200	567	10
John	Kite	57	160	6,000	200	866	7
Martin	Kite	36	75	1,672	120	378	4
Mary	Kite	128	140	2,500	102	120	4
Noah	Kite	81	130	6,000	200	462	4
Reuben	Kite	85	140	4,500	75	440	5
William	Kite	20	164	6,000	25	400	3

Name	Surname	Milk Cows (No.)	Other Cattle (No.)	Sheep (No.)	Wool (Lbs.)	Pigs (No.)	Value Animals Slaughtered ($)
Abraham	Kite	3	4	10	15	14	72
Daniel	Kite	3	2	8	18	10	45
Daniel	Kite	5	9	24	50	18	175
David	Kite	6	6	0	0	25	125
Elizabeth	Kite	2	3	4	8	1	24
Henry+Adam	Kite	10	8	8	36	45	160

TABLE C-1, *continued*

Name	Sur-name	Milk Cows (No.)	Other Cattle (No.)	Sheep (No.)	Wool (Lbs.)	Pigs (No.)	Value Animals Slaugh-tered ($)
Isaac (of H)	Kite	3	2	20	33	15	60
Jacob	Kite	6	22	0	0	27	185
James	Kite	6	8	22	50	30	180
James A.	Kite	3	2	0	0	8	72
John	Kite	4	1	1	4	30	140
John	Kite	7	15	0	21	63	160
Martin	Kite	4	5	8	23	13	14
Mary	Kite	1	0	6	13	12	76
Noah	Kite	6	10	42	100	40	180
Reuben	Kite	3	6	9	24	21	165
William	Kite	3	10	0	0	6	90

TABLE C-2.

CROPS, HOME MANUFACTURES

Name	Sur-name	Wheat (Bu.)	Rye (Bu.)	Corn (Bu.)	Oats (Bu.)	Buck-wheat (Bu.)
Abraham	Kite	148	0	130	30	0
Daniel	Kite	30	0	150	50	0
Daniel	Kite	400	0	100	50	0
David	Kite	350	0	300	0	0
Elizabeth	Kite	24	14	50	18	0
Henry+Adam	Kite	350	10	500	300	0
Isaac (of H)	Kite	102	40	150	20	0
Jacob	Kite	800	100	500	0	0
James	Kite	576	60	400	200	0
James A.	Kite	0	0	200	200	0
John	Kite	430	75	400	100	0
John	Kite	500	0	400	100	0
Martin	Kite	145	20	75	20	15
Mary	Kite	330	0	150	20	0
Noah	Kite	250	50	500	74	0
Reuben	Kite	350	30	500	65	0
William	Kite	60	0	200	0	0

TABLE C-2, *continued*

Name	Sur-name	Apples (Bu.)	Butter (Lbs.)	Flax (Lbs.)	Pota-toes (Bu.)	Value Home Manu-factures ($)	Hay (Tons)
Abraham	Kite	0	150	0	16	30	5
Daniel	Kite	60	20	0	15	40	1
Daniel	Kite	0	150	0	30	40	12
David	Kite	0	104	0	15	0	5
Elizabeth	Kite	60	50	0	22	0	1
Henry+Adam	Kite	520	100	0	23	10	12
Isaac (of H)	Kite	250	400	5	28	37	0
Jacob	Kite	0	300	0	15	100	13
James	Kite	200	100	0	55	25	15
James A.	Kite	250	104	0	12	0	2
John	Kite	500	208	0	70	92	20
John	Kite	0	150	0	57	40	3
Martin	Kite	0	50	10	24	10	5
Mary	Kite	250	104	5	20	69	1
Noah	Kite	100	200	10	18	50	20
Reuben	Kite	150	52	0	15	40	15
William	Kite	0	52	0	5	5	0

SOURCE: U.S. Census of Agriculture, Page County, Virginia, 1850.

Appendix D

Household Agricultural Inventories, Mountain Farmers
(Page County, Virginia, Shenandoah Iron Works District,
Breeden, Cubbage, Lamb, Meadows Households,
1850, 1860, 1870, and 1880)

TABLE D-1. Acreage, Livestock, Etc., 1850

Name	Surname	Year Born	Unim-proved Acres	Im-proved Acres	Value Farm ($)	Value Tools ($)
James	Breeden	1767	1,450	50	500	0
Elijah	Breeden	1792	1,000	20	150	5
Jacob	Cubbage	1795	90	30	300	20
Richam	Breeden	1796	125	35	500	0
Allison	Breeden	1797	1,640	200	1,000	67
Thomas	Meadows	1802	480	20	400	2
Jeremiah	Breeden	1803	0	0	0	5
Paschal	Breeden	1808	133	20	153	3
Elias	Breeden	1811	122	53	177	10
William	Breeden	1817	500	5	100	0
James	Cubbage	1818	90	30	300	30
Henry	Cubbage	1819	710	40	300	5
Mitchel	Meadows	1823	0	0	0	5
Sanford	Breeden	1824	0	0	0	0
Samuel	Breeden	1829	496	3	100	5

Name	Surname	Year Born	Value Live-stock ($)	Horses (No.)	Milk Cows (No.)
James	Breeden	1767	30	1	1
Elijah	Breeden	1792	105	1	2
Jacob	Cubbage	1795	50	1	2
Richam	Breeden	1796	133	1	3
Allison	Breeden	1797	215	2	1
Thomas	Meadows	1802	38	1	1
Jeremiah	Breeden	1803	65	1	2
Paschal	Breeden	1808	83	1	2
Elias	Breeden	1811	198	1	2
William	Breeden	1817	16	*	1

TABLE D-1, *continued*

Name	Surname	Year Born	Value Live-stock ($)	Horses (No.)	Milk Cows (No.)
James	Cubbage	1818	60	2	1
Henry	Cubbage	1819	150	2	2
Mitchel	Meadows	1823	70	1	1
Sanford	Breeden	1824	66	1	0
Samuel	Breeden	14	*	1	

Name	Surname	Year Born	Other Cattle (No.)	Sheep (No.)	Wool (Lbs.)	Pigs (No.)	Value Animals Slaughtered ($)
James	Breeden	1767	1	0	0	4	40
Elijah	Breeden	1792	0	6	16	4	34
Jacob	Cubbage	1795	0	6	0	6	*
Richam	Breeden	1796	2	11	16	16	20
Allison	Breeden	1797	5	3	52	21	72
Thomas	Meadows	1802	0	0	0	12	12
Jeremiah	Breeden	1803	1	6	8	13	24
Paschal	Breeden	1808	0	3	11	19	32
Elias	Breeden	1811	3	18	19	18	40
William	Breeden	1817	*	2	*	*	4
James	Cubbage	1818	2	0	0	8	*
Henry	Cubbage	1819	5	7	0	5	48
Mitchel	Meadows	1823	0	0	0	8	22
Sanford	Breeden	1824	0	0	0	3	20
Samuel	Breeden	1829	*	*	*	7	*

* No information available in this category for this household.
SOURCE: U.S. Census of Agriculture, Page County, Virginia, 1850.

TABLE D-2. Acreage, Livestock, Etc., 1860 and 1870

Name	Surname	Year Born	Census	Unim- proved Acres	Im- proved Acres	Value Farm ($)
Richam	Breeden	1796	1860	91	30	700
Elias	Breeden	1811	1860	220	80	700
James	Cubbage	1818	1860	155	40	500
Henry	Cubbage	1819	1860	345	200	1,500
Mitchel	Meadows	1823	1860	200	40	400
Hamilton	Cubbage	1824	1860	155	40	500
Sanford	Breeden	1824	1860	55	14	200
William	Cubbage	1828	1860	40	60	1,200
Richam	Breeden	1796	1870	150	30	620
James	Cubbage	1818	1870	100	60	600
Hamilton	Cubbage	1824	1870	20	20	200

SOURCE: U.S. Census of Agriculture, Page County, Virginia, 1860; 1870.

TABLE D-3. Acreage, Livestock, Etc., 1880

Name	Surname	Year Born	Unim- proved Acres	Im- proved Acres	Value Farm ($)	Value Tools ($)	Value Live- stock ($)
Richam	Breeden	1796	56	40	600	5	20
Nancy	Cubbage	1801	34	22	300	4	40
James	Cubbage	1818	70	55	600	20	175
Thomas	Cubbage	1823	200	24	800	5	100
Matthew	Lamb	1825	0	0	0	5	110
James	Meadows	1826	65	21	350	12	140
William	Cubbage	1828	175	160	3,600	75	500
Thomas	Meadows	1831	155	43	600	10	80
Nathaniel	Breeden	1832	0	13	300	3	35
Wesley	Breeden	1834	260	44	300	50	150
Amanda	Cubbage	1835	30	16	350	6	75
William B.	Meadows	1839	30	30	300	25	120
Joseph	Cubbage	1839	0	5	150	1	25
Henry	Meadows	1840	200	110	1,000	20	195
Early	Cubbage	1843	5	44	400	3	20
James H.	Cubbage	1843	62	78	500	5	20
Wesley	Cubbage	1845	20	105	1,500	20	200
Hiram F.	Meadows	1849	2	19	200	5	30

Value Tools ($)	Value Live-stock ($)	Horses (No.)	Milk Cows (No.)	Other Cattle (No.)	Sheep (No.)	Wool (Lbs.)	Pigs (No.)	Value Animals Slaugh-tered ($)
20	117	1	1	2	5	10	12	25
60	146	2	2	0	5	16	10	126
24	40	1	1	0	0	0	0	56
100	374	2	4	2	8	23	7	117
6	173	2	2	3	15	12	10	90
5	100	1	1	0	0	0	4	10
75	120	1	2	0	4	8	13	70
60	202	2	3	3	0	17	11	80
0	100	2	1	0	0	0	1	10
5	100	1	2	0	0	0	1	20
5	85	1	1	0	0	0	4	18

Horses (No.)	Milk Cows (No.)	Other Cattle (No.)	Sheep (No.)	Wool (Lbs.)	Pigs (No.)	Chickens (No.)	Eggs (Doz.)	Value Farm Production ($)
0	1	0	0	0	1	3	10	80
1	1	0	0	0	5	8	50	125
2	2	0	0	0	8	8	100	325
1	1	0	0	0	2	6	75	175
1	2	1	8	24	12	15	100	175
2	2	1	0	0	18	8	75	105
6	5	16	0	0	3	10	50	700
2	1	1	0	0	20	12	50	150
0	1	0	0	0	0	8	10	56
3	1	4	3	10	15	20	125	160
2	1	0	0	0	1	10	50	125
2	1	0	3	15	10	15	50	115
0	1	0	0	0	2	5	25	25
3	2	1	15	60	12	20	125	170
0	1	0	0	0	2	8	75	75
0	1	0	0	0	0	20	50	175
2	2	2	0	0	2	15	100	300
0	1	0	0	0	5	10	75	140

TABLE D-3, *continued*

Name	Surname	Year Born	Unim-proved Acres	Im-proved Acres	Value Farm ($)	Value Tools ($)	Valu Live stoc ($)
James S.	Meadows	1851	96	10	225	5	50
Thomas W.	Meadows	1854	15	11	150	5	80
Richard	Breeden	1855	1,135	30	375	8	180
Daniel	Breeden	1858	0	0	0	10	120
Zechariah	Meadows	1859	60	22	200	12	65
Simeon	Breeden	1859	0	0	0	3	52

SOURCE: U.S. Census of Agriculture, Page County, Virginia, 1880.

TABLE D-4. Crops and Home Manufactures, 1850

Name	Surname	Year Born	Wheat (Bu.)	Rye (Bu.)	Corn (Bu.)	Oat (Bu.
James	Breeden	1767	0	0	50	0
Elijah	Breeden	1792	60	15	15	0
Jacob	Cubbage	1795	60	50	100	0
Richam	Breeden	1796	0	60	65	30
Allison	Breeden	1797	50	90	500	0
Thomas	Meadows	1802	6	15	100	0
Jeremiah	Breeden	1803	0	14	50	21
Paschal	Breeden	1808	0	60	50	0
Elias	Breeden	1811	0	75	200	40
William	Breeden	1817	*	*	*	*
James	Cubbage	1818	50	50	80	0
Henry	Cubbage	1819	250	80	75	0
Mitchel	Meadows	1823	15	15	75	0
Sanford	Breeden	1824	0	30	75	0
Samuel	Breeden	1829	*	*	*	*

*No information available in this category for this household.
SOURCE: U.S. Census of Agriculture, Page County, Virginia, 1850.

rses (No.)	Milk Cows (No.)	Other Cattle (No.)	Sheep (No.)	Wool (Lbs.)	Pigs (No.)	Chickens (No.)	Eggs (Doz.)	Value Farm Production ($)
1	0	0	0	0	0	0	0	80
1	1	0	0	0	4	7	50	75
1	2	5	8	24	30	10	75	170
1	1	0	3	12	12	10	75	100
1	1	0	0	0	7	14	75	75
1	1	1	6	18	18	20	125	65

uck-heat (Bu.)	Butter (Lbs.)	Flax (Lbs.)	Potatoes (Bu.)	Value Home Manufactures ($)
0	52	30	20	25
0	52	8	12	0
0	0	0	20	0
0	20	0	2	10
0	52	6	0	34
0	26	0	0	0
20	30	4	0	0
6	26	0	10	25
24	52	10	6	35
*	*	*	*	*
0	0	0	0	0
0	0	0	30	0
0	30	5	16	0
0	0	0	7	0
*	*	*	*	*

TABLE D-5. Crops and Home Manufactures, 1860 and 1870

Name	Surname	Year Born	Census	Wheat (Bu.)	Rye (Bu.)	Corn (Bu.)	Oats (Bu.)	Buck-wheat (Bu.)
Richam	Breeden	1796	1860	0	60	60	0	0
Elias	Breeden	1811	1860	0	115	100	10	30
James	Cubbage	1818	1860	4	110	150	0	0
Henry	Cubbage	1819	1860	13	295	200	60	0
Mitchel	Meadows	1823	1860	12	100	50	25	6
Hamilton	Cubbage	1824	1860	0	0	200	0	0
Sanford	Breeden	1824	1860	0	20	100	15	0
William	Cubbage	1828	1860	30	30	350	40	0
Richam	Breeden	1796	1870	0	30	40	0	0
James	Cubbage	1818	1870	0	50	50	0	0
Hamilton	Cubbage	1824	1870	0	20	75	0	0

Name	Surname	Census	Year Born	Butter (Lbs.)	Flax (Lbs.)	Pota-toes (Bu.)	Value Home Manu-fac-tures ($)
Richam	Breeden	1796	1860	100	0	10	0
Elias	Breeden	1811	1860	150	0	12	35
James	Cubbage	1818	1860	25	0	5	0
Henry	Cubbage	1819	1860	240	10	80	8
Mitchel	Meadows	1823	1860	50	10	0	8
Hamilton	Cubbage	1824	1860	125	0	0	0
Sanford	Breeden	1824	1860	150	0	5	0
William	Cubbage	1828	1860	200	0	50	20
Richam	Breeden	1796	1870	0	0	0	0
James	Cubbage	1818	1870	25	0	15	0
Hamilton	Cubbage	1824	1870	50	0	3	0

SOURCE: U.S. Census of Agriculture, Page County, Virginia, 1860; 1870.

TABLE D-6. Crops, 1880

Name	Surname	Year Born	Wheat (Bu.)	Rye (Bu.)	Corn (Bu.)	Oats (Bu.)	Buck-wheat (Bu.)
Richam	Breeden	1796	12	10	50	10	0
Nancy	Cubbage	1801	0	10	80	0	0
James	Cubbage	1818	0	60	250	0	0
Thomas	Cubbage	1823	0	25	150	0	0
Matthew	Lamb	1825	50	80	100	10	10
James	Meadows	1826	0	35	100	10	0
William	Cubbage	1828	240	20	1,000	40	0
Thomas	Meadows	1831	14	20	150	18	0
Nathaniel	Breeden	1832	0	0	50	0	0
Wesley	Breeden	1834	25	80	100	0	0
Amanda	Cubbage	1835	0	20	100	0	0
William B.	Meadows	1839	12	25	78	0	0
Joseph	Cubbage	1839	0	0	5	50	0
Henry	Meadows	1840	0	100	50	0	10
Early	Cubbage	1843	12	15	60	0	0
James H.	Cubbage	1843	25	115	10	0	0
Wesley	Cubbage	1845	32	60	300	0	0

Name	Surname	Year Born	Apples (Bu.)	Butter (Lbs.)	Flax (Lbs.)	Pota-toes (Bu.)
Richam	Breeden	1796	300	0	0	5
Nancy	Cubbage	1801	500	80	0	10
James	Cubbage	1818	1,000	400	0	20
Thomas	Cubbage	1823	20	100	0	10
Matthew	Lamb	1825	0	80	0	0
James	Meadows	1826	100	180	0	14
William	Cubbage	1828	500	100	0	5
Thomas	Meadows	1831	100	40	0	10
Nathaniel	Breeden	1832	0	0	0	9
Wesley	Breeden	1834	250	180	0	0
Amanda	Cubbage	1835	300	50	0	10
William B.	Meadows	1839	250	25	0	6
Joseph	Cubbage	1839	10	25	0	5
Henry	Meadows	1840	150	180	0	20
Early	Cubbage	1843	50	75	0	0
James H.	Cubbage	1843	20	200	0	10
Wesley	Cubbage	1845	200	250	0	10

TABLE D-6, *continued*

Name	Surname	Year Born	Wheat (Bu.)	Rye (Bu.)	Corn (Bu.)	Oats (Bu.)	Buck-wheat (Bu.)
Hiram F.	Meadows	1849	0	80	125	10	0
James S.	Meadows	1851	18	20	40	0	0
Thomas W.	Meadows	1854	0	15	50	0	0
Richard	Breeden	1855	37	67	80	0	0
Daniel	Breeden	1858	0	75	100	0	0
Zechariah	Meadows	1859	0	20	75	30	0
Simeon	Breeden	1859	0	18	65	0	0

Name	Surname	Year Born	Apples (Bu.)	Butter (Lbs.)	Flax (Lbs.)	Pota-toes (Bu.)
Hiram F.	Meadows	1849	0	75	0	20
James S.	Meadows	1851	0	0	0	20
Thomas W.	Meadows	1854	100	100	0	20
Richard	Breeden	1855	0	100	0	10
Daniel	Breeden	1858	0	75	0	0
Zechariah	Meadows	1859	50	20	0	25
Simeon	Breeden	1859	100	25	0	5

SOURCE: U.S. Census of Agriculture, Page County, Virginia, 1880.

Appendix E

Recordings and Interviews

Summary of Field Tape Recordings, Fellowship Independent Baptist Church, Documentary Project

I. Airchecks, WRAA radio, Luray, Virginia, Christmas 1971–June 1972. Ten broadcasts, 1 hour each, "Bible Way Gospel Time," Bro. John Sherfey. Recorded by Cameron Nickels.

II. Studio recordings, WRAA radio, Luray, Virginia, summer 1977 and April 1978. Eight broadcasts, 1/2 hour each, "Bible Way Gospel Time," Bro. John Sherfey. Recorded by Ken George and Jeff Titon.

III. Worship services, Fellowship Independent Baptist Church, Stanley, Virginia, Bro. John Sherfey, pastor. Thirty-nine Sunday morning and night services, 1975–1985. Recorded by Barry Dornfeld, Ken George, Tom Rankin, and Jeff Titon.

IV. Prayer meetings, Fellowship Independent Baptist Church, Stanley, Virginia. Six prayer meetings, summer 1977. Recorded by Ken George and Jeff Titon.

V. Hymn sings, Fellowship Independent Baptist Church, Stanley, Virginia. Two hymn sings, summer 1977. Recorded by Ken George and Jeff Titon.

VI. Tape-recorded interviews with congregation members, Fellowship Independent Baptist Church, 1975–1985. Interviewed by Barry Dornfeld, Ken George, Tom Rankin, and Jeff Titon.

[The above tape recordings are housed and may be heard at the Archive of Folk Culture, Library of Congress, Washington, D.C., and also in the Folklore Archives of the University of North Carolina at Chapel Hill.]

Recorded Interviews

(*Page references in text citations of these interviews refer to my transcriptions, which are on deposit at the Library of Congress along with the tapes.*)

Breeden, Tom. August 4, 1977. At home, Luray, Virginia. Interviewed by Ken George.

Cave, Betty, Arthur Cave, Wellford Cave, and Rosalee Cave. April 4, 1978. At Belvin Hurt's home, Etlan, Madison County, Virginia. Interviewed by Jeff Titon.

Comer, Jesse. July 21, 1977. At home, near Verbena, Page County, Virginia. Interviewed by Jeff Titon and Ken George.

———. October 23, 1985. At home, near Verbena, Page County, Virginia. Interviewed by Jeff Titon and Barry Dornfeld.

Cubbage, Edith, and Clyde Cubbage. August 12, 1977. At home, Stanley, Virginia. Interviewed by Jeff Titon and Ken George.

Dove, Allen, and Goldie Dove. August 4, 1977. At home, Timberville, Rockingham County, Virginia. Interviewed by Jeff Titon.

Hughes, Thurston. July 12, 1977. Old schoolhouse, Luray, Virginia. Interviewed by Jeff Titon and Ken George.

Hurt, Belvin. August 11, 1977. At home, Etlan, Madison County, Virginia. Interviewed by Jeff Titon and Ken George.

Jenkins, Harry, and Minnie Meadows Jenkins. October 26, 1985. At the Jenkins' home in Pine Grove Hollow, near Stanley, Virginia. Interviewed by Tom Rankin, Barry Dornfeld, and Jeff Titon.

Jenkins, Harry, Minnie Meadows Jenkins, and John Sherfey. October 26, 1985. At the Jenkinses' Home in Pine Grove Hollow, near Stanley, Virginia. Storytelling session.

Lam, Rastus. July 8, 1977. At home, near Stanley, Virginia. Interviewed by Jeff Titon and Ken George.

Meadows, Vernie. July 15, 1977. At home, Pine Grove Hollow, near Stanley, Virginia. Interviewed by Jeff Titon and Ken George.

———. March 16, 1982. At home, Pine Grove Hollow, near Stanley, Virginia. Interviewed by Jeff Titon.

———. November 21, 1985. At home, Pine Grove Hollow, near Stanley, Virginia. Interviewed by Jeff Titon.

Sherfey, Charles, and Pammie Sherfey. November 20, 1985. At home, Stanley, Virginia. Interviewed by Jeff Titon, Tom Rankin, and Barry Dornfeld.

Sherfey, Dana, Sharon Painter Sherfey, John Sherfey, and Pauline Sherfey. November 16, 1985. In Dana and Sharon's house trailer, Inwood, West Virginia. Interviewed by Jeff Titon and Barry Dornfeld.

Sherfey, Donny, and Charles Sherfey. July 17, 1977. In the Fellowship Independent Baptist Church, Stanley, Virginia. Interviewed by Ken George.

Sherfey, Donny, and Jeannie Sherfey. November 18, 1985. At home, Stanley, Virginia. Interviewed by Barry Dornfeld, Jeff Titon, and Tom Rankin.

Sherfey, John. July 28, 1975. At home, Falls Church, Virginia. Interviewed by Ken George.

———. July 9, 1976. At home, Falls Church, Virginia. Interviewed by Jeff Titon.

———. July 17, 1977. In the Fellowship Independent Baptist Church, Stanley, Virginia. Interviewed by Jeff Titon.

———. July 23, 1977. In the Fellowship Independent Baptist Church, Stanley, Virginia. Interviewed by Jeff Titon.

———. December 13, 1982. At home, Stanley, Virginia. Interviewed by Jeff Titon.

———. November 21, 1985. At home, Stanley, Virginia. Interviewed by Tom Rankin and Jeff Titon.

Sherfey, John, and Belvin Hurt. July 3, 1977. Kentucky Fried Chicken restaurant, Luray, Virginia. Lunch conversation among Sherfey, Hurt, Carl Fleischhauer, Ken George, Jeff Titon.

Sherfey, John, and Pauline Sherfey. August 14, 1977. At the Dixie Diner, Luray, Virginia. Interviewed by Jeff Titon and Ken George.

———. April 2, 1978. In the Sherfeys' house trailer, Stanley, Virginia. Interviewed by Jeff Titon.

———. December 3, 1979. At home, Stanley, Virginia. Interviewed by Jeff Titon.

————. October 7, 1985. At home, Stanley, Virginia. Interviewed by Jeff Titon.

————. November 7, 1985. At home, Stanley, Virginia. Interviewed by Jeff Titon.

Sherfey, Josie Coffey, Elsie Sherfey McNally, and Archie Jenkins. August 7, 1977. Homecoming dinner, Fellowship Independent Baptist Church, Stanley, Virginia. Interviewed by Jeff Titon.

Stroupe, Kenny, and Todd Stroupe. November 21, 1985. At home, Pine Grove Hollow, near Stanley, Virginia. Interviewed by Tom Rankin, Barry Dornfeld, and Jeff Titon.

Turner, Earl, and Ella Turner. April 8, 1978. At home, Stanley, Virginia. Interviewed by Jeff Titon.

Turner, Janice. August 9, 1977. In the Fellowship Independent Baptist Church, Stanley, Virginia. Interviewed by Jeff Titon and Ken George.

Interviews Cited from Notes

(No tape recordings exist for these.)

Gordon, Bertha Jenkins. June 6, 1983. At home, Luray, Virginia. Interviewed by Jeff Titon.

Meadows, Howard. October 4, 1985. At home, Jollett Hollow, Virginia. Interviewed by Jeff Titon.

References Cited

In addition to the works listed here, sources cited in the book include:

County records, including county atlases and maps, deed books, tax records, probate inventories, will books, court records, marriage licenses, and vital statistics for Culpeper, Madison, Orange, Page, Rockingham, and Shenandoah counties, Virginia, and Monroe County, West Virginia.

John W. Keyser diary, Personal Papers Collection, Accession 24023. Archives Branch, Virginia State Library and Archives, Richmond, Virginia.

Recordings and interviews listed in Appendix E above.

Records of the Fellowship Independent Baptist Church, Stanley, Virginia.

U.S. population, agricultural, and industrial census records for Virginia, 1790–1910, especially agricultural censuses for Page County in 1850, 1860, 1870, and 1880.

Adams, James Truslow, ed. 1943. *Atlas of American History*. New York: Scribner's Sons.

Agricultural Statistics, 1982. Washington, D.C.: U.S. Government Printing Office.

Armstrong, Robert Plant. 1971. *The Affecting Presence*. Urbana: University of Illinois Press.

Atack, Jeremy, and Fred Bateman. 1979. "The Profitability of Northern Agriculture in 1860." *Research in Economic History* 4:87–125.

———. 1984. "Self-Sufficiency and the Marketable Surplus in the Rural North, 1860." *Agricultural History* 58:296–313.

Austin, J. L. 1975. *How to Do Things with Words*. Cambridge: Harvard University Press.

Ayer, A. J. 1946. *Language, Truth and Logic*. 2d ed. New York: Dover.

Battalio, Raymond C., and John Kagel. 1970. "The Structure of Southern Antebellum Agriculture: South Carolina, a Case Study." *Agricultural History* 44:25–37.

Bauman, Richard. 1984. "Verbal Art as Performance." In *Verbal Art as Performance*, edited by idem, pp. 3–58. Prospect Heights, Ill.: Waveland Press.

Bauman, Richard, and Americo Paredes, eds. 1972. *Toward New Perspectives in Folklore*. Austin: University of Texas Press.

Bauserman, Gary. 1976. "History of Page County." In *Page: The County of Plenty*, pp. 11–29. Luray, Va.: Page County Bicentennial Commission.

Baxter, Norman Allen. 1957. *History of the Freewill Baptists.* Rochester: American Baptist Historical Society.

Bellah, Robert N. 1984. "Civil Religion in America." In *Religion North American Style,* edited by Patrick H. McNamara, 2d ed., pp. 39–51. Belmont, Calif.: Wadsworth Publishing Company.

Bennett, Merrill, and Rosamond H. Pierce. 1961. "Changes in the American National Diet, 1879–1959." *Food Research Institute Studies* 2:95–119.

Berkland, J. O., and L. A. Raymond. 1973. "Pleistocene Glaciation in the Blue Ridge Province of the Southern Appalachian Mountains in North Carolina." *Science* 181:651–653.

Berry, Wendell. 1981. "Discipline and Hope." In his *Recollected Essays, 1965–1980,* pp. 151–220. San Francisco: North Point Press.

Boles, John B. 1972. *The Great Revival, 1787–1805.* Lexington: University Press of Kentucky.

Booth, Mark W. 1981. *The Experience of Songs.* New Haven: Yale University Press.

Breeden, Shirley Seal. 1978. *The Descendants of Francis Meadows of Orange and Rockingham Counties.* Boyce, Va.: Carr Publishing Co.

Bruce, Dickson D., Jr. 1974. *And They All Sang Hallelujah: Plain-Folk Camp-Meeting Religion, 1800–1845.* Knoxville: University of Tennessee Press.

Bryant, F. Carlene. 1981. *We're All Kin.* Knoxville: University of Tennessee Press.

Buzzell, John. 1827. *The Life of Elder Benjamin Randal.* Limerick, Maine.

Caldwell, Patricia. 1983. *The Puritan Conversion Narrative: The Beginnings of American Expression.* Cambridge: Cambridge University Press.

Campbell, John C. 1969. *The Southern Highlander and His Homeland.* [Originally published in 1921.] Lexington: University Press of Kentucky.

Cartwright, Peter. 1856. *Autobiography of Peter Cartwright, the Backwoods Preacher.* Edited by W. P. Strickland. New York: Carlton & Lanahan.

Cash, W. J. 1941. *The Mind of the South.* Garden City, N.Y.: Doubleday.

Chase, Gilbert. 1955. *American Music: From the Pilgrims to the Present.* New York: McGraw-Hill.

Clark, Christopher. 1979. "Household Economy, Market Exchange and the Rise of Capitalism in the Connecticut Valley, 1800–1860." *Journal of Social History* 13:169–189.

Clark, Walter Houston. 1958. *The Psychology of Religion.* New York: Macmillan.

Clements, William M. 1974a. "The American Folk Church: A Characterization of American Folk Religion Based on Field Research among White Protestants in a Community in the South Central United States." Ph.D. dissertation, Indiana University.

———. 1974b. "The Rhetoric of the Radio Ministry." *Journal of American Folklore* 87 (1974):318–327.

———. 1975. "The Folklorist and the Study of Religion." Paper read at Annual Conference of the American Folklore Society, New Orleans.

———. 1976a. "Conversion and Communitas." *Western Folklore* 35:35–45.

———. 1976b. "Faith Healing Narratives from Northeast Arkansas." *Indiana Folklore* 9:15–39.

————. 1979. The Base-Sinner Persona in Oral Conversion Narratives. Unpublished paper.

————. 1980a. "The Pentecostal Sagaman." *Journal of the Folklore Institute* 17:169–195.

————. 1980b. "Public Testimony as Oral Performance: A Study in the Ethnography of Religious Speaking." *Linguistica Biblica: Interdisziplinaere Zeitschrift für Theologie und Linguistik* 47:21–32.

————. 1984. "'I once was lost': Oral Narratives of Born-Again Christians." *International Folklore Review* 4:105–111.

Cohen, Norm, and Anne Cohen. 1973. "Tune Evolution as an Indicator of Traditional Musical Norms." *Journal of American Folklore* 86:37–47.

Cook, Frederick A., et al. 1983. *The Cocorp Seismic Reflection Traverse across the Southern Appalachians*. Tulsa: American Association of Petroleum Geologists.

Couper, William. 1952. *History of the Shenandoah Valley*. New York: Lewis Historical Publishing Co.

Coxe, Tench. 1814. *A Statement of the Arts & Manufactures of the United States of America, for the Year 1810*. Philadelphia: A. Cornman.

Crèvecoeur, J. Hector St. Jean de. 1961. *Letters from an American Farmer* (1782) and *Sketches of Eighteenth Century America* (1925), edited by Albert E. Stone. New York: New American Library.

Crites, Stephen. 1971. "The Narrative Quality of Experience." *Journal of the American Academy of Religion*, September 1971, pp. 291–311.

Cummings, Richard O. 1940. *The American and His Food*. Chicago: University of Chicago Press.

Dorson, Richard M. 1972. "Africa and the Folklorist." In *African Folklore*, edited by idem, pp. 3–67. Garden City, N.Y.: Anchor Books.

Edwards, Jonathan. 1979. "Personal Narrative" (written ca. 1740). In *The Norton Anthology of American Literature*, edited by Ronald Gottesman et al., 1:207–219. New York: Norton.

Ergood, Bruce, and Bruce E. Kuhre, eds. 1976. *Appalachia: Social Context Past and Present*. Dubuque, Iowa: Kendall/Hunt Publishing Co.

Erikson, Erik H. 1967. "Growth and Crises of the Healthy Personality" (1959). In *Personality*, edited by Richard S. Lazarus and Edward M. Opton, Jr. Baltimore: Penguin.

Fenneman, N. M. 1938. *Physiography of the Eastern United States*. New York: McGraw-Hill.

Flint, J. Wayne. 1979. *Dixie's Forgotten People: The South's Poor Whites*. Bloomington: Indiana University Press.

Foote, Henry Wilder. 1968. *Three Centuries of American Hymnody*. [Originally published in 1940.] New York: Archon.

Ford, Thomas R., ed. 1962. *The Southern Appalachian Region: A Survey*. Lexington: University Press of Kentucky.

Frost, William Goodell. 1899. "Our Contemporary Ancestors in the Southern Mountains." *Atlantic Monthly* 83:311–319.

Frye, Northrop. 1982. *The Great Code: The Bible and Literature*. New York: Harcourt Brace Jovanovich.

Garland, Jim. 1983. *Welcome the Traveler Home*. Edited by Julia S. Ardery. Lexington: University Press of Kentucky.

Geertz, Clifford. 1973. "Religion as a Cultural System." In his *The Interpretation of Cultures*, pp. 87–125. New York: Basic.

George, Kenneth Martin. 1978. "'I Still Got It': The Conversion Narrative of John C. Sherfey." M.A. thesis, University of North Carolina, Chapel Hill.

———. 1980. "Speakin' from the Heart: The Role of Autobiography in Southern Evangelical Oratory." Paper read at the 1980 Annual Meeting of the American Folklore Society, Pittsburgh.

Gerlach, Luther. 1974. "Pentecostalism—Revolution or Counter-revolution?" In *Religious Movements in Contemporary America*, edited by Irving I. Zaretsky and Mark P. Leone, pp. 669–699. Princeton: Princeton University Press.

Gerrard, Nathan L. 1978. "Churches of the Stationary Poor in Appalachia." In *Religion in Appalachia*, edited by John D. Photiadis, pp. 271–284. Morgantown: West Virginia University.

Gewehr, Wesley M. 1930. *The Great Awakening in Virginia, 1740–1790*. Durham, N.C.: Duke University Press.

Glassie, Henry. 1982. *Passing the Time in Ballymenone*. Philadelphia: University of Pennsylvania Press.

Goodenough, Ward. 1981. *Culture, Language and Society*. Menlo Park, Calif.: Benjamin/Cummings Pub. Co.

Gordon, Michael, ed. 1973. *The American Family in Social-Historical Perspective*. New York: St. Martin's.

Graham, Keith. 1977. *J. L. Austin: A Critique of Ordinary Language Philosophy*. Atlantic Highlands, N.J.: Humanities Press.

Grant, Charles S. 1961. *Democracy in the Connecticut Frontier Town of Kent*. New York: Columbia University Press.

Gray, Lewis Cecil. 1933. *History of Agriculture in the Southern United States to 1860*. 2 vols. Washington, D.C.: Carnegie Institution.

Greven, Philip. 1970. *Four Generations: Population, Land and Family in Colonial Andover, Massachusetts*. Ithaca, N.Y.: Cornell University Press.

Griffin, Emilie. 1980. *Turning*. New York: Doubleday.

Hale, John S. 1978. *A Historical Atlas of Colonial Virginia*. Verona, Va.: McClure Press.

Hall, Connor, ed. 1951. *Church Hymnal*. Cleveland, Tenn.: Tennessee Music and Printing Company.

Hammond, Paul Garnett. 1974. "Music in Urban Revivalism in the Northern United States, 1800–1835." D.M.A. thesis, Southern Baptist Theological Seminary.

Hammons Family, The. 1973. Two 12″ discs. Recorded by Carl Fleischhauer and Alan Jabbour. Booklet edited by Carl Fleischhauer and Alan Jabbour. Washington: Library of Congress AFS L6.

Harrell, David E., Jr. 1971. *White Sects and Black Men*. Nashville: Vanderbilt University Press.

Hatch, Charles E. 1968. *Alexander Spotswood Crosses the Blue Ridge: A Great Discovery of the Passage over the Mountains*. Washington, D.C.: National Park Service, U.S. Department of the Interior, Office of Archeology and Historic Preservation.

Heiler, Friedrich. 1958. *Prayer: History and Psychology.* [Originally published in 1932.] Translated and edited by Samuel McComb. New York: Galaxy Books.

Henretta, James A. 1978. "Families and Farms: *Mentalité* in Pre-Industrial America." *William and Mary Quarterly* 35:3–32.

Herberg, Will. 1955. *Protestant-Catholic-Jew.* New York: Doubleday.

Hicks, George L. 1976. *Appalachian Valley.* New York: Holt, Rinehart and Winston.

Hill, Samuel S., Jr. 1967. *Southern Churches in Crisis.* Chapel Hill: University of North Carolina Press.

Hilliard, Sam. 1972. *Hog Meat and Hoecake.* Carbondale: Southern Illinois University Press.

Hitch, Margaret A. 1931. "Life in a Blue Ridge Hollow." *Journal of Geography* 30:309–322.

Horn, Dorothy D. 1970. *Sing to Me of Heaven.* Gainesville: University of Florida Press.

Hymes, Dell. 1974. *Foundations in Sociolinguistics.* Philadelphia: University of Pennsylvania Press.

———. 1978. "The Grounding of Performance and Text in a Narrative View of Life." *Alcheringa,* n.s. 4, 1:137–140.

———. 1981. *In Vain I Tried to Tell You.* Philadelphia: University of Pennsylvania Press.

In the Good Old Fashioned Way. 1973. 16mm film. Color, 30 min. Directed by Herb E. Smith. Appalachian Film Workshop/Appalshop. Whitesburg, Ky.

Ives, Edward D. 1977. *Argyle Boom. Northeast Folklore,* vol. 17.

Jackson, George Pullen. 1965. *White Spirituals in the Southern Uplands.* [Originally published in 1933.] New York: Dover.

Jansen, William Hugh. 1957. "Classifying Performance in the Study of Verbal Folklore." In *Studies in Folklore,* edited by W. Edson Richmond. Bloomington: Indiana University Press.

Jenkins, J. Geraint. 1972. "The Use of Artifacts and Folk Art in the Folk Museum." In *Folklore and Folklife,* edited by Richard Dorson, pp. 497–516. University of Chicago Press.

Johnson, Paul. 1978. *A Shopkeeper's Millennium.* New York: Hill & Wang.

Jones, Loyal. 1977. "Old-time Baptists and Mainline Christianity." In *An Appalachian Symposium,* edited by J. W. Williamson, pp. 120–130. Boone, N.C.: Appalachian State University Press.

Joy Unspeakable. 1981. Videotape. Color, 58 min. Directed by Elaine Lawless and Betsy Peterson. Bloomington: Indiana University Media Center.

Kaplan, Berton H. 1965. "The Structure of Adaptive Sentiments in a Lower Class Religious Group in Appalachia." *Journal of Social Issues* 12:126–141.

———. 1978. "Religion—the Traditional and the Modern: A Study of Three Churches in the Blue Ridge Mountains." In *Religion in Appalachia,* edited by John D. Photiadis, pp. 255–270. Morgantown: West Virginia University.

Kelley, Dean M. 1972. *Why Conservative Churches Are Growing.* New York: Harper and Row.

LaBarre, Weston. 1969. *They Shall Take Up Serpents: Psychology of the Southern Snake-Handling Cult*. New York: Schocken Books.

Lawless, Elaine. 1982. "Making a Joyful Noise: An Ethnography of Communication in the Pentecostal Religious Service." *Southern Folklore Quarterly* 44:1–21.

Lederer, John. 1902. *The Discoveries of John Lederer*. [Originally published in 1672.] Rochester, N.Y.: George P. Humphrey.

Lemon, James T. 1967. "Household Consumption in Eighteenth-Century America and Its Relationship to Production and Trade: The Situation among Farmers in Southeastern Pennsylvania." *Agricultural History* 41: 59–70.

———. 1972. *The Best Poor Man's Country: A Geographical Study of Early Southeastern Pennsylvania*. Baltimore: Johns Hopkins University Press.

———. 1980. "Early Americans and Their Social Environment." *Journal of Historical Geography* 6:115–131.

Lomax, Alan. 1968. *Folk Song Style and Culture*. Washington, D.C.: American Association for the Advancement of Science.

Lord, Albert B. 1968. *The Singer of Tales*. [Originally published in 1960.] New York: Atheneum.

Lumpkin, William L. 1959. *Baptist Confessions of Faith*. Philadelphia: Judson Press.

McDonald, Forest, and Grady McWhiney. 1980. "The South from Self-Sufficiency to Peonage: An Interpretation." *American Historical Review* 85:1095–1118.

Malpezzi, Frances M., and William M. Clements. 1985. "Tropological Allegory in Pentecostal Radio Sermons." *Midwestern Journal of Language and Folklore* 11:31–38.

Marsden, George M. 1980. *Fundamentalism and American Culture*. New York: Oxford University Press.

Marty, Martin S. 1976. *A Nation of Behavers*. Chicago: University of Chicago Press.

Mathews, Donald G. 1977. *Religion in the Old South*. Chicago: University of Chicago Press.

Merton, Thomas. 1971. *Contemplative Prayer*. New York: Doubleday Image Books.

Miller, J. Hillis. 1981. "The Two Allegories." In *Allegory, Myth, and Symbol*, edited by Morton W. Bloomfield, pp. 355–370. Harvard English Studies 9. Cambridge: Harvard University Press.

Miller, Terry. 1983. Review of *Powerhouse for God* (recording). *Ethnomusicology* 27:390–393.

Mitchell, Robert D. 1977. *Commercialization and Frontier: Perspectives on the Early Shenandoah Valley*. Charlottesville: University Press of Virginia.

Morrison, I. B. 1940. *Feeds and Feeding*. Ithaca, N.Y.: Morrison Publishing Co.

Mullen, Patrick B. 1983. "Ritual and Sacred Narratives in the Blue Ridge Mountains." *Papers in Comparative Studies* (Ohio State University) 2: 17–38.

Mutch, Robert E. 1977. "Yeoman and Merchant in Pre-Industrial America: Eighteenth-Century Massachusetts as a Case Study." *Societas* 7:279–302.

Newcomb, Robert M., ed. 1976. "Carl O. Sauer, Teacher." *Historical Geography Newsletter* 6:21–30.

Newton, Milton, Jr. 1971. "The Annual Round in the Upland South: The Synchronization of Man and Nature through Culture." *Pioneer America* 3: 63–73.

Norris, Christopher. 1982. *Deconstruction: Theory and Practice.* New York: Methuen.

Open Bible, The. 1975. Nashville: Thomas Nelson Publishers.

Page Co., Va., Overall Economic Development Program. 1977. Luray: Page County Board of Supervisors.

Peacock, James L. 1971. "The Southern Protestant Ethic Disease." In *The Not So Solid South,* edited by J. Kenneth Morland, pp. 108–113. Athens: University of Georgia Press.

Pennington, Jean A. T., and Helen Nichols Church. 1985. *Food Values of Portions Commonly Used.* New York: Harper & Row.

Perdue, Charles L., Jr., and Nancy Martin-Perdue. 1979–1980. "Appalachian Facts and Fables: A Case Study of the Shenandoah National Park Removals." *Appalachian Journal* 7:84–104.

Phillips, D. Z. 1966. *The Concept of Prayer.* New York: Schocken.

Photiadis, John D. 1978. "A Theoretical Supplement." In *Religion in Appalachia,* edited by idem, pp. 7–27. Morgantown: West Virginia University.

———, ed. 1978. *Religion in Appalachia.* Morgantown: West Virginia University.

Photiadis, John D., and Harry K. Schwarzweller, eds. 1970. *Change in Rural Appalachia: Implications for Action Programs.* Philadelphia: University of Pennsylvania Press.

Pope, Liston. 1965. *Millhands and Preachers.* New Haven: Yale University Press.

Powerhouse for God. 1982. Two 12″ discs, recorded by Jeff Todd Titon and Kenneth Martin George. Edited with booklet by Jeff Todd Titon. Chapel Hill: University of North Carolina Press.

Primitive Baptist Hymns of the Blue Ridge. 1982. 12″ disc. Recorded by Brett Sutton and Peter Hartmann. Edited with booklet by Brett Sutton. Chapel Hill: University of North Carolina Press.

Propp, Vladimir. 1968. *Morphology of the Folktale.* Translated by Laurence Scott. 2d ed. Austin: University of Texas Press.

Quilligan, Maureen. "Allegory, Allegoresis, and the Deallegorization of Language." In *Allegory, Myth, and Symbol,* edited by Morton W. Bloomfield, pp. 163–186. Harvard English Studies 9. Cambridge: Harvard University Press.

Reed, John S. 1974. *The Enduring South.* Chapel Hill: University of North Carolina Press.

Reeder, Carolyn, and Jack Reeder. 1978. *Shenandoah Heritage.* Washington, D.C.: Potomac Appalachian Trail Club.

Ricoeur, Paul. 1976. *Interpretation Theory.* Fort Worth: Texas Christian University Press.

Rodeheaver, Homer, and Charles B. Ford, Jr. 1941. *Song Leadership.* Winona

Lake, Ind.: Rodeheaver/Hall-Mack Co.

Rohrbough, Malcolm. 1978. *The Trans-Appalachian Frontier.* New York: Oxford University Press.

Rosenberg, Bruce. 1970. *The Art of the American Folk Preacher.* New York: Oxford University Press.

Rothenberg, Winifred B. 1981. "The Market and Massachusetts Farmers, 1750–1855." *Journal of Economic History* 41:283–314.

Ryan, Mary P. 1981. *Cradle of the Middle Class: The Family in Oneida County, New York, 1790–1865.* Cambridge: Cambridge University Press.

Sallee, James. 1978. *A History of Evangelistic Hymnody.* Grand Rapids, Mich.: Baker Book House.

Scheiber, Harry N., Harold Vatter, and Harold U. Faulkner. 1976. *American Economic History.* New York: Harper and Row.

Scofield, C. I., ed. 1945. *The Scofield Reference Bible: The Holy Bible, Containing the Old and New Testaments* . . . [Originally published in 1909.] New York: Oxford University Press.

Searle, John. 1969. *Speech Acts.* London and New York: Cambridge University Press.

Seeger, Charles. 1950. "Oral Tradition in Music." In *Funk & Wagnalls Standard Dictionary of Folklore, Mythology and Legend.* New York: Funk & Wagnalls.

———. 1977. "Contrapuntal Style in the Three-Voice Shape-Note Hymns of the United States" (1940). In his *Studies in Musicology, 1935–1975,* pp. 237–251. Berkeley: University of California Press.

Shapiro, Henry D. 1978. *Appalachia on Our Mind.* Chapel Hill: University of North Carolina Press.

Sherman, Mandel, and Thomas Henry. 1973. *Hollow Folk.* [Originally published in 1933.] Berryville, Va.: Virginia Book Co.

Sizer, Sandra S. 1978. *Gospel Hymns and Social Religion: The Rhetoric of Nineteenth-Century Revivalism.* Philadelphia: Temple University Press.

Smart, Ninian. 1968. *The Experience of Religion.* New York: Scribner's.

Smith, Dorothy Noble. 1983. *Recollections: The People of the Blue Ridge Remember.* Edited by James F. Gorman. Verona, Va.: McClure Printing Co.

Somerville, Wilson, ed. 1981. *Appalachia/America.* Johnson City: East Tennessee State University.

Stadtfeld, Curtis. 1972. *From the Land and Back.* New York: Scribner's.

Stahl, Sandra K. D. 1977. "The Personal Narrative as Folklore." *Journal of the Folklore Institute* 14:9–30.

Stanley, David. 1982. "The Gospel-Singing Convention in South Georgia." *Journal of American Folklore* 95:1–32.

Stephenson, John B. 1968. *Shiloh.* Lexington: University Press of Kentucky.

Strickler, Harry M. 1924. *Massanutten.* Strasburg, Va.: published by the author.

———. 1952. *A Short History of Page County.* Richmond, Va.: Dietz Press.

Tallmadge, William. 1975. "Baptist Monophonic and Heterophonic Hymnody in Southern Appalachia." *Yearbook for Inter-American Musical Research* 11:106–136.

———. 1984. "Folk Organum: A Study of Origins." *American Music* 2:47–65.

Tedlock, Dennis. 1983. *The Spoken Word and the Work of Interpretation.* Philadelphia: University of Pennsylvania Press.

Temperley, Nicholas. 1979a. "The Old Way of Singing: Its Origins and Development." Abstract for paper read at Symposium on Rural Hymnody, Berea College, Berea, Ky.

———. 1979b. *The Music of the English Parish Church,* vol. 1. Cambridge: Cambridge University Press.

———. 1981. "The Old Way of Singing: Its Origins and Development." *Journal of the American Musicological Society* 34:511–544.

Thompson, Frank Charles, ed. 1964. *The Thompson Chain-Reference Bible.* 4th ed. Indianapolis: Kirkbride Bible Co.

Thornbury, W. D. 1965. *Regional Geography of the United States.* New York: Wiley and Sons.

Titon, Jeff Todd. 1969a. "Calling All Cows: Lazy Bill Lucas." *Blues Unlimited,* nos. 60–63 (March, April, May, and June).

———. 1969b. "All Pretty Wimmens: The Story of Jo Jo Williams." *Blues Unlimited,* nos. 64–65 (July and September).

———. 1975. "Tonal System in the Chanted Oral Sermons of the Rev. C. L. Franklin." Paper read at Annual Conference of the Society for Ethnomusicology, Middletown, Conn.

———. 1976a. "Intonation as Constraint on Diction and Syntax in the Chanted Oral Sermons of the Rev. C. L. Franklin." Paper read at Annual Conference of the American Folklore Society, Philadelphia.

———. 1976b. "Son House: Two Narratives." *Alcheringa,* n.s. 2(1):2–9.

———. 1977. *Early Downhome Blues: A Musical and Cultural Analysis.* Urbana: University of Illinois Press.

———. 1978a. "Some Recent Pentecostal Revivals." *Georgia Review* 32: 579–605.

———. 1978b. "Every Day I Have the Blues: Improvisation and Daily Life." *Southern Folklore Quarterly* 42:85–98.

———. 1980a. "Prayer: Native Viewpoints and Oral Theory." Paper read at Annual Conference of the American Folklore Society, Pittsburgh.

———. 1980b. "A Song from the Holy Spirit." *Ethnomusicology* 24:223–231.

———. 1980c. "The Life Story." *Journal of American Folklore* 93:276–292.

———. 1982. "Identity in the Religious Life Story." Paper read at Annual Conference of the American Folklore Society, Minneapolis.

———. 1985. "Stance, Role, and Identity in Fieldwork among Folk Baptists and Pentecostals in the United States." *American Music* 3:16–24.

Titon, Jeff Todd, ed. 1974. *From Blues to Pop: The Autobiography of Leonard "Baby Doo" Caston.* JEMF Special Series, No. 4. Los Angeles: John Edwards Memorial Foundation at the Folklore and Mythology Center, University of California.

———. 1984. *Worlds of Music.* New York: Schirmer Books.

Titon, Jeff Todd, and Kenneth Martin George. 1977. "Dressed in the Armor of God." *Alcheringa,* n.s. 3(2):10–31.

———. 1978. "Testimonies." *Alcheringa,* n.s. 4(1):69–83.

Toelken, Barre. 1979. *The Dynamics of Folklore.* Boston: Houghton Mifflin.

Tryon, Rolla Milton. 1966. *Household Manufactures in the United States,*

1640–1860. [Originally published in 1917.] New York: Augustus M. Kelley.

Tuan, Yi-Fu. 1974. *Topophilia.* Englewood Cliffs, N.J.: Prentice-Hall.

Tufte, Virginia, and Barbara Myerhoff. 1979. *Changing Images of the Family.* New Haven: Yale University Press.

Turner, Victor. 1969. *The Ritual Process: Structure and Anti-Structure.* Chicago: University of Chicago Press.

van Gennep, Arnold. 1960. *The Rites of Passage.* Translated by Monika B. Vizedom and Gabrielle L. Caffee. Chicago: University of Chicago Press.

Wallace, Anthony F. C. 1966. *Religion: An Anthropological View.* New York: Random House.

Watts, May Thielgard. 1975. *Reading the Landscape of America.* Rev. ed. New York: Collier.

Wayland, John. 1930. *Virginia Valley Records.* Strasburg, Va.: Shenandoah Publishing House.

———, ed. 1925. *The Journal of Thomas Lewis.* New Market, Va.: The Henkel Press.

Weatherford, W. D., and Earl D. C. Brewer. 1962. *Life and Religion in Southern Appalachia: An Interpretation of Selected Data from the Southern Appalachian Studies.* New York: Friendship Press.

Weller, Jack E. 1965. *Yesterday's People.* Lexington: University Press of Kentucky.

Wilhelm, E. J. [Gene], Jr. 1967. "Folk Settlement Types in the Blue Ridge Mountains." *Keystone Folklore Quarterly* 12:151–174.

———. 1975. "Folk Culture History of the Blue Ridge Mountains." *Appalachian Journal* 2:192–222.

———. 1978. "Folk Settlements in the Blue Ridge Mountains." *Appalachian Journal* 5:204–245.

Williams, Peter A. 1980. *Popular Religion in America.* Englewood Cliffs, N.J.: Prentice-Hall.

Williamson, J. W., ed. 1977. *An Appalachian Symposium.* Boone, N.C.: Appalachian State University Press.

Wilson, Walter Lewis. 1957. *Wilson's Dictionary of Bible Types.* Grand Rapids, Mich.: Eerdmans.

Wolfe, Charles. 1982. "Gospel Goes Uptown." In *Folk Music and Modern Sound,* edited by William Ferris, pp. 80–100. Jackson: University Press of Mississippi.

W.P.A. Virginia. 1940. *Virginia: A Guide to the Old Dominion.* American Guide Series. New York: Oxford University Press.

Wright, Gavin. 1978. *The Political Economy of the Cotton South.* New York: Norton.

Yoder, Don. 1974. "Toward a Definition of Folk Religion." *Western Folklore* 33:2–15.

———. 1976. "Folklife Studies in American Scholarship." In *American Folklife,* edited by idem, pp. 3–18. Austin: University of Texas Press.

Zwelling, Shomer. 1977. *Working in Rural New England, 1790–1840.* Sturbridge, Mass.: Old Sturbridge Village.

Index